HINDU POLITY
(The Ordinances of Manu)

HINDU POLITY

(The Ordinances of Manu)

TRANSLATED FROM THE SANSKRIT.
With an Introduction

BY THE LATE

ARTHUR COKE, BURNELL, Ph.D., C.I.E.

COMPLETED AND EDITED BY

EDWARD W. HOPKINS, Ph.D.
OF COLUMBIA COLLEGE, N.Y.

GYAN

Published by

Gyan Publishing House
5, Ansari Road
Daryaganj, New Delhi-110002
Phone: 011-47034999, 9811692060
E-mail: books@gyanbooks.com

Distribution Network
gyanbooks.com
India, USA, Canada, UK, Australia, France

ISBN : 978-81-212-2221-1 (HB)
First Published, 1884

2nd Impression 2021

Printed at: Gyan Press, Delhi.

Hindu Polity
(The Ordinances of Manu)
Completed and Edited by: Edward W. Hopkins

HINDU POLITY
(The Ordinances of Manu)

TRANSLATED FROM THE SANSKRIT.

With an Introduction,

BY THE LATE

ARTHUR COKE, BURNELL. PH.D., C.I.E.

COMPLETED AND EDITED BY

EDWARD W. HOPKINS, PH.D.

OF COLUMBIA COLLEGE, N.Y.

CONTENTS.

PREFACE BY THE EDITOR.

The late Dr. Burnell had, as is well known, begun a new translation of the Mānava-dharma-çāstra, based on the more accurate knowledge we now possess of Indian literature, as compared with that obtainable by the early translators. This work the author unhappily did not live to finish. A year ago it was proposed to the editor to complete the undertaking, and deeming it a pleasure to feel that the last labours of an honoured scholar, such as was Dr. Burnell, might be preserved and handed down through his instrumentality, he cheerfully consented to undertake the preparation of the work for the press.

The present volume contains this final memorial of Dr. Burnell, and is now offered to the public with such additions only as appeared to the editor to be absolutely necessary. Of the lessened worth unavoidably arising from the transfer of the work to one lacking the skill and scholarship of the author of the translation, the editor himself is fully aware.

The book's plan and purpose have been sufficiently discussed by Dr. Burnell in the following Introduction, and nothing further is needed on that score except in so far as the editor may have laid himself open to the charge of deviating from the method proposed by the author. On that point he would remark: the author of the translation has defined the line of interpretation as based on the text of Kullūka, over against modifications of that text by acceptance of the varied readings found in Medhātithi. He has not, however, always complied with this rule;

and if here and there the editor has altered the *textus receptus* of Kullūka to suit a reading preferred by Medhātithi, and seemingly better, he has but followed where the author led. In so far as there were sufficient data to indicate a line of action, the practice pursued by Dr. Burnell has been uniformly followed. As indicative of the course which in certain cases would originally have been taken by him, the following facts have been noticed. Differences of opinion on the part of the commentators, when based on a desire to reconcile the text with itself, or with other tradition, are seldom noticed; occasionally special remarks only are noted; the explanation of one commentator is sometimes omitted entirely when that of another is preferred; no one word or phrase is persistently rendered in the same way (i. 21; ii. 1, 3–6; i. 58; *dharma*, rule, law, duty, ii. 3, 45, 61, 229, 235). In short, the aim was practical, and Dr. Burnell has grasped the real value of the commentators, viz., to show us the original form of the text, and to indicate the Indian understanding of passages which might, through his foreign tone of thought, be misunderstood by an Occidental. On the forced and sometimes impossible meanings got from the text by expositors theoretically obliged to make it conform to certain opinions held by themselves, little weight is laid by Dr. Burnell, and the editor has, therefore, tried to submit his choice of extracts from the commentators to this principle of excerption.

A decided leaning, however, will be noticed in Dr. Burnell's translation to an interpretation based on the unanimous explanation of the commentators on points where it might be questioned whether these scholiasts are not all wrong. This has been conspicuous in the treatment of the first Lecture, where much of late philosophy has crept into the translation on account of the commentators, though such interpretation has been objected to by European scholars. In no such case has the editor felt himself at liberty to alter the phraseology of the translation, though he has sometimes added in the notes what he conceived to be a truer rendering of the original text. He has, indeed, been particularly cautious not to offend the intention of the author in this respect, since it is possible that, in conformity with the late origin assumed by the latter for the work, this very style of translation may have been his deliberate choice, aside from the remarks of the Vedantic commentators. In regard to other portions of the translation less scruples have been felt, and occasionally changes in the wording have been made by the editor. As a matter of course, these have, however, been as infrequent as possible, and no change has been made without due remark and explanation in the notes. In general, nothing has been altered which the editor did not believe would have been altered by Dr. Burnell, had he lived to complete and revise his work. The few exceptions to this statement are justified by the fact that such cases are chiefly due to a simpler arrangement of the too literal translation sometimes employed. It was thought unnecessary to call attention to such changes at each occurrence, as the alterations were made merely to simplify, not to change, the original thought.

To separate the original translation and notes of Dr. Burnell from the part which the editor added for the purpose of completing the translation and filling out points left untouched in the notes, the following method has been employed:—From i. 1 to viii. 16 the translation is Dr. Burnell's; from viii. 16 to the end, the editor's. Every note on the first part of this translation (from i. 1 to viii. 16), unless enclosed in square brackets, is Dr. Burnell's; for those on the same portion included in square brackets the editor is responsible. A note at viii. 16 indicates that the portion from viii. 16 to the end, both translation and notes, has been done by the editor; a bracket at each verse and note of this portion seemed unnecessary. It has not seemed advisable to burden the translation itself with brackets, and therefore, as said above, any alteration made by the editor in the first part (to viii. 16) has been made without indicators, but immediately explained in the bracketed note at the foot of the page. The only remaining sign used is the parenthesis, ( ), employed, not, as in the old translation, to insert the added explanation of the commentator, but to indicate merely that which was needed in converting the idiom of the Hindu into English, and which every translator must employ irrespective of the commentators. The Introduction has, with one bracketed exception, explained there, not been altered at all. It was complete, and to change so important a part of Dr. Burnell's work would have been, to say the least, indiscreet. The editor is aware, however, as every reader must be, of its somewhat fragmentary condition. The abrupt transitions in it seem to indicate intended additions. Yet no sign of this was given in the smooth and fair manuscript left by Dr. Burnell. In the notes to this Introduction the bracketed portions are again the editor's.

The disappointment to be felt by all on discovering what portion of the work had been left untouched by Dr. Burnell is shared by the editor. When the latter received the first communication in regard to completing the translation, he understood that it was already nearly finished. Had he known what his own share was to be, he would have been reluctant to assume such a responsibility; for it was exactly where a master-hand was most needed that the master's hand was wanting. To supply this deficiency the editor has done what he could, but it must be to all a source of regret that those portions of the work where Dr. Burnell's acquaintance with practical Hindu law would have been of the utmost value have been left to one who knows it in theory only.

Mention has been made above of Dr. Burnell's method of employing the commentators; a word may here be added respecting his choice among them. The editor noticed that Dr. Burnell makes little use of Rāghavānanda, more of Medhātithi, most of Kullūka. In Lectures viii. and ix. the editor has added the "Nandinī" to these. Govindarāja he has, to his great regret, been able to quote from fragmentary sources only, no manuscripts being at his disposal; the same may be said of the scant use of Nārāyaṇa in Lecture viii., though he doubts if much has been lost by this commentator's absence. Of Medhātithi several very fair copies were obtained; also a complete one of Rāghavānanda. The last is helpful in establishing the text, but is otherwise seldom worth special quotation, as nine-tenths of what he says has been said by older commentators. It is the lack of Govinda that the editor most regrets. It would have been interesting at least to note how many of Medhātithi's *eke* and *anye* referred to his school; and as a rival of the latter he should be entitled to equal consideration. The editor doubts, however, whether Dr. Burnell would have felt his loss much, or taken into his notes very many of the discussions between the two opposing interpreters.

As the text from which the translation should be made had been laid down by Dr. Burnell to be that of Kullūka, seemingly later additions supported by him are merely touched upon in the notes, and the numbering of the verses remains substantially the same as in the old translations.

All the varied readings quoted by Loiseleur in the notes to his edition—readings gathered from a number of manuscripts—have been compared with what has been found by the editor in his own manuscripts, and specially referred to where even one seemed plausible. Changes from the received text have been seldom made unless supported by strong authority; no single copy of Rāghavānanda, or even Medhātithi, would justify the substitution of new readings, though such were not infrequently offered.

The manuscripts of Medhātithi referred to by the editor are those belonging to the India Office (Colebrooke's collection), marked No. 989 (Lectures vii., viii., x., xi., xii.), a much-altered copy, where the original text has been frequently changed by a later hand; No. 935 (vii.–xii.), copied apparently from the following, and much tampered with; No. 1551 (vi.–xii., *saṁvat* 1648, Lois. v.), clean, and but little revised; also Dr. Burnell's copy (marked "from Colebrooke"), containing Lectures i.–viii. One fair complete copy of Rāghavānanda (i.–xii.) was supplemented by the commentary of the same author on Lecture viii., bound with the Nandinī (Grantha MS. of Nandanācārya's gloss) on Lectures viii. and ix., both from Dr. Burnell's collection. In regard to this last commentator the editor would modify somewhat the depreciatory remarks made respecting him by Dr. Burnell, since, although modern and unscrupulous, his version often gives support to the oldest readings, the more valuable as showing that the Medhātithi text was not entirely supplanted by that of Kullūka. For Kullūka's text and commentary the editor has used the various published editions, that of Loiseleur Deslongchamps and Haughton being supplemented by the commentary as given in the Calcutta edition. As much of the work of Govindarāja as was offered by the numerous citations of this author by Kullūka and Rāghavānanda has been compared and noted along with the works of the other commentators. It is hoped, therefore, that nothing of importance has been omitted in the notes embodying the native interpretations of the text.

In conclusion, the editor feels constrained to say that he has not felt it his right to expand, still less his duty to criticise, the views advanced in the Introduction, whether relating to the origin of the work or to the use of the commentators; here and there the same may be said of the notes. It has been his object to complete what was left him by another to be completed in the way the author himself would have adopted, and he declines to be regarded as more than the *persona* whereby the opinions of Dr. Burnell are given to the public. That the work was not issued at a much earlier date is due to the dilatoriness of others in returning to the India Office certain indispensable manuscripts.

To Dr. Rost, librarian of the East India Office, the editor gives his hearty thanks. With no little trouble to himself Dr. Rost has most kindly aided this work, and by the loan of manuscripts rendered it possible for the present volume to be published; for this and for other assistance rendered by the same scholar the editor begs leave to express here his grateful acknowledgment.

E. W. H.

NEW YORK, *April* 1884.

INTRODUCTION

TO THE

MĀNAVA-DHARMA-ÇĀSTRA.

No Indian book has been better known for the last hundred years[1] nearly than the so-called "Laws of Manu," and to many people it is still the decisive authority respecting India.[2] Numerous and important as have been the discoveries in Sanskrit literature during this century, and through which a new world has been rediscovered by European scholars, these laws still hold their old place in the popular estimation. This is partly owing to the circumstances under which Sir William Jones brought out his translation, and it is partly owing to the high estimate which, in comparatively modern

[1] Sir William Jones' translation (Calcutta, 1794) became at once famous; it was reprinted at Calcutta (1796) and London in 1796 (Gildermeister, p. 125). It was early translated into German by Hüttner (1797), and several essays were written on the matter it furnished (Gildermeister, p. 126).

[2] See, *e.g.*, the large use made of it in S. Johnson's Oriental Religions (1879), vol. i. p. 169 ff. M. Lafitte has taken the author of the Mānava-dharma-çāstra as a type of the theocratic stage of civilisation (Les Grand Types de l'Humanité); Professor Thonissen has also largely used the text in his treatise on early criminal law (Etudes [sur l'Histoire du Droit Criminel des Peuples Anciens], 2 vols., 1869); and a recent writer in the Calcutta Review (No. cxxi., 1875) on crimes and punishments under Hindu law relies solely on it. All these are instances since ample materials have become available. For the earlier time, when this was not the case, it is sufficient to quote Mill's History of British India (2d ed. of 1820), vol. i. bk. ii. pp. 133 ff. (especially pp. 192–246), and Elphinstone's History of India, i., chaps. i.–iii. On the other hand, the appearance of the name Manu in the Positivist Calendar for the tenth day of the first month of the year is in every way suitable; it is the only possible representative in such a place of Indian theocracy.

times, has attached to the book in India for perhaps nearly fourteen hundred years. But the grounds assigned for this, as usual in India, are not satisfactory. Sir W. Jones' translation was the first real translation of a Sanskrit work,[1] and for this reason deservedly attracted notice. It threw a flood of real light on Indian notions which had been hitherto imperfectly represented in Europe,[2] and for which the metaphysical philosophers of those days were most curious. Again, a systematic judicial administration was just then begun in the British province of India, and the Mānava-dharma-çāstra, as translated by Sir W. Jones, at once became, and has remained, an authority on the laws of the so-called Hindus for the uncritical lawyers who attempted the task, and are still carrying it on. It was not suitable for this purpose, for to make it *the* authority was to take a retrograde step, as even Sir W. Jones soon discovered,[3] and no real paṇḍit

[1] All that had been done before was the translation of Bhartṛhari's poem in Rogerius, Open-Deure, 1651 (into Dutch).

[2] The accounts of Hindu mythology, etc., by Rogerius (1651) and Baldæus (1672) were, *e.g.*, mostly through Tamil, and these influences are visible in most of the early Portuguese accounts (see Couto, Dec., v. 6, 3, and cf. my paper on early knowledge of existence of the Vedas in the sixteenth century, in the Indian Antiquary, vol. viii. pp. 98 ff.) The later Portuguese accounts, such, *e.g.*, as those in the first vol. of the Collecção de Memorias para a Historia de Nações ultra-Marinas Portuguezas, pp. 1–126) are from Mahrāṭha sources. Lord's Display (1630) is second-hand and from Gujarati: he says (Introd. B. 2), "I . . . essayed to fetch materials for the same out of their manuscripts, and by renewed accesse, with the help of interpreters, made my collections out of a booke of theirs called the SHASTER, which is to them as their Bible, containing the grounds of their religion in a written word." But it is plain from what follows that he had to rely on so-called interpreters, who misled him, as they have done other inquirers. His book is very inferior to those by Rogerius and Baldæus. The first real attempt to give an account of Hindu law was in the Digest translated by Halhed (1776), but this was not an original Sanskrit work.

[3] When he got Jagannātha to compile the Digest which was translated by Colebrooke. This, however, Colebrooke from the first rightly condemned, and eventually expressed a stronger opinion on. He says (Preface to Mitākṣarā and Dāyabhāga, p. ii.): "In the preface to the translation of the Digest . . . I hinted my opinion unfavourable to the arrangement of it as it has been executed by the native compiler. I have been confirmed in that opinion of the compilation since its publication; and indeed the author's method . . . renders his work of little utility to persons conversant with the law, and of still less service to those who are not versed in Indian jurisprudence; especially to

would ever have suggested it; but accident has given it this supreme position, which is, even now, hardly weakened, owing to the general ignorance of the history of Sanskrit law.

In India a high position has been claimed for the book for at least several hundred years. This opinion is very fully set forth by the later commentators,[1] who lived within the last few centuries; it is chiefly based on references to Manu in the Vedas, Mahābhārata, Bṛhaspati-Smṛti, etc., such as: "Whatever Manu said is curative;" "Manu divided his property among his sons;" "A Smṛti opposed to Manu is not approved."[2]

But the myth connecting this law-book with the Manu referred to in the Vedas is recent, as the real nature (to be explained) of the book will show. That the text owed its popularity in India chiefly to its completeness, orderly arrangement, and intelligibility, cannot be doubted; and there are other causes connected with the origin of the text, as we now have it, which, as I hope to show farther on, probably contributed to the same result. The fabulous antiquity assigned to it from Sir William Jones' time[3] (1250–500 B.C.) had little weight except in India. All Indian books of a sacred character prefer precisely the same claims.[4]

the English reader, for whose use, through the medium of translation, the work was particularly intended." The real systematic study of Hindu law became possible with his translation of the Mitākṣarā and Dāyabhāga (Calcutta, 1810), which introduced the scientific Digest to Europeans. Compare also the Life of this illustrious man by his son, p. 74 ff.

[1] *E.g.*, Kullūka and Rāghavānanda, in their commentaries on i. 1; even Medhātithi quotes the first saying given above. [Rāgh.'s quotations are most complete; besides the above he gives: *Bhārate'pi* (!) *Purāṇaṁ, mānavo dharmaḥ, sāṅgo Vedaç, cikitsitaṁ / ājñāsiddhāni catvāri na hantavyāni hetubhiḥ.*]

[2] Tait. Saṁ. ii. 2, 10, 2, iii. 1. 9. 4; Ait. Br. v. 14; Bṛhaspati Smṛti.

[3] Sir William Jones' reasoning is to be found on pp. xi. and xii. of the preface to his translation (Haughton's ed., vol. ii.) Professor Monier Williams (Indian Wisdom, p. 215) puts it at about 500 B.C. Johaentgen (Ueber das Gesetzbuch des Manu, p. 95) puts 350 B.C. as the latest date possible. Schlegel confidently asserted it not to be later than 1000 B.C. [Dr. B.'s own opinion, being known before the publication of this work, has already been anticipated in print by Nelson, Scientific Study, p. 37, and Müller, India, p. 366.]

[4] [The bracketed paragraph following, crossed through in Dr. B.'s MS., was evidently intended to be

[It is time now to explain the real nature of the Mānava-dharma-çāstra. This has been proved[1] to be no original treatise, but a versified recension of an older treatise in prose. It is now well known that there were several recensions of the texts of each of the Vedas as used in ancient India, and that people who followed these different recensions split up into other schools in the course of time by the modification of the chronologically secondary Vedic or Brāhmaṇa literature; and still later, and in a still larger degree, by teachers compiling Sūtras or manuals for the sacrifice, etc., and laws which differed more or less from one another,[2] and thus instituted different schools. Such Sūtra works were very numerous in the early centuries A.D.,[3] and some fifteen still remain, in a more or less complete condition. There is every reason from analogy to believe that each such contained a section on traditional law and custom. The Mānava-dharma-çāstra is to be traced back to such a work belonging to the Mānavas, one of the six subdivisions of the Maitrāyaṇīya[4] school of the Black Yajur Veda, of which

revised, as it contained a few errors of authorities, etc., and was perhaps to be completely altered; this has not been done, however, and it may stand, in brackets, as some introduction is necessary to what follows. The brackets shall include also the notes. One or two errors of reference have been silently bettered.]

[1] Professor Weber, in the first volume of Ind. Studien (in an essay written prior to 1850); Professor Max Müller, Letter (1849) to Professor Morley (in the Digest by the latter, and reprinted by Professor Bühler in his and West's Digest and his translation of the Āpastamba-dharma-sūtra); and Ancient Sanskrit Literature (2d ed.), pp. 61, 200 ff. Cf. also Weber, Indische Literaturgeschichte, p. 296; Professor Goldstücker (1860) in "Remains," vol. i. p. 61; Professor Whitney, Sanskrit Grammar, p. xviii.

[2] These differences often were very slight, and in some cases went little beyond a difference of arrangement. See my Classified Index to the Tanjore MSS., p. 21, as regards the relation between parts of the Bharadvāja and Hiraṇyakeçin Sūtras.

[3] Kumārila Bhaṭṭa (c. 700 A.D.) says, "*Dharma-çāstras* and *Gṛhya* books are studied in each *Caraṇa* like the rules of the Prātiçākhyas." Here, as the *Dharma-çāstras* are mentioned with the *Gṛhya-sūtras*, only *Dharma-sūtras* can be intended.

[4] See my Index to the Tanjore MSS., p. 9, *b*. That the Mānava-dharma-çāstra is a work attached to the Black Yajur Veda is also apparent from the frequent citation of and reference to this Veda, and even to its late Āraṇyaka, as will be shown below. It also cites one of the latest of the B. Y. V. sūtras, the Vaikhānasa (vi. 21). The last statement is open to question, as

a few adherents still exist in the Bombay Presidency and in Northern India. Large fragments of the Kalpa portion of their Sūtra have long existed in England,[1] and Dr. Haug recovered the whole, as well as the Gṛhya-sūtra. These MSS. are now at Munich, and of the last there is also a MS. in the University Library at Bombay.[2] So far as we have them, these works are precisely similar to the other sūtras. The Dharma-sūtra has not yet been recovered, and is probably lost for ever; but there can be little doubt that it was turned into verse and added to, and that this is the actual Mānava-dharma-çāstra. That this was done with other such works is also certain.[3] Professor Whitney gives the final results of these researches as follows: "Out of the last two (Gṛhya- and Dharma-sūtras), especially the last, come by natural development the law-books (Dharma-çāstra) which make a conspicuous figure in the later literature: the oldest and most noted of them being that called by the name of Manu (an out-growth, it is believed, of the Mānava Vedic school); to which are added that of Yājñavalkya and many others."[4]

The Manu Smṛti is, then, plainly later than the Sūtra period, as it quotes books of this kind,[5] and this conclusion furnishes the first element by which to fix the date

the word *vaikhānasa* may be otherwise taken in this passage. To this note Dr. Burnell had added a pencil reference to Dr. Schroeder's proposed edition of the Maitrāyaṇī Saṁhitā. Two books of this work are now before the public.]

[1] Together with the commentary of Kumārila Bhaṭṭa (c. 700 A.D.) in the I. O. library, edited (in *facsimile*) by Dr. Th. Goldstücker (1861). The whole text with another commentary has since been discovered at Bombay by Professor Bühler. [This is really nothing more than a commentary to part of the Çrauta-sūtra; cf. Von Bradke's remarks in Z. D. M. G., xxxvi. 448.]

[2] [For the MSS. of the Çrauta- and Gṛhya-sūtra, with a discussion of their mutual relations and their relations to the text, we may now compare the essay by P. v. Bradke, Ueber das Mānava-gṛhya-sūtra Z. D. M. G., xxxvi. pp. 417-477.]

[3] Compare Weber's Ind. Literaturgeschichte, p. 296 note. This matter has been worked out by Weber, Stenzler, Müller, and Bühler.

[4] Sanskrit Grammar, p. xviii.; compare also Whitney's Oriental and Linguistic Studies, i. p. 72.

[5] [Our text quotes Dharma-çāstra, but not Dharma-sūtra; the argument is not wholly convincing, for the metrical Çāstra may have existed contemporaneously with the sūtra.]

of the text. The Sūtra stage of the early Sanskrit literature is the latest, and has been put at from 600 B.C. to 200 B.C.)[1] The first explicit mention of Dharma-sūtras is in the Mahābhāṣya of Patañjali, or in the second century B.C.[2] It is therefore obviously impossible to put a metrical work,[3] such as our text is, earlier than the first or second century B.C. But a close examination of the text furnishes other important information, which enables us to fix its date much more precisely. Medhātithi—and he was not the first commentator on it, as I shall show—lived about 1000 A.D., and this circumstance fixes the lowest possible date at about 500 A.D.; for it is impossible to suppose that the earliest commentators came nearer than 250 or 300 years after the text.

Let us first consider the form and language of the book. The first striking fact is that it is in *çloka* verse, and in very simple and modern language.[4] The style of the verses is not at all that of real old *çlokas,* but is that of the epics, and a good deal is sacrificed for the sake of the metre. Again, the most modern forms of compound words are freely used.[5] The text thus closely resembles the

[1] Max Müller, Ancient Sanskrit Literature, 2d ed., pp. 244 ff. [These limits are not fixed with any great certainty; in fact, the Sūtra period probably extended to a later time.]

[2] Goldstücker, "Pāṇini's Place," p. 234 ff.; Weber, Ind. Studien, xiii. p. 457 ff. The earliest date is the middle of the second century B.C.; the latest the end of the first century A.D.

[3] The style of the Sūtras is still to be traced in the Mānava-dharmaçāstra, in, *e.g.,* the constant use of the third person optative, "one ought to," . . . "one should," . . . which occurs in nearly every verse of most of the chapters.

[4] American scholars (Professors Avery and Lanman) have introduced a new and important branch of Sanskrit scholarship—the examination, statistically, of the grammatical forms in Sanskrit texts. This laborious form of research promises most brilliant results, and has already definitely settled the character, so far as verbs are concerned, of the language of different periods. Mr. Edgren has examined the verbs in the text, and has fixed the language as modern (see pp. 320–321 of Prof. Avery's paper, Journal American Oriental Society, vol. x.)

[5] Whitney, Sanskrit Grammar, p. 424 ff. "There is, however, a marked difference between the earlier and the later language as regards the length and intricacy of the combinations allowed. In Veda and Brāhmaṇa it is quite rare that more than two stems are compounded together, except that to some much used and familiar compound, as to an integral word, a further element

versified forms of ritual Sūtras, the composition of which appears to have chiefly occurred in the early centuries A.D., and of which we have at least one, the metrical form of the Āçvalāyana-gṛhya-sūtra by the well-known Kumārila Bhaṭṭa, of which the date, viz., about 700 A.D., is beyond doubt.[1]

This singular development of Sanskrit literature has continued down to the present time,[2] and I have myself seen the Indian Penal Code put into Tamil verse by a pettifogging native lawyer. It is not out of the way to notice that there are traces of a similar practice among the lawyers of old Rome, who had a metrical version of the Laws of the Twelve Tables.[3] Thus both in language and in form the Mānava-dharma-çāstra decidedly belongs to a relatively late development of Sanskrit literature.

If we turn to the matter of the text, the same conclusion is necessarily arrived at.

Compared with the older Dharma-sūtras, two important additions are seen at once in the text: first, chapters i. and xii., which form an explanatory philosophical framework to the whole; second, chapter vii., which is an abstract of polity and conduct of life and affairs for kings, such as is

is sometimes added. But the later the period, and especially the more elaborate the style, the more a cumbrous and difficult aggregate of elements, abnegating the advantage of an inflective language, takes the place of the due syntactical union of formed words into sentences. . . . In the oldest language copulative compounds, such as appear later, are quite rare, the class being chiefly represented by dual combinations of the names of divinities and other personages and of personified natural objects" (pp. 424–425, 429). Even in later Vedic works, such as the Atharva Veda, the class of neuter singular collectives is almost wanting (*ib.* p. 430). Now the Mānava-dharma-çastra is distinctly modern in these respects [as compared with the Vedic language].

[1] I was able to fix this date by Tibetan documents. See p. 6 of the preface to my edition of the Sāmavidhāna-Brāhmaṇa. For an account of the versified Āçv.-gṛhya-sūtra, which I discovered in 1871 among the Tanjore MSS., see p. 14 of my Classified Index. The Āçvalāyana-smṛti is a similar versification of the Āçvalāyana-gṛhya-sūtra (do. pp. 124–126).

[2] See examples in my Catalogue, and (pp. 14 and 17) Classified Index. Max Müller (Anc. Sansk. Literature, 2d ed., p. 257 ff.), has discussed the object of the Pariçiṣṭas and such easily intelligible versions of difficult Sūtras.

[3] Schöll, Legis Duodecem Tabularum Reliquiæ, p. 4: "Etiam in metricam formam aliquando xii tabulas fuisse redactas." [A vague

found in the Rāja-dharma[1] section of the Mahābhārata and in the Nīti-çāstras of perhaps later times; such matter is *entirely foreign*[2] to the original Sūtras.

The philosophical additions are very characteristic. The dialogue[3] introducing the substantial matter is quite in the style of the Purāṇas, as is the philosophical system used, which is slightly different from the well-known Sāṅkhya system, as was long ago pointed out by Colebrooke, and distinguished by him as the Purāṇic Sāṅkhya.[4] There cannot be any doubt that this is the system followed in the text, for the commentators have uniformly recognised it to be so.

Now, fortunately, the dates between which this system was in vogue can be satisfactorily established.

The late Professor Goldstücker pointed out that Pāṇini did not know this system;[5] it is, therefore, subsequent to

statement to this effect occurs in a note of Rudorff's to Puchta's Inst., i. p. 112, quoted from Nicolas Antonius, Biblioth. Hisp. vet. vi. 14, 350 (i. p. 518, ed. 1788); but cf. Ihering, Geist des Röm. Rechts, ii., p. 585.]

[1] See [parvan xii. of] the epic. Prof. Weber (Ind. Lit., p. 297) considers that the text is more recent than the latest parts of the Mahābhārata. The Çaiva parts are among the latest, if not the latest. [This is not precisely what Prof. Weber means, for he expressly says "the text as it (now) lies before us." *In this form*, he adds, the text is later than the Mbhā., *unless* the similar *çlokas* found therein *be due to misquotation* (which often happens in Indian literature). Prof. Weber by no means commits himself to the statement that the text of the Mānavadharma-çāstra is absolutely posterior to the Mbhā.]

[2] [This seems to be rather an extreme statement; the duties of the king form, for instance, an integral part of Āpastamba's work, ii. 10, 25.]

[3] Even Medhātithi recognised this as introductory, and that the book really commenced with chap. ii.

[4] Essays, vol. i. p. 249 (ed. Cowell). Goldstücker, "Remains," vol. i. p. 174. Nearly half the existing Purāṇas, including the oldest, follow this system, and are also Vaiṣṇava. The philosophical part of the text has in more recent times been discussed in a most scholarly way by Dr. Johaentgen, Ueber das Gesetzbuch des Manu, Berlin, 1863. [Cf. Weber's review, ii. bd. Ind. Streifen.]

[5] "Pāṇini's Place," p. 151. "Sāṅkhya is a peculiar form. It comes from Saṅkhyā. . . . Its very name shows that it is the counterpart, as it were, of Nyāya. . . . For while the former builds up a system of the universe, the latter dissects it in categories, and 'enters into' its component parts. Yet a grammatical rule would have to explain why the name of the former system is not a *kṛt*-formation. . . . It had not been noticed by Pāṇini. Nor does he teach—as he probably would have done had this philosophy existed in

about 300 B.C., when Pāṇini probably lived,[1] and no trace of it appears in the Mahābhāṣya, about 150 years later, so the earliest date for these chapters cannot be before the first century A.D. Again, it was entirely supplanted and out of fashion by the introduction of the Vedānta (by Gauḍapāda and the great Çaṅkarācārya) in the seventh and eighth centuries A.D.[2] Thus we get the period 1 A.D. to 700 A.D. as that within which the composition of the Mānava-dharma-çāstra must have taken place.

But the text furnishes other information which can be turned to account.

It states expressly[3] that Çiva is the god of the Brahmans, Viṣṇu of the Rājas, etc.; and in accordance with this we find (i. 10) the active Being developed from matter (*prakṛti*) is called Nārāyaṇa, *i.e.*, Viṣṇu. Here again there is a point of contact with the epics[4] and similar compositions.[5] Now all this class of literature has been recognised in India as of a popular character and intended for women and the lower classes, who were not allowed immediate access to the more original sources of information;[6]

his time—that the same word means, as a masculine, a follower of the Sāṅkhya philosophy."

[1] See my Aindra Grammarians, pp. 44. 103; Weber, Ind. Lit., p. 236.

[2] Hiouen-Thsang does not mention these great reformers and their work, which he would certainly have done had they lived before or during his visit to South India in the middle of the seventh century A.D. They must, therefore, as other facts indicate, have lived after 650 A.D.

[3] [Where? i. 10 may have been taken from these same Vaiṣṇava portions of the epic; the same derivation is there often given. The first quotation is a mistake, and the argument will have to rest on i. 10.]

[4] The Çaiva parts of the Mahābhārata, as A. Holtzmann has seen (Arjuna, p. 13), are interpolations, and it will now be evident, if verse 10 of the text be considered, that these are late Brahmanical interpolations, made not earlier than the tenth century A.D., after the Çaiva reaction had begun.

[5] Inscriptions which quote the metrical Smṛti occasionally refer to them as Vaiṣṇava-dharma-çāstra, or quote the verses as by Vyāsa, the author, according to vulgar opinion, of much of this class of literature. These are not quotations of the actual Vyāsa-smṛti, and therefore refer to the mythical Vyāsa. In one case an almost unchanged dharma-sūtra has lost its proper name—Kāṭhaka—and appears as Viṣṇu-smṛti.

[6] *E.g.*, Sāyana's commentary on the Black Yajur Veda (Bibl. Ind., vol. i. p. 2) says that the Bhārata and Purāṇas are intended to teach women and Çūdras their duty, as they may not learn the Vedas. Commentary on the Ṛg-Veda (ed. Müller, i. p. 33).

and the Vaiṣṇavism of the authentic works of this class marks that they were intended for the class of Rājas, on whose behalf only it is likely that Brahmans would in those times have taken the trouble to popularise their learning.

The interpolation of chapter vii. (which treats of matters relating solely to polity and the life of kings), confirms decisively the conclusion that the text was intended for Rājas. A question may perhaps arise here: If the text is intended as a manual for kings, why should so many details which refer solely to Brahmans be inserted? The conclusive answer to this is that kings are bound to see that all do their *dharma* or duty.[1]

That the text has been universally received, though a Black Yajur Veda treatise and not of universal significance, is to be attributed to the fact that this Veda is still the most commonly followed one: in South India about eighty-five per cent. of the Brahman population adheres to it.

The above arguments lead, I think, to the safe conclusions:—

1. The text, as it is,[2] was compiled between about 1 A.D. and 500 A.D.

2. It is a popular work, intended for Rājas and similar persons, and was not originally intended for the use of Brahmans.

It now remains to be seen if it is possible to determine

[1] This duty of a king is fully laid down in the Gautama-dharma, viii. 1; xi. 1–10: *e.g.*, he shall protect the castes in accordance with justice, and those who forsake duty he shall lead back (xi. 9–10). Compare also I. S., x. pp. 29, 60. The Nārada-smṛti is very full on this point; see xi. 1–7; xvii. 5, 12–16; and 15 is: "The Brahman would forsake *his brother Brahman*, the Kṣatriya his brother Kṣatriya, and the stronger would devour the weaker like fish on a spit;" *i.e.*, if the king did not punish evil-doers "of any class" (Jolly). [The same idea is found already in Mānava-dharma-çāstra, vii. 20–24.]

[2] Excluding the verses on which Medhātithi's commentary throws doubt, and which are, therefore, interpolations subsequent to about 1000 A.D. These are, however, of no importance as rega ds the present argument.

still more exactly the date and circumstances of the composition of the text. I think this can be done with a considerable amount of certainty. In the first place, it is sufficiently certain that the greater part of India was in great trouble in the first century A.D., and that it is impossible to suppose that such a work as the text, which could only be done under a powerful prince and in peaceful times, could have been written then. Thus the time is further limited from about 100 A.D. to about 500 A.D.

To what king or dynasty in this period is it likely the text could owe its origin? This also can, I think, be inferred with tolerable certainty.

It is well known that in India the kings adopted the *gotra* of their *purohita* or domestic priests.[1] Now it is quite certain that the text is called Mānava, not from a mythical Manu, as stated in the first chapter,[2] but that it is so called from the Mānavas, a Brahman *gotra* and division of the followers of the Black Yajur Veda.[3] Now, in the period in question there arose a great and powerful dynasty, which ruled over the Deccan and Gujarat, and at times over nearly all India, and which (the inscriptions show) claimed to be Mānavyas[4]—I mean the Cālukyas.

[1] Authorities for this are I. S., ix. p. 325; x. p. 83.

[2] This mythical synonym, Manu, occurs in the Vedic literature as the seer of hymns (R. V. viii. 27), and in the legend of the deluge in the Çatapatha Brāhmaṇa (I. S. i. 1–10), translated by Professor A. Weber (Indische Streifen, i. p. 9 ff), and it also occurs in the Matsyapurāṇa. There are other Vedic allusions (*vide* above, p. xvii.) Goldstücker was clear that the name "belongs, properly speaking, to ancient Hindu mythology, and it was connected with the renowned law-book in order to impart to the latter the sanctity on which its authority rests" (Remains, i. p. 107).

[3] The Mānavas as a Çākhā formed (as already said) one of the six subdivisions of the Maitrāyaṇīyas, and were probably a Sūtra division. The Maitrāyaṇīya (Vedic) Saṁhitā is still in existence, and was discovered by the late Dr. M. Haug. See his Ueber das Wesen und den Werth des Wedischen Accents, p. 27 ff. An edition by L. v. Schroeder is in progress.

[4] The epithet "*Mānavyānām . . . Cālukyānām*" occurs in several inscriptions, *e.g.*, one of c. 600 A.D. (I. A., ix. p. 124). So down to the eleventh century A.D. Of these, there are some which are Vaiṣṇava as far as the kings are concerned, and confer gifts on Çaiva Brahmans, a remarkable proof that the verse . . . in the text represented a fact

Three great branches of this family are known: that which ruled in Gujarat and the west; that of the Deccan, or the central branch, which ruled at Kalyāṇapurī in the Deccan;[1] that which ruled on the Telugu sea-coast, and was from the Deccan. The last arose in the beginning of the seventh century, and is therefore too late. The choice, accordingly, must rest between the western and central branches.

Now the inscriptions show that these branches became important about the sixth century A.D.,[2] and they also appear to show that some of these kings were Jains.[3] This is no difficulty, for the Jains and Vaiṣṇavas were always closely connected in belief and worship, and are so still;[4] but a Hindu king would be a more probable patron of such a work as the text, and such an one is not far to find.

The founder of the dynasty is one Pulakeçī or Polakeçī, according to the inscriptions, and he must have flourished about 500 A.D.

Is it possible to trace anything about the author? The text, I think, suggests that he was a North Indian, and probably a Punjab Brahman. In verse 20 of the second Lecture a Brahman from that part is declared to be the most proper and best teacher, and presumably the author wrote this to recommend himself. He was therefore most likely one of the learned Brahmans (*e.g.*, Gauḍapāda, and later Bilhaṇa) who came down from the north and helped

then in existence. It is hardly necessary to remark here that Mānavya is a patronymic from Manu (Pāṇini iv. 1, 105). It is, however, noteworthy that the selection of Mānavya in preference to Mānava points to the fact that the Mānavas had at the time of the composition of the text already arrived at the legend connecting themselves with the later Manu, as given in the first chapter of the text.

[1] This was first discovered by Sir Walter Elliot. For the present information regarding it, which is chiefly due to Mr. J. E. Fleet, see his articles in the Indian Antiquary and my South Indian Palæography (2d ed.), p. 18 ff. Dr. Bühler has discussed the inscriptions of the Western branch.

[2] *Loc. cit.*, and Fleet, The Dynasties of the Kanarese Districts, p. 18 ff.

[3] See the quotations in p. 134 of A. Barth, The Religions of India.

[4] Cf. Colebrooke, Essays, vol. ii.

to civilise the south. If verses 123 and 126 of Lecture ii. be considered, it is evident that he then lived in a country where little was known of Sanskrit; and this also points to a place in the Deccan [1] as the locality where the work was composed.

It thus appears that the text belongs to an outgrowth of the old Brahmanical literature, which was intended for the benefit of the kings, where the Brahmanical civilisation had begun to extend itself over the south of India,[2] and to pursue the giant's course which rendered it the great fact in Eastern history, and when, but for untoward circumstances, it would probably have eventually welded the different races and dynasties of the vast continent of India into a homogeneous whole. It also appears highly certain that it was composed about 500 A.D., under the Cālukya sovereign Pulakeçī at Kalyāṇapurī, and that to the subsequent great extent and power of the west Cālukya dynasty it chiefly owes the wide and great

[1] It must be remarked that Kumārila Bhaṭṭa, who lived about the time at which I put the composition of the text, considered Tamil and Telugu to be Mleccha languages (see my paper in I. A., i. p. 310); and this would account for the rule in vers. 123 and 126 of Lecture ii. of the text, for to accost in these languages would thus be indecent. [K. lived, according to Dr. Burnell (*loc. cit.*), two hundred years (700 A.D.) after this date.]

[2] An important distinction is to be made between the original literature of the Brahmans, written for themselves in their North Indian home, and the literature which arose on their settling in South India and Malaya, where a modified Brahman civilisation arose, with many essential differences as compared with their source, and which gave rise to an enormous secondary Sanskrit literature, of which, *e.g.*, my Classified Index will afford some notion. It is difficult to carry back these settlements farther than the third century A.D., and the mention of Āpastambīya Brahmans in the inscriptions is later still. I am, then, unable to agree with Dr. Bühler in his theory (Preface to Āpastamba's translation) that the Āpastamba Sūtras could have been composed in the Āndhra (? Telugu) country; for they must, though late among the Black Yajur Veda Sūtras, have been composed at least B.C., and the wide use of the book both in North and South India can only be explained by its being in existence already in the North before Brahman emigration began, and its importation into the South by a majority of the emigrants. As regards the form Āpastambha (Ind. Ant. v. 135; ix. 103), I can only view it as an instance of the Dravidian inability to distinguish between aspirated and unaspirated letters; or perhaps here it may have been caused by a false etymology.

repute it has held, and still holds, in the continent of India.[1]

At the time it was composed, colonies of Indian emigrants were occupying Burmah[2] and the Malay islands, and continued to settle there for several centuries. They took with them the Mānava-dharma-çāstra, which exists in a loose Burmese paraphrase[3] and in Sanskrit (or Kavi) in the island of Bali.[4]

Thus much being determined, it is now possible to discuss the text and its nearer relations to other parts of the Sanskrit literature, as well as to consider it critically, and its use and influence in the later stages of Sanskrit jurisprudence, including the Indian views in respect of its authority.

To make a right use of the Mānava-dharma-çāstra, the consideration of these details is obviously requisite; but it has been used by the mere English lawyer for nearly a century in a random way, without the slightest regard to these points.

(*a.*) The first point to be considered is the transmission of the text down to the present time.

The MSS. of the texts now existing are written in a multitude of different characters, but when the book was

[1] Till the West Cālukyas were defeated by the Coḷas (in the eleventh century A.D), they were almost the masters of India. About the eleventh century our Mānava-dharma-çāstra was well known, not only to the lawyers, but also to writers on other branches of Sanskrit literature in very different parts of India, *e.g.*, to Kṣira-Svāmin (a North Indian commentator on the Amarakoṣa), who quotes it together with Yājñavalkya and Nārada, and to Vardhamāna (a Gujarat grammarian) in the beginning of the twelfth century.

[2] Buddhaghoṣa's mission was about 430 A.D.

[3] It has been published in Burmese, and translated into English by Richardson. It bears about the same relation to the text as the Tamil and vernacular Rāmāyaṇas do to the Sanskrit, *i.e.*, it is not, properly speaking, a translation at all. [Since the "Menu Kyay" (1847), we have (1882-83) other works of the same sort translated by Forchhammer, Wonnana Dhammathat, etc.]

[4] Friederich, "Voorloopig Verslag," in the Transactions of the Batavian Society (xxii.); translated into English by Logan in his Journal of the Indian Archipelago (1849); and again in the J. R. A. S. (N.S., vols. ix. and x.), and into German in Professor Weber's Ind. Stud. (vol. ii. pp. 124-149). [It is doubtful if our Mānava-çastra was known in the island of Bali.]

composed these did not exist, and it was beyond doubt written in a variety of the "Cave character."[1]

This character was then in use over nearly all Brahmanised India, so the text would at once be widely disseminated, and to this fact must be attributed the trivial *varietas lectionis* between the Bengāli, *e.g.*, and South Indian MSS.[2] But when our oldest authority for the text, the commentator Medhātithi, wrote, about 1000 A.D., this state of things was already much altered; the Nāgarī character was fully developed in North India, and in the South what became the Telugu and the Grantha characters were already perfectly distinct. Medhātithi probably used what I have termed elsewhere[3] the Cālukya character, which was the direct predecessor of the modern Telugu.[4] But the difference between this and the Cave character is not of a nature to allow of much alteration in the text, and the small *var. lec.* mentioned by Medhātithi[5] are certainly to be attributed to the errors of copyists rather than to an alteration of the text by mistakes made in reading one letter for another. Medhātithi's text also shows that there are some interpolations,[6] but these are generally of an explanatory nature, and are *prima facie* open to suspicion, though Kullūka and the later commentators accept them. There is then no doubt that the *textus receptus*, viz., that of Kullūka Bhaṭṭa, as adopted in India and by European scholars, is very near on the whole to the original text.

A few other slight interpolations, before the time of Medhātithi, may be, perhaps, suspected, but nothing of

[1] See my South Indian Palæography, 2d ed., p. 13 ff.

[2] See the account of an old Bengāli MS. in "Notices," vol. iii. p. 117 ff. The *v. l.* given is always, at first sight, preferable to the text of Kullūka; but it must be noticed that of the *v. l.* as given, slightly less than half are only supported by Medhātithi, and that the rest are evidently arbitrary emendations.

[3] Elements of South Indian Palæography, 2d ed. p. 17 ff.

[4] See below (p. xli) for reasons for believing that Medhātithi lived in the Deccan.

[5] So far as my MS. will allow, I have noticed the *v. l.* in my notes to the translation.

[6] I have carefully marked these in the notes, so far as the poor MS. of Medhātithi accessible to me goes.

real importance.[1] With this view of the history of the text I have unhesitatingly adopted the recension of Kullūka, marking the verses which Medhātithi does not support; and of the only two attempts at critical editions, those by Sir G. C. Haughton[2] and Loiseleur Deslongchamps, I have used the first.

(*b.*) As has already been pointed out, the text belongs to the second class of Sanskrit law-books: that is to say, to the books which were intended to popularise the earlier Dharma-çāstras, and for practical use in tribunals. The number of these, including the spurious compilations foisted into this rank, is very considerable.[3] The composition of these works probably extended to about 900 A.D., and some show most decided evidence of the Vedānta[4]

[1] *E.g.*, the first four verses of ch. i., as, according to Nārada-smṛti (Introd., § 4, p. 2, of Jolly's translation), the original form of the text began with our fifth verse. Medhātithi, however, fully accepts these four *çlokas*. As regards the vv. ix. 64-68, which Dr. Jolly (p. xiii.) rightly explains as an interpolation, see the note in that place. According to the questionable authority of the introduction to Nārada, the text has been abridged from far more extensive compositions in 100,000, 12,000, and 4000 verses. It is possible that there is a grain of truth here, and that the text was not brought at once into its present form, but the story is purely mythical, and a specimen of Brahmanical systematising. Not only is the existence of such enormous works on such subjects almost impossible to conceive, but there is also not a jot of evidence to support the assertion: cf. Jolly's remarks, pp. xi.-xii.

[2] The memory of this scholar, who helped to a considerable extent the study of Sanskrit law, should not be so much forgotten as it is. He was born in Ireland in 1789, and entered in 1809 the East India Company's Bengal army, and was stationed at Rangpūr. He got permission to study in the civilians' college at Calcutta, and in 1813 finished his course with great success. In 1815 his health compelled him to leave India, and in 1817 he was appointed Professor of Sanskrit and Bengali at the Haileybury College. Here he published a Bengali Grammar and his edition of Manu (1825). In 1825 his weak health forced him to resign his appointment, and he went to London, where he printed his Sanskrit-Bengali-English Dictionary (1833). In 1839 he settled in Paris, and his weak eyesight not allowing him to continue his Oriental studies, he turned his attention to electricity and physics, but could publish little. He died at St. Cloud on the 28th August 1849. (Mohl, "Rapport," 1850, where a full list of his publications is to be found in a note.)

[3] See the list by Professor Stenzler in Ind. Stud., i. p. 232 ff., and in West and Bühler's Digest, i. p. xiii. ff.

[4] As I first pointed out in 1868 (Dāyavibhāga, pref., p. ix.) The Dharma-smṛtis are most clear in this way. One, Hārīta-smṛti (Classified Index, p. 128), cannot be earlier than 1200 A.D., as it represents a late form of Vaiṣṇavism.

doctrines, which came into vogue about the eighth century A.D. But of the more important works of this class, the Mānava-dharma-çāstra is decidedly the earliest[1] and most important; the Yājñavalkya-smṛti comes next,[2] and the Nārada-smṛti is later than that.[3] These books all embody, here and there, verses which are certainly much older, but these do not affect the actual dates when these books assumed their present actual forms. Some of these verses are probably popular proverbs or sayings of a great age.[4]

Another point in these texts is that all have a number of verses verbally or substantially in common. Manu (as we have it) contains some 2685 verses; the Yājñavalkya-smṛti, out of 1009 verses, has more than half the same or like these, and the Nārada-smṛti, out of 859[5] verses, has 37; Manu also occurs in the Viṣṇu and other Smṛtis. Copying is in this case the most likely cause, but that will not explain the same fact as it occurs in the Brāhmaṇas, which also have many passages in common.[6]

Thus the only possible explanation seems to be that the Brāhmaṇas have been compiled from old material, probably in a different form to what it has now assumed. But Professor Whitney thinks that the bearing of this fact is not determined.[7] In considering the nature of this fact as displayed in the law-books and epics, etc., the

[1] Excluding, of course, such unmodified Dharma-sūtras as the real Viṣṇu-smṛti, which cannot be said to belong to this class.

[2] See p. ix. of Prof. Stenzler's preface to his edition; also Jolly's Nārada, p. xvii.

[3] See Prof. Jolly's remarks in the preface to his translation (pp. xv.–xix.): "It becomes, indeed, apparent from a more general survey of the latter code (Yājñavalkya) that it must be younger than Manu's, but earlier than Nārada's" (p. xvii.)

[4] *E.g.*, the verses ii. 114 and 144, which are found in the Saṁhitopaniṣad-Brāhmaṇa (pp. 29, 30 of my edition), and the Nirukta (ii. 4). They also occur in the Viṣṇu and Vasiṣṭha-Smṛtis.

[5] I take these from Stenzler's and Jolly's respective works.

[6] *E.g.*, the Aitareya and Gopatha Brāhmaṇas; so also the Jaiminīya (Talavakāra) and Çatapatha.

[7] Sanskrit Grammar, p. xvi. "To a certain extent there is among them (the Brāhmanas) the possession of a common material; a fact the bearings of which are not yet fully understood."

existence of the same state of things in the Brāhmaṇas must not be overlooked: though similar, the explanation is probably different. The law-books have also verses in common with the Mahābhārata.

(*c.*) The most superficial examination of the text proves at once that the Vedic literature in its entirety, even down to a late Sūtra, as well as later developments, was known to the compiler.[1] It repeatedly refers to previous legislators, tradition, and to the "Wise,"[2] and is, therefore, fully entitled to the epithet *smārta* or "traditional," which it claims. To Indian theories this fact offers no difficulty, but to the critical student it is significant in a totally different manner. The Indian theory is that Çruti, or revelation eternally existing,[3] and Smṛti, or tradition based on Çruti, are the authoritative sources of the conduct of life in all matters.[4] Though there may be no actual authority in the Çruti for a practice declared by the Smṛti, it is strangely assumed that such practice is based on a Çruti not actually existing among mortals.[5] The important bearing of this belief (which is taught by the Mīmāṁsā system of exegesis of the Vedic literature) has not been hitherto noticed in regard to its effect on Sanskrit law. Here is to be found the possibility of development and of personal influence, to an almost un-

[1] *E.g.*, reference to Atri, iii. 16; Atharva, xi. 33; Āraṇyaka, iv. 123; Asacchāstra, xi. 65; Itihāsa, iii. 232; Upanishads, vi. 29, xi. 262 (*rahasya*); Ṛg-Veda, i. 23, 93, ii. 77, iii. 145, iv. 123–124, xi. 261, 264, xii. 112; Gautama, iii. 16; Tarka, xii. 111; Taittirya Āraṇyaka (quoted), ii. 181; Dharma-çāstra, ii. 10, iii. 232, viii. 3, xi. 60, xii. 106, 109, 111 (*Dharma-pāṭhaka*); Nirukta, xii. 111; Nyāya (?), xii. 111; Purāṇa, iii. 232; Bhṛgu, iii. 16; Manu ii. 7, iii. 35, 150, 222, iv. 41, 103, v. 131, vi. 54; Yajur Veda, i. 23, iii. 145, iv. 123–124, vi. 21, 38, ix. 18, xi. 261–264, xii. 112; Yoga, vi. 65; Vasiṣṭha, viii 140; Veda-çāstra, iv. 260, xii. 99–102, 106; Veda-saṁhitā xi. 77, 258, 262; Vaikhānasa, vi. 21; Çāstra, ii. 16, 70; Ṣaḍaṅga, ii. 105, 109, 111, iii. 185, iv. 19, 98; Sāmaveda, i. 23, iii. 145, 185, 232, iv. 123–124, xi. 262.

[2] *E.g.*, ii. 12, 14, 32, 59, 89, 171; iii. 14, 26, 53, 284; iv. 18, 55, 178; vi. 89.

[3] For a full account of the Indian ideas on this subject see Muir's Sanskrit Texts, vol. iii. p. 1 ff.

[4] See Gautama Sūtra, i. 1–3; Āp. Sūtra, i. 1, 1, 2; Text. ii. 6; Yāj. i. 1.

[5] So here (ii. 7), all that Manu directed is said to be based on the Veda.

limited extent, in what would otherwise have been the most hopelessly stereotyped and rigid system ever seen. But it must be noticed that even this could be but for a short time, *i.e.*, during the final consolidation of the Vedic religion and system. The Mīmāṁsā and other systems once in full swing, matters became again hopeless, and all that was possible was to rearrange old materials, to which additions then became impossible. All that now remained feasible was to harmonise these materials by means of one of the philosophic systems.[1] This was done by the Nibandhas or Digests, and from difference of method a difference of result followed in some cases; but there was no liberty of interpreting, and the adherence to the chosen system was most rigid; all Indian ingenuity could do was but little, and (except in analysis and precision) practically unimportant.[2] The authors of the Digests were, in fact, in precisely the same position as their European contemporaries, the schoolmen. The Indian system was thus originally, and throughout its course, theocratic. English lawyers, even with the Pentateuch[3] before their eyes, have as yet failed to see that law is in India not differentiated from what is elsewhere matter of religion.[4] The Mānava-dharma-çāstra is then essentially a religious book, and not, as in England and most of Europe, a profane treatise on mere law. The ordeals[5] mentioned are all, *e.g.*, religious ceremonies.

[1] In Bengal Jīmūtavāhana used the Nyāya; in the Deccan and South India, Medhātithi and Vijñāneçvara and his imitators used the Mīmāṁsā. Hence the different views as regards the time when a right to an interest in the family property arises; the former holding that it arises on birth, the latter on conception.

[2] In effect, it was only on doubtful or disputed points that anything could be done. Such are, *e.g.*, the number of *vyavahārapadas* or topics of law; *niyoga*, or a brother taking a deceased brother's wife; the nature of *strīdhana*, etc.

[3] The late S. Monk's comparison between the Pentateuch and Mānava-dharma-çāstra is still of interest.

[4] It is owing to the peculiar nature of theocratic civilisations that no names of the founders and promoters of these systems have been preserved. It was the work of the priestly caste rather than of individuals, and education consisted in imitation rather than in instruction.

[5] The use of torture to extort evidence or confessions is still com-

(*d.*) A brief survey of the development that can actually be traced will perhaps not be useless here.

Sanskrit literature has preserved traces of an early stage of development of law, viz., between the Brāhmaṇa and Sūtra periods. This unfortunately only refers to criminal law, not to civil law. In the Sāmavidhāna Brāhmaṇa[1] is a considerable list of crimes there treated as to be expiated by religious ceremonies. In the Sūtras we find the same crimes punished by temporal penalties. It is thus obvious that what afterwards became crimes against the state were at first merely a matter of concern to the individual and his family or tribe.[2]

There is also ample evidence to prove that criminal law was always but little administered, and that much was left to local usage. Thus a common punishment of adulterous wives in India has always been to cut off their noses. The Pañca-tantra mentions it,[3] and so do the old travellers of the sixteenth century, but this is not mentioned in the law-books. It is evident that these punishments were left to be carried out by the heads of castes and similar authorities in accordance with their own customs.

There is also a great development traceable in the different Smṛtis as regards, *e.g.*, the use of ordeals, and in definition and systematisation of crimes.

It is remarkable that the only account we have of a trial in ancient India is that of a criminal trial in the early drama, the Mṛcchakaṭikā,[4] and (much earlier) in the fourth century B.C. little but criminal law was administered by the sovereign, and civil suits seem hardly to have been known.[5]

mon in India, but if such cases are examined a little closely, it will always, I think, appear that they are cases of the use of the old ordeals. When, as is often the case, such practices are resorted to by the police, it is of course a different matter.

[1] See p. xiii. ff. of the preface to vol. i. of my edition.

[2] The earliest trace of law that we find in India is of criminal law. In the Ṛg-Veda times thieves were seized and beaten and tied to posts. H. Zimmer, "Altindisches Leben" (1879), p. 181 ff.

[3] i. 4.

[4] See Acts ix. and x.

[5] Megasthenes, Fr. xxvii. (Schwanbeck). The cases tried seem to have

(*e.*) Books on the Dharma-çāstra were used in the tribunals,[1] and these must have been such as our text; for about 320 B.C. the Greeks found that the Indians had no written laws,[2] but some Smṛtis mention such books. It must, however, be once more clearly and distinctly asserted that these books were merely consulted[3] in order to ascertain the law as it was divinely fixed from all time. They were not codes, nor were they promulgated by the authority of any sovereign; indeed, such a supposition is impossible to any one who has some acquaintance with Indian ideas.[4] The king was to ascertain the law, and to aid him he had Brahman assessors.[5] Now, it is certain, that, at least in later times, there were men to educate men for this office. Inscriptions show that there were provisions made for the study of the Dharma-çāstra in the Brahman settlements, and a relic of the employment of such assessors was to be seen within twenty years ago in the Sudder pandits. That the practice actually coincided with the rules of the Dharma-çāstra all over India is evident, *e.g.*, in the case of deeds of gifts, etc.[6]

One remarkable fact in the history of Indian law is the early occurrence of what is now generally termed "con-

been chiefly of theft, violent assault, and false statement, and mutilation or death the chief punishments.

[1] Text, viii. 3 (not necessarily written); Nārada (ed. Jolly), i. 16. Here there can be no doubt that a written book is intended.

[2] Megasthenes, Fr. xxvii.

[3] I first drew attention to this fact in the preface to my Dāyavibhāga (1868); cf. Nārada Smṛti, i. 31 ff.

[4] *E.g.*, Gautama, xi. 23–24: "Reasoning is a means for arriving at the truth; coming to a decision through that, he shall decide properly." The final decision was with learned Brāhmans (ib. 25).

[5] Mānava-dharma-çāstra, viii. 1; Yāj. ii. 2; Nārada, i. 16. This is also hinted at in the still earlier Sūtras, *e.g.*, Āpast. ii. 11, 29, 5; Gautama, xi. 25.

[6] This is apparent from the way in which such deeds are drawn up, as I have shown in my South Indian Palæography (2d ed., p. 119). Bernier's account of the schools at Benares, and Adams' and (later still) Professor Cowell's description of the Nuddea *tols* (J. As. Soc. Beng.) exactly illustrate this. A few such schools still exist at Benares, though in much diminished numbers. See Sherring's Benares, pp. 345–346.

flict of laws." This is to be first traced in the Dharma-sūtra, or more than two thousand years ago. In the Dharma-çāstra principles are laid down for the decision of such questions, but they have been entirely neglected by the English lawyers, as well as the rules about local laws and customs.[1] The recognition of local laws is very early, and occurs in full already in the Dharma-sūtras.[2]

(*f.*) As regards the use of such books there is something to be said. The king, as chief judge, had to ascertain the law from the Vedas, etc., and the numerous Dharma-sūtras; and again, with reference to local laws, he had to gather it from adequate evidence of experts.[3]

Now the sacred texts he had to refer to were numerous and more or less conflicting; and the local laws and customs were also numerous and varying, but recognised. The authority of the inferior castes to make their own laws was early admitted.[4] Neither were the Sanskrit Brahman laws forced on them, nor were their own customs ignored, as is now the case.[5]

But it is only in the Dharma-çāstra that the difficulties hence arising are treated in a rudimentary manner, which

[1] The existence of these rules was first brought to the notice of the legal world in J. H. Nelson's "View" (1877). See i. 118 of the text for a very explicit enumeration of what was recognised in this way in the Smṛtis.

[2] Baudhāyana, [i. 1. 2. 1–7]; Āpast. ii. 6. 15. 1; Gautama, xi. 20–21. Cf. chapter i. v. 118, and viii. 3 of the text, [although it is a disputed point as to the extent of recognition to be shown. Cf. Baudh. ib. 7.]

[3] In the fourth century B.C. we find the king much occupied in judicial functions, but there were no written laws to refer to. He went forth from his palace to act in this capacity (Megasth., Fr. xxvii., ed. Schwanbeck). The official recognition of books to consult certainly is not earlier than the early centuries A.D.

[4] Gautama, xi. 21. "Cultivators, traders, herdsmen, money-lenders, and artisans (have authority to lay down rules for their respective classes" (Bühler).

[5] Goldstücker, "On the Deficiencies," etc., 1870 (reprinted in his "Remains," p. 145 ff.), pointed out the misuse and misinterpretation of the Indian Sanskrit law-books by the superior courts; and other similar errors have been fully explored by Nelson in his "View."

becomes fully developed in the Nibandhas or Digests. In the Smṛti-Candrikā (about 1200 A.D.), and the Mādhavīya (fourteenth century), *e.g.*, we find chapters on *Deçadharma* or local laws. These display a marked development as compared with the Smṛtis. The earliest recognition of local laws, as already mentioned, is in the Dharma-sūtras, but this refers rather to the differences of the Brahmanical *çākhās* than to local laws proper; but Baudhāyana, beyond doubt, refers to the last,[1] and the Smṛtis do not go much farther than he does. In the Digests we find a provision and limitation unknown to the earlier books, and which is unquestionably due to the progress of Brahmanical civilisation in the South of India. Here we find also almost the only trace of a desire to make Sanskrit law paramount, and to exclude all in local customs inconsistent with it. The *siddhānta* or conclusion at which Devaṇṇa, the author of the Smṛti-Candrikā, and Mādhava-Sāyaṇa, the author of the Mādhavīya, arrive is, that local laws, to be recognised by lawyers, must not be inconsistent with Sanskrit (or Brahmanical) law.[2] But this principle has never, in reality, obtained much influence. Even among South Indian Brahmans numberless usual practices are opposed to the Sanskrit law; and in Malabar, Cochin, and Travancore this is so much the case, that a small manual called the Anācāranirṇaya has been composed to enumerate them,[3] and these are now enforced by the courts, so far as they come within their cognisance. This

[1] [A blank; but probably the passage above, Baudh. i. 1. 2. 1–7, is referred to.]

[2] [A blank where a note was to be, followed by these words :—] . . . Here at last we find a decided step made, and Indian social existence has at last progressed from the family or tribal state to the civic form in which a conception of the state is evident. Further progress would, no doubt, have been made, but for historical events, on which it would be out of place to enlarge here.

[3] This tract is attributed to Çaṅkara, of course, but it cannot be more than a few centuries old. It is, however, an unquestionably respectable authority for the peculiar customs of Malabar, and (somehow) has never been noticed by the high court as such. On the other hand, a ridiculous forgery of this century, which pretends to do the same for Canara, is taken for what it pretends

is, no doubt, a retrograde step, and it is hard to see how tribes now addicted to polyandry and similar customs will ever be able to free themselves, though an inclination to do so has already begun to display itself in a few cases, and attempts are constantly being made to evade its consequence. But the English tribunals are sadly careless in the matter of local customs, and nothing like an attempt has yet been made (except Steele's work) to observe and record such facts. The Portuguese, however, already in the sixteenth century[1] did this well, and the Dutch and French have also taken the same course.

The above will suffice to show how much the Mānava-dharma-çāstra has been misunderstood and misused by the English lawyers.

On perusing the text and similar works, including the Dharma-sūtras, carefully, an impression of unreality arises which casts serious doubts on the reality of these works. We meet with so much that is inhuman,[2] and such a hideous and cynical contempt for the human body, that we are tempted to believe that these books are the insane ideal of crazy fanatics or the foolish reveries of besotted ascetics. But there is too much external evidence[3] that

to be, and is quoted by judges with a serious face! (Madras High Court Reports.) We shall soon see "Jack the Giant Killer" received as an authority on the law of homicide.

[1] M. J. C. Loureiro's "Memorias dos estabelicimentos Portuguezes a Leste do Cabo da Boa Esperança," Lisbon, 1855, contains a Goa "customary" of 1526. F. Nery Xavier has (lately) published others. The Dutch at the beginning of the eighteenth century had the customs of the Jaffna country drawn up. The French courts nearly follow the precepts of the Sanskrit law as regards the customs of the different castes, and the evidence to prove them.

[2] *E.g.*, Āpast., i. 9. 25. 12. . . . "Such a sinner may tear from his body and make the priest offer as a burnt-offering his hair, skin, flesh, and the rest, and then throw himself into the fire" (Bühler). Cf. Yājn. iii. 247. Prof. Bühler considers that this "is not altogether a mere theory of Āpastamba" (p. 83, note). See especially ch. xi. of the text; Vasiṣṭha xx.; Āpast. i. 9, 24 to 25; Gautama xxii. and xxiii.

[3] Compare the suicide by fire of Καλανος, which astonished the Greeks of Alexander's army (Meg. Fr. x. from Strabo xv. 1); Bardesanes (ed. Hilgenfeld). The practice of *satī* (suttee) was very early (Barth., Religions of India, p. 59 ff.) Several remarkable instances of self-torture

such enormities were commonly done to allow us to accept this easy explanation.

The real explanation may be readily seen by a consideration of the frequency of hysteria and analogous disorders among the natives of the present day. Hardly a day passes in even small villages without a case of this kind, which passes among the people as diabolical possession.[1] In some parts men are habitually reduced to this state artificially in order to deliver oracles.[2] This, the true and satisfactory explanation of the sorcery and witchcraft of the Middle Ages, is, no doubt, the true explanation here also. The partial or total anæsthesia, a characteristic of hysteria, which was known in the Middle Ages as the "Devil's mark," is also adequate to account for the insensibility to pain which is implied.[3]

There is, however, a striking difference in one respect between India and other countries. Whereas in other countries such hideous displays of human weakness have been dreaded, and even put down with frightful cruelty, in India they have been encouraged, and even made a part

and insensibility to pain are mentioned by the early Arab travellers, edited and translated by the late Abbé Reinaud (Voyages Arabes). In modern times several well-observed cases occur. As. Res. v. contains a case of a man who lay on a couch covered with iron spikes! The habits of the Aghorapanthas and other Yogins are well known. Compare also the swinging by hooks, etc., and the walking over fire, still practised in some parts. The poems (*e.g.*, the bed of arrows on which Bhīṣma lay, in the Mahābhārata, and the stories about ascetics in the Purāṇas, etc.) all display a fondness for such repulsive scenes. The carvings on temples, etc., also display the same tendency, and excited the horror of the Portuguese Camões Lusiadas, vii. 47 ("as abominaveis esculpturas"). See also Trans. R. A. S. for a disgusting case of a Yogin who ate a whole sheep raw!

[1] Hysteria of this kind was known in the Vedic times; compare the girl *gandharva-gṛhītā* of the Ait. Br.

[2] In the Bhūta worship of South Canara. [After this sentence occurs the remark: "Another widespread indication of it is the prevalent mendacity;" but, as Dr. B. cannot have meant this to be antecedent to "this . . . explanation . . . of sorcery," it appears to have slipped in by mistake.]

[3] The fact that primitive and little developed races display great physical insensibility is now fully recognised, and should not be forgotten here.

of religious worship. The way of producing them has been reduced to an art in the Yoga and Tantric systems, and a good Hindu is surrounded by provocations of these melancholy diseases.

If anywhere, we must find a Brahman ideal in the endless and stringent rules which would take up every moment of an Indian's life in frivolous ceremonies, and which can never have been carried out even in India, and are now entirely obsolete.

As the text is, it is one of a large class of works[1] of much the same character, to which a few late forgeries have been added for sectarian purposes. But many of these are mere fragments,[2] and others can be shown to be abridgments which have supplanted older and more copious texts.[3] It is on these that the authors of the Digests have chiefly based their works, and the Mānava-dharma-çāstra takes a prominent place among these; it has not, however, like the text of Yājñavalkya in Vijñāne-çvara's hands, become the foundation of a Digest.

The history of the text in recent times is tolerably complete. The earliest existing commentary that we have is the Manubhāṣya by Medhātithi, the son of Vīra-svāmin. His date, about 1000 A.D., can be safely inferred from the following circumstances. He is quoted already by Vijñāneçvara of about 1200,[4] and it is not, therefore,

[1] Upwards of fifty are now enumerated. See Yājñ. i. 4, 5, where twenty are mentioned. This is probably the oldest list. Devaṇṇa, the author of the Smṛticandrikā, accepts thirty-six Smṛtis on the authority of Paiṭhīnasi, and sixteen Upa-smṛtis on the authority of Aṅgiras. See p. 133 of my "Classified Index." Compare the lists by Europeans in I. S., i. p. 232 ff. (by Stenzler); in West and Bühler's Digest, i. p. xiii. ff.; Stokes, Hindu "Law-book," p. 5, note, which collects the results of the Indian lists.

[2] Such are Laghu Ātreya-smṛti, Dakṣa, Devala, Pulastya, Budha, Bṛhaspati, the two Yamas, Vyāsas, etc.

[3] Dr. Führer has, *e.g.*, restored in an able manner part of the real Bṛhaspati-smṛti (Darstellung der Lehre von den Schriften, etc., 1879). The work that now passes under this name (see Smṛti-saṅgraha, Calcutta, 1876, pp. 644–651; Tanjore Cat., p. 125) is quite a modern and wretched substitute.

[4] As proved by Bühler. The passage in the Mitākṣarā referring to

too much to allow 200 years before this date. But he was not the earliest commentator, and in doubtful passages he often quotes the explanations of others.[1] He was probably a native of the Deccan,[2] and we often find such names as his father's in the Cālukya inscriptions. His reputation has always been enormous, and he often is mentioned as "Asahāya" or the "Peerless."[3] He has had a number of successors, who have generally adopted his words, and who seldom differ in interpretation from him. Unfortunately manuscripts of his work are rare, and that accessible to me is not good.[4] Modern scholars will find his work often diffuse, tedious, and obscure, but its practical use is considerable, as he occasionally notices a *v. l.*, and his commentary enables us to trace subsequent interpolations.[5] He followed the Mīmaṁsā system in his explanations.[6]

His next follower was Govindarāja, whose work I have been able to examine cursorily in a MS. discovered by Professor Bühler, and belonging to the Bombay Government. It is quite evident that Govindarāja established the *textus receptus* as adopted by Kullūka, and found everywhere in India, and that he was rival to Medhātithi.

Medhātithi is iii. 24. Medhātithi is also quoted by Mādhava-Sāyaṇa in his Parāçara-smṛti-vyākhyā (fourteenth century), and by the Smṛti-kaumudī (fifteenth century), etc.

[1] iii. 15, 5; vii. 139 (*anye tu*); 255 (*anye tu vyācakṣate*); 271, 274; iv. 19 (*ye tu vyācakṣate . . . tadayuktam*). [No predecessor is found mentioned by name (viii. 46, another?). Opposed we often find *pūrve, eke,* and *pare* (*apare*), *anye*, etc., and the expression quoted, *ayuktam*, followed by Med.'s view, occurs very often. He also touches on the relative position of the verses and notes arrangements of the same from which he differs. He quotes often Gautama, ii. 60; iv. 9; v. 141 (*eke*); Vasiṣṭha, Baudhāyana, Gautama, iv. 136; the Mahābhārata, Mahābhāṣya, Pāṇini (v. 111 Sūtrakārī), and many later Smṛtikārāḥ.]

[2] See his explanation of *kutapa* (= a blanket) in his comment on iii. 234. *Kutapaḥ . . . udicyeṣu kambala iti prasiddhaḥ. Udicya* can here only mean "Northerner," and the word is said to mean a Nepal blanket.

[3] Varadarāja calls him by this epithet (see my "Vyavahāra Nirṇaya," p. 30).

[4] It is from the Colebrooke collection in the I. O. Library. [Cf. also Preface, p. xii.]

[5] He often quotes other Smṛtis, and evidently had a large acquaintance with Sanskrit literature.

[6] Compare his Commentary on iv. 19.

He seems to have differed much from Medhātithi, and Kullūka occasionally quotes contrary opinions of the two. His name points to about the twelfth century at the earliest.

After him came a commentary by the famous Mādhava-Sāyaṇa, who lived in the fourteenth century.[1] This work appears to be in existence, but I have not been able to find it or trace it in any library. I have met one pandit who told me he possessed it, but I never could get a sight of it.

After him came Kullūka Bhaṭṭa, whose brief commentary (chiefly taken from Medhātithi) is the commonest and most popular one in existence.[2] He tells us that he was a native of Benares, and he probably lived in the sixteenth or seventeenth century A.D. This commentary is a concise practical work.

After him came a Nārāyaṇa, quoted by Rāghavānanda, but of whom I can learn no more.[3]

Then came Rāghavānanda, whose very brief commentary (Manvarthacandrikā) chiefly follows Kullūka. He refers to all the commentators already mentioned except Sāyaṇa-Mādhava, and seems to have been a native of South India. At least one manuscript of his work is in the great Paris Library, and was used by Loiseleur Deslongchamps for his edition.

Besides these there is a commentary by a Nandanācārya among the Tanjore manuscripts.[4] As his name shows, he was a native of South India; his work appears to be modern and of small value. I can find nothing in it to enable me to fix his date. Perhaps he was the Nanda who wrote on adoption.

Editions of the text are quite recent.[5] Sir William

[1] See the preface to my edition of the Vaṁça Brāhmaṇa, p. xx.

[2] It is a *vṛtti* called Manvarthamuktāvalī.

[3] [MSS. of this work are still extant.]

[4] See p. 126 of my Tanjore Catalogue.

[5] The first, with Kullūka's commentary, was in 4to, Calcutta, 1813. This was printed by Colebrooke's protégé, Bābu Rām, and, like all the

Jones' translation appeared in 1794. The means of acquiring a knowledge of Sanskrit were then very small, and the author deserves the greatest credit for his generally successful attempt. The chief defects in it are due to the prejudices of the day; it is diffuse and rhetorical, and largely interpolated with passages from Kullūka's commentary; the *a priori* and metaphysical theories of the time show their influence in every line, and the translation of such terms as *ātman* will not now pass muster. Sir William Jones has converted the materialist Sāṅkhya system of the text into the metaphysical deism that he and his associates had so largely adopted. But any correct notion of the Indian systems was then impossible.

Since 1813 numerous reprints of the text, with and without Kullūka's commentary, have appeared at several times in India, but they are all uncritical. Two editions have appeared in Europe, in which a critical restoration of the text has been attempted—that by Sir G. C. Haughton in 1825, and that by Loiseleur Deslongchamps in 1830–33. Haughton gives Sir William Jones' translation, again collated with the Sanskrit; Loiseleur Deslongchamps gives a version of his own in French,[1] but it agrees tolerably closely with that of Sir William Jones.[2] A revised text of Sir William Jones' translation was begun (about 1840) at Calcutta, but continued only down to iii. 33; Dr. Goldstücker expresses a high opinion of it.[3]

productions of his press, is full of serious misprints. For other (especially the recent editions), see the Catalogue of Sanskrit and Pali Books in the British Museum, by Haas, pp. 86–87.

[1] Goldstücker termed Sir William Jones' translation "excellent," and that of Lois. Deslongchamps "very good" (Remains, i. p. 108). Professor Monier Williams (Two Addresses, 1881) also praises Sir William Jones' version as "admirably translated."

[2] Haughton's edition of Sir William Jones' translation was reprinted at Madras (1863), and by Grady at London (1869), and Deslongchamps' translation [of the text] was reprinted at Paris in 1850.

[3] Remains, ii. p. 148, note. The differences from Sir William Jones' version are numerous and striking. All the information I have respecting this translation is derived from the above passage. I have not been able to procure a copy.

Dr. J. Muir has given model translations of numerous passages of the text in his "Sanskrit Texts" and "Metrical Translations from the Sanskrit." Many points connected with the text have been fully discussed by Johaentgen, "Ueber das Gesetzbuch des Manu" (1863).[1] "The Mutual Relations of the Four Castes according to the Mānava-dharma-çāstra" have been fully treated by Dr. E. W. Hopkins (Leipzig, 1881).

This summary of original work up to the present will show that there is room for much more to be done. A new critical edition of the Sanskrit text, with the aid of South Indian manuscripts, is to be desired; but it appears to me it is to be wished that the *textus receptus* of Kullūka should still be followed, and the discrepancies merely pointed out. The reason for this is to be found in the fact that a critical text would in reality present no considerable *v. l.*, and though some changes in the order of the verses would have to be made, and interpolations omitted, yet it is not advisable to change the well-known numbers of the verses as found in Sir William Jones' translation, for the inconvenience thereby caused would be great. This applies equally to a new translation, which is equally necessary, for the reasons I have already mentioned.

I have therefore followed in the following pages the text after Kullūka as edited by Haughton, and noted the chief discrepancies in the notes. The manuscript of Medhā-

[1] [More important than anything since Johaentgen as regards articles concerned directly with the text is Bradke's Mānava-gṛhya-sūtra, in which the relations of our text are discussed from many sides, to the Gṛhya Sūtra as well as to the Maitrāyaṇī Saṁhitā. A special translation of most of book viii. has been given by Professor Jolly (iii. bd. Zt. für Vergleichende Rechts Wissenschaft). A special but popular essay on Manu will be found I. A., vol. ii. More has been done indirectly in the introductions to the law-books published by Bühler and Jolly. Critiques of special passages are given in Bühler's Digest, Mandlik's ed., of the Vyavahāra Mayūkha; and more general critique in Nelson's Scientific Study of Hindu Law and Müller's India. The works of Professor Bühler and Professor Jolly (Āpastamba, Gautama, Vasiṣṭha, Baudhāyana, Viṣṇu), the latter's text of Viṣṇu and translation of Nārada, have done much for the study of Hindu law, and, indirectly, for the Mānava-çāstra.]

tithi which I have been able to use is unfortunately not a good one, but I have extracted the more important *v. l.* noted by the writer.[1]

As the text has been so often referred to by the courts in India and the ultimate Court of Appeal, the Privy Council in England, it might be expected that some useful help would be got from the law reports; but this is not the case. Most of the cases decided are evidently wrongly decided,[2] and others really need no elucidation; the decision may be very able, but (as an eminent writer has said) "life is not long enough to study able demonstrations that the moon is made of green cheese." I therefore do not refer to this branch of literature referring to Sanskrit law.

It is not often given to any man or class of men to carry out crucial experiments in sociology, though such a course has been, one might think, rendered impossible in India by royal proclamation[3] and actual law; here, however, it cannot be doubted that the result will confirm the conclusion that only a natural and spontaneous development is of use and value, and that imitation is sterile.

The preceding pages will show that Sanskrit law was pursuing a course of spontaneous development; this has

[1] It is the one used by Haughton (i. p. 322–323), and forms part of the Colebrooke collection now in the India Office Library. It is recent (about 1800), and is in 4 vols., but does not include the commentary on chap. xii. I owe the power to use this MS. in India to the kind help of Dr. Rost, the chief librarian of the India Office (London).

[2] The most glaring instance is the so-called "chastity" case, in which the Privy Council has lately confirmed the decision of the Bengal High Court. The question here was: whether a widow, holding property as such, and having (admittedly) ceased to be chaste, could retain it? She was allowed to do so by both courts. It is obvious that under Sanskrit law she would not; for a property being held for the benefit of her deceased husband by means of religious ceremonies, with the loss of her virtue she could no longer do so. In fact, she lost her position in the caste altogether, and her existence as a member of the family ceased utterly.

[3] On the resumption of the Government of India by the Crown (Proclamation of Nov. 1, 1858), Her Majesty said: "We disclaim alike the right and desire to impose our convictions on any of our subjects. . . . We will that generally in framing and administering the law due regard be paid to the ancient rights, usages, and customs of India."

been interrupted, and English doctrine has been pitchforked into Sanskrit texts. Is it likely that a satisfactory result will ever follow? The whole subject is now in a chaotic state, and so great is the uncertainty that valuable property is commonly sold for a thousandth part of its value. So far the present policy cannot be viewed with complacency.

As regards my translation, I have endeavoured to make it as literal and concise as possible. With [the] greater part of the text, *i.e.*, chapters ii. to x., or the really important part of the book, this is not a matter of much difficulty. The case is different with chapters i. and xii. These, as has already been said, are metaphysical, and follow the Sāṅkhya system. Much labour has been bestowed on this subject by Colebrooke, and after him by Dr. F. Hall, but it must be admitted that it is all but impossible to express the terms of this system in a European language. All possible renderings convey much more than the primitive and rude original signifies, and it is impossible to limit each word so as to provide against a too wide signification being attached to it. Language cannot go back to suit primitive and barbarous ideas.[1]

The rudimentary metaphysics of India are solely of interest now as showing the development of Indian conceptions, and that, in this respect, there is no difference between India and other countries. Here, as elsewhere, a fictitious stage of conceptions, such as is found in the Upanishads, has been followed by an abstract stage, such as is found in the metaphysical systems. Intrinsically they possess nothing of permanent value, and vanish like

[1] Mr. Nelson ("View") has exposed fully the delusion of "apt equivalents" for the Sanskrit technical law-terms; his remarks apply equally to the philosophical terms, as Dr. F. Hall has noticed (Rational Refutation, pp. viii. to x.): "There are scores of terms belonging to the nomenclature of Hindu philosophy, precise equivalents of which have not yet been wrought out for us with the help of the Latin and Greek. . . . Colebrooke and his successors have indeed elaborated many close and felicitous renderings; still they have left much unattempted, and something to be amended."

mists before the sun when confronted with the results of positive science. To those persuaded of the truth of the axiom, "No force without matter, and no matter without force," the vague *a priori* dreams of India are, and must remain, without any intelligibility or importance beyond their historical connection; even in this respect they lead to no new laws, but merely confirm what is already established.

But all this [metaphysical] part of the text is an excrescence, and really independent of the subject-matter of the book.

[NOTE.—Here, somewhat abruptly, Dr. Burnell's Introduction to Manu is brought to a close. Immediately following is a fragmentary Introduction to Yājñavalkya, which work was apparently to be translated and published with the Manu, the general heading of the whole-MSS. being "Mānava-dharma-çāstra and Yājñavalkya-smṛti." The translation of the latter work was not begun, and the introduction offers nothing new, so that it would be useless to reproduce it here. In regard to the precise dates assumed in this discussion, it may be necessary to remark that many of them are not so undisputed as could be wished; especially in the inscriptions with the various eras in vogue when they were written we are often at a loss. Criticism of the above argument is at present waived by the American editor, who has felt it his duty simply to follow in his predecessor's steps, and fill the lacunæ left in his MS., while abstaining from individual comment, except where it seemed necessary in assertions of facts; although he may at times have questioned whether the theories advanced are based upon sufficient data.]

CORRIGENDA.

Page 1, note 1, p. 9, vss. 61, 63, p. 13, vs. 102, for *Syayambhū* and *Svāyambhuva* read *Syayam°* *Svāyam°*.
Page 9, vs. 62, insert) after *i.e.*
Page 19, vs. 28, for *Bráhman* read *Bráhma*.
Page 24, vss. 64, 66, and p. 29, vs. 105, for *texts* read *mantra*.
Page 32, vs. 130, before *priest* insert *sacrificial*.
Page 45, note 2, for *ṣākhā* read *çākhā*.
Page 59, vs. 121, for *texts* read *mantra*.
Page 62, note 4, dele *p*.
Page 68, vs. 194, before *Hiraṇyagarbha* insert *son of*.
Page 72, vs. 232, for *Dharmā-çastra* read *Dharma-çāstra*.
Page 73, vs. 239, for *Caṇḍāla* read *Cāṇḍāla*.
Page 106, vs. 232, for *Brahma* read *Brahmā*.
Page 119, note 4, read *Govindarājā-dayaḥ*.
Page 124, note 1, for *Dimba* read *Ḍimba*.
" " 3 and 4, read third line as second.
Page 139, note 3, dele] after *paçuḥ*.
Page 144, vs. 70, for *Vyāhṛti* read *Vyāhṛtis*.
Page 146, vs. 94, for *Brahman* read *Twice-born man*.
Page 152, vs. 37, before Vedas insert *three*.
Page 158, note 1, and p. 213, note 8, for *Ṛtvig* read *Ṛtvij*.
Page 196, first line of notes, for *Viçvamitra* read *Viçvā°*.
Page 215, vs. 226, for *anantra* read *mantra*.
Page 217, note 7, for *Ap.* read *Āp.*
Page 244, note 4, for *world of Brahm* read *Brhama-world*.
Page 294, note 6, for *Courān* read *Caurān*.
Page 309, vs. 36, after *Niṣāda* insert semicolon, and for *Vaid°* read *Vaid*.
Page 315, note 4, for *Brahm* read *Brahma*.
Page 328, vs. 29, for *Sādyas* read *Sādhyas*, and in note 3, *Viçva°* for *viçra°*.
Page 337, note 3, for *often Bṛhaspati* read *after Bṛhaspati*.
Page 342, vs. 125, for *heating* read *burning*.
Page 349, vs. 176, for *Cāṇḍala* read *Cāṇḍāla*.
Page 351, vs. 183, for *ṛtvig* read *ṛtvij*.
Page 353, vs. 201, enclose *of the Veda* in ( ).
Page 364, vs. 4, for *worlds* read *world*, and in note 4, for *minds* read *mind*.

THE ORDINANCES OF MANU.

LECTURE I.

THE SOURCE OF THIS WORK, AND AN ACCOUNT OF THE ORIGIN OF THE UNIVERSE; WITH A SUMMARY OF THE CONTENTS OF THE WHOLE BOOK.

1. THE great Seers having approached Manu seated intent, having reverenced him, duly spoke this speech.[1]

2. Lord! deign to tell us truly in order the rules of all the castes,[2] and of all the castes that arise between (them).

3. For thou, Lord, alone knowest the true sense of the objects of this universal, self-existent system,[3] unattainable by (simple) reason, not to be reasoned out.

4. He whose glory is unmeasured, being duly questioned by those magnanimous ones, having saluted all the great Seers, answered them: Hear!

5. This (All) was darkness, imperceptible, without

[1] In some MSS. (including two in the I. O. which belonged to Sir W. Jones) there is an additional verse at the beginning which runs: "Having reverenced Svayaṁbhū and Brahman of unlimited glory, I shall declare the various eternal laws directed by Manu."

This verse is supported by Rāghavānanda's commentary, and is probably authentic, though not noticed by Medhātithi; it points to the real character of this book, viz., that it is a compilation from and a redaction of older matter. [The first four verses of this lecture are prefixed by a late compiler; the work really begins with vs. 5, as is formally stated in the opening of Nārada.]

[2] Medhātithi says these laws refer to only the Brahmans, Kṣatriyas, and Vaiçyas; not to the Çūdras. Cf. iv. 80–81, from which it is evident that this is correct. Medhātithi might have quoted the Āpastamba dharmasūtra (i. 1, 5) to the same effect, also vs. 91 of this lecture.

[3] "System"—*vidhāna*. This is explained by Medhātithi by *çāstra*, or a body of teaching on the subject either revealed or human.

definite qualities, undiscoverable, unknowable, as if wholly in sleep.[1]

6. Then the self-existent Lord became manifest, making this undiscrete (All) discernible with his power, unobstructed by[2] the chief elements and the like, removing the darkness.

7. He who can be apprehended by the suprasensual,[3] (who is) subtile, undiscrete, eternal, who consists of all elements, incomprehensible, he verily[4] became manifest of himself.

8. Wishing to produce different beings from his own body, he having desired,[5] first[6] created water alone; in that he cast seed.

9. That became a golden egg,[7] like in splendour to the thousand-rayed (sun); in that was born spontaneously Brahmá, the grand parent of all the worlds.

10. Waters are called *nārāḥ*, for they are the offspring of Nara; and since they were his first abode (*ayana*), he thence is called Nārāyaṇa.[8]

[1] This description of the creation is, generally, in accordance with the Sāṅkhya system, as it is already recognised by the Indian commentators. The whole has been discussed in great detail, and with reference to the philosophical treatises, by F. Johaentgen (Ueber das Gesetzbuch des Manu, 1863). The whole of this lecture calls to mind what Megasthenes says of Indian speculations at an earlier period: "Their notions about physical phenomena . . . are very crude, for they are better in their actions than in their reasonings, as their belief is mostly based upon fables" (Fr. xli., ed. Schwanbeck). [A similar description occurs xii. 29 of *darkness* as a metaphysical quality (*guṇa*), where *b*. 1 is identical with this passage.]

[2] [Perhaps better, "unfolding that not (yet) unfolded (All), the self-existent Lord, whose power is contained in the great existent (elements)," etc.] Medh. gives this reading, while K. reads, "The . . . Lord, the undiscrete, became manifest." [And Medh. in (*b*) gives another reading, *mahābhūtānu-vṛttaujaḥ*, while the translation in the text rests on K.'s assumption that *vṛtti* = *apratighāta*, the old translations making *vṛttaujaḥ* one word, and uniting the preceding as epithet to the foregoing.]

[3] "Powers beyond the senses," *i.e.*, can be inferred.

[4] [*Eva* or (Medh., cf. Beng. MS.) *eṣa*, "this one before spoken of."]

[5] [*I.e.*, by merely intending it (cf. vs. 12), he thus produced water (Medh., K.)]

[6] [Literally "in the beginning."]

[7] This egg of Brahmá plays a great part in the Puranic mythology, but does not appear, properly, to belong to the Sāṅkhya system [which it really contradicts]. It can be traced in the Vedic literature (see Kellgren's essay, "Mythus de Ovo Mundano").

[8] *Nara* or *puruṣa*, *i.e.*, Brahmá. The appellation "Nārāyaṇa" is foreign to the Sāṅkhya system,

11. That which is the undiscrete Cause, eternal, which Is and Is not, from It issued that male who is called in the world Brahmá.

12. That Lord having dwelt in that egg for a year, spontaneously, by his own meditation, split that egg in two.

13. And with those two shares he formed the heaven and the earth, in the middle the sky and the eight regions,[1] and the perpetual place of waters.

14. From himself[2] he created mind,[3] which is and is not; and from mind egoism,[4] the ruler,[5] the lord.

15. And likewise the great self, and all (things) with the three qualities, and, severally, the five organs of sense, the apprehenders of sensible objects.[6]

16. He also, having made the subtile parts of those six, of unmeasured brightness, to enter into the elements of self,[7] created all beings.

and betrays Vaiṣṇava influences. [In the Mbhā. this derivation is several times repeated, *e.g.*, iii. 189, 3, where Viṣṇu says, "I called the name of water *nārā* in ancient times, and am hence called Nārāyaṇa, for that was always my abode, *ayana*."]

[1] Eight regions, *i.e.*, points of the compass.

[2] [Or "from self," *ātmanaḥ*.]

[3] "*Manas* = mind, situated in the *hṛdaya* or breast." "Mind, serving both for sense and action, is an organ by affinity, being cognate with the rest" (Colebrooke).

[4] [Self-consciousness (egoism) is produced from mind; Medh. says it means the converse of this, that the former is produced after the latter. Cf. vs. 15.]

[5] [According to Medh., "the one conscious of the I."]

[6] [Cf. ii. 89–92. The above interpretation follows the text and the note of Medh., while K. Rāgh. endeavour to fill out the missing *tanmātra* and organs of activity by giving an impossible extension of meaning to the word "and" (*ca*); thus making the text accord with the developed system of later times. The word *ca* does not imply the *tanmātra*; the text itself does not make a distinction between sensations and the organs of sense.] The order of the evolution is very much confused. See for a better account of these Sāṅkhya reveries Colebrooke [ed. Cowell], Essays, pp. 239–280; and Hall's "Rational Refutation," pp. 79–103.

[7] "Into the elements of self." K. has *ātmamātrāsu*, as translated above; Medh. would read *mātrābhiḥ*, "by elements;" thus the whole verse would be: "He having pervaded the subtile parts of those six, of unmeasured brightness, by elements of self, created all beings." "Those six" [are according to K.], the five *tanmātra* or subtile elements and *ahaṁkāra* or egoism [*i.e.*, self-consciousness, which it is safe to say were *not* intended by the text. Vs. 14 does not hang together with vs. 15, nor does vs. 15 with vs. 16. The six appear rather to be the *manas* plus the five principles of ether, air, fire, water, earth; "having united fine portions of these six with the spiritual elements, he (thus) created

17. As the subtile elements[1] of bodily forms of This One depend on these six, so the wise call his form *çarīra.*[2]

18. From it proceed the great[3] elements with their action, and mind, by (its) subtile parts, (is) the perpetual creator of all forms.[4]

19. This non-eternal (universe) arises then from the eternal, by means of the subtile elements of forms of those seven very glorious principles.[5]

20. Of these,[6] then, that which succeeds partakes of the quality of that which goes before; such as each one is in order, so, and with such qualities, it is traditionally held to be (endowed).

21. He, in the beginning, from the words of the Vedas, appointed the names and functions of all beings severally, and their several conditions.

22. And the Lord created a subtile host of divine beings which have breath (and are) active,[7] and of *sādhyas*, and the eternal sacrifice.

all existent things" (cf. the discussion of this passage in Johaent., p. 24–25); *ātmamātra* is therefore the spiritual atom as opposed to the elementary, not reflexive "elements of himself"].

[1] ["Elements" means here portions, "as the fine portions of form of this (Brahmá, the creator) depend on the six." I have ventured to make *asya* depend on *avayavāḥ* instead of *saḥ*, Dr. B.'s text giving "these six *in him*." Dr. B. appears to have attached himself quite closely to K.'s interpretation, and I do not feel at liberty to alter his words, though it may be pointed out that "subtile elements" is more in accordance with the commentator's explanations than the text. The technical *tanmātra* is not found in the original, and the word translated "element" is literally a "part."]

[2] [*I.e.*, "depends on six" (according to K.), *ṣaḍāçrayaṇa*, as if this were near enough in sound to *çarīra* to cause the verbal derivation. The parts of the body (*çarīra*) of Brahmá are portions of the six (*manas* and the five elements). After this verse appears to have once followed another, quoted by Vij. on Kap. iii. 10.]

[3] "Great" or grosser. [Perhaps better not translated at all, the *bhūtāni mahānti* being "the elements;" the translation follows K. Literally, "Into this (body) enter the elements with their acts, and mind by means of the fine portions (as in 17)." K.'s translation of *āviçanti* (enter into, constitute) as (*tebhya*) *utpadyante* has been (unfortunately) followed by Dr. B.]

[4] [All created things].

[5] "Principles"—*puruṣa* is here put for *tattva*, according to Medhâtithi. [The five elements plus mind and self-consciousness are probably meant; "subtile elements" as before "fine portions of form."]

[6] [These (elements, *manas* and self-consciousness) seven *puruṣa*.]

[7] [A *var. lec.* recorded by Medh. (*karmātmānaṃca*); this may mean "he created the active-soul (self) of

23. He (Brahmá), for the perfection of sacrifice, from fire, wind, and the sun, milked (out) the eternal threefold Veda (Bráhma), which consists of the Ṛig-, Yajur-, and Sāma- (Vedas).[1]

24. He created time and the divisions of time, the lunar zodiac, also the planets; rivers, oceans, rocks, plains, and uneven ground;

25. Austerity, speech, and sexual enjoyment,[2] desire also as well as anger: and desiring to create these beings, he created this creation.

26. And he made distinct *dharma* and non-*dharma*[3] in order to a distinction of deeds. And he endowed these beings with the pairs—pleasure and pain, and the like.

27. But of the five (elements), those which are called the atomic destructible[4] elements,[5] by these this All arises in successive order.

28. Now in what action that Lord first employed any (creature), that (creature) being reproduced again (and) again, spontaneously followed just that (course of action).

29. Baneful (or) harmless; gentle (or) savage; right (or) wrong; true (or) false; whatever he, at the creation, assigned to any that quality spontaneously entered it.

30. As the seasons acquire their own characteristics in (their) course, so beings with a body (acquire their characteristic) acts.

31. Now for the prosperity of the worlds, he from his mouth, arms, thighs, and feet created the Brahman, Kṣatriya, Vaiçya, and Çūdra.[6]

the divine beings (gods) (or "of the Vedas"), and the subtile host of Sādhyas. The Sādhyas are a secondary order of divine beings.]

[1] This myth of the creation of the Vedas differs from the Sāṅkhya account, according to which they are eternal and issue from Brahmá's mouth at each successive *Kalpa*-creation, or rather evolution.

[2] [According to Medh. and K., "satisfaction of mind."]

[3] "*Dharma*, non-*dharma*." The first is derived from √*dhṛ*, to hold or retain; it thus means a man's whole duty or order of conduct, including both secular and religious duty. I retain *dharma*, and coin the word non-*dharma*, to prevent a very general term from being understood in a limited sense.

[4] [Therefore distinct from the atoms of the *nyāya*.]

[5] [Portions.]

[6] The nearest approach to this myth in the Vedic literature is

32. Having divided his own body into two, he became a male by half, by half a female: on her that Lord begot Virāj.

33. But, O best of twice-born men! know that I am he, the creator of all this world, whom that male Virāj, having practised austerity, spontaneously produced.

34. Now I, desirous of creating beings, having performed very severe austerity, first created the ten lords of beings, great Seers.

35. (Viz.) Marīci, Atri, Aṅgiras, Pulastya, Pulaha, Kratu, Pracetas, Vasiṣṭha, Bhṛgu, and also Nārada.

36. They, very glorious, produced seven other Manus,[1] together with gods and the abodes of gods, and great Seers unlimited in glory.

37. Yakṣas, Rakṣasas, Piçācas, Gandharvas, Apsarasas, Asuras, Nāgas, serpents, eagles, and the different hosts of Manes.[2]

38. Lightnings, thunderbolts, and clouds, Indra's bent and unbent[3] bows, meteors, comets, and various luminaries.

39. Kinnaras, apes, fishes, and all kinds of birds;

found in the recently recovered Talavakāra Brāhmaṇa (ii. 3-4). See also Muir's "Sanskrit Texts" (2d ed.), i. p. 22, &c., for other similar myths. [It is spoken of in R. V. x. 90, 12, K.]

It is necessary to remark that in the oldest times there was no hard and fast line between the different three superior classes; the names indicated a rough classification of a rude population, such as is now to be found in Russia, and not distinct genealogical descents. In course of time myths arose which made a man's caste a matter of descent, but as Brahman civilisation extended over alien races, different classes were brought under the four heads, and hence arises the great number of subdivisions of each which have no intercourse with one another. Lord ("Display"), 1830, already found eighty-two subdivisions of Brahmans in Gujarat, and mentions nearly similar numbers for the other three castes; many more are known now. I know some families in Southern Canara which now claim to be Brahmans, and are called so, but inscriptions show that 500 years ago they were Jains. Much doubt is thrown on the origin of the Gurukkal or Çaiva priests of the Tamil country, and some wealthy traders in Madura have suddenly set up a claim to be Brahmans. Wilson ("On Caste," 2 vols.) and Sherring's works throw much light on these endless divisions in Northern India; for the Madras Presidency, the introduction to the Census Report by Dr. Cornish is invaluable.

[1] Some MSS. for *manūn* read *munīn* = devotees.

[2] *Pitaras*, lit. "fathers." Like "manes," this is always plural.

[3] "Bows . . . of Indra" = rainbows. [The commentators explain the "unbent bow" as "staff-shaped and variegated, blue and red" (Medh.)]

cattle, deer,[1] and men, beasts of prey, and animals with two rows of teeth.

40. Worms, grubs, and winged insects, lice, flies, and bugs, with all biting gnats, and innumerable things of different kinds.

41. Thus was this All, (consisting of things) stationary and movable according to (their) acts,[2] created by those great beings at my command, through the force of austerity.

42. What kind of acts is ordained for what creatures here, that I shall declare to you, also (their) order in origin.

43. Cattle and also deer, and wild beasts with two rows of teeth, demons and devils,[3] and men, are born from a caul.

44. Produced from eggs (are) birds, snakes, crocodiles, and fish, and tortoises; and likewise all other kinds (of reptiles which are) produced on land or (are) aquatic.

45. From moisture are produced gnats and flies, lice, fleas, and bugs; and from heat is produced whatever else is of this kind.[4]

46. All plants (which are) fixed grow from seed or slips. Herbs (are) those which perish with ripening of fruit, (and) abound in flowers and fruit.

47. Those (trees) which have no flowers (but) have fruit, are called *vanaspati* (forest-lord); those that have flowers, and also those that bear fruit, (are) both called trees.

48. Plants with one stem and many stems[5] are of many kinds; so also grasses: but convolvulus and creepers spring from seed or a slip.

49. These (creatures), enveloped by a manifold darkness

[1] [Or "forest animals."] Animals with two rows of teeth, *i.e.*, the carnivora. Cf. vs. 43, below.

[2] "According to their acts," *i.e.*, "with reference to their acts in a former existence" (Medh.)

[3] [Rakṣas and Piçācas.]

[4] It is difficult to a resident in the tropics not to agree with Miss Martineau's conclusion respecting vermin in hot countries; it comes to much the same as the text.

[5] "One stem" (*guccha*), "many stems" (*gulma*). Medhātithi explains these terms as meaning "one root" and "many roots." Indian botany and zoology are, it is needless to say, utterly fanciful and unscientific. [K.'s explanation is plain: where a shoot springs right up from the root and there are no boughs, that is a *guccha*; where a clump of shoots come up from one root, that is a *gulma*.]

caused by (past) deeds, have an internal conscience,[1] and are endowed with pleasure and pain.

50. The existences, beginning with Brahmá and ending with those (plants), which occur in this terrible, ever-progressive[2] transmigration of beings, have (thus) been related.

51. Having thus created all This and me, he of unthinkable powers was again absorbed into himself, alternating a time of (creation) by a time (of repose).

52. For when that Divine Being wakes, then this world is active; when he, peaceful, sleeps, then all sleeps.

53. Now when he sleeps in repose, those active beings with a body cease from their own proper acts, and the mind becomes powerless.

54. And when, in due course, they are lost in that great being, then this self of all beings sleeps pleasantly in rest.

55. This one with its organs long remains (inactive), having returned to darkness, nor does it perform its proper acts; then it issues forth in forms.[3]

56. When, having become elemental (and) emanate, it enters into seeds of plants or animals, it assumes a form.

57. Thus he, by wakefulness and sleep, vivifies, and, imperishable (himself), destroys perpetually all This movable and immovable.

58. Now he, having made this science[4] spontaneously, duly taught it to me in the beginning, but I (taught it) to the devotees Marīci and the rest.

[1] [*I.e.*, are possessed of consciousness.]

[2] [At all times its nature is to go on, that is, ever vanishing (*vināçini*) Medh.; so K.]

[3] [*Mūrtitaḥ*, or "it takes its exit from the body;" cf. Medh. (who, we must remember, was a Mimāṃsist): "It goes forth from the body (*çarīrāt*), but truly this all-pervading self is, like the atmosphere, everywhere; what sort of an *exit* then has it? Its exit is merely the abandonment of a body induced by activity, . . . or, now, as certain ones explain, there is another fine body existing within (soul); it is the exit of this only; but by others this is not allowed, as Vyāsa has said, 'When the body has passed away the organs occupy another body; there is thus no soul.' Even some Sāṅkhyas will not allow a soul, those living in Vindhya and others; . . . others say this *mūrti* is a form of the highest soul (*ātmā*); out of it living creatures make their appearance and are each (individual soul) endowed with bodies."]

[4] [*Çāstram* is the treatise here proclaimed. Medh. says, "This book (*grantha*) containing law and prohibitions is called the Mānava code

59. This Bhṛgu shall cause you to hear that science in its entirety; for that devotee learnt it all, complete, entire, from me.

60. Then that great Seer Bhṛgu being thus addressed by that Manu, said with pleased mind to all those Seers: Let it be heard!

61. There are six other Manus in successive generations sprung from this Manu Svāyaṁbhuva (born of the self-existent); they, magnanimous and of great glory, created their own several offspring.

62. They are: Svārociṣa, Auttami, Tāmasa, Raivata also, and Cākṣuṣa, and the son of the sun (*i.e.*, Vaivasvata very glorious.

63. The seven glorious Manus, of whom Svāyaṁbhuva is the first, having produced all this (world) of moving and stationary beings, ruled (it each) in his own period.[1]

64. Eighteen winkings[2] of the eye make one *kāṣṭhā*; thirty *kāṣṭhās* (one) *kalā*; thirty *kalās* one *muhūrta*; and so many (*muhūrtas*) one should know to be a day and night.[3]

65. The sun causes day and night, divine and human. Night is for the sleep of beings, and day for the performance of their acts.

66. A (human) month (is) a day and a night of the

because Manu made it." In Medh.'s time the double authorship of the work seems to have been looked on with disfavour, not by him, but by opponents; for he says, "Certain persons say it was made by Hiraṇyagarbha but was revealed by Manu, the fact of the case being that the work is like the Ganges, which has its source elsewhere, though first discoverable in the Himālayas, so that it is an idle question whether the Deity or Manu made it." Medh. adds that Nārada says, "A book composed of 100,000 (verses) was made by Prajāpati, and abridged by Manu and others" (Nārada coming first in our version).]

[[1] "Period"—*antara*. This makes a *manvantara* (cf. vs. 79). Some say that the word "period" (*antara*) is, like the word "month," expressive of a mere division of time; but this is wrong, for the time implied by the word *manu* is different, and to this the word *manvantara* refers; it is not ordinary time (Medh.)]

[[2] *Nimeṣa*. Two explanations are given by Medh., one (so K.) as translated, and one given by "others" as "the time necessary to articulate a syllable."]

[3] This system of reckoning time, except that fifteen winkings are put for eighteen, is the same as that of the Viṣṇu Purāṇa. Several such systems are mentioned in the Purāṇas, etc. See Hall's edition of Wilson's Viṣṇu Purāṇa, i. pp. 47–50 *note*.

manes, and the division is by the lunar fortnights. The dark (half), (beginning with the full moon, is their) day for actions; and the bright (half, beginning with the new moon), is their night for sleep.

67. A (human) year is a day and a night of the gods. Again their division (is this): their day is the northern, and their night is the southern course of the sun.

68. Learn now summarily the measure of a day and a night of Brahmá, and of the several ages in order.

69. They call *kṛtayuga* (a period containing) four thousand years; the twilight (preceding it consists) of as many hundreds, and the twilight (following it) of the same number.

70. In the other three (ages), with their twilights preceding and following, the thousands and hundreds are diminished by one.

71. Twelve thousand of the four *yugas* just now reckoned are called a *yuga* of the gods.[1]

72. But a thousand of (such) divine *yugas* in number is to be known to be a day of Brahmá, and a night also is the same (in length).

73. They (who) understand a holy day of Brahmá, which ends with a thousand *yugas*, and the night also of the same extent, (are) people who know (the divisions of) days and nights.

74. At the end of His day and night, He, being asleep, awakes, and awaking creates mind, which is and is not.

75. Mind, urged on by (His) desire to create, effects again) the (work of) creation; and thence is produced the

[1] The translation is literal. According to the commentators it should be translated, "The four *yugas* just reckoned, (consisting of) twelve thousand years, are called a *yuga* of the gods." The lengthening of ordinary into divine years is probably (as Prof. von Roth considers) the work of commentators. When the end of the imaginary period, as first invented, arrived, and nothing happened, such a fiction would naturally arise and be adopted. Similar ideas may be found to have arisen in Europe in the Middle Ages, and even in the present century. In India these enormous periods are of comparatively modern invention, and were unknown in the fourth century B.C. Cf. Arrian, "India," ix. (on authority of Megasthenes).

ether, which (the learned) know (to have) the quality of sound.

76. Now from ether transforming itself springs the pure and potent air, a vehicle of all odours; and that is held to be endued with the quality of touch.

77. Then from air transforming itself arises light, illuminating (objects), dispelling darkness, shining; and it is declared to have the quality of form.

78. But from light transforming itself, water with the quality of taste is said (to arise); and from water (arises) earth with the quality of smell: such is the creation in the beginning.

79. The before-mentioned age of the gods of twelve thousand (years), if multiplied by seventy-one, is here named a *manvantara*.[1]

80. (Such) *manvantaras* are countless, as (are) also the creations and destructions; the Supreme Being does this again and again as if in sport.[2]

81. In the *Kṛta* age, *dharma* stands on four feet, and is complete, as is truth also; and (in that age) no advantage accrues to men by non-*dharma*.[3]

82. But in the other ages, owing to accession of (wrong), *dharma* is deprived successively of one foot; and *dharma* disappears foot by foot, through the prevalence of theft, falsehood, and frand.

83. Men free from disease, and with all sorts of prosperity, live four hundred years in the *Kṛta* age; in the *Tretā* and other (ages) their life[4] becomes shorter by a fourth.

[1] According to the Amarakoça, an account of the *manvantaras* should form one of the five topics treated in Purāṇas; this is not, however, the case.

[2] [The idea of the Supreme Being *parameṣṭhin*) amusing himself by his creations is found elsewhere; it is not only the ease that is implied, but also that it is done for sport, as, *e.g.*, Mbhā. xii. 308, 3 (in a different connection) *ajasraṁtviha krīḍārthaṁ vikaroti.*]

[3] [*Uparastate* (Medh.): the image of the four-footed *dharma* may be united, according to the commentators, with that of the bull in viii. 16 (cf. *ib.* note), or the four feet may refer to the four virtues in v. 76, or to other fourfold things.]

[4] [(*Āyuḥ*, *vayaḥ*, Medh.)]

84. The life of mortals, as mentioned in the Veda,[1] the blessings (resulting) from (good) works, and the powers of embodied beings bear fruit according to the ages.

85. Other are the laws for men in the *Kṛta* age; other in the *Tretā* (and) in the *Dvāpara;* other in the *Kali* age, in proportion to the decrease of the ages.

86. In the *Kṛta* age, the chief (virtue) is declared to be austerity; in the *Tretā,* knowledge; in the *Dvāpara,* sacrifice; the only duty of the *Kali* is generosity.[2]

87. Now, for the sake of preserving all this creation, the most glorious (Being) ordained separate duties for those who sprang from (His) mouth, arm, thigh, (and) feet.

88. For Brahmans he ordered teaching, study, sacrifice, and sacrificing (as priests) for others, also giving and receiving (gifts).

89. Defence of the people, giving (alms), sacrifice, also study, and absence of attachment to objects of sense, in short, for a Kṣatriya.

90. Tending of cattle, giving (alms), sacrifice, study, trade, usury, and also agriculture for a Vaiçya.

91. One duty the Lord assigned to a Çūdra—service to those (before-mentioned) classes, without grudging.

92. Man is declared purer above the navel; therefore the purest (part) of him is said by the Self-Existent to be his mouth.[3]

93. Since he sprang from the most excellent part, since he was the first-born,[4] and since he holds the Vedas, the Brahman is, by right, the lord of all this creation.

94. Him the Self-Existent, after having performed penance, created in the beginning from his own mouth, for presentation of oblations to the gods and offerings to the manes, (and) for the preservation of all this (world).

[1] [That is, of one thousand (Medh.) or one hundred years (K.), as "others" say (Medh.)]

[2] [Literally "giving," and "to the Brahmans" may be supplied as the real thought of the maker.]

[3] [Cf. v. 132.]

[4] [Literally, his pre-eminence of birth, as it is expressed in full in the similar verse, x. 3.]

95. What being is then superior to him, by whose mouth the gods eat oblations and the manes offerings?[1]

96. Of beings, the most excellent are said to be the animated; of the animated, (those which) subsist by intelligence; of the intelligent, men; of men, the Brahmans.

97. But of Brahmans, the learned (are most excellent); of the learned, (those who) know their duty; of those who know it, (such as) do it; and of (those who) do it, (those who) know the Vedas.

98. The birth of a Brahman is a perpetual incarnation of *dharma*;[2] for he exists for the sake of *dharma*, and is for the existence of the Vedas.[3]

99. When a Brahman is born, he is born above the world, the chief of all creatures, to guard the treasury of *dharma*.

100. Thus, whatever exists in the universe is all the property of the Brahman; for the Brahman is entitled to it all by his superiority and eminence of birth.[4]

101. The Brahman eats his own alone, wears his own, and gives away his own: through the benevolence of the Brahman, indeed, the other people enjoy (all they have).

102. For the ascertainment of his duties (and those) of the other (castes) in order, the prudent Manu Svāyaṁbhuva composed this treatise.

103. This treatise must be strenuously perused by a learned Brahman and explained rightly to the pupil, but not by any other (person).

104. A Brahman who studies this treatise[5] (and) who

[1] *Havya* and *kavya*. These two terms are continually put together by way of contrast. *Havya* is an oblation to the gods; *kavya* an offering to the Manes.

[2] *Dharma*: see the note to vs. 26.

[3] [Or, "He is *fitted* for Brahma-existence" (when he has acquired knowledge of *dharma*. It is doubtful if "Vedas" is the correct translation of *bráhma*; it probably refers to the substance from which the world is developed; not even meaning the spiritual absolute being; see note on ii. 28, 82.]

[4] As the commentators admit, this is mere figure of speech. Brahmans could commit theft just as well as people of lower caste (see ch. ix.), under Hindu laws just as under the Penal Code. They were, however, formerly let off very easily.

[5] "Treatise" = *çâstra*, or a body of teaching on any subject, either of divine or human origin. It may

has performed (his) vows, is never defiled by defects arising from mind, speech, or body.

105. He purifies his associates[1] and seven of his kindred, (both) ascending and descending; and, verily, he alone deserves all this earth.

106. This (treatise is) a cause of prosperity, most excellent, (and) increases intelligence; this treatise brings fame (and) long life; this (treatise is) the best (source of) knowledge which brings deliverance.

107. In this (treatise) *dharma* (is) fully declared, also the good and bad qualities of actions; likewise also the perpetual usages of the four castes.

108. Usage is highest *dharma*, (it is) mentioned in the Vedas and approved by tradition;[2] therefore, a prudent twice-born (man) should ever be intent on this.

109. A Brahman who has fallen away from usage gets not the fruit of the Veda; but (if he be) attached to usage, he enjoys the full fruit.

110. Thus devotees having seen (that) the course of *dharma* is according to usage, comprehended usage to be the final root of all austerity.

111. Manu has declared in this sacred treatise[3] the origin of the world and the rules of the sacramental rites; also vows, conduct, and service (as due by a pupil to his teacher), and the best rule for the ablution (by a student on finishing the pupil stage of his life);

112. The taking a wife also, and the definition of the (kinds of) marriages; the rules also for (the five) ceremonies, and the perpetual order of funeral rites;

113. Also the description of modes of livelihood, and the vows of a householder; also what may and may not be eaten, ceremonial purity, and the purification of chattels;

be asserted that written books are intended, but of this there is no direct proof till late times.

[1] "Associates," lit. "line," *i.e.*, those who sit in the same line with him in meals on solemn occasions. By being allowed to sit in the same line with others, men are, even now, restored to caste.

[2] [*Çruti* and *Smṛti*; cf. ii. 12.]

[3] The words—"Manu has declared . . . treatise"—are from vs. 118.

114. The application of *dharma* regarding women, the duties of ascetics, final bliss and renunciation (of the world); the whole *dharma* of kings and the decision of legal disputes;

115. Also the rules for examining witnesses, and the laws concerning husband and wife; the *dharma* of partition (of heritage); (about) gambling, and (that of) chastisement of criminals;

116. (The rules regarding) the service (due by) Vaiçyas and Çūdras, and the origin of mixed castes; also the law of castes in times of distress, and the rules of expiation;

117. Also the threefold state of existence[1] which arises from actions; and final bliss, and the examination of good and bad qualities of actions;

118. The eternal *dharma* of countries,[2] castes,[3] families;[4] also the *dharmas* of heretics[5] (and) of guilds.[6]

119. Just as Manu formerly, when questioned by me, declared this body of teaching, so learn ye it to-day from me!

END OF THE FIRST LECTURE.

[1] "Threefold state of existence," *i.e.*, being born again as an animal or in some higher form of existence—high, medium, or inferior. See xii. 51 and the matter before it, in which the three degrees are further subdivided, each into three.

[2] "*Dharma* of countries" [or districts], followed in some particular country, not in all the world (Medh.) Rāgh. gives the Holi festival as an example, which varies much in different localities.

[3] "Castes," Brahmans, etc.

[4] "Families," established by famous families (Medh.)

[5] "Heretics." Medhātithi explains this by *vikarmastha*, *i.e.*, who do what is wrong, "as Buddhists," etc.

[6] "Associations," as of traders, smiths, actors (Medh.)

It is worth while to compare the twelfth lecture with the first, on which it throws considerable light in parts. [The twelfth lecture appears more uniform, and is based on one system almost entirely; the first lecture appears to contain much more mingling of various philosophical views, as its whole character is that of a later prefix to the work. Aside from the Puranic mythology, I find it difficult to bring such verses as 55 ff. in harmony with Sāṅkhya doctrine.]

LECTURE II.

SOURCES OF THIS SYSTEM AND THE COUNTRIES WHERE IT OBTAINS; ON THE FIRST CONDITION OF LIFE OF A BRAHMAN, OR THAT OF A STUDENT.

1. LEARN the *dharma* which is followed by the learned (and) good, by those ever free from spite and passions, (and) which is acknowledged by the mind:[1]

2.[2] Selfishness (is) not praiseworthy, yet unselfishness exists not here; for the study of the Vedas is for selfish ends, and the practice of rites according to the Vedas.

3. Selfishness certainly has its root in the hope of a reward; sacrifices have their origin in selfishness; all vows and prohibitive rules[3] are said to arise from a hope of reward.

4. Any act of an unselfish man is never at any time seen here; for whatever one does, that is the act of selfishness.

[1] According to Medhātithi the first chapter is to be regarded as introductory; the real treatise begins here. The words, "*hṛdayenā 'bhyanujñātaḥ*" = "acknowledged by the mind," have much exercised the commentators. I take *hṛidaya* to be put for *manas*, of which it is the seat. This is much as Medhātithi explains it: "*hṛdayaçabdena cittam.*" Rāghavānanda says: "*Hṛdayene 'ti çāstradvaidhe sati sādhūnām manasy atīve 'ṣṭo yaḥ sa dharmaḥ / tathā ca Vyāsaḥ: Vaikalpike ātmatuṣṭiḥ* [*pramāṇam iti:* that is, the doctrine that where there is no fixed rule in the treatises one should follow his own inclinations. Cf. 6.]

[2] Vss. 2–5. These are clearly an interpolation in later times, when the doctrine of *bhakti*, or faith, had arisen. In the old Vedic religion, all ceremonies and sacrifices were avowedly performed in order to gain desired objects of different kinds. [We may compare Cic., Fin., 3. 5. 16: "Ex quo intellegi debet principium ductum esse a se diligendo,"—the principle of all action is derived from self-love. In the text, *self* is to be inferred; literally, "To be devoid of desire is something that does not exist in this world."]

[3] "Prohibitive rules," such as not to injure any one (Medh.)—[Gov.]

5. (Yet) one rightly occupied in those (acts) goes to the world of the immortals, and gets all (his) desires here as hoped for.

6.[1] The entire[2] Veda is the root of law, (so also) tradition and the practice[3] of those that know it; (also) the custom of the good, as well as satisfaction of (one's) self.

7. Whatsoever *dharma* was proclaimed by Manu for any one, that is all directed in the Veda; he (was) possessed of all knowledge.

8. So a learned man, having viewed by the eye of knowledge all this complete (system) as according to the authority of revelation, should certainly be firm in his own *dharma*.

9. For a man performing the *dharma* declared by revelation and tradition obtains fame here, and after his death extreme happiness.

10. Now the Veda is to be understood as "revelation," but the law-treatises[4] (*dharma-çāstra*) as "tradition;" these two are irrefutable[4] in all matters, for by these two virtue arose.

11. A Brahman who, from adherence to rationalism,[5] shall despise these two sources, he, an infidel blamer of the Vedas, is to be banished by the just.

12. The Veda, tradition, good custom, and (what is) pleasing to one's self, that (the wise) have plainly declared to be the fourfold definition of *dharma*.[6]

13. A knowledge of *dharma* is ordained for men not given up to wealth and pleasure; of those who would know *dharma*, the Veda (is) the supreme authority.

[1] Cf. Gautamadharma, i. 1. 2; Āpastamba, i. 1. 1, 2.

[2] [Medh. says some consider the Atharva as not a Veda at all, and hold only the threefold knowledge (of Rik, Yajus, Sāma) as binding.]

[3] [This may mean either practice as manners or good morals. Thirteen kinds of the latter are quoted by K. from Hārita, who adds that Gov. defines it as freedom from affection and hate.]

[4] "Law-treatises;" not necessarily, though very probably in this case, written books are intended. [Perhaps better, "These two are not to be discussed in any respect."]

[5] "Rationalism" [*hetuçāstra*]; Buddhist and Cārvāka, etc., doctrine (Medh.) [The *hetuçāstra* implies the *hetuka* (xii. 111), who is a very worthy person; but cf. iv. 30.]

[6] [Cf. i. 108.]

14. Now where there may be an opposition (of texts) of the Veda, both (inconsistent passages) are declared (to be) *dharma;* for both those *dharmas* were regularly declared by the wise.

15. (Thus there is) this Vedic revelation: "The sacrifice takes place at all times; when (the sun) has risen, also when (the sun) has not risen; so, too, when neither sun nor stars are seen."

16.[1] Authority (to study) this science is to be recognised (as belonging) to him whose sacramental course of life, from conception to cremation, has been declared (to be) by *mantras*,[2] but of no one else.

17. The (country) which is between the divine rivers Sarasvatī and Dṛṣadvatī, that land, fixed by the gods, (the wise) call *Brahmāvarta.*

18. What custom of the (four) castes (and) the mixed castes has been handed down by course of succession in that country, that is called good custom.[3]

19. *Kurukṣetra, Matsya, Pañcāla, Çūrasenaka,* (are) indeed *Brahmarṣi* land, next[4] to *Brahmāvarta.*

20. All men in the world should learn their own proper behaviour from a Brahman born in that country.

21. The country between the Himālaya and Vindhya (mountains), which is to the east of *Vinaçana* and to the west of *Prayāga*, is called the central country.[5]

22. (The land) indeed between those two mountains, (extending) to the Eastern and to the Western Sea, the wise call *Āryāvarta.*

[1] In Vedic times the reception of outsiders into the community was, to a certain extent, recognised, and ceremonies (*e.g.*, the *vrātyastoma*) were in use for this purpose. This verse is rather in the spirit of the exclusive Brahmans of modern times. [The ceremonies at this time were more for the purpose of readmitting outcast members than to admit new ones; cf. vs. 39 note. The general meaning of the verse may be "those whose course of life is such as the holy texts ordain.]

[2] *Mantras, i.e.*, Vedic texts.

[3] [Medh. observes this is a general rule, not specially, *e.g.*, to forbid marriage with a cousin on the mother's side, as some say.]

[4] "Next;" the commentators say "inferior." There is a map of India according to the text by Mr. E. Thomas in the new edition of the "Numismata Orientalia" (edited by him), Part I.

[5] [*Vinaçana, i.e.*, the terminus of the Sarasvatī; *Prayāga*, the place where the Yamunā meets the Ganges.]

23. Where the black antelope[1] is indigenous, that country is to be known as a land fit for sacrifices; the Mleccha land (is) beyond it.[2]

24. Let the twice-born (Brahmans, Kṣatriyas, and Vaiçyas) strenuously resort to those countries; but a Çūdra distressed for a livelihood may abide in any (land) whatsoever.

25. The source of *dharma* has been concisely told you, also the origin of all this (universe; now) learn the *dharmas* of the castes.

26. The conception-rite, &c., of the twice-born is to be effected by meritorious Vedic rites; (this) bodily sacrament (is) purificative both here and after death.[3]

27. By fire-offerings during the pregnancy, by the rite on birth, the shaving of the head to form a tuft, (and) by binding on the *muñja* string, the seminal and uterine sin of the twice-born is wiped away.

28. By study (of the Vedas), by vows, by fire-offerings, by the *traividya* (vow), by offerings, by offspring, and by the great sacrifices, as well as the (other) sacrifices,[4] this body is made united[5] with *Bráhman.*

29. Before cutting the umbilical cord of a male (child), the birth-rite is ordained (to be performed), and he (must)

[1] *Kṛṣṇamṛga.* What animal is intended it is impossible to say. In Southern India a pretty little, but rare, gazelle is taken for it. It does not, however, answer to the name so far as its colour (light brown) goes. The earliest mention of the animal by a European that I know is by Barbosa (circa 1516).

[2] "Beyond it," *i.e.*, sacrifices may not be performed there. [Medh. enumerates among Mlecchas the Meda Andhru (*sic*) Pulinda Çavara, &c. (cf. Medh. x. 48), as outsiders from the castes. The order to dwell in this land is construed to mean that if a king conquers the Mlecchas, he should make the kingdom like this land of sacrifice.]

[3] These verses enumerate the ten first sacramental rites, to which also are to be added the (11) *samāvartana*, or ceremony on a student's return home, and his (12) marriage. The first three rites (during pregnancy) are: (1) *garbhādhāna*, or sign of conception; (2) *puṁsavana*, or quickening, and (3) *sīmantonnayana*, or parting the mother's hair in the fourth, sixth, or eighth month of her first pregnancy. The best account of these rites is in the *prayogaratna* for the present time.

[4] [Such as the *jyotiṣṭoma* (Medh., K.)]

[5] [Another reading is neuter, "becomes a thing united to," etc. The word *brahma*, which has been left untranslated, is neuter, and means probably the world-substance, not as a spiritual, but as a physical force.]

eat honey and ghee in a gold (spoon) to (the accompaniment of) *mantras*.[1]

30. Now one should have his (the child's) name-rite performed on the tenth or twelfth day (after birth), or on a merit-giving lunar day or hour, or under a lucky star.

31. Let a Brahman's (name) be auspicious, a Kṣatriya's full of power; let a Vaiçya's mean wealth, a Çūdra's, however, be contemptible.[2]

32. Let a Brahman's (distinctive title) imply prosperity, a Kṣatriya's safeguard, a Vaiçya's wealth, a Çūdra's service.

33. Let women's (names) be pleasant, not harsh, plain of meaning, charming, auspicious, ending in a long vowel, (and) like words of benediction.

34. The infant's going out from the house should be done in the fourth month; (his) eating food in the sixth month,[3] or what auspicious (practice) is preferred in the tribe.[4]

35. The *cūḍā*[5]-rite of all[6] the twice-born must be done according to law in the first or third year (after birth), as ordered by revelation.

36. One should perform the investiture of a Brahman (with the sacred string) in the eighth year from conception; of a king (Kṣatriya) in the eleventh; of a Vaiçya in the twelfth.

[1] [The *mantras* are those used by his sect, his father's, or his Guru's; *male* is emphatic according to Medh. (This commentator's use of "some think," "some explain," is such as in this passage to suggest that they are occasionally used hypothetically, a possible view being set up and overthrown, rather than an actual statement that other commentators explain the passage so and so; a modification of meaning that would somewhat affect the amount of criticism devoted to the text before Medh.'s day).]

[2] This is obsolete. The names of the different castes are now usually epithets or titles of some favourite deity. The caste is known only by the suffixed title.

[3] There is more or less laxity allowed in these matters at present, [as permitted by the text and emphasised by the commentators; the tribal or family custom refers to the variation of time or of the practice. Medh. says "food" means other than milk which the child takes the first five months.]

[4] "In the tribe." This is an example of *kuladharma* alluded to in i. 118. A "tribe" is a lesser division than a caste, and more corresponds to a family.

[5] *Cūḍā*, *i.e.*, forming a tuft on the head; a kind of pigtail.

[6] Or "this rite is for all the twice-born only," *i.e.*, not the Çūdra, who, according to Medh., is included in vs. 34.

37. (The investiture) of a Brahman desirous of divine knowledge is to be done in the fifth year; of a king who seeks power, in the sixth; of a Vaiçya who wishes for wealth here, in the eighth (year).

38. The (communication of the) *gāyatrī*[1] does not, for a Brahman, take place after the sixteenth year; for a Kṣatriya, after the twenty-second; for a Vaiçya, after the twenty-fourth.

39. After that, (men of) those three (castes) who have not been invested at the proper time are *Vrātyas*,[2] degraded from the *gāyatrī*, (and) despised by the respectable.[3]

40. Let not a Brahman at any time, even in time of distress, form ties legally with those not purified according to rule; either (spiritual, by teaching them) the Veda, or by kinship.

41. Let students wear (outwardly) skins of the *kṛṣṇamṛga*, deer, or goats; (as under-garments,) stuff of hemp, *kṣuma*, or wool, in order (of the castes).[4]

42. The girdle of a Brahman is to be made of a triple cord of *muñja*, smooth[5] and pliable; but of a Kṣatriya it (should be) a bowstring of *mūrvā*; of a Vaiçya, a triple thread of hemp.[6]

43. If *muñja* cannot be had, (their girdles) are to be made of *kuça*, *açmāntaka*, (or) *valvaja*, threefold, with one knot, (or) three, or even five.

44. The sacred thread of a Brahman (must be) of cotton, put on (over the left shoulder), threefold; of a Kṣatriya (it must be) of hemp-thread; of a Vaiçya, a woolen thread.

45. A Brahman should, by law, have a staff of *bilva* or

1 *I.e.*, the investiture.

2 *Vrātyas*, an old term for Aryans not Brahmanised. Such people were admitted to the Aryans community by the ceremony called *vrātyastoma*. In later times *vrātya* came to mean people who were deficient as regards the sacramental rites as above.

3 [Ārya.]

4 Cotton and silk (with the well-to-do [Ārya] cloth and velvet) are alone used now for outer garments. Silk (as pure) is the only cloth used by some Vaiṣṇavas while eating.

5 [Or according to Medh., of like size, *i.e.*, "not small in one part and smaller in another."]

6 This girdle is now only used at investiture with the thread, or on occasion of its renewal every year by a *Brahmacārin* (student). For a description of *muñja* ("Saccharum sara" of botanists), see Stewart's "Punjab Plants" (1869), p. 261.

palāça (wood); a Kṣatriya, of banian (wood) or acacia; a Vaiçya, a reed or *udumbara* (staff).[1]

46. A Brahman's staff is to be made, according to rule, to reach (his) hair; a king's, as high as his forehead; a Vaiçya's, to reach his nose.

47. Let all these staves be straight, without blemish, fair to look at, not weapons of offence against men; with their bark, (and) not spoiled by fire.

48. Having taken a staff to his liking, and standing opposite to the sun, let (a student), having circumambulated the (sacred) fire to the right, go for alms[2] according to rule.

49. Let an invested Brahman go for alms, (using) *bhavat* at the beginning (of his request); let a king (do so, using) *bhavat* in the middle; but a Vaiçya with *bhavat* last.[3]

50. He should first beg alms of his mother, (his) sister, or the own sister of (his) mother, or (of a female) who will not insult him.[4]

51. Having gathered those alms as much as he wants, having informed his *Guru* (of it) without deceit, let him eat it after rinsing his mouth, (sitting) facing the east, (and) pure.

52. For one facing the east eats (food) conducive to long life; facing the south, conducive to fame; facing the

[1] Natives, except old and low-caste people, do not, in Southern India, carry staves. In Malabar the length of the stick (or handle) of the palm-leaf umbrella carried by every one denotes the caste. Brahmans have it nearly as long as they are tall; low-caste people have it only a few inches long. *Bilva*, the "Ægle Marmelos;" *Palāça*, the "Butea frondosa;" *Udumbara*, "Ficus glomerata."

[2] "Alms," articles of food, etc.

[3] *Bhavat*, *i.e.*, sir or madam, as the case may require; *e.g.*, "Sir! give alms;" "Give, sir! alms," etc. [King, *i.e.*, Kṣatriya.]

[4] This begging alms by a Vedic student is, I believe, everywhere obsolete. Such students are now almost unknown, for Brahmans are always married while yet boys. The practice of students going about to beg food, etc., arose, there can be little doubt, from the fact that the Brahman teachers were mostly poor men, and that they taught gratis. Students at the Government schools of the present day in Southern India think it no shame to follow the old custom, though they meet with the smallest success.

west, he eats prosperous (food); facing the north, he eats (food) conducive to truth.

53. Let a Brahman always eat his food after having rinsed his mouth, and (in a) collected (state of mind); having eaten, let him thoroughly rinse his mouth, and sprinkle with water the hollow parts.[1]

54. Let him ever reverence food, and let him eat without finding fault with it; having seen it, let him rejoice and be satisfied, and let him always receive it gladly.

55. For food that has been reverenced ever bestows strength and power; but that which has not been reverenced, (if) eaten, destroys both.

56. Let him not give the leavings to any one, and let him also not eat between (times);[2] let him not eat to excess, and let him not go anywhere with a morsel in his mouth.

57. Over-eating is unwholesome, prejudicial to long life and to (attainment of) heaven; (it is) vicious (and) detested by people; let him therefore avoid it.

58. Let a Brahman always perform the rinsing of his mouth with (the part of his hand called) *brāhmatīrtha*,[3] or with the *kāya* or *traidaçika;* never with the *pitrya.*

59. (They) call *brāhmatīrtha* (that part) which is on the surface of the root of the thumb; (that) at the root of the little finger, *kāya;* that at the tips (of the fingers), *daiva; pitrya,* that below those two.

60. Let him first thrice rinse his mouth with water, then twice wipe his mouth; and let him also touch with water the hollow parts,[4] the breast,[5] and also the head.

[1] "Hollow parts," *i.e.*, eyes, ears, nostrils, mouth, and excretory organs.

[2] "Between (times)." Medhātithi says [in giving the best of different explanations of "between"] that there are two times for eating—morning and evening, and that one should not eat at any other. Cf. Āp. Dh. S. i. 6, 18, 4, by which only enough food to support life is allowed to be eaten.

[3] *Tīrtha*, or "pool," is used as these several places are those from which the water is thrown or taken in the ceremonies.

[4] [Of the head. Cf. Gaut. i. 36 (K., Medh.)]

[5] [Literally, self-soul, "place of heart," or the navel; and I think this means the navel, because it is somewhere recorded that one should lay hold on the navel; the Mbh. commands also bathing of the feet.—Medh. (cf. Mbh. xiii. 104. 39.)]

61. One who knows the law (and is) desirous of purity should ever rinse his mouth by means of the *tīrtha*,[1] (and) facing the east or north, in a solitary place, (and) with water neither warm nor frothy.

62. A Brahman is purified by water that reaches his breast; a king by (water) that reaches his neck; a Vaiçya by (water) swallowed; but a Çūdra by (water merely) touched by the extremity of (his lips).

63. A Brahman is said (to be) *upavīta* when his right hand is lifted up (so that the sacrificial thread rests on his left shoulder and passes under his right arm); if his left (be extended, so that it rests on his right shoulder and passes under his left arm), *prācīnāvīta*; when it is round his neck (and is not under either arm), *nivīta*.

64. Having thrown into water his girdle, skin (outer garment), staff, sacrificial thread, (and) water-pot, (when) worn out, let him take others with texts of the Vedas.

65. The *keçānta* (tonsure-rite) is ordered (to be done) in the sixteenth year of a Brahman, in the twenty-second of a Kṣatriya, and in two years more after that for a Vaiçya.

66. This course, but without sacred texts, is all to be performed for females, at the due time, and in due order, for the consecration of (their) bodies.[2]

67. The marriage ceremony is said to be the Vedic consecration for women; (also) attendance to (their) husbands, subjection to the Guru, household affairs, (and) attention to the (household sacred) fire.

68. That holy rule regarding the investiture of the twice-born which distinguishes (their second) birth has been declared; learn next the course of their acts.

69. The teacher, having invested a pupil, should first teach him ceremonial purity, custom, and the attending to the (sacred) fire, also the *sandhyā* devotions.[3]

70.[4] Now when about to recite (the Veda) he is to be

[1] *Tīrtha*, see vs. 58.

[2] The only real sacrament (*saṁskāra*) for women is marriage. See next verse.

[3] [The twilight devotions, morn and eve.]

[4] 70 ff. Cf. another account of this curious scene in the *Prātiçākhya* of

taught, after he has rinsed his mouth, sitting with his face to the north,[1] as is prescribed, and having made[2] homage to the Vedas, with a light garment[3] on, and his senses regulated.

71. At the beginning and end (of recitation) of the Veda, the teacher's two feet are always to be clasped; he must recite having closed both hands, for that is called homage to the Vedas.

72. The clasping of his teacher's (feet) is to be done by him with the hands crossed,[4] the left (foot) is to be touched by the left (hand), the right by the right.

73. Let then the teacher, at all times unwearied, say to the (pupil) about to recite, "Ho! recite!" and let him rest (if he says), "Let there be a pause!"

74. A Brahman should always say *ōm* at the beginning and end (of a recital) of the Veda; without *ōm* before, it slips away; and without it after, it disappears.

75. Sitting on (*kuça*-grass) with the points to the east, and made pure by purifications,[5] purified (also) by three suppressions of breath, one is then fit (to pronounce) the syllable *ōm*.

76. Prajāpati milked from the three Vedas the letter *A*, also the letter *U* and the letter *M*,[6] and (the words) *bhūḥ, bhuvaḥ, svaḥ.*"

77. Also from the three Vedas Prajāpati, the Supreme Lord, milked part by part this *ṛc*, beginning with *tad*, (called) *gāyatrī*.[7]

the Rigveda, ch. xv. (Lect. iii. ch. 3), vol. iii., pp. 92-98 of M. Regnier's edition.

[1] [K. quotes Gaut. i. 54 to show he may stand facing east as well.]

[2] [Or "making" (°*kṛd*); *pāṭha* (Medh.); Vedas, literally Bráhma.]

[3] [One explanation of this is, according to Medh., that purity is shown by the lightness of the garment.]

[4] [Some read *vinyasta* (for *vyatyasta*), that is, the hands are to be spread out and lightly rested, so as not to hurt, touching merely with the finger-tips (Medh.)]

[5] ["Grass rings on his third finger," is Dr. B.'s translation (K. and Rāgh. say on the two hands), for which I have ventured to substitute the literal meaning, as these words are evidently explanatory.]

[6] These three letters form *ōm*.

[7] Rigveda, iii. 62, 10. *Tat savitur varenyam / bhargo devasya dhimahi / dhiyaḥ yo naḥ pra cadoyāt.* [This verse is one of the most famous in Hindu literature. Prof.

78. A Brahman who knows the Vedas, if he mutter that syllable (*ōm*) and that (verse) preceded by the three words (mentioned) at both *sandhyās* (or morning and evening), is endowed with the merit of the Vedas.

79. But a twice-born (man), having repeated those three a thousand times outside the (town[1]), is freed in a month from even a great sin, like a snake from its slough.

80. A Brahman, Kṣatriya, (or) Vaiçya not endowed with that *ṛc* and his proper sacraments at their due times, becomes an object of contempt among the good.

81. The three imperishable great words preceded by *ōm*, and also the *sāvitrī*, consisting of three lines,[2] is to be considered the mouth of the Vedas.

82.[3] He who, unwearied, repeats day by day those (words and text) for three years, goes, with an etherial body,[4] to the supreme *Bráhma*, becoming (like) air.

83. The one syllable *ōm* (is) the supreme *Bráhma;* suppressions of breath (are) the highest austerity; but there is (nothing) higher than the *sāvitrī:* truth is better than silence.

84. All the Vedic rites, oblational (and) sacrificial, pass

Whitney has discussed it in vol. i. p. 111-112 of the new edition of Colebrooke's Essays. His translation runs as follows:—"Of Savitar, the heavenly, that longed-for glory may we win, and may himself inspire our prayers!"]

[1] "Outside the town," *i.e.*, on a river island and the like (Medh.); "on the bank of the river, or in a jungle and the like" (K.) [This is undoubtedly a general statement offering purification on slight terms. Medh. has an amusing discussion of this point, comparing this purification with other severer ones. Who, he says, would be such a fool as to undergo severe penance and bodily mortification when he can get purified by merely muttering prayers? As a verse says, "If honey is found in the sunbeam, what use to go to the mountain?" Again, "That which can be got for a penny, no sensible man buys for ten." The real meaning is that the regular purification must be done; this is for general absolution when sins are done unintentionally.]

[2] [The *sāvitrī* (*gāyatrī*) has three *pādas*, cf.. vs. 77. Vedas, literally Bráhma.]

[3] 82 ff. This is quite recent in idea; substitutes for sacrifices in this style are found in relatively recent treatises only, such as the Sāmavidhāna-brāhmaṇa and Ṛgvidhāna.

[4] [That is to say, his body is destroyed; he is like the atmosphere, devoid of a real body (Medh., K. Rāgh.) On Bráhma, cf. vs. 28, note. I have here again ventured to change the translation of Dr. B. ("goes in *his own* body"), convinced that it is a mere mistake through reading *sva* for *kha*.]

away; but this imperishable[1] syllable *ōm* is to be known to be *Bráhma* and also *Prajāpati.*

85. The sacrifice of muttering (this word, &c.) is said to be better by tenfold than the regular sacrifice; if inaudible, it is a hundredfold (better); a thousandfold, if mental.

86. The four household sacrifices accompanied by the regular sacrifices,[2] all those are not worth the sixteenth part of the sacrifice by muttering.

87. But by (such) muttering even a Brahman (becomes), there is no doubt, perfect; whether he perform anything else or not, a Brahman is called *maitra* (or well disposed to all things.)[3]

88. Let a wise man, like a driver of horses, exert diligence in restraint of his senses straying among seductive sensual objects.

89. Those eleven senses which former wise men have mentioned, I will declare rightly in due order.

90. Ears, skin, the two eyes, the tongue, and the nose also (as) fifth, the anus and generative organ, hand and feet; speech is said (to be) the tenth.

91. The ears, &c., in succession, (viz.) five of these (ten

[1] "Imperishable." Medhātithi reads *akṣaram*, which he explains by "imperishable." *Akṣayam* is given by Kullūka, which means the same; Haughton reads *duṣkaram*, or "hard to make," which is unintelligible.

[2] "Four household sacrifices," *i.e.*, the *pākayajñas* called *Vaiçvadeva-homa, balikarman; nityaçrāddha*, and *atithibhojana*. "Regular sacrifices," *i.e.*, new and full-moon sacrifices, etc. (*darçapūrṇamāsa*, etc.) [The *pākayajñas* are called "the great sacrifices;" omitting the *brahmayajña*, there are the (above-named) four (Medh.) According to K. the *pākayajñas* are these four of the five *mahāyajñas*, great sacrifices.]

[3] [As this is carefully punctuated in Dr. B.'s MS., I allow the translation to stand as his, though it seems to me rather to reverse the original meaning; for the tenor of these verses is, as he has pointed out above (82 note), that just as much good is done by prayer as by destruction of life in sacrifices. The translation would, therefore, be perhaps better if we translated *eva* in its usual sense, rendered *saṁsidhyet* according to the commentators, and connected (*b*, 1) with (*a*) thus: "Now there is no doubt that a Brahman would attain complete happiness by merely muttering prayers, whether he perform anything else or not (*i.e.*, slay animals at a sacrifice), [for] a Brahman is called one who is friendly (to all creatures)." Rāgh. also seeks a connection between Maitra and Mitra, the sun-god; cf. xi. 35.]

the wise) term organs of sense; the anus, etc., viz., five of them (they term) organs of action.

92. Mind is to be known (as) the eleventh, which by its own nature partakes of both (sense and action), which being conquered, those two sets of five are also conquered.[1]

93. Without doubt, one incurs fault by attachment of the senses (to sensual objects); but having subdued them, then one gets perfection.

94. Desire never rests by enjoyment of lusts, like as fire surely[2] increases the more by butter (offered in it).

95. He indeed who may attain all those desires, and he who may forsake them entirely, (as for both these) the renunciation is better than attainment of all lusts.

96. Those (organs) attached to sensual objects cannot be curbed so much by non-indulgence as ever by knowledge.

97. The Vedas, liberality also and sacrifices, observances also and austerities, never make for the perfection of one who is of depraved nature.

98. That man who, having heard and touched, seen and eaten and smelled, neither rejoices nor ever is sad, he is to be known (as a man) who has conquered his senses.

99. But among all the senses, if one sense fails, by that his wisdom fails; as water (runs out) by one hole from a leather bag.[3]

[1] [These eleven organs of sense and action plus the two principles of intelligence and consciousness make the "thirteen instruments of knowledge" of the Sāṅkhya doctrine. Cf. with this elaborate interpolation (?) the vss. i. 14, 15.]

[2] [Just as a fire merely grows greater if a melted oblation is poured upon it, so lust, etc.; a proverbial verse in the epic poetry.]

[3] Medh. reads *dṛtcḥ pādāt, i.e.*, from the bottom of a leather bag. K. has *dṛtcḥ pātrāt, i.e.*, from a vessel of leather. [Medh. means, I think, literally one *foot* of the bag. He says the vessel is one made of a goat's hide, and adds, "All the water could escape from one foot, even if all the other feet are securely fastened." Rāgh. renders *pādād* directly by "from a hole." The hide often is used in Oriental countries complete, each leg being made water-tight. Though Dr. B. prefers Medh.'s explanation, he has kept that of K. It is possible, however, that K.'s *pātrāt* may merely explain *dṛtcḥ*, and both words may be ablatives, *chidra*, as in Rāgh., paraphrasing *pādāt*, "from a leather vessel out of a hole."]

100. Having restrained the host of senses, and having also subdued the mind, (even though) not wasting his body by asceticism, a man may attain all objects.[1]

101. At the morning twilight let him stand muttering the *sāvitrī* till he has seen the sun; at the evening, (let him) seated (mutter it), till the constellations clearly appear.

102. Standing and muttering (the *gāyatrī*) at the morning twilight, he removes nocturnal sin; but seated at the evening twilight, he destroys sin done by day.

103. But he who stands not at the morning and sits not at the evening (twilight) is to be expelled, like a Çūdra, from every ceremony of the twice-born.

104. Subdued near water, let him engaged in the obligatory ceremonies repeat the *sāvitrī*, having gone to a forest, (being) self-possessed.

105. There is also no prohibition of study for the *vedāṅgas*[2] or the obligatory recitation, so also as regards the texts for offerings to fire (*homa*).

106. There is no prohibition of the obligatory recitation, for that is called the Veda sacrifice;[3] the Veda sacrifice is meritorious with (the word) *vaṣaṭ*, which should not be uttered.[4]

107. He who, restrained and pure, goes over the recitation according to rule for a year, for him it ever flows with milk, curds, butter, honey.

108. Let a twice-born man who has been invested (with the sacred string) collect fuel, go begging, sleep low on the ground, do what pleases (his) teacher, till he (the pupil) returns home.

[1] [K. understands by this that a man accustomed to pleasures should give them up gradually, so as to do himself no harm. Medh. offers two explanations of *yogataḥ*, uniting it with *akṣiṇvan*, or with *vaçekṛtvā*.]

[2] *Vedāṅgas*. So Medhātithi explains *upakaraṇa* = helping, assisting, apparatus. [In (*b*) Medh. notes *na virodha iti vā pāṭhaḥ*.]

[3] [Which never has an end (Medh.)]

[4] [This may be the sense, but it seems better to render: "the Veda-sacrifice (recitation) is meritorious, though the signal for completion has been given." The second Veda-sacrifice means here the recitation, which is meritorious although the word *vaṣaṭ*, indicating the end of the sacrifice (here the reading), has been pronounced. *Vauṣaṭkartum* is to pronounce the benediction, to end the work.]

109. Ten are legally to be instructed—the son of (one's) teacher, an obedient (youth), one who communicates knowledge, one who is virtuous, one who is pure, one who is trustworthy, one who is able, one who gives wealth, one who is good, one's own (relative).

110. Let not a prudent man unasked tell any one (the Vedas), nor (tell) one who asks improperly; though he knows, let a wise man act like a dumb man in the world.

111. He who declares illegally and he who asks illegally, one of those two dies or incurs hatred.

112. Where there are not virtue and wealth or suitable obedience, learning is not to be sown there, just as (one does not sow) good seed in barren soil.

113. Rather a teacher of the Veda should die with his knowledge; even (if) in distress,[1] he may not sow it in wild salt soil.

114.[2] Learning went to a Brahman (and) said, "I am thy treasure! Guard me! Give me not to a scorner! so I shall be strongest.

115. "But him whom thou knowest (to be) a pure student subdued, declare me to him, a Brahman, a protector of (this) treasure, (and) not self-willed."

116. Now he who may acquire the Veda without permission from one reciting (it), he is guilty of theft of the Veda, (and) goes to hell.

117. One should salute first him from whom one gets secular, Vedic, or also transcendental[3] knowledge.

118. Better a well-behaved Brahman who knows only the *gāyatrī*, than one ill-behaved, who eats all (kinds of

[1] "Even (if) in distress," *i.e.*, he must not communicate it to an unworthy person for a reward.

[2] This, with vs. 144 [which appears to have originally followed these verses as a whole], constitutes a very favourite saying of the Brahmans. These verses, in an older form, are quoted in the Nirukta (ii. 4), and (more like this present text) they occur also in the Viṣṇu and Vasiṣṭha *smṛtis*. They also occur in the Saṁhito-panishadbrāhmaṇa of the Sāmaveda, see pp. 29–30 of my edition. [The older form of these two verses, 114, 115 (as well as 144), was in the *triṣṭubh* metre, as in the *smṛtis* just referred to.]

[3] [Knowledge concerning one's self (*adhyātman*; cf. Jobaent., p. 58), as opposed to the outer world.]

food) and sells all (kinds of articles), though he knows the three Vedas.

119. One should not sit down on a bed or couch on being approached[2] by a superior, and one sitting on a bed or couch should arise and salute him.

120. For at an old man's approach the vital breath[2] of a youth goes out upwards; by rising and saluting he gets it again.

121. Of one who has the habit of saluting always (and) reverencing the aged, four (things) increase—life, knowledge, glory, (and) strength.

122. After saluting, a Brahman addressing an elder should declare his own name, saying, "I am such a one!"

123. Those who understand not[3] salutation by name, let a wise man say to them, "It is I." So also to all women.

124. In salutation one should utter the word "*bhoḥ*" at the end of one's name; for the nature of "*bhoḥ*"[4] has been held by the seers (to be the same as) the nature of names.

125. In salutation a Brahman is to be addressed, "Live long, sir!" at the end of his name the vowel[5] with its preceding letter is to be uttered prolonged.

126. The Brahman who knows not the (form of) answer to a salutation is not to be saluted by a wise man; as a Çūdra, so even (is) he.

127. One should ask a Brahman on meeting (him) after (his) happiness; a Kṣatriya, (after his) welfare; a Vaiçya, (after his) prosperity; a Çūdra, (after his) health.

128. A person initiated (for a sacrifice) is not to be

[1] On a bed or couch occupied by (K.); or according to Medh., one should not sit down alongside a superior on a prepared bed or couch.]

[2] "Breath," lit. "breaths;" "it," lit. "them."

[3] "Understand not," *i.e.*, from ignorance of Sanskrit.

[4] [*I.e.*, *bhoḥ*, when used for names of persons, is the form of the name.]

[5] [Lit. the vowel *a* which stands for *i*, and the others; this is in the salutation in return, and the rule is for Kṣatriyas and Vaiçyas as well as priests (Medh.)]

addressed by name, even though he be the younger; but let one who knows law accost him with *bhoḥ* or *bhavat.*

129. The wife of another and women not relatives, one should address by *bhavatī*, *subhagā*, or *bhaginī.*

130. One's maternal and paternal uncles, wife's father, priests, teachers (though) younger, one should, standing up, accost by "I am such an one."

131. A mother's sister, a maternal uncle's wife, a mother-in-law, and a father's sister are to be reverenced like a teacher's wife; they are equal to a teacher's wife.[1]

132. A brother's wife of the same caste is to be saluted even every day; but kinswomen are to be saluted after an absence from home.

133. To his father's sister, (and) his mother's sister, and (his own) elder[2] sister, one should behave as to (one's) mother; (but) a mother (is) more venerable than they.

134. The equality of fellow-citizens is for (a difference in age of) ten years; of artisans, (for) five; of priests, (for) three; but among blood-relations for a short while.[3]

135. Now one should consider a Brahman ten years old and a Kṣatriya a hundred years old as father and son; but of them the Brahman (is) the father.

136. Wealth, kindred, age, acts, (and) knowledge as the fifth; those are causes of respect; the most important (is) the last (mentioned).

137. In whom among the three (higher) castes the most and the best of (those) five may be, he is here worthy of respect; even a Çūdra, (if) he has attained the tenth (decade of his life).

138. Way is to be made for one in a carriage, one in his tenth (decade), a sick person, one carrying a load, a woman,

[1] [This rule applies even if the women are younger (than the speaker).—Medh. The teacher is here the Guru.]

[2] [Accidentally omitted in Dr. B.'s MS.]

[3] *I.e.*, a small difference in age constitutes among relatives a difference in position; but in other cases only a considerable difference as specified. [This "equality" refers to the form of salutation among equals. Cf. Gaut. vi. 15 ff.]

also for the king and a student who has returned home, and for a bridegroom.[1]

139. But of (all) those (if) met together, the student who has returned home and the prince[2] are to be honoured (with the right of way); but of the prince and the student who has returned home, the student receives this honour from the prince.

140. Now the twice-born man who having invested a pupil (with the sacred string) teaches him the Veda with its ritual and *upaniṣads,*[3] him (the learned) term teacher (*ācārya*).

141. But he is called sub-teacher (*upādhyāya*) who for (his) livelihood teaches a single portion of the Veda, or again the Vedāṅgas.

142. That Brahman is called Guru who performs according to rule the rites on conception and the like, and feeds (the child) with rice (for the first time).

143. He who, chosen by any one, performs the *agnyādheya,*[4] *pākayajñas,* and *agniṣṭoma,* and other sacrifices, is called here the sacrificial priest (*ṛtvij*).

144. He who fills[5] duly both ears with the Veda is to be considered (like one's) father and mother; him one should never injure.

145. A teacher surpasses in venerableness ten sub-teachers; a father, a hundred teachers; but a mother (surpasses) a thousand fathers.

146. Of the natural father and the giver of the Veda, the more venerable (is) the father who gives the Veda; the birth of a twice-born man through the Veda is eternal, here and after death.[6]

1 "Bridegroom," *vivāhāya pravṛttaḥ.*—Medhātithi.

2 "Prince," not a mere Kṣatriya, [because of vs. 135, K.]

3 [Lit. "its mysteries," cf. vs. 165.]

4 *I.e.*, the establishment of the sacred fires. It must be remarked that the first three terms here defined (and especially *ācārya* and *guru*) are not used in this book with the precision one might expect after this definition; at the end of this lecture *ācārya* and *guru* are used as equivalent.

5 "Fills," *ātṛṇoti* or *āvṛṇoti*; both readings occur. Medhātithi supports the first. [Cf. Yāska's *ātṛṇatti*, vide note to 114.]

6 *I.e.*, by a knowledge of the Vedas one profits not only here, but ever after in successive conditions of existence, whereas the effect of the natural birth ceases with death.

147. As his father and mother beget him mutually out of lust, one should know that (birth to be merely) his cause of existence, when he is born from the womb.

148. But the birth which the teacher[1] who has completed the Veda, duly brings about for him by the *gāyatrī*, that is the true (birth), free from old age, eternal.

149. He who confers the benefit of the Veda (*çruta*) on any one, be it little or be it much, he should know him to be here his Guru, by reason of that benefit through the Veda.

150. The Brahman who is the cause of the Vedic birth and the director of one's duty, even though a youth, is legally the father of an old man (whom he teaches).

151. Āṅgirasa[2] Kavi, a child, taught his elders,[3] (and) said to them, "Children!" having received them (as pupils) by reason of his knowledge.

152. They, indignant, asked the gods about that matter; and the gods having assembled, said to them, "The child has spoken to you correctly."

153. An ignorant man is verily a child; one who communicates the *mantra* is a father; for (the wise) have called an ignorant man a child, but one who communicates the *mantra* a father.

154. For not by years, nor by grey hair, not by wealth or kindred (is superiority); the seers made the rule—Who knows the Veda completely, he is great among us.[4]

155. Of Brahmans superiority (is) by knowledge, but of Kṣatriyas by valour; of Vaiçyas by reason of property (and) wealth, and of Çūdras by birth.

156. One is not, therefore, aged because his head is grey; whoever, although a youth, has perused (the Vedas), him the gods consider an elder.

157. Like a wooden elephant, like a leathern deer, so a

[1] [Ācārya; so in the following, if not used technically.]

[2] [Cf. Baudh. i. 3. 47. The sentiment is opposed by Āp. i. 13, 15.]

[3] "His elders," *pitaraḥ*. Medhātithi explains this by "uncles, their sons, and the like." [Cf. Āp. i. 13, 15.]

[4] [This verse with the following is proverbial, and is repeated several times in the Mbhā. and the other law-books.]

Brahman who has not perused (the Veda): those three carry the name only.[1]

158. As a eunuch (is) unproductive with women, and as a cow (is) unproductive with a cow, and as a gift to a fool (is) futile, so a Brahman who knows not the (Veda) verses (is) useless.

159. Teaching for good is to be effected without injury to creatures;[2] and by one desiring his duty, also, sweet low speech must be used.

160. He whose speech and mind (are) pure and ever properly guarded verily obtains all the fruit derived from the completed Veda.[3]

161. Let not a man, even though pained, be sour-tempered, nor devise a deed of mischief to another; let not a man utter improper (sayings), by which utterance another is made uneasy.[4]

162. A Brahman should ever shrink from honour as from poison, and should always be desirous of disrespect as if of ambrosia.

163. For though despised, one sleeps with comfort, with comfort awakes, with comfort goes about in this world; (but) the scorner perishes.

164. Purified in self by this course of acts, a twice-born (student) should gradually, while dwelling with his Guru, accumulate austerity according to the Veda.

165. By different kinds of austerities and by various vows prescribed by rule the whole Veda with its esoteric teaching[5] is to be studied by a twice-born man.

166. So let a Brahman ever study just the Veda, when

[1] Probably allusions to old stories. Cf. the Bṛhatkathā for a wooden elephant. Medhātithi takes it literally. [In Mbhā. xii. 36, 46 ff., the same idea as this is expressed in slightly different words (but *yathā* still retained!) and with added similes.]

[2] "Creatures," *i.e.*, pupils, who are to be chastised by a rope or bamboo! (Medhātithi and Kullūka).

[3] [Or (Medh.) "first recognised in the Vedānta."]

[4] [In Mbhā. xiii. 104, 31, this verse occurs as Triṣṭubh, which may indicate the older form. This is not necessarily the case, however, as some of the latest verses in the Mbhā. are in that measure.]

[5] [What in vs. 140 is translated *upaniṣads*; lit. mystery.]

about to practise austerity; practice of the Veda is here termed a Brahman's best austerity.[1]

167. The twice-born man who, though wearing a garland, daily repeats the Veda as well as he can, to the tips of his nails performs the highest austerity.

168. The twice-born man who not having gone over the Veda makes diligence in other matters,[2] he with his progeny, even when living, speedily attains the condition of a Çūdra.

169. By rule of revelation (*çruti*) a twice-born man's first birth (is) from a mother; the second, on binding on the girdle; the third, on initiation for a sacrifice.[3]

170. Of these, his Veda-birth is marked by the binding on of the girdle; in it the *gāyatrī* (is) the mother, but the teacher is said to be the father.

171. (The learned) term the teacher father by reason of his communicating the Veda; for no rite is proper for him (the student) up to the fastening of the girdle.

172. Let him not use[4] the Veda except for funeral rites; for he is like a Çūdra so long as he is not born by the Veda.

173. Of him who has been invested the performance of vows is required, and also the reception of the Veda in due order with rites.

174. Whatever skin(-garments), whatever thread, and whatever girdle is ordered for any one, whatever staff and whatever clothes, that (is) for him even in (the performance of) vows.

175. Now let a student of the Veda living with his Guru follow these rules, having restrained the host of his senses for the sake of the increase of his austerity.

176. Being bathed[5] (and) pure, let him ever make

[1] [Cf. Āp. i. 12, 1 ff.]

[2] [Women's knowledge, etc. Cf. Āp. ii. 29, 11; Vas. iii. 2.]

[3] [So the *twice*-born has *three* births! Viṣṇu xxviii. 37 gives only two.]

[4] [*I.e.*, peruse for himself as well as employ at rites; for it is elsewhere said, *Na Brahmā bhiryāharet*; therefore the opinion some hold that it is no fault to peruse by himself is incorrect.—Medh.]

[5] [He should bathe for cleanliness, not for pleasure, according to Gaut. ii. 8, 9, and ix. 61; Baudh. i. 2. 3, 39; and Viṣṇu xxviii. 5 (K.).

libation of water to the gods, seers, and manes; also (let him do) worship of the gods, and collecting of fuel.

177. Let him avoid honey and flesh, perfumes, garlands, (sweet) juices, women; all sweets turned sour, and injury also to living beings;

178. Ointments, collyrium for the eyes, shoes, carrying an umbrella; lust and anger and greed, dancing and music;

179. Gaming also, and disputes between people, gossip and falsehood; looking at and touching women also, and striking another (person).

180. Let him sleep by himself always; let him never spill (his) seed; for one who voluntarily spills (his) seed destroys his vow.

181. A twice-born student having involuntarily spilt (his seed) in sleep, having bathed and having worshipped the sun, should thrice mutter the text, "Again to me,"[1] &c.

182. Let him, well-disposed,[2] collect the water-pot, cow-dung, earth, *kuça* (grass), as much as necessary (for his Guru), and let him, day by day, go to beg.

183. Let a student, restrained, gather alms every day from the house of persons not wanting in the Vedic sacrifices who are famed in (respect of) their acts.

184. Let him not beg in the family of his Guru, nor from his kinsmen or relatives; but if there be not other houses, let him avoid the first.[3]

185. Or let him, in the absence of those mentioned formerly, go to the whole village, restrained, having repressed (his) speech; but let him avoid accursed (sinners).[4]

186. Having gathered fuel from afar, let him lay it

[1] 'Again to me.' '*Punar mām aitv indriyam*,' "Again to me may strength return" (Taitt. Āraṇyaka, i. 30). Such uses of texts are frequent in the later Vedic works, *e.g.*, the *Sāmavidhānabrāhmaṇa* and the several *Rigvidhānas*.

[2] [*Sumanasaḥ* (?), better *flowers* (K.) Let him collect the water-pot, flowers, etc.]

[3] [*I.e.*, each first; in other words, he should not resort to any of these unless he must; then let him begin with the last mentioned. According to Medh., in this inverse order: his Guru's relatives, relatives on the father's side, those on the mother's side, *i.e.*, her brother, etc.]

[4] [In the language of the *Sūtras* we have here *abhiçasta* for *mahāpātakin*; cf. Āp. i. 21, 8.]

down in the air,[1] and, evening and morning, let him, unwearied, offer with it to fire.

187. Not having begged, and not having fed the fire for seven days, if not sick, (a student) should perform the vow of an unchaste student.[2]

188. Let him ever subsist by alms; let one under a vow eat not the food of one person; the subsistence by alms of one under a vow is said to be equal to fasting.

189. But he may eat at his will, so far as his vow will allow, when invited for a ceremony to the gods, and abstinently[3] (in a ceremony) to the manes; (so) his vow is not broken.

190. This conduct is, indeed,[4] indicated by the wise for a Brahman; but this conduct is not ordered thus for a Kṣatriya or Vaiçya.

191. Directed by (his) Guru, (and) even if not directed, let him ever exert[5] himself in study and in (what is) grateful to his teacher.

192. Having restrained both body and speech, (his) organs of sense (and his) mind, let him stand with the palms of his hands together regarding the face of (his) Guru.

193. He should ever have his arm bare,[6] (be) well-behaved and composed; if addressed, "Be seated!" let him sit opposite (his) Guru.

194. In his Guru's presence let him always have the worse food, clothes, and garments; let him stand up[7] before him, and go to rest last.

195. Let him not, when lying down, listen to[8] and

[1] [*I.e.*, out-doors.]

[2] '*Avakīrṇin*,' *i.e.*, a student who has failed in chastity, etc. [cf. xi. 121; the expiation, ib. 119. "Sick," *i.e.*, ill.]

[3] [Literally, "like a seer" (*ṛṣivat*). Medh. says this and the foregoing *vratavad* are "two words with one meaning."]

[4] [(*eva*), perhaps better "for a Brahman alone."]

[5] [Medh. reads *yogam* for *yatnam*.]

[6] [Literally, hand. K. says, "His right arm outside of his outer garment." Medh. remarks that some think the application of this rule is at the moment of address by the Guru, "he should have his body covered up in the Guru's presence (should not remove the outer garment) and stand thus; but the rule takes effect the moment the Guru by word or wink indicates that he is to be seated." (Cf. Āp. i. 2. 6, 18.)]

[7] [*I.e.*, get up in the morning.]

[8] [*I.e.*, in effect, he should not recline, &c., when listening or conversing.]

converse (with his Guru), nor seated, nor eating, nor standing with his face turned aside.

196. Let him do so standing (if his Guru) be seated, but approaching him if standing; meeting him if he advance, and running after (him) if he run;

197. Facing him if (his face) be turned away; going near if he be standing far off; but reverencing him if lying down, and in his proximity if standing.

198. Let his bed and seat be always low in (his) Guru's presence; let him not sit as he likes within eyesight of (his) Guru.

199. Let him not utter his (the Guru's) mere name [1] even behind his back; [2] let him not imitate his gait, speech, acts.

200. Where there is detraction or even blame of (his) Guru, he must there stop both ears, or go from thence elsewhere.

201.[3] By detraction (of his Guru) he becomes (when born again) an ass; a blamer (of his Guru) becomes indeed a dog; one who appropriates his goods becomes a worm; (if) envious, he becomes an insect.

202. Let him not when at a distance salute him, nor if angry,[4] or in proximity of a woman; [5] and so, if on a vehicle or seat, having descended, he should accost him.

203. Let him not sit with (his) Guru to the leeward or windward (of him); and let him not even tell anything out of hearing of (his) Guru.[6]

204. He may sit with his teacher in a bullock-, horse-, or camel-carriage; on a terrace, pavement, and mat; and on a rock, plank, (or) boat.[7]

205. (His) Guru's Guru being near, let him behave as if

[1] It is remarkable that this notion is still current, and it is thought even now in Southern India highly indecent to mention direct the names of certain persons. A married woman who is a witness in court (*e.g.*) will never mention her husband's name, but will (if possible) get some bystander to tell it.

[2] [That is, he should put a respectful epithet before the name even when speaking of him behind his back (K.)]

[3] [Each half of this verse has a syllable over.]

[4] [Or when the Guru is angry (*kruddham*) (Medh.)]

[5] [*I.e.*, when he (the Guru) stands in the presence of his wife (K.)]

[6] [*I.e.*, he should not say anything at all in a tone too low for his Guru to hear.]

[7] [Medh. says the word carriage is to be taken with bullock, horse, etc., for it is not permitted to sit alongside the teacher on the backs of these ani-

(his) Guru (were present); and if not permitted by (his) Guru, let him not accost his own elders.[1]

206. So (should be) his constant behaviour to (his) Gurus in learning,[2] to his own blood-relatives, to those who forbid him from wrong, also to those who indicate (his) good.

207. Let him also ever behave towards the excellent as toward (his) Guru; also toward (his) Guru's worthy sons, and toward (his) Guru's own kinsmen.[3]

208. The Guru's son, (whether) younger or of equal age, or a pupil, if he in sacrificial rites teach the Vedas, deserves the same honour as the Guru.

209. But let him not shampoo (his) Guru's son's limbs, nor bathe him, nor eat his leavings, nor wash his feet.

210. The Guru's wives of equal caste are to be reverenced like the Guru; but those of different caste are to be reverenced by rising and salutation.

211. Anointing, bathing, as also shampooing the limbs and dressing the hair, are not to be done (by him) for a Guru's wife.

212. A youthful wife of a Guru is not to be saluted here by a student of full twenty years old, who discerns good and evil, by (touching her) feet.[4]

213. This is the nature of women, to seduce men here; hence the discerning are not in effect[5] careless towards wantons.

214. For a wanton can lead astray in (this) world an ignorant, or, again, even a learned man when subject to lust and anger.

mals (consequently the words do not mean *on* a bullock, etc., and *in* a carriage). This permission would indeed be given if "carriage" could be understood as an independent word, but general custom forbids it. Terrace means the earth at the top of the house, "pavements" of grass, &c.; plank, *i.e.*, wooden settee.]

[1] [Gurus, *i.e.*, father, mother, etc. (Medh.); those to whom respect is due.]

[2] [*I.e.*, the *upādhyāna*, etc., other than the *ācārya* (Medh.)]

[3] [Medh. reads *guruputre tathācārye* (as Rāgh.), but knows K.'s reading; 207, 208, are in translation based on K.]

[4] [Gaut. ii. 33, contradicts this (as a youth of twenty is *vyavahāraprāpta*), and says some prohibit it.]

[5] [For this reason (*ato arthāt* Medh., K.) cf. Mbhā. xiii. 48, 38, idem, except v. l. *atyartham na prasajjante*, *i.e.*, the wise are not over-fond of wanton women.]

215. One should not be seated in a secluded place with a mother, sister, or daughter; the powerful host of the senses compels even a wise man.

216. But a youth may, at his will, make reverence duly (by prostration) on the ground to the youthful wives of (his) Guru, saying, "I am such an one."

217. Having been from home, he should, remembering the duty of the good, touch the feet of his Guru's wives, and salute them every day.

218. As a man digging with a spade comes to water, so an obedient (student) attains unto the knowledge attained by (his) Guru.

219. Be he shaven[1] or long-haired, or be his hair fastened in a knot, let not the sun set or rise on him (asleep[2]) in the village.

220. If without his knowledge the sun rise or even set while he is asleep voluntarily, let him fast a day, muttering (the *gāyatrī*).[3]

221. For one caught asleep by the sun rising or setting, if he does not penance, incurs great sin.

222. Having rinsed the mouth, one should, restrained and composed, ever at sunrise and sunset be seated, muttering, according to rule, in a pure spot, (the texts) to be repeated.

223. If a woman or a low-caste man do any good act, (the twice-born) should (also) do it all with energy, or (that) in which his mind may delight.

224. "Good" is said to be duty and wealth combined, pleasure and wealth combined, or even duty or wealth here is "good;" but the right opinion (is) that it consists of all three.[4]

1 "Shaven," etc., *i.e.*, a student.

2 [So K., or "he may be," etc.; "long-haired" (*jaṭa*), cf. iii. 151 note. Others, says Medh., give a different interpretation, referring it to his duties out of the village, which he is to quit at the twilight. Cf. Āp. i. 30, 8; and Gaut. ii. 10.]

3 [Gaut. xxiii. 21, gives fasting as the expiation for neglect when the sun rises, muttering the *gāyatrī* when it sets. Cf. Āp. ii. 12, 13.]

4 [Four schools are noted. The first say good (or happiness) consists of duty and wealth (*artha*, gain, cattle, land, gold — Medh.); the second of pleasure and wealth; the third of duty alone (*eva*); the fourth

225. A teacher[1] (is) the image of Brahma; a father (is) the image of Prajāpati; a mother (is) the image of the earth; one's own brother (is) the image of one's self.

226. So a teacher, a father, a mother, and an elder brother, are not to be disrespectfully treated, especially by a Brahman,[2] even though injured.

227. The pain that a father and mother endure in producing human beings, of that acquittance cannot be made even by hundreds of years.

228. One should ever do what is pleasing to them and to a teacher always; for these three[3] being satisfied, all austerity is accomplished.

229. Obedience to these three is called the highest austerity; except permitted by them,[4] one should not perform other religious duties.[5]

230. For they themselves are the three worlds, they are also the three orders;[6] they are the three Vedas, (and) they also are called the three fires.

231. The father indeed is the *gārhapatya* fire, the mother is said to be the *dakṣiṇa* fire, but the Guru is the *āhavanīya*;[7] this fire-triad is most venerable.

232. A householder not neglectful to those three will conquer the three worlds; like a god, illuminated by his own body, he rejoices in the sky.[8]

of wealth alone. The last would include the *Cārvāka* (the Epicurean of that time), who, as Medh. says, makes happiness consist of pleasure alone.]

[1] *Ācārya*. See the definition in vs. 140 above. [Medh. and K. make "self" the *kṣetrajña*, observing that these are all divinities.]

[2] [Medh. takes this expression differently, "No one at all is to be disrespectfully treated, especially, however, these." My MS. of Medh. makes 225 follow 226.]

[3] [Alone.]

[4] "Permitted by them." Medh. reads *anabhyanujñātaḥ*; Haughton adopts Kullūka's reading, *abhyanujñātaḥ*.

[5] Cf. 235. One should not undertake a pilgrimage [or practise asceticism if it interferes with attendance on these three (Medh.)]

[6] "Three orders." See this and following lectures. They are: studentship, condition of a householder, and that of a hermit who lives in the jungle or woods. [Or, omitting the student, the Yati, ascetic, makes the third.]

[7] For the arrangement of these three fires, see the plan at the end of the first volume of Haug's Aitareya Brāhmaṇa, and that at page 191 of Hillebrandt's Das Altindische Neu- und Vollmondsopfer. These fires are on circular, semicircular, and square altars respectively. [The same comparisons, otherwise employed, are found Āp. ii. 7, 2.]

[8] [A remnant of the old concep-

233. By devotion to (his) mother he obtains this world; by devotion to (his) father, the middle (world); but by obedience to (his) Guru, the Brahma-world.

234. All religious duties are fulfilled (by him) by whom those three (persons) are respected; but of him by whom those are not respected, all acts are fruitless.

235. As long as those three live, so long let him do no other (religious duty);[1] he should, devoted to (their) desires, ever do obedience to just those (three).

236. Whatever act he may do with a view to a future state, by mind, word, or deed, (and) without derogation to them, let him tell them that.[2]

237. (By acting thus) toward those three, the obligation of a man is indeed completed; that (is) plainly the highest religious duty; other (duty) is called subordinate religious duty.

238. A faithful man may receive pure knowledge even from a low-caste man; the highest virtue from the lowest,[3] a jewel of a woman even from a bad family.

239. Ambrosia can be extracted even from poison; elegant speech, even from a child; good conduct, even from an enemy; gold, even from impurity.

240. From all[4] are to be accepted, women, gems, knowledge, duty, purity, good speech, and the various arts.

241. In time of distress[5] learning the Veda from one not a Brahman is enjoined, and attendance and obedience[6] to (him as) to a Guru as long as the study (lasts).

tion of God as light and the sky as the place of light. Literally, these words might be rendered, "shining . . . like the Shining One (God) in the shining (sky)."]

[1] *Dharma;* cf. vs. 229.

[2] ["But he should not inform them if he does anything derogatory"—Medh.]

[3] [That is, a man who has faith may acquire the highest religious duty (*dharma*) from the lowest man, as, *e.g.*, a Cāṇḍāla (K.) This rule is not for ordinary times, but for times of distress; pure knowledge is said in distinction to that of Çambara, *i.e.*, magic; the "highest" dharma, as opposed to the other of worldly affairs, is that pertaining to the Vedas, Smṛti, etc. (Medh.)]

[4] [From all people without regard to caste (Medh.)]

[5] [Medh. notes a *var. lec. āpatkalpaḥ*, *i.e.*, (this practice) is enjoined as an arrangement for (times of) distress.]

[6] [According to Medh. his obedience, *i.e.*, servile attendance to this man, who for the nonce is his Guru, consists only in following him about; washing his feet, and the other observance towards a brahmanical Guru

242. But if the Guru be not a Brahman, the pupil should not live all his life with him, nor (even) with a Brahman who has not thoroughly studied (the Veda), (if) he desire the best way.[1]

243. But if he desire to live all his life in the family of (his) Guru, attentive he should serve him till he is released from his body.

244. Now the Brahman who obeys (his) Guru till the end of his body goes straight to the eternal abode of Brahma.[2]

245. Let not one who knows his duty offer anything earlier to (his) Guru, but when, dismissed by (his) Guru, he is about to bathe (on his return home), let him, as he best can, present property to (his) Guru.

246. A field, gold, a cow, a horse, an umbrella, shoes, a seat, grain and vegetables, clothes—such let him offer[3] to (his) Guru as (a mark of) affection.

247. But, truly, after his teacher is dead, let him serve as (he would his) Guru the Guru's son endowed with good qualities, the Guru's wife, or Sapiṇḍa.[4]

248. If these do not exist, let him perfect his own body, occupying (his Guru's) place, seat, and occupations, and practising attendance on the fires.[5]

249. The Brahman who thus uninterrupted passes his studentship, goes to the highest place, and is not born here[6] again.

END OF THE SECOND LECTURE.

are excluded. This rule is denied Baudh. i. 4, 23. The words "not a Brahman" K. restricts to Kṣatriya or Vaiçya; but this is evidently not intended.]

[1] [*I.e.*, the way to the highest happiness.]

[2] [Doubtful if person or substance (as in 28).]

[3] [*Āharet* (*var. lec.* Medh.) or *ārahet.*]

[4] [*Sapiṇḍas* are kinsmen to the seventh degree according to vs. 60.]

[5] "Fires," *i.e.*, the three fires just mentioned, which a Brahman should keep burning.

[6] "Here," *i.e.*, in this world. He is born in a superior world for the future. [For rules in regard to student life in other works, cf. Āp. i. 1–8; Gaut. i.–iii.; Vas. vii.; Baudh. i. 3; Viṣṇu xxviii. ff.; Yāj. i. 1–50. Rules in regard to the different rites as limited by caste in still older literature will be found in the 10th vol. of the Indische Studien, collated by Prof. Weber.]

LECTURE III.

ON MARRIAGE, AND ON THE RELIGIOUS DUTIES OF A HOUSEHOLDER, OR THE SECOND STATE OF LIFE.

1. THE course of study of the three Vedas to be gone through in the (house of the) Guru (is) for thirty-six years, the half of that, or a quarter, or only until mastery.

2. One who has not broken his rule as student,[1] having duly studied the (three) Vedas, or two Vedas, or one,[2] should enter the condition of life of a householder.

3. Let (his Guru) first honour him wearing a garland, (and) seated on a couch, by (a gift of) a cow,[3] when he is accomplished in his own duty,[4] (and) has received the inheritance of the Veda from his father.[5]

4. Let a twice-born man dismissed by (his) Guru, having bathed according to rule, having returned home, marry a wife of the same caste endowed with (good) marks;

5. And who (is) not a Sapiṇḍa of (his) mother, who (is) not also of the same tribe (*gotra*) as his father; such a one is approved for twice-born men for marriage duties (and) intercourse.[6]

6. Though great (and) prosperous, with cows, goats,

[1] "Rule as student," *i.e.*, rule of chastity.

[2] [This means the ancestral recension (*ṣākhā*) studied in the family (Medh.) A later view; cf. Āp. ii. 6, 5.]

[3] [This is to be understood as meaning a *madhuparka* (Medh., K.)]

[4] This long course of study by even grown-up men brings to mind what Cæsar says of the Druids, and which existed in Ireland down to recent times: "I have seen where they kept school ten in some one chamber, . . . being the most part lusty fellows of twenty-five years and upwards." Campion (in 1571), quoted in *Westminster Review*, No. ciii. p. 140. The discipline of the Egyptian pupil "scribes" was much the same.

[5] "Father" here includes a spiritual father or teacher.

[6] [Medh. identifies the *pravara* of Gaut. iv. 2 with the *ārṣa* of "another" Smṛti. *Vide* Āp. ii. 11, 15, with Bühler's note. Cf. Laghu Hārita, iv. 1. Cf., however, Jolly's note to Viṣṇu, xxiv. 9.]

sheep, wealth, and grain, let him avoid, for marriage ties, these ten families:

7. That by which rites are neglected, which has no males, which possesses not the Vedas (*chandas*) (the members of) which are hairy, or have piles; also families (afflicted) with consumption, dyspepsia, epilepsy, albinoism, and leprosy.

8. Let him not marry a tawny[1] maiden, nor one with superfluous members, nor a sickly (maiden), nor one without hair, or with excessive hair, nor a chatterbox, nor one red-(eyed).

9. Nor one called after a star, a tree, (or) a river; nor one called after barbarians[2] or a mountain; nor one called after a bird, snake, or slave; nor one with a terrifying name.

10. Let him marry a woman not malformed, with a prosperous name, that walks like a *haṁsa*[3] or elephant, with slender hair-locks[4] and teeth, (and) soft-bodied.

11. But she who has not a brother, (or whose) father is not known, let not a wise man marry her, through fear of the law about a daughter's son.[5]

12.[6] For twice-born men, at first, a woman of the same caste is approved for marrying; but of those who act from lust, those of lower caste may in order (be wives).

13. A Çūdra woman alone (is) a wife for a Çūdra; both she and a woman of his own caste (are) legally (wives) of

[1] [A tawny maiden, Medh. says, is one whose hair is auburn or golden.] Lombroso finds that female criminals are often marked by excessive growth of hair on the head.

[2] [*Antya.*] Indian women of the lower castes have still very extraordinary names; I have met with "Insect," "Spittle," and "Privy," as names of women on the Malabar coast. Brahmans have still in Southern India some names of the same kind, if their relatives fear for their luck or health. *E.g.*, if a man has lost several children, the next son born to him is called by a name which means "refuse;" but this is his name by which he is commonly known, his real (or "*Çarman* name," as it is called) is kept more or less a secret, and is used only for ceremonies. As regards the best-known name of this class, "Sāyaṇṇa," see my "Vaṁçabrāhmaṇa." Some prohibited names are used for women nowadays: *e.g.*, *Gaṅgā*, which is inadmissible as the name of a river.

[3] *Haṁsa*, a kind of mythical flamingo or goose.

[4] [Or, according to some MSS. (emended *metri causâ*), "with thin lips, fine hair and teeth."]

[5] *I.e.*, a daughter's son is like a son [cf. ix. 127 ff., and Gaut. xxviii. 20.]

[6] 12, 13. All this is obsolete. Marriages are now-a-days strictly be-

a Vaiçya; they two and also a woman of his own caste (are wives) of a Kṣatriya; both they and a woman of his own caste (are wives) of a Brahman.

14. A Çūdra wife is not indicated in any history for a Brahman and Kṣatriya, even though they be in distress.[1]

15. Twice-born men marrying a casteless woman out of infatuation surely bring quickly (their) families and descendants to the condition of Çūdras.

16. According to Atri and Utathya's son,[2] one who marries a Çūdra woman falls by the act; according to Çaunaka, (he falls) by the birth of a son; according to Bhṛgu, by the birth of his (the son's) son.

17. A Brahman having taken a Çūdra woman to his bed goes the lower course; having begotten on her a son, he is surely deprived of his Brahmanhood.[3]

18. Now of (a man) whose offerings towards gods, manes, and guests depend on her, the manes and gods eat not that offering, nor does he go to heaven.

19. An expiation is not prescribed for him who has drunk the moisture on a Çūdra[4] woman's (lips), who has been reached by her breath, and who has also begotten a son on her.

20. Learn summarily these eight (ways of) marriage with women for the four castes, (which are) good and bad here and in a future existence.

21. These are the Brāhma, the Daiva, the Ārsha, the

tween members of the same division of a caste. In Southern India differences of religion (Vaiṣṇavism, Çaivism, etc.), and even narrower divisions, are a bar to marriages between members of what is strictly the same caste. The so-called Rājas, however, have wives of their own caste, and concubines of any other, often hundreds.

[1] [Cf. Mbhā. xiii. 47. 8, "The Çūdrā can be a Brahman's (wife) by lust, desire, or irregular conduct (only, but) she is not enjoined for the sake of example" (*dṛṣṭāntataḥ smṛtā*). Cf. ib., 47, also *Kṣatriya.*]

[2] "Utathya's son," *i.e.*, Gautama. Cf. Gautama (ch. iv.), for the rules about marriage. The above opinion is not found here, but only a statement that sons of a Çūdra woman by men of higher caste are outside the law (vss. 25-26). [The present Atri Smṛti contains no corresponding rule.]

[3] [A significant alteration in Mbhā. xiii. 47. 9, makes the last part of this verse read, "He is nevertheless purified by a ceremony known in law."]

[4] [Vṛṣalī, cf. iii. 119; expiation (!), xi. 179.]

Prājāpatya, the Āsura, the Gāndharva, and also the Rākṣasa; the Paiçāca,[1] the eighth, (is) lowest.

22. Which is legal for which caste, and what are the good and bad qualities of which—all that I shall tell you, (and) the good and bad qualities of the progeny.

23. One should know that, legally, the six (first) in succession are for a Brahman the four last for a Kṣatriya, and the same for a Vaiçya and Çūdra, except the Rākṣasa (form).

24. The poets have recognised that the first four are approved for a priest, the Rākṣasa alone for a Kṣatriya, the Āsura for Vaiçyas and Çūdras.[2]

25. But of the five (last) three are here said (to be) legal, two (to be) illegal. The Paiçāca and also the Āsura (forms) are never to be done.[3]

26. Whether separately or mixed, two (forms of) marriage—the Rākṣasa and Gāndharva—are ordered by the former (lawgivers). Those two are said (to be) legal for a Kṣatriya.[4]

27. The gift of a maiden spontaneously, after clothing and reverencing her, to one learned in the Veda and of good character, having invited (him), is called the Brāhma rite.

28. But they term the Daiva rite the gift of a daughter, after having adorned her, to a sacrificial priest rightly doing his work in a sacrifice begun.[5]

29. The gift in due form of a maiden is called the

[1] The intention seems to have been much that of the canon law, viz., that a contract followed by cohabitation is what constitutes a marriage, here the contract being expressed or implied.

[2] ["For Vaiçyas and Çūdras are not particular about their wives" (Baudh. i. 20, 14). Cf. the following passages for the different rules in this respect. Vas. i. 27–28 gives six equivalent to these eight; so Āp. ii. 12, 3, who admits three as good. Baudh. i. 20, 10, gives eight and permits but four; so Viṣṇu, xxiv. 27. Gaut. gives the eight, admits four, and says some admit six (iv. 14, 15). The Mbhā. i. 73, 8 ff., ascribes descending virtue to each "according to Manu," and mixing up the words and sense of vs. 23 and vs. 27, allows four for a Brahman and six for a Kṣatriya.]

[3] [This rule is for the Kṣatriya, etc., not for a Brahman (Medh.)]

[4] A famous Gāndharva marriage or seduction occurs in the Çakuntalā. Cf. also vs. 32 below.

[5] [*I.e.*, the priest who performs a sacrifice receives a maiden as part of the fee.]

Ārsha rite,[1] when a pair or two of cattle have been legally received from the bridegroom.

30. The gift of a maiden is called the Prājāpatya rite, (when the gift is made) after reverencing and addressing (the pair) with the words, "Together do ye both duty."

31. The gift of a maiden voluntarily after having presented to the kinsmen and the maiden wealth as much as he (the suitor) can, is called the Āsura rite.[2]

32. The voluntary connection of a maiden and a man is to be known as a Gāndharva union, which arises from lust.

33. The forcible abduction from home of a maiden crying out and weeping, after slaying and wounding (her relatives) and breaking in, is called the Rākṣasa form.

34. Where (a man) secretly approaches (a girl) asleep, intoxicated, or confused, that, the most sinful of unions, is the Paiçāca, the eighth and lowest (form).

35. The gift of a maiden by water[3] alone is approved for Brahmans; but for the other castes (the rites are) according to their several fancies.

36. What quality has been declared by Manu for each of these marriages, hear all that, O Brahmans! from me relating (it) all.

37. The virtuous son of a (wife married by the) Brāhma rite frees *pitṛs*[4] from sin—ten ancestors, ten descendants, and himself as the twenty-first.

38. The son born of a (wife) married by the Daiva (rite) also (frees) seven ancestors (and) seven descendants; the son born of a (wife) married by the Ārṣa (rite), three and

[1] This is perhaps the most common form now.

[2] [A recognised sale is meant.] This form is also practised at the present day by people claiming to be Brahmans, *e.g.*, the Çaiva Brahmans, called "Gurukkal," in Southern India, who seldom can get wives for less than a thousand rupees. It often happens that low-caste girls are palmed off on them!

[3] "By water," *i.e.*, by pouring out water. This or some similar ceremony forms part of the symbolic procedure on transfer of property under Hindu law. See my "Elements of Southern India Palæography," second edition, p. 105, note 3.

[4] ["*Pitṛ* (father) has here the meaning deceased" (Medh.), *i.e.*, includes descendants.]

three; the son of a (wife) married by the Prājāpatya rite, six (and) six.[1]

39. Of the four marriages Brāhma and the like in order, are born sons learned in the Vedas, approved by good men,

40. Endowed with beauty (and) the quality of goodness, rich, glorious, possessed of enjoyments, most dutiful; and (they) live a hundred years.

41. But of the other remaining bad marriages are born cruel, untruthful sons, hating the Vedas (and) duty.

42. A blameless offspring arises from blameless marriages of women among mortals; from blameworthy (marriages) a blamable (offspring is born) to men; therefore one should avoid the blamable (marriages).

43. The sacrament of joining hands is directed for women of the same caste (as the bridegroom); this rule (as follows) is to be recognised for marriages with women not of the same caste.

44. By a Kṣatriya woman an arrow is to be held at (her) marriage with a higher caste man; by a Vaiçya maiden, a goad; by a Çūdra woman, the skirt of a garment.

45. Let a husband devoted to his wife approach (her) in (due) season; and he, being fond of her,[2] may approach her with desire for intercourse at all times, except at the *parva* days.

46. The natural time of women is said (to be) sixteen (days and) nights (in a month), together with other four days avoided by the virtuous;[3]

47. But of those, the first four and the eleventh and thirteenth are blamed; the remaining ten, however, are allowed.

48. On even nights sons are begotten, daughters on odd; therefore one desirous of a son should approach (his) wife on even (nights) in the season.

[1] [Gaut. iv. 30 ff. gives a different table.]

[2] [Or "adhering to this observance." The *parva* includes the eighth, fourteenth, and fifteenth days of each half month. Cf. Baudh. i. 21, 22.]

[3] *Prathamaçoṇitadarçanāt prabhṛti ahargrahaṇaṁ ca sarvāhorātropalakṣaṇārtham* (Medh.)

49. (In reality), a male is produced if the semen of the male is in excess,[1] a female, if that of the female; if equal, a eunuch, or a male and a female; if weak or scanty, the contrary (no conception takes place).

50. One who avoids women on the blameworthy nights, and on eight others, is like a student,[2] in whatsoever order (he may be) living.

51. A learned father of a maiden should never take a consideration, not even a tittle,[3] (on her marriage); for a man who takes a consideration through greed is a seller of (his) child.

52. Sinful relations, who, through delusion, subsist on a woman's property, (or take) a woman's vehicle or clothes, go to hell.[4]

53. Some say that the pair of cattle (given) at an Ārsha (marriage is) a consideration; that is false.[5] Be it even small or great, it is indeed a sale.

54. For whom[6] relatives do not take a consideration, it is not a sale; it is merely a token of affection for them, and is harmless.

55. Women are to be honoured and adorned by fathers and brothers, by husbands, as also by brothers-in-law, who desire much prosperity.

56. Where women are honoured, there the gods rejoice; but where they are not honoured, there all rites are fruitless.

[1] *Adhikyaṁ cā 'tra na parimāṇataḥ kiṁ tarhi sārataḥ*—Medhātithi. For "same" he mentions a *var. lec.*, *sāmye* [*çuklaṁ vījaṁ puruṣasya retaḥ striyāḥ çoṇitam.*]

[2] Brahmacārin, a student under obligation of chastity.

[3] "A tittle," even a little property (Medhātithi). [Cf. ix. p. 98.]

[4] [Literally, "the downward path," the "lower course," as in vs. 17.] "Woman's property," *i.e.*, *strīdhana*. The Indian lawyers have much discussed the meaning of this word, whether it has a technical meaning or is an ordinary word. In Southern India, the Mitākṣarā and its commentaries leave no doubt that it is an ordinary word, and that all property which comes to a woman anyhow is *strīdhana*. The courts, however, hold the contrary and erroneous view, for reasons which (as urged) are no reasons. It would be useless to mention them here. On this subject see Sir H. Maine's "Early Institutions," p. 254, &c. [Manu restricts *strīdhana* to six kinds in ix. 194, see note.]

[5] "False," according to Manu [for it is nothing but a sale.]

[6] "For whom;" the conclusion is that for whom, etc.

57. Where women grieve, that family quickly perishes; but where they do not grieve, that (family) ever prospers.

58. Houses which women, not honoured, curse, those, as if blighted by magic, perish utterly.[1]

59. Therefore they are ever to be honoured at ceremonies and festivals, with ornaments, clothes, and food, by men who desire wealth.

60. In what family the husband is pleased by his wife, and so also the wife by the husband, truly prosperity is ever firm there.

61. For if the wife be not pleased, she cannot please (her) husband; from displeasure of the husband, again, progeny does not arise.

62. But if a wife be pleased, all the house[2] is pleased; and if she be not pleased, all is not pleased.

63. By bad marriages, neglect of rites, and want of study of the Vedas, by violence to Brahmans also, families decay.

64. By mechanical arts, by trade, and by Çūdra offspring alone, by (dealing in) cattle, horses also, and carriages, by agriculture, by attendance on a king;

65. By sacrificing for those who have not the right, and by incredulity (as regards the effect) of works—(by these) families quickly perish, (and) such (as are) wanting in the *mantras*.

66. Prosperous by the *mantras*, families, though of little wealth, attain respectability and attract great glory.

67. Let a householder perform the household rites according to rule with the marriage fire, and the accomplishment of the five sacrifices, and the daily cooking.

68. A householder[3] has five instruments of killing (insects, etc.), the hearth, the grindstone, the besom, the

[1] Vss. 58 to 66 are, apparently, not known to Medhātithi [and are therefore very probably a later addition. The corresponding passage in the Mbhā. xiii. 46 adhy. stops right here also (including, however, the verses corresponding to vs. 58 and vs. 61), and goes over to another topic.]

[2] [*I.e.*, household, family.]

[3] [Probably one of the three upper castes is meant, though not explicitly stated. Cf. Medh.]

pestle and mortar, the water-pot; using which he is fettered (by sin).

69. For expiation of all these in due course, the five great sacrifices were ordered for householders[1] every day by the great seers.

70. (These are as follows): Teaching the Veda (is) the Veda sacrifice; offering cakes and water (is) the sacrifice to the manes; an offering to fire (is the sacrifice) to the gods; offering of food[2] (is the sacrifice) to all beings; honour to guests (is) the sacrifice to men.

71. He who, as he best can, fails not in those five great sacrifices, though he always abide in his house, is not polluted by the sins (caused) by the (five) instruments of killing.

72. Whoever presents not food to those five, the gods, guests, dependents, the manes, and himself, though he breathe, lives not.

73. (Some) term the five sacrifices *ahuta*, *huta* also, as well as *prahuta*, *brāhmya huta*, and *prāçita*.

74. *Ahuta* is muttered recital; *huta* is fire-offering; *prahuta* is offering to beings; *brāhmya huta* is reverence to excellent twice-born (people); *prāçita* is offering to the manes.

75. One should be ever occupied here in study of the Vedas and in offerings to the gods; for one occupied in offerings to the gods supports this movable and immovable (world).

76. An offering duly thrown into fire goes to the sun; from the sun is produced rain; from rain, food, and thence human beings.[3]

[1] See previous note.

[2] "Offering of food," *i.e.*, the fragments of morning and evening meals are thrown up in the air at the house-door, with some sentences addressed to inferior gods. It appears to me that this is one of the chief causes which make India a land of vermin; crows, squirrels, ants, and all kinds of pests exist there in surprising numbers, which are not found in other tropical countries, *e.g.*, Java.

[3] [*Prajāḥ* may be taken in a wider sense as all beings having life (so Medh., Rāgh.) The causal nexus explains vs. 75, for animal life is supported by food, food comes from rain, rain is produced by the sun, which is supplied by burnt sacrifices, therefore he who sacrifices supports the world.]

77. As all beings depend on air, so all orders [1] depend [2] on the householder.

78. Because men of the three (other) orders are daily supported by the householder alone with knowledge and food, therefore the householder (is) of the chief order.

79. That order must be upheld strenuously by one desiring an imperishable heaven, and who here desires perpetual happiness. (It is an order) which cannot be obtained by those with weak organs.[3]

80. The seers, manes, gods, beings, and guests also pray [4] to those heads of families (for support). (This duty must, therefore,) be done by a man of discernment.

81. One should daily honour the seers by study of the Veda, the gods by offerings, the manes by funeral oblations, man by food, beings by offerings.

82. Daily one should make funeral oblations with food and the like, or water; or even with milk, roots, (or) fruit, bringing gratification to the manes.

83. One should feed one Brahman, at least, at the ceremonies to the manes included in the five sacrifices; but one should not feed here even a single Brahman at the ceremony to all the gods.

84. Let a Brahman [5] make daily an offering to these deities according to rule in his (sacred) household fire (used) for dressing food for all the gods.

85. To fire, and to the moon also, first, and to both of them also together; to all the gods, and also to Dhanvantari: [6]

86. To Kuhū [7] also, and Anumati,[8] and also to Prajāpati, and to sky and earth together, and likewise to Sviṣṭakṛt [9] last.

[1] The four orders are the student, householder, hermit, and mendicant.

[2] [Literally, "exist (by) depending on." Cf. vi. 89.]

[3] [*I.e.*, with organs uncontrolled, sensual in eating, unchaste, etc. (Medh.)]

[4] ["Offer entreaties to," not pray = worship. "They long for study of Veda, *çrāddhas*," etc. (Rāgh.)]

[5] [This means any upper-caste man (Medh., K., Rāgh.) Cf. vs. 121.]

[6] [The sun rising.]

[7] [The new moon.]

[8] [Goddess of love-reproduction (also a phase of the moon).]

[9] [Fire personified as "successful sacrificer." Cf. Gaut. v. 10; Āp. ii. 3, 16.]

87. Having thus properly offered butter (in the fire), one should bring an offering (*bali*) in all the quarters, from the east southwards,[1] to Indra, Death, Varuṇa, the Moon, and to their followers.[2]

88. Saying "(Honour) to the Maruts!" one should throw (the offering) by the door; saying, "(Honour) to the waters!" one should throw (it) in water; saying, "(Honour) to trees!" one should throw it on the pestle and mortar.

89. And one should do (it) in the north-east to Çrī, in the south-west to Bhadrakāli; but in the middle of a brahmanical abode one should make the offering to the two lords.[3]

90. One should[4] throw up in the air (one) offering to all the gods; to spirits that go about by day (one should offer by day), and to those that go about at night (by night).

91. One should make an offering for the welfare of all beings on the house-top;[5] but one should present all the remainder of the offering to the manes, (casting it) to the south.[6]

92. One should throw gradually on the ground (the offering) for dogs, outcasts, keepers of dogs, those having grievous illnesses,[7] to large birds, and insects.

93. The Brahman who thus ever honours all beings goes with glorious form to the best place by a straight road.

94. Having then performed those offerings, one should let the guest eat first, and give alms[8] to a beggar who is a student of the Veda according to rule.

[1] [In the east to Indra, south to Yama, west to Varuṇa, north to Soma (and to the followers of each), according to their position (*pratidiçam iti pāṭhāt*) (K.)]

[2] [Slightly altered from Dr. B.'s text, who takes this as meaning the deities just mentioned; but cf. *Anugāḥ anucarāḥ yat puruṣās tathā c'endra puruṣebhya ityādi prayogaḥ* (Medh.)]

[3] [Or: on the pillow to Çrī (goddess of good-luck), at the feet to B. (goddess of bad-luck), but in the middle of the house to the two lords of a Brahman house. Some define these terms as parts of the house. Medh. and K. make the last mean "to Brahm and to the lord of the house."]

[4] [After coming out of the house (Medh.) The last parentheses are from K., an interpretation denied by Medh.]

[5] ["Or to the west" (K.)]

[6] [*I.e.*, he should stand facing south (Medh.)]

[7] [*Pāpa rōgiṇām.* I venture to change B.'s translation, "lepers and so forth, cows (!)" for the literal meaning. Medh., K., and Rāgh. say lepers or consumptives; cows for crows (?).]

[8] [K. quotes Çātātapa as saying the beggar is to ask only for food, but adds that one may give more.]

95. What good fruit one gets having given duly a cow to (one's) Guru, that a twice-born householder gets having given alms.

96. One should, having first reverenced (him) duly, give alms or a pot of water to a Brahman that knows the real meaning of the Veda.

97. The oblations to the gods or manes (made) foolishly by ignorant men perish, (if) given by the offerers to Brahmans (like) ashes.

98. An offering in the fires of a Brahman's mouth, which are kindled by austerity and knowledge, frees from misfortune and even from great sin.

99. To a guest that has arrived one should give a seat and water, and food also as he best can, having reverenced (him) first duly.

100. A Brahman guest not reverenced takes away all the good deeds of even one who always gleans ears of grain (for his support),[1] or even sacrifices in five fires.

101. Grass, earth, water, and kindly speech as a fourth; even these are never wanting in the house of the good.[2]

102. Now a Brahman staying one night is called *atithi* (guest); as he stays not always, hence he is called *atithi*.[3]

103. One should not think a Brahman of the same village (to be) a guest, nor one come on business,[4] (though) he have arrived at the house where one's wife and (sacred) fires are.

[1] [On this mode of life, cf. iv. 5 ff.; cf. Viṣṇu, lxvii. 33. This is a proverb often found in other literature.]

[2] [That is, they are always given to the guest (Medh.) Cf. Hit. i. 33; Āp. ii. 4, 14.]

[3] [Cf. Vas. viii. 7; Viṣṇu, lxvii. 34. Medh. quotes Āp. ii. 7, 16, as showing that guestship is not restricted to so short a time. As *atithi* means guest and *tithi* a lunar day, K. connects the two, meaning "not over a day;" but the text derives the word merely from *sthā*, abide, and the negative prefix, so that a nearer translation would be: as he does not stay long, he is a "not stayer" (guest).]

[4] [According to Medh. and K., his business is here merely friendly conversation to pass the time. Medh. also renders *sāṅgatika* by *sahādhyāyī*, so that the sense of the whole passage is simply that one need not feel obliged to go through the formalities ordained for receiving a guest if a neighbour or comrade drops in about meal-time just to have a chat. Dr. B's translation, unless thus understood, rather destroys the real state of affairs, for a Brahman who came on business was very ceremoniously received.]

104. Senseless householders who seek[1] another's food, by that (sin) become after death cattle of the givers of (such) food and the like.

105. A guest brought by the (setting) sun is not to be turned away at evening by a householder; if he came in time or out of time, let him not remain without food in his house.

106. One certainly should not oneself eat that which one does not give to a guest;[2] reverence[3] to a guest brings wealth, glory, long life, and heaven.

107. One should supply (to guests) seats, resting-places, couches, attendance, and reverence; to the highest, the best; to the lowest, the lowest; to equals, an equal (sort).[4]

108. But if another guest arrive after the offering to all the gods is finished, one should give him food as one best can, (but) should not make (another) offering.[5]

109. Let not a Brahman for the sake of food proclaim his family and tribe; for one who proclaims those (particulars) for the sake of food is called by the wise "an eater of vomit."

110. Now a Kṣatriya is not called a guest in a Brahman's house, nor a Vaiçya, nor a Çūdra; neither is a friend, the kinsmen, nor a Guru (of the householder).[6]

111. But if a Kṣatriya come as a guest to the house after the said Brahmans have eaten, one should give him food (if) he wishes.[7]

[1] ["Seek," *i.e.*, go here and there merely with this purpose in view (Medh.)]

[2] [*I.e.*, if the guest is not allowed to eat dainties which the householder has in store, he must not eat them himself. Medh. mentions cakes, ghee, sour milk, sugar, etc., as examples.]

[3] [Or "feasting a guest," according to another reading.]

[4] [This verse refers to a number of guests received at the same time; the honour given them is then in accordance with their rank (Medh., K.)]

[5] [*I.e.*, the *pākabali* (food-offering to the deities)—Medh. He must cook a supper for the guest, but need not a second time go through the all-gods (*vaiçvadeva*) ceremony.]

[6] [For the under castes are inferior; friends and kinsmen are the same as one's self; the Guru is superior: the like holds for each caste towards those lower (Medh., K.)]

[7] [*I.e.*, "if the host wishes to do so;" or "as much as he (the guest) wishes to eat." The latter appears to be the meaning which K. and Rāgh. give the expression; the former is given by Medh. (*Kāmam iti niyamābhāvam āha kāmyo' yaṁ vidhir na nitya ity arthaḥ.*) So Nand. to Viṣṇu, lxvii. 36.]

112. If even a Vaiçya (or) Çūdra come to the house as guests,[1] one should give them food with the servants, using kindness.

113. One should give food as one best can with (one's) wife even to others[2]—friends and the like—who have come to the house through affection, after having kindly received them.

114. One should, without hesitating, give food to brides, children, sick people, so also to pregnant women, even before[3] the guests.

115. For he who, without discernment, not having given food to them, eats first, knows not while eating that he will be food for dogs and vultures.[4]

116. Now after the Brahmans and one's own servants also have eaten, then afterwards the husband and wife should eat what is left.[5]

117. After having worshipped gods, seers, and men, the manes, and one's household gods, then the householder should eat the rest.[6]

118. He eats sin only who cooks for himself (only); but that food which remains after the sacrifice is termed the food of the good.

119. After a year[7] one should again honour a king, a sacrificial priest, a student who has returned home, a Guru,

[1] [*Atithidharminaḥ* are those who "have the rights (*dharma*) of guests" (Medh.), a Hindu form of the universal and ancient *gastrecht*. Cf. Āp. ii. 4, 19.]

[2] [Literally "even others . . . one should permit to eat along with his wife," *i.e.*, as Medh. and K. say, quoting vs. 116, "along with himself;" but "along with" does not mean off the same plate—Medh.]

[3] [That is, before the other guests are fed (K.), or, according to the reading preferred by Medh., let them be fed, *even if they come later*, at the same time as the other guests. (Dr. B.'s MS. reads *agra*, but has K.'s quotation!).]

[4] [That is, after death (K.)]

[5] [Cf. Yāj. i. 105.]

[6] [This is nothing more than a repetition of the foregoing rule in regard to the five sacrifices (the householder includes the two subjects of vs. 116)—Medh.]

[7] [*Parisaṁvatsarāt* (preferred by K.), or *parisaṁvatsarān* (preferred by Medh.) The meaning is the same, that inside a year they are not to be thus honoured (but cf. Medh.) The Mbhā. has here *parisaṁvatsaroṣitān*, "Gone a year on a journey" (xiii. 97, 21). Cf. with this and the next verse, Gaut. v. 27–28. The *madhuparka* is a mess made of milk or curds and honey or butter. Āp. ii. 8, 78; Āçv. Gṛh. Sūt. i. 24, 5–6.]

a beloved (son-in-law), a father-in-law, and a maternal uncle with a honey-mixture (if they come to the house).

120. A king and a learned (priest) also who have come at the (time of) sacrifice are to be honoured with a honey-mixture, but not when there is no sacrifice;[1] (this is) the rule.

121. Let a wife make an offering of prepared food in the evening without (reciting any) Vedic texts;[2] that is called (the offering) to all the gods; it is prescribed in the evening and morning.

122. Now having finished the (daily) sacrifice to the manes, a Brahman[3] who keeps a (sacred) fire should offer every month, during the moon's wane,[4] the *piṇḍānvāhārya çrāddha.*

123. The wise call *anvāhārya* the monthly *çrāddha* to the manes,[5] and it is to be carefully done with excellent meat.

124. What best[6] Brahmans are to be fed then, and what are to be avoided, and how many also and with what food, I shall fully tell (you) those (details).

125. One should feed two at the feast to the gods,[7] three at that to the manes, or one in both cases; even if one be rich, one should not be fond of large company.

126. A large company destroys these five things—reverence, (suitable) time and place, purity and prosperity of Brahmans; therefore one should not desire a large company.

127. That ceremony to the dead at the moon's wane[8] (is) famed as the manes' (feast). (This) usual ceremony to the dead ever benefits one intent upon it.

[1] [Cf. Gaut. v. 29; 'before the year is over' is meant.]

[2] [She gives the offerings and simply calls out the name of the deity, as "Honour to Indra" (K.)]

[3] [That is, any twice-born man (Medh., K.) Cf. vs. 91.]

[4] [That is, when the moon is reduced, at the time of the new moon.]

[5] [Medh. and K. note a reading, *piṇḍānām* for *pitṛṇām*, "a feast of rice-balls," which means the rice-balls offered to the manes, and amounts to the same thing.]

[6] [*Dvijottama* means "Brahman" (so Medh.), as well as "best among the twice-born;" *varjyāḥ* seems to restrict the meaning here to Brahman; cf. viii. 73, note.]

[7] [The feast in honour of the gods, *daiva.*]

[8] [*Vidhukṣaya. Vidhu* is moon, its *kṣaya*, lack, *i.e.*, on the day of the new moon. Another reading noticed by Medh. is *tithikṣaye;* a reading noted by K. as Govindarāja's, *vidiḥ kṣaye* (= *candrakṣaye* or *gṛhe*), is also noticed by Medh. K. says he rejects

128. The offerings to the gods and the manes[1] are to be presented by the offerers only[2] to a learned (man), a most worthy priest. What is given to him (bears) great fruit.

129. One should feed[3] at least one learned man at the feasts to the gods and the manes; so one gains excellent fruit, (but) not (by entertaining) many even who do not know the *mantras*.

130. One should inquire, even at a distance, for a Brahman who has read all the Vedas;[4] he is a fit receptacle on the presenting the offerings to gods and manes; he is said to be a guest.

131. For where even a thousand thousands of persons who do not know the (Veda) verses are fed, one learned in the *mantras* (and) content[5] is properly worth all those.

132. The offerings to the manes and to the gods must be given to one excellent by (his) knowledge; for both hands smeared with blood are not purified by blood.[6]

133. As many mouthfuls as a man ignorant of the *mantras* eats at the offerings to the gods and manes, so many hot iron balls (the giver) swallows in the next world.

134. Some Brahmans are intent on knowledge, others are intent on austerity; and some are intent on austerity and study (of the Vedas), so also others are intent on works.

it, as it is awkward, and is not the traditional reading accepted by Medh. and the following commentators *older than* Govinda.]

[1] [*Havya* and *kavya*.]

[2] [Dr. B's. translation omits "only," and reads, "to a most worthy Brahman priest," which I venture to change as above, in accordance with his usual rendering of *çrotriya*. Cf. vs. 97.]

[3] [Govinda understands the meal given to a wise Brahman to be the chief act, the *pinda* gift as secondary; K. thinks otherwise, and gives a long quotation from Ap. ii. 16, 1–5, to prove himself right in his argument.]

[4] [This translation seems discordant with the view held by the commentators, that "one should thoroughly examine (the family and relations of) a Brahman." Medh. renders *durāt* by *nipunataḥ* (thoroughly), and quotes a passage to show that it is not sufficient for the man invited to be wise, but one's ancestors both on the mother's and father's side must be carefully looked into. Cf. vs. 149.]

[5] [*I.e.*, content with food = "if one learned in the Veda has been fed" (Medh., K.)]

[6] [This is, as K. says, merely a rhetorical figure—as blood is not cleansed by blood, but by pure water, so a fool is not purified by feasting a fool, but by feasting a man of pure knowledge.]

135. The offerings to manes are strenuously to be presented to those intent on knowledge; but the offerings to gods, as is right, even to all four.[1]

136. (If there be) a father not learned (in the Veda), whose son has completed a Veda, or if there be a son unlearned (in the Veda), whose father has completed a Veda,

137. One should recognise as the better of these two (him) whose father is learned (in the Veda). The other, however, for sake of reverence to the *mantras*, deserves respect.

138. One should not feed a friend at a *çrāddha;* his friendship is to be gained by (other) wealth. One should at a *çrāddha* feed a Brahman whom one considers neither foe nor friend.

139. He whose *çrāddhas* and oblations depend on friendship has no fruit in the next world, either for his *çrāddhas* or oblations.

140. The man who, through folly, makes friendship by a *çrāddha,* falls down from the heaven-world (as) a friend by *çrāddhas* (and) the basest of Brahmans.

141. That feast (for friends) is termed by the Brahmans a gift to the devils; it remains in this world like a blind cow in a single abode.[3]

142. As a sower gets not again if he sow seed in salt soil, so the giver gets no fruit if he give an offering to (one) unlearned in the (Veda) verses.

143. A gift duly presented to a wise man renders the giver and receiver (alike) partakers of the fruit both here and in the next world.[4]

[1] [But the *kavya,* like the *havya,* are to be given to all four if those intent on knowledge are not present (Medh.)]

[2] [A "friend by *çrāddha*" is one who prostitutes the ceremony to the purpose of making friendships. According to Medh., this is a possessive compound, "one who possesses a *çrāddha* friend, *i.e.,* the feast is the reason he obtains the friend."]

[3] [Dr. B. has, "that gift is . . . a devil's feast," which is incorrect. Beginning with vs. 138, we find possibly older forms of some of these verses in the Mahābhārata, xiii. 90 adhy., where Mbhā. 42 tṛṣṭubh = Manu 140 çloka; Mbhā. 43 tṛṣṭ. = M. 138 çl.; Mbhā. 44 tṛṣṭ. = M. 142 çl.; Mbhā. 46 tṛṣṭ. = M. 141 çl. This last verse is also found as tṛṣṭubh in Āp. ii. 17, 8, whence the full force of *chaira* in our text is apparent—"it stays just here in this world," *i.e.,* here *alone,* for such a feast does not reach the departed spirits.]

[4] [The reward in this world is

144. One may (if need be) reverence a friend at a *çrāddha*, but not an enemy, even if a suitable person; for an offering eaten by an enemy is fruitless in the next world.

145. At a *çrāddha* one should feed carefully (a priest) who knows well the Ṛg. (Veda verses) and has completed the (Ṛg.) Veda; or an Adhvaryu (priest of the Yajur Veda) who has gone to the end of his recension; or a Chandoga (priest of the Sāmaveda) who has acquired it all.[1]

146. He whose *çrāddha* any one of those may eat after being honoured, his ancestors to the seventh degree are ever content.

147. This is the primary rule for presenting the offerings to the gods and manes; but this (following) subsidiary (rule) is to be recognised (which is) ever observed by the good:

148. [Viz.] one may feed a maternal grandfather, a maternal uncle, a sister's son, a father-in-law, a Guru, a daughter's son, a son-in-law, a kinsman, and a sacrificial priest, together with the performer of the sacrifice.

149. One who knows the law need not scrutinise[2] a Brahman on occasion of a ceremony to the gods; but for a rite to the manes one should scrutinise (him) carefully.

150. Those Brahmans who are degraded on account of theft, or are eunuchs,[3] and those who are unbelievers, Manu has declared unworthy of the offerings to the gods and to the manes.

151. One should not feed at a *çrāddha* a wearer of the *jaṭa*,[4] one who does not study the Veda, one without a

reputation and fame, like that got by one's being proficient in the *çāstras* (Medh.) Medh.'s explanation is incorrect; the reward meant is that declared by Yāj. i. 269, long life, progeny, etc. (K.)]

[1] [Medh. and Rāgh. say some think this çloka implies the exclusion of the followers of the Atharva-veda (*ātharvaṇika*).]

[2] [Cf. vs. 130. Medh. notes that there are conflicting views as to what "scrutinise" means. He regards it as pertaining to the bodily and moral soundness, etc., of the guest, not, as in vs. 130, of the family. Rāgh. takes it as a simple extension of the former; "repeating the 'examination of the Brāhman' at the rite to the manes, he says it does not take place at that to the gods."]

[3] [Medh. separates these into three classes—"degraded (*i.e.*, those who have committed any one of the great sins), thieves, and eunuchs." *Nāstika*, atheist in Dr. B.'s version.]

[4] The *jaṭa* is hair allowed to grow long, and twisted round the head so as to look like a turban. Medhātithi says that a (brahmacārin) student is intended. [Cf. ii. p. 219.]

prepuce,[1] so also a gambler and those who sacrifice often[2] (for others).

152. So also physicians, those who worship idols for a living,[3] and those who sell meat. Those who live by trading are to be avoided at the offerings to the gods and to the manes;

153. A servant of the village or of the king, a man with deformed nails or black teeth, and an opponent of (his) Guru, also, as well as one who neglects the (sacred) fire, and a usurer;

154. A consumptive man, a cattle-herd, a younger brother married before an elder, one who does not perform his religious duties, a hater of Brahmans,[4] an unmarried elder brother whose younger brother is married, and also one who is a member of an association;

155. A dancer,[5] and one who has broken the rule of his order,[6] the husband also of a low-caste woman,[7] the son of a woman twice married, a one-eyed man also, and one whose fellow-husband (is) in (his) house;

156. One who teaches for hire, also one who is taught for hire; the pupil of a Çūdra, and (a Çūdra) Guru; one who speaks roughly,[8] a son of an adulteress born before, and also one born after her husband's death;

157. Those forsaken[9] without cause (even) by mother,

[1] [Medh. reads *durvāla* for *durbala* (cf. Har. to Gaut. xv. 18), and explains as either a bald-headed or a red-headed man, or one wanting in manly strength (*vikalendriyo vā*).]

[2] [The meaning given by the commentators is "those who sacrifice for many, for anybody, outcasts, etc." Medh. and K. quote a verse from Vas. to the effect that one who sacrifices for the many is not admitted to *çrāddha*. In explanation of *çrāddha*, Medh. says that some confine the word to the feast for the manes, but that it includes the feast to the gods also.]

[3] [That is, one who earns a living out of idols, whether by serving in a temple (?) or by travelling around with idols (to sell ?). Cf. B. R., *s. v.* It might mean an idol-manufacturer.]

[4] [Or of the Veda (Medh.)]

[5] [Or singer (so Medh. and K., otherwise Nīl. to Mbhā. xiii. 90, 11, "One who supports himself by cutting clods;" *kāṣṭhacchedanopajīvin* by a forced derivation from *kuçi* and *phāla* = *lava* and *chedana*).

[6] [*I.e.*, has become unchaste.]

[7] [Of a Vṛsalī.]

[8] ["Or one who lies" (Medh.); though some say "one cursed" (Medh., K.) Cf. vs. 174.]

[9] [Dr. B. translates *parityaktā* as a participle, but all the commentators interpret as *nomen agentis*, "one who deserts mother, father, or Guru,"

father, or Guru; and one who has entered into connection with degraded (people, either) by spiritual or marriage ties;

158. One who burns houses, a poisoner, one who eats with the son of an adulteress,[1] one who sells the soma plant,[2] one who goes on sea-voyages, and a panegyrist,[3] an oilmonger, and a suborner of perjury;

159. Also one who disputes with his father, gamblers,[4] also one who drinks spirituous liquors, one with a disgraceful[5] disease, one of bad character, a swindler, one who sells liquids;

160. A maker of bows and arrows also, and a husband of a younger sister married before her elder sister,[6] one who injures a friend, one who lives by gambling, so also one whose son is his teacher;

161. One distraught,[7] one who has scrofula also, so also a white leper, an informer also, a madman, one who is blind also are to be shunned, as also one who finds fault with the Vedas;

162. A trainer of elephants, cattle, horses (or) camels; one who lives by the stars also; a keeper of birds also; so also a fencing-master;[8]

i.e., fails to render obedience, etc. (Medh., K.) "Spiritual," literally "Vedic" (*brāhmya*).]

[1] [See Medh. and K. Rāgh. says the same, "or a great eater, from the saying a *kuṇḍāçi* is a coward;" otherwise Nil. (Mbhā. xiii. 143, 24, *Kuṇḍāçī: kuṇḍe pākapātre açnātīti kuṇḍāçī*), and Har. to Gautama, xv. 18).]

[2] [Medh. says some explain otherwise, as sellers of sacrifice where *soma* is used.]

[3] [Later the name of one of the mixed classes (Vandin, bandin).]

[4] [*Kitava*, or, according to some, *kekara*, squint-eyed (Medh., K.); the last is perhaps better, as *kitava* appears in vs. 151, and the explanation of Medh. and K., that it here means, in distinction from the former, "one who makes others gamble," is scarcely allowable.]

[5] [Or "grievous disease," cf. vs. 92, as consumption (K.) Cf. ii. 185 note.]

[6] [Cf. Gaut. xv. 16, and see B. R. sub *agredidhiṣū*. (Medh. says there is no such person as an *agredidhiṣūpati*, and maintains that this word must be divided into two parts, one being *agredidhiṣu* (sc. *pati*), and the other *didhiṣūpati* (defined in vs. 173), as in the passage of Gautama).]

[7] [Perhaps, as Medh. speaks of this as a disease, "one who lost his memory."]

[8] [One who gives instruction in *dhanurveda* (Medh.) This science was naturally highly esteemed among the Kṣatriyas, and its acquisition was procured not only by practising arms, but by mystic rites, prayers, etc.]

163. A diverter of watercourses, and he who is accustomed to obstruct them, a designer of houses, a messenger, and a planter of trees (for hire);

164. A seller[1] of dogs, and one who lives by falcons, a seducer of maidens also; a mischievous fellow, one being a Brahman who lives by a Çūdra's[2] occupation; also a sacrificer to the *gaṇas*;[3]

165. (One) who follows not established custom, and a eunuch; so one who constantly begs, one who lives by agriculture, and a club-footed[4] man also; one censured by the good;

166. One who deals in rams, one who keeps buffaloes, the husband of a woman married before; also one who removes corpses;—(all these) are to be carefully avoided.

167. Those lowest of Brahmans whose customs are despised, who are not fit to take part (in a solemn feast), a good Brahman (who is) wise should reject for both (ceremonies).

168. Now a Brahman who does not study (the Vedas) is quenched like a fire in grass;[5] to him the oblation to the gods is not to be given, for one does not sacrifice on ashes.

169. What result is for the giver in the next life if (food) be given to an unfit person at the oblation to the gods or manes, that I shall now fully declare.

170. Whatever (offering) has been eaten by Brahmans who have broken their vows, by younger brothers married before the elder and the like; whatever (has been eaten) by others (who are) unfit, that indeed evil demons devour.

171. He who, his elder brother not having done so, takes a wife and (performs) *agnihotra* (offerings), is to be

[1] [Rather one "who sports with dogs," or "raises them for pleasure" (Medh., K.)]

[2] [Literally, a Vṛṣala's; by another reading, "the son of a Vṛṣala."]

[3] [Troops of deities.]

[4] A Grantha MS. reads *çilpajīvī* for *çlīpadī ca*, *i.e.*, lives by mechanical arts

[5] [Not being fed like a holy fire, it is not able to burn. According to the commentators, some say that it is an unlearned man alone who is to be excluded at the gods' feast where the *havya* is offered, while those physically deformed are excluded from that to the manes only.]

known as a *parivettar* (one who marries before his elder brother), but the elder brother is a *parivitti*.[1]

172. The *parivitti*, the *parivettā*, and she by whom this is caused, all those go to hell, five in number (by the addition of) the giver and sacrificer.

173. He who out of lust is devoted to the wife of a deceased brother, even if she be legally appointed, is to be known as the husband of a *didhiṣū*.[2]

174. Two sons, the *kuṇḍa* and *golaka*, are born of other men's wives: the *kuṇḍa*, if the husband be alive; if he be dead, the *golaka*.

175. Those two beings, born of another's wife, when dead and (when alive) in this world also, destroy the offerings given to gods and manes of those who present (these offerings).

176. As many fit persons as a man unfit (for the feast) sees eating, of so many the foolish giver does not get the reward after death.

177. A blind man being present destroys the giver's reward for ninety, a one-eyed man for sixty, and a white-leper for a hundred; one afflicted with elephantiasis[3] for a thousand.

178. As many Brahmans as a sacrificer for a Çūdra could touch on their limbs, of so many there is no meritorious fruit to the giver of the gift (at a *çrāddha*).

179. And, though he knows the Veda, if a Brahman, out of greediness, receive a present (from such a man), he quickly goes to destruction, like an unburnt pot in water.

180. (Food) given to a seller of the *soma* plant (becomes) ordure; to a physician, blood; (it is) lost (if given to) an attendant on idols; but it is without foundation (if given) to a usurer.

181. But what is given to a trader, that exists not either

[1] [According to a Smṛti quoted by Medh., he need only wait six or eight years for the elder brother to marry, unless the latter is on a journey.]

[2] [Cf. vs. 160. Medh. says another Smṛti defines these in the following manner, which is here inapplicable: *Parapūrvāpatiṁ dhīrā vadanti didhiṣūpatiṁ; yas tv agredidhiṣur vipraḥ sai'va yasya kuṭumbinī.* This verse does not forbid *niyoga*, but its abuse.]

[3] [Literally, one with an evil, severe, disease. Cf. note to vss. 92, 159. Medh. says "leper."]

here or in the next world; so (what is given) to a son of a remarried woman is like an oblation to the gods offered on ashes.

182. Now the learned say that (food given) to other base men unfit (for the feast), such as have been indicated, (is) fat, blood, flesh, marrow, (and) bones.[1]

183. By what Brahmans a company polluted by unfit persons is purified, learn now completely those best of Brahmans, purifiers of the company.

184. The most learned in all the Vedas and in all the Aṅgas, as well as also those descended from learned (priests), are to be known as purifiers of the company.

185. A Triṇāciketa, one who keeps up the five fires, one who knows the Trisuparṇa, one who knows the six Aṅgas, a son of a woman married by the Brāhma ceremony, one who knows the Jyeṣṭha-Sāman;[2]

186. One who knows the meaning of the Vedas, and who teaches it, a student who gives a thousand (cows as fees to his teacher), one a hundred years old[3] also, (such) Brahmans are to be known as purifiers of the company.

187. The *çrāddha* rite being prepared, on the day before or the next day one should duly invite three at least of such Brahmans as have been described.

188. A Brahman invited for a rite to the manes should always be self-restrained; he should not peruse the metrical[4] Veda. This should be also the (rule) for the performer of the rite.

189. The manes indeed stand by those invited Brahmans, and follow (them) like wind; likewise sit by them when seated.

190. Now a Brahman duly invited for offerings to the gods and manes, if anyhow soever he fail,[5] sinful, he becomes a hog (in another birth).

[1] [With vss. 180-182 cf. iv. 220-221.]

[2] [Regarding the meaning of these terms see Bühler's note to Āp. ii. 17, 22. Mbhā. xiii. 90, 27, has *Brahmadeyānusantānaç chandogo jyeṣṭha-sāmagaḥ.*]

[3] [This means a very old man, not precisely 100 years old (Medh.)]

[4] [Chandāṁsi; cf. iv. 111.]

[5] [This means if he is not present at the time for eating the feast (Medh., K.) Some say it means to refuse an invitation; but this is wrong.]

191. But he who, invited to a *çrāddha*, dallies with a Vṛṣalī woman, acquires for himself all that which has been done wrong by the giver.[1]

192. The manes are primitive [2] gods, who are free from anger, intent on purity, ever chaste, who have laid down arms, (and) possess great qualities.

193. From what (is) the origin of them all, who (they are), and by what ceremonies they are to be worshipped, learn this completely.

194. Marīci and other (seers) who (are) the sons of Manu Hiraṇyagarbha,—the sons of all those seers are called the hosts of manes.

195. The Somasads, sons of Virāj, are said (to be the fathers) of the Sādhyas; and the Agniṣvāttas, sons of Marīci, (who are) famed in the world, (are said to be the fathers) of the Devas.

196. The Barhiṣads, sons of Atri, are said (to be the fathers) of the Daityas, Dānavas, and Yakṣas, of the Gandharvas, Uragas, and Rakṣasas, and of the Suparṇas and Kinnaras.

197. The Somapas, indeed, of the Brahmans, the Havirbhujs of the Kṣatriyas, the Ājyapas too of the Vaiçyas, but the Sukālins of the Çūdras.

198. Now the Somapas (are) sons of Kavi, the Haviṣmants (are) sons of Aṅgiras, the Ājyapas are sons of Pulastya, the Sukālins of Vasiṣṭha.

199. The Agnidagdhas and Anagnidagdhas, the Kāvyas, the Barhiṣads, the Agniṣvāttas, and the Saumyas, one should certainly indicate (as the parents) of Brahmans.

200. But these which are famed as the chief hosts of manes, of them even in the world the sons and grandsons without end are to be known (as manes).

201. From the seers were begotten the manes, from the

[1] [Cf. vs. 19 and xi. 179. The Vṛṣalī woman stands for any woman whatever (Medh.)]

[2] [The manes are called primitive because they were reverenced in ancient times (Medh.)]

manes the gods and demons;[1] but from the gods all the universe moving and stable, in due order.

202. Mere water offered with faith to these (manes) by means of silver vessels, or (vessels) adorned with silver, fits (one) for incorruption.

203. The offering (given) by the twice-born to the manes is more excellent than (their) offering to the gods; that to the gods is called the prelude and close[2] of the offering to the manes.

204. Now one should perform first an offering to the gods as a preservative (of these offerings to the manes), for the evil demons destroy a *çrāddha* without a protective.[3]

205. One should make an offering therefore to the gods at the beginning and end;[4] it should not be with an offering to the manes at the beginning and end. One who does it with an offering to the manes at the beginning and end quickly perishes with his offering.

206. One should smear with cow-dung a pure and lonely spot; and one should carefully select a place sloping to the south.

207. The manes, indeed, ever are pleased with what is given in pure open spaces, also on river-banks and in lonely places.

208. One should seat those Brahmans, after they have properly made ablution, separately[5] on seats which have been prepared (for them), and have *kuça*-grass[6] on them.

209. Having seated those venerable[7] Brahmans on their seats, one should honour them after the gods with perfumes and sweet-smelling garlands.

[1] [Dēvas and Dānavas.]

[2] [*Āpyāyana*, which in vs. 211 means "(having made) satisfaction," may here also be taken in the sense of "making complete." Medh. says, "It causes the increase of the sacrifice to the manes; it is not for itself, but only to exalt the sacrifice to the manes;" so that we may translate, "Since the ceremony to the gods preceding that to the manes is said to render the latter complete" (and consequently is subordinate to it).]

[3] [*Ārakṣavarjitam* is merely a pun on *Rākṣasas*, demons.]

[4] [Of the *çrāddha*.]

[5] [That is, in such a way that they do not touch each other (Medh.)]

[6] [*Kuça* is the sacred grass used in ceremonies.]

[7] [Literally, "unblamed;" those who cannot be objected to, such as have already been described (Rāgh.); or it may mean he should not insult them after he had seated them, *i.e.*, he should honour them (Medh.)]

210. Having brought water for them with *kuça*-grass and sesamum seeds, the Brahman authorised by the Brahmans should make (the oblation) in fire.[1]

211. At the beginning, having satisfied in due form Agni, Soma, and Yama by the gift of an oblation, afterwards one should satisfy the manes.

212. But if there be no (consecrated) fire, let him put it in the hands of a Brahman; for it is said by the priests (who are) seers of the *mantras* that fire is a Brahman.

213.[2] They term gods of *çrāddhas* those best of Brahmans who are free from wrath, gentle, primitive, engaged in the satisfaction of the world.

214. Having completely circumambulated (the fire with the right hand toward it), and thrown in the fire all the offering, one should sprinkle water on the ground with the right hand.

215. Having made three balls from the remainder of that oblation, one should, composed in thought and facing the south, offer (them) in the same way as the water.

216. Then, attentive, having offered those balls according to the rite, one should wipe the hand on those *kuça*-grass (blades) for those (ancestors who eat) the wipings.[3]

217. Having rinsed (the mouth), having returned to the north, having thrice restrained the breath slowly, one knowing the *mantras* should also reverence the six seasons and the manes as well.

218. One should again put slowly the rest of the water near the balls, and, composed (in mind), should smell those balls as they were offered (in order).

219. Then having taken in succession a little bit from the balls, one should first in due order cause the seated Brahmans to eat those (balls).

220. But if the father be alive, one should only offer

[1] [*Pavitra* means *darbha* (Medh.) Water-bringing is a Northern custom according to Ap. ii. 17. 17.]

[2] Medhātithi omits vss. 213-214.

[3] The balls are offered to the father, paternal grand- and great-grandfathers; the wipings to the ancestors in the fourth, fifth, and sixth degrees.

to (those) before him, or should cause him to eat at the *çrāddha* like a Brahman.[1]

221. But he whose father is dead and (paternal) grandfather is alive, having mentioned the name of his father, should mention (his) great-grandfather.[2]

222. Either the grandfather, said Manu, should eat that *çrāddha*, or (the grandson) alone, being authorised by him, may of himself perform (it) voluntarily.

223. Having put water with *kuça*-grass and sesamum in their (the Brahmans') hands, one should give (them) the top of those balls, saying "Hail to those (manes)."

224. Then having himself taken with both hands a (dish) full of cooked rice, meditating on the manes, he should put it down leisurely near the Brahmans.

225. That rice which is offered held loosely[3] by the hands, the evil-minded Asuras carry off by force.

226. One should ordinarily, intent (and) composed in mind, place sauces, broth, herbs, and the like, milk-pudding, curds, ghee, (and) honey, properly only on the ground.

227. (One should prepare) cakes and milk-puddings[4] of various kinds, also roots and fruits, also favourite meats and well-smelling drinks.

228. Having brought all that gradually and composed in mind, one should present them intent (and) proclaiming all the qualities.

229. One should never drop a tear, be angry, or say what is untrue, nor touch the rice with (one's) foot, nor shake it.

230. A tear sends (the offering) to ghosts; anger, to enemies; falsehood, to dogs; contact with the foot, to the evil demons; shaking, to evil-doers.

231. Whatever pleases Brahmans one should give with-

[1] [And in this case he offers of course but two balls.]

[2] [Govindarāja, relying on Viṣṇu lxxv. 4, says that he must first offer to his father and then to the two ancestors who precede his grandfather (K.). Cf. this chapter of Viṣṇu for other parallels.]

[3] Medhātithi says it must be held by both, not by one hand only. [So that "held loosely by (freed from) the *hands*" means held in one hand (Medh. and Rāgh.) Asuras are evil spirits.]

[4] ["Things to be eaten and enjoyed," which are explained by K. as above.]

out envy, and one should tell Vedic stories,[1] (for) that (is) desired by the manes.

232. And at a ceremony to the manes, one should cause to be repeated the Vedas, the law-treatises (Dharmā-çastra), tales (Ākhyāna), epics (Itihāsa), legends (Purāṇa), and the supplements (Khila).[2]

233. Delighted, one should please Brahmans, and cause them to eat by degrees, and entice them frequently by the cooked rice, and by the curries.[3]

234. At a *çrāddha* one should strenuously give food to a daughter's son, even though (he be) engaged in a vow;[4] one should give (a guest) a blanket[5] for a seat, and sprinkle the ground with sesamum.

235. Three (things) are purifying at a *çrāddha:* a daughter's son, a blanket, and sesamum. And (the learned) praise three (things) in it: purity, absence of anger, and freedom from haste.

236. All the cooked rice should be very hot, and (the Brahmans) should eat it in silence. The Brahmans must not tell the qualities of the oblation if asked by the giver.

237. As long as the cooked rice is hot, as long as (a Brahman) eats in silence, so long the manes eat (it), (and) as long as the qualities of the oblation are not mentioned.

238. What one eats with the head covered, what one eats facing the south, and what one eats with sandals[6] on, that the evil demons eat.[7]

[1] [Tales which are told in the Veda (Brahma), as of the deeds of Saramā, &c., or of the highest spirit, Brahma (Medh.)]

[2] *Dharma-çāstras* of Manu, etc.; tales, Sauparna, Maitrāvaruṇa, etc.; *itihāsas*, the Mahābhārata, etc.; *purāṇas*, that by Brahma, etc.; *khilas*, the Çrisūkta [R. V. i. 165 (?)], Mahānāmika (Sāmaveda, Ar.)—Medh.

[3] ["By (telling them) the qualities (of the food)" seems to be the literal meaning, that is, the ingredients.]

[4] [That is, if he is still a student (K).]

[5] "Blanket," in Sanskrit, *kutapa*. Medhātithi explains it thus; Kullūka says "a Nepal blanket." This word also occurs in Vardhamāna's "Ganaratna-mahodadhi" (ed. Eggeling, p. 104), who explains it by (1) *çrāddhakāla* [midday]; (2) *chāgaromamayo vastraviçeṣaḥ*. The second meaning is the only one possible here. [That is, it is a kind of garment made of goats'-hair. By his note on this verse Medh. shows he is a Southerner, since he speaks of a *var. lec.* called *kambala* "among the Northerners;" cf. Introduction. Another reading has "a blanket and a seat." This is given to every guest (Medh.) Otherwise see Vas. xi. 35.]

[6] [Some say this means leather shoes (Medh.)]

[7] [The same verse in the Mbhā. ends

239. A Caṇḍāla and a boar, a cock and also a dog, and a woman in her courses and an eunuch, may not see the Brahmans eating.

240. What is seen by these during an oblation,[1] at a gift, and at a meal, at rites to the gods, or in a ceremony to the manes, that becomes unprofitable.

241. The boar destroys[2] by smelling, the cock by the wind from (his) wings, the dog by the cast of a look, the low-caste man by touch.

242. If a lame man or a one-eyed man be merely a servant of the giver, or one with a limb deficient or in excess, even him let (his master) remove from thence.[3]

243. Permitted (to do so) by the Brahmans (already there), one should honour according to one's power a Brahman or a beggar[4] who has come for food.

244. Having brought all kinds of cooked rice and food and the like, having sprinkled it with water, one should put (it) down before these who have eaten, scattering (it) on the ground.

245. What remains and what is scattered on the *kuça*-grass is the portion of those dead without investiture (with the sacred string), and of those who desert the women of their family.[5]

246. The rest which has fallen on the ground at a ceremony to the manes, that (the learned) declare (to be) the share of the servants who are not crooked (by nature) and deceitful.

247. But up to the ceremony of making a *sapiṇḍa*

sarvaṁ vidyāt tad āsuram (xiii. 90, 19), "belonging to the Asuras."]

[1] [*Agnihotra* or *Çānti* oblation (Medh).]

[2] [*I.e.*, renders the ceremony useless (K.)]

[3] [Perhaps better, "If there be present a lame man, or a man who is one-eyed, or a slave, even if he belong to the giver of the *çrāddha*, or a man who has deficient or too many limbs, one should exclude him." Medh. and K. say a Çūdra is meant, implied by the servitude, and any Çūdra is to be excluded, even if he is the servant of the man who is performing the ceremony.]

[4] [*Bhikṣuka*, a religious mendicant.]

[5] [Or, "Those who desert their Gurus, and those who have unmarried women in their houses" (when they ought to be married), according to a forced interpretation mentioned by K. Rāgh., or "untrue wives" (Govind.), or "deserters of women of good family." Partly quoted as Manu's remark in Vas. xi. 23.]

for a deceased Brahman,[1] one should have the *çrāddha* eaten without the ceremony to the gods, and one should offer a single ball.

248. But when the *sapiṇḍa* rite has been properly done for him, the offering of balls is to be made by the sons in this manner (as directed before).[2]

249. Having eaten a *crāddha*, that fool who gives what remains to a Çūdra goes head foremost to the hell Kālasūtra.

250. If an eater of a *çrāddha* on that day approaches the bed of a Çūdra woman,[3] for that month his manes sleep on her ordure.

251. After having asked, "Have you eaten well?" one should cause (those who are) satisfied to rinse their mouths, and say to them when they have done so, "Rest!"

252. The Brahmans should reply to him after that, "Hail be it," for in all ceremonies to the manes the word "hail" is the best blessing.

253. Then one should inform those who have eaten of the remainder of the cooked rice; then he should do as they say, being ordered by the Brahmans.

254. In (a *çrāddha*) to the manes (the word) *svaditam* is to be uttered; in a *goṣṭha* (the word) *suçrutam;* in an *abhyudaya* (the word) *sampannam;* but in one to the gods (the word) *rucitam.*[4]

255. The afternoon[5] as well as the *kuça*-grass, the clear-

[1] [Cf. Viṣṇu, xxi. 11 ff., for a description of this *ekoddiṣṭa* ceremony on making a sapiṇḍa (relative) for him. It implies that the deceased died without any family to offer the *çrāddha* for him. According to Viṣṇu the rite is the same when a deceased woman is to be invested with relationship.]

[2] Vs. 248 is, apparently, omitted by Medhātithi.

[3] [Vṛṣala and Vṛṣalī, cf. iv. 88.]

[4] [There are different *çrāddhas* for different purposes: the *abhyudaya* is for increase, the *goṣṭha* for purity. So in the former the greeting is "success" (*sampannam*); in the latter, "heard with pleasure" (*suçrutam*); *rucitam* means brilliant (as does *deva*, god); *svaditam* is "well-eaten." K. says Medh. and Govind. wrongly say that the greeting is to be offered by anybody at the *çrāddha*, but he does not believe it.]

[5] [The afternoon is not for all *çrāddhas*, for another Smṛti says, *Pūrvāhne daivikaṁ kāryam aparāhne tu paitṛkam ekoddiṣṭaṁ tu madhyāhne prātar vṛddhinimitta-*

ing of the site, the sesamum, the giving (of food), the preparation (of food, and) eminent Brahmans are prosperity in *çrāddha* rites.

256. The *kuça*-grass, the purifying (texts), the forenoon and the oblations entirely, (and) the purification as already mentioned, are to be known as prosperity in the oblations.

257. Hermits' food,[1] milk, *soma*, meat not forbidden,[2] and natural salt[3] are termed oblation by nature.

258. Now having dismissed these Brahmans, restrained, silent, pure, looking to the south, one should supplicate these best manes (saying):

259. "May the generous increase among us! May the Vedas and progeny also! May faith never leave us! May also much to give away[4] be with us!"[5]

260. Having thus made the offering, one should after it cause a cow, a Brahman, a goat, or fire to consume those balls, or one should throw them into water.

261. Some perform the offering of the balls just after[6] (the feast); others cause birds to eat (it), or throw (it) into fire or water.

262. A lawful wife devoted to her husband, intent on the worship of the manes, should then duly eat the middle cake, (if) desirous of offspring.[7]

263. (Thus) she brings forth a long-lived son, endowed with fame (and) intelligence, wealthy, having offspring, truthful, (and) also righteous.

---

kam" (the feast to the gods in the forenoon, to the manes in the afternoon, at mid-day to one just deceased, early in the morning when for gain)—Medh.]

1 The hermits (Munis) are supposed to live on wild rice.

2 [Medh., "not made up" with forbidden things.]

3 [K., see note to v. 73.]

4 [This may mean "may much to be given (to us) be ours" (may we receive much). See Stenzler, Yāj. i. 245.]

5 [One MS. has a new verse following this, and found Viṣṇu, lxxiii. 30: "May we have much food and obtain guests; have those who beg (of us), but never beg (ourselves")."]

6 [Dr. Burnell says "before," reading *purastāt*; but it is plain, on comparing K. with Rāgh., that the former as the latter read *parastāt*. The sense is the same according to Medh., if we read with him *purastād*, *i.e.*, *kṛte brāhmaṇabhojane* (which comes "before").]

7 There are many such magical ceremonies in the Sāmavidhāna and Ṛgvidhāna.

264. Having wiped (one's) hands and rinsed (the mouth), one should prepare (food) for (paternal) kinsmen; having given it to (those) kinsmen with reverence, one should cause (one's maternal) relatives to eat.

265. Let the rest remain until the Brahmans are dismissed, then one should perform the household rites.[1] Thus is the rule established.

266. I shall now fully declare what oblation duly presented to the manes is for a long time, and what for endless (time).

267. The manes of men are delighted for a month by sesamum, rice, barley, pulse, water, roots, (and) fruit duly given;

268. For two months by fish (and) flesh, but for three months by venison; also for four (months) by mutton, but for five (months) indeed by birds' flesh;

269. For six months by goat's flesh, and for seven (months) indeed by spotted deer's (flesh); for eight months by *ena's* flesh; for nine months by *ruru's* flesh;[2]

270. But for ten months (they) are pleased by the flesh of hogs (and) buffaloes, and for eleven months also by the flesh of hares and tortoises;

271. But a year by cow's milk and milk-pudding. The pleasure by flesh of the rhinoceros[3] endures for twelve years.[4]

272. The *kālaçāka*[5] and *mahāçalka*,[6] the flesh of a rhinoceros and red goat,[7] (and) honey (are productive of satisfaction) for endless time indeed, and hermits' food (also) universally.

[1] ["The offering" (*bali*) to beings, though this is only a type of all the rites, such as offerings, hospitality, etc., not strictly, as some say (Medh.)]

[2] The *ena* and *ruru* are, apparently, kinds of deer. [So K. and Rāgh., *mrgajātiviçeṣau*.]

[3] "Rhinoceros" or "white goat." [So Medh. and K., or "crane;" see Jolly, Viṣṇu, lxxx. 14. Medh. reads (with some K. MSS.) *vā*, "or," not "and."]

[4] ["For a year" (Dr. Burnell), evidently an error.]

[5] *Kālaçāka* is a plant [sacred basil].

[6] What *mahāçalka* is the commentators cannot determine. The prevailing opinion is that it is a kind of fish [viz., prawn. This is K.'s opinion, and that of "others" quoted by Medh., who defines as porcupine, *çalyaka*. Rāgh. says it is a fish "according to Yama"].

[7] "Red goat;" Medhātithi says "black."

273. Whatever (food) mixed with honey one may present on the thirteenth (lunar day) in the rains or under (the lunar asterism) Maghā is even imperishable.

274. "May one be born of our race who will give us on the thirteenth milk-pudding with honey and ghee, and when an elephant's shadow is to the east!"[1]

275. Whatever one who has faith properly offers according to rule, that becomes endless, undecaying for the manes in the other world.

276. The most excellent lunar days for a *çrāddha* (are) the tenth, and so on of the dark fortnight, excluding the fourteenth. As they (are), so (are) not the rest.

277. He who performs (*çrāddhas*) on even lunar days, and under even asterisms, obtains all desires; (if) on odd (lunar days, and under odd asterisms he offers to) all[2] the manes, he obtains an illustrious progeny.

278. As the dark fortnight is better than the bright fortnight, so for a *çrāddha* the afternoon is better than the forenoon.[3]

279. Rites to the manes are to be duly performed to the end by one (who has) *kuça*-grass in the hand, with his sacred thread over his right shoulder, going to the right and unwearied.

280. One should not perform a *çrāddha* at night, for it is said to be of the evil demons; nor at sunrise or sunset also; so also when the sun has not long risen.[4]

[1] The commentators seem unable to make any sense of the latter part of this verse. [Medh. says this refers to the (eastward-going shadows that mark the) afternoon. Kull. quotes Viṣṇu, lxxviii. 52–53, where the (afternoon) time of lengthening shadows is mentioned for the Kārttika month especially, the rainy season of vs. 273 being also only one month. Is *dakṣiṇāyana* to be so taken in Mbhā. xiii. 88, 12? Cf. for the days Āp. ii. 16, 20–21; Viṣṇu, *loc. cit.*, vs. 50. The thirteenth day is lucky, the fourteenth not so for Brahmans, but for Kṣatriyas.]

[2] [Medh. and Rāgh. read with MS. Beng. *arcan* (revering), for *sarvān*, (all), "if (on the odd) he revere the manes."]

[3] [In the original strengthened by the fact that the dark fortnight is called the "*after*-part" (*aparaḥ pakṣaḥ*), and its effect is like that of the "*after*-noon." Cf. Āp. ii. 16, 5.]

[4] [Cf. ii. 15. Viṣṇu, lxxvii. 8, permits a *çrāddha* at twilight or at night if an eclipse has taken place; *vide* next. Cf. Āp. ii. 17, 25.]

281. One may by this rule perform here a *çrāddha* thrice a year, (viz.) in winter, the hot weather, and the rains; but one should make the five sacrifices every day.

282. The offering[1] to the manes is not prescribed in ordinary fire, (and) the *çrāddha* of a Brahman who has established the (sacred) fire is not (prescribed) except at the conjunction of the sun and moon.[2]

283. If a good Brahman, having bathed, offers to the manes by (means of) water, by that alone he obtains all the fruit of a sacrifice to the manes.[3]

284. They (the learned) term fathers Vasus, and grandfathers Rudras, but great-grandfathers Ādityas. This is an everlasting Vedic text.[4]

285. One should always eat *vighasa*, or always eat *amṛta*. *Vighasa* (is) the remains of a (*çrāddha*) feast; *amṛta* is likewise the remains of a sacrifice.[5]

286. All this system of the five sacrifices has been told you; hear the rules about the occupations of the chief of the twice-born.[6]

END OF THE THIRD LECTURE.

[1] [Medh. calls attention to the fact that the oblation (offering) is the only thing forbidden, so that "all else" may be performed. The dependent genitive is to be construed with each clause.]

[2] [*Na darçena vinā; darça* sacrifice is one on the day of the "appearance" (of the new moon). Several opinions are broached here by Medh. in regard to the meaning; he quotes three sets of commentators, "some," "others," and "the ancients."]

[3] [This remark makes the regular daily *çrāddha* optional (Medh.)]

[4] [*Çruti*. The object of this verse is to inspire those who through dislike of the manes have grown averse to their sacrifice with the due feeling of reverence for them as divinities (Medh.) K., quoting this, inserts (through dislike of manes) "or through infidelity" as part of Medh.'s explanation: he himself takes it in a more mystical sense: "the manes are to be thought of under the form of Vasus," etc., and quotes an old teacher, Paiṭhinasi, in support of this view.]

[5] ["Read *bhṛtyaçeṣa*, a feast by one's dependents; there is another reading, *bhukta-çeṣa*, which conveys the same idea of a feast by guests, etc. Some say it refers only to the feast at *çrāddha*"—Medh. In Mbhā. xiii. 93, 13 and 15, these terms are defined: one who eats the portions left from feasts to manes or gods they call an eater of *vighasa*, while one who always eats after his dependents and guests eats pure *amṛta*. Cf. below, iv. 5].

[6] [Āp. ii. 16 refers the origin of the *çrāddha* to Manu; the Mbhā. has a different account. Much of the above occurs in the sūtra literature; most fully in Viṣṇu lxxiii. ff.]

LECTURE IV.

ON A HOUSEHOLDER'S DUTY AS REGARDS SUBSISTENCE AND PRIVATE MORALS.

1. A BRAHMAN having lived the first quarter of his life with a Guru, should live, having taken a wife, the second quarter of his life in (his own) house.

2. A Brahman should live, except in distress, following the calling which is his, without (doing) any injury to beings, or with little injury.

3. He should make accumulation of wealth, without pain of body, by his own (proper) blameless occupations, as much as is necessary for subsistence.

4. Now one may live by *ṛta* and *amṛta*, or by *mṛta* and *pramṛta*, or even by *satyānṛta*; never at any time by *çvavṛtti*.

5. *Ṛta* (truth) is to be understood as living by gleaning; *amṛta* (undying) is (what is given) unasked, but *mṛta* (dead) is alms begged; agriculture is *pramṛta* (dead).

6. *Satyānṛta* (truth and lying) is trading; even by that also one lives. Service is termed *çvavṛtti* (dog's livelihood), therefore one should avoid that.[1]

[1] [These are evidently technical terms, and will scarcely bear a literal translation. Gleaning is the true (right) way to live; living by unasked alms is of more merit than living by alms begged, and one is therefore immortal as compared to the other, which is "mortal;" agriculture is "dead," probably because it results in the death of creatures in the ground (cf. x. 83); "truth and lying" is a plain hit at trading; and service as dog's livelihood needs no exposition. Cf. to *amṛta*, iii. 285, where it is used in a different sense. K. says the word "and" (*ca*) in vs. 6 means that money-lending is included under the word agriculture, as expressly stated by Gaut. x. 5, 6, who says in the same place that agriculture is permitted a Brahman if he does not do the work himself. *Çvavṛtti* is like *çvacaryā* in Mbhā. xiii. 101, 15 (*nīcasevā*). In spite of the famous dog in the epic, the animal was one much despised: "he that goes about with dogs or is bitten by one" is excluded from *çrāddha*, and "the wise hold a dog as lower than a jackal" (Mbh. xiii. 90, 10; xii. 141, 157).]

7. One may have grain for three years or for one year, or for three days, or not have (enough) for the next day.[1]

8. Now of these four householder Brahmans, the last in order is to be known as the better; by law[2] he has most overcome the world.

9. One of them subsists by six ways, another lives by three, one by two, but the fourth lives by *brahmasattra*.[3]

10. One living by gleaning ears and kernels, intent on the *agnihotra*, should always perform merely the sacrifices belonging to the *parvan* and (time of) solstice.[4]

11. For the sake of a livelihood one should never by any means follow a worldly occupation, but should live a Brahman life, not crooked, free from fraud, pure.

12. One seeking happiness should be firm, practising perfect content. Happiness is, indeed, based on content; the contrary is the origin of unhappiness.

13. Hence a twice-born man returned home from his studies who lives by any of the (above) occupations must perform these (following) ceremonies, which bring fame, longevity, and heaven.

14. He must ever, unwearied, perform his duty (as) related by the Veda; for, doing that as well as he can, he obtains the highest course (of happiness).

15. One must not eagerly desire wealth (by music, etc.[5]),

[1] Cf. Baudhāyanadharmasūtra [iii. 2, and iii. 3 (21). This translation rests on K.'s arbitrary interpretation of the time implied by the first words in the verse, which mean literally no more than "he may have a storehouse of grain" or "a measure of grain." K. bases his translation on xi. 7 and Yāj. i. 124, but admits that other commentators give different times. Probably no specific period is meant.]

[2] [*I.e.*, by reason of the religious merit gained by his law of life.]

[3] [K. and Rāgh. define this as study. This verse connects the four persons of vs. 7 with the six occupations of vs. 4, according to Medh. K., as above, inserts money-lending as one of them, but does not make the four represent those of vs. 7. Both commentators decide arbitrarily what are the omitted ones in order. Some regard the occupations as the six regularly ordained for a Brahman (study, teaching, giving, receiving, etc.)]

[4] [That is, he should perform the sacrifices which come at the day of the new moon, at the day of the full moon, and at the solstices (*ayana*). (I have ventured to change Dr. Burnell's reading here, as it does not seem to give the right meaning and omits *ayana*; it is "(the sacrifices) ending with the ones at the *parvan*.")]

[5] [*Prasangena* means "by (following some pursuit with too much) devo-

nor by any prohibited deed; nor whether one have wealth or be in distress, (may he gain it) from any source (not permitted).

16. One should not from sensuality be addicted to any of the objects of the senses, and excessive addiction to them one should cause to cease by the mind.

17. One should forsake all wealth that obstructs study (of the Veda), and (be always) properly teaching (the Veda), for that is (one's) duty done.

18. One should live in this world bringing about conformity of (one's) clothing, speech, (and) intelligence to (one's) age, calling, wealth, knowledge, and family.

19. One should ever regard (those) treatises which quickly cause increase of knowledge, conduce to wealth, and are beneficial, as well as the Vedic *nigamas* (exegetical and explanatory treatises).[1]

20. For just as a man gets acquainted with a treatise, exactly so he becomes discerning, and his discernment shines forth.

21. So much as one can, one should never at any time neglect the offerings to seers, gods, beings, men, and the manes.[2]

22. Some people who understand the rules of offerings, not performing those great sacrifices, ever sacrifice in their own organs of sense alone.

23. Some sacrifice breath in speech, and ever again (sacrifice) speech in breath, seeing the imperishable result of a sacrifice in (their) speech and breath.

24. Other Brahmans ever sacrifice with those sacrifices by knowledge alone, seeing by the eye of knowledge that the doing of them is based on knowledge.

tion, K. illustrates by citing music as an example. I have supplied "eagerly" in Dr. B.'s translation, and enclosed the last words in parentheses, as they are from the commentator. His own translation, "one must not desire wealth by music, etc.," is a little misleading. The true meaning of *prasaṅga* is apparent from vs. 186.]

[1] Medhātithi explains *nigama* by *nirukta*, grammar, and *mīmāṁsā*. [The treatises do not imply writings; they are treatises either on law or on other subjects. Medh. refers to those of Bṛhaspati and Uçanas.]

[2] *I.e.*, the five ceremonies the subject of the last lecture [cf. iii. 81].

25. One should always make the *agnihotra* at the beginning and end of day and night, and (sacrifice) with the *darça* at the end of the half-month, and also with the *paurṇamāsa*.[1]

26. A twice-born man (should) at the end of the (old) grain (offer) with a sacrifice of new grain; so at the end of the season, with the *adhvaras*;[2] at the beginning of the solstice, with cattle; at the end of the year, with *soma* sacrifices.

27. A twice-born man who keeps (sacred) fires, (if he) desires long life, should not eat new grain or flesh if he has not sacrificed with the new grain or cattle.

28. For his fires, not honoured with new (grain) or an offering of cattle, being eager for new (rice)-food and flesh, desire to devour his breath.[3]

29. Let no guest abide in his house not honoured, as well as may be, with a seat, food, bed, (and) water, and with roots and fruit.

30. But he should not honour, even by speech, heretics, those who do wrong acts, pretenders to virtue,[4] the fraudulent, rationalists, and hypocrites.[5]

31. One should adore with oblations to gods and manes learned Vedic (priests) who are householders,[6] who have

[1] The *agnihotra* is an offering of milk morning and evening. This sacrifice is practically obsolete. [The *darça* is a sacrifice at the beginning of the new moon, the *paurṇamāsa* the one offered when the moon is full. "At the end of the half-month" is to be construed with each clause.]

[2] [*Adhvara* are sacrifices which come every four months at the end of a season (K.) Medh. gives two quotations from a Sūtrakāra, the first of which refers to the sacrifice of grain—"one should not eat grain without offering an *agnihotra*;" the second, that he should offer sacrifice each six months, or yearly.]

[3] "Breath" is plural, to express the "five breaths" attributed to man.

[4] ["Those who act like cats" (cf. vs. 192 and the definitions in vss. 195 and 196).]

[5] ["Those whose habits are like the *baka*" (a kind of crane). Medh. renders "heretics" by "those who bear the token of outcasts" (*vāhyaliṅgin*), and "rationalists" by "unbelievers" (*nāstika*). Cf. note on ii. 11.]

[6] "Householders." A Grantha MS. reads *gṛhamāgatān*, "come to the house," which is preferable in sense, but probably not the original reading, as it is unsupported by other MSS. or by the commentators. "Vedic priests who have studied," etc., should, according to the commentators, be divided into those priests who have both finished the Vedas and completed their vows; such priests should be honoured at sacrifices to manes and to deities.]

studied the Vedas and returned home (from their teacher's house), and should avoid those who are the contrary.

32. According to his ability a householder must give to beggars,[1] and a portion is to be made for beings (as well as he can) without inconvenience (to his family).

33. A (Brahman) returned home (from his teacher's), if wasting with hunger, may seek wealth from a king, or from a sacrificer or pupil, but not from any other. Such is the rule.

34. An able Brahman who has returned home (from his teacher's) must never anyhow[2] waste with hunger; he must never wear worn-out dirty clothes if he have property.

35. Having his hair, nails, and beard trimmed, subdued, with white clothes (and) pure, he should be ever devoted to study (of the Veda) and to what is beneficial to himself.

36. He should have a bamboo staff, and a pot with water in it, a sacred thread, and (a handful of *kuça*) grass,[3] also a pair of bright gold earrings.

37. He should not at any time look at the rising or setting sun, nor when it is eclipsed or (reflected) in water, nor when it is at the zenith.

38. He should not step over a calf's rope,[4] nor may he run when it rains, nor may he look at his own form (reflected) in water. Such is the rule.

39. He should circumambulate to the right[5] a mound,

[1] ["Beggars," literally "those who do not cook for themselves;" students and wandering (religious) mendicants, even of heretical sects, are understood by the commentators, though no such idea is in the text. The "beings" are probably, in accordance with the use of this word, the ghosts and spirits to whom offerings are made.]

[2] [Or "if able in any way (to prevent it)."]

[3] [Dr. B. reads *védam* for *vedàm*, and translates "and the Veda," which I venture to change, as this is not upheld by the accent, and is expressly explained as grass, *kuça*, *darbha* (*muṣṭi*), by K. and Medh.; and cf. Rāgh.'s *çruti*, "*Vedaṁ kṛtvā vediṁ karotîti.*" Medh. quotes from Vas. xii. 15 ff. to show for what purpose the water-pot is enjoined.]

[4] "Calf's rope," by which it is tied; [or it may mean "he should not pass through (?) a company of calves" (*vatsa paṅkti*, Medh.); cf. Gaut. ix. 52. The same commentator construes the final words to mean "the rule in the *çāstras*" (pl.), not "the rule as enjoined by Manu."]

[5] *I.e.*, in token of respect [he should, in passing by, keep these objects at his right hand. Well-known or "conspicuous trees are meant, such as the *udumbara*, etc." (Medh.)]

a cow, an idol, a Brahman, ghee, honey, a meeting-place of four roads, as also well-known trees.

40. Although wild with passion, he must not approach (his) wife on the appearance of her courses; nor must he even sleep with her on a common bed.

41. For of a man who approaches a woman when menstruating, the learning, glory, strength, sight, and also longevity, are destroyed.

42. But of him who avoids her when menstruating, the learning, glory, strength, sight, and longevity increase.

43. One should not eat with (his) wife, nor look at her eating, sneezing, yawning, or sitting at her ease.[1]

44. A good Brahman desirous of glory may not see her adorning her eyes (with collyrium), smeared with oil, naked, or bringing forth (a child).

45. One should not eat food with one cloth on; one should not go naked to the bath; one should not make water[2] on a road, on ashes, or in a cow-pen;

46. Nor on cultivated ground, nor in water, nor on a pile (of fuel), nor on a mountain, nor in a ruined temple, nor by any means[3] on an ant-hill;

47. Nor in pits with living beings in them, nor (when) walking, or even (when) standing,[4] nor (when) sitting on a river's bank; nor on the top of a mountain.

48. Nor (when) beholding the wind, fire, a Brahman, the sun, water, or also cattle, should one ever anyhow perform excretion.

49. Restraining his speech, subdued, his breast covered (and) head veiled, he may void (his excrement), having

[1] [According to Viṣṇu's commentator (lxviii. 46), a low-caste wife; eating with his wife is eating off the same dish (K.); or it is at the same place and time (Medh.)]

[2] [Void excrements or make water (Medh., K.)]

[3] [Literally "at any time," but this is to be taken with the whole verse.]

[4] [Medh. discriminates here between these ideas and sitting. "By forbidding one walking and standing, permission (is here given) to one who is sitting," with deference to which finical distinction I have supplied "sitting" in the next clause, as it is in the text, but omitted by Dr. B.]

covered the earth with wood, clods, leaves, grass, and the like.[1]

50. He should void his excrements by day with his face to the north, during the night facing the south, but at day-dawn and at nightfall as by day.[2]

51. A twice-born man in shade or in darkness, by day or night, should do it facing as he likes; so (when) in fear for his life.

52. The intelligence of one who pisses against fire, against the sun, against the moon, against water, against the twice-born, against a cow, and against wind, perishes.

53. One should not blow fire with the mouth; one should not look at a naked woman; one should not throw an unclean (thing) into fire, nor warm (one's) feet (at it).

54. One should not put (it) below,[3] nor should one step over it, nor put it at (one's) feet, nor do any injury to life.

55. One should not eat at day-dawn or nightfall, nor go forth, nor even lie down; and one should not scratch lines on the ground, nor take off from oneself[4] a garland.

56. One may not discharge into water[5] either urine, or ordure, or spittle, or anything smeared with (what is) unclean, or blood, or poisons.[6]

57. One should not sleep alone in an empty house, nor awaken a sleeper, nor talk with a woman in her courses, nor go to a sacrifice (when) not invited.[7]

[1] After vs. 48 Medhātithi has vss. 52, 49, 51, 53, &c.

[2] Medhātithi omits this verse. [His gloss on vs. 52 (beginning *nanu co'd-inmukhasya mehanavidhānāt*) seems to imply it, however. The verse occurs in Mbh. xiii. 104, 76, following the one (75) that is equivalent to Manu 52, but with the *var. lec.* (*a*) *ubhe mūtrapurīṣe tu;* (*b*, in second *pāda*) *tathā hi ayur na riṣyate.*]

[3] "Below." Medhātithi and the commentators subsequent to him understood this to mean making use of a fire-pan under a bed.

[4] [This means one is not to take it off himself, but have it taken off by some one else (K.) The first three of these rules are set just for the (*sandhi*) twilight-time. "Connection with a woman is also forbidden, as it is said in another Smṛti: One should avoid these four acts at the *sandhi* time — eating, cohabitation, sleep, and study" (Medh.)]

[5] [Paying attention to the Çruti that says waters are divinities (Rāgh.)]

[6] [Poisons in the plural shows that all the different kinds are meant, natural and artificial (Medh., K.)]

[7] [*Avṛta.* In ii. 143 we have *yaḥ karoti vṛtaḥ*, "he who performs (a

58. In a fire-shrine, in a cow-pen, and in the presence of Brahmans, in reciting (the Veda), and also in eating, one should hold out the right hand.

59. A wise man should not restrain a cow when drinking, nor should he tell it to any one; nor having seen Indra's weapon[1] in the sky, should he show it to any one.

60. Let him not dwell in an unrighteous village, nor very long in one where there is much disease; nor let him alone set out on the road; let him not dwell long on a mountain.

61. He may not dwell in the kingdom of a Çūdra, nor in one full of unrighteous people, nor in one invaded by hosts of heretics, nor in one possessed by low-born men.

62. Let him not eat that from which the oil is extracted, nor let him eat to excessive fulness, nor very early or very late, nor in the evening (if) he has eaten in the morning.

63. Let him not make effort[2] in vain, nor drink water from the hollow of his hands, nor eat food[3] from (his) lap; let him never be inquisitive.

64. Let him not dance nor sing, nor play on musical instruments, nor clap his hands, nor gnash his teeth, nor, though in a passion, let him roar out.

sacrifice) when chosen," as definition of *ṛtvig*, "sacrificial priest." So in vii. 78 the same verb for choosing a priest. K. refers to Gaut. ix. 55 as meaning when *not* chosen as priest, he should not go to a sacrifice except, if he wishes, to look on. Medh. construes *avṛta* differently, as when not invited he shall not go to take part in the eating; but both agree that *avṛta*, whether to the dinner or to the post of priest, means chosen, invited; so that I have ventured to alter the translation given by Dr. B., "nor unattended go to a sacrifice."]

1 "Indra's weapon," the rainbow. [Medh. (if the text of Dr. B.'s MS. is correct) says that among the inhabitants of Kashmir one is accustomed to call attention to the rainbow. The word *divi*, in the sky, merely emphasises the idea, though some hold that this refers to the appearance in the mid-day heaven, as distinct from the appearance at the end, where it is not wrong to show it. Cf. Gaut. ix. 22.]

2 [*I.e.*, take exercise with his bodily organs for no purpose.]

3 [Water is to be distinguished from milk, etc., to which the prohibition does not apply; so "food" (rice, etc.) is to be distinguished from fruits (Medh.)]

65. Let him never, by any means, wash his feet in a bell-metal vessel, nor eat from a broken dish, nor when (his) mind is disturbed.[1]

66. He must not wear sandals, cloths, a sacred thread, an ornament, a garland, or a water-pot borne by others.[2]

67. He must not journey with[3] unbroken beasts, nor with those tormented by thirst or disease, nor with those with injured horns, eyes, or hoofs, nor with those with deformed tails.

68. But let him ever journey with trained, quickly going (beasts), that bear (good) marks, that are endowed with (good) colour and shape, not striking (them) excessively with the goad.

69. The sun in Virgo,[4] smoke from a corpse (being burned), are to be avoided, likewise a broken seat. One should never cut (one's own) nails and hair,[5] nor break (one's) nails with the teeth.

70. One should not break clods also, nor break grass with one's nails, nor do a useless act,[6] nor one which will bring discomfort in future.

71. A man who is a breaker of clods, a cutter of grass, a biter of (his) nails, goes quickly to destruction, as also a betrayer and an impure (person).

72. One should not talk scandal, nor wear a garland

[1] "Nor when his mind is disturbed." This is how Medhātithi, and Kullūka following him, understand it; but it would be better to translate, "nor in a (vessel) polluted by nature."

[2] [But some say there is no prohibition of wearing jewellery (which has been worn)—(Medh.)]

[3] [That is, literally, "he must not go." According to another Smṛti, even mounting them is forbidden (Medh.)]

[4] [The three commentators, Medh., K., Rāgh., afford an idea of the development of this explanation of (not *kanyā* but) *bālātapaḥ*. "The designation *bālātapa* means a period of three hours (*muhūrta*) after the sun is up" (Medh.) "As Medh. explains it, (or), as others say, the sun in Virgo" (K.) "The sun in Virgo, or, as others say, the early morning heat for three hours" (Rāgh.) I have not changed Dr. B.'s translation, as it affects his theory of the antiquity of the text; but it is proper to say that probably no allusion to the western zodiacal sign is intended.]

[5] [He should not foolishly cut his hair and nails himself, but, when they are too long, have them cut by a barber (Medh.)

[6] [This differs from the bodily act of vs. 69 by including mental action (Medh., K.)]

outside (the clothes [1]). Riding on the back of cattle is in every way blamed.

73. One should not enter a village or an enclosed house except by the gate; and at night one should keep far from roots of trees.

74. Now one should at no time play with dice,[2] nor take off one's sandals (with the hands), nor eat (when) on a bed, nor what is in (one's) hand, nor (when) on a seat.

75. Nor after sunset should one eat anything mixed with sesamum, nor should one sleep naked here (in the world), nor set out with food in (one's) mouth.

76. Now one may eat if one's feet are wet, but not lie down if one's feet are wet. But one who eats with wet feet attains long life.

77. One should never enter a difficult place not exposed to the sight; nor look at ordure and urine, nor cross a river with his arms (by swimming).[3]

78. One desirous to live a long life should not stand on hair, nor on ashes, bones, or potsherds, nor on cotton seeds or chaff.

79. One may not abide with outcasts, nor Cāṇḍālas, nor Pukkaças, nor idiots, nor proud (people), nor with low-born (people), nor with Antyāvasāyins.[4]

80. One may not give advice[5] to a Çūdra, nor (give him) the remains (of food), or (of) butter that has been offered. And one may not teach him the law or enjoin upon him (religious) observances.

[1] [Medh. offers three explanations of *bahirmālyaṁ na dhārayet.* As above, or, as others say, "in an open place;" or it is equivalent to *bahirgandha*, meaning he should not wear one with a weak perfume; as another Smṛti has it, "one should not wear a garland without perfume, except it be of gold." Cf. Āp. i. 31, 23.]

[2] [This excludes the possibility of the later licensed gaming-houses.]

[3] [Most of these are precautionary rules against danger, as Medh. remarks at this verse, not of religious moment. "The difficult place is a thick, dark jungle."]

[4] [In x. 12, 39, 40, we have the exact definition of these low castes according to the scheme of the law-book. The commentators say the meaning of "abide" in this verse (as distinct from the injunction in vss. 60, 61) is that one should have no friendly or commercial intercourse with these people, or should not live in the outskirts where they do.]

[5] [Advice means in regard to his conduct, not simply friendly advice (Medh.) Discrepancies between this verse and others in the work (cf. ix. 125) are explained by the commentators, who say that the Çūdra men-

81. For he who tells him the law and he who enjoins upon him (religious) observances, he indeed, together with that (Çūdra), sinks into the darkness of the hell called Asaṁvṛtta.[1]

82. One may not stroke (one's) own head with both hands joined, nor touch it (if) food is in one's mouth, nor bathe without (bathing) it.[2]

83. One should avoid taking hold of the hair and (inflicting) blows on the head.[3] If one's head has been rubbed with sesamum oil, one should not touch any limb (with oil).

84. One must not accept (a gift) from a king not born of the royal (caste),[4] or from owners of a slaughter-house or an oil-press, or from those who have a flag as a sign (*i.e.*, are venders of liquor), or from those who live by wages of prostitution.

85. An oil-press is equal to ten slaughter-houses, a (liquor seller's) flag to ten presses, a house of prostitution to ten flags, (such) a king (as above described) to ten houses of prostitution.[5]

86. A butcher who maintains ten thousand slaughter-houses, with him (such) a king is said to be equal: his gift is terrible.

87. He who receives (a gift) from an avaricious king (who) acts in opposition to the treatises goes in succession to these twenty-one hells:[6]

tioned in the other rules is a family servant.]

[1] [Unbounded.]

[2] [That is, without having first bathed the head. Medh. explains that bathing with oil is meant.]

[3] [As a result of anger is meant. Some say this means his own head or that of another; others say it means another's (only)—(Medh.)]

[4] [For instance, a Çūdra king. Such kings appear to have been not uncommon (cf. vs. 61). The commentators point out that this is a restriction of vs. 33. Medh. on x. 113 says that this prohibition is restricted to a bad king (*duṣṭarājaviṣayaḥ*), *i.e.*, his birth is not good.]

[5] [*Daçavreçasama* (Medh., K.) or *daçaveçyāsama* (Govind.)]

[6] [These hells all have a meaning more or less clear, conveying an idea of their properties. They may be rendered by Darkness, Dense-darkness, Very-frightful (or Howling), Frightful, Hell, Thread of Death, Great-hell, Quickener, Great-billowless, Burning, Consuming, Compression, Place of Rodents, Gaping, Stinking-earth, the Place of Iron Spikes, Frying-pan, (Hard)-path, the River of Hell (?) or Thorny *çalmali* tree, the Sword-leafed Wood, the Place of Iron Fetters. Medh. has *lohacāraka* for the last, found also in Viṣṇu, where more are added. A varied list, though very similar, is found Yaj. iii. 222 ff.; Viṣṇu, xliii. 1 ff. Others occur in our text (cf. iii. 249; xii. 76; above, vs. 81, and below, vs. 197.]

88. Tāmisra, Andhatāmisra, Mahāraurava, Raurava, Naraka, Kālasūtra, and also Mahānaraka;

89. Sañjīvana, Mahāvīci, Tapana, Sampratāpana, Saṁhāta, Sakākola, Kuḍmala, Pūtimṛttika;

90. Lohaçaṅku, and Ṛjīsa, Panthāna, the river Çālmalī, also Asipatravana, and also Lohacāraka.[1]

91. Wise Brahmans who know that, (and) who recite the Veda, desiring happiness in the other world, do not accept (gifts) from (such) a king.

92. (A householder) should awake at the *brāhmī*-time,[2] and should think on law and wealth, on the troubles to the body which arise from them, and also on the true meaning of the Veda.

93. Having arisen, having done what is necessary, purified, self-contained, he should long stand muttering (the texts) during the former twilight, and during the last twilight also at its own time.[3]

94. The seers got long life by long twilight (recitations); (they got) wisdom, glory, and fame, and also holiness.

95. Having duly done the *upākarman*[4] at the Çrāvaṇa (full moon), or in Prauṣṭhapada,[5] intent, a Brahman should recite the metrical Veda for four and a half months.

96. Now a twice-born man should make *utsarga* of the Vedas outside (the village) in Puṣya, or on the first day of the bright fortnight of Māgha[6] in the forenoon.

97. Having so done, according to the treatises, the

[1] [Dr. B. transcribes *lohāṅgāraka* on the authority of one MS., for which I have given the one supported by more MS. authority and by my MS. of Medh. Other inferior readings are also found.]

[2] [The night has three periods; the last of them is called (the period translated above, in accordance with K.) the *brāhmī*-time (*brāhmyo muhūrta*)—(Medh.) The *brāhmyo muhūrtaḥ*, therefore, corresponds to the period embraced by our "last watch of the night," though Govindarāja restricts it to the "last hour."]

[3] [That is, at the gloaming, morn and eve.]

[4] *Upākarman*, a ceremony on beginning the [annual] course of Vedic study.

[5] [That is, on the day of the full moon in July-August or August-September.]

[6] *Utsarga*, a ceremony on completing (the annual course of) Vedic study. [Puṣya corresponds to December-January, Māgha to January-February. According to Āp. i. 9, 1–2, the Vedic term lasts five months. He alludes to the term of four months and a half as commanded by "some." Cf. Gaut. xvi. 2, and Vas. xiii. 1.]

utsarga of the metrical Veda outside (the village), one should rest for a night with a day before and after,[1] (or) also for that one day and night.

98. But then after that one may, intent, recite the metrical Veda in the bright fortnight; in the dark fortnight one should recite all the Vedāṅgas.

99. One should never recite (the Vedas) indistinctly or in presence of a Çūdra; nor having recited the Veda at the end of the night, (though) fatigued, may one sleep again.

100. A twice-born man must, intent, ever recite in the way directed the metrical Veda, and, when not in trouble, the Veda and also the metrical part.[2]

101. One reciting (the Veda) and duly making the pupils to recite (it) must ever avoid those days on which recitation is prohibited.

102. When wind is audible at night, when dust is collected by day, those are two occasions during the rainy season not fit for recitation: (so) declare those who understand recitations.

103. During lightning, thunder, rains, and the fall of great thunderbolts, Manu[3] has declared that the recital (is to be adjourned) to the same times (next day).[4]

104. But if one know those (accidents) to have occurred when his (sacrificial) fires are made to blaze up, then he should know that there is no recital; also when rain-clouds are seen in the wrong season.

105. When there is a storm, an earthquake, or an eclipse of the heavenly bodies, even in season, one should know recitals to be unseasonable.

106. But if when his fires are blazing up there is a sound of lightning and thunder, there is no recital till the sunrise; in the evening it is by night as by day (*i.e.*, till the stars appear).[5]

107. There should be in villages and towns perpetual

[1] ["A winged night," the night with the day before and after; "metrical veda," cf. p. 67, note 4.]

[2] [Medh. and K. explain *chandāṁsi* here as *gāyatrī*, etc., and Veda (brahma) as "a brāhmaṇa."]

[3] [Manu is mentioned for the sake of (showing that this is an) old verse; some (say) for the sake of (showing) a difference (between his ordinance and that in v. 102)—(Medh.)]

[4] [So Medh. and K. For like rules, cf. Āp. i. 9-12; Vas. xiii.; Viṣṇu xxx.]

[5] The commentators differ greatly in their interpretations of the last

non-recital of those who desire completeness of virtue; also, always, if there be a stinking smell.

108. In a village through which a corpse has passed, and in the presence of a Vṛṣala, there is non-recital; so where there is weeping, and in a crowd of people;

109. In water,[1] and at midnight, during execretion of urine and ordure also. Let no one with food in his mouth or one partaking of a *çrāddha* even meditate with his mind (the texts).

110. A wise twice-born man having accepted an invitation to a *çrāddha* to one recently deceased,[2] may not recite the Veda for three days; nor on (the impurity caused by) the birth of a king's (son), or by the birth of Rāhu.[3]

111. As long as the scent and ointment remain on the body of an invited wise Brahman, so long may he not recite the Veda.[4]

112. One may not recite (the Veda) when lying down, when with the feet raised, or having put a cloth over the loins, nor having eaten meat or rice and food at events involving pollution;[5]

113. Nor if there be a fog, or sound of arrows,[6] nor at the morning and evening twilights, nor at the conjunction (of sun and moon), nor on the fourteenth (lunar) day, nor on the day of the full moon, nor on the eighth (lunar) day.

part of this verse [as the word *çeṣe* may refer to the rest of the day or to the omitted disturbance, rain, among the triad thunder, lightning, and rain. The sense is given most clearly by K. and Rāgh., either as "if these sounds are heard in the morning twilight, there is no study as long as the sun is up, and when heard in the other time (the evening twilight), there is no reading so long as the stars are up," or "if the two disturbances occur, the intermission lasts as long as the sun or stars, but if it also rains, as long as a day and night." The latter explanation is given by Medh., who refers to v. 103, on which this forced explanation rests.]

[1] [Or at sunrise (*udaye*), according to a *var. lec.* noted by Medh.]

[2] ["To one recently deceased," *ekoddiṣṭa*. I have changed for this the translation of Dr. B., "to one ancestor."]

[3] "By Rāhu," *i.e.*, by an eclipse.

[4] [Cf. iii. 188; "invited," *i.e.*, as in vs. 110.]

[5] "Events involving pollution," *i.e.*, births or deaths in the family. [Literally, "birth-food," which Medh. says includes food eaten at a time when impurity is caused by a death; cf. vs. 110. "When with the feet raised" or "with the feet on a seat."]

[6] [May be a musical instrument (Medh., K.) The eighth, fourteenth, and fifteenth of the half month are the *parva* days; cf. Baudh. i. 21, 22.]

114. The day of conjunction destroys the Guru, the fourteenth destroys the pupil; the eighth and full moon day (destroy) the Veda. Therefore one should avoid those (days).

115. A twice-born man should not recite during a dust shower, (or) redness of the quarters (of the horizon); so when a jackal howls, or dogs, asses, and camels bray, and in a company.

116. One may not recite (the Veda) near a burning-ground, near a village, or even in a cow-pen, when one has put on a cloth worn in copulation, and when one has received a present at a *çrāddha*.

117. Whether (it be) a living thing or not living, whatever be the present at a *çrāddha*, having accepted it, there is non-recital; for a twice-born man is said to have his hand as his mouth.[1]

118. When a village is invaded by robbers, and in a tumult caused by fire, and during all portents, one should know that recital is to be adjourned.

119. At the (time of) *upākarma* and *utsarga*[2] the suspension is directed for three nights, but on eighth (lunar days) for a day and night, and on nights at the end of the seasons (also).[3]

120. One should not recite (when) mounted on a horse, and (on) a tree (or on) an elephant; nor on a ship, nor on an ass, nor on a camel, nor standing on a salt waste, nor riding in a vehicle;

121. Nor in a dispute, nor in a fight, nor with an army, nor in battle, nor having just eaten, nor during indigestion, nor having vomited, nor in (a state of) pollution;[4]

122. Nor without having warned a guest, nor when a wind blows strongly, nor when blood flows from a limb, nor when wounded by a weapon.

[1] [Quoted Vas. xiii. 16.]

[2] [That is, at the beginning and at the completion of the annual Vedic study.]

[3] [There are six (Medh.), as usually reckoned: Çiçira (the cool season), Vasanta (spring), Grīṣma (summer), Varṣa (rain), Çarad (autumn), Hemanta (winter). Çiçira begins in the middle of January, and each season lasts two lunar months. Cf. Sūryasiddhānta, xiv. 10.]

[4] [Also indigestion (Medh.)] The commentators [K., Rāgh.] under-

123. In the sound of the Sāman one may not recite the Ṛg or Yajus by any means, or when also one has gone over the end of the Veda and has read an Āraṇyaka.

124. The Ṛgveda is sacred to the gods, but the Yajurveda belongs to men; the Sāmaveda is said to belong to the manes, therefore its sound is impure.[1]

125. The wise, knowing this, having first every day, in due order, repeated the extract from the three (Vedas),[2] recite the Veda.

126. Should a cow, a frog, a cat, a dog, a snake, a mongoose, a rat, come between (the teacher and his pupil), one must know that there is non-recital for a day and night.[3]

127. A Brahman should ever strenuously avoid two (occasions for) non-recitals: viz., (when) the place for recital (is) impure and he himself (is) defiled.

128. On the (night of) new moon and the eighth (lunar day), and also on the (night of) full moon and the fourteenth (lunar day), let a Brahman who has finished his student's course be always (as) a student,[4] even in season.

129. One should not go to bathe having eaten, or (when) suffering, nor at midnight,[5] nor ever with (several) cloths (on), nor in an unknown pool.

130. One should not voluntarily step over the shadow of gods,[6] a Guru, a king, a student returned home, or

stand *sūtaka* to mean here "heart-burn" or "sour eructation." [There are various readings.]

[1] What this impurity of the sound of the Sāmaveda may mean, no one can now say. [It seems to result simply from the fact that connection with the dead, as by sacrifice, etc., makes purification necessary; thus the Veda which has the dead as its divinity has a sound impure in relation to the others.]

[2] [That is, they do not repeat the Veda unless they preface it by the word *om*, the words *bhūs, bhuras, svar*, and the *gāyatri* (Medh., K.)]

[3] [Cf. Gaut. i. 59, where a different rule is given (though harmonised by the commentators), and Viṣṇu xxx. 22.]

[4] "Be always (as) a student," *i.e.*, "must remain chaste" [according to Medh., K., and Rāgh., who say he must not have intercourse with his wife. Cf. Vas. xii. 21. Medh. notes that *anye* (other commentators) gave different renderings, as "he must avoid flesh," etc.]

[5] [K. defines as a period embracing two *prahara* (six hours) in the middle of the night. According to Medh., some appear to have interpreted *mahāniçi* by "at the time when the night is long"—winter.]

[6] [Idols of stone (K.)]

likewise of a spiritual teacher, of a red-(haired) man,[1] and of one initiated (for a sacrifice).

131. At noon and at midnight, and[2] having eaten flesh at a *çrāddha*, and at both twilights, one should not stay where four paths meet.

132. One should not voluntarily stand near (used) unguents and bath-water, ordure and urine, or blood also, (or) phlegm, (or) what has been spit out (or) vomited.

133. One should not honour an enemy, nor an enemy's companion, nor a vicious person, nor a thief,[3] nor the wife[4] of another (man);

134. For there is nothing in the world so prejudicial to long life as a man's honouring[5] here another's wife.

135. One desirous of prosperity should certainly never despise a Kṣatriya, also a snake or a learned Brahman, however mean (they be);[6]

136. For that trio (if) despised can consume a man; therefore a wise man should never despise that trio.[7]

137. Nor should one despise himself for former failures, (but) should desire good fortune till death, nor think her hard to attain.[8]

138. One should speak truth, and speak (what is) pleasant; one should not speak unpleasant truth: one should not speak pleasant falsehood. This is fixed law.

139. One should say, "Well, well!"[9] or may say merely "Well!" One should never have fruitless enmity and disputation with any one.

[1] [One "of red-brown colour" (*babhru*) might refer to skin.]

[2] [No peculiar force is claimed by Medh. and the following commentators for this "and;" but (as Medh. tells us) the older ones (*kecid*) get out of it an artificial extension of meaning.]

[3] [Or a wicked thief (Medh. *taskaraç cauraḥ asmād eva ca bhedo'pālanāt, adhārmiko na sarvaḥ*).]

[4] [*I.e.*, One should not pay her attention, or even *dishonour* her, as in vs. 134.]

[5] [Having carnal intercourse with her (Medh., K.)]

[6] [*I.e.*, even if they are not able to do one any service at the time (Medh., K.) Cf. Gaut. viii. 1.]

[7] [The snake and Kṣatriya by their evident power, and the Brahman by incantations and prayers (Medh., K.)]

[8] [Cf. ix. 300.]

[9] [The commentators explain the first "well" (*bhadra*) to be used in the sense of *abhadra*, "unlucky," and render the rule: he shall call an unlucky thing lucky, or use the word *bhadra*. This implies a *naja̤da* (Medh.) not in the text. K.

140. One should never travel very early or very late, nor very much at midday, nor with an unknown (man), nor alone, nor with Çūdras.[1]

141. One should not find fault with (those) deprived of a limb (or) who have one in excess, those who have no learning or who are advanced in age; also those deprived of beauty and wealth, and those deprived of caste.[2]

142. A Brahman with food in his mouth should not touch with his hand a cow, a Brahman, (or) fire; nor may he in good health, (if) impure, look at the hosts of the heavenly bodies in the sky.

143. But having (when) impure touched them, he should ever sprinkle with water, by the palm of his hand, his organs,[3] and also all (his) limbs (and his) navel.

144. When not diseased, one should not causelessly touch one's hollow parts,[4] and one should avoid also all concealed hair.

145. One should be devoted to fortunate usages,[5] devout, (and) with subdued senses, and should ever recite (the *gāyatrī*) and also sacrifice to fire, unwearied.

146. For those devoted to fortunate usages and ever devout, who repeat (the *gāyatrī*) and also sacrifice, there is no misfortune known.

147. One also should ever practise the Veda, unwearied, at the proper time, for (the wise) have declared that to be one's chief duty; (any) other is said to be subordinate.[6]

148. By practice of the Vedas constantly, by purity, and also by austerity, by not doing injury to (any) beings, one remembers one's former birth.

149. Remembering (one's) former birth, one again prac-

refers to Āpast. i. 31, 13, *nābhadram abhadraṁ brūyāt* (sic).]

[1] [Vṛsalas.]

[2] [Or "of a low family."]

[3] "Organs" [*prāṇa*], *i.e.*, eyes, etc. [so Medh. and K.; and cf. Nil. to Mbhā. xiii. 104, 5. *Prāṇa* = the nose, etc.]

[4] "Hollow parts," or, perhaps, "apertures." These are reckoned to be nine, viz., the two eyes, two ears, two nostrils, mouth, penis, and anus.

[5] [Such as carrying the yellow pigment of the cow (*gorocanā*), sesame, and lucky fruits, etc. (Medh.)]

[6] [Cf. ii. 237.]

tises the Veda, and by practice of the Veda continually one attains endless happiness.

150. At the *parvans* one should always perform the *sāvitra* (offerings) and expiatory rites; one should ever reverence the manes also on the eighth and ninth (lunar days).[1]

151. Far from the place of the sacred fire one must put urine, far (from it) water in which the feet have been washed;[2] far also remains of food and seminal discharge.

152. In the forenoon one should discharge excrement,[3] comb, bathe, rub (one's) teeth, use ointment (for the eyes), and worship the gods;

153. But at the *parvans* one should go to the images of gods, and virtuous Brahmans, and the king for protection; also (to) Gurus.[4]

154. One should salute old men (if they come), and one should give them one's own seat. One should sit near (them) with the hands joined,[5] and go after them (as) they walk.

155. One should for one's own acts unwearied follow the good custom, rightly coherent, declared by the Çruti and Smṛti, the root of virtue.

156. By (right) custom one attains (long) life; by (right) custom, desired offspring; by (right) custom (one gets) imperishable wealth; (right) custom destroys bad luck.

157. But a man with bad customs is blamed in the world, and (is) ever subject to misfortune, (is) diseased and lives but a short time.

158. But he lives a hundred years who, though he has no lucky marks, follows good custom, and is full of faith, and not envious.[6]

[1] *Parvans*, *i.e.*, days of new and full moon (K.); *sāvitra*, *i.e.*, offerings accompanied by the *gāyatrī*. ["Expiatory" or "preventive of evil" (Çānti.)]

[2] [K. Other explanations are offered by Medh.]

[3] [*Maitra* some construe as worship of the sun-god, Mitra (Medh.)]

[4] [Vss. 153–155 are omitted in Dr. B.'s MS. of Medh.; as also vs. 158. In vs. 155, 'good custom,' *i.e.*, of the good.]

[5] "The hands joined," with the palms upward, as if to receive something.

[6] [The lucky marks on the hands, etc., are meant; so in vs. 156. Cf. Vas. vi. 7, 8, with Bühler's note.]

159. Whatever act depends on another, one should avoid that with effort; but what may depend on (one's) self, one should follow that strenuously.

160. All that depends on another (is) pain; all that depends on (one's) self (is) happiness. One should know this (to be) a definition in brief of pleasure and pain.

161. What act may be a delight to the inner feelings of the doer, that he should do with energy, but should avoid the contrary.

162. One should never injure (one's) teacher, a man who declares (the Veda), a father, mother, Guru, Brahmans, and cows, and also all ascetics.[1]

163. One should avoid materialism,[2] and censure of the Vedas, and reviling of the gods, hatred, fraud, and pride, anger, and cruelty.

164. Even when angry one should not lift a stick against another, nor smite (any one) except a son or pupil; but those two one may beat for correction-sake.[3]

165. A Brahman[4] having merely assaulted[5] a Brahman out of desire to slay him, abides a hundred years in the hell Tāmisra.

166. Having designedly struck him out of anger, even with a straw, for twenty-one births he is born (again) from sinful wombs.[6]

167. A man having, through want of discernment,

[1] [Govindarāja takes this as an universal rule, and asserts that even when the Guru and others attack one with a drawn weapon one should not injure them. This is evidently false, as will be seen by comparing viii. 350: the true meaning is that he should not injure them by unfamiliar practices (K.), or by false reports and evil words (Medh.) G.'s interpretation is, however, older than Medh., since he notes it as the opinion of some (*kecit*).]

[2] [Saying, "There is no other world" (K.); but Medh. takes *nāstikyam* in the sense of denial of the authority of the Vedic rules. The word is used of one who denies anything, in the Mbhā. being applied even to one who denies having anything to give away. Materialism and atheism are too special translations of *nāstikyam*, which would be best rendered by "unbelief."]

[3] [Cf. the restriction to this rule in viii. 299; cf. also below, vs. 175.]

[4] [A Brahman, lit. one of the twice-born, while the recipient is specially designated as a Brāhmaṇa.]

[5] ["Assault" here means raising a staff, etc., to strike, as K. remarks on this passage. Such is the apparent meaning also in vs. 169.]

[6] [Cf. with vss. 165–166 the corresponding verses in xi. 206–207.]

drawn blood from the limbs of a Brahman not fighting in battle obtains great sorrow in the next life.

168. As many (grains of) dust as the blood gathers up from the ground, so many years in the next world the shedder of blood is devoured by others.[1]

169. Therefore a wise man should never at any time even assault a twice-born man, nor strike (him) even with a straw, nor draw blood from his limbs.

170. For a vicious man, and he whose wealth is unjust,[2] and one who ever delights in injury, such a one gets not happiness (even) here.[3]

171. Though perishing through virtue, one should never turn his mind to vice, observing the speedily (obtained) fate[4] of the vicious and wicked.

172. Vice practised in the world does not at once bear fruit like the earth, but, proceeding by degrees, it tears up[5] the roots of the doer;

173. If not of himself, of (his) sons; if not of (his) sons, of his grandsons: wrong done never, in truth, fails to bear fruit to the doer.

174. One prospers for a time by wrong, (and) then sees good things; then one conquers foes, but (at last) is destroyed from the root.[6]

175. With speech, arms, and belly restrained, one should ever delight in truth, virtue, (and) noble[7] customs and purity; one should justly[8] punish pupils.

176. One should forsake wealth and pleasure which may be devoid of right; and even right (acts) which result in pain and[9] are also reproved by the world.

1 [Cf. xi. 208.]

2 [Medh. takes *anṛta* (untrue) literally, and defines this wealth as that obtained by making a false statement when called upon to speak in a legal action, etc.]

3 [In this world.]

4 [Fate (*viparyaya*) means *reverse* of fortune (Medh., K.) Dr. B.'s text I have altered slightly, as it is ungrammatical,—"fate (which is) speedily of."]

5 [Literally, "cuts."]

6 [Literally, "together with (his) root," *i.e.*, root and all.]

7 [*Ārya*, *i.e.*, the customs of the twice-born.]

8 [That is, in a just or proper manner. Medh. and K. refer to the rule in viii. 299; cf. above, vs. 164.]

9 ["And" is here disjunctive—"and likewise those which are," etc. Medh. and K. instance as an act which gives pain the giving away of all

177. One should not be restless with hands and feet, nor restless in the eyes, (crooked) in behaviour, or talkative, or meditative on mischief to others.

178. (In the path) by which one's father walked, by which one's grandparents walked, by that one should go the way of the good;[1] going by that one does no wrong.

179. One should never have a dispute with a sacrificial priest, a domestic priest, and a teacher; with a maternal uncle, with a guest, with dependents,[2] with a child, with an old or sick person, with a physician,[3] with paternal relatives, kinsmen, or maternal connections;[4]

180. With (one's) mother (and) father, with female relatives, with a brother, son, (and) wife, with a daughter, (or) with servants.

181. A householder (who) leaves disputes with these is freed from all sin; by these (disputes being) overcome, he conquers all these worlds.

182. The teacher (is) lord of the Brahma-world;[5] the father (is) ruler in that of Prajāpati; but a guest (is) lord of Indra's world, and sacrificial priest of the Deva-world.

183. Female relatives[6] (are chief) in the world of the Apsarasas; maternal connections (in the world) of the All-gods (Viçvadevas); kinsmen, indeed, in the world of waters; a mother (and) maternal relatives (are powerful) over the earth.

one's wealth when one has a family, and as an act right in itself, but to be avoided, because reproved by the world, the sacrifice of a cow on certain occasions.]

[1] [Medh. emphasises the way *of the good*—"if any one should say in regard to the rule in the first part of this verse, How can then anything be wrong which has been practised by our ancestors? the answer is that it is the path of the good (ancestors) we are to follow."]

[2] [So K.; according to Medh., refugees who have sought shelter with him. Rāgh. gives both explanations.]

[3] "A physician." The original has "physicians," an honorific plural to save the metre. [The word may mean learned men of any sort, which is preferred by Medh.; literally "experts."]

[4] [K., *jñātayaḥ pitṛpakṣāḥ . . . bāndhavā mātṛpakṣāḥ;* so Medh., and both explain "kinsmen" as relations by marriage.]

[5] [The application of these statements is, that if the teacher and so forth are not quarrelled with, the world in Brahma and the other worlds are secured. Cf. ii. 244 for Brahma.]

[6] [*Yāmayaḥ* or *jñātayaḥ*, paternal relations (*pāṭha*, Rāgh., perhaps thinking of the Mbhā. ending of this line, *vaiçvadeve tu jñātayaḥ*).]

184. Children, old people, the poor and sick are to be known (to be) lords of the sky; an elder brother is equal to a father; a wife (and) son (are) one's own body.

185. And (one's) servants (are) one's own shadow; a daughter is the chief miserable object.[1] Therefore, offended by these, one should always bear (it) without heat.

186. Though allowed to receive gifts, one should avoid eagerness[2] for them, for by receipt of gifts a man's Vedic glory quickly abates.

187. A wise man should never accept a gift, even if fainting from hunger, (if) he does not know the lawful manner as regards acceptance of things.

188. An unlearned man (who) accepts gold, land, a horse, a cow, food, clothes, sesamum seeds, (or) ghee becomes ashes like a tree (in the fire).

189. Gold and food consume his life;[3] land and a cow, also (his) body; a horse, (his) eyes; clothes, (his) skin; ghee, (his) beauty; sesamum seeds, (his) offspring.

190. But a twice-born man, not austere, not a reciter (of the Veda), who delights in taking a gift, sinks with it as with a stone boat in the water.

191. Therefore let an unlearned man fear accepting presents from any one (not suitable); for an unlearned man even by a small (gift) perishes like a cow in a morass.

192. Now one knowing (this) rule should not give even water to a cat-like twice-born (Brahman), nor to a Brahman like a crane, nor to one who knows not the Veda.[4]

193. For wealth, even if duly gained, when bestowed on those three, in the other world is no good to the giver or to the receiver.

194. As one crossing by a stone boat sinks in the water, so the ignorant giver (and) receiver sink down.

[1] [Cf. Ait. Br., vii. 13, or "objects of pity."]

[2] [Cf. *prasaṅga*, iv. 15.]

[3] [So K. Eight things, gold, etc., consume six, life, etc. (Rāgh.) Dr. B.'s MS. of Medh. has a lacuna here; but, on the strength of the above commentators, as well as on other grounds, I have not hesitated to change Dr. B.'s translation, "gold consumes (his) food."]

[4] [Cf. vs. 30, note.]

195. One who (puts forth) the flag of virtue, ever covetous, a hypocrite, a deceiver of the world, is to be known to be a cat-like (man); he is mischievous, a calumniator of all.[1]

196. A twice-born man with downcast eyes, malignant, intent on gaining his own ends, fraudulent, and falsely humble, is like a crane.

197. Such Brahmans as act like a crane and those that have the character of cats fall by that sinful conduct into (the hell) Andhatāmisra.

198. Let no one, having done sin, perform a vow under pretence of virtue, and, concealing (his) sin by the vow, deceive women and Çūdras.

199. These Brahmans both after death and here are despised by the utterers of the Vedas, and a vow performed by fraud[2] goes to the evil demons.[3]

200. He who not (being qualified) to wear a distinguishing mark,[4] lives by wearing such a mark, takes (to himself) the sin of those who wear such a mark, and is born (again) in the womb of an animal.

201. Also one should never bathe in another's pools; for, having bathed, one is defiled by part[5] of the sins of the maker of the pool.

202. One who uses a carriage, bed, seat, well, garden, or house not given (to him) takes a fourth of the sin of the owner.

203. One should ever bathe in rivers, natural pools, tanks and lakes, in pits and springs also.

204. A wise man should ever attend to the (great) moral duties, (though) not always (following) minor rules. One

[1] [At this place Medh. says that some read a verse: *yasya dharmadhrajo nityaṁ sura* (sic) *dhraja iro 'cchritaḥ / prachannāni ca pāpāni, baiḍālaṁ nāma tad rratam / iti;* which occurs in the fifth book of the Mbhā. Cf. B. R. *s. baiḍāla.*]

[2] [That is, with intent to deceive.]

[3] [Evil demons, *i.e.*, bears no fruit (Medh.)]

[4] "A distinguishing mark." Medhātithi gives as examples, among others, the fraudulent wearing of a *Brahmacārin's* girdle, or a *vānaprastha's* (tiger) skin and matted hair, or a *parivrājaka's* brown dress and staff, etc. "Animal," deer, etc.

[5] [A fourth part according to K.]

who performs not the moral duties, attending to the mere minor rules, falls.[1]

205. A Brahman may never eat of a sacrifice performed by one not a priest,[2] nor of one performed by a village priest, (or) offered by a woman or a eunuch.

206. When these sacrifice (any) offering, that (is) unlucky to the good, that is displeasing to the gods; therefore one should avoid (it).

207. One should never eat (food) of the insane, violent, (or) sick, and that on which there are lice,[3] and what has been voluntarily touched by the foot;

208. Also what has been beheld by a procurer of abortion,[4] or has been touched by a menstruating woman, or pecked by a bird; also what has been touched by a dog;

209. Also food smelled by a cow, and especially food proclaimed (to be given away); food for a number of persons, and harlots' food, and (food) blamed by the learned;[5]

210. Also food of a thief, a singer, a carpenter and a usurer; of an initiated person, of a miser, and one bound (or) in chains;[6]

211. Of an accursed (person), of a eunuch, of an adulteress, and of a hypocrite, acid (things), and stale food also, as also the leavings of a Çūdra;[7]

[1] [K. and Medh. give different definitions of what these rules are, the former holding to the explanation given by Yāj. iii. 313–314. The text seems simply to refer in general to the great rules of morality and the lesser observances, such as those enjoined in this book; neither *yama* nor *niyama* are defined in Manu.]

[2] [Literally "by one not learned."]

[3] [*Keçakīṭa*, hair-lice; otherwise Medh., who takes a *kīṭa* as a dead creature, *keça* as embracing other impurities.]

[4] [*Bhrūṇaghna*. Medh. *bhrūṇaha* (sic) *brahmaghnaḥ*, etc. So K. extends this term in viii. 317 to the meaning "one who slays a Brahman," the middle step probably being "the procurer of abortion if the fœtus belonged to Brahman parents;" but cf. Vas. xx. 23.]

[5] [Medh. has the *v. l.*, found in most MSS. and supported by K., *viduṣā* (not *viduṣām* as above), "by a learned man."]

[6] [K. says the genitive is for the instrumental and rendered "bound by fetters." The exact meaning of *nigaḍa* is uncertain (cf. B. R., *s. v.*); Medh. defines "restrained by voice alone" (*baddha*), and "confined with a cord;" Rāgh. as one "confined for punishment (on account of a light crime) or tormented by darts, *çaraiḥ* (on account of a great one). Medh. notes a *v. l.* *viçada*, explained as *kaṣṭa* (*viçada ity eke paṭhanti kaṣṭaṁ ca viçadam ācakṣate*.)]

[7] [According to K. this means "food of a Çūdra (left stale) overnight, and the leavings of anybody's food. Govind. defines as a Çūdra's

212. (Nor food) of a physician and hunter, of a cruel man, (and) of an eater of leavings, (nor) the food of a wrathful[1] (man), nor food of a woman in child-bed;[2] nor of one who has rinsed his mouth (and left it), or whose ten days (of purification have not passed after a death);[3]

213. (Nor what is) offered without reverence, unsacrificed flesh, (food) of a woman who has no husband,[4] food of an enemy, town-food, food of an outcast, what has been sneezed on;

214. (Nor) food also of a slanderer and liar, so also of a seller of (the benefits of) sacrifices; nor food of a mountebank or tailor, also the food of an ungrateful person;[5]

215. (Nor) food of a blacksmith, of a Niṣāda, of an actor,[6] of a goldsmith, of a worker in bamboo; so also of a seller of arms.

216. (Nor food) of owners of dogs and of sellers of liquor,[7] and of a washer of cloths, of a dyer, of a mischievous[8] man, and his who (allows) a gallant in (his) house;

217. And (of those) who put up with a paramour (of their wives),[9] and (the food) of men always subject to their wives, and food for the dead without ten days having passed, and what also does not please one.

leavings and food tasted by him even in the pot; to which explanation Medh. alludes. "Accursed," *i.e.*, a great criminal.]

[1] [*Ugra*, or cruel, while *krūra* (above "cruel") is according to Medh. and K. a man of bad (violent) nature from which this differs; Govind.'s explanation (K. "*Mañjaryāṁ ugram rājānam uktavān*"), though astonishingly novel to K., is at least as old as Medh., who compares vs. 218. Rāgh. defines as cruel, or according to x. 9.]

[2] [Sūtakānna (Medh. *v. l.*); K. has the better word, *sūtika*, "food (defiled because) of woman with child."]

[3] [Cf. Yāj. i. 161–168.]

[4] [Or sons (Medh., K.); lit. manless.]

[5] [According to the commentators and the literal sense, *kṛtaghna* is one who returns evil for good; not ungrateful only, but by a base return actively showing it.]

[6] [*Raṅgāvatāraka*, the word also occurs in the Mbhā. xii. 294, 5.]

[7] [So Medh. and K.; but the former gives first "those addicted to liquor."]

[8] [*Nṛçaṁsa* is, according to Medh. and K., a man devoid of compassion, but the former gives first "he who praises (*çaṁsati*, *stauti*) men," that is, he who is known in the world as a *vandin* (a professional encomiast). Cf. B. R. *s. v.*)]

[9] ["The case in vs. 216 is where the paramour is known (to exist). This person is one who winks at the fact and does not put his wife in confinement" (Medh.)]

218. King's food takes away beauty; a Çūdra's food (takes away) spiritual eminence; a goldsmith's food (takes away) long life, and that of a leather-worker (takes away) fame.[1]

219. An artisan's food destroys offspring, and a washerman's (food destroys) strength, and food of a company (or) of a harlot excludes from the (other) worlds.

220. The food of a physician is pus, and the food of an unchaste woman is semen; the food of an usurer is ordure, that of a seller of arms is foul.[2]

221. But the food of those who (are) other than these[3] mentioned in succession as those whose food is not to be eaten, the wise say is skin, bones, and hair.

222. Hence, having unintentionally eaten the food of any one (of these), there is a fast[4] for three days; having intentionally eaten (it) and semen, ordure, urine also, one must perform the simple penance.

223. Let not a learned twice-born man eat the cooked food of a Çūdra who does not perform *çrāddhas;* but he may take raw (food) from him enough for one night if he has no subsistence.[5]

224. The gods having considered the food of a miserly learned (priest) and of a liberal usurer, made both equal.[6]

225. But Prajāpati went and said to them, "Make not the unequal equal." The food of a liberal man is purified by faith, the other is destroyed by want of faith.[7]

226. Unwearied, one should ever perform with faith the *iṣṭa* and *pūrta* ceremonies;[8] for these two done with faith, by means of well-earned wealth, are undecaying.

[1] [Cf. vss. 186 and 189. The leather-worker has not been mentioned in the above list.]

[2] [Or, as substantive, bodily impurities. With vss. 220–221 cf. iii. 180, 181.]

[3] [Read *ebhyo'nye*, which is supported by Medh. and K.'s gloss.]

[4] [*Kṣapaṇa*. So Medh. and K. Cf. vs. 71, note.]

[5] [Raw food alone is what he may take, not cooked food. Rāgh. adds, in explanation of this verse, another, which, coming from a commentator on Manu, is interesting: *Kaṇḍū-yuktaṁ snchayuktaṁ pāyasaṁ dadhisaktavaḥ—etāni çuddhānna-bhujām bhojyāni Manur abravīt; iti* (*kaṇḍūpayuktam* is the reading in Dr. B.'s MS.) Cf. vss. 24, 25.]

[6] [Cf. x. 73.]

[7] [Given in Mbhā. xii. 264, 11 ff. as *gāthā brahmagītāḥ*.]

[8] [Ordinarily defined as *sacrifice*, and (excluding this) all other acts of piety.]

227.[1] One should, having met with fit subjects,[2] ever pursue the virtue of liberality at *iṣṭa* and *pūrta* ceremonies, with glad disposition and according to (one's) power.

228. Whatsoever is given [3] without grudging by a person asked, that goes to a fit subject who saves (the giver) from all (sins).

229. A giver of water gets satisfaction ;[4] a giver of food, undecaying happiness ; a giver of sesamum seeds, desired offspring ; a giver of a lamp,[5] best eyesight.

230. A giver of land gets land ; a giver of gold, long life ; a giver of a house, best abodes ; a giver of silver, excellent beauty ;

231. A giver of clothes, the same world with Candra ; a giver of a house, the same world with the Açvins ; a giver of a bull, full good fortune ; a giver of a cow, the abode of the sun ;

232. A giver of a vehicle or bed, a wife ; a giver of indemnity, lordship ; a giver of grain, everlasting happiness ; a giver (teacher) of the Veda, equality with Brahma.[6]

[1] [Between 226 and 227, Medh., in discussing kinds of property, inserts an explanatory verse to the effect that property gained by cheating, force, pretence, theft, *ura*, or by doubtful means (*pārçvika*, bribery, etc.) is termed dark (dubious).]

[2] [That is, a learned and ascetic Brahman (K.)]

[3] [*Yatkiṁcid api dātavyam . . . hi tat* ; perhaps better, something, even if it is a trifle, should be given, etc.; *since* that, etc. Cf. Yāj. i. 203.]

[4] [Freedom from hunger, thirst, &c. (Medh., K.), and thereby health and wealth (Medh.)]

[5] [In a place where four roads meet, or in an assembly of Brahmans (Medh.) Mbhā. xiii. 57, 22, makes the giver of lamp-light *cakṣuṣmān*.]

[6] [The connection between some of the gifts and their corresponding rewards is occasionally more apparent in the original than in the translation, thus the reason a giver of silver gets beauty is because silver (*rūpya*) and beauty (*rūpa*) are of like sound ; so in the last Veda is *brahma*, while Brahmā is the divinity. Others are more obscure, but might perhaps be cleared up by more knowledge of the peculiar significance of the rewards, as the cow-giver getting the abode of the sun is cleared up by Medh.'s note to the effect that the abode of the sun may mean a special home of the cows in heaven (*smṛtyantare, goviçeṣāçrayaḥ*). Another explanatory verse is inserted between 231 and 232, to the effect that the cow to be given must have golden horns, etc., the verse being the same as Yāj. i. 204, with *v. l. rupyakhura . . . saṁvṛtā* (cf. Viṣṇu, xcii. 8), and parts of *ib.* 205–208 ; Dr. B. marks Brahma, as person ; it may be as in ii. 28).]

233. Thus of all gifts—water, food, cows, land, clothes, sesamum seeds, gold, ghee—that of the Veda is the best.

234. But with what disposition[1] one gives any gift, honoured in return with just the same disposition one gets the same (gift).

235. He who receives with reverence, and he also who gives with reverence, both these go to heaven; but those who are the reverse go to hell.

236. One may not be proud of austerity; having sacrificed, one should not tell an untruth; though injured, one may not abuse Brahmans; having made a gift, one should not boast (of it).

237. A sacrifice perishes by untruth; austerity perishes from pride; life (is shortened) by abuse of Brahmans, and a gift (perishes) by boasting.

238. One should accumulate virtue by degrees, as the white ants their hillock, not vexing any creatures for the sake of a helper in the other world.[2]

239. For in the next world neither father nor mother are (there) as helpers, nor son, wife, (or) kinsman; (his) virtue alone is (there).

240. Each creature is born alone, dies also alone; alone each enjoys (his) good deeds; alone, also, (his) bad deeds.

241. Leaving (his) dead body on the ground like a log or clod, with averted faces (his) kinsmen go away; his virtue follows him.

242. Therefore one should accumulate virtue by degrees

[1] [Whatever be his purpose in giving (whether for his own good or simply to do good to another), he is in his next birth the recipient of a like gift given with the like intent (K.) Gifts are of three kinds: given in fitting time and place, without expectation of return, to a good man, which partake of the quality of absolute goodness; given with hope of return, which partake of the quality of passion; given to bad men in despite, which partake of the quality of darkness (verses quoted by Rāgh.)]

[2] [The late Ahiṁsā doctrine, that spiritual merit is not to be quickly gained by sacrifices involving slaughter, but slowly by austerity, etc. The clause, "for the sake of a helper," gives the general reward for practising this virtue, which consists from the negative side in doing no harm to any creature, and results in this virtue itself becoming one's companion and helper after death.]

for the sake of a helper; for with virtue as a companion one crosses darkness hard to cross.

243. It quickly leads to the other world[1] a man virtuous at the bottom,[2] whose sin has been destroyed by austerity, (in a) resplendent (form), with an ethereal body.

244. One desirous to bring (his) family to eminence should ever form relations with the best, and should avoid the low.

245. A Brahman who resorts to the best and avoids the low reaches eminence; by the contrary (he reaches) the state of a Çūdra.

246. One firm in action,[3] gentle, subdued, who associates not with people of savage customs, not mischievous, such a one conquers heaven by restraint and liberality.

247. Fuel, water, roots, fruits, food, and what is presented one may accept from all, also gifts of honey and security.[4]

248. Prajāpati considered alms brought (and) presented, (if) not previously demanded, to be accepted even from a doer of evil.

249. The manes eat not for ten and five years his (offerings), nor does fire convey (his) oblation, who despises such (alms).

250. One should not reject (as gifts) a bed, houses, *kuça*-grass, scents, water, a flower, jewels, curds, rice-flour, fish, milk, flesh, and greens also.

251. When desirous to assist his Gurus[5] and depen-

[1] [Or *paralokais*: *paraloka* is "the world of Brahmā," as *para* is Brahmā (Rāgh.)]

[2] [Or, "A man whose base (of action) is virtue, not one whose base (of action) is the fruit (derived from virtue)"—(Rāgh.)]

[3] [One who completes what he has to do and does not leave one thing uncompleted to begin something else, a man of perseverance (Medh. "Mischievous," *i.e.*, injurious to life.]

[4] [K. refers to Yāj. i. 215 for limitations to this rule, with vss. 248–249. Cf. Āp. i. 19, 14.]

[5] [Medh. says: *Gurava, upadeçāpadeçair* (*atideçair*, sic) *bahavaḥ: bhṛtyāḥ āçritāḥ; Smṛtyantare tu saṅkhyātāḥ, "Vṛddhau tu mātāpitarau bhāryā sādhvī sutaḥ çiçuḥ."* (Dependents are reckoned as "aged parents, wife, and infant" in another Smṛti. Dr. B. appears to have misunderstood the commentator, for he gives here a note (which I have omitted) to show that, according to this "other Smṛti" mentioned by Medh., the term Guru was used to embrace all

dents, or about to reverence gods and guests, one may receive from all, but may not satisfy oneself by such (gifts).

252. But the Gurus being dead, or he living without them in the house, one should accept always from the good, if one desires one's own support.

253. (A cultivator) who has a half (share of the produce), and a family friend, a herdsman, a slave, a barber, these among Çūdras (are those whose) food may be eaten,[1] also one who may present himself (for work).

254. What sort of person he may be, and what he desires to do, and how he may serve him, so let him present himself.[2]

255. He who untruly declares himself, being otherwise, to good men, he is the most sinful thief in the world—a thief of self.

256. All matters are fixed in speech, have (their) root in speech, issue from speech; he, then, who steals speech is a man who steals all.

257. Having duly paid (his) debts to the great seers, the manes, (and) the gods,[3] having delivered all to (his) son, he may abide (as) an umpire (in the house).

258. Alone, in a secluded place, he should ever meditate on what is beneficial to himself, for meditating (thus) alone he attains supreme bliss.

hose enumerated above. In commenting on the next verse, Medh. says that the word Guru (does not mean, but) indicates the dependents (one word being used here for all those in vs. 251).]

[1] [*Bhojyānnāḥ*, cf. Yāj. i. 166. The old translation, "may eat the food of their superiors," may have prompted Dr. B.'s translation, "are to be fed," which I have changed as above, since it is plainly wrong.]

[2] [This exegetical verse with the following seems a late addition; it is simply a business-like explanation of the *ātmanivedana*, defining the meaning of "present himself" in v. 253. The servant who seeks a situation in a new family must declare, first, what his disposition is, what family he used to belong to, etc.; secondly, what kind of work he is looking for; and, thirdly, how well able he is to be of use (Medh., K.) Medh. mentions another absurd explanation of "others," based on *ātman* being a synonym for son and daughter. Much of his lengthy commentary is occupied in refuting such earlier mystical explanations, which in K.'s time seem to have died out.]

[3] "His debts" to the seers by Vedic studies; to the manes by begetting a son; to the gods by sacrifices.

259. The eternal rule of life of a Brahman householder has been declared; also the rule for a student returned home[1] which increases goodness (and is) prosperous.

260. A Brahman living by this conduct, who knows the Veda (and) treatises,[2] freed from sin, is ever glorified in the Brahma[3]-world.

END OF THE FOURTH LECTURE.

[1] "*Snātaka*," a Brahman who has finished his studies.

[2] ["Treatises of the Veda" may be the meaning.]

[3] [Brahma; cf. ii. 244. Cf. with these rules those of Āp. i. 15, 16, 18, 31, 32 kh.; Viṣṇu lxxi.; and Yāj. i. 200 ff. The other works of the same sort have less in common with our text on this subject. The rules for the "student returned home" apply to those who have completed their studentship and are about to marry (which may not, but generally should, happen at once); but the term is also employed for the householder.]

LECTURE V.

ON FOOD, CEREMONIAL PURIFICATION, AND THE DUTIES OF WOMEN.

1. THE seers having heard these laws duly declared for a student returned home, said this to magnanimous Bhṛgu sprung from fire:

2. Lord! how does death prevail over Brahmans who fulfil their law as declared (and) who know the Veda (and) the treatises ?[1]

3. He, Manu's son, Bhṛgu, whose self is virtuous, said to the great seers: Hear by what fault death desires to slay Brahmans.

4. Death desires to destroy Brahmans because of (their) neglect to study the Vedas and disuse of (established) customs, because of laziness and faults in food.

5. Garlic, onions also, leeks and mushrooms, are not to be eaten by the twice-born, as well as things arising from impurity.

6. Red gums from trees, also exudations from incisions, *çelu*, and cow's biestings, one should avoid with care.

7. (Also), if for no (sacred) purpose, kitchery,[2] frumenty rice-milk and cakes, flesh not offered (to gods), and food for gods and offerings;[3]

8. Milk from a cow which has not passed the ten days (of impurity after calving), camel's milk, (milk of an

[1] [Or the Veda treatises.]

[2] "Kitchery," rice and pulse boiled together, a common Indian dish. [Cf. vi. 14.]

[3] [In Mbhā. xiii. 104, 41, some of these are ordered to be prepared for the gods, but not for oneself, which, according to Medh. and K., is here expressed by *vṛthā* ("if for no purpose," which I have thus supplied, the word being left untranslated by Dr. B.), which excludes cases where the food is prepared for guests or gods (Medh.) It may mean food prepared without due circumspection. Cf. xii. 2.]

animal) with a solid hoof also, ewe's milk, (milk of a cow) in heat,[1] or milk of a cow that has no calf;

9. Also (that) of all forest animals except the buffalo: women's milk also, and all sour (liquids) must be avoided.[2]

10. Of sour (liquids), curdled milk and all produced from it, and all (liquids) pressed from pure flowers, roots, and fruits (may be drunk).

11. One should avoid all carnivorous birds, so also those that abide in towns, and beasts with solid hoofs not permitted (by this law), *ṭiṭṭibhas*[3] also.

12. The sparrow, *plava*, flamingo, the cuckoo, the (tame) town-cock, the *sārasa*, and *rajjuvāla*, the parrot and *sārikā*;[4]

13. (Birds) that peck, and web-footed (birds), the paddy-bird, (birds) that tear with their claws, fish-eating divers; butcher's meat and dried meat also;

14. Also the crane, the small crane, and the raven, *khāñjarīṭaka*, fish-eaters, tame swine, and fish of all kinds.

15. Who eats the flesh of any creature, he is called the eater of it (the animal); a fish-eater (is) the eater of all flesh, therefore one should avoid fish;

16. (But) the fishes *pāṭhīna* and *rohita*, used for *havya* and *kavya* (offerings), *rājīva* and *simhatuṇḍa* and scaly fish also, (may be eaten) everywhere.[5]

17. One may not eat solitary (animals) or unknown beasts and birds, so also all those, though indicated among eatable (animals), which have five toes.

18. The wise have pronounced eatable, among five-toed (animals), the hedgehog (or boar) and porcupine, the iguana, rhinoceros, tortoise, and hare also, and, except camels, (animals) which have one row of teeth.

[1] [Or "a cow that has adopted another's calf" (Medh.) Cf. Viṣṇu, li. 40; Āp. i. 17, 23.]

[2] [Cf. Çat. Br. i. 2, 3, 9, for an early list of animals whose flesh is forbidden.]

[3] *Ṭiṭṭibha.* This seems to be a kind of wagtail.

[4] It is hopeless to identify most of these birds. [Cf. Āp. i. 17; Gaut. xvii.; Vas. xiv.; Viṣṇu, li.]

[5] So K., but Medh., allowing the last everywhere, limits the two first to use at sacrificial ceremonies.

[6] [The rhinoceros is a disputed animal. Cf. Baudh. i. 12, 5.]

19. A twice-born man having intentionally eaten a mushroom, tame swine, garlic, a tame cock, onions, or leeks, falls.

20. Having unintentionally eaten those six, one should perform the *sāntapana* penance or the *yati-cāndrāyaṇa;* for the rest one should fast a day.[1]

21. A Brahman should perform the (simple) penance[2] once a year at least, in order to purify himself from unknown (impurity) from what he has eaten, but for what is known he must (do it) specially.

22. The prescribed beasts and birds are to be slain by Brahmans for the sacrifice, and also for support of dependents; for Agastya did (so) formerly.[3]

23. There were, indeed, offerings of eatable beasts and birds in the ancient sacrifices and in the oblations[4] of Brahmans and Kṣatriyas.

24. Whatsoever edible food smeared with grease (is) not forbidden, that, even if kept over a night, is to be eaten, also remains of offerings.

25. Stale[5] food can also be eaten by the twice-born, even if not smeared with grease, (also) all made from barley or wheat and forms of milk.

26. The food of the twice-born and what is not to be eaten has been completely declared;[6] next I shall tell you the rule what flesh to eat and avoid.

[1] [Cf. xi. 155. For an explanation of the penances cf. ib. 213-219.]

[2] [Cf. xi. 212. The penance called Prājāpatya (Medh., K.)]

[3] [Agastya was an ancient seer and Nimrod, who was a famous character in the epic (cf. Der Heilige A., by Holtzmann). That he did this formerly is here used as an argument for the sacrificial use of slaughter, a point in which the text contradicts itself by enjoining no harm to any creature, and then limiting the slaughter of animals to sacrifice. The old custom of killing animals being revolting to the later Brahmans, the substitution of harmless offerings was attempted, as is illustrated by the pretty tale in the Mbhā. xii. adhy. 337 (cf. Medh.) In xiii. 116, 15-17, Agastya is cited as authority for the Kṣatriya caste on killing animals in hunting. So, too, Vas. xiv. 15. On this point cf. Vas. iv. 5 ff., with Dr. Bühler's notes.]

[4] [Ceremonies (*saveṣu*). Rāgh. interprets "in the legends" (Purāṇas), which is only implied by Medh.]

[5] [Kept several nights (K.)]

[6] [Or perhaps (cf. Medh.), "This (rule) of what is to be eaten and not eaten has been declared (exclusively) for the twice-born;" but the implied exclusion of Çūdras is denied by Rāgh.]

27. One should eat flesh which has been consecrated,[1] and at the desire of Brahmans, and when duly required,[2] and in danger of life.

28. Prajāpati made all this food for life; both movable and immovable, all is food for life.[3]

29. The immovable (things are) food of those that move about; the toothless, of those with teeth;[4] those without hands, of those with; the cowardly, of the bold.[5]

30. An eater who even day by day eats eatable living beings is not polluted, for the eatable living beings were created by the creator as well as the eaters.[6]

31. "The eating of flesh is at the sacrifice"—such is said to be the divine rule; hence the use of it in any other way is called the rule of evil demons.[7]

32. Having reverenced the gods and manes,[8] one who eats flesh he has bought, or has got himself, or which has been merely furnished by another, is not polluted.

33. Let no twice-born (man) who knows the rules, except in distress, eat flesh against the rule; for having eaten flesh irregularly, he in the next world is eaten by those (animals) against his will.

34. The sin of a slayer of animals for grain is not such as is (the sin) in the next world of one who eats flesh in vain.

35. But a man who, duly required, eats not flesh, he in the next world becomes a beast for twenty-one births.[9]

[1] [That is, *only* consecrated flesh (Medh., K.)]

[2] "When (the eater) has been duly authorised."]

[3] [Or "appointed this All, both movable and immovable, as food for living creatures," *i.e.*, whatever exists, animals or plants, may be eaten by living creatures. Medh: *Idam iti sāmānyato nirdiçya viçeṣeṇa nirdiçati sthāvaraṁ jaṅgamam iti.*]

[4] [Or fangs, tearing teeth.]

[5] [Thus herbs are eaten by deer, deer by tigers, fish by man, and elephants by lions (K.)]

[6] [Medh. and K. explain the incongruous rule of these three verses by making it apply to the last clause in vs. 27, "when in danger of life," which *ahany ahany api* alone would refute.]

[7] [Cf. with this and ff., Mbhā. xiii. adhy. 114–116. In ib. 116, 15, this is quoted as Çruti, but in 115, 53, its gist is ascribed to Manu.]

[8] [The reverence paid the gods may consist in the house-offering of part of the food or (*anye . . . āhuḥ*, Medh.) the sacrifice at a *çrāddha*.]

[9] [This verse gives the reward for not performing the rule in vs. 27 (K.), *i.e.*, at a *çrāddha* or other rite, it is a sin not to eat flesh, or, in Medh.'s paraphrase, "not to honour the gods."]

36. A Brahman should never eat beasts unconsecrated by *mantras*, but may, following the eternal rule, eat those that are consecrated by *mantras*.[1]

37. If he long (to eat meat), he should make beasts of ghee, also of dough. He should never desire to vainly kill an animal.[2]

38. As many as (are) the hairs on the beast, so many times in the next world does one who slaughters beasts in vain obtain a violent death from birth to birth.[3]

39. By Svayambhū[4] beasts were indeed voluntarily created for the sake of sacrifices; sacrifice is for the existence of all this (universe), therefore slaughter at a sacrifice (is) no slaughter.

40. Plants, beasts, trees, amphibious animals, so also birds, that have attained death for the purpose of sacrifice, attain exalted births again (in the next world).

41. When the honey-mixture (is given) at a sacrifice and in rites to the manes and gods, on these occasions only, cattle are to be slain, not on any other—so said Manu.[5]

42. A twice-born man who knows the real meaning of the Veda, (if) he slay cattle for those purposes, causes himself and the cattle to reach the best happiness.

43. Whether he live in (his own) house, or with his Guru, or in the jungle, let no careful twice-born (man),

[1] [Another allusion to the rule in vs. 27, "one should eat consecrated flesh" (K.)]

[2] [So K. "To vainly kill" means to slaughter for his own use, without reference to the gods. Medh. makes the verse apply to women and Çūdras who are not acquainted with the Vedic ritual: "If one has desire to kill cattle, he should sacrifice to the gods with kine made of ghee," in his explanation of *sañge*, &c. (*paçuvadhaprasañge*), not for eating, but for sacrificing. Cf. Cat. Br., i. 2, 3, 5.]

[3] [That one may become a *vṛthāmāṁsāçanaḥ* is one of the curses we find uttered upon a sinner in Mbhā. xiii. 93. 121. The simile of the hairs is often found.]

[4] ["*Ity api çrūyate çrutiḥ*" is the end of this verse (instead of *svayam eva svayambhuvā*), as found Mbhā. xiii. 116, 14. Quite a number of Manu's verses are cited as Çruti in the epic.]

[5] [Cf. Çāñkh. Gr. ii. 16, 1; Vas. iv. 6; Viṣṇu li. 64. The rites to the gods, as distinct from sacrifice, means the regular sacrifice called *daivyam* (K.) Bühler (note on Vas. iv. 6), agreeing with Medh.'s explanation, prefers to take it as "a rite where the manes are divinities," to distinguish it from *yajña*. For the honey-mixture, cf. iii. 119.]

even when in distress, do any injury (to animals) not directed by the Veda.[1]

44. The injury directed by the Veda, (and which is) done to (things) movable and immovable, one should indeed know that to be no injury; for virtue arose from the Veda.[2]

45. He who, to please himself, injures harmless creatures, does not, living or dead, anywhere increase (his) pleasure.

46. He who desires not to cause confinement, death, and pain[3] to living beings, (but is) desirous of the good of all, gets endless happiness.

47. He who injures nothing attains, without effort, what he meditates, what he does, and what he takes delight[4] in.

48. Without doing injury to animals, flesh is nowhere to be had, and the slaughter of animals is not conducive to heaven; therefore one should avoid flesh.

49. Having considered the source of flesh, and the slaughter and confinement of animals, one should cease from eating all flesh.

50. He who eats not flesh, forsaking rule like a Piçāca,[5] in the world gets affection, and is not tormented by disease.[6]

51. The consenter, the slaughterer, the butcher, the

[1] [Limited by Medh. to cases where life is not to be preserved. If it comes to saving his life, the Çruti says he should eat flesh. In discussing the point whether this applies to the Vānaprastha, etc., Medh. here sets the opinion of the "teacher" over against that of "some" (*iti kecid upādhyāyas tv āha.*]

[2] [Since the law of right and wrong (Medh.) originated from the Veda, therefore what is there enjoined must be right, even if it is opposed to what is otherwise right; therefore injuring animals is right where it is prescribed in the Veda, though elsewhere injury (slaughter) is wrong. With this and vs. 48 cf. Vas. iv. 7.]

[3] [Or "pains caused by confinement and death" (Medh.)]

[4] [*Ratim*—Medh. and most MSS. of K.]

[5] A kind of demon, who, of course, does not observe the rules either of eating, or, according to Medh., of honouring the gods. Cf. vss. 31 and 52.

[6] [Cf. Mbhā. xiii. 114, 12, where this man is then "declared by Manu to be a friend of all creatures." "Like a Piçāca—so he says; Piçācas are a kind of beast (? *tiryagjātiviçesāḥ*); they eat flesh without regard to the rule, so anybody else eating thus becomes like a Piçāca" (Medh.)]

buyer and seller,[1] and the cook and the server up and the eater are slayers.

52. Than the man who desires to increase his own flesh by the flesh of another, without reverencing the manes and gods, there is no other (more) wicked.[2]

53. He who for a hundred years sacrifices every year with a horse-sacrifice, and he who eats not flesh, the fruit of the virtue of both is equal.

54. One attains not such fruit by pure feeding on fruits and roots, or by eating hermit's rice, as by avoiding flesh.

55. The learned declare that the meaning of *mām̐sa* (flesh) is, "he (*sa*) will eat me (*mām*) in the other world whose flesh I eat here."[3]

56. There is no fault in eating flesh, nor in (drinking) intoxicating liquor, nor in copulation, (for) that (is) the occupation of beings, but cessation (from them produces) great fruit.[4]

57. I shall (now) duly declare purification[5] for the

[1] [Or "he who has bought it and sells it" (Govind.) The "slaughterer" is he who, after the animal has been killed, divides the pieces (Medh.) The passage is of course to be taken freely; those who in any way effect the death or have anything to do with the dead animals are (as sinful as) slayers. Medh. seems to have had a shoal of literal-minded interpreters to deal with, who could from their standpoint easily prove that these agents only were not slayers, which leads him into discussing the use of words by Bhagavān Pāṇini, Manu, and others, beside the application of penance, and other points not hinted at in the text. In Mbhā. (xiii. 114, 36–49) this is "as told of old by Mārkaṇḍeya."]

[2] [In the Mbhā. (*loc. cit.*, vs. 14) this verse is ascribed to Nārada, while the next is the speaker's own (*matam mama* / but *māse* for *varṣe*), as differing from the quotation from "Manu" noticed above, vs. 50.]

[3] [Given in varied form, Mbhā. xiii. 116, 35; cf. above, vs. 15.]

[4] [This rule (*pravṛttau ca nirvṛttau ca vidhānam ṛṣinirmitam*, as it is called in Mbhā. xiii. 115, 85) reaches its height in the Nīti, where most of the sins a king can commit are declared of no account if he does not hold fast to them. Cf. the Kām. Nītisāra, i. 47. "The king should cultivate vices on occasion, avoiding their being the chief thing." Medh., after basing his general exposition on the Mīmām̐sakas dictum, quotes the Āyurvedakṛt as saying, "*Āhāro brahmacaryam̐ ca nidrā ce'ti trayam̐ matam̐ / madakam̐ ca striyaç cai'vam upastambhanam āyuṣaḥ*," adding "But if one can live without these, his abstinence bears great fruit." A quotation from Vyāsa (?) adds that continence in things not forbidden, such as scratching and laughing, etc., is also virtuous.]

[5] [This also implies the circumstances which produce impurity (Medh. and K.)]

dead, and also the purification of substances, for the four castes in order.

58. When a child teeths, and on the after-teething, when his top-knot is formed, and when he is invested (with the thread),[1] all his relatives are impure, and so (is the case), it is declared, on a birth.

59. There are ten days' impurity from a corpse ordered for Sapiṇḍas, or (there is impurity) before the gathering of the bones, (or) three days, or one day.[2]

60. Now Sapiṇḍa-ship ceases with the seventh person (in ascent or descent), but the relationship of a Samānodaka (ends) with the ignorance of birth and name.[3]

61. As this impurity from a corpse is ordered for Sapiṇḍas, so it should also be on a birth for those who desire complete purity.

[1] [I think Dr. B. is wrong in this translation, for "invested with the thread" must be due to K.'s note (*cakārāt kṛtopanayane ca*, so Medh.), in which case *saṁsthite* is not translated at all. According to B. R., *anujāte* means what K. here finds expressed by *ca*. It is possible, however, that Dr. B. chose to translate *saṁsthite* in this way (?), and I therefore leave his translation as I find it, although Medh. and K. render *saṁsthite* by "on his dying" (*Sarvavyāpāranivṛtyā mṛta ucyate saṁ-pūrvasya tiṣṭhater vyāpāra (nivṛti) pradarçanāt*—Medh. *Anujāte* is translated by Medh.) *dantajātād balatare;* Viṣṇu xxii. 27, says *adantajāte bāle prete*, etc.; Yāj. iii. 18, 23, *çāvamāçaucam;* v. 57 of the text says *preta*çuddhi. I therefore translate: All the relatives (are rendered) impure (if a child) dies at teething and (if it dies) after it has teethed (or "before," see below), and (if it dies at the time when) its tonsure is made, and likewise (they are also made impure) at the birth (of a child). The word "relatives" includes both kinds mentioned in vs. 60 (K). Yāj., *loc. cit.*, gives the time for the impurity which Medh. tries to construct out of various Smṛtis. The text has nothing to say on this subject, or on the different castes of the child, and the rules thereon differ according to circumstances. If *anujjāte* were possible, we should have a text, as Rāgh. says, agreeing with Yāj. He renders *anutpannadante* as he does *dantajāte* by *utpanna*° (*pūrvasya paççād bhāvini*). Cf. vss. 7, 8, and Āçv. Gṛh. Sūtra (Lanm. p. 101) *saṁsthite*, "if he dies."]

[2] [Following K. we have the ten days prescribed for a Brahman; four days elapse till the bones are collected (Viṣṇu), and the number of days depends on what sort of a man the relative is (Dakṣa, Parāçara).]

[3] [This verse is in the Mitākṣ. ascribed to Bṛhan Manu, with the *var. lec. nivartetā 'caturdaçāt / janmanāmno smṛter eke tat paraṁ gotram ucyate* (*iti*), in which *iti* closes the whole quotation, and the opinion of Manu is thus that of *eke*, from which the Great Manu differs! The fourteenth degree here closes the list of relations called *samānodaka* (having common water-libation), of which the synonym is *gotraja* (gentilis). Other degrees for maidens, etc., are noted by Medh., depending on quotations from other works, as Vas. iv. 18, etc. Cf. Gaut. xiv.]

62. Impurity from a corpse is for all, but (that) on a birth for the mother and father; (ten days') impurity is for the mother;[1] the father, having sipped water, is pure.

63. But a man having emitted semen becomes pure having bathed; he should observe three days' impurity after sexual connection.

64. (Sapiṇḍas) touching a corpse becomes pure by one day and a night and three three-nights,[2] the Samānodakas after three days.

65. But a pupil performing the *pitṛmedha*[3] of his dead Guru becomes pure by ten nights, like those who lift the corpse.

66. (A woman) on miscarriage becomes pure by (a number of) nights equal to the months (she was pregnant). A virtuous woman in her courses (is purified) by bathing when the courses have ceased.[4]

67. For males who have not had the *çūḍā* rite[5] preformed, purity is said to be (after) a night; but for those who have had it performed, purity is allowed after three nights.

68. A corpse (of a child) under two years (old) the relatives should deposit outside[6] in pure ground, having adorned it, without collecting the bones (afterwards).

[1] [(Helped out by the commentators K. and Rāgh., but) literally: "The birth (impurity) would be the mother's only." Rāgh. says "he makes a distinction," and explains, as K., that the mother's impurity lasts ten days, and the father is pure on sipping water or bathing. There seem to be alternatives offered: "but impurity for birth extends only to the parents, (or) the impurity may be for the mother only." This agrees with Vas. iv. 20–22; Gaut. xiv. 15–16; Baudh. i. 5. 11. 20.]

[2] [That is, in ten days (Medh. and K.)]

[3] [The ceremony for the dead (manes). The pupil is not a relative of the Guru, which means here merely a teacher (K.) But others declare that all the ceremony (*sarvaṁ karmaiva*) is designated (not *carameṣṭi*) (Medh.)]

[4] [K. quoting Medh. and Gov. on this verse says "*navamāsād arvāk.*" The words of Medh. are "*srāvastu garbhasya māsatrayād ūrddhvaṁ prāg daçamān māsāt kecit tu prāg navamād ity āhuḥ;*" a small point, but, like his reference to them (Medhātithi and Govindarājā, *Aayaḥ*), of historical worth.]

[5] [The rite of cutting the hair (*akṛtamuṇḍanam*) (Medh.)]

[6] [Outside the village (Medh., K.), in a grave (Medh.), adorning it with wreaths (K., or) with the ornaments of the dead child (Medh.) Pure earth is where no other person's bones are (Medh., K.)]

69. For him the consecration by fire is not to be done, nor the rite with water;[1] leaving[2] (him) like a log in the jungle,[3] they should also fast three days.

70. The rite with water is not to be done by the relatives for a (child) not three years old, but they may optionally do it for one whose teeth are grown, or if the name-ceremony has been done (for him).

71. One day's impurity[4] is directed if a fellow-student be dead, but on the birth of Samānodakas purity is allowed after three nights.

72. Now relations[5] of unmarried women[6] become pure after three days, but uterine kind[7] become pure by the same rule[8] also.

73. They should eat food without (fictitious) salt,[9] they must bathe for three days, must not eat meat, and must lie separate on the ground.

74. This rule for impurity produced by a corpse is directed (for cases) when near (the survivors); when at a distance, this (following) rule is to be followed by the kinsmen and relatives.[10]

75. Now whoever hears within ten days[11] that (a relative) in a foreign country[12] is dead, is impure for so long as what remains of the ten days.

76. But if the ten days be past, he is impure for a

[1] [That is, the *çrāddha* ordained for the adult dead is here omitted (Medh.)]

[2] [That is, they should leave him without weeping and grieving (K.)]

[3] [They should bury him, as Yāj. says (iii. 1), though Manu does not specify this (K.)]

[4] [*Kṣapaṇa* (rendered "fast" in iv. 222) is here translated "impurity" by Medh. and K.]

[5] [In the would-be husband's family (Medh., K.)]

[6] [Women who have not received the sacrament of marriage but who are betrothed (Medh., K.)]

[7] [Relations by blood on the father's side (Medh., K.)]

[8] ["By the rule just as declared," *i.e.*, in the last verse, viz., in three nights (K.), or by the rule in the last part of vs. 67 (also three nights).]

[9] [K. Medh. says, *yavakṣārādi kṣāraṁ lavanaṁ saindhavādi tan na bhuñjīran, lavaṇaviçeṣaṁ kṣāragrahanaṁ tena saindhavasya pratiṣedhaḥ.*]

[10] [*Sambhandhi* and *bāndhava* are according to K. *sapiṇḍas* and *samānodakas*; according to Medh., the other way about.]

[11] [Literally, "Heard of a dead man for whom the ten (days of impurity regularly enjoined on a death are) not (yet passed)."]

[12] ["In another district," *i.e.*, village or town (Medh.)]

space of three nights; if, however, a year be past, having touched[1] water, he is pure.

77. Having heard, after ten days, the death of a kinsman or the birth of a son, a man having plunged into water with his clothes[2] on becomes pure.

78. A boy[3] in another country, or a Samānodaka, being dead, (the relative) having plunged into water with his clothes on becomes indeed[4] pure.

79. If within the ten days a death or birth again[5] occur, a Brahman is impure till the ten days are over.

80. (The learned) say that a teacher being dead, the pupil's impurity is for three nights; and if his son or his wife (have died), for a day and night; such is the rule.

81. But a learned (Brahman) being dead, one is impure for a space of three nights; a maternal uncle (being dead), for a night with the day before and after;[6] so also for a pupil, a sacrificial priest, and (distant) kinsmen.

82. A king being dead in whose kingdom one is, (impurity lasts) during sun- or star-light; on the death of a

[1] [*I.e.*, bathed (Medh., K.) This rule is for all four castes (K.)]

[2] [Or, "with a cloth about him."]

[3] A boy (*bāla*), *i.e.* [a son (Medh.)] under five years of age. *Samānodaka*, so the commentators [Medh., K.]; it probably means a distant kinsman who makes separate funeral offerings. [The ordinary interpretation of *bāla* in a legal sense is up to the sixteenth year (cf. Medh. on vs. 58: *Prāg aṣṭamāc chiṣuḥ prokto anyais tv āṣoḍaçād bhaved bāla iti*). I do not know where Dr. B. gets five years as the limit; both Medh. and K. specify a child whose teeth are not cut (cf. vs. 58, also Gaut. ii. 1, Bühler's note). "A young son or a distant kinsman (who is not a Sapiṇḍa) having died in another country" is the meaning of the first clause.]

[4] [Rather "becomes pure at once."]

[5] [The word "again" signifies the (case is the same, and the death) one of a relative (Medh., K.)]

[6] [Cf. iv. 97 (note). The translation in the preceding passage I have here substituted for the less good one given here, "for a day, night, and day." The "learned Brahman" is the Çrotriya, the "sacrificial priest" the Ṛtvig. There are two points open to discussion in the above reading: *Upasampanne* may mean "dead" (Medh., B. R.), or (with *dead* supplied) "connected by friendship and intimacy" (Medh., K.), or "being a man of good character" (*çīlena yukto vā*—Medh.) Again, some construe the "uncle" as in apposition to Çrotriya, *i.e.*, "If a maternal uncle . . . (who is) a learned Brahman," etc., because the word "kinsmen" includes "uncle," and therefore it is unnecessary to mention him in the second clause, or supply "other" with "kinsmen" (Medh.) The word "kinsmen," (? *bāndhava*) = Çālaka's mother's sister's son (Medh.), father's sisters (Rāgh.) Cf. Gaut. xiv. 20.]

(Brahman) not learned, for the whole day;[1] so for a Guru who studies the Veda.[2]

83. A Brahman becomes pure in ten days,[3] a king (Kṣatriya) in twelve, a Vaiçya in fifteen, a Çūdra in a month.

84. One should not increase the days of impurity, or interrupt the rites or the (sacred) fires; for even a kinsman within seven degrees[4] when performing that rite is not impure.

85. One becomes pure by bathing if one has touched a Paria,[5] or a woman in her courses, an outcast, also a woman lying-in, a corpse, or one who has touched it.[6]

86. Having rinsed the mouth, one should mutter always intent (the sacred texts); on sight of (anything) impure one should repeat the *Saura mantras*,[7] as well as one can, and the *pāvamānīs*.[8]

87. A Brahman who has touched a greasy human bone, having bathed becomes pure; but if a dry (bone), by touching a cow, or looking at the sun after only rinsing (his) mouth.

88. One engaged in any vow[9] should not offer water (at funerals) till he has finished his vow; but when it is finished, having offered water, he becomes pure in a space of only three nights.[10]

89. The ceremony with water is not applicable in the case of those born in vain of a mixture of castes, and

[1] [K. says the impurity is here as in vs. 81 for one who dwells in his house.]

[2] [Like K., Medh. restricts this to one learned in a part only, but offers other explanations as a secondary teacher(?); some say the negative in *açrotirya* is carried over here).]

[3] [On the birth or death of a relative (K.)]

[4] [*Sanābhya.*]

[5] [*Divākīrti*, a Cāṇḍāla (Medh., K.)]

[6] [Some say *it*, the corpse; others, *them*, the foregoing objects (Medh., K.)]

[7] [Various hymns to the sun.]

[8] [Purificatory verses in the ninth book of the Rigveda. A more natural construction would be, "After rinsing the mouth on sight of anything impure, one should, always intent, mutter the hymns to the sun and the purificatory verses."]

[9] [Or one who receives instructions, *i.e.*, a Brahmanical student (Medh., K.)]

[10] [This rule does not apply in case of the death of either parent or a teacher (K. from Vas.)]

those who abide with religious mendicants, and also for suicides;[1]

90. And for (women who) resort to a heretic[2] (teacher), and (those that) follow their own pleasure,[3] and (women who) cause abortion, or injure (their) husbands also, and women who drink intoxicating liquor.

91. But one under a vow having carried out (his) own dead teacher,[4] sub-instructor, father, mother, Guru, is not free from his vow.[5]

92. One should carry out by the southern town-gate a dead Çūdra, but the twice-born by the western, northern, and eastern (gates) respectively.[6]

93. There is not (ceremonial) impurity of kings, those under a vow, and those engaged in a *sattra*,[7] for they are seated on Indra's seat; they are ever one with Brahma.

94. Purity is declared at once of a king on the glorious throne. The throne is for protection of the people; (it is) the cause of (their) food.[8]

[1] [Some say this rule is for Sapiṇḍas, but not for their sons; but in the case of suicides it affects even the sons; the ceremony with water is the offering of the rice-ball and water to the manes (Medh.) According to Medh. and K. there should be a comma after the word "vain," "born in vain, (or born) of a mixture of castes," the former designating those who neglect their religious duties. "Those who abide with religious mendicants" are those who live in a state of religious vagabondism, wearing unauthorised apparel, etc. (Medh., K.) No limitations in the case of suicides is suggested by the text.]

[2] [As in vs. 89, those who wear unauthorised red garments, etc. This may be "heretical teaching" (Medh.) as well as "heretic teacher."]

[3] [Who, heretically inclined, wanton about at pleasure (Medh.)]

[4] "Teacher" (*ācārya*), who teaches the whole Veda, etc. "Sub-instructor" (*upādhyāya*), who teaches a part only. "Guru," who performs the sacramental rites. See ii. 141. [The one under a vow is the student. The word *own* goes with each member (K.) Others say it is used substantively, "his own relative," which is wrong, as some relatives are mentioned (Medh.)]

[5] [*Na luptavrato bhavati* (K.) *Vrataviyogo nāsti* (Medh.) His vow is not broken.]

[6] [A Vaiçya by the western, Kṣatriya by the northern, Brahman by the eastern gate.]

[7] [Impurity on the death of a kinsman and other (causes of impurity) is meant (K.) Those under a vow are both students and those performing a vow of penance (Medh., K.) Those performing a "session," *sattra* (a great sacrifice) are, according to some, those who are ever bestowing gifts (Medh.) This vs. is quoted from Yama by Vas. xix. 48; so the inscriptions, often.]

[8] [It seems a pity that Dr. B. should have adopted the unauthorised *anna* (*kāraṇam*) reading. The true reading is *atra* (so Medh.), and the sense is, "The throne is for the

95. (There is) also (purity) of those slain in battle,[1] by lightning, and by a prince (in course of justice), and (of those slain) for a cow or Brahman,[2] and (of him of whom) the prince desires (it).[3]

96. A sovereign has a body (composed of) Soma (the Moon), Fire, the Sun, the Wind, Indra, the two Lords of Wealth and Water, and Yama[4]—the eight protectors of the world.

97. A king is presided over by (these) lords of the world; impurity is not declared of him, for purity and impurity of mortals arise from and disappear by the lords of the world.[5]

98. The sacrifice is at once perfect, as also the purity of (a warrior) slain in Kṣatriya duty, his weapons being raised in war.[6] Such is the rule.

99. A Brahman who has performed (funeral) rites[7] becomes pure having touched water; a Kṣatriya (having touched) his vehicle and weapons; a Vaiçya (having touched his) goad (or) halter-ropes; a Çūdra (having touched his) stick.

protection of the people, and *then* (while engaged in protecting his people) it is the cause (of the king not becoming impure)."]

1 [*Dimbāhavahatāḥ* is, according to K., those killed in a tumult when the king is not present. According to Medh. it means those killed in a *ḍimba* (crowd of many persons, or weaponless strife), and in battle, *i.e.*, "slain in a quarrel or in war."]

2 [Cf. xi. 80.]

3 [Any one is rendered at once

4 [Dr. B. inserts *and* after Yama, pure if the king wants him to be so.] which must be an accidental error. The lord of wealth is Kubera; of water, Varuṇa.]

5 [So K., but some MSS. have with Medh. *prabhavāpyayau*, of which he makes two clauses: *yato martyānām...ābhyām* (purity and impurity) *adhikāraḥ, tāyoç ca prabhavāpyayau pravṛttinivṛtti lokeçebhyaḥ sakāçān martyānām, na tu lokeçānām.* Neither purity nor impurity affect the gods; man alone is affected thereby; and since the king is identified with the gods, he has it in him to produce purity and destroy impurity instantaneously.]

6 [Dr. B. seems to take this as explanatory of the Kṣatriya duty. The commentators say this duty is to die facing the foe, and the upraised weapons seem to belong to the enemy, "slain by upraised weapons," *i.e.*, sword, etc., not stones (K.) The *çastra* (weapon) is one with which one is cut and slain (Medh.) "The sacrifice is perfect," *i.e.*, he obtains the same holiness as one would get from a sacrifice (Medh.)]

7 [That is, on the expiration of the time enjoined for impurity after having performed the *çrāddha*, etc. (K.), or the bath alone (Medh.)]

100. O Brahmans, this (way of) purity has been told you for Sapiṇḍas; learn now purity as regards a corpse for all not Sapiṇḍas.

101. A Brahman having carried out, like a kinsman, a dead Brahman[1] not a Sapiṇḍa, or kinsmen by his mother,[2] becomes pure by three nights.

102. But if he eats their food, he becomes, indeed, pure in just ten days; but if he does not eat the food, in a single day only, provided he lives not in the house.

103. Having voluntarily followed a corpse,[3] whether a (paternal) kinsman or not, having bathed with (his) clothes (on), having touched fire and eaten (some) ghee, one becomes pure.

104. One should not, when his own relatives are by, cause a dead Brahman to be carried out by a Çūdra; for the offering[4] defiled by a Çūdra's contact is not conducive to heaven.

105. Knowledge, austerity, fire, food,[5] earth, mind, water, plastering with cow-dung,[6] wind, deeds,[7] the sun, and time are the cause of purity of living beings.

106. Of all purities, indeed, purity of wealth is said to be the highest; he who is pure as regards wealth is indeed pure; he is not pure (who is) pure by earth and water.[8]

107. The learned become pure by tranquillity;[9] those doing what is not to be done, by gifts; those with concealed sin, by muttering (sacred texts); the most learned in the Vedas, by austerity.

108. By earth and water what is to be purified is made

[1] [*Dvija.*]

[2] [Maternal uncle, etc. (Medh.), more strictly K., "own brother or sister."]

[3] [This causes the impurity, the other acts purify again.]

[4] [The offering implies the burning of the body (when carried out) (Medh.); the corpse should be carried out by a Brahman; if there is none, by a Kṣatriya; if there is none, by a Vaiçya; and if there is no Vaiçya, by a Çūdra. The word *sveṣu*, rendered "relations" above, is said by Medh. and K. to mean also those of his own caste.]

[5] [Sacrificial food is a cause of purity (Medh., K.)]

[6] [From its sacred character cow-dung is purificatory.]

[7] [Sacrifice is meant (K.), or the acts appointed by the law.]

[8] [While impure in respect to wealth (K.)]

[9] [Patience, long-suffering, even when injured by another (K.)]

pure; a river becomes pure by (its) velocity; a woman defiled by her mind becomes pure by (her) courses; a Brahman, by renunciation (of the world).

109. The limbs become pure by water; the mind becomes pure by truth; the self of beings[1] by knowledge[2] and austerity; the intellect becomes pure by knowledge.

110. This rule as regards bodily purity has been told you, hear (now) the rule for purity of various articles.

111. Purity of metal articles, gems, and every stone article,[3] has been said by the learned (to be) by ashes, water, and earth also.

112. A golden vessel without soil becomes pure by water alone; so also everything produced by water,[4] or of stone, and unworked silver.

113. Gold and silver arose from a union of water and fire; therefore their purification is most efficacious just by their own source.

114. Purification of articles of copper, iron, bell-metal, brass, lead, and tin is to be made properly by alkali, acids, and water.

115. The purification of all liquids also is said to be straining;[5] of folded (cloths),[6] sprinkling; and of wooden (articles), planing.

116. But purification of sacrificial vessels, *camasas*, and *grahas*[7] is by wiping with the hand in the sacrificial ceremony or washing.

117. Of *carus, srucs, sruvas*, purification is by hot water;

[1] [*Bhūtātmā* is here pretty nearly our *soul*, the "true self" according to Medh.]

[2] [This knowledge, *vidyā*, is the knowledge of the meaning of the sacred books (Medh, K.) Cf. Vas. iii. 60.]

[3] [When defiled by remnants of food (Medh., K.)]

[4] [As shells (Medh., K., Rāgh.)]

[5] [*Utpavanam kasyacid aṁçasya*' (of impurities), '*panayanam* (with *kuca*-grass), *anye tu plāvanam āhuḥ* (Medh.) That is, if I understand his process, letting the impure particles in the liquid settle, and then pouring the pure part into another vessel, or straining. The quantity is limited by the commentators.]

[6] [According to Medh., liquids (such as ghee, syrup, *āmikṣā*, etc.), of which the part that is *sam*° or *upa-hata* (contaminated) is to be drawn off while the remnant is pure; or, he says, it may mean separate things of different parts of like or unlike sort clumped together, as seats, couches, etc.; so K. and Rāgh.]

[7] [The *camasa* is a wooden drinking vessel; the *graha* is a kind of dipper; both are employed in the sacrificial ceremonies.]

so of the *sphya*,[1] winnower and cart, and pestle and mortar.

118. But sprinkling with water (is) the purification of much[2] grain and (many) cloths; but purification by washing with water is ordered for small (quantities).

119. The purification of leather (articles)[3] as also of rattan (goods) is as of cloths; and the purification of herbs, roots, and fruit is directed (to be) as (that of) grain.

120. (The purification) of silk and woollen (is) with salt earth; of blankets (of goat's hair) by *ariṣṭaka* seeds; of different silks[4] by *çrīphala* fruits; of flaxen (goods), by *gaurasarṣapa* seeds.

121. The purification of chank or horn (articles) and (those) of bone or ivory is to be done by a discerning man like (that of) flaxen (stuffs or) with cow's urine or water.

122. Grass, wood, and straw are indeed purified by a sprinkling; a house by rubbing and smearing (with cow-dung); (pots of) earth by baking again.

123. But an earthen (pot) cannot be thus purified by baking again if touched by spirituous liquor, urine, ordure, spittle, pus, and blood.

124. Land becomes pure by five[5]—sweeping, smearing with cow-dung, sprinkling,[6] by digging, and by cows staying on it.[7]

125. (Anything) pecked by birds, smelt by a cow, shaken (by the foot), sneezed on, and polluted by head-lice, becomes pure by throwing earth (on it).[8]

[1] [(*Caru*), kettle; (*sruc*), ladle; (*sruva*), spoon; and (*sphya*), wooden sword, are with the others all used at sacrifices, and when thereby made greasy, etc., are to be thus cleansed; otherwise soiled, as ordinary articles (Medh.)]

[2] [More than a *droṇa* of grain, and more than three garments, or according to circumstances (Medh.)]

[3] [Medh. distinguishes between leather made of pure and impure beasts, such as the dog and jackal.]

[4] [*Aṁçupaṭṭa* may mean *aṁçu* and *paṭṭa*, clothes, pieces of (woollen) cloth (?) (K. and) Rāgh. define this as *paṭṭaçūtau*. Medh. gives *ūṣa* as *kāñcana*. The untranslated words are names of trees; the last is mustard. Cf. Baudh. i. 8, 40 ff.]

[5] [In five ways.]

[6] [With water or cow-urine, or even with milk (Medh.)]

[7] [A day and night (K.) The land is defiled by impure substances, by Çūdras dwelling on it, etc. (K.)]

[8] [As is his custom, Medh. adduces several "other Smṛtis" to modify this verse, specifying the kind of birds, etc., meant.]

126. As long as the smell and smear caused by pollution do not leave (an article) soiled by an impurity, so long are earth and water to be applied in all purification of things.

127. The gods made three things pure for Brahmans[1]—what is not seen (to be defiled), what is purified with water, and what is commended by (their) speech.

128. Waters which pass over earth are pure, in which a cow[2] quenches (its) thirst, if (they are) not pervaded by impurity, and possess (good) smell, colour, and taste.

129. The hand of an artificer is always pure (when working at his craft); and so is everything exposed for sale: alms given to a student (are) always pure—thus is the rule.

130. A woman's mouth is always pure;[3] (so) a bird on the fall of a fruit (it has pecked); (so) a calf on the flowing forth (of the milk it sucks); a dog is pure on catching deer.

131. Manu declared the flesh of (a beast) killed by dogs (to be pure); also the flesh of an animal killed by other carnivorous (animals), (or) by Parias[4] (and) other Dasyus.

132. All the hollows above the navel are everywhere pure: those which are below (the navel) are impure; as also all excretions fallen from the body.[5]

133. Mosquitoes, drops, a shadow, a cow, a horse, rays of the sun, dust, earth, wind, and fire, one should declare to be clean on contact.

134. Earth and water are to be used as necessary for purification on discharge of ordure and urine, and also on purification from the twelve bodily impurities, (that is to say):

[1] [For all the castes is meant (Medh.)]

[2] "In which a cow," to indicate the quantity (Medh.) [For if they contain no impurity and have a good smell, etc., they are pure any way, even though of small amount (Medh.)]

[3] [The mouth of a wife is pure for the husband to kiss, is what is meant (Medh.)]

[4] [*Parias, i.e., Cāṇḍālas* and so forth, may explain *Dasyus*, though Medh. takes this as Niṣādas, Vyādhas, etc. Cf. Viṣṇu, xxiii. 50, where Manu is not given the credit of the rule.]

[5] [Cf. i. 92. "Hollows" denote the *indriyāṇi* places according to their respective positions (ear, nostril, etc. (Rāgh.)]

135. Oiliness, semen, blood, scurf, urine, ordure, ear-wax, nails,[1] mucus, tears, rheum of the eyes, sweat—these are the twelve impurities of men.

136. One (piece of) earth is to be applied to the penis, three to the anus, likewise ten for one hand,[2] seven for both, by one desiring purity.

137. That is the purification of householders; it is twofold (that) for students, threefold for hermits,[3] but fourfold for ascetics.

138. One should rinse (the mouth) and wash the cavities after having passed urine or ordure; (so) when about to recite the Veda, and always when (going to) eat food.[4]

139. Firstly, one should thrice take water (in the mouth and) then twice wipe the mouth, if desirous of bodily purity; but a woman and a Çūdra (should do so) only once.

140. By Çūdras living properly a monthly shaving[5] is to be performed,[6] and (their) rule of purification (is) like Vaiçyas, and their food the leavings of twice-born (men).

141. Drops of spittle from the mouth which fall on a limb do not make (it) impure,[7] nor (hairs of) the beard that have got into the mouth, nor (food) that has stuck between the teeth.[8]

142. The drops which fall on the two feet of one serving water to others to rinse their mouth with are to be known as the same with (water flowing) on earth; one is not impure by them.[9]

[1] [Or excretions of nose and ear (for ear-wax and nails), according to another reading.]

[2] [The left hand (Medh., K.); the only real limit is that in vs. 134, "as necessary" (Medh.) Cf. vs. 126 (K.); and Vas. vi. 18, 19; Viṣṇu, lx. 25, 26.]

[3] [The four orders of a Brahman's life are here given,—student, householder, hermit in the wood (Vanastha); last and highest, ascetic who has renounced the world (Yati).]

[4] [This addition (in regard to eating) is meant for women and Çūdras (Medh.)]

[5] [Of the head.]

[6] [Literally, "of Çūdras a shaving is to be performed." Medh. says the agent is doubtful, as it may be taken in a double sense, since the genitive may stand for the instrumental, or the act is for the Brahmans to perform.]

[7] "Impure," *i.e.*, like the hands soiled by food.

[8] [Cf. Gaut. i. 41, where *na ced aṅge patanti*; ib., 38–40, a restriction to the last clause is given (quoted by Medh. as *eke*). Cf. Āp. i. 16, 13.]

[9] [Literally, rendered unfit for the ceremony.]

143. But one having an article in his hand, if touched anyhow by an impure thing, becomes pure by rinsing his mouth, without, indeed, putting down that article.[1]

144. Having vomited (or) purged, one should bathe and eat ghee; but having eaten (rice) food,[2] one should merely rinse the mouth. Bathing (is the purification) for one who has had sexual intercourse.

145. Having slept and sneezed, having eaten and spit, and having told lies, having drunk water, and being about to recite (the Veda), although pure,[3] one should rinse the mouth.

146. All this system of purification, as well as the purification of things, has been pronounced for all castes; hear now the laws for women.

147. No act is to be done according to (her) own will by a young girl, a young woman, or even by an old woman, though in (their own) houses.[4]

148. In her childhood (a girl) should be under the will of her father; in (her) youth, of (her) husband; her husband being dead, of her sons; a woman should never enjoy her own will.

[1] [There are two views on this subject, some texts enjoining that the article is to be put down. The text here says it needs not to be placed on the ground. "How then," says Medh., "can he sip water (for which the two hands are necessary)?" Let him put it in his lap, or rest it in the hollow of the arm. He then tries to explain away the contradiction in Gaut. by making it depend on the weight of the article. Cf. the notes of Prof. Bühler and Jolly on Gaut. i. 28, and Viṣṇu xxiii. 55. Medh. takes *ucchiṣṭa* not of an impure article, but as "a man who not having performed the purification of rinsing the mouth for acts demanding it, is burdened with this penance."]

[2] [Two explanations are possible; one, recommended by Medh., makes this clause dependent on the preceding, "if, after eating (rice) food, vomiting and purging take place on the same day, he has merely to rinse the mouth;" but Medh. admits that this is explained independently by others.]

[3] ["Fit for the ceremony" (cf. vs. 142). This refers to the last clause only (Medh.) Cf. ii. 70. It may be taken, however, with all in the sense of *ācānta*, as Yaj. i. 196 ("although he has rinsed the mouth, let him do it again"). Each clause seems to be grammatically independent, though K. renders "after sleeping, etc., being desirous of reciting, let him." Cf. for these rules Vas. iii.; Gaut. i. 30 ff.; Viṣṇu, xxii., xxiii.; Yāj. i. 180 ff.]

[4] [Cf. ix. 2, 3. Medh. quotes a "saying" attributed to Nāranda (cf. xiii. 29) by K., to the effect that the king is the (husband) supporter of a woman who has lost all her relatives, *i.e.*, she is under his care, and not independent.]

149. She must never wish separation of her self from her father, husband, or sons, for by separation from them a woman would make both families contemptible.

150. She must always be cheerful and clever in household business, with the furniture well cleaned, and with not a free hand in expenditure.

151. But him to whom her father gives her, or (her) brother with the father's consent, she must obey alive, and dead must not disregard.[1]

152. The *svastyayana*[2] is used in marriages for their (the brides') prosperity, (as is) the sacrifice of Prajāpati; the giving away is the cause of the (husband's) lordship.

153. Out of season and in season a husband who performs the sacrament by *mantras*[3] is ever a giver of happiness to a woman here and in the next world.

154. Though of bad conduct or debauched, or even devoid of (good) qualities, a husband must always be worshipped[4] like a god by a good wife.

155. For women there is no separate sacrifice, nor vow, nor even fast;[5] if a woman obeys her husband, by that she is exalted in heaven.

156. The good wife of a husband, be he living or dead, (if) she desire the world (where her) husband (is), must never do anything disagreeable (to him).[6]

157. But she may at will (when he is dead) emaciate her body by (living on) pure flowers, fruits, (and) roots. She

[1] [She must be devoted to him in his death as in his life, by no means implying the burning of the widow, but plainly forbidding her second marriage.]

[2] [Wishes for good-luck. The Prajāpati sacrifice implies also offerings to other deities (Medh.)]

[3] [*I.e.*, the husband who marries her by the proper ceremony.]

[4] [Rather "served" (*upacaryaḥ*, rendered by Medh. and K. *ārādhanīyaḥ*); "like a god" may, but does not necessarily, imply "worship." The comparison seems rather to be of the constant attendance of a priest on an idol. The rule here given is found more in detail in ix. 78 ff., with some restrictions.]

[5] [Without consent of the husband (Medh. and K.)]

[6] [Cf. with the expression *sādhvī* (the good) the explanation in ix. 29. She does a disagreeable thing when she omits the prescribed ceremonies for the dead (K.) Medh. gives the simpler explanation that what pleased him for her to do when he was alive should still be done after his death.]

may not, however, when her husband is dead, mention even the name of another man.[1]

158. She must be till death subdued, intent, chaste, following that best (law) which is the rule of wives of a single husband.[2]

159. Many thousands of Brahmans chaste from youth[3] have gone to heaven without leaving children to continue the family.

160. (Her) husband being dead, a virtuous[4] wife, firm in chastity, goes, though childless, to heaven like those chaste (men).

161. But the woman who, from desire of offspring, is unfaithful to (her dead) husband, meets with blame here, and is deprived of her husband's place (in the next world).

162. There is no offspring here begotten by another (than the husband),[5] nor even on marrying another; nor is a second husband anywhere permitted to good women.

163. She who, having left (her) own base (husband), attaches herself to an excellent one, is blamable indeed in the world, and is called *parapūrvā*.[6]

164. Now a woman from unfaithfulness to her husband gets blame in the world, is born of a jackal (on being

[1] [Medh. recognises the rule "declared by Aṅgiras," *women should follow their husband in death;* but introduces it by the rule that suicide is forbidden women as well as men.]

[2] [The widow must support herself, if in need of subsistence, by blameless acts (Medh. to vss. 157, 159).]

[3] [*I.e.*, unmarried (Medh., K.) Medh. says the object is to show the reason why the woman should not of herself form a *niyoga* connection (such as enjoined in the ninth lecture) to raise up seed for her husband. It is not necessary, for men have gone to heaven without children.]

[4] [*Sādhvī.*]

[5] [No such offspring is permitted by law. Cf. R. V. vii. 4, 7. This rule refers to cases other than the *niyoga* connection (K.) Medh. makes the rule more general. "The offspring born of other than the husband is not the wife's, and born of other than the wife is not the husband's" (Medh.)]

[6] [("She who has had) another (husband) before." "Is blamable indeed," or "is only to be blamed" (*nidyaiva*): *i.e.*, in taking another husband, even of higher caste, she does not do well. K.'s commentary and other passages seem to require that we read "left a low-caste husband for one of high caste." Rāgh. says only "left one who is poor."]

born again), and is tormented by diseases (produced) by[1] sin.[2]

165. She who, restrained in mind, speech, and body, is not unfaithful to (her) husband, attains the abode of (her) husband, and is called virtuous by the good.

166. By this conduct for women, (she who is) subdued in mind, speech, (and) body gets here prominent fame and the abode of (her) husband in the next world.[3]

167. A twice-born man must burn a wife of such behaviour (and) of the same caste, (if) dying before him, by means of the sacred fire and sacrificial vessels, according to rule.

168. Having used the fires for the last rites to his wife dying before him, he may marry again, and again establish (the sacred fires) also.

169. By this rule he should never fail in the five sacrifices, and, married, should live the second part of his (life) in (his) house.[4]

END OF THE FIFTH LECTURE.

[1] [*Pāparogāḥ* may mean "evil diseases." Cf. iii. 92, 159.]

[2] [" By this rule the raising up of offspring in time of need is forbidden; but by the Niyoga-smṛti the same thing is again allowed; which of the two Smṛtis is the more authoritative? It is not possible to decide; In such a case both are good" (Medh.) "Unfaithfulness" means not remaining chaste to her husband. This view is repeated at ix. 30.]

[3] This verse is omitted by Medhātithi, and is clearly an interpolation. Part of the first line is word for word the same as in the last. [Dr. B.'s MS. of Medh. omits also vs. 165, which is repeated in ix. 29.]

[4] [For these rules cf. Viṣṇu xxv.; Gaut. xviii. 1-3; Vas. v. 1-2.]

LECTURE VI.

ON THE THIRD AND FOURTH ORDERS OR STAGES OF LIFE.

1. LET a twice-born man, who has completed his studentship and has lived, according to rule, in the householder's order, abide in a forest, intent, his organs truly subdued.[1]

2. But when a householder sees wrinkles and grey hair on himself, and (also sees) the child of his child, then let him go to the woods.[2]

3. All food from towns is to be given up, and all utensils as well.[3] He may go to the jungle, having given his wife over to (his) sons, or with her also.

4. Having taken with (him his) sacred fire (*agnihotra*), and the household pot[4] of fire, going forth from the village to the wood, let him dwell (there) with his organs subdued.

5. With hermit's (wild) rice, with various pure (substances), or with herbs, roots, and fruits, he should offer the (five) great sacrifices[5] according to rule.

6. Let him wear a skin or bark; let him bathe in the evening and also in the morning; let him ever wear long hair, beard, and nails.

7. Of what may be eatable (for him), of that let him

[1] All this chapter is nearly obsolete; the first part is totally so (vss. 1–33).

[2] [Some say this means a grandson only, but not a grand*daughter*, while others correctly regard these expressions as merely denoting the proper age of the man, not that he must positively possess a grand*son* (Medh.)]

[3] [Literally, "after he has given up."]

[4] ["The fire-furniture" is more literal, *i.e.*, according to the commentators, the sacred implements, spoons, etc., used in sacrifice.]

[5] "The (five) great sacrifices." See iii. 69–71.

give offerings[1] and alms as best he can; let him honour (people who have) come to his abode with alms of water, roots, (and) fruit.

8. Let him be ever applied to recital (of the Veda), subdued, well-disposed, composed; ever a giver, not a taker; compassionate to all beings.

9. And let him duly offer the *agnihotra* (sacrifice) with the three fires,[2] not neglecting at the proper time the (offering at) new and full moon.

10. Let him perform the *ṛkṣeṣṭi*, the *āgrāyaṇa* also, and the *cāturmāsyas*, the winter and summer solstice (ceremonies), in order.[3]

11. With pure spring and autumn[4] hermit's rice gathered by himself, he should separately offer cakes and messes according to rule.

12. But having offered to the gods that purest offering from the forest, he should use for himself the rest, and salt made by himself.[5]

13. He should eat herbs that grow on land or in water, flowers, roots, and fruits, and what is produced by pure trees, and oils produced by fruits.

14. He should avoid honey and meat and mushrooms

[1] [To the divinities; "what may be eatable," fruits, etc., if not forbidden.]

[2] [*Vitāno vihāras tatrabhavaṁ vaitānikaṁ, tretāgnivisayaṁ* (Medh.) If, as said above, he goes alone into the wood, he is to perform the sacrifice in the same way he would when all alone on a journey (Medh.), or when his wife is impure (K.) Medh. in a long note branches into a discussion of the food, whence he gets it, and other questions, in which so many points seem undecided that we might be led to think this part of the work was already "obsolete" in his time and mere matter of speculation. Cf. iv. 25 for the (*darça*) new and (*paurṇamāsa*) full-moon sacrifices.]

[3] [The *ṛkṣeṣṭi* is a sacrifice to the heavenly bodies (*nakṣatreṣṭi*, K.; Dr. B.'s MS. of Medh. has *darçeṣṭi* without commentary); the *āgrāyaṇa* is the sacrifice at the time of new grain; the *cāturmāsya* (to all the gods) are sacrifices coming every four months (K.) The reading is not certain in (*b*); *turāyaṇam* is the reading of Medh. and Rāgh. (according to Dr. B.'s MSS.), *i.e.*, a modification of the *paurṇamāsa*. K. says some think on account of spare food they are not to be performed at all (*vanāprasthasya stutyarthaṁ na tv asyā 'nuṣṭheyaṁ*). Some of these are explained in the fourth book (iv. 26). Cf. Viṣṇu, xciv. ff.]

[4] [Spring and autumn rice, *i.e.*, rice that springs up or is ripened (*paçyante?*) at this time (Medh.)]

[5] [This prohibits sea-salt (Medh.); it is made of salt earth (K.)]

coming from the ground,[1] the *bhūstṛṇa*,[2] *çigruka*[3] also, and the fruits of the *çleṣmātaka*.[4]

15. In the month Āçvayuja[5] he should throw away the hermit's rice previously collected, also (his) worn garments, and (his) herbs, roots, and fruits.

16. He may not eat produce of agriculture though thrown away by any one; nor, even if in distress, either roots[6] or fruits produced in town.

17. He may eat what is cooked by fire, or eat only what is ripened by time; he may either use a stone-pounder, or else make use of his teeth as a pestle.

18. He may either gather (food) for a day,[7] or even collect for a month, or accumulate for six months or for a year.[8]

19. Having gathered, as he best can, (rice)-food, he may eat it by night or by day; or he may (omit three meals and) eat at the fourth (meal)-time, or even (omit seven and) eat at the eighth.[9]

20. Or he may, in the bright and dark lunar fortnights,

[1] [Mushrooms, cf. v. 5. "Since these grow in the trees or on the ground, the adjective designating the latter excludes the former, but mushrooms are all forbidden by the common practice; therefore the word *bhaumāni* (on the ground) must be taken alone as a noun, and mean some plant, as the *gojihvikā*" (Medh.) "I do not believe that one plant would be left unnamed among so many names, therefore I take it as merely introducing the class (mushrooms on the ground, etc.) . . . Govind. even says that tree-mushrooms may be eaten, which is against the law of Yama" (K.) It does not appear to have occurred to any of the commentators (Rāgh. follows Medh.) that "mushrooms on the earth" may be poetical, and not precise. This being a repetition of the law in v. 5, K. adds that they are mentioned to show the same penalty for eating the other plants.]

[2] [*Andropogon schoenanthus*, Lin.]

[3] [Horse-radish tree.]

[4] [(The sticky) *Cordia latifolia*, Roxb. The *bhūstṛṇa* and *çigruka* are words for plants understood among the Vālhikas (Medh.) K. and Rāgh. say the *bhūstṛṇa* is current in Mālavadeça, the *çigruka* as in Medh.]

[5] [Begins the middle of September.]

[6] [Medh. reads *puṣpāṇi*.]

[7] [So Medh. and K. interpret *sadyaḥ prakṣālaka*, "he who washes at once" the grain, and does not store it up. Cf. with this verse iv. 7.]

[8] [Storing up for a year refers here to some grain that will keep, as the *nīvāra*, or wild-rice (K.), which it is permitted to eat.]

[9] [There are two meal-times a day, morning and evening; he may, therefore, fast one day and the next morning, eating in the evening of the second day, or fast three days and the following morning, eating in the evening of the fourth day (Medh., K.) Fasting half the day any way is enjoined by the first clause (Medh.)]

live according to the moon-course (*cāndrāyaṇa*,[1] penance), or at the two ends of the fortnights he may even eat once[2] boiled rice-gruel.

21. Or he may, firm in the opinion of Vaikhānasa,[3] live always on mere flowers, roots, and fruits, ripened by time (and) withered[4] of themselves.

22. He may roll on the ground or stand a day[5] on tip-toe, or occupy (himself) by sitting and standing, going to waters (to bathe) at morning, noon, and evening.[6]

23. In the summer, also, he should be exposed to five fires;[7] in the rains (he should) have the clouds for shelter; he should have wet clothes in winter, gradually increasing his austerity.

24. Rinsing his mouth[8] at morning, noon, and night, let him offer water to the manes and gods;[9] practising more cruel austerity, he should dry up the body of himself.

25. Having according to rule deposited those (three) fires in himself, without fires, without abode, he should be silent,[10] living on roots (and) fruits.

26. Without efforts for means of pleasure, chaste, sleeping on the ground in hermitages, indifferent, living at the roots of trees;

[1] [That is, a mouthful a day more and then less; cf. the explanation in xi. 217.]

[2] [That is, either morning or evening (Medh., K.)]

[3] "Vaikhānasa" is the reputed author of *sūtras* used by a few followers of the Black Yajur-veda. I possess a fragment. [Medh. says on this word "(There is) a treatise called Vaikhānasa (*vaikhānasaṁ nāma çāstram*) wherein the rules of a hermit in the wood are laid down; by the teaching of *these* (rules let one abide." He does not hint at Vaikhānasa (Vikhanas (?)) being a person, and it is not necessary to suppose a person is meant here, as *vaikhānasa* is synonymous with a *hermit-in-the-wood*. The use of (*teṣāṁ*, male) the plural by Medh. shows he regards this as meaning "firmly abiding by the teaching *of the rules* (laid down in the treatise on hermits)." But cf. Vas. xxi. 23; Baudh. ii. 11, 14, iii. 3, 15 ff.]

[4] [Or fallen (to the ground).]

[5] [The commentators say this is one of the rules referred to in vs. 21. Cf. xi. 225.]

[6] [Avoiding meal-time and resting-time (Medh.)]

[7] "Exposed to five fires," *i.e.* [according to the commentators], with four around him and the sun above. I have seen a North Indian Brahman doing this, but he was a maniac.

[8] [*Upaspṛçan*, according to the commentators, "bathing."]

[9] [*Pitṛs and devas*. Dr. B. sometimes translates these terms and sometimes not. I have uniformly thus rendered them.]

[10] [*Muniḥ* is so interpreted by Medh. and K.]

27. Let him take alms for (his) subsistence only from austere Brahmans, and[1] from other twice-born householders living in the forest.

28. Or having received (food) from a town, he may, living in the forest, eat eight mouthfuls, having received (it) in a leaf basket alone, or in (his) hand, or in a potsherd.

29. A Brahman living in the forest must follow these and other self-devotions.[2] For perfection of his self (he must study) also the different Upanisad (parts) of the Vedas;[3]

30. Studied by seers and Brahmans also, and householders also, for increase of knowledge (and) austerity and purification of the body.

31. Or he should go straight to the unconquered region[4] till his body decay, resolute, feeding on water (and) air.

32. Having forsaken (his) body by one or the other of these[5] practices of the great seers, free from sorrow and fear, a Brahman is magnified in the Brahma-world.[6]

33. But having thus spent the third part of his life[7] in the forests, let him, forsaking (all) affections, wander about for the fourth part of (his) life.

34. He, having gone from stage to stage (of life), having offered sacrifices, with his organs subdued, (if) when weary of alms (and) offerings he wanders, is glorified when dead.

35. Having paid (his) three debts, he should fix (his)

[1] [For "or" (Medh.) If he cannot get alms from the first, let him get them among (locative for ablative, Medh.) the second (K.)]

[2] [*Dīkṣāḥ* = *niyamāḥ*, (rules) (Medh., K.), religious practices.]

[3] [Literally, "the different Çruti (contained) in the Upaniṣads."]

[4] "Unconquered region," *i.e.*, the north-east, or of Yama, the cause of death. [? (Yama's district is the south); the unconquered district is the north-east according to the commentators (cf. Ait. Br. i. 4). This is that journey called by the Yoga-çāstra the "Great journey" (Medh.)]

[5] [K. refers only to "those declared above;" Medh. adds, as a means of ending life resorted to by the seers, "drowning (*bhṛgu-prayata* (?)), burning, starving."]

[6] [This clearly points to a consolidation of the two last orders, as no argument can show that the ordinary Brahman of the third order is not here instructed to end his life in the third stadium and get rewarded for it, unless, which I think likely, vss. 31 and 32 be later additions.]

[7] [No set time is given for the end of the third order; it depends on his progress in austerity (Medh., K.)]

mind on final deliverance;[1] for one who, not having paid (his debts), seeks deliverance goes downward.

36. Having duly studied the Vedas, and begotten sons according to law, and sacrificed according to (his) ability with sacrifice, he should fix (his) mind on deliverance.[2]

37. A twice-born man not having studied the Vedas, and not having begotten a son, and also not having sacrificed with sacrifices, (who) desires deliverance, goes downward.

38. Having done the Prājāpatya[3] sacrifice with a fee of all (his) property, having established the (sacred) fires in himself, a Brahman should go forth from (his) house.[4]

39. If one having given indemnity to all beings goes forth from (his) house, of him, an utterer of the Veda, the abodes become glorious.

40. To the twice-born, from whom not even the least fear is caused to beings, there is no fear from any cause when separated from (his) body.[5]

41. Going forth from his house, silent, furnished with

[1] [The commentators tamely take this to mean that when a man has completed three orders he should enter the fourth. (The wandering order is denoted by the word "final-deliverance" (Medh.) The three debts are generally debts to the gods, paid by sacrifice; debts to the manes, paid by funeral feasts; debts to the seers, paid by purity of life, etc. They are here given differently in the next verse. Cf. Gaut. iii. 1.]

[2] [Medh. and K. quote the Tait. S. 6. 3. 10. 5, with the *var. lec.* *svādhyāyena ṛṣibhyaḥ* (for *Brahmacaryeṇa*) to bring it into conformity with the text. Accordingly, the three debts are sacrifice, offspring, and study, which are owing to gods, manes, and seers.]

[3] [A sacrifice to Prajāpati, accompanied by giving up all his goods to the priests, as prescribed in the Yajur-veda (K.) Medh. hints at quite a different meaning: "But others say that the sacrifice called *prājāpatya* is a human sacrifice, as it is said, 'He shall sacrifice a Brahman to Brahmā.' The Brahman is the sacrificial beast (*paçu*) and Prājāpati is Brahmā;" or (the Brahman is) the first sacrificial beast, but *prathamaḥ paçuḥ* in Dr. B.'s MS. must be for *Brāhmaṇaḥ paçuḥ*.] This human sacrifice (*puruṣamedha*) was anciently offered in India, and seems to be not entirely unknown or unused in the time of the great epic.]

[4] [This means (what is said in the Jābālaçruti) that one may go straight from the second order (householder) to the fourth without passing through the stage of being a dweller in the woods (K.) Cf. Gaut. iii. 2.]

[5] [The Mbhā. reading grants it before (*mohād* for *dehād*), "released from distraction, ignorance," a mere epithet, as in v. 39.]

pure things,[1] regardless of objects of desire presented (to him), let him set out.[2]

42. Let him ever go quite alone, without a helper,[3] for the sake of perfection; seeing the perfection of one alone, who forsakes not, nor is forsaken.

43. Being without fire, without an abode, he may go to a town for the sake of food, being indifferent (to disease), not fickle-minded, silent, (and) composed in resolution.[4]

44. A potsherd,[5] roots of trees,[6] common clothes, loneliness, equanimity also to all, that is the sign of one freed.

45. He should not desire death, nor should he desire life; let him, indeed, expect the time as a servant (his) orders.[7]

46. He should put down his foot purified by seeing (that there is no impurity in the way); he should drink water purified by a (straining) cloth; he should utter speech purified by truth; he should have his mind purified.[8]

[1] [*Pavitra:* according to K., the staff, water-pot, etc.; according to Medh., the addition would be the sacred grass, and the skin of the black antelope; or he takes it more spiritually as mutterings of hymns; or *pavitra* may be for *pāvana*, penances of purification. I have therefore substituted the above for Dr. B.'s "implements," which is the only translation he gives of the word.]

[2] [*Parivrajet*, literally "wander about," the mark of the fourth order.]

[3] [*Asahāyavān* means scarcely more than *eka*, "let him go quite alone, without having a companion," *i.e.*, as the commentators say, having with him neither servants nor sons.]

[4] "Composed in resolution." The commentators say, "With mind fixed on Brahmā!" ["Being without fire," literally "let him be," etc. The fire is either the sacred fire or fire for cooking (Medh.) "Indifferent," *i.e.*, not attempting to ward off disease (Medh. and K.), or not caring to clean his water-pot, etc. (Medh.) "Not fickle," or, according to a *var. lec.* noted by Medh. and K., "not keeping a store (of food, etc.)" (*asañcayika*). "Silent" (*muniḥ*), here rendered by Medh. "restrained in voice and in senses." K. gives the explanation of *bhāva* as Brahmā, which Dr. B. notes, but Medh.'s is different: "composed in thought and mind, not in voice alone" (*bhāvena cittena . . . manasā vikalpān varjayet, bhāvenaiva samāhito na vāṅmātrena*). Rāgh. follows K.'s interpretation.]

[5] [Perhaps only a dish, not necessarily a potsherd. Cf. vss. 53, 54, and cf. Medh., "the begging-dish for food."]

[6] [The roots of the tree make his house (Medh. and K.)]

[7] [*Nirdeça* (or *nideça*, some MSS. and Bomb. Mbhā.); a better reading seems to be that of Medh., *nirveça*, *i.e.*, his reward. "Time" (of death, K.) is thus explained by Medh.: "Let him think, whatever is going to happen at any time, then let that happen."]

[8] [Cf. vs. 68. *Manaḥ pūtaḥ samācaret* can perhaps only be fully rendered by a paraphrase, "Let all his actions be purified by his possessing a pure mind."]

47. He should endure abuse; he should despise no one; and he should not be at enmity with any one with reference[1] to this body.

48. He may not be angry again with an angry man; abused, he should speak fair; he may not utter untrue speech spread through the seven gates.[2]

49. Delighting in the supreme self, seated, indifferent (to mundane objects), without lusts,[3] with his own self[4] alone as a companion, he, seeking happiness, should exist here.

50. He must never gain alms by (expounding) portents and omens, nor by astrology, nor by preaching and expounding.[5]

51. He may not go (to beg) at a house frequented[6] by (persons) practising austerity, or by Brahmans, or by birds and dogs, or by other (religious) beggars.

52. With his hair, nails, (and) beard trimmed, bearing a dish, a stick, and a water-pot, he should ever wander, intent, not injuring any creatures.

[1] [So the commentators render *āçritya;* but they hold that every clause must have some particular meaning in connection with the whole. The words seem to mean no more than "while he occupies this (earthly) body," *i.e.*, so long as he lives.]

[2] [What gates? The commentators only show their ignorance of what was once a term understood by all in offering us the following explanations (Medh., Govind.): A sevenfold basis of speech lies in duty; gain; desire; duty and gain united; gain and desire united; duty and desire united; duty, gain, and desire united; untruth may come in either division; or (Medh.) the seven gates refer to the seven breaths; or (Medh.) to the six organs of sense plus intelligence (*buddhiḥ*) as seventh. The last is the first explanation given by K., who only changes it by making five organs of sense and adding the dual *antaḥkaraṇa*, composed of mind and intelligence (*re-dāntadarçane*). Still others say that the gates refer to the seven *bhuvanāni*. Rāgh. as K.'s first, but he adds the meaning is, "let him keep silence." Apropos Baudh. (i. 1, 12) speaks of the treatises as the "many gates of the law."]

[3] [(*Nir*)*āmiṣa*, "desire of flesh; a too great eagerness for living things" (Medh.)]

[4] ["Self" is probably the inner self here, though K. renders it "his own body as only companion." The *adhyātman* (supreme self) may be himself as individual (cf. vs. 82).]

[5] [He must not in this period of life direct the king what ought to be done, or give instruction in the meaning of different treatises; preaching, *i.e.*, giving directions, orders, advice.]

[6] [*Āgāra* is not translated "house" by Medh., but "locality" (*pradeça*), and "frequented" he explains, "where many dependents (come) for the sake of getting food." A courtyard is perhaps meant.]

53. His dishes must not be bright[1] or cracked. The purification of them is directed (to) be by (means of) water, like (that) of the *camasas*[2] in the sacrifice.

54. A gourd and a wooden bowl, an earthen (pot), and likewise a rattan (vessel), those Manu son of Svayambhū declared to be vessels for religious duties.[3]

55. He should go once (in a day) for food. He must not be addicted to much (food), for an ascetic addicted to (much) alms is ever addicted to objects of the senses.

56. When there is no smoke, when the pestle is quiet, when there is no burning charcoal, when people have eaten, when the removal of dishes has been done, the ascetic should always go for alms.

57. If he get none, he should not despair. If he get (some), he should not rejoice. He should have only enough to support life, free from attachment to materials.[4]

58. But he should indeed always despise food got by cringing, for by food so got an ascetic is fettered, though free.[5]

59. He should restrain, by eating little food and by sitting in a secluded place, the organs which are influenced by objects.

60. By opposition to the organs, and by decay of passion (and) hatred, and by harmlessness to beings, he becomes fit for immortality.

61. He should contemplate the existences of men which

[1] [Gold and silver ware, etc. (K.)]

[2] [Cf. v. 116 note ("purified by hand or by water"). The verse appears to be a late addition.]

[3] [Medh. has no note on this verse. Govind. explains rattan (*vaidala*) as "bark." "For religious duties" is a free translation of *yati* (which means "for an ascetic of the fourth order"), as if Dr. B. had read *dharma*, but I know of no such reading. The *alāru* (gourd) is forbidden as food at a *çrāddha* (Mbhā. xiii. 91, 39). It is not elsewhere spoken of in Manu.]

[4] [That is, he should have no desire for a new staff, water-pot, etc. (Medh., K.)]

[5] [Although his soul is in the condition of freedom (it is not necessary for the man to die in order to become "freed") it is fettered again by this act.]

arise from faults in acts and their falling into *niraya*,[1] and their torments in Yama's abode;

62. And (he should contemplate) also separation from friends, and union with the hated, and victory (over himself) by old age, and pain from diseases;

63. And (let him contemplate) the leaving this body, and again being produced in the womb, and the going of this internal self through a thousand millions (of passages) in the womb;

64. And the pain of living creatures arising from sin, and also the eternal pleasure arising from righteousness.

65. He should also consider by means of *yoga*[2] the subtileness of the supreme self, and (its) inherence in bodies, both high and low.

66. Even though calumniated,[3] he should follow virtue in whatever stage of life he be occupied,[4] equable to all beings: a mark (is not) a cause of virtue.[5]

67. Though the fruit of the strychnine tree clears (muddy) water, water does not settle down by merely mentioning its name.[6]

68. Ever by night or day, for the protection of creatures, he should walk looking at the ground, even in pain of body.[7]

69. For purification for the creatures that an ascetic injures ignorantly, by day or night (as he moves about), he should, having bathed, make six suppressions of breath.

[1] *Niraya*, a hell [literally, "exit." The commentators understand no special hell, but all the different ones.]

[2] [*Yoga* is concentrated meditation. The appearance of the Vedantic Paramātmā (all-soul), in opposition to the internal self (vs. 63), is not in harmony with the philosophical views of the rest of the work.]

[3] [Or adorned (*bhūṣita*) *v. l.* (in some MSS. so Medh.)]

[4] [*Vasan* (cf. iii. 50; xii. 102), or (*v. l. rataḥ*), "pleased in any order").]

[5] [That is, the mark of his order alone (to carry a staff, etc.), is not enough to produce virtue (K.) Cf. Yāj. iii. 65.]

[6] "Mention of its name," *i.e.*, it is necessary to actually rub the inside of the pot with it. [Thus carrying the mark of an ascetic does not produce virtue (Medh.)]

[7] [Medh., K. Cf. vs. 46.]

70. Even three suppressions of breath duly made, accompanied by the *vyāhriti* and *praṇava*, is to be known as the highest austerity of a Brahman.[1]

71. For as the dross of ores being melted is burnt, so faults of the organs are consumed by suppression of breath.

72. He should burn faults by suppression of breath, and sin by abstraction, attachment by restraining (the senses), and the uncontrolled qualities[2] by meditation.

73. He should, by means of meditation,[3] see the course of this internal self through high and low beings, (a course) difficult to be recognised by those whose self is not (rightly) formed.

74. A man endowed with correct insight is not bound by acts,[4] but one deprived of insight attains (successive stages of) existence.[5]

75.[6] By harmlessness, by non-attachment of the organs, and by acts taught by the Veda,[7] by severe courses of austerity, men here attain the condition (or world) of That.[8]

76. He should forsake this abode of the elements (the body) with pillars of bones, joined by tendons, with flesh and blood for plaster, covered by skin, full of stinks, (and) of urine and ordure;

[1] *Vyāhṛti, i.e., bhūḥ bhuvaḥ svaḥ; praṇava, i.e., om.* Cf. ii. 74. [The word Brahman is used to show that this rule is not confined to the ascetic (Medh., K.)]

[2] [According to Medh., the three qualities (goodness, passion, darkness) which depend on things other than themselves (*paratantrāḥ*). Various expositions of the other words are given by the same commentator.]

[3] [*Dhyānayogena* is taken by some as "by means of meditation and abstraction" (Medh.) Or it may mean "the practice of meditation."]

[4] [To be "bound by acts," is to feel in after life the effects of acts done or undone in this, or, in other words, to pass through successive existences. "Correct insight" means as taught by the Vedānta respecting the supreme self (Medh.)]

[5] [The mere performer of acts (without knowledge) enters transmigration (*saṁsāra*) (Medh.)]

[6] [Final deliverance is brought about by union of acts and knowledge. The necessity of knowledge being declared in the last verse, *acts* are now spoken of (Medh.)]

[7] [Not acts of pleasure, but sacrificial acts, taught in the Veds.]

[8] [That highest, viz., Brahma (Medh., K.), or universal sovereignty independence (Medh.)]

77. Penetrated by the sorrows of old age, disturbed by sickness, diseased, full of passion, and not lasting.

78. As a tree (falls) on a river bank, or as a bird (deserts) a tree, so, leaving this body, one is freed from a savage monster.[1]

79. Leaving his good deeds to his loved ones and his evil deeds to his enemies,[2] by force of meditation he goes to the eternal Brahma.[3]

80. When he is truly indifferent to all emotions,[4] then, here and when dead, he gains everlasting happiness.

81. Having in this way gradually relinquished all attachments, freed from all duality, he is firm in Brahma[5] alone.

82. All this depends on meditation, whatsoever has been declared; for no one who knows not the supreme self[6] obtains the fruit of (his) deeds.

83. He should mutter the Veda (*brahma*) relating to sacrifices, and also that relating to the gods, and ever that relating to the supreme self,[7] and that set forth in the Upaniṣads.[8]

84. This is the refuge of the ignorant, this also of the discerning, this is (the refuge) of those who desire heaven, this of those who desire eternity.

85. The twice-born who wanders (as an ascetic) in due

[1] [*Grāha*: The continuation of births is meant (K.) I doubt if there is anything in the commentator's distinction between the voluntary and involuntary act intended here.]

[2] [So K. On the other hand, Medh. renders, "considering among the things pleasing and unpleasing that which is really good and ill to himself," etc.; in other words, "he should not be pleased with him who does him a pleasure, nor angry with him who does anything unpleasant." In this the phrase "by force of meditation" is to be construed with the participle, which in Dr. B.'s MS. is *vimṛçya*, "considering by force of meditation," which, as a rule, Medh. paraphrases by *citte bhāvayet*, "let him realise;" but K. seems to confound his own reading with Medh.'s interpretation.]

[3] [Neuter, as in ii. 28; the Brahma as world-substance.]

[4] [*I.e.*, literally, "When he by his condition (of mind) becomes indifferent to all conditions" (*bhāveṣu*, or to all things).]

[5] [Neuter, world-substance.]

[6] ["He who does not meditate on the Paramātmatva (supreme selfship)" is K.'s rendering of *anadhyātmavit*. Medh. has besides various explanations. Here and in vs. 83 the commentators, all Vedantists, are not to be trusted, cf. vs. 49; the *adhyātman* is probably the man's self as distinguished from the outer world.]

[7] [Cf. note to vs. 82.]

[8] [*Vedāntābhihitañ ca yat*, "the teaching of the Vedānta," may refer to the system of philosophy, but probably not. So "Vedanta" in vs. 94.]

course, having here shaken off sin, goes to the supreme Brahma.[1]

86. This rule for ascetics whose self is restrained has been taught you; learn (now) the practice of Vedasannyāsins.[2]

87. A student and a householder, a hermit (dweller in the forest), as also an ascetic, those four separate orders arise from the householder.

88. And all these observed in due order, according to the treatises, conduct a Brahman who does what is taught to the highest course (of existence).

89. But of all of them, according to the system of the Veda and Smṛti,[3] the householder is declared the best, for he supports those (other) three.

90. As all rivers, female and male (small or large), go to (their) resting-place in the ocean, so men of all orders depend on the householder.

91. By the twice-born, ever members of those four orders, a tenfold law is to be strenuously followed.

92. Resolution, patience, self-restraint, honesty, purity, restraint of the organs, devotion, knowledge (of the Veda), truth, absence of anger, are the tenfold law.

93. Brahmans who study the ten constituents of law, and, having gone over (them), act up (to them), attain a supreme course (of existence).

94. A Brahman who has discharged his (three) debts, who, steadfast, practises the tenfold law, having duly heard the Upaniṣads, may become a Sannyāsin.

[1] [The world-substance.]

[2] [Ascetics who have given up all pious acts (Veda) except muttering prayers and meditating on the supreme self (Medh.) Cf. vs. 94, after the interpolated (?) digression, which has been said in substance before, iii. 77–78. The Sannyāsin is, in fact, as distinguished from the Vanaprastha (hermit) and Yati (*pravrājaka*), not so much a special kind of Yati as a Brahman in a fifth stage of life. Vs. 33 completes the third, and vs. 86 the fourth stage of life. Here the sixth lecture should end, for the text nowhere else recognises a distinct fifth order, and *sannyāsa* (as in v. 108) is employed as a general term; while originally three orders were more apt to be reckoned (ii. 230). To correct this impression, I fancy vss. 87 ff. were inserted till vs. 94 picks up the Sannyāsin again.]

[3] [Or, "the Çruti of the Veda." There are two readings; the latter is Medh.'s.]

95. Having given up[1] all acts, and thrusting away the faults of acts, restrained, having practised the Veda, he may live at ease in dependence on his son.

96. Having thus relinquished[1] acts, occupied with (his) own duty, without desire, having destroyed sin by renunciation, he obtains the highest course (of existence.)

97. This fourfold law of the Brahman has been told you, (that is) virtuous, that brings endless fruit after death. Learn the laws for kings!

END OF THE SIXTH LECTURE.

[1] [*Sannyasya*, whence *sannyāsin*, "he who gives up."]

LECTURE VII.

ON THE DUTIES OF KINGS, AND ON THE SECOND CASTE.

1. I SHALL declare the laws[1] for kings, how a sovereign should be occupied, and what his origin (is), and how his supreme perfection[2] (is effected).

2. Protection of all this (his realm) according to justice is to be done by a Kṣatriya who has duly received the Vedic initiation.

3. For, this world being without a king, it trembles everywhere from fear; the Lord,[3] then, created a king for the protection of all this (world).[4]

4. Having taken eternal elements from Indra, Wind, Yama, the Sun, from Fire and Varuṇa, the Moon and Kuvera.

5. Because a king is formed from parts of these chiefs of the gods, therefore he excels in glory all beings.

6. And he burns, like the Sun, the eyes and minds, nor can any one on earth even behold him.

7. He is Fire and Wind; he (is) the Sun, the Moon, the King of Justice;[5] he (is) Kuvera, he Varuṇa, he great Indra in grandeur.[6]

8. Though a child, a king is not to be despised as a

[1] [*Dharma*. Medh. here paraphrases this word simply by "duties" (*dharmaçabdaḥ kartavyatā vacanaḥ*), and it often means no more.]

[2] [Or, "complete success" (as a conqueror)—(Medh.)]

[3] "The Lord," *i.e.*, Prajāpati; see i. 6 ff.

[4] [" When the world was without a king, and trembling (or going to pieces) with fear," is the literal sense of the first part.]

[5] [*I.e.*, Yama.]

[6] [Compare ix. 303 ff. "In grandeur," *i.e.*, (*prabhāvataḥ*) by virtue of his supernatural power (Medh.)]

human being,[1] for he is a powerful divinity in man's form.

9. Fire burns only the individual who approaches (it) carelessly; the fire of the king burns the race,[2] with (their) cattle and accumulation of wealth.

10. He having truly considered the matter, (his) power, and the place and time, again and again takes, in order to the perfection of justice, all forms.[3]

11. In whose favour best good fortune[4] abides, in (whose) heroism victory, in whose wrath death, he indeed consists of all glory.

12. But he who hates him out of folly perishes certainly; for the king quickly turns his mind to his destruction.

13. Therefore let the king never alter the rule, (either) the law he arranges for those he loves, or the punishment, for those he dislikes.

14. On his[6] account Îçvara formerly created Punishment, his son, (as) the protector of all beings, consisting of the glory of Brahma, (criminal) law.[7]

15. From fear of him, all beings, immovable and movable, are fit for enjoyment, and wander not from (their) law.

16. Having truly considered him (Punishment), (as well as) place and time, and (his)[8] power and knowledge, (the) king) should suitably[9] punish evil-doing men.

[1] [Literally, (by one thinking thus: "he is only) a human being."]

[2] [The whole family (*kula*), his children and relatives (Medh.)]

[3] [That is, he is friend, foe, or neutral, as occasion requires (Medh., K.) All forms of the gods are perhaps meant.]

[4] "Best good fortune," *Padmāçrī*; "*padmā-çabdo mahatvapratipādanārthaḥ*" (Medh., etc.)

[5] [*Aniṣṭa*, any disagreeable regulation, as "no communication must be had with this man," "he must not be allowed to enter the house," etc. (Medh.)]

[6] [Medh. reads *tadartham* in the first pada.]

[7] [*Dharma*, *i.e.*, as a personification of *dharma* (K.); opposed to injustice (*adharma*), for punishment should not be unjust (Medh.)]

[8] [*I.e.*, the criminal's (K.) Dr. B. takes it as explanatory of the personified punishment. The other substantives, especially *vidyā*, knowledge (of Veda), would seem to support K.]

[9] [*Yathārhataḥ* (Medh.)]

17. He, Punishment,[1] (is) a royal person;[2] he (is) a guide and ruler; he is said to be the surety for the law of the four orders.

18. Punishment rules all men; punishment alone protects them; punishment is watchful while they sleep; the wise know punishment (to be) justice.[3]

19. Inflicted properly after consideration, (punishment) delights all people;[4] but, inflicted without consideration, it altogether destroys (them).

20. If the king did not untiringly inflict punishment on those to be punished, the stronger would roast the weak like fish on a spit.[5]

21. The crow would eat the sacrificial cake, and the dog would likewise lick the offering; there would be no lordship in any one; all would be upside down.[6]

[1] "Punishment," literally a club or stick, which is here personified as punishment. Such personifications are very common in Sanskrit literature; we find even different metres thus dealt with. Compared with the present instance may be Rāma's slippers, which struck against one another when injustice was done; and this occurs in the Buddhist Jātaka, which is the foundation of the Rāmāyaṇa (see Prof. V. Fausböll's "The Dasaratha Jātaka," 1871), and has been adopted in the diffuse epic. There is an actual instance of what is done in the text at Benares in the worship of Daṇḍapāṇi, properly the name of an attendant of Çiva, but "the true character of this personage has been forgotten, and his emblem has been elevated to the rank of a substantive deity." This emblem is "a veritable cudgel, of enormous thickness; not, indeed, of wood, but . . . of stone. . . . Bhairo has issued his commands to it to beat any person who may be found working mischief" (Sherring, "Benares," pp. 62 and 63).

[2] [Both Medh. and K. take *puruṣa* as a second attribute, "he is a king; he is (like) a man," *i.e.*, he has manly strength, others being (in comparison) as women (K.); his strength is not as a woman's (Medh.)]

[3] ["Justice" (*dharma*), translated "criminal law" in vs. 14. "It is not the king and the treatises, but punishment alone," says Medh. on *daṇḍa eva*. Both Medh. and K. call attention to the fact that punishment is of two sorts, here and hereafter, Rājadaṇḍa and Yamadaṇḍa.]

[4] [Punishment which has been inflicted after (the king) has carefully considered what is to be considered, according to vs. 16, makes the whole realm happy (Medh.)]

[5] [Medh. and K.; the latter notes another reading (*jale matsyān ivā 'hiṁsyuḥ*), which would mean "destroy as fishes in water." Medh. does not know this reading, which was probably substituted after his time, because the other was "une image bizarre," as Schlegel, rejecting it, calls it. As the "spit" (*çūla*, stake) was used to torture human beings upon, the comparison is not so unhappy.]

[6] [Even the Çūdra caste would be above the Brahman, etc. (Medh., K.)]

22. The whole world is mastered by punishment; a pure man is hard to find: from fear of punishment, indeed, all the world is fit for enjoyment.[1]

23. Gods, devils, Gandharvas, evil demons, birds, and snakes—even they, ruled by punishment, become fit for enjoyment.[2]

24. All castes would be perverted, all landmarks would be broken down, there would be mutiny in all the world from perversion of punishment.

25. Where dark, red-eyed Punishment, destroying sin, advances, there the people are not confounded, if the leader[3] discerns well.

26. (The wise) declare a truth-speaking king, one who acts after consideration, discerning, wise in virtue, pleasure, and wealth, to be the (proper) inflictor of this (punishment).

27. A king properly inflicting it (punishment) prospers in all three (virtue, pleasure, and wealth[4]); but a sensual,[5] unfair, and base (king) verily perishes by punishment.

28. For punishment, very glorious, and hard to be borne by the undisciplined, destroys a king, together with his kin, when he has indeed departed from justice;

29. Also (it destroys his) castle, and kingdom, and land, with immovable and movable things, and vexes the Munis gone to heaven, and the gods also.[6]

[1] [Cf. vs. 15; Mbhā. xii. 15, 34. "A pure man," *i.e.*, a man pure by his own natural condition; fear of punishment is necessary to make him pure (Medh.) It seems as well in most cases to let Punishment drop into punishment, as Dr. B. has indicated by dropping the capital; the personification is too awkward.]

[2] [It is only because it is oppressed by fear of punishment that each creature gives up its own desires, and so all are kept in peace and happiness. As to the heavenly beings, a Çruti is quoted that says all the divinities perform their functions through fear alone, "for if the sun followed his own inclination, he would not get up" (Medh.) The Gandharvas are heavenly singers, Dānavas and Rākṣasas evil spirits.]

[3] [*Netā* (leader), like *saṁpraṇetā* (inflictor), in the next verse, is the one who guides (inflicts) punishment.]

[4] K.

[5] [*Kāmātmā* (K.); or "blind with lust," *kāmāndho* (Medh. *v. l.*, noted by Rāgh.)]

[6] "The Munis," because they and the gods get no offerings. [B. R. understand the Munis gone to heaven (*antarikṣa*) as the Great Bear. Munis are the departed saints. Quotations from the *Purāṇa-kārāḥ* are given by Medh. to show that the power of the celestials depends on the sacrifice and offerings given them by man.]

30. It (punishment) cannot justly be inflicted by (a king who is) without a helper, (who is) foolish, covetous, undisciplined, and devoted to sensual objects.

31. By (a king who is) pure, truthful, (who) exactly follows the treatises, who has good helpers and is prudent, may punishment be inflicted.[1]

32. He should act justly in his own kingdom[2] and (be) very severe to enemies, straightforward to loving friends, patient to Brahmans.

33. The fame of a king who does so, though he live by gleaning,[3] is spread in the world like a drop of oil on water.

34. But the fame of a king the opposite of this[4] (in conduct), of unconquered self, is congealed in the world like a drop of ghee in water.

35. The king is created the protector of the castes and orders, each being devoted to its own duty[5] in order.

36. What is to be done by him with (his) ministers to[6] protect the people, that I shall declare to you duly in order.

37. The king, having arisen early, should reverence Brahmans learned in the Vedas (and) wise,[7] and he should stand (firm) by their decision;

38. And he must ever honour old[8] Brahmans who know the Veda (and are) pure; for one who honours the old is worshipped even by evil demons.

[1] [The "helpers" are his ministers, generals, priests, etc. (K.) Medh. renders the word in vs. 30 and here by *çobhanāḥ.*]

[2] [Or "according to the laws in his own kingdom," whether he be an inhabitant of Kashmir or a Pañcāla. The reading is either *nyāyavṛttaḥ* or *nyāyavṛttiḥ* (Medh.)]

[3] [Figurative for "however poor he may be" (Medh., K.)]

[4] [*Atas tu viparītasya.* Dr. B. translates *atas tu* simply "hence," which is clearly wrong.]

[5] [(*Sve sve dharme niviṣṭānām*) *atha vā na tatra praçliṣyate aniviṣṭānām iti.* As a prefix to this alternative interpretation, Medh. says that the king's sin is great if he does not protect the castes (in which he includes all the women, children, and old people) while firm in their duty; if they err from it his sin is greater.]

[6] [Medh.]

[7] [Medh. understands "learned" (literally "old") as those who have read; "wise," as those who understand the Vedas. K. and Rāgh. make the latter refer to wisdom in other works, as the treatises on polity.]

[8] [A repetition of the sense of the foregoing (Medh.)]

39. From them he should always learn good conduct, though disciplined; for a well-behaved[1] king never perishes.

40. Many kings with their attendants have perished from want of good conduct;[2] and even dwellers in the forest have gained kingdoms by discipline.

41. Vena was ruined by bad conduct, and also the king Nahuṣa, and Sudās Paijavana,[3] also Sumukha and Nimi.

42. But Pṛthu by good conduct got a kingdom, and Manu and Kuvera (got) lordship over wealth, and Gādhi's son (got) even Brahmanhood.

43. He should learn the threefold knowledge (of the Vedas) from those who possess the knowledge of the three (Vedas), and the eternal (art of) policy,[4] logic, and knowledge of self; but business from the people.[5]

44. Let him day and night apply himself to the conquest of his organs; for one whose organs are conquered is able to bring the people under control.

45. Let him avoid with effort ten vices which arise

[1] ["Disciplined" and "well-behaved" are the same in the original (*vinīta* = directed, under control), to which *vinaya* ("good conduct") is the substantive.]

[2] [*Vinaya*, see last note. "Dwellers in the forest," *i.e.*, (kings) deprived of resources (Medh.)]

[3] [For Sudāso Yavana, as Dr. B. has it, cf. B. R., and our text, viii. 110. Vena or Vena (cf. ix. 66). Vena is often taken as a type of an undisciplined king. He was son of Sunīthā and father to Pṛthu. As a mixed class the Vena appears x. 19. Nahuṣa, son of Āyus (Mbhā. i. and v.), was ruined by love and ambition. Ruling in Indra's stead, he was finally changed to a snake. Sudās (spoken of as a Çūdra in the epic) was king at the time of the great Vasiṣṭha, and a leader of the Tṛtsu (R. V. vii. 18). Sumukha, as king, is unknown to me. Nimi in the epic is said to be a Videha king. Pṛthu (cf. ix. 44) was the title of several gods as well as kings. The one meant is probably he whose happy reign is described in the 7th and 12th books of the Mbhā. Manu needs only an exclamation. There is a tale in the epic of his ruling as king, but only as incarnate deity. Kuvera was god of wealth, and Gādhi's son was Viçvāmitra, who was born a Kṣatriya.]

[4] [*Daṇḍanīti* is rather the science of subjugation (punishment) of friends or foes. They say *daṇḍa* is from *damana* (restraint)—(Medh.)]

[5] [By the Bārhaspatya (Medh., treatise of Bṛhaspati mentioned in the epic) Medh. unites "from the people" with all three last, "learn these from any one who knows them." The first two in (*b*) should be in apposition, and *ānvīkṣikī* is not logic as a system—"introspection (a seeking after), knowledge of self."]

from lust, and eight which arise from anger; (these) end ill.

46. For a king devoted to vices which spring from lust is deprived of his wealth and virtue; but (if addicted) to those which arise from anger, of his self.

47. Sport,[1] dice, sleeping by day, gossip, women, liquor, song, dance, (and) music, and vain wandering about, are the tenfold class (of vices) arising from lust.

48. Malice, violence, injury, envy, calumny, mischief to property, abuse, and assault are the eightfold class (of vices) arising from anger.

49. But covetousness, which all bards have recognised as the root of both those, he should overcome with effort; for both those classes (of vices) spring from it.[2]

50. Drink, dice, women also, and hunting, let him know to be, in order, the worst four in the class arising from lust.

51. Let him know infliction of violence, also abuse, and mischief to property to be the worst three in the class arising from anger.

52. Of this class of seven everywhere prevailing, a self-possessed king should know the prior sin to be the worse.

53. Of vice and death, vice is said (to be) the worst; a vicious man, when dead, sinks down (and) down;[3] a virtuous man goes to heaven.

54. (The king) should appoint seven or eight carefully examined ministers, (who are) hereditary, learned in the treatises, brave, skilled in the use of weapons,[4] and well-descended.

55. Even an easy deed is difficult to be effected by one

[1] [*Mṛgayā*, hunting for pleasure only (not for sacrifice), resulting in the death of animals (Medh., K.)]

[2] [Cf. ii. 2, where all is derived from the principle of lust (*kāma*).]

[3] [*I.e.*, goes to hell (Medh.); to different hells (K.)]

[4] [So K. to *labdhalakṣa*; Rāgh., "skilful in war;" Medh., more according to the literal sense, "those who have received distinction for what they have done."]

only, especially by one without a helper; still more a very prosperous kingdom (is hard to rule).

56. With them he should ever deliberate ordinary matters[1] of peace and war, the condition of the kingdom,[2] wealth,[3] protection, and the pacification of acquired (territory).[4]

57. Having separately got from (each of) them his opinion, and then from them all,[5] let him arrange in affairs what is good for himself.

58. But let the king think over most important designs referring to the six matters[6] with a learned Brahman distinguished from all.

59. Always trusting him, (the king) should devolve (on him) all matters; having determined (them) with him, he should then begin[7] the affair.

60. He should also appoint other ministers, pure, discerning, firm, gatherers of wealth properly,[8] well-tried.

61. As many men as by whom the business to be done for him may be effected, so many, unwearied, clever, discerning, let him appoint.

62. Of them he should appoint over (his) gains the brave, clever, and well-descended; the pure, over mines;[9] the fearful, in the interior of the palace.

[1] [Perhaps better (*sāmānyam*), "in common with these (ministers) let (the king) discuss peace and war." But the commentators take it as a substantive, "what is not too secret" (Medh.), and reckon seven divisions (Rāgh.)]

[2] [*Sthāna* is, according to B. R., any event which occurs. Medh. and K. both explain it as "of four sorts, consisting of army, treasury, capital, realm, for the welfare and protection of which he must consult." In accordance with this I have prefixed to Dr. B.'s translation ("the kingdom") the words conveying the commentator's meaning, though Medh. has another explanation whereby "defences" (stability) would be the right word.]

[3] [Medh., K.]

[4] [Property (K.)]

[5] [First the opinion of each in secret, and then of them all assembled in council together (Medh.)]

[6] "Referring to six matters," see vs. 56.

[7] [Dr. B.'s MS. Medh. has *samācaret* (for *samārabhet*) with the Beng. MS., "he should carry on the affair after determining," etc.]

[8] [Medh. renders *arthasamāhartar* by *nidhātar*. The office of the *samāhartar* appears to be that of royal coactor, or collector of revenues, who collects them when due (*samyag*).]

[9] [So B. R. It seems odd to have the mines, which we must suppose to be in different parts of the country, introduced in this way. By following Medh. we get a simple meaning, where all are town officials.

63. He should also appoint an ambassador learned in all the treatises, who understands gestures, expression, and acts, pure, clever, well-descended.

64. The ambassador of a king is praised (who is) liked, pure, clever, with a (good) memory, who knows place and time, personable, fearless, eloquent.

65. The army (is) dependent on the minister;[1] disciplinary administration on the army; the treasury and kingdom on the prince; peace and the opposite on the ambassador.

66. For, verily, the ambassador alone unites, (and) divides also the united; the ambassador conducts that business by which they are divided or not.

67. In affairs he (the ambassador) should know by (his) obscure signs and acts the emotions, intentions, and efforts of him (the other king), and (should learn) what he intends to do from (his) dependents.

68. And having known truly (from the ambassador) all that is intended by the other king, (the king) should so make effort that he does not vex himself.[2]

69. He should inhabit a country with waste ground, supplied with grain, inhabited by Āryas chiefly, not marshy, delightful, with subdued neighbouring (kings), yielding a living.[3]

70. Let him dwell in a town fortified by a desert,[4] or

He should appoint pure (not greedy) men, etc. (including all the adjectives but the last), to take charge of the business of his income and expenditure (*artha, āyavyayavyavahāre*), viz. (to explain the places connected therewith he adds), in the places for preparing (*saṁskāra*) gold and silver, and for receiving goods resulting from (hand) labour; *i.e.*, these officials superintend the workers in gold and the grain market, which gave heavy revenues to the king. Cf. vs. 80. For *saṁskāra* (Medh.), K., and Rāgh. have *utpatti*, "production." *Artha* is what they superintend, *ākārakarmānte* is where.]

[1] [General of the army (Medh., K.)]

[2] ["So as not to cause himself injury," is the literal meaning.]

[3] "Āryas," *i.e.*, people of the higher castes. ["With waste land," *i.e.*, in respect to water, as Medh. defines: *parvatāntapānabahurṛkṣo deço jāṅgalam ucyate*; "not marshy," according to K., "healthy," according to Medh., "not filled with quarrelsome people," literally, "not disturbed;" according to Medh., Āryas are "instructed."]

[4] [Five yojana in extent.]

by earth,[1] or by water,[2] or even by trees, by (armed) men, or by mountains.

71. But let him with all efforts occupy a hill-fort;[3] for a hill-fort by its many (good) qualities is the best of them.

72. The first three of them, beasts, rats, and water animals occupy; the last three, monkeys, men, and immortals, in order.[4]

73. As enemies hurt them[5] not when they have occupied (their) forts, so enemies hurt not a king in his fort.

74. One archer on the wall fights a hundred (below); a hundred, ten thousand; therefore a fort[6] is directed.[7]

75. That (fort) should be furnished with weapons,[8] with wealth, grain, and animals to ride, with Brahmans,[9] artisans, machines,[10] fodder, and water.

76. In the middle of it he should have a well-built[11] house made for himself, protected, suitable for all seasons,[12] beautiful, with water and trees.

77. Having occupied it, he should marry a wife of the

[1] [A circular wall of brick or stone raised twelve cubits.]

[2] [A moat (Medh., K., Rāgh.) These are, of course, the late views of the commentators only.]

[3] [The one last mentioned, vs. 70, as "fortified by mountains."]

[4] [The desert is occupied by (beasts, *i.e.*) deer, the (earth) wall by rats, etc., the water by crocodiles, etc., the woods by monkeys, the (outposts of) men by men, while the gods reside on the mountain (hill), (K.) All the qualities, bad and good, of these occupants become those of the king (Medh.)]

[5] [The creatures residing in these various strongholds are safe from attack by the enemies peculiar to themselves; so the king is safe when in his fort or stronghold (K.)]

[6] [The mountain stronghold is meant (Medh.)]

[7] [*Vidhīyate*; or "is best" (*viçiṣyate*) (Rāgh.); or, "therefore let him erect forts" (*durgāṇi kārayet*) (Medh.)]

[8] [That is, offensive weapons, swords, darts, etc., not defensive weapons, as helmets, etc. (Medh.)]

[9] [As priests or enchanters to slay the enemy, remove illness, etc., according to the commentators, or to settle what the king's duties are when the readings of the commentators (*ṭīkā*) differ (Medh.)]

[10] [Machines, *i.e.*, divine projectiles made of iron (Rāgh.) There is no possibility of determining what "machines" are meant by the text; the word denotes elsewhere "bands" and even "amulets."]

[11] [Or commodious.]

[12] [Literally "making all seasons" (*sarvartukam*), by employing fruits, flowers, etc., of different sorts, or (*sarvartugam iti vā pāṭhaḥ*) "receiving all" (*i.e.*, "suitable for all seasons")—(Medh.)]

same caste, with good marks, born of a great family, dear, endowed with beauty (and) good qualities.

78. And he should appoint a domestic priest, and choose a sacrificial priest; these should perform the domestic and sacrificial[1] rites for him.[2]

79. The king should offer by various sacrifices with proper[3] gifts (to the priests), and should also give, for virtue-sake, to Brahmans both means of enjoyment and wealth.[4]

80. He should cause to be collected by fit (persons) the yearly tribute from the kingdom, and should be thoroughly conversant with the holy texts in the world;[5] he should behave to men as a father.

81. He should appoint several clever superintendents in different places; they should inspect all the acts of the men doing his work.

82. He should reverence Brahmans returned from their Guru's family, for that is laid down as the undecaying Brahmanic treasure of kings.[6]

83. Neither thieves nor enemies take it, and it perishes not; therefore (this) undecaying treasure is to be deposited by a king with Brahmans.

84. What is offered in a Brahman's mouth is better than *agnihotras*;[7] it never is spilled, nor dries up, nor perishes.

[1] [*Purohita* (*cohen*), family priest; *Rtvig*, sacrificial priest. Medh. says the latter must be chosen, *i.e.*, carefully selected, as he should not be very short or very tall, nor very old nor very young, etc.]

[2] [*Vaitānikāni*. In the Mbhā. xiii. 61, 4, the *vaitānikam karma* and gifts are the purification for the Ksatriya's "eternal deeds of cruelty" (*raudravat karma*).]

[3] [Medh. slyly observes that proper gifts means many gifts.]

[4] [Wreaths, perfumes, etc., and gold, etc. (Medh.)]

[5] [I have taken the liberty of changing entirely Dr. B.'s translation of this clause, for which I see no more support in the commentators than in the text (unless it be a very free rendering of K.): "He should be intent on usage; in the world he should behave to men as a father." *Āmnāya* does not mean usage, and *loke* goes with the first clause in its current meaning of (in the world), "among men," customary. Following K., we should have the meaning "he should be conversant with the customary rules (in regard to taxation")."]

[6] [Reverence means bestow gifts These gifts to Brahmans are the king's undecaying treasure (Comm.)]

[7] [Oblations (offerings) to fire. Better than these is the gift to a Brahman, for the latter offering has none of these faults; the "mouth"

85. A gift to a non-Brahman (produces) equal (fruit); to one who calls himself a Brahman, twofold; to a learned (Brahman),[1] a hundred thousand-(fold); to a student[2] of the Vedas, endless (recompense).

86. For the fruit, small or great, of a gift to one specially fit and given with faith also, is obtained after death.[3]

87. A king challenged by (kings of) equal, greater, (or) less power, giving protection to his people and remembering his duty as a Kṣatriya, may not cease from battle.[4]

88. Never ceasing from battle, protection also of the people, (and) obedience to Brahmans (are) the chief cause of bliss to kings.

89. Kings who, desirous to slay one another, fight with their greatest strength in battles and without turning away, go to heaven.

90. One should not, fighting in battle, slay enemies by concealed weapons, nor with barbed or poisoned (weapons), nor with fire-kindled arrows.

91. Nor should one (mounted) slay an enemy down on the ground, a eunuch,[5] a suppliant, one with loosened hair, one seated, one who says "I am thy (prisoner);"

92. Nor one asleep, one without armour, one naked,[6] one without weapons, one not fighting, a looker-on, one engaged with another;

is the hand, as is said (iv. 117), "The Brahman is one whose mouth is his hand" (Medh.)]

[1] [Or to an instructor, *ācārye* (*sic*), Medh. noted as *v. l.* by K.]

[2] [That is, one who has completed one entire Veda in all its parts.]

[3] [I see no reason for rejecting the verse (kept and commented on by Medh. and Rāgh., but not by K.) found after vs. 86 as follows (86 *b*): "If an article presented with faith be given to a fit person, according to rule (of) place and time, this (gift) causes the perfection of duty."]

[4] [*Saṅgrāma*, conflict, engagement. This is probably said of the army headed by the king; it might, however, be taken as referring to the king's personal conflicts hand to hand, as in the epic often. Medh. favours this explanation; those of less power being a personally weak adversary, or robbers and other law-breakers. It is K.'s note that makes the "challenger" a king in Dr. B.'s translation.]

[5] [Or one wanting manliness, a coward (Medh.) Cf. Āp. ii. 10, 11.]

[6] [*Nagna* or (*var. lec.*) *bhagna*, "one dashed down," overcome, though the words "one without armour" do not include *nagna* (γυμνος), as the defensive armour may be open in only one place (Medh.)]

93. Nor one who has his arms broken, a distressed man, one badly hit, one afraid, one who has fled; remembering virtue, (one should not slay) them.

94. But he who in fear flying is killed by others, whatever ill has been done by (his) chief, he acquires all that;[1]

95. And whatever good the slain coward has acquired for the future life, the chief takes all that from him.

96. He who captures car and horses, elephants, umbrella, wealth, grain, women, property, and base metals, of him is that.[2]

97. 'But they must give a special portion[3] (of the booty) to the king;' such is the Vedic revelation (Çruti); and (that) which is not separately captured is to be given by the king to all the soldiers.

98. This real[4] and eternal law for soldiers has been declared; from this law a Kṣatriya slaying enemies in battle should not fall away.

99. He should also desire to gain what (he has) not gained, (and) should with effort guard what is gained; he should also increase what is preserved, (and) bestow on the worthy what is increased.

100. He should know this fourfold (rule to be) useful for human objects,[5] (and), unwearied, should ever properly effect its accomplishment.

101. He should desire (to get) by force what (he has)

[1] [K. (Rāgh.), who quotes vi. 79 in support of the theory that one man can receive the good and evil of another. Medh.'s differing explanation (supported by Govind.) of the passage in the sixth lecture is continued here, and he explains *bhartar* (supporter, chief) as one who is able to support arms, *i.e.*, as a mere epithet of the soldier. K.'s explanation seems better.]

[2] [These belong to the one who captures them.]

[3] [Dr. B. has "give the sixth part to the king." This is neither in the text nor gloss, and I have ventured to change it. The *uddhāra*, part to be taken out, is the best of the booty, silver, gold, land, etc. (Cf. chariots and steeds, Gaut. x. 21.) The soldiers may not have all they get (*na sarvaṁ tair gṛhītavyam ity eṣā vaidikī çrutiḥ* (Medh.) The authority for this is a like demand for a special portion made by Indra after killing Vṛtra (Medh., K.)]

[4] [According to Medh. *anupaskṛta* is blameless (so K. and Rāgh.) or simple.]

[5] [*Artha*, perhaps better, "productive of gain to men" (*upakāra-vacano 'rthaçabdaḥ*)—(Medh.)]

not got; he should guard with care what he has got; what is guarded, he should increase by interest; what is increased, he should bestow in gifts.[1]

102. He should ever have his sceptre erect, his manliness evident; what is to be concealed, concealed; (he should) ever be seeking out his enemy's weak points.

103. The whole world trembles at a king with ever-erect sceptre; therefore let him subdue all beings by (his) very sceptre.

104. He should indeed act guilelessly, never by guile; but he, self-guarded, should be aware of the frauds used by his enemy.

105. Let not another know his weak point, but let him know the other's weak point; like a tortoise, he should protect his members, and guard his own defect.[2]

106. Like a crane, he should meditate gain; like a lion, he should advance; like a jackal, he should rush on; like a hare, he should fly.

107. These who are the opponents of him thus victorious, he should bring under his power by conciliation and the like expedients.[3]

108. But if they do not stand (firm)[4] by the three first means, he must surely bring them into subjection by gradual force, having conquered them.

109. Of the four expedients, conciliation and the like, the learned ever praise conciliation and force for the increase of a kingdom.

110. As a cultivator pulls up the grass and protects the grain, so a prince should protect (his) kingdom and should slay (his) opponents.

[1] [Did this verse get smuggled in between the time of Medh. and K.? The former has no note upon it, and it seems like a mere variation of vs. 99. It is in all the MSS., however.]

[2] [With this and the following similes compare Mbhā. xii. 140, 24 ff.]

[3] "The like," *i.e.*, liberality [bribery], dissension, and force [K.]

[4] [*I.e.*, cease their enmity, *tiṣṭheyuḥ* (if they cannot be subdued by the first three means—Medh.); "by gradual force," or: "he should gradually bring them into subjection, overcoming them by force alone, if they will not come to a standstill (in their enmity) when he employs the first three means." *Daṇḍenaiva* shows force as the one last resource.]

111. If the king, through folly, harasses by carelessness his own kingdom, he, with his kin, soon loses (his) kingdom and life.

112. As the lives of living beings perish from harassing the body, so the lives even of kings perish from harassing the kingdom.

113. Let him ever follow this system[1] for the protection of his kingdom; for a king whose kingdom is well protected gains happiness.

114. (As) a protection of the kingdom, let him station in the middle of two, three, five, or a hundred towns an army division[2] (properly) commanded.

115. Let him appoint a chief of a town, as well as a chief of ten towns, a lord of twenty, a lord of a hundred, and also a chief of a thousand.[3]

116. Let the head of a town frequently[4] of his own accord acquaint the lord of ten towns with the evils arisen in the town; let the lord of ten (towns) acquaint the lord of twenty;

117. But the lord of twenty should give notice of all that to the lord of a hundred, and the lord of a hundred should, of his own accord, acquaint the chief of a thousand.

118. What food, drink, (and) fuel are to be daily given by the inhabitants of a town to the king, let the head of the town take.

119. Now (a lord) over ten (towns) should enjoy two ploughs' land;[5] and (a lord) over twenty (towns) ten

[1] [Rule.]

[2] [*Gulma.* The number varies according to the force of robbers (barbarians) in the district (Rāgh.)]

[3] [Chief, *pati* or *adhipati;* lord, *adhyakṣa, īça.* The titles appear to be used without technical distinction.]

[4] [*Çanakaiḥ*, slowly, *i.e.*, methodically, regularly (?).]

[5] [*Kula*, mass, family, etc.; the translation follows K.'s explanation of the word, which is, "as much land as can be turned by a plough drawn by six head of cattle is a *kula*" (so Rāgh.) Medh. says it is "a portion of a town, in some places termed a *ghaṭa.*" It would be better perhaps to keep the term in the translation, "He of ten (towns) should enjoy (one) *kula;* he of twenty (towns), five *kula.*" The general meaning of *kula* being "family," we might possibly take it as "the tax levied on one family," as the superintendent of a hundred takes the tax of a town; for the verse seems to supplement vs. 118, and not to denote the use of special tracts of land. But this tax in "food, drink, and fuel," from one

ploughs' land; the superintendent of a hundred towns, a town; the lord of a thousand, a city.

120. (As for) the affairs of those (towns), and also those to be done separately, let another faithful minister of the king, unwearied, see to them.

121. And he should make in every city an overseer of all matters, exalted in position, terrible in appearance, like a planet among the stars.

122. He[1] should of himself ever visit all those (chiefs, and) discover duly their behaviour in (their) provinces by his spies.

123. For those servants appointed by the king for protection (are) mostly takers of the property of others (and) cheats; from them he should protect these people.

124. Those sinful-minded (servants) who take property from suitors,[2] the king, having taken all their property, should banish.

125. He should arrange daily[3] a maintenance for women employed in the king's affairs, and for his messengers,[4] according to their position and work.

126. A *paṇa* is to be given as salary of the lowest, six to the highest, with clothes[5] every six months, and a *droṇa* of grain every month.

family seems rather small. Rāgh. says expressly that "enjoy" means "he should take so much land as a means of subsistence." He adds a *Bhṛgu* verse defining a town as a place occupied by priests and their servants, and likewise the home of Çūdras. It must be a medium (sized) town, say K. and Rāgh.]

[1] [The superintendent of the city (K.)]

[2] [Those who bring suits at law and are unrighteously deprived of property by the king's servants (K.)]

[3] [Medh. says it is given them once a year; so perhaps better, "appoint for each day."]

[4] [Servants.]

[5] By "clothes" the commentators understand two pieces of stuff, just as is still the case in India; one being worn round the middle, the other over the shoulders. A *paṇa* is the copper "*fanam*." [The *paṇa* is the *daily* wage; the lowest servant (house-cleaner, water-carrier, &c.) gets one *paṇa* a day, one pair of cloths every six months, a *droṇa* of grain every month; the highest servant gets six *paṇas* a day, six pairs of cloths every six months, and six *droṇa* of grain every month; a middling servant gets three of each: the *droṇa* = 4 *āḍaka* = 16 *puṣkala* = 128 *kunca* = 1024 *muṣṭi* (handfuls) (K.) (Cf. Colebrooke, Essays, i. 534.) The cloth is twelve cubits long (Rāgh.) Medh. does not mention the increase in aught but money; Rāgh. makes it optional. The *droṇa* of Medh. and Rāgh. agrees with that of K.]

127. (The king) should make the traders pay taxes, after having considered the purchase and sale (of their goods), the journey (they have made), the food and condiments[1] (they use), and the means for security (they employ).[2]

128. Having considered (the matter), let the king ever arrange the taxes in (his) kingdom, so that the king and the business-men may get profit.

129. As the leech,[3] calf, and insect eat little by little (their) food, so yearly taxes are to be taken little by little from the kingdom by the king.

130. A fiftieth part of cattle and gold is to be taken by the king; the eighth part of grain, or the sixth or twelfth.[4]

131. He may also take a sixth part of trees, meat, honey, (and) ghee; also of perfumes, medicines, and liquids, and of flowers, roots, and fruits.[5]

132. And of leaves, herbs, (and) grass, of hides, and of rattan work; of earthen pots, and of all stoneware.

133. Though dying (from hunger), a king may not take taxes from a learned (priest);[6] and a learned (priest) living in (his) jurisdiction must not perish from hunger.

[1] [Rather "side expenses" in obtaining food.]

[2] [This is evidently the meaning of *yogakṣema*, and is so explained by the commentators; it has also just such a meaning in viii. 230. I have therefore substituted "means of security" (that is, the efforts necessary to protect their goods from robbers, etc., Medh., K.) for Dr. B.'s translation, "the insurance and grain" (*sic*), as the last word must surely be an error, and the word "insurance" has with us a technical sense not intended by the text.]

[3] ["Water animal" may be fishes; cf. Rāgh. "They drink very little for fear of drinking up their home" (viz., the water they live in). Medh. inverts the order of vss. 128 and 129.]

[4] These moderate rates have been in use nowhere for the last thousand years in India. The Cola kings of Southern India certainly took a half of all produce, the rate which now obtains. But these plundering robbers, the Vijayanagara Telugu kings, and the Mahrathas after them, raised the rates considerably for a time. [When Manu became a king on earth, the people he governed offered him only one-tenth of the grain crop according to the Mbhā. xii. 67 adhy.; cf. Viṣṇu, iii. 22–25 and 29; Gaut. x. 24, 25. Vas. i. 42 makes it one-sixth; so Baudh. i. 10. 18. 1. The grain-tax varies according to land, crop, etc. (Medh., K.) Cf. viii. 398, and x. 120. This tax is an annual one apparently, on the whole amount held, both stock and gain being probably reckoned. Medh. and K. observe that this is where the cattle and gold (at the end of the year) are more than the original stock (*mūlādadhikayoḥ*), *i.e.*, there is no tax if there has been no increase (?).]

[5] [Cf. Viṣṇu, *loc. cit.* Gaut. x. 27 makes it one-sixtieth per cent.]

[6] [Cf. viii. 394. Other needy or pious persons are also exempt from taxes (Gaut. x. 10; Viṣṇu, iii. 80.]

134. Now if in any king's territory a learned (priest) perishes with hunger, his kingdom will soon perish with hunger.

135. Knowing his learning and behaviour, let him arrange (for him) a proper maintenance; and protect him wholly, as a father his own son.

136. Protected by the king, the religious duty which he does daily increases the life of the king, (his) wealth, and the kingdom also.

137. Let the king cause the low people in (his) kingdom who live by trade[1] to pay something called tax every year.

138. Let the king cause skilled workmen and artisans also, and Çūdras living by their own (labour), to work (for him) a single day in each month.[2]

139. Let him not cut off his root and (the root of) others through much covetousness; for cutting off his root, he would torment himself and them.

140. The king, considering the matter,[3] should be severe and mild also (by turns); a king both severe and mild is approved.

141. When wearied of regarding the affairs of men, let him put in that place the chief of the ministers, knowing law, discerning, subdued, born of (a good) family.

142. Having thus disposed of all this to be done by himself, devoted, and also not careless, he should protect the people.

143. That (king is) dead and lives not, from whose kingdom the people crying out are carried off by savages,[4] while he with (his) ministers look on.

144. The chief duty of a Kṣatriya is simply the protec-

[1] [Peddling vegetables, feathers, and other things of very little value (K.) "Trade" is almost too dignified an expression for the text.]

[2] [Workmen and Çūdras who do not live under a master, but support themselves (as porters, etc., Medh. and K.), substitute a day's labour a month for a tax. The loss of wages thereby incurred would render this a much lighter tax than that on the tradespeople of vss. 131, 132.]

[3] [*Kāryam*, what ought to be done (in each case). This question of whether a king should be severe or mild forms one of the great discussions on the king's duty in the epic.]

[4] [*Dasyus.* Medh., K., and Rāgh. understand "robbers."]

tion of the people, for a king who receives the recompense mentioned is bound by law.[1]

145. Having risen in the last watch[2] (of the night), purified (and) composed, having sacrificed by fire,[3] and having reverenced the Brahmans,[4] let him enter his splendid assembly-room.

146. Standing there, after he has pleased[5] all the people, he may dismiss (them). Having dismissed all the people, he should consult with his ministers.

147. Having gone up a mountain-back, or gone privately to the roof-terrace, or in a solitary wood, let him consult unperceived.

148. Whose deliberations the low people, having come together, do not know—that prince, though deprived of treasure, enjoys the whole earth.

149. At deliberation-time he should expel the foolish, dumb, blind, and deaf; birds;[6] the aged; women; the impure,[7] diseased, and deformed.[8]

150. The despised disclose counsel, so also do birds, and especially women; therefore among these let him be careful.[9]

[1] [*Dharmeṇa yujyate* = *sambadhyate* (K.) From Medh.'s remark (*anyathā tu grahaṇaṁ kurvan, pratyavaiti*) the meaning would seem to be that the king who receives the recompense (tax) mentioned does (gets) his duty (cf. vs. 128, *phalena yujyeta*, get profit). Literally the words mean, "is joined to *dharma*," and *dharma* should mean in (*b*) what it does in (*a*), "duty" or moral merit. "He who draws (no more than) the tax mentioned (by law) does right," seems to be the meaning, and "protection" would then mean not overloading with taxes. If the proximity of vs. 143 (though that in such a work as this has little meaning) makes *pālana* necessary to be taken in the sense of physical protection, we may supply it in (*b*), "for the king does right who draws the tax mentioned (if he protects his people)." It is the want of this ellipsis, apparently, that makes Dr. B. translate *yujyate* "is bound" and *dharma* "law."]

[2] ["Watch" is a period of about three hours.]

[3] [Poured the oblation to the gods upon the fire. As no such oblation is enjoined for the last watch (*brāhmyo muhūrtaḥ;* cf. iv. 92), Medh. says the text means it should be done at the last end of the watch, at dawn (*vyuṣṭāyām rātrau*).]

[4] [Not as in vs. 82 (*pūj*), in the sense "bestow gifts," though the commentators paraphrase this word (*arc*) by that.]

[5] [By greeting and conversing (Medh. and K.)]

[6] [Parrots, crows, etc., which reveal his plans (Medh.)]

[7] [Mlecchas — literally "barbarians."]

[8] [This verse may mean he should not admit these creatures as counsellors (Medh.)]

[9] [Dr. B. has "he should be

151. At noon or midnight let him, having reposed and overcome (his) weariness, think on duty, pleasure, (and) wealth,[1] with those (ministers), or all alone;

152. And on the attainment[2] of these (things) when mutually opposed, and on the giving of (his) daughters (in marriage), and on the protection of his sons;[3]

153. Also on ambassadors (and) messengers, and the result of his acts also; on the behaviour of the harem,[4] and the doings of (his) spies;

154. On all the eightfold acts (of a king), and on the fivefold class (of spies) exactly; on affection and disaffection also, and on the behaviour of neighbouring states.[5]

honoured there;" but *ādṛta* means careful. "The despised" means the unfortunates of vs. 149. The word *tiryagyona* means beasts or birds in vs. 149 and here, but Medh. refutes as silly the idea of its meaning (men disguised as) "beasts," and its literal sense is impossible.]

[1] [Or gain. Cf. the discussion in ii. 224, with the note.]

[2] [Attainment, *samupārjanam* (K. *arjanopāya*; Medh. *saṅgrahaṇa*). I have substituted this word for Dr. B.'s "reconciliation of them," which is an error based on K.'s *virodhoparihāreṇa*, expressing the means.]

[3] [Protection of sons, *i.e.*, training, education, etc. (Medh., K.)]

[4] [These three terms may be interpreted differently. Instead of "ambassadors and messengers," the literal meaning (upheld by Yāj. i. 327) is preferable, "the sending forth of ambassadors." The expression *kāryaçeṣa* means not "result," but literally "the rest of what is to be done," that is, "the completion," which is the meaning held also by the commentators. "Behaviour of the harem" is the meaning given by the commentators to *antaḥpura-pracāra*, and is probably correct, though the literal meaning is "behaviour of the inner city," which may include the conduct of his city officials. As meaning harem, Medh. and K. give instances to show that the women, the queen, etc., should be watched, as otherwise they might poison or otherwise kill the king, Vidūratha and the king of the Kāçi having been slain thus. Cf. Kām. Nīt. vii. 52, 4.]

[5] [Medh. and K. give together three explanations of these divisions. The latter adopts that given by Uçanas, and which he regards as intended by the text respecting the "eightfold acts," viz.:—(1) Reception of taxes; (2) expenses; (3) commands to ministers; (4) prevention of wrong; (5) decisions in regard to doubtful caste-duty; (6) inspection of judicial affairs; (7) punishment; (8) purification from sin (though Medh. interprets (3) *praiṣa* as *duṣṭatyāg*). Medh. prefers one of two explanations founded on data given in the text, the first of which seems more reasonable, and is thus:—(1) Attempting what is still undone; (2) completing what has been done; (3) bettering what is completed; (4) reaping the fruits of his acts (cf. vss. 99 and 101); (5, 6, 7, 8) = the four "means" (taken for granted in vs. 107), viz., conciliation, bribery, dissension, and force. Rāgh. follows K. As Medh.'s other explanation is still more arbitrary, it is plain that there was no certainty felt in his time as to what the "eightfold"

155. (Let him) strenuously (watch) the behaviour of (a king of) middle position,[1] and the attempts of (an aggressive power) desirous to conquer, the conduct of one who is neutral, and of (his) enemy.

156. Those elements (are) the root, in short, of the surrounding country; and eight others are reckoned:[2] those twelve are said to be (the concern of a king[3]).

157. And (there are) five other (elements), (viz.) ministers, kingdoms, forts, wealth, forces; these, told separately,[4] (amount), in brief, (to) seventy-two.

158. A king should know the next (king to him to be) an enemy, as also the adherents of (that) enemy; the (one) next to the enemy (to be) a friend; the one beyond both[5] (to be) neutral.

meant. The fivefold class (of spies) is given by the commentators with probably the same arbitrariness:—(1) Ordinary detectives disguised; (2) fallen priests employed as spies; (3 and 4) decayed farmers and merchants; (5) priests under guise of religion. The guiles employed by them are explained by the ingenious commentators.]

[1] [*Madhyama* is the king lying between two foes, whose position and disposition is neutral. This technical meaning (as the commentators explain it) is the same as that found in Kām. Nīt. viii. 18, and means the king whose land borders on that of an ordinary foe and one aiming at universal sovereignty (desirous to conquer). Dr. B., overlooking this part of the technical meaning, has rendered it "a king of moderate power," which is a secondary point with Medh. and K. It may mean literally, "in the middle," or stratagetically, *i.e.*, a neutral between two foes (as above), since *udāsīna* (neutral) refers not to two foes, but to all the "circuit" (*maṇḍala*, "neighbouring states," vs. 154) of the king and really lies outside the circuit. The "enemy" (*çatru*: cf. Kām. Nīt. viii. 14) is, according to Medh. and K., either one of the same family, a factitious foe, or one whose land lies next, though the Kām. Nīt. gives but two kinds, the *sahaja* and *kāryaja* (= *kṛtrima*), *i.e.*, family and unrelated foe (viii. 56).]

[2] [According to K. the eight others are (in front):—The ally, foe's ally, ally's ally, ally of foe's ally; (in the rear) the heel-catcher (cf. vs. 207), his attacked neighbour, the outlying neighbour of the heel-catcher, and of the neighbour of the heel-catcher; these, with the four of vs. 155, make twelve (cf. Kām. Nīt. viii. 17).]

[3] [Or: "and eight others are reckoned with them, and these are called The Twelve." The twelvefold realm is meant, as Uçanas says (Kām. Nīt. viii. 22). According to the same work (xi. 67), the "province of consultation" of a king with his ministers extends over twelve, sixteen, or twenty subjects," as say Manu, Bṛhaspati, and Uçanas respectively; others say, "according to occasion"—possibly this verse is referred to.]

[4] [Cf. ix. 294. Each of these things "told (*i.e.*, counted) separately" or "for each one" (of the twelve in vs. 156), makes sixty things to be attended to; adding the twelve king's themselves makes seventy-two (K.)]

[5] [Friend and foe (Medh., K.)]

159. All those he should gain by conciliation [1] and the like means, separate or together; also by valour and policy.

160. He should ever think of the six tactics of (a king), alliance, war, marching, encampments, stratagems,[2] and recourse to protection.

161. Having considered what is to be done, he should employ encampment, marching, alliance, war, stratagems, and recourse to protection.[3]

162.[4] But a king should know that alliances (are) of two kinds, (as is) also war; both marching (and encampment) also, and stratagem; and recourse to protection (is) also said to be of two kinds.

163. Alliance, connected with present or future (gain), is to be known as of two kinds: (first) when one acts[5] in conjunction, and (second) the opposite also.

164. War is said to be of two kinds: (first) when made of one's own accord, in season or out of season, on account of one's object, and (second) also (when made) on occasion of injury to a friend.[6]

165. Expeditions are said (to be) of two kinds; (first) when (the king marches) alone, some affair admitting of no delay having unexpectedly arisen;[7] and (second) when he is accompanied by an ally.

166. Encamping is said to be of two kinds; (first)

[1] "Conciliation and the like means," *i.e.*, conciliation, dissension, liberality (bribery), and force. [Cf. vs. 107.]

[2] "Stratagems," literally, dividing a hostile [? his own] army into two bodies (in order to engage the one while the other is out of position). ["Alliance" (union); "war" (separation) is its opposite (Medh.) The word *dvaidhībhāva* (stratagem) is explained in the Kām. Nit. (xi. 27) as "twofold, on his own and on his enemy's side." K. and Rāgh. take it here as on his own.]

[3] [Or, "on making alliance and on making war, let one employ encampment, or marching, division and recourse, after inspection of what is needful." The paraphrase *sandhāya ca vigṛhya ca* is Medh.'s and K.'s. *Dvaidha* seems certainly opposed to *saṁçraya* (recourse), and seems to me to be so in vs. 160. Cf. note to vs. 173 and vs. 167.]

[4] [Medh. has no note on this (late) verse, and the word "king" is in some MSS. omitted. The last pada in most MSS. repeat that of vs. 161.]

[5] Literally, "makes an expedition in conjunction (with the ally)." As the commentators say, both go together, or one goes in one direction and the other in another.]

[6] [*Mitrasya* (= friend, ally) or (*var. lec.* not preferred by Medh. and K.) *mitreṇa caiva* (Govind.), *i.e.*, war made by an ally against a distressed foe, or "when injury is done by an ally."]

[7] [*Ātyayikaṁ kāryaṁ parasya vyasano'tpattiḥ; tadā'bhiyamanīyatamo bhavati* (Medh.), *i.e.*, some affair such as a sudden attack.]

when the king is by degrees weakened by chance or by former deeds, and (second) to help an ally.

167. Stratagem is declared (to be) of two kinds by those who know the sixfold characteristics of tactics:[1] the placing (first)[2] of the army, and (second) of the king to gain (his) ends.

168. Recourse is said (to be) of two kinds: (first) when (a king is) oppressed by enemies (and takes refuge) to save (his) wealth,[3] and (second) (when he is among) friends (and takes refuge) in order to forestall (danger).[4]

169. Whenever (a king) infers a sure increase (of power) of himself in future, and at the present time (suffers) little annoyance, then let him have recourse to an alliance.

170. Whenever he thinks all the elements of the state[5] very exalted, likewise himself very mighty, then let him make war.

171. Whenever he thinks his own force pleased in disposition (and) prosperous, and (that) of the enemy the opposite, then let him march against the enemy.[6]

172. But whenever he is feeble in carriage[7] and force,[8] then he should encamp strenuously, conciliating the enemy by degrees.

173. Whenever a king considers the enemy in every respect more powerful (than himself), then, having divided his army, let him accomplish his own object.[9]

[1] [Cf. v. 160, where the six are given.]

[2] [Part of the army, being commanded by the general, is sent in one direction, and the king is posted in his fortress to defend it with another part (K.)]

[3] [Or (more literally and generally) to accomplish some good, as K. and Rāgh. say, "to guard against this present oppression by the enemy."]

[4] [*I.e.*, according to Medh. and K. (cf. vs. 174), recourse at any time, even when not oppressed, as an excuse (escape) when in fear of coming danger. Medh. notes that *vyapadeça* is another word expressing the motive of, and implying "recourse."

[5] For the five elements of a state see [vs. 157, and cf. Kām. Nit. viii. 4.] They are the minister, treasure, kingdom, fortress, and army. [The text elsewhere reckons seven (ix. 294), *i.e.*, these five *plus* king and ally; here, where the king is specially mentioned, all the others are probably meant. Cf. Yāj. i. 347.]

[6] [Cf. Kām. Nit. x. 26 ff.]

[7] [*Vāhanam* (vehicles), *i.e.*, including elephants, horses, chariots, etc.; "conciliate," by honours, gifts, etc. (Medh. and K.)]

[8] [*Bala*, *i.e.*, ministers, etc. (K.), or infantry and cattle (Medh..), or treasure (Rāgh.), or it may mean his own personal strength (Rāgh.)]

[9] "His own object," *i.e.*, distract

174. But whenever he is most accessible to the enemy's forces, let him then quickly resort to a virtuous (and) powerful prince.

175. Let him ever, with all his might, have recourse as to a Guru, to him who can effect control of (disobedient) elements (in his) state[1] and of the enemy's forces.

176. If even then he perceive injury caused by (his) taking refuge, he should, even in that position, fearlessly[2] fight a good battle alone.[3]

177. A prince skilled in polity should by all means so arrange that friends, neutrals, (and) enemies may not be his superiors.

178. Let him truly consider the future and present of all matters,[4] and the good and bad (sides) of all past (deeds).

179. He who knows the good and bad to come, who quickly decides as to the present, and who knows the result of past actions,[5] is never overpowered by enemies.

180. Let him so manage all that neither friends, neutrals, (nor) foes may prevail over him; that is polity in brief.

181. When a chief begins an expedition against the kingdom of (his) enemy, he should then march gradually against the enemy's city in this system.[6]

182. Let a king go on an expedition in the clear month Mārgaçīrsha, or about the (time of) the two months Phālguna and Caitra, according to his forces.[7]

the attention of the enemy by a part of his forces to enable himself to get into a safe position. [This, as the order shows, as well as the words (*dvidhā balaṁ kṛtvā*), proves that what has been translated "stratagem," means always this stratagem of dividing forces.]

1 "Elements (of state)," see note to vs. 170 above.

2 ["Without doubting" (K.); or "without change" (*nirvikāraḥ*), Medh.; or "without questioning" (*nirvitarkaḥ*), Rāgh.]

3 [Recourse to another is his last hope; if that causes evil results (to the other king, Rāgh.), let him fight bravely, even to the death (though *doṣa* may mean expose himself to evil).]

4 [*Kārya* = *agenda*, with present and future time, opposed to *atīta* = *acta* of the past; he should study his errors of the past, and weigh the prospects of future acts.]

5 [Cf. note to vs. 153 on *kārya-çeṣa*.]

6 [*I.e.*, according to the following directions.]

7 "In the month Mārgaçīrsha,"

183. Or even at other times, when he sees certain victory, let him set out (against the enemy), waging war, or when also (his) enemy is in trouble.[1]

184. Having made arrangement at home, and for the expedition in due form, having collected supplies[2] also, and having properly placed (his) spies;

185. Having prepared the threefold way and sixfold forces,[3] let him gradually advance by military rule to the enemy's city.

186. Let him be more (than ordinarily) watchful, both of an ally who secretly favours the enemy, and also of (a man who has) returned (to him) after going (away to the enemy),[4] for such an one is an enemy more (than ordinarily) dangerous.

i.e., when the crops are ripe and the weather is fine, or [in Phālguṇa and Caitra, *i.e.*] the spring. [The first month mentioned comes at the middle of November, the others at the middle of February and March. The stores of food to be found in the enemy's realm, the kind of army that is to march, and the distance of the journey, are all implied in the words "according to his forces." K. observes that Yāj. i. 347 gives the gist of the matter in directing the expedition to be made whenever the enemy's kingdom is supplied with grain and advantageous factors of any sort. Cf. vs. 171, and Viṣṇu, iii. 40.]

[1] [Dr. B.'s translation ("let him set out, or when also (his) enemy is defeated after fighting") I have been obliged to change somewhat. The general meaning of *yāyād vigṛhya* is "he should make a war expedition," and the participle cannot be construed with "the enemy." *Vyasana* is not "defeat" but "distress." Cf. Medh., *vigṛhy'eti yātavyam evā 'vaṣṭabhyā'hūya yāyāt*, and he defines *vyasana* as "weakened in treasury or army." Cf. also the technical *vigṛhyayānam* in Kām. Nīt. xi. 3.]

[2] ["Collected supplies" (?), or "having secured a position," *i.e.*, by winning over malcontents from the other side, he should secure a foothold in (his enemy's) kingdom (Medh., K.) The "arrangement" is one for defence (Medh.)]

[3] "The threefold way" is by level land, marshes, and through woods. [Medh., K., Rāgh.; (cf. Kām. Nīt. xviii. 2. 24.) Cf. vs. 192. "Preparing" means clearing, leveling, etc.] The "sixfold force," *i.e.* [according to K. the army, comprising elephants, horses, chariots, infantry, the general, and the workmen. Medh. gives as the opinion of "others" that the two last are "workmen and treasure." The army is prepared by furnishing it with food, medicine, etc. (K.)]

[4] [This translation is mine. Dr. B. has "let him be most intent on the adherent of (his) enemy, and on the secret friend (of his enemy), and on goers and comers also." The translation I have substituted follows Medh., K., and Rāgh., as well as the evident sense. Medh. classifies the returned deserters as of four sorts, according to the reason of both actions. Rāgh. makes all the epithets refer to one person: "an ally both secretly favouring the foe and (acting like a friend) by going away (openly but) coming (back by a secret way)." *Sa* in the next clause seems to favour this. K. takes them separately, as in the translation, and makes *sa* refer to both.]

187. He should march upon the road with the troops distributed like a staff, or a waggon, or a boar, or a Makara, or a needle, or a Garuḍa.[1]

188. And from whence he may suspect danger, to that (point) let him expand his forces; and let him ever himself be[2] in (the centre of) a body distributed like a lotus.

189. Let him place his general and commanders[3] in all parts, and whence he fears danger (there) let him arrange his force to the front.[4]

190. And let him on all sides place fit bodies of men, distinguished (by uniform),[5] clever in standing firm and in fighting, brave, unchanging.

191. Let (him) make a few fight in serried rank; at his will he may spread about many. And thus having arranged them in the needle, or also the thunderbolt form, let (him) cause (them) to fight.[6]

192. He should fight with chariots and horses on level (ground), so with boats and elephants on marshes; on

[1] Like the altars in the sacrifices with *cayana*, bodies of troops were arranged in forms of animals, etc. The only representations I know of such figures are to be found in Raffles's "Java." In my "Catalogue" I gave a plan of such an altar, and Professor Thibaut has since given others. [Like a "staff" is in straight columns; the "waggon" has a sharp van with a broad rear; the "boar" has a sharp van and rear with a broad centre; the "makara" (sea-beast) is the opposite of this, having a narrow centre with a broad van and rear; the "needle" is a long, thin, sharp-pointed row; the "garuḍa" (mythological bird) has a very wide centre, but is otherwise like the "boar" (K.) The commentators give also the disposition of the forces. Cf. Kām. Nīt. xix. 40; and the plans, ib. p. 130 (ed. Cal. Bib. Ind.)

[2] [*I.e.*, takes his position (*niviçeta* = *niveçaṁ kuryāt*, Rāgh.) The army is spread out in a circle about the king in the middle (Rāgh.) Medh. has a *var. lec. āçaṅket tu bhayaṁ yasmāt.* Another interpretation is "let him lead the attack himself with an encompassing army."]

[3] [According to K. the commander has a command equal to ten generals.]

[4] [Literally, "put that place ahead."]

[5] [Distinguished by their musical instruments, banners, etc., according to the commentators. These outposts (*gulma*) serve to warn of danger. They are posted at a distance of four thousand rods (*daṇḍa*) from the main force (Medh.) (The rod is about four cubits in length.)]

[6] [If he has but a few soldiers, they should be made into one compact body; if he has many, he should mass them, or distribute them about as he chooses. The needle array has been explained in vs. 187. The thunderbolt array is where the army is drawn up in three divisions (K., Rāgh.) by separating the two flanks (Medh.)]

(ground) covered by trees (and) shrubs, with bows; on cleared (ground), with weapons, swords and shields.[1]

193. Let him cause Kurukṣetras, Matsyas, Pañcālas, and natives of Çūrasena, and tall and light men also, to fight in the van.[2]

194. Having arranged (his) forces, let (him) cheer them up, and let him properly try[3] them; and he should find out their deeds when they are fighting the enemy.

195. Having obstructed the enemy, let him encamp and harass his kingdom, and ever spoil his fodder, food, water, (and) fuel.

196. Let (him) also burst tanks, enclosures, as well as trenches; let (him) assail him, and also terrify (him) by night.

197. Let him bring over (those that) can be seduced, and let (him) be aware of what is done (by the enemy), and let him fight, desirous of victory, and without fear, when a fortunate (time) occurs.

198. He should endeavour to overcome (his) enemy by alliances, bribery, and treachery[4]—all together or separate—never by battle.

199. For since victory or defeat in battle is seen to be not permanent between (two forces) fighting, therefore he should avoid a battle.

200. But in case the three expedients already mentioned do not suit, let (him), prepared,[5] fight, so that he may conquer (his) enemies.

201. Having conquered, let (him) worship the gods and righteous Brahmans also; let him grant immunities, and proclaim indemnities.[6]

[1] ["As weapons," or "with swords, shields, and (spears, and other such) weapons" (Medh., K.)]

[2] [Cf. ii. 19. All places in Northern India along the Ganges, from Delhi down. Most MSS. have Kauruksetra and Pañcāla, but not Mātsya.]

[3] [Or "inspect."]

[4] [Or "by conciliation, bribery, and dissension," as in v. 107, note, which seems right here also.]

[5] [*Saṁyattaḥ*, (°*pannaḥ*), or *saṁyuktaḥ* (Medh.) Some K. MSS. and Dr. B.'s MS. of Medh. have *parikṣaye* for *asambhave*.]

[6] "The gods," according to K. the gods of the conquered country. "Immunities," according to Rāgh. gifts, such as clothes and ornaments.

202. But having completely known the intention of all of them, let (him) station there (as ruler) one of that race, and give precise directions.[1]

203. And let (him) make authoritative their laws as declared, and let (him) honour him (the new king) with jewels, together with the chief persons (in the country).

204. The taking of desired things produces disaffection, but liberality (is) productive of loyalty; (either) is proper if used in season.

205. All this action depends on divine or human design); but of the two, the divine is unthinkable; in human (affairs), action is known.[2]

206.[3] Or he may act with (the conquered), having carefully made an alliance (with him), (and) considering an ally, gold, territory, (as) the triple fruit (of a victory).

207. And, considering (his) heel-catcher,[4] as well as the attacker (of that heel-catcher) in the adjacent region, let him reap the fruit of the expedition from friend and from foe.

208. A (conquering) sovereign prospers not so much by gain of gold (and) territory as by gaining a firm ally, though (now) insignificant, (yet) capable in the future.

209. An insignificant ally, who knows duty and is grateful and contented,[5] devoted and firm in (his) endeavours, is preferred.

[1] [Literally, "stipulations."] That this policy was actually carried out is amply proved by the South Indian inscriptions.

[2] [Cf. xi. 47 note. Every act on earth is established by fate, (divine) or human, (*i.e.*, earthly action); fate cannot be known, but the deed produced by human action is apparent to all. Moral: do not trust to fate, but to your own ability (K.) The divine power, fate, is regarded as the after-working power of deeds done in a former life. Cf. Yāj. i. 348.]

[3] Medh. appears to omit this verse as well as verses 207 to 210. Kullūka has them all, as well as Rāgh. [Medh.'s discussion of vs. 205 ends with the following verse: "A human act which is produced through great effort by one who is united to fate's law causes success."]

[4] [The "heel-catcher" as well as "attacker" are technical names (not elsewhere in Manu, and probably late) for the king who is in the rear and threatens attack, and the one next beyond him and adverse to him. I have substituted the literal meaning "heel-catcher" for Dr. B.'s erroneous "supporter." Cf. note to vs. 156.]

[5] [K. and Rāgh. take *prakṛt* in the sense of ministers, etc., "one whose realm is contented."]

210. The wise declare an enemy who is discerning, of (high) race, brave, clever, liberal also, grateful and firm, (to be) a difficulty.

211. Nobility, knowledge of men, heroism, mercifulness, and constant magnanimity[1] are the fruit of virtues of a neutral.

212. A king should, to save himself, unhesitating, abandon even a prosperous land, furnishing grain, and plentiful in cattle.

213. Let (him) preserve wealth against misfortune; let (him) preserve his wife even by wealth; let (him) ever[2] save himself, even at the cost of wife (and) wealth.

214. Let a wise (king), seeing all calamities arisen together in excess, apply, together or separate, all means.

215. The doer,[3] what is to be done, and the means, as a whole—keeping in mind those three, let him strive for the accomplishment of the business.[4]

216. Let the king, after he has thus considered all this (business) together with the ministers, taken exercise and bathed, enter at noon the harem to eat.

217. There let (him) eat food well tested by faithful attendants, (who are skilled in times[5] (and) not to be seduced, (which has been enchanted) by *mantras* which counteract poison.

218. Let (him) use all his (useful) articles with drugs[6] destructive of poison; and let him, ever attentive, wear gems destructive of poison.[7]

219. Let attentive women, who have been tested, and

[1] ["Or generosity" (K.) Medh. and Govind. erroneously interpret as "subtilty" (K., Rāgh.) "nobility," *āryatā*.

[2] "Ever," *i.e.*, *satatam* (K.); Medh. reads *sarvato* = in every way. [So Dr. B.'s MSS., but other MSS. are like K.]

[3] [*I.e.*, himself.]

[4] [*Prayetā 'rthasiddhaye* (K.), or (Medh. *var. lec.*) *sādhayet kāryam ātmanaḥ.*]

[5] [Meal-times (K.)]

[6] "Drugs." Medh. reads *udakaiḥ* or waters; "gems destructive of poison." Medh. mentions the *garuḍodgīrṇa* or emerald, and *nāgaramaṇi* or snakestone (?).

[7] "Use," *yojayet* = *çodhayet* (Medh.), "wash with waters."

[8] "Tested," *i.e.*, to prevent their concealing weapons about them. The *viṣakanyā* also, or poisoned maiden, was a favourite way of destroying enemies in India. [Cf. note to vs. 153.]

pure in dress and ornaments, attend him with fans, water and perfumes.

220. Thus let (him) take care of vehicles, couches, seats, food;[1] of baths, anointing also, and all ornaments.

221. Having eaten, he should also sport with women in the harem; having sported, he should, according to the time, again think of business.

222. Dressed, he should again inspect the armed forces, and all vehicles,[2] weapons, ornaments.

223. Having performed the evening devotion, bearing arms, let (him) hear in the inner apartment what has been done by the reporters of secrets and also the spies.

224. Having dismissed these people, having gone to another private apartment, surrounded by women, let (him) again enter the harem for food.

225. Having there again eaten something, cheered by instrumental music,[3] let him go to sleep in due time, and rise with fatigue gone.

226. A healthy king should pursue this system; unwell, he may depute all that to (his) dependents.

END OF THE SEVENTH LECTURE.

[1] [Medh. has *āsanādiṣu* (seats, etc.) for *āsanāçane*, as food has already been mentioned. "Bath" means in bathing the head (Medh.)]

[2] "Vehicles," elephants, horses, etc. (K.)

[3] [Soft sounds of (*tūrya*, *i.e.*) flute, lute, drum, or horn (Medh.) The Mbhā. distinguishes the last from the *tūrya*. These last rules are found in much the same form in Yāj. i. 324–330.]

LECTURE VIII.[1]

CIVIL AND CRIMINAL LAW.

1. Now a king, desirous to inspect suits, should, subdued, enter the assembly with Brahmans and ministers who know *mantras*.[2]

2. There, seated or standing, having stretched forth his right hand, with humble vesture (and) ornaments, he should inspect the affairs of the parties.[3]

3. Day by day (he should judge) separately (cases) under the eighteen titles[4] by reasons (drawn) from local usage and the treatises.[5]

4. Of these (titles), the first is non-payment of debt; (next) pledges; sale without ownership; partnership and non-delivery of what has been given;

5. Also non-payment of wages; breach of contract;[6] revocation of sale (and) purchase; disputes between master (and) servant;

6. Also the law of disputes (about) boundaries; assault (and) slander; theft; violence; also adultery;[7]

[1] The eighth and ninth chapters of the text correspond to all Nārada and the second book of Yājñavalkya. [Cf. also Viṣṇu, iv.-xviii.; Āp. ii., kh. 13, 14, 26-29; Gaut. x. xii. xiii. xviii. xxviii.; Vas. xv. xviii.; Baudh. ii. 3, par.]

[2] Who know *mantras*, *i.e.*, the Vedas. [This may mean ministers, advisers, who know how to advise.]

[3] Kings used in the fourth century B.C. to be much occupied with criminal, but little with civil law (Megasthenes, Fr. xxvii., ed. Schwanbeck); but the strict decorum here directed was not observed.

[4] "Eighteen titles." This is not a part of the original system of law; it appears only in the Smṛtis, and its later development is easily traced. Nārada (i. 17-20) has the same number [but these are again subdivided]. The later books multiply these divisions, and thus afford signs of progress toward a more rational classification.

[5] *Çāstras*, *i.e.*, a body of teaching on a subject, whether ascribed to divine or human origin.

[6] [Perhaps better, with Nārada, breaking the customary ordinances that govern a guild, or family community, corporation, etc.]

[7] [So K. It may mean improper connection with women in general.]

7. The law between man and woman; partition; dicing; and games with animals.[1] These eighteen topics occur in the settlements of suits here.[2]

8. Let (the king), relying on eternal law, determine the affairs of men, who mostly dispute on these topics.[3]

9. But when the king does not himself inspect (such) affairs, then he should appoint a learned Brahman for the inspection of affairs.

10. Let him, accompanied by three[4] members of the court, view his affairs,[5] having entered the high court, (and) seated or standing.

11. In what country three Brahmans learned in the Veda and the king's learned deputy[6] sit, (the wise) have said that assembly (is) of Brahmā.

12. Now when Dharma pierced by non-Dharma has recourse to (that) court, and they do not extract the arrow from him, there the judges are pierced (also).

13. One should not enter the court[7] or (what is) correct must be spoken; a man who speaks not, or speaks perversely,[8] is sinful.

14. When Dharma is slain by non-Dharma, and truth by the untruth of the parties there, the members of the court (are) slain.

15. Dharma slain verily slays, (but) Dharma protected protects; therefore Dharma is not to be injured. May not injured Dharma slay us!

16. For lord Dharma is a bull (*vṛṣan*), and the gods take

[1] [Cf. ix. 223. Games with animals means betting on them in fights.]

[2] This division is very confused and unsatisfactory; the confusion is partly owing to the theocratic nature of the work. J. Mill remarks, "It is not easy to conceive a more crude and defective attempt at the classification of laws than what is here presented (History of India, book ii. ch. 4). All his remarks on this subject are still worthy of attention.

[3] [Nand. omits this verse. Cf. Viṣṇu, iii. 72–74.]

[4] [Medh. says three is stated to exclude a smaller number.]

[5] "His affairs." The king's affairs, as he should decide the suits.

[6] [Either *adhikṛta* or *prakṛta*. Medh. reads the latter, but knows the former. The verse is omitted by Nand.]

[7] [*Sabhā-praveṣṭavyā* (Medh., Rāgh., and Nand.)]

[8] [Contrary to what has been seen or heard (Rāgh.)]

one who injures him (to be) an outcast (*vṛṣala*).[1] One should not then cause dharma to fail.

17. Dharma (virtue) is the one only friend who even in death follows after (us), for all else goes to destruction along with the body.[2]

18. One-fourth of the non-Dharma (wrong) comes upon the doer,[3] one-fourth comes upon the witness, one-fourth comes upon all the members of the court, one-fourth comes upon the king.

19. But the king is sinless, and the members of the court are free (from sin), and the sin comes upon the doer (alone), where one worthy of censure is censured.

20. He who can claim to be a Brahman merely on account of his birth, or he who only calls himself a Brahman, may be, if desired, the declarer of law for the king, but a Çūdra never.[5]

21. If a king looks on while a Çūdra gives a judicial decision, his realm sinks into misfortune, like a cow in a quagmire.[6]

22. A realm which consists chiefly of Çūdras and is overrun by unbelievers[7] and destitute of twice-born men is soon totally destroyed, oppressed by famine and disease.

23. After the king has seated himself on the seat of justice and paid reverence to the guardians of the world, let him, (being properly) clothed and with strict attention, undertake the inspection of affairs.

24. Considering what is useful or not useful, and what

[1] This is a fanciful explanation of *vṛṣala*, as one who does *alam* (or injures) *vṛṣa*. [Cf. i. 81, 82. In the Mbhā. we find these figures united, and *dharma* is a four-footed bull. In Nand. *kurute* (*layam* in text !); *'lam* (Comm.) is paraphrased "prevent" or "hinder."]

[2] Quoted Hit. i. 59. *N.B.*—For the rest of the translation and for all further notes the editor alone is responsible, and [ ] are not used.

[3] "Doer" is the one who, either as plaintiff or defendant, has caused the decision to be wrong (Medh., K.)

[4] Or the Brahman appointed by v. 9 (Medh.) Medh. reads *arhati*, "deserves."

[5] The commentators all say that the two middle castes, since they are not forbidden to do so, may declare law. The later law so modified the stricture on the Çūdra that, if he were appointed, his judicial decision was regarded as valid. The "Brahman by birth" is one by whom the proper ceremonies have not been performed.

[6] Nand. transposes the position of Çūdras and *rājño*.

[7] Who say there "is not," *i.e.*, according to Medh. and K., deniers of another world.

is in itself right or wrong, let him inspect all the affairs of the parties in the order of the castes.[1]

25. Through the outward signs (manifested in) voice, colour, gesture, appearance, eye and movements, let him clearly ascertain the true inward nature of men.[2]

26. Through (his) appearance, gestures, gait, movements and speech, and by the contortions of (his) eye and mouth, the mind in its inner action is comprehended.

27. An inheritance received by a child the king should have guarded till such time as (the owner's) course of study is completed, or till he has passed beyond the age of childhood.[3]

28. Like protection (of property) should be (given) in (the case of) barren women, or such as have no sons,[4] or have no families, or (who are) true to the conjugal vow,[5] or (are) widows or ill.[6]

29. But if while these women are alive their relatives should take away this (property), let a just king punish those (relatives) with the punishment awarded to thieves.[7]

30. The king should cause to be kept for three years (all) property of which the owner is unknown. The owner may have it inside the period of three years, (but) at the end of that time the king may take it.[8]

31. One who says, "This belongs to me," must be strictly examined according to rule; and on his declaring correctly the shape, number, and other[9] (characteristics of the lost goods), he ought as owner to receive those goods.

[1] Beginning with the Brahman (K., Rāgh., and Nand.)

[2] "Gestures" are involuntary motions; "movements" are spasmodic clenchings of hand or feet (Medh., K.)

[3] Nārada says the age of childhood is up to the sixteenth year (K.) This clause applies to the lower castes, who do not study (Medh., Rāgh.) The completion of his studies may last till he is a man grown.

[4] These two classes refer to women put aside by their husbands because of their barrenness (Medh., K.), as allowed in ix. 81.

[5] "True to conjugal vow," *i.e.*, when the husband is away on a journey (not as widows)—(Nand.)

[6] This applies to these women only when they have no relatives to take care of their property for them (Medh.) Cf. Vas. xix. 37; Gaut. x. 48; Viṣṇu, iii. 65.

[7] Not open robbery, but by plausible pretences (Medh., K.) Medh. refers to viii. 334 (cf. viii. 193) for punishment.

[8] See note to vs. 34. Cf. Yāj. ii. 33.

[9] "The other characteristics," *i.e.*, place and time of loss (Medh., K.) Nand. reads *saṁvedya*.

32. If he does not declare in accordance with the facts the place and time (of his losing),[1] the colour, shape, and dimensions of his lost (goods), he deserves a fine equal in amount to the value of these (goods lost).

33.[2] Property which has been lost and found again should be placed under the guard of persons thereto commissioned; thieves whom he catches about it he should have trampled on by an elephant.[3]

34. The king may take from an article (thus) lost and found again the sixth part (of its worth), or the tenth, or only one-twelfth,[4] being mindful of the law of good men.

35. If a man say with truth in regard to a treasure-trove,[5] "This is mine," let the king take a sixth, or only a twelfth part of it.[6]

36. But on his speaking an untruth in regard to it, he should be fined an eighth part of his property, or (at least a sum equal to) a rather small part of the treasure, after an estimate has been put upon it.

37. But a wise Brahman, on finding a treasure which has been previously hidden away, may take possession of it even without leaving any (for the king), since he is lord of all.[7]

38. Now if a king discover any ancient treasure hid in

[1] *Avedayan pranaṣṭasya deçakālau ca . . . varṇarūpaṁ* (Nand.); *deçakālau* (Rāgh.)

[2] In K. vss. 33 and 34 have been transposed in position; the text follows the order of Medh.

[3] If he catch thieves stealing it (Medh.); when the property has been found by king's servants (K.) Govind. restricts the sum.

[4] In the first year one-twelfth, in the second one-tenth, in the third one-sixth (Rāgh.) So Medh.; or, the difference depends on the injury it has received. In this and vss. 35, 36, K. and N. make the difference depend on the merit or demerit of the owner. M. supports this view in vss. 35, 36. So in May. p. 75, the rule in vs. 30 is made to apply only to priests, and the sum here deducted is according to the years, *after* the first one-twelfth, etc.; but if the owner is known, even after three years, it must be returned to him. Cf. Gaut. x. 36 ff.

[5] Treasure-trove (*nidhi*) is what has been found hid in a hole in the ground (Medh.)

[6] The rest he must give to the owner (K.) The May. (p. 76), reads *ca* (and a twelfth) "for the finder of the treasure." Cf. Viṣṇu, iii. 63–64.

[7] Medh., G., and N. regard the treasure as one hid by his ancestors, that is, his any way by inheritance; but K. quotes Yāj. ii. 35, M. I. 100, and again Yāj. ii. 34, to show that this is not so; also, declaring this view opposed to ancient usage, he remarks that he does not care for what Medh. and Govind. say.

the ground, after giving half of it to the twice-born (Brahmans), he should store up[1] the other half in his treasury.

39. For of old treasures and metals in the earth the king, because he guards (his people), should have a half share,[2] since he is the lord of the earth.

40. Property seized by thieves must be restored by the king to (men of) all castes;[3] if the king takes possession of it, he incurs the sin of stealing.[4]

41. (A king) knowing what is right (*dharma*)[5] should cause his own law (*dharma*) to be established, after making careful inspection of the laws (*dharma*) of the different castes[6] and country-folks, and of the laws of the (different) guilds,[7] and of the laws of the (different) families.[8]

42. Men who attend to their own occupations, performing each his own occupation, become dear to the world even though they are far away.[9]

43. The king should not himself instigate a law-suit,[10] neither should his representative;[11] nor should he at any time set at naught a suit begun by some one else.[12]

[1] Nand. reads *vinikṣipet*; Rāgh., *niveçayet*. Cf. Gaut. x. 43 ff.; Viṣṇu, iii. 56 ff.

[2] That is, if not taken by a wise Brahman (K.) Rāgh. and Nand. read *hi* for *tu*, which explains vs. 38, and gives more favour to K.'s "he is also lord," etc.

[3] After taking it from the thieves (Medh., K.)

[4] This may mean he receives the sin of that thief on his own soul. If it is impossible to return it to the owner, Medh. says the amount of the theft should be paid out of the king's treasury; so N., *koçād vā*; so Gaut., Viṣṇu, *loc. cit.*; cf. Kṛṣṇa-dvaipāyana in May. p. 76.

[5] Nand. reads *çāçvatān* for *dharmavit*.

[6] Or tribes, subdivisions of castes. Cf. Bühler's note to Vas. i. 17.

[7] Of merchants, etc. (Medh., K., and Rāgh.)

[8] The "country-folks" are the inhabitants of any one district (Medh., K., and Rāgh.) That is, if these laws are not repugnant to the law given by tradition (Medh., K.) The laws which the castes and families already have are meant; cf. viii. 203. the principal verb may mean "these (laws of) castes, etc.), he should establish *as his* law." Some MSS. read "he should have protected" (*paripālayet*, Rāgh., or *pratipālayet*); cf. vs. 46.

[9] From relatives (K.); "world," *i.e.*, everybody (Medh.) This verse seems to me to refer to the king, introducing vs. 43; the *dūre* would then refer to distance by exalted station. Nand. reads: *loke'smin, sve sve dharme vyavasthitāḥ*.

[10] Lawsuit, affair, as in vs. 2. Medh. and K. explain the instigation as one proceeding from greed.

[11] Literally, his man, *i.e.*, one commissioned by him (K.); his representative in court (Medh).

[12] The latter part of this verse, couched in not technical language, may, as Medh. remarks, mean simply that the king should not take possession of another man's property, as *artha* (*grastārtham* (*sic.*) Medh.) may mean "goods" or "suit." K.

44. As the hunter directs (his) step by the blood-drops of the beast, so should the king direct the course of justice by means of inference.[1]

45. Abiding by the rule of legal suits, let (the king) examine the truth, the thing, himself, the witnesses, the place, the time, and the form.[2]

46. Whatever may be practised by good and virtuous men of the twice-born castes, let (the king) cause that to be ordained (as law), if it does not conflict with (the laws of) districts, families, (and) castes.[3]

47. When the king is besought by a creditor for the recovery of his property from a debtor, he should cause the property to be given to the creditor by the debtor, (after it has been) proved (by the former to be his).

48. A creditor may make a debtor pay after coercing (him) by any means whereby he can obtain his property.

49. By negotiation of friends,[4] by legal action,[5] by trickery, and by received fashion,[6] and, fifth, by force may a creditor get back the money he has lent.

quotes similar language from Kātyāyana, and the alternative meaning of *grazed* is given by Rāgh.

[1] This (*anumāna*, "inference") is one of the three means of arriving at a conclusion; cf. xii. 104. It may be based on what is seen or what is inferred (Medh.) The verse is probably proverbial; cf. Mbhā. xii. 132, 21. K. makes *nayati* mean "gets," and takes *padam* with *mṛgasya*.

[2] The *thing* (or property) is the object of the controversy, which may be too unimportant to permit a suit; the *form* may, according to different commentators, refer to the nature of the suit or of the object contested, or may refer to the appearance of the parties. "Place, form, and time" is the accepted reading, but the other is Medh.'s (*deçaṁ kālaṁ ca rūpaṁ ca*), and K.'s comment seems also to support this (*deçaṁ kālaṁ ca . . . svarūpaṁ*). It is further supported by Rāgh. and Nand.

[3] Medh. quotes an older (?) commentator (*anyas tv āha*), who affirms that a sacrifice customary in the north, but not in the south, east, and west, must (according to this verse) be ordained in these districts, since the northern custom agrees with tradition and the Veda. Medh. does not agree with this. K. refers the verse merely to settling a lawsuit.

[4] Literally, by right or justice (*dharma*); so explained by Bṛh. in K. (where *dharma* changes to *sāman*, and in Kāty. *sāntva* is used as equivalent); by some regarded as like the fourth means, consisting of persistent persecution of the debtor by dogging him about.

[5] *Vyavahāra* is, according to Medh., the proceeds of compulsory labour (cf. vs. 177), while K. incorrectly understands (the usual sense) a mere suit at law. (Nand. says *vyavahārapradarçanena*.)

[6] Rāgh. and Nand. read *vā* for *ca*. The "received fashion" is generally explained as an allusion to what is now known as performing

50. A creditor who recovers his goods himself from his debtor is not to be prevented [1] by the king from recovering his own property.

51. When (a debtor) denies (a debt) and it is proved by (some) means [2] to have been contracted, the king should cause the money to be paid to the creditor, and have (the debtor pay) a small fine [3] in proportion to (his) ability (to pay it).

52. When the debtor still denies, after being admonished to pay in court, the one who brings the suit should point out the place (where the debt was contracted), or exhibit some other proof.[4]

53. He who points out an impossible place,[5] and he

dharna (cf. Maine, Early Inst., p. 297); the word used, *ācarita*, would thus correspond to *ācāra*, the usual practice. K. and Rāgh. support the "door-sitting" theory, relying on Bṛh. (cf. the later additions of other law-books in Jolly's Ind. Schuldrecht, § 7). The word itself has no such meaning as that given it by Mandlik (Mayūkha, ii. 109), "confinement," and it is to be noticed the door-sitting (*drāropaveçanam*) is only half the process, the first being the theft of the debtor's "wife, son, or cattle." I doubt if Ap. i. 19, 1, refers to this practice at all. In Mit. the word is translated "fasting," referring to the same thing. Nand. says that of these five the first is first to be tried, then the others in order. The difference between the *vyavahāra* and *karma* of vs. 177 is that the latter is compulsory labour confined to the three lowest castes, while the former appears to be a legal attempt to compel (any man) to engage in trade, etc., for the benefit of the creditor, but not to do menial work in his house. Cf. Jolly (Ind. Schuldr.), § 7.

[1] So K. Or, "since he is only recovering his own property, he is not to be put on trial." Cf. with this vs. 176.

[2] The "means" are the proofs necessary to establish a statement (the MSS. vary between *karaṇam* and *kāraṇam;* in vs. 52 Medh. has both). These are naturally said by the commentators to be documents in writing. This is plainly not the case, however, in vs. 52, and neither here nor in *ācarita* of vs. 49 is it necessary to assume for a vague term the precise sense which a perhaps later usage has fastened upon it. Writing is mentioned but once in the text, and then probably interpolated. Cf. notes to vss. 154 and 168. In vs. 57 *kāraṇa* is not writing, and vs. 200 shows plainly that it has no such meaning. Of all places, this last would be the one for "documents" to be mentioned; instead of this, we find the word said to mean document used simply as the predicate subject—"the (*kāraṇam*) *proof* (of ownership in anything) is acquisition," where, if writing were used, we should expect to have the word for "document" used quite otherwise.

[3] The small fine is said by the commentators, in accordance with vs. 139, to be 10 per cent.

[4] *Karaṇaṁ* (*kāraṇam*) *va samuddiçet* is Medh.'s reading; K. is as translated; Nand. follows Medh. The place (*deça*) of Medh. is preferable to K.'s (*deçyam*) witness (K. and Rāgh.) Cf. the following verse.

[5] *Adeçam* (Medh.) Nand. in vv. 52 and 53 has also *deçam* and *adeçam;* in Rāgh. (*deçyam* and) *adeçayam* . . . *cpahnavec ca.*

who denies (it) after indicating (it), and he who does not perceive that (his) earlier and subsequent statements are discordant;[1]

54. He who declares what it is necessary to declare, and then retreats again (from his statement); and[2] he who, on being questioned in regard to a duly acknowledged statement, does not uphold it;

55. He who converses with the witnesses in a place where he ought not to talk;[3] he who is not willing (to reply to) a question addressed him, and he who even runs away;

56. He who does not speak when (the judge) says "Speak," or does not prove what he has said; he who does not know (what comes) first and (what comes) last,[4]—these all lose their suits.

57. If a man says, "I have witnesses," but does not exhibit them when told to exhibit them, the judge[5] should declare that he has lost his suit by the (same) means.[6]

58. If he who brings a suit does not speak, he must, in accordance with justice, be corporally punished or fined; if (his opponent) does not respond within three half months, he justly loses his case.[7]

59. As large a sum as a man (falsely) denies or falsely

[1] The *var. lec.* found in Nand., *āhitān*, seems a mere error.

[2] Or, "in regard to a matter which has been already duly discovered by spies" (B. R.), which seems to be the meaning of Nand., though the text is corrupt. The latter's interpretation of (*a*) seems also to be strange: (*apadeçyam*) *avaktavyam uktvā tat sādhane yaḥ punar . . . upasarati* (*upa-dhāvati*).

[3] Nand. reads *asaṁbhāvye*, "in an improper place," which may be an allowable *var. lec.*, as he has also *saṁbhāvite* (*sic*) for *saṁbhāṣate*, which would give the meaning, "if he meets (them) in a place where he ought not to meet (them)," *i.e.*, as he explains, "in a secret place."

[4] That is, he who does not know what his proofs are, or how they are to be disposed (K.), or what he has said first and last (Nand.; so N.)

[5] So the commentators, though the epithet (*dharmastha*) may be a mere epithet of the king, who is, in reality, generally the judge.

[6] "By reason of the proofs aforementioned" (Medh., K.) The other reading for *sākṣiṇaḥ santi me*, quoted by K. and Rāgh., is found in Medh. (in Dr. B.'s MS. in inverted order). Nand. also has *santi jñātāra ity uktvā*, omitting the objectionable *me ity* as dissyllable. For *kāraṇaṁ* Nand. reads *hetunā 'nena* (on this ground), "because he does not exhibit the witness."

[7] Literally, "he is conquered." Medh. omits vss. 59-61.

claims (as a debt), twice this amount these two men should be fined by the king, (since they are) ignorant of the right.

60. Now if a man on being questioned denies (a debt) when he has been compelled to appear (in court) by him who wants the property, he must be convicted by at least three witnesses in presence of the king and the Brahmans.[1]

61. What sort of persons in cases at law may be made witnesses by the creditors I will now explain, and also how the truth is to be declared by these (witnesses).

62. Householders, men with sons, men of (ancient) stock,[2] whether of the Kṣatriya, Vaiçya, or Çūdra caste, when called upon by the creditor, may bear witness (in court); not, however, any one at random, except in case of necessity.[3]

63. Worthy persons of all the castes may be made witnesses in cases[4] (at court), those conversant with all (kinds of) duty and free from covetousness; but one should avoid (witnesses) of an opposite nature.

64. Neither persons (interested) in the trial, nor friends,[5] nor companions,[6] nor enemies, nor (such as) have had sins (formerly) exposed,[7] nor those distressed by illness, nor those (who are) blameworthy[8] should be allowed to serve (as witnesses).

65. The king must not be made to serve as witness, nor a workman nor an actor,[9] nor a learned (Brahman), nor an

[1] K. refers this to the king's representative as alternative. "Either the king or the Brahman appointed as judge," as the word may be singular or plural.

[2] K. and Rāgh. explain this as men born in that part of the country; Nand. as men who from family or guild are important.

[3] Cf. vs. 72, which, according to the Comm., is here meant. It may mean where no other witnesses can be obtained, as in vs. 70.

[4] Nand. reads *sākṣyeṣu sākṣiṇaḥ*. The list in vss. 63–67 is in Kāty. used to restrict sureties.

[5] So K. The word is the same as the first general division in vs. 63.

[6] By Medh. explained as sureties; by K., G., and N. as servants.

[7] Detected in perjury (Medh., K., and Rāgh.), or in other sins (Medh. and Nand.) Cf. Viṣṇu viii.; Gaut. xiii.

[8] Capital offenders (K.)

[9] So Medh. and K., or, in a restricted sense, a dancer; literally a "man of bad habits." Nand. explains only as singer, *gāyaka*. A

ascetic, nor one (who has) shaken off all connection with the world;[1]

66. Nor a slave,[2] nor a notorious man, nor a Dasyu,[3] nor one who does what he ought not, nor an old man, nor a child, nor one man (alone), nor a man of the lowest (classes), nor a man defective in the organs of sense;

67. Nor a man in distress, nor one who is drunk, nor a crazy man, nor one oppressed by hunger and thirst, nor one distressed by weariness, nor one distressed by lust, nor an angry man, nor a thief.

68. For women, women should serve as witnesses; for twice-born men, twice-born men of like sort; for Çūdras, good Çūdras; and for those of lowest (birth) those of lowest birth.[4]

69. But in a case (where the crime has been committed) in the interior of a house, or in a forest, or where death has (in consequence) ensued,[5] any one who has been present may bear witness for the disputing parties.

70. (Testimony) may be given, when (other witnesses) are not forthcoming, even by a woman, a child, or an old man; or by a pupil, a relative, a slave, or a servant.[6]

very different sense is, however, given to the word by other commentators. Cf. Nil. to Mbhā. xiii. 90, 11 (where the *kuçilava*, is one who practises a trade that deprives him of the right of *çrāddha*), who gives the derivation explained above in note to iii. 155, and renders "clodcutter."

[1] Instead of ascetic, K. understands the Brahmanic student; the other commentators seem right in taking *liṅgastha* as ascetic (cf. *Na liṅgam dharma - kāraṇam*, vi. 66). So that three grades of Brahmans in ascending scale are represented—the scholar, hermit, and the one who has passed beyond the needs of asceticism and has reached complete subjugation of the senses. Nand. paraphrases *liṅgastha* by *sannyāsi*, and Rāgh. says that as the latter is implied in the former, he will not translate *vinirgata* as some do by *sannyāsi*, but by "sundered from the household."

[2] So K. and Medh., or a son, student, etc., dependent on the teacher (Medh.) Nand. quotes K. as the opinion of "some," but does not give the opinion of the "others" mentioned by Medh.

[3] *Dasyu*, a non-Aryan, a barbarian; in general, a robber, murderer, cruel man, etc. (Medh., K.), or simply a servant (Medh., G.); casteless (Nand.) The meaning varies between a barbarian and a barbarous person; it seldom requires the late modification of meaning as "servant."

[4] Like in caste or in other respects. Medh. gives the more general similarity, such as like in caste, study, habitation, etc. K., G., N., and Nand. limit it to caste equality.

[5] Rāgh. and Nand. MSS. have *çarīrasyai'va* for *'api*.

[6] Like the cases in the last verse (K.)

71. But one should know that the statement of children, old men, and diseased (persons), as also that of weak-minded (persons), is not to be relied upon, (since they often)speak falsely while giving testimony.[1]

72. In all cases of violence,[2] theft, (illegal) intercourse (with women), and injury by word or by deed, one need not examine the witnesses very carefully.[3]

73. In a case where the testimony is divided, the king should accept the greater number (of witnesses); where (the number of witnesses) is the same, those who have qualities superior (to the others); where those having (good) qualities are (equally) divided, those of the twice-born (who are) most exalted.[4]

74. Testimony based on seeing as an eyewitness, or on hearing, is to be received; and a witness who speaks the truth on such an occasion is deprived neither of (the reward of) virtue nor of (his) goods.[5]

75. A witness who in an assembly of honourable men[6] declares anything contrary to what he has seen or heard goes headlong to hell, and, after passing (this), is (still) deprived of heaven.[7]

76. When any one, (although) not held (as a witness), has seen or heard anything, and is questioned about it, he should declare it just as (it was) seen, just as (it was) heard.[8]

[1] A totally different meaning in Nand.: "Even when speaking truth, regard their testimony as untrue, and not accept it from the mere statement;" doubtless an error.

[2] Such as house-burning and the like (K.)

[3] Examine either into their mental condition or inquire whether they would naturally be excluded by their social status. The verb is the same as that used in the "inspection" before inviting to a *çrāddha*.

[4] The commentators are divided as to whether this means simply "the Brahmans," or those members of the twice-born castes who are in general most attentive to their duties. The earlier commentators Medh., G., (and Nand.), hold the former, K. the latter. K. quotes G., but anticipates by a contradictory quotation from Bṛhaspati. Rāgh. unites the two by defining as "priests of conspicuously good qualities."

[5] Nand. omits this verse.

[6] The "assembly" means here the court, and the sentence may mean "a court of the Aryans."

[7] *Pretya*, usually meaning gone forth from (life), *i.e.*, "after death," seems here to refer to passing through hell; even then, as Medh. remarks, he does not reach heaven.

[8] *Vikṣeta* is the reading of Rāgh. and Nand.

77. Now one man (alone) may be a witness, (if) free from covetousness; but not (even) several women, although (they may be) pure, on account of the lack of reliableness[1] of woman's mind; and also other men who are involved in sins (may not be witnesses).

78. Only what (the witnesses) declare of their own accord is to be accepted as having bearing on the case; if, however, they declare anything other (than this[2]), that does not affect the consideration of justice.

79. When the witnesses are collected together in the court in the presence of the plaintiff and defendant, the judge[3] should call upon them to speak, kindly addressing (them) in the following manner:

80. Whatever you know has been done in this affair by one or the other of these two parties, declare it all in accordance with the truth, as it is here your (duty) to give testimony.[4]

81. A witness who in testifying speaks the truth reaches (hereafter) the worlds where all is plenty,[5] and (even) in this world obtains the highest fame. This declaration (of truth) is honoured by Brahmā.

82. One who in testifying speaks an untruth is, all unwilling, bound fast by the cords of Varuṇa till a hundred births are passed. Therefore one should declare true testimony.[6]

83. Through truth is the witness made pure, through truth is right increased; therefore among all the castes truth, indeed, should be spoken by witnesses.

[1] The noun to the adjective found in v. 71. A *var. lec.* occurs in Medh. and G., *eko lubdhas tv asākṣī syāt.* This is supported by Nand., and it is known to K. and Rāgh. For *api na* Nand. reads *api ca* in (*a*), and *ca* for *tu* in (*b*).

[2] That is, as K. remarks, (because they are frightened or) from any other cause. *Svabhāvena* seems better rendered in its usual sense than "in accordance with the truth," which goes without saying. Medh. supposes a lie out of pity in the second case; and Nand. takes *svabhāvena* simply as *satyena*, "in truth." "In accord with nature" is the literal meaning, *i.e.*, nature of case or of witness.

[3] The judge is the Brahman who has been appointed to represent the king (K.)

[4] Nand. reads *yatra* for *hy atra*.

[5] The worlds of Brahmā and the other divinities (K.) This verse is omitted by Nand. Medh. says the goddess of truth, Saravastī, is meant.

[6] Nand. has the locative, "the truth in (giving) testimony," *sākṣye*.

84. For self alone is the witness for self, and self is likewise the refuge of self. Despise not, therefore, (your) own self, the highest witness of men.

85. Verily the wicked think, "No one sees us," but the gods are looking at them, and also their man within.[1]

86. Sky, earth, the waters, (man's own) heart, the moon, the sun, the fire, Yama,[2] and the wind, night and the twilights twain, and Dharma,[3] (are) aware of the conduct of all corporate beings.

87. In the presence of the gods and the Brahmans, (the king), being pure, should, early in the day, call upon the twice-born, (being also) pure, to speak the truth, after they have turned their faces toward the north or the east.[4]

88. "Speak," thus let him ask a Brahman (for his testimony). "Speak the truth," thus (let him address a warrior (Kṣatriya). (He should conjure) a Vaiçya by his cows, his seed, and his gold; but a Çūdra by all evil acts.[5]

89. The worlds which are declared (to exist) for one who slays a Brahman, or for one who kills women and children, injures a friend, or shows ingratitude—all these would be (the home after death) of one who speaks falsely.

90. All thy pure deeds done by thee from thy birth up,

[1] The reading of Nand., *svaçcaira*, is supported by Rāgh. Nand. reads also *ca* for *tu*, *i.e.*, "both the gods and the man within," conscience.

[2] God of the lower world. He seizes upon the soul when the body dies, and no entreaties will induce him to give up his prey.

[3] *Dharma*, as personification, or as an abstraction, right. It is sometimes difficult to say which is intended.

[4] The purity enjoined refers probably to the completion of the morning ablutions. It is not necessary to regard the "gods" as meaning "idols" (K., Nand.), which would be contradicted by the sentiment of the preceding verse. Idols, images of divinities, are, however, mentioned in Manu. Cf. ix. 285, "a breaker of images" (K., small idols), and *devalaka*, iii. 152, 180; cf. also iv. 153, 39.

[5] That is, he should explain to the Vaiçya that the punishment in a future world for speaking falsely is as severe as for stealing cows, etc. (K.), or as severe as any sin which can be committed in respect to these things (Medh.) In the case of the Çūdra, the evil deeds with their results are depicted in the following verses (Nand.) Cf. vs. 113; Mutual Relations, p. 7; Viṣṇu, viii. 22 ff.

O good man, would go to the dogs if thou shouldst speak falsely.[1]

91. Although thou, O good man, regardest (thy) self, thinking, "I am alone," (yet) that wise seer who sees the evil and the good stands ever in thy heart.

92. It is the god Yama, the son of Vivasvant,[3] who resides in thy heart. If thou beest not at variance with him, go not to the Ganges and Kurus.[4]

93. Naked and shorn, and begging for food with the potsherd, hungry and thirsty and blind, shall he who gives false testimony come to the house[5] of his enemy.

94. Headlong, in darkness and gloom, that sinner shall go[6] to hell who makes a false statement when questioned in a legal examination.[7]

95. As a blind man eats up fishes and fish-bones together, so (does) that man who having entered the court

[1] Literally, "otherwise" (than truly). A *var. lec.* in Nand., *puṇyabhadram* (*sic*) *ca yat kṛtam*, is partly supported by Rāgh., *bhadram;* so that we may read, "whatever pure, whatever excellent (thing) thou hast done." In Yāj. ii. 75 the fruit of the perjurer's good deeds goes to the man whom he overpowers by his false testimony. Cf. with this passage iii. 230, where a lie sends the food to the dogs. In xi. 122 the virtue of the sinner goes to the gods. From the connection here we might imagine the dogs of Yama to be meant, "who guard (the under world), four-eyed guardians of the path, who gaze upon men" (Ṛgveda, x. 14, 11); though the dogs are probably a general term, as Yama has but two.

[2] This verse appears in more antique (*triṣṭubh*) form in the Ādiparvan of the Mbhā. i. 74, 28 (Çak.), where the neighbouring verses are also found (*triṣṭubh*) with a slight change of arrangement.

[3] Vivasvant, (god of) gleaming, is the father of the twins Yama and Yamī, the primeval parents.

[4] The Kurus, that is, the plains of the Kurus, were regarded as sacred. Cf. ii. 19. This district and the Ganges were favourite places of pilgrimage. As a general thing, all such holy spots seem held in equal veneration, as K. says of these two. Later still, the "holy pools" eclipsed the older places, if we may judge by Mbh. xii. 152, 11, where we read, "Holy, they say, is Kurukṣetra, holier still Sarasvatī, and the pools (holier) than Sarasvatī." This passage of ours has been quoted to show that Manu deprecates pilgrimages, *i.e.*, that they were not yet in favour. But the words taken in their connection negatively oppose this view. The man who has made himself pure needs not to go to the Ganges, and he purifies himself by speaking the truth (K.) Were he at "variance with Yama," however, *i.e.*, had he perjured himself, it would then be necessary. Cf. xi. 76, 78. Medh. and G. take a less metaphysical view of the divinity than K. Cf. xi. 76, 78.

[5] Or family (*kula*) (K.) "House" (*gṛha*) is the reading of Medh. and Nand., and (in the Comm.) of Rāgh.

[6] Rāgh. reads *patet*, "fall."

[7] Literally, "at a decision in regard to right" (*dharma*).

says anything different from the real fact, or declares what he has not actually seen.[1]

96. The gods know no other better man in the world than he of whom his own wise soul has no apprehension while he is speaking.[2]

97. Hear now in order, good man, how many in number the relatives are whom a false witness destroys, and in what cases (he destroys them).

98. By untruth in regard to small cattle (he destroys) five; ten, by untruth in regard to cows; one hundred, by untruth in regard to horses; a thousand, by untruth in regard to men.[3]

99. Speaking an untruth for the sake of gold, he destroys those born and those (yet) unborn. By an untruth in regard to land he destroys everything. Speak thou not then an untruth in regard to land.

100. They say (false testimony) in regard to water[4] is like (that in regard to) land; so also (is false testimony) in regard to carnal pleasures, in regard to gems (produced by) water, and all (gems) made of stone.[5]

[1] Nand. and Rāgh. read *kanṭakaiḥ sa naraḥ saha* /

[2] He whose soul is not obliged to ask itself, "Will he say a truth or a lie?" (K.) The word for "soul" is here *kṣetrajña*. It is the intellectual self, as said in the Mbhā. The *kṣetrajña* is the perceiver (masc.) and truth is its object (*viṣayi* and *viṣaya*, xiv. 1374).

[3] Cf. Gautama, xiii. 14, 15, and Vasiṣṭha, xvi. 34, where "maiden" takes the place of cattle. It is odd that that holy animal the cow should fall below the horse. "Kill," K. says, means he sends ten relatives, etc., to hell, or his reward for the sin of perjury is as great as if he killed them. Medh. and Nand. explain the untruth in regard to men as referring to the ownership of a slave.

[4] K. refers this to the water in pools and ponds. As we learn in the epic, these were regarded as sacred, and especially so to the cows. The necessity of providing a constant supply of water during the hot season led to the extraordinary reverence with which the cow-pools were looked upon. The possession of them secured to the owner freedom from sin, and gave him sure passage to heaven. Cf. Mbhā. xiii. 58, 19, "Eternal happiness is secured by a gift of something to drink, for water, my child, is hard to get (especially in the next world);" and our text, ix. 279, 281, 286, for the high value put on the precious fluid, even though unconsecrated.

[5] That is, all gems whatever, even including water-gems (pearls). In Nand., 100 comes after 98, and 99 follows as the second verse after 100. Between these occurs the following verse, which ought, if anywhere, to stand after 96. *Na tu tuṣyati yasyaiva puruṣasya durātmanaḥ / tasya putrān vaçrān (pitṛn ?) hanti, sapta sapta parāvarān.* Cf. i. 105.

101. Considering all these sins which (are committed) when falsehood is spoken, declare thou quickly everything just as (it was) heard, just as (it was) seen.[1]

102. Priests (living as) cowherds, traders, workmen, actors,[2] servants, and money-lenders one should treat[3] like Çūdras.

103. A man who, knowing the matter is not as he states it, makes a (false) declaration in a case (purely) out of consideration for (what he thinks) is right,[4] is not (on that account) shut out from the heavenly world; (on the contrary,) they call this the speech of the gods.

104. Wherever a truthful declaration would be the death of a Çūdra, Vaiçya, Kṣatriya, or Brahman, there falsehood should be spoken, for (in such a case) it is better than truth.[5]

105. Let those who desire to make full expiation for the sin of such a falsehood bring a sacrifice to Sarasvatī, with cakes sacred to the divinity of speech;[6]

106. Or let one pour ghee upon the fire according to rule, accompanied by the Kūṣmāṇḍa (verses); or that verse addressed to Varuṇa which begins "Off;" or the three verses addressed to the divinity of the water.[7]

[1] Nand. reads *etān sarvān avekṣyai'va doṣān*; and in (*b*) *satyam* for *sarvam*.

[2] Actors, as in vs. 65.

[3] That is, he should address them thus (K.)

[4] *Dharmataḥ*, out of pity, etc. (Medh., K.) Nand. places this verse after 104.

[5] Nand. offers a slight *var. lec.*, *uktarte ced vadho bhavet*, and in (*b*) *taddhitatra*. This same sentiment is found in Yāj. ii. 83. K. restricts this to cases where a petty offender is liable to lose his life through the severity with which the king is apt to punish criminals. It must not be assumed, he says (quoting Gaut. xiii. 24, 25), that this rule is to be applied in the case of a very wicked man unless he be a Brahman, for by Manu viii. 380, the life of a Brahman is never to be taken, whatever his sins. K. adds that the other castes are included because of the general inauspiciousness of capital punishment. This is only one case of the venial lies permitted by all the law-books (cf. vs. 112 note), as an exception to the universal rule given in the Hindu adage, "No duty greater than truth." For other texts of like sort cf. Müller, India, note D. In Greek literature we find the same rule in Sophocles' remark that it is no disgrace to tell a lie, *εἰ τὸ σωθῆναι γε τὸ ψεῦδος φέρει* (Phil. 108).

[6] *I.e.*, to Sarasvatī herself. Nand. reads *atas te'sya* (*dharmahetoḥ*.)

[7] The Kūṣmāṇḍa, according to K., mean the Kūṣmāṇḍī, Vāj. Saṁh. xx. 14–16; or Taitt. Araṇy. x. 3–5. Rāgh. and Nand. say this applies to the members of the twice-born

107. If a man, without being ill, should give no testimony (when summoned as witness) in suits for debt and similar cases, he would himself, when three half-months had expired, incur the whole of that debt, (and in addition) a tenth of the whole sum as fine.[1]

108. That witness to whom, within seven days of the time when he has made his statement, there comes sickness or fire or the death of a relative, shall be made to pay the debt and receive a fine.[2]

109. But in cases where witnesses are wanting, and the two parties mutually contradict each other, let the (king), being thus ignorant of the true facts of the case, discover (the truth) even by means of an oath.[3]

110. By the great seers and by the gods have oaths been taken in order to determine cases;[4] even Vasiṣṭha swore an oath before the king descended from Pijavana.[5]

castes. A Çūdra's expiation is a gift. The verse to Varuṇa reads (Ṛgveda i. 24, 15): "Loose off from us, O Varuṇa, thy fetter; the highest, lowest, and the midmost loose. Within thy realm, O Son of the Unending, may we rest sinless, and be free for ever." The reading *tad ity* for *ud ity* implies, as Rāgh. says, the Gāyatri, though he finds this verse in the "Vāruṇyā," and gives it also. The verses addressed to the waters (Ṛgveda, x. 9–13) are as follows:—(1) "O waters who refreshment give, ye who bestow upon us strength, that we great happiness behold; (2) distribute here to us on earth your liquid streams beneficent, as kindly mothers, willingly; (3) before him may we straight appear, unto whose house ye urge us on, O waters, and produce us there." The eighth verse of this hymn has more explicit reference to the case in hand—"Bear off, ye waters, far away, whatever wickedness is mine, whatever wrong I have performed, whatever falsehood I have sworn." This text is also enjoined in xi. 133 for expiation on killing a cat, etc.

[1] The detention by illness is not excepted by Yāj. (ii. 76), who has the man fined any way on the forty-sixth day. There may be an error in the text, as Nand. reads *gato naraḥ* for *naro'gadaḥ*. The fine is to be paid to the king (K.)

[2] *Dṛçyate yasya* is Nand.'s order. The relatives whose death convict him of perjury are, according to Medh., wives, sons, etc. K. says sons, etc.

[3] Or by an ordeal (see below), as Medh. understands *çapatha*. It may mean that they should imprecate curses on their own heads. Cf. the following explanation and the case in vs. 256. Dr. B.'s MS. of Rāgh. has *avindaṁs* for *na vindaṁs*.

[4] Probably no definite cases are meant. The epic has many such tales, though Medh. gives us an example of each in the oaths taken by the seven seers at the theft of the lotus stalks, and the oath of Indra to clear himself of an accusation of seducing Gautama's wife. Both are from the Mbhā.

[5] That is, Sudās; cf. vii. 41. K. says that Vasiṣṭha gave an oath to clear himself when accused of hav-

111. A wise man should never take an oath in vain when the occasion is only a small one, for he who takes an oath in vain is lost both after death and here.[1]

112. In (regard to) love affairs, marriages, food for cows, fuel, and in giving aid to a Brahman, there is no sin in an oath.[2]

113. (The king) should cause a Brahman to swear by truth; a Kṣatriya by his steed and his weapons; a Vaiçya by his cows, his seed, and his gold; but a Çūdra by all wicked deeds.[3]

114. Or he may cause him to hold fire,[4] or cause him to dive into the water, or even let him touch the heads of his wife and son one after the other.[5]

115. He whom the lighted fire does not burn, he whom the water does not cause to rise (to the surface),[6] and he

ing eaten the sons of Viçvamitra. Medh. says this accusation was united with another, namely, that Vasiṣṭha was a demon, on which the latter took an oath, "May I die if," &c. In the Mbh. account the king is changed into a demon.

[1] Medh. and Nand. differ from Rāgh. in taking this to mean "a false oath," connecting it with the following verse. The translation here given rests on the meaning of *vṛthā* as "vain," that is, as explained in *alpe arthe*, on a trifling occasion, such as the word has in v. 38, *vṛthā paçugha*. In Medh.'s translation we should expect not "even in a small," but "even in a great" matter. Rāgh. quotes the following verse to elucidate the passage, which is thus connected with the preceding verse: "If one in the presence of God, fire, and teacher takes an oath even with truth (*satyenāpi çapet*), King Vaivasvata destroys half his (reward for) virtue."

[2] Parallel passages from Vas. xvi. 35 and Gaut. xxiii. 29 show that here a false oath is meant. Gaut. says "some" say this, but such a lie must not be made to a Guru. The importance of the circumstances here mentioned make the oath necessary, and therefore right—"the sin is thus destroyed" (Rāgh.); "the sin (of taking an oath is thus) a duty" (Nand.); the wood is for a sacrifice (K.) I regard this verse as a proverbial saying, independent of the position in which it is found, like many others in our text.

[3] Cf. vs. 88. K.'s explanation is here that the cattle, etc., of the Vaiçya will yield no fruit; the Çūdra is to imprecate all evils upon himself if he lies.

[4] Rāgh. reads *apsu vai'nam* (and in (*b*) *vāpi*).

[5] That is, instead of an imprecation on himself alone, he may involve his whole family. The ordeal by oath was the substitute in the case of the Brahman in later times for the sacred libation, which was forbidden to be used for a Brahman (Viṣṇu ix. 17).

[6] B. R. translate "drown," but the test seems to be whether he can stay under water. Medh. paraphrases *unmajjayanti* by *ūrdhvaṁ plāvayanti*, "makes swim upwards." A general statement in Mbhā. (xiii. 1, 22) makes the good swim and the evil sink in the floods of evil that one meets in life (*plavante dharmalaghavaḥ . . . majjanti pāpaguravaḥ*).

who within a short time[1] meets with no misfortune,—these must be recognised as pure in respect to their oath.[2]

116. For when Vatsa of old was accused by his younger brother, the fire, (which is the) witness[3] of the whole world, burned not even one of his hairs, on account of his truthfulness.[4]

117. In whatever dispute (at law) false testimony has been given, (the king) should reconsider that affair; and even what has been done is to be (regarded as) not done.[5]

118. That testimony is called false (which has been given) through avarice, error, fear, friendship, love, anger, or, again, through ignorance or foolishness.[6]

119. I will now declare in order the varieties of punishments that a man receives who gives false testimony in any one of these cases.

120. (If one gives false testimony) through avarice, he should be fined[7] one thousand (*paṇas*); if through error, the first fine; if through fear, two medium fines; if through friendship, four times the first.

[1] *I.e.*, according to Medh., fourteen days, or (Rāgh.) three half months.

[2] This subject has been treated by Stenzler, Z. D. M. G. bd. ix., and by Schlagintweit "Ueber die Götterurtheile der Indier." Besides these verses and vs. 108, we find the custom of ordeal, including imprecation, spoken of in viii. 90 (178) and 256. The ordeal is an ancient custom. A hymn of one undergoing trial by fire is given in the Atharva Veda (ii. 12), and directly mentioned in the Chandogya Upaniṣad, vi. 16, 1. It began apparently with the simpler imprecation, and extended to physical proof. The later down we come the more kinds of tests we find. Yāj. ii. 99 restricts the fire and water proof to Çūdras. In the water test there is some doubt whether the meaning may not be, as indicated above, drown; but it seems more probable that it is the innocent one who sinks. Such was the early custom in Germany, and two hundred years ago in America in the test for witches . . . Viṣṇu says he is guilty "even if one limb is seen (above the water")—(xii. 6).

[3] So two MSS., *spaçaḥ*.

[4] The story, as told in the Pañcatviṅça Br. of the Sāma Veda, is that Vatsa was accused by his step-brother of being the son of a Çūdra woman. He proved he was not by walking through the fire unharmed (cf. Weber, Ind. Stud., ix. 44); so the commentators. A small *var. lec.* occurs in Nand., *vatsyasyaivābhi*.

[5] Or perhaps better, with Rāgh. (*kṛtaṁ vāpy*), "he should reconsider the affair (law-case), or (else) the decision of the affair would be without effect. In (*a*) Nand. also reads (for *vivāde tu*) *kṛte kārye*, in whatever *settled* law-case.

[6] Or childishness, perhaps better "being a child;" "less than sixteen years old" (Nand.)

[7] Or "the fine is," *daṇḍas tu* (Nand.) Rāgh. has *ca*.

121. If through love, ten times the first; if through anger, three times the highest;[1] if through ignorance, a full two hundred; but if through foolishness, one hundred only.[2]

122. They say these punishments for giving false testimony (were) proclaimed by the wise in order to secure the sure advance of right (*dharma*) and the suppression[3] of wrong.

123. A just king should have three (of the) castes banished after administering the fine, when they have given false testimony, but a Brahman he should have banished (without having administered a fine).[4]

124. Manu, son of the Self-Existent, declared ten places of punishment which should be (selected) in (punishing) three (of the) castes; (but) a Brahman should go[5] uninjured;

125. (Namely), the privy parts, the belly, the tongue, the two hands, and, fifthly, the two feet; also the eye, the nose, the two ears, the property, and (tenth) the body.[6]

126. After carefully considering the purpose (of the crime), the place, and the time,[7] exactly (as they were), and after examining the property[8] (of the criminal), and

[1] So G. and N.; but, according to K., three times the medium fine. Nand. and Rāgh. support the former view.

[2] As the first (lowest) fine is 250 *paṇas* (vs. 131 ff.) the medium 500, and the highest 1000 (vs. 138), the fines would be as follows: For testimony falsified through foolishness, 100 *paṇas*; through ignorance, 200; through error, 250; through avarice, fear, or friendship, 1000; through love, 2500; through anger, 3000.

[3] Nand., *nidhanāya* (*nivṛttaye*).

[4] The word here used of the Brahman, *vivāsayet*, in distinction from the "three (lower) castes," has given trouble to the commentators. Govind. says (in K.) that the Brahman is to be fined (like the other castes) and stripped naked (*vivāsaḥ*); Medh. says this means taking away his *vāsa*, *i.e.*, deprivation of home. Banishment is the meaning given by K., who quotes (as does Rāgh.) vs. 380 to prove that the Brahman is to lose neither life nor property, and this agrees with vs. 124. Nand. says merely that both verbs mean to remove one from the country.

[5] Out of the country (K.) Nand. reads *tāni* for *yāni*; his meaningless *v. l. akṣato vrajed vivaset* probably denotes no more than a note of the commentator which has slipped into the text.

[6] The importance and trivial nature of the crime are in each case to be taken into consideration (K.) That member of the body with which the crime is committed should be mutilated; the "body" in the text means capital punishment (Medh., K.)

[7] That is, whether the crime was committed in a town or in a wood, by day or by night (Medh., K.)

[8] So B. R.; perhaps better "the natural ability."

the crime itself, let (the king) cause punishment to fall on those that deserve it.[1]

127. The infliction of unjust punishment injures the reputation (of the king) among men, is destructive of (future) fame, and even in the next world prevents his entrance into heaven; therefore let him avoid it.

128. A king punishing those undeserving of punishment, and even failing to punish those deserving of punishment, attains great infamy, and also goes to hell.

129. Let (the king) inflict first punishment of the voice; next, that of reproof; thirdly, that of property; then, last, that of corporal injury.[2]

130. But if even by corporal injury he be unable to restrain them, then let him employ upon them all these four (kinds of punishment).

131. The names given on earth to (weights of) copper, silver, and gold, when used among men for traffic, I will now declare in full.

132. The fine particle of dust which is seen in a beam of light as it enters a lattice-window, is taken as the first standard, and is called an atom.[3]

133. Eight atoms are considered in respect to weight (as equal to) one egg of a louse; three of these (are equal to) one grain of black mustard; three of these (are equal to) one grain of white mustard.

134. Six grains of (white) mustard (are equal to) a medium-sized barley-corn; three barley-corns (are equal

[1] An interesting *var. lec.* occurs here, and makes the exactness of this translation not quite certain; the word translated "purpose" Rāgh. refers to the frequent repetition of the crime, not to the intent, as Medh. does, and Nand. reads (instead of the accepted *anubandha*) *aparādha*, while in (*b*) he reads *sārāsāraṁ tathā'lokya*. Rāgh.'s version differs from K. only in having *vijñāya* for *ālokya* (which Medh. notes as a *var. lec.*) Nand. explains his reading as *daṇḍyasya balābalam*, "the strength and weakness of the criminal;" the same form is found ix. 331; Yāj. i. 367 has *aparādha* in (*a*).

[2] By punishment of the voice a mild and kind exhortation is intended; by reproof or contempt is meant bringing the criminal to shame by speaking sharply to him. The word *vadha*, "corporal injury," has two meanings in the law-books, either corporal or capital punishment. Medh. and K. remark that the latter is here excluded by the next verse.

[3] *Trasareṇu*, trembling dust-speck.

to) one *kṛṣṇala* (berry); five *kṛṣṇala*[1] constitute in (weight) a bean (*māṣa*); sixteen *māṣa* (are equal to) a gold-piece (*suvarṇa*).

135. Four *suvarṇa* (are equal to) a *pala;* ten *pala* to a *dharaṇa;* two *kṛṇṣala* of the same weight should be regarded as a silver *māṣaka.*

136. A *dharaṇa* or silver *purāṇa* would be sixteen of these; a copper *paṇa* weighing the same as a *karṣa* should be known as a *kārṣapaṇa.*

137. Ten (silver) *dharaṇa* make a silver *çatamāna;* a weight of four *suvarṇa* is called a *niṣka.*

138. Two hundred and fifty *paṇas* are termed "the first fine;" the "medium fine" is known as five hundred, and the highest as one thousand.[2]

139. When (a debtor) has acknowledged (in court) that a debt is really due, he deserves a fine of five in the hundred; if he has denied the debt, (he should be fined) twice as much. This is an ordinance of Manu.[3]

140. A money-lender, to increase his capital, may take the interest declared (legal) by Vasiṣṭha, (namely) an eightieth part of one hundred a month.[4]

141. Or, reflecting on the duty of good men, he may take two per cent., for (even) taking two per cent. (a month) he does not become a wrong-doer for gain.[5]

142. He may take a monthly interest of two per cent.,

[1] The *kṛṣṇala* was practically the smallest weight used; it was also termed a *raktikā*, and its weight was 0.122 grammes. The fines in court were reckoned as so many *paṇas*, one *paṇa* being the same as a *karṣa* = 16 *māṣa* = 80 *kṛṣṇala.* Some of the weights mentioned are confined to gold—*suvarṇa*, and *niṣka;* some to silver—*purāṇa* and *çatamāna;* and some are used of both—*kṛṣṇala, paṇa, māṣa,* (*māṣaka*), *pala, dharaṇa;* the last at times of copper (v. Colebrooke, Essays, i. p. 531, and Jolly, *ad loc.* from whom this note).

[2] Nand., *sahasraṁ tv ekam.* Copper *paṇas* are meant.

[3] That is, the debtor who obliges the creditor to bring him into court, pays on there denying it a fine of ten per cent. It is doubtful if this verse is not a late addition. Jolly notes that N. says it is wanting in some MSS., and, besides being out of place, it contradicts vs. 59. Medh. says "others" think the "twice as much" means the debt doubled.

[4] So stated in the existing law-book of Vasiṣṭha, ii. 51. This rate is equal to 15 per cent. per annum. K. says this is when a pledge is given (vs. 142).

[5] When he has no pledge as security. So in vs. 142 (K.)—(*kurvita*, Nand.)

three per cent., four per cent., or five per cent., according to the order of the castes (beginning with the Brahman).

143. But he may not increase his capital by taking interest if a pledge has been given him of which he has had free use; nor may he dispose of or sell the pledge,[1] although (it has been in his possession) for a long time.

144. A pledge should not be made use of by force;[2] if one makes use of it, he must relinquish the interest; and he must gratify that one (the owner) by a payment;[3] otherwise, he would be a pledge-stealer.

145. Neither a pledge nor a deposit are lost through lapse of time, (for) both of them may be taken back (although) kept for a long time.

146. A milk-cow, a camel, a draught-horse, and (an animal) which is being broken in (are never lost) to the owner when they are made use of with the (owner's) good will.[4]

147. When the owner stands by and sees (his property) used by others for ten years while he says nothing, he does not deserve to recover it, whatever it may be.[5]

148. If the property of a man who is neither under age[6] nor weak-minded is made use of while he is in the vicinity, by the general practice (of business people[7]) that property is lost (to the owner), and the user has a right to have it.[8]

149. A pledge, a boundary, the property of children, an

[1] The pledge just described, of which he may make use (K.) In the last three verses the explanation given by Medh. and G. differs from that of K. The former considers the highest interest as allowed when the lender requires it in support of his family, etc. K. regards the pledge or absence of pledge as making the difference, and quotes Yāj. ii. 37 to prove it. In v. 143 K. holds the second pledge mentioned as one for use, not for safe-keeping, as do Medh. and G.

[2] *I.e.*, against the owner's consent, but cf. vs. 150.

[3] By paying the original value to compensate for injury received by its use (Medh. and K.), or by paying over the profit such use has given him (N. and Nand.)

[4] The commentators regard this as a restriction to the following verse.

[5] Except land (Rāgh.); for this some claim twenty years (Medh.)

[6] A child is under age up to his sixteenth year, Nārada (3, 37) in K.

[7] *Vyavahārena*, by business custom, or by legal usage.

[8] It is possible that a verse after 147 has been omitted, enjoining the punishment of a thief for one who wrongly uses for many years what is not permitted.

open deposit or one sealed up, women, the property of the king, and the property of a learned (Brahman), are not lost (to the owner) through being used (by other people).[1]

150. He who is so foolish as to make use of a pledge without the owner's permission shall be made to give up one-half the interest (he would have received) to make up for this use.[2]

151. Interest on money, if paid all at once and at the same time (as the debt), should not be more than enough to double (the principal);[3] and (the sum of the interest and principal) should not be more than five times (the principal, when this interest is paid on) corn, fruit, wool, or draught animals.

152. Excessive (interest) made higher than the regular rate is not lawful, and they call this usury; (the lender) may take five per cent.[4]

153. One should neither take interest which extends over a year,[5] nor interest unrecognised (by law); wheel-interest, periodical interest, stipulated interest, and corporal interest (should also not be taken).

154. He who, being unable to pay a debt, desires to renew the obligation, must cause the proof[6] (of the obliga-

[1] Rāgh. reads *upabhogena jīryati* (!).

[2] Medh. and K. observe that this command differs from that of vs. 144, in that the use is forcibly made, while here only secretly; a distinction, which, as Jolly remarks, is insufficient to explain the difference.

[3] That is, the sum of interest *plus* principal must not exceed twice the original debt. On the meaning of *kusida*, cf. Jolly, Ind. Schuldrecht, § 3, where the variations of the later lawgivers are added.

[4] That is, according to vss. 140–142, five per cent. (a month) is the very highest interest he is permitted to take; a rate which is here made legal (so G.) apparently for all castes, though by vs. 142 confined to the Çūdra.

[5] Gaut. (xii. 30) quoted this as the opinion of "some." A *var. lec.* in Nārada (iv. 34) falsely attributes to Manu the doctrine that the interest is unlimited for certain objects (so declared by Viṣṇu, vi. 16). K. explains that when a year is passed the creditor who has agreed to receive monthly payments of interest can demand no more. "Wheel-interest" is compound; "periodical" is where the debt is increased on non-payment at the time due, or simply monthly interest (so in N. and Bṛh.; but cf. p. 239, Bühler's Gautama); "stipulated" is forced interest, when one is pressed by need; "corporal" interest is when the interest is paid by labour of (the borrower or his cattle) (Medh.), or, according to Nārada, is "daily" interest. This verse Jolly regards as not genuine (Ind. Schuld., § 3, 4).

[6] *Karaṇam*, as in vs. 52, is proof, instrument. The meaning "docu-

tion) to be repeated after he has paid the interest due (on the debt).

155. When he has not paid the interest, he should cause the (agreement in regard to the) principal to be renewed, and ought at the same time to promise a sum equal to the accumulated interest.[1]

156. He who has agreed upon a price to be paid on delivery,[2] with a definite understanding in regard to the time and place, shall not receive the reward if he fails to keep the agreement in regard to time and place.

157. The price which men conversant with ocean travel and skilled in time, place, and goods set upon ware, this shall in that case be established as the gain (allowed the seller).

158. Any man who acts in this world as surety for the appearance (of a debtor) shall, on failure to produce him, pay[3] the debt out of his own money.

159. The son ought not (to be compelled) to pay (his father's debts when contracted) through offering surety, through foolish gifts,[4] through playing with dice, or through drinking intoxicating liquors; and (he need not pay money) remaining (due) from a fine or a tax.[5]

ment," which the commentators give the word, is not here necessary, and seems improbable. The proof of the debt must be renewed; that is, the creditor brings again witnesses to hear the (renewed verbal) agreement. (Nand., MS., has *kāraṇam.*)

[1] *I.e.*, this sum forms part of the capital in the new agreement.

[2] Perhaps better "agreed upon compound interest" (as in vs. 153). So in vs. 157, N. regards the *vṛddhi* (price) as interest, the rate of which in cases of dangerous travel, etc., may be stipulated in each case. The other commentators read as translated.

[3] There are three kinds of sureties, those of appearance, trust, and money-payment, therefore "appearance" is specified (Medh.) Cf. Yāj. ii. 53, 54. The later writers divided sureties into three, four, and five classes, and Nārada (xiii. 39) restricts them in kind, not permitting the nearest relations in a family. One of these is in Kāty. a surety for ordeals, and his list of forbidden sureties agrees with Manu's forbidden witnesses (cf. vs. 63).

[4] Gifts promised to persons of low birth (Medh., K.), or bribes made by the father and not yet paid (Medh.) To the Brahman all gifts not made to himself were, since they were thus wasted, idle or foolish. In the Mbhā. (xiii. 93, 121), this expression is used as a curse (*vṛthādānaṁ karotu*). The son in general does not inherit liabilities arising from his father's sins, nor taxes not paid at the time of his death (except as in vs. 160). Vas. (xvi. 31) gives this verse as a well-known quotation, so Gaut. (xii. 41), but neither recognises a distinction between the kinds of uninherited or inherited surety.

[5] Or marriage-money still remaining due.

160. The rule declared above should hold in the case of surety for appearance; but if a man who has given surety for payment has died, one should cause payment to be made by the heirs.

161. On what ground may the lender of money demand the money owing him back again after the death of a surety, who was not a surety for payment, and whose position (in this respect) was well known?

162. If money has been paid over to the surety,[1] and he has (in this way received) money enough (to pay the debt),[2] let (the heir of him who has been paid) pay the money out of his own property alone; so stands the law.[3]

163. A business transaction is not legal when it has been performed by a drunken person, a crazy person, a person in distress, a slave,[4] a child, an old man, or one not duly authorised.

164. A verbal agreement, even if it be upheld[5] (by evidence), is not a true (agreement) if what has been said (in this agreement) is opposed to the law which has been established, and which is usually acted on in business transactions.[6]

[1] By the debtor in order to pay the debt (Medh., K.)

[2] Lit., "having money enough." Medh. says if he has received the full amount necessary to pay the debt; if the heir receives but a trifle paid over for this purpose, he is not obliged to pay a debt that is large. K. understands merely that the heir should have money enough any way to pay the debt.

[3] From the connection the son (heir) must be intended (as the surety is dead)—(Medh., K.)

[4] Instead of "slave" it is possible that "dependent," including younger brothers, etc., is meant, as no one but the head of the family was independent, *i.e.*, could be responsible for business acts, except as in vs. 167.

[5] The commentators regard this as an agreement proved by written documents (K.), or also proved by sureties (Medh., Nand.) From the text it is impossible to say which is meant, but probably only sureties are here intended.

[6] Medh. explains this last part as "out of *dharma* (*dharmabāhyam*), *i.e.*, what is opposed to the practice of the law-books," and gives instances of such illegal agreements. As *dharma* means legal rule as well as rule of right, and *bhāṣā* (speech, *i.e.*, verbal agreement) indicates that it is a matter of words, we might possibly translate the *bahis* literally also, as in *bahiṣkṛta*, "excluded," and render the passage word for word: "The speech is not true (*i.e.*, binding), even when attested, if (what is said) is said outside the legal rule (*i.e.*, form), which has been established and generally used in business transactions." Such was the early custom at Rome, where the

165. When (the king) sees that anything has been pledged[1] or sold through artifice, or anything has been given or accepted through artifice, or wherever he sees any cheating, he should cause the whole transaction to be annulled.

166. If the receiver (of money) is dead, and the money has been spent for the good of the household, this (debt) must be paid by his[2] relatives out of their own (property), even if they (have lived with property) divided.[3]

167. If even a slave[4] makes a business transaction for the sake of the household, his superior,[5] whether present or absent (at the time), must not rescind it.

168. What is given by force, used by force, and also what is written by force—(in short) all things done by force, Manu said, (are as if) not done.[6]

169. Three are afflicted for the sake of another—witnesses,

slightest deviation from the prescribed forms of speech invalidated the act (cf. Ihering, Geist des Röm. Rechts., ii. 577–598); it is, however, perhaps too much to extract such *leges contractus* from an isolated passage, even assuming it to be more primitive than the other laws on agreements. *Bahis . . . vyāvahārikam* may mean merely "opposed to good custom" (cf. vs. 78).

[1] *Ādhamana*, Medh., K., and Rāgh. render as "pledge;" B. and R. incline to the meaning, "puffing" wares by fraud.

[2] *Tasya* (Medh., Nand.)

[3] "Divided" means having a divided property; the word "even" implies, as a matter of course, that this should be done when they live (in the united household), as common proprietors (Medh.) Yāj. ii. 45, specifies that in the latter case the same rule holds when the master of the house is on a journey; so Rāgh. and Nand.

[4] Or "a dependent," perhaps a younger brother (cf. vs. 163.)

[5] *I.e.*, the master (K.) of the house (Medh.) Jolly notes that G.'s text requires the meaning, "the slave must wait till the master returns." Nand. reads, *(Na)vicārayet* ("*na kuryāt*"). Cf. Jolly, Ind. Schuldrecht, § 6 (p. 309 note).

[6] Cf. vs. 144; and Yāj. ii. 89. An agreement written with one's own hand is valid, unless done by trickery (cf. above, vs. 165) or force. This is the only passage in Manu where positive reference to writing can be claimed (cf. above, notes on vss. 52, 154). It is probably one of the latest additions to the text, as we find the same verse in Nārada, iv. 55 (cf. Viṣṇu, vii. 6); cf. Jolly, Ind. Schuldrecht, § 2. Müller (India, p. 92) regards it as "recognising the practical employment of writing for commercial transactions." Writing was long used before it was recognised in the literature of India; it appears to have been first used for grants and deeds; not till much later was it employed for literary purposes. The next law-books in time after Manu speak of and enjoin writing in business acts, but its existence in the time of the body of the text would seem, from negative data, to be unknown.

a surety, and a family;[1] four enrich themselves (by means of others)—a priest, a creditor,[2] a merchant, and a king.

170. A king, even if deprived of resources, should not receive what he ought not to take; and even when he is in prosperity, he should not reject what he ought to take, even if it be a little thing.

171. By taking what ought not to be taken, and by neglecting to take what ought to be taken, the weakness of the king is proclaimed,[3] and he is lost in this world and in the next.

172. But by taking what is (properly) his, by caring for his duties,[4] and by protecting the weak,[5] the king obtains strength and flourishes in this world and in the next.

173. Therefore, like Yama, let the ruler lay aside his own pleasure or displeasure (in any matter), and act after the fashion of Yama, with wrath subdued and organs of sense subdued.[6]

174. Now if any evil-hearted king conducts his affairs with injustice, through want of discernment, his enemies[7] quickly get him in their power;

[1] Or "judges," according to Medh. and K., but (as in v. 201) this is not necessary. The literal meaning is known here to some commentators. N. refers it to the family embarrassed by debts left unpaid by some one member; Rāgh. remarks in explanation that one bad boy is the ruin of a family, while Nand. takes it to mean a friend (*kulaçabdena kulīno' bhipretaḥ*). Although the verse is probably a proverb, the commentators agree that it means here, first, that the "three" may not be made to serve by force; second, the "four" must not make money unlawfully.

[2] Literally, "a rich man" (*āḍhya*); so *dhanika* is used in the same double sense.

[3] Or "produced" (*jāyate*)—(Nand.)

[4] Or "by preventing mixture of the castes," as K. explains by a rather forced construction of a *var. lec.* (*varṇa* for *dharma*); Nand. reads *varṇa*, and explains (cf. K.) as "by showing kindness to castes." Rāgh. knows and rejects *varṇa*, preferring *dharma*, which, it seems to me, is better suited to the place, and is more appropriately read with *saṁsargāt*. The meaning of this word in Manu is "connection, intercourse, close acquaintance" (cf. xi. 47), which with *varṇa* gives no sense, while with *dharma* in the same sense (whether as love or understanding) the meaning is good. In a somewhat similar situation the word is used of a *person* in Mbhā. xv. 10, 44: *Vipriyam . . . janasya . . . saṁsargād dharmajasya . . . na karisyanti;* "(the princes) will, through affection for Dharma (Yudh.), do nothing unpleasant to the people."

[5] K.'s paraphrase, *durbala*, is Nand.'s text (also in Rāgh.)

[6] That is, he must be as impartial as Yama, the judge of the dead.

[7] *I.e.*, his estranged people support him.

175. But if, restraining lust and anger, he views all things with justice, his people hasten toward him as rivers do towards the sea.[1]

176. He who accuses a moneyed-man (a creditor) before the king (because of his) compelling the payment of a debt in any way he chooses,[2] shall be fined one-fourth part of the debt by the king, and (be made to pay) the money to the creditor.

177. The debtor may liquidate the debt due the creditor even by (corporal) labour, provided he be of the same or of lower caste; but if he belong to a higher caste, he should pay off the debt by degrees.[4]

178. By this rule let the king make an equitable decision in regard to the affairs of two parties mutually at strife,[5] when these affairs have been made plain by witnesses or by ordeals.[6]

179. A wise man should deposit a deposit with a man of (good) family, of good habits, who is conversant with the rules of right, who speaks the truth, who has a large retinue, who is wealthy and honourable (*ārya*).[7]

180. In whatever condition a man has deposited anything in any one's hand, in just the same condition he must receive it back again; as the delivery, so the receipt.[8]

181. He who, being asked (to give up) a deposit, does

[1] The image may be the Vedic one (*e.g.*, R. V. i. 32, 3) of the lowing cows and the "waters running to the sea." The commentators say the people become one with the king (in desires, &c.), their union is perfect, as rivers lost in the sea.

[2] Literally, "according to his pleasure."

[3] Cf. vss. 49, 50.

[4] Cf. viii. 49, ix. 229. In viii. 153 corporal *interest* is nevertheless forbidden (?). In viii. 415 such a one is a slave; the labour is menial work, and apparently all members of lower castes might, if insolvent, be held as temporary slaves till the debt was paid.

[5] Nand. and G. read *vivadamānayoḥ* (dual) for the ordinary plural.

[6] Nand. and G. explain *pratyaya* as oath; Medh. as ordeal (*anumānaṁ daivī kriyā*).

[7] *Ārya* may mean simply a twice-born man.

[8] Cf. ver. 195. In text and comm. of Nand., *yathā dānam*, etc. "In whatever condition" means whether sealed or not, etc. (Medh., K., and Rāgh.) "Whether it has the same appearance" (Nand.), literally "as the giving so the taking."

not make it over to the depositor, should be questioned about it by the judge, the depositor being absent.

182. In the absence of witnesses (the judge) must, under some pretext, make an actual deposit of gold with him by means of spies who are of (proper) age and appearance.[1]

183. If he returns this latter deposit in the same condition it was in when it was deposited and received,[2] the accusation of his enemies fails completely;

184. But if he does not return them[3] their money as he ought,[4] he must by compulsion be made to pay both (deposits): so is the rule of right (*dharma*).[5]

185. Neither open nor sealed deposits should ever be delivered to the next successor[6] (of the depositor); both are lost (to the owner) if the receiver dies, but if he does not die they are not lost.[7]

186. But if he makes over (the deposit) voluntarily to the next successor of the deceased (depositor), he should not be brought to examination[8] by the king or by the relations of the depositor.[9]

187. And without any trickery one should pleasantly ask for the thing (deposited), or by kind words alone prevail upon him after examining his mode of life.[10]

[1] Nand. regards the spies as "like in age and appearance to the former depositor;" reads *satyasya* (*nidhānasya*) for *sannyasya*, and takes the verb from the preceding verse, his whole idea being that the man is to be examined by spies (when there are no witnesses) of like sort with the former depositor, and also by pretexts (he is to be examined) in regard to the money of the real deposit.

[2] So Medh (*yathāgṛhītam*). Nand. reads *pratidadyāt tu* and *yat pareṇābhi* [*pūjyate* !].

[3] The spies.

[4] Literally, "as is the rule."

[5] From ver. 180 on there seems to have been a doubt as to the proper order. Jolly notes that N. has 181, 183, 182, 184, while G.'s order is 181, 183, 184, 182. In Nand. the disorder is more extensive, though these four verses are themselves in regular position, but they fall as a group after (K.'s) 187 and before 196. Nand.'s arrangement is as follows: 180, 195, 188, 185-186, 189, 194, 187, 181-184, 196, 190-193, 197, 198; new v. 201, 202, 199, 200, 203-230 (231 after 244), 232, etc., as in K. (though after 187 the commentator implies 188 as following!). Medh.'s order is like that of K.

[6] His heir, son, brother, or wife (Medh.)

[7] *Anāçitau* (Medh, Rāgh.)

[8] Medh., Nand., and Rāgh. read *abhiyoktavyaḥ*, and Nand. *sa rājñā n'ābhi*.

[9] In order to test his truth as to the amount of the claim (Medh.)

[10] Or his means of life, wealth.

188. Let this be the rule in all these (cases where there are) unsealed deposits, and one tries to adjust the matter but where a deposit has been sealed, no blame should attach (to the receiver) unless he has extracted something from it.[1]

189. (The receiver of a deposit) need not return what has been stolen, washed away by water, or burned by fire, unless he has extracted something from this (deposit).

190. One who has stolen a deposit, as also one who is not really a depositor,[2] the king should examine by all methods,[3] and also by administering the oaths[4] of the Veda.

191. He who does not return a deposit, and he who without having made a deposit (falsely) claims one, are both to be punished as thieves, or fined a sum equal (to the amount involved).[5]

192. The king should cause the man who takes from an (unsealed) deposit to be fined a sum equal in value to it; also him, without distinction, who takes from a sealed deposit.[6]

193. If any man should by fraud steal the goods of another, he ought, along with his companions, to be killed openly,[7] by means of different (corporal) injuries.

194. If a deposit of a certain value has been made by

[1] This means after changing the seal (to conceal what he has taken) —(K.)

[2] But claims to be (all commentators).

[3] Medh. and K. give four kinds of "methods," but do not agree with each other. Nand. says "all not spoken of."

[4] Cf. note to vs. 115. K. says by holding fire, etc.; probably ordeals are implied.

[5] (Mutilated) as thief if the deposit is valuable, otherwise the fine (K.), (*çiṣyau*, Nand.)

[6] Medh. and K. make the distinction between vss. 191 and 192 to be, that in 191 the fine is for the sake of freeing the Brahman from the mutilation, and the severer law appertains to cases of repeated crime; while in 192 (Nand. reads in (*b*) *hartāraṁ cāpy upanidher*, etc., and explains *aviçeṣena* as "without any distinction in regard to caste") they refer to the different kinds of deposit whether valuable or not (as in 191), as the "distinction."

[7] That is, on the royal highway (Medh.) Nand. places the three following verses before this by no accident, for in commenting on this verse he says: "Here ends the deposit; now the sale of property not owned," and passes to vs. 197.

any one in the presence of the family,[1] it must be acknowledged (to be) of just[2] that value, and (if the receiver) denies[3] (this) he deserves punishment.

195. If the delivery and receipt (of goods) have been confidentially made by any person, the goods must be returned in confidence also: as the delivery, so the receipt.[4]

196. The king, without oppressing the holder of the loan, should render his decision in regard to money deposited and a deposit made for friendship.[5]

197. If a man, not being himself the owner, sells the property of another without the owner's permission, one should not allow him to be a witness,[6] (since he is) a thief, (although) he may think he is not a thief.

198. He should be held to a fine of six hundred (*paṇas*) if he is a near relation; if he is not a near relation and has no excuse,[7] he would incur the sin of a thief.

199. If a delivery or sale[8] has been made by any one

[1] *Kula*, according to Medh., K., and Nand., is "witnesses" (cf. 201); Medh. and K. have before (169) made it mean "judges." Why should it not have its usual meaning?

[2] Just that and no more (Nand.)

[3] (Falsely), and his statement is overborne by witnesses (Medh., K.)

[4] Cf. 180, which this verse follows in Nand.

[5] The deposit made for friendship is one for friendly use (Medh., K.)

[6] Cf. 67. Medh. and K. remark that he is incapacitated for any acts that good people can perform; in short, he is *intestatus* in its widest sense.

[7] If he give no excuse, such as that it has been received from a relative, etc., or openly done, so that no evidence of guilt is seen (Medh., K.) Rāgh. observes that the "sin of a thief" means he would be fined one thousand (*paṇas*). After this verse, Nand. has another like it:

(*b*) *Anena vidhinā çiṣyaḥ kurvann asvāmivikrayaṁ /*
Ajñānāt, jñānapūrvaṁ tu cauravad vadham arhati //

("By this rule a man who sells what he does not own is to be punished if he does it unwittingly, but if he does it on purpose, he deserves death.") To which he adds: "This rule" means the "fine of six hundred." It is no "sin" (*doṣa*) if it is done unknowingly (so he does not deserve to die, but must pay the fine). A slight *var. lec.* also occurs in 198: *Avahāryas sa tu bhavet* (and in (*b*) *sāpasaraḥ !*). Nand. disagrees from Medh. and K. in their explanation of *sānvayaḥ* as "relative:" he gives simply that *sānvaya* means when there is a companion (cf. 193), and in this case he adds, each of them receives the full 600; *niranvaya* means "without a companion," but he does not try to define *sāpsaraḥ*, which may be a mere error.

[8] Or purchase (*krayaḥ*), as Nand. and Rāgh. read.

who is not the real owner, it should be regarded as not made at all, according to the rule in business transactions.

200. If a man has clearly possession (of property), but (his) acquisition (of it) is not clear, in this case the proof (of ownership) is acquisition, not possession.[1] So stands the rule.

201. When a man gets any property by a sale in the presence of the family,[2] he receives property (which) by this (open) purchase is clearly and legally his.

202. If the seller[3] cannot be produced, but the purchase has been made openly,[4] (the purchaser) is (to be) released by the king, (as he does) not deserve a fine, and the (owner) who has lost (it) receives the property.[5]

203. One thing should never be sold mixed with another,[6] nor (should anything be sold) damaged,[7] deficient, far away, or concealed.[8]

204. If one girl is given away (in marriage) to a wooer after letting him see another,[9] he may marry both of them for the same price:[10] so said Manu.[11]

205. If a girl is crazy or leprous or has lost her virginity, and the one who gives her away (in marriage) has

[1] The fact of possession (enjoyment) cannot make a man owner; he must have something to prove it by, as sale, etc. (Rāgh.) "Acquisition" means the manner or proof of acquiring, *i.e.*, his title.

[2] *Kula*, as in vs. 196; according to the commentators, "in the presence of witnesses, in the market-place." This "purchase" is the "acquisition" of vs. 200.

[3] So Medh. and K., "the seller who is not the owner." B. R. translate "the instigator (of the sale)." According to Nand. the meaning is that the (*mūlyam* = *dhanam*) property if not producible after open sale returns to the former owner, while the buyer is released (from the purchase). Cf. Viṣṇu, v. 164, 165.

[4] *Çodhitam*, Medh., Govind., and Nand.; *dhanam*—Nand. has *vahate ca tat.*

[5] K. says he gives half to the buyer (!), which is a mere attempt to bring this verse into harmony with contradictory injunctions of Bṛh.

[6] In such a way as to deceive the customer, as is seen in the examples given by the commentators.

[7] *Sāvadyam* (Medh., G., N., and Rāgh.) Kashm. MS. *asāraṁ* (Cal. and Nand.)

[8] By covering it over, by concealing (Medh., N., and Nand.), or by dyeing it (M., G., and K.)

[9] This is equivalent to promising in marriage.

[10] This rule holds in the sale of a girl, but not in the case of cows, horses, and other such chattels (Medh.)

[11] Yet he has emphatically inveighed against the sale of women, iii. 51, ix. 98.

exposed (these) defects before (marriage), he deserves no punishment.[1]

206. If a priest selected for (performing) sacrifice should fail to complete his work,[2] a part (only of the reward) should be given him by his co-workers, in proportion to the work he has (done.)

207. If he fails to complete his work when the rewards have already been given, he may keep the whole of his share, and have (the rest of his work) done by some one else.

208. If in any ceremony[3] certain rewards have been declared for each part, should this (priest) alone receive these rewards, or should all the priests share them?

209. The Adhvaryu should take the chariot, the Brahman at the laying on of the fire[4] (should take) the steed, the Hotar should take also a horse, the Udgātar, too, should take the waggon (used) at the sale (of *soma*).[5]

210.[6] The first (four) of them all[7] should have half,[8] the other (four) a half of that, the third division (should have) a third share, and those to whom a fourth is allotted should have a fourth share.

[1] For the alternative, cf. 224. A similar rule occurs ix. 73; and a similar form of expression occurs ix. 262.

[2] Because he is ill (K.) Cf. vs. 388.

[3] That is, such a ceremony as a coronation, as in regular sacrifices the exact division in like parts is subject to no change (Medh.) A *jyotiṣṭoma* celebration and such like (Nand.)

[4] So N. and Nand. (? *anyādhāne*, slip for *agnyādhāne*), while Rāgh. says "at a ceremony," with Medh. and K., "in some sects at the ceremony of birth" (*kāsucic chākhāsu ādhāne*, see B. R., *s. v.*)

[5] *I.e.*, the waggon for transporting the soma (K.); and Medh. knows this, for "some" say "*soma* cannot be sold," though he says it is the waggon for selling; so too Rāgh. and Nand. (The MS. of Nand. has in the text *kratau* for *kraye*.) Medh. says of the two horses that the second may be a steer instead. These are the four high-priests, each of whom has three underlings. The Adhvaryu repeated verses from the Yajurveda, and had the mechanical part of attending to the fire and pouring offerings; the Brahman was the presiding priest who overlooked the whole; the Hotar repeated verses from the Rg-, and the Udgātar from the Sāma-Veda.

[6] N. says this verse is an alternative to vs. 209.

[7] The first four are those mentioned in vs. 209 (Medh., K., Nand., and Rāgh.)

[8] The division is not explained by all commentators alike: G., N., K., and Rāgh. explain that of 100 (cows) the first group take 48, the next 24, the next 16, the last 12. Medh. supposes 112, of which the divisions are in turn 56, 28, 16, 12. Nand. says, "If 25 are to be divided among

211. The arrangement of shares is to be made by the application of this rule by men who join together in this world to perform their various tasks.[1]

212. If goods have been promised[2] to a man who has asked for them for some worthy act, and that (act for which the goods were promised) is not afterwards so (performed), the goods should not be given to this man.[3]

213. But if through pride or avarice he should again (try to) make (his claim) succeed,[3] he should be fined one *suvarṇa* by the king as expiation for his theft.

214. Thus is the lawful and proper non-delivery of (what has been) promised declared; and now, furthermore, I will proclaim the (lawful and proper) non-payment of wages.

the *ṛtvigs* (*i.e.*, one high-priest with his underlings), the first would have 12 shares, the second 6 shares, the third 4 shares, the fourth 3 shares—and a like division of 12 among the other groups of four," *i.e.*, each high-priest receives 12 (=48), each next 6 (=24), each next 4 (=16), each next 3 (=12), (=100). In the *açva-medha* sacrifice, told of in the Mbhā. xiv. 72, Yudhiṣṭhira gives the sixteen Brahmans (*ṛtvigs*) their reward divided into four parts (*cāturhotra-pramāṇataḥ*). The remark here made (*brāhmaṇā hi dhanārthinaḥ*) reminds one that in four MSS. (two of Medh., one of Rāgh. and Nand.) this adjective takes the place of *ardhinaḥ* in the text, though not so explained.

[1] Any sort of co-operative labour, such as that of carpenters, etc., is meant (Medh., K.) Rāgh. has *kramayogena* for *vidhi-*.

[2] Literally "given;" so in vs. 214.

[3] The worthy act is explained by Medh. and K. as a sacrifice, a wedding, or something of the sort; Medh. suggests a literal interpretation of the text, in that if already given it shall be regarded as not given and may be taken back. K. quotes a general rule from Gautama (given without authority by Medh.), to the effect that one should not give to an unworthy person, even if he has promised (Gaut. v. 23; dative by the reading of Medh., K.), and Medh. gives "the opinion of Nārada," he may go to the man's house and take it from him. Medh. reads (without alteration of the sense), *Kasmaicid yācamānāya dattaṁ dharmāya yad bhavet* (cf. K.) Nand. follows K. in (*a*), but in (*b*) reads: *Tasmai deyaṁ na tena tat*, and so Nand. has the remarkable explanation: "The words 'and it is not afterwards so,' mean 'if the giver says, I did not give them for this worthy act,' and when he has said this the *receiver must* give the property back to him (*tasmai*), *i.e.*, the giver, or, in other words, the giver must not *take* it back (*pradātrā nāpahāryam*)."

[4] If he brings the matter to the king for trial (Medh.); if he has received a promise only and takes them by force (K.) Nand. reads *mānavaḥ* for *vā punaḥ*, and in accordance with 212 understands, "if (the giver) should (*apaharet*) take the goods back" (instead of waiting for them to be given?). It will be observed that Nand. translates in each case "gift," and not "what is promised." With him it is an accomplished fact; his general sense is, "Now if any man give a present and take it back again, he is to be fined."

215. If a hired man, (although) not ill, insolently fail to work as agreed upon, he should be fined eight *kṛṣṇala*,[1] and his wages should not be paid him.

216. But if he is ill, and, when he is himself again, does the work as originally agreed upon, he should in that case receive his wages even after a very long time (has passed).[2]

217. But if he does not have the work done as agreed upon, whether he be ill or well, the wages (promised) should not be given him, even if the work lacks but little (of being finished).[3]

218. Thus is completely declared the law in regard to non-payment of wages; and now I will proclaim besides the law in regard to those who violate their agreements.

219. If a man has sworn[4] to observe the compact of a corporation in a village[5] or in a district, and then through avarice does not hold to his compact, (the king) should banish him from the realm.

220. (The king) should arrest such a breaker of an agreement and have him fined six *niṣkas*, (each) of the value of four *suvarṇas*, and one silver *çatamāna*.[6]

221. Thus[7] let a just ruler establish the rule of punishment for those who break compacts of village or caste communities.

222. Whoever feels regret in this world after buying or[8] selling anything may within ten days give (back) or take (back) the goods.[9]

223. But after the period of ten days is passed he

[1] Of gold (K.); or, according to circumstances, silver or copper (Medh.)

[2] *Sudīrghasya*, Medh., G., N., Nand., Rāgh., and K., Kash. MS.

[3] Omitted in Medh.

[4] K.

[5] The inhabitants of a village who are embraced in a village community as one corporation (Medh.)

[6] Cf. vs. 137. The reason why the *niṣka* is defined as containing four *suvarṇa* is that there are other *niṣkas* of different value. "Some say there are three punishments intended, four *suvarṇas*, six *niṣkas*, or a *çatamāna*" (Medh.), which may be imposed separately or together (K., Rāgh.)

[7] Medh. and Nand., *eva*. "This rule" (*etam*)—(K.)

[8] But not, say the commentators, if liable to be injured by keeping this length of time.

[9] *Ādadīta ca*, Medh. and Nand.; *vā*, K.

may neither give them (back) nor take them (back);[1] and if he take them (back) or give them (back), he should be fined six hundred (*paṇas*) by the king.

224. If a man give away (in marriage) a girl who has a defect, without first making (the defect) known, the king himself should impose a fine of ninety-six *paṇas* upon this man.[2]

225. When a man, because he dislikes her, says of a maiden that she is no (longer a) maid, he should receive a fine of five hundred (*paṇas*) if he does not prove her defect.

226. Marriage hymns (*anantra*) have been ordained for virgins only, but never among men for (those who are) not virgins; since these women are debarred from all legal[3] ceremonies.

227. The marriage hymns (*mantra*) are the established token whereby a (legitimate) wife may be recognised, and the completion of those (ceremonial rites) must be recognised by the wise (as occurring) at the seventh step.[4]

228. If any one feels regret at having performed any business whatever,[5] (the judge) should by this rule set that man upon the path of duty.[6]

229. I will now proclaim exactly, in accordance with the principles of duty, the disputes in (regard to) cattle (which arise) on occasion of some fault (either) of the owners or of the keepers (of the flocks).

230. The responsibility in (regard to) the safety (of the cattle) rests by day with the keeper, but by night with the owner (if the cattle are) in his house; otherwise[7] the keeper should be made responsible.

[1] Nand. reads *nādadīta ca* (as in 222), which, although unsupported, seems better than *nāpi dāpayet* (Medh. and K.), on account of the parallel *ādadānaḥ*.

[2] Cf. vs. 204, where the defects are mentioned (Medh., K.), though here that of vs. 225 is more particularly intended.

[3] Or, "holy" (*dharma*).

[4] The marriage pair take seven steps around the fire; before the last step is taken the marriage is incomplete.

[5] *Dharma;* so vs. 229.

[6] Such as agreements, etc., where "this rule" of vs. 222 is in force, and he has ten days to consider the matter (K.)

[7] That is, when the cattle are not housed at night, but remain out of doors in a wood (Medh.) with the keeper (Medh., K.)

231. A cowherd who is paid by milk may milk the best of ten (cows), being supported in this way by the owner's consent; this should be the support for a keeper not (otherwise) supported.[1]

232. The keeper alone should restore (the value of) cattle which have been lost, or destroyed by worms, or slain by dogs,[2] or killed (by tumbling) in a hole (because they were) deprived of (this) man's care.

233. If the keeper gave an alarm when the cattle were fallen upon by thieves, he is not in fault,[3] provided he give notice to the owner at the (proper) place and time.[4]

234. When cattle die (a natural death), he should present to the owners the two ears, the hide, the tail, the bladder, the sinews, the gall-yellow, and let them see the proofs.[5]

235. When goats or sheep are attacked by wolves and the keeper does not come up (to protect them), if a wolf should seize and kill one of them, the fault would lie with the keeper.

236. But if, while grazing in a wood, and united into a herd,[6] a wolf should spring[7] upon and kill one of them, the keeper is in that case not in fault.

237. Round about (every) village there should be a strip of land one hundred bows,[8] or even three casts of a

[1] This verse is here omitted in Nand. and placed between 244 and 245. Medh. observes that other arrangements may be made at discretion.

[2] Or "such animals," *e.g.*, jackals. So in vs. 235 (Medh.)

[3] *Na pālas tatra kilbiṣī* (Medh.), or the keeper ought not to pay (K.; so Nand.)

[4] That is, (K.) at once, or (Medh.) that evening, and the place where it happened (K.), or where the owner is (Medh.)

[5] *Aṅkāṁç ca* (Medh.), "show in general some proofs" (Jolly). Nand. reads in this with K., but in (*a*) has *vastisnāyūni* with Medh., and differs from both in reading *carma karṇau sakthivālau*, increasing the list by "a thigh-bone." The slight differences, other than these, between Medh. and K. do not change the sense.

[6] Medh. and K.; but B. R., "hedged in."

[7] *Utpatya* (Medh., Rāgh.), *utplutya* (Nand.); K. in commentary defines by *utplutya*.

[8] On all four quarters (Medh.) A bow is four cubits (*hasta*)—(Medh. and K.) Nand., on the contrary, regards the bows as bow-casts, defining the enclosure round a city as *dhanupātāḥ çatatrayaḥ* in extent, which, however, varies with the size of the town. He reads, too, *parivāra* for *parihāra*. Medh. (and K.) explain better by the length of the bow.

staff[1] (in width); around a city (it should be) three times (as wide).[2]

238. If the cattle (which pasture) in this place should injure a grain crop which was not enclosed, the king should not in this case allow punishment to fall on the guardians of the cattle.

239. (The owner of the field) should in such a case make a hedge (so high that) a camel could not look over it,[3] and have every hole closed, through which a dog could thrust his muzzle, or a boar his snout.

240. (But if the damage be done by cattle) in an enclosed field (bordering on) a road,[4] or again (in one) lying on the outskirts of the village, the keeper[5] should be fined one hundred (*paṇas*), (and the field owner[6]) should drive them off[7] if they are destitute of a keeper.

241. In other fields (the one responsible for) the cattle ought to pay a fine of one *paṇa* and a quarter, but in all cases[8] (the value of) the crop (destroyed) must be paid the owner[9] of the field: so is the rule.

242. A cow with a calf not ten days old, bulls, and also the cattle of the gods, whether with a keeper or without a keeper, Manu said, ought not to be punished.[10]

[1] Medh. says of the staff that one casts it with the hand, picks it up where it fell, and so on three times.

[2] This land is intended for a common, and is not to be tilled (Medh.)

[3] *Nāvalokayet* (MS. Bomb.), Medh. Rāgh., Nand. Medh. observes that this fence or hedge is of thorns and boughs. A slight *var. lec., āvārayet* in (*b*) of Dr. B.'s MS. of Medh. is supported by Nand.

[4] *I.e.*, a field bordering on a public road.

[5] "The cattle when with a keeper," *i.e.*, the keeper receives the fine if he is appointed to watch and is absent (K.)

[6] Medh., K.

[7] *Vārayet* is the reading of Medh. (Dr. B.'s MS.) and Nand. (Rāgh.) "they may be enclosed." Cf. vs. 242. (Medh.) "This is no crime" (Nand.); cf. Ap. ii. 28, 5. Medh. supports the general tenor of the text by quoting Gaut. xii. 21. According to Yāj. ii. 162, "there is no crime" in this case if the damage was done without (the owner's) wish, otherwise he is to be punished as a thief.

[8] With or without a keeper (Medh.); at the outskirts (of the village), etc. (Nand.)

[9] Dat. in Medh. By the keeper or by the owner of the cattle (K.)

[10] The beast doing the damage is here, as in the foregoing, represented as paying the penalty, meaning that the cattle-keeper receives the punishment (fine). In Yāj. ii. 163 this is only said of those who have *not* a keeper —they are to be released (*mocyāḥ*). The cattle of the gods are those ordained for sacrifice (Medh.) Neither Vas., Baudh., Āp., nor Gaut. have

243. When the owner of the field is in fault, the punishment should be ten times as great as (this portion[1]), but half of this sum should be the fine if the fault lay with the servants and the owner of the field knew nothing about it.

244. This rule[2] let a just king maintain in (regard to) faults committed by owners, cattle, and keepers.

245. If a dispute has arisen between two villages in regard to a boundary, the king should determine the boundary in the month Jyaiṣṭha;[3] as the boundary marks[4] are then very plain.[5]

246. One should make as boundary trees the ficus indica, ficus religiosa, butea frondosa, bombax heptaphyllum, valica robusta, palms, and milky trees;

247. Thickets, different kinds of bamboo, prosopis spicigera, running plants, mounds, reeds, and thickets of trapa bispinosa: a boundary-line thus (made) is not destroyed.[6]

248. Ponds, springs, long ponds, (dammed) brooks, and temples are to be made at the points of union of the boundary.

249. And one should make other boundary marks which are concealed; considering the constant mistakes occurring among men in this world, when they are settling a boundary.

250. Stones, bones, cow-tails, hulls, ashes, potsherds, dry cow-dung, tiles, coals, gravel, and sand,

any mention of this. Gaut. (xii. 22) says in general that a cow is to be fined. Viṣṇu gives the same rule, but only for bulls and lately-calved cows (v. 150).

[1] According to Medh. and K. the sin here spoken of is the neglect to plant crops in proper season. From these crops the king takes a portion (cf. vii. 130), and if through neglect of the owner he is deprived of this income-tax, it should be increased tenfold as a penalty. As the king's share on grain was generally one-sixth, the penalty paid would be nearly half as much again as the whole crop, to obtain the value of which we must suppose an average taken from the crops of former years. Nand.'s explanation seems more natural, "ten times the amount the owner has spoiled by neglect," with no reference to the king.

[2] After this verse Nand. places 231.

[3] From the middle of May to the middle of June.

[4] Medh. has *hetuṣu* (the means of proof).

[5] The grass is then dried up by the hot sun, and therefore the boundary marks are easily seen (Medh. and K.)

[6] These trees are all tall, or otherwise conspicuous, or very enduring.

251. And all kinds of things which the earth could not devour even after a long time; these he should have put out of sight at the points of union of the boundary.[1]

252. By these marks he should determine the boundary of the two disputing (villages); or[2] (he may determine it) by priority of occupation[3] (which has lasted) for ever; or by a stream of water.

253. If there should still be a doubt, even where the marks are visible, the decision in regard to the discussion[4] of the boundary should be settled by an appeal to witnesses.

254. In the presence of all the families in the villages and the two opponents,[5] the witnesses in regard to the boundary must be questioned concerning the boundary marks.

255. In accordance with the decision which they, on being questioned, have unanimously rendered, let (the king) make certain the boundary, and also all these (witnesses) by name.[6]

256. Placing earth on their heads, be-crowned, and wearing red garments, they should determine correctly the course (of the boundary), after each has been sworn by his good deeds.[7]

257. If they determine (the boundary) truthfully, they are made pure, (being) witnesses of the truth; but if they determine (it) contrary (to truth), they shall (each) be fined two hundred (*paṇas*).

258. In the absence of witnesses, four men who live on

[1] Gen. in Medh.

[2] And.

[3] Priority of occupation must have lasted from immemorial times; cf. 149. This is an alternative to 250–251, when the boundary-lines do not exist (Medh.)

[4] *Viniççayaḥ* (Medh.); (so Bomb. MS.); *vâda-vinirṇaye* (Nand.); (so the Wilkins MS.)

[5] The two men commissioned to represent the villages (Medh., K.)

[6] Both Medh. and K. refer this to writing down the limits of the boundary and the names of the witnesses. It probably refers simply to calling on the witnesses by name. The whole account precludes the idea of documents. In (*a*) Nand. reads *samâseṣu tu lakṣaṇaṁ*, cf. 262.

[7] They imprecate a curse on their acts that they may be fruitless hereafter if they lie now (Medh., K.) The crowns are of flowers (K.)

the outskirts of the village[1] may, having been instructed to do so, settle the question[2] of the boundary in the presence of the king.

259. But in the absence of neighbours, and of men who have lived (in the village) for a long time, (and who might have served as) witnesses in (regard to) the boundary, let (the king) call upon these (following kinds of) men who live in the woods:

260. (Namely), hunters, bird-catchers, cowherds, fishermen, root-diggers, snake-catchers, gleaners,[3] and other men who wander about the woods.[4]

261. In accordance with what they, on being questioned, shall declare (to be) a mark on the boundary-lines, shall the king establish it between the two villages according to law.[5]

262. A decision in regard to the boundary-lines of a field, spring, pond, garden, or house, shall be established by an appeal to the neighbours.[6]

263. If the neighbours lie concerning the boundary (over which) men are disputing, each one of them shall be fined the medium fine[7] by the king.

264. The man who by frightening (the owner)[8] takes possession of a house, pond, garden, or field, should be fined five hundred (*paṇas*); but if (he has taken possession) through ignorance, the fine (should be) two hundred.

[1] *Grāmasīmanta°*, *i.e.*, on all parts of the village, not "the neighbour's" alone, (as K. says). (Medh.) (Nand. = K.)

[2] *Sīmā viniçcayam* (Nand.)

[3] The men are connected with those in the village, but gain a livelihood in the woods; the gleaners are of any village, poor beggars, who pick up what they can get (Medh.)

[4] K. and Nand.; or perhaps better, with Medh., "and likewise others by the hundred" (*çataças tathā*), though Medh. and K. both explain as "flower and fruit dealers, and wood-gatherers," etc. Nand. reads (repeating vs. 259) *vanagocarān*, thus tacitly agreeing with Medh., G., and K., while N. alone thinks it means "wild tribes of the woods."

[5] *Dharmeṇa*, according to Medh., to be joined to the participle, "being lawfully questioned." Nand. says only "this is self-evident."

[6] These cases are confined to the circuit of one village (K.) [Nand., (cf. vs. 255) reads *samāseṣu tu nirṇayaṁ*].

[7] Five hundred *paṇas*.

[8] Threatening him with thieves or a suit at law (Medh.); with fetters and death (K.) This is a special case, not coming under vs. 193, where death would be the result (Rāgh.)

265. If it is impossible to settle the boundary-line, a king who knows the right should himself, (and) alone, in order to do them a kindness,[1] point out the ground:[2] so stands the law.

266. Thus is the law completely established regarding the determining of boundaries. I will now, furthermore, proclaim the determining of verbal injuries.

267. A Kṣatriya who reviles a Brahman ought to be fined one hundred (*paṇas*); a Vaiçya one hundred and fifty or two hundred;[3] but a Çūdra ought to receive corporal[4] punishment.

268. A Brahman should be fined fifty if he has thrown insult on a Kṣatriya, but the fine should be a half of fifty if on a Vaiçya, and twelve if on a Çūdra.[5]

269. If one of the twice-born abuses a man of like caste, (he should be fined) twelve, but (the fine) should be twice this (amount) for words that ought never to be spoken.[6]

270. If (a man) of one birth[7] assault one of the twice-born castes with virulent words, he ought to have his tongue cut, for he is of the lowest origin.[8]

271. If he make mention in an insulting manner of their name and caste, a red-hot iron rod, ten fingers[9] long, should be thrust into his mouth.

[1] With justice and kindness towards each party, regarding the qualities of the land (Medh.)

[2] The ground about which they dispute (K.), or the ground belonging to each party (Medh.)

[3] The difference in the fines of the Vaiçya depends on the enormity of the crime (K., Nand.) Nand. and Rāgh. read *adhyardhaçataṁ;* with the Beng. MS. Medh. has *sārdha°*.

[4] So the commentators; "beating," etc. (K.); beating, mutilation, or death, according to the offence (Medh.); perhaps capital punishment is alone intended, as the word *vadha* has either meaning; Nand. limits to beating.

[5] Gautama, xii. 13, seems to say that the Brahman pays nothing for insulting a Çūdra; (so Har., who adds that this implies that the Kṣatriya and Vaiçya *are* fined); but Medh. quotes this as meaning that in the case of a Çūdra the fine is according to circumstances, *i.e*, "nothing (is settled)."

[6] Such as insults to the wife, mother, sister, etc. (Medh., K.) This refers not to those of equal caste, but to members of any caste (Medh.)

[7] "*I.e.*, a Çūdra, for he lacks the initiation" (that makes the second birth)—(Nand.)

[8] "For it is said in i. 31 that the Çūdra was created from the feet of Brahmā, and in x. 4 that there is no fifth caste" (Medh.) Medh. reads *dvijātim*.

[9] Or thumb-joints, inches. Nand. (and Rāgh.) read *nikheyo* with the Beng. MS.

272. If this man through insolence gives instruction to the priests in regard to their duty, the king should cause boiling-hot[1] oil to be poured into his mouth and ear.

273. If one through insolence denies their learning, country,[2] caste, or bodily ceremonies,[3] he should be fined a fine of two hundred.[4]

274. (If he insults) a one-eyed man, or a lame man, or any other person deformed in like manner, he should be fined a fine of at least one kārṣāpaṇa, even if he speaks the truth.[5]

275. He who slanders[6] his own mother, father, wife, brother, son,[7] or spiritual teacher, should be fined one hundred, and (also) he who does not give the right of way to his spiritual teacher.

276. The fine to be imposed by a wise (king) on a Brahman and Kṣatriya (for mutual insults) is the first[8] in (the case of) the Brahman, and the medium (fine) in (the case of) the Kṣatriya.

277. Exactly thus and in accordance with the caste of each (should be) the application of punishment (in the case) of a Vaiçya and Çūdra,[9] except the cutting of the tongue:[10] thus is the decision.

278. Thus has the rule of punishment in regard to verbal injuries been declared in accordance with truth.

[1] *Tapta;* the hot oil drunk as a penance was called simply hot (*uṣṇa*), though the penance itself was termed *tapta.* Cf. xi. 215.

[2] Brahmans born in certain districts were specially honoured; cf. ii. 19–22.

[3] The Brahman lost caste if initiation with the accompanying "bodily ceremonies" were not performed at the right age; cf. ii. 38, 39.

[4] The lightness of the fine shows this verse refers to those of like caste, not to the Çūdra (K.); to all castes say we, but others say it refers to the Çūdra (Medh.) Nand. notes nothing on this point. When it is done in ignorance or in joke it is no sin (Medh.)

[5] This fine is for the Çūdra or for all, as before (Medh.)

[6] Causing hate in the family by making slanderous statements (Medh.), cursing (K.) It may mean charging with adultery and the like (N.) Angry vituperation (Nand.) Cf. note to vs. 354.

[7] *Tanayam*, or "father-in-law" (*çvaçuram*), according to the reading of the Mitākṣ. and May. (p. 83).

[8] That is, the lowest (250 *panas*), while the medium fine is 500.

[9] That is, the Vaiçya receives the lowest, the Çūdra the middle fine. Cf. for these rules Gaut. xii. 8 ff.; Yāj. ii. 206; Viṣṇu, v. 35, 36.

[10] Cf. ver. 270. The mutual abuse softens the offence.

Now, furthermore, I will proclaim the law of corporal injuries.

279. If a man of the lowest birth should with any member injure one of the highest station,[1] even that member of this man shall be cut (off): this is an ordinance of Manu.

280. If he lift up his hand or his staff (against him), he ought to have his hand cut off; and if he smites[2] him with his foot in anger, he ought to have his foot cut off.

281. If a low-born man endeavours to sit down by the side of a high-born man, he should be banished after being branded on the hip, or (the king) may cause his backside to be cut off.[3]

282. If through insolence he spit[4] upon him, the king should cause his two lips to be cut off; and if he make water upon him, his penis; and if he break wind upon him, his buttocks.[5]

283. If he seize him by the locks, let the king without hesitation cause both his hands to be cut off; (also if he seize him) by the feet, the beard,[6] the neck, or the testicles.

284. A man who tears (another's) skin and one who causes blood to be seen[7] ought to be fined one hundred (*paṇas*); if he tears the flesh (he should be fined) six *niṣkas*, but if he breaks a bone he should be banished.[8]

[1] Any one of the three upper castes (Medh.); one of the twice-born (K.); (*çreyāṅsam*), "any one better than his own caste" (Nand.)

[2] Medh. and Nand. say this is not an actual kick, but simply raising the foot in order to kick. The protest will hardly stand, as *praharan* in vs. 300 shows.

[3] In such a way that death shall not ensue. K., Nand., with Bomb. MS. *apakṛṣṭajaḥ*.

[4] Or towards him, and so in ff. (Medh.) For *meḍhram* Medh. has *çiçnam*.

[5] This is only when it is done to insult, not when it is the result of carelessness (Medh., K.)

[6] *Nāsikāyāṁ ca* (by the nose) is Nand.'s reading for the obscure *dāḍhikāyām* (beard or whisker).

[7] *I.e.*, to flow (from the surface, not from the nose or ear) — Medh.)

[8] This refers, not, as in the above, to a Çūdra injuring a Brahman, but to men of like caste injuring each other (Medh., K., Nand.) Banishment is for the Brahman, death for the other castes (Medh.) This is tacitly contradicted by N., who assumes the confiscation of the goods along with banishment (which is forbidden in the case of a Brahman). Cf. Yāj. ii. 215 ff.; and *ib.* 227 for the next rules.

285. A fine must be imposed for injuring all (kinds of) trees, in exact accordance with their usefulness:[1] thus is the rule.

286. (The king) should impose a fine in exact proportion to the amount of hurt caused when a blow has been given to the hurt of either men or beasts.

287. When injury has been done to a limb, when a man's strength[2] has been impaired or his blood shed, he (who caused the injury) shall be made to pay the expenses of restoring him to health, or shall pay the whole as a fine.[3]

288. Whoever injures any man's goods, whether wittingly or unwittingly, must give this (owner) full satisfaction, and pay to the king a sum equal to this (fine paid to the owner).

289. But the fine should be five times the real worth[4] (when damage is done) to leather, utensils of leather, wooden or earthen ware, and to flowers, roots, and fruits.

290. They say there are ten (cases when), in respect to a waggon, a driver, and an owner of a waggon, (the fines for damage) may be remitted; in every other case a fine is ordained.

291. When the nozzle-rope is cut, the yoke broken, when (the waggon)[5] slips sideways or backwards,[6] when there is a break in the axle of the waggon, or likewise one in the wheel;

292. When the straps, girth, or reins break,[7] and when (the driver) has called "Out of the way," Manu said, (there is) no fine.

[1] Cf. Viṣṇu Sūtra, v. 55–58 (K.) The difference in value is according to products (K.) and position (Medh.)

[2] *Prāṇa* = *bala* (Medh., G., Kash. MS., and Rāgh.) for *vraṇa*. Nand. supports Medh. and resembles him in his whole gloss.

[3] If the injured man will not accept the payment for his recovery the whole must be given to the king (Medh., K., Nand.)

[4] In addition to payment for damage (K.)

[5] So Medh., G., N., and Nand.

[6] "Others" explain this as "running against something" (Medh.)

[7] This hemistich (*a*) is omitted in Medh.'s gloss.; so in Yāj. (ii. 299) the substance of it is also omitted.

293. But if the waggon be upset through the unskilfulness of the driver, and any injury has been done, the owner should be fined a fine of two hundred (*paṇas*).

294. If the driver was a capable person, the driver deserves the fine;[1] but if the driver was incapable, all those in the waggon ought to be fined one hundred (*paṇas*) each.

295. But if he, being detained upon the way by cattle or by a chariot, should thereby cause the death of animate creatures,[2] a fine should without hesitation[3] be imposed.

296. If (thereby) the death of a man should occur, his crime would at once become like that of a thief;[4] in (the case of) large animate creatures, such as a cow, elephant, camel, horse, etc., half (of this fine should be imposed).

297. A fine of two hundred (*paṇas* is set) for the killing[5] of small[6] animals, and the fine should be fifty (*paṇas*) in (the case of) propitious forest animals and birds.[7]

298. The fine (for killing) asses, goats, and sheep should amount to five *māṣaka*, but one *māṣaka* should be the fine for destroying a dog or a boar.

299. A wife, son, slave, pupil, and own brother[8] should, when they have committed faults, be beaten with a cord or a bamboo-cane;[9]

300. But on the back of the body (only), never on a noble[10] part: if one should smite them on any other part than that, he would incur the sin of a thief.

[1] As in vs. 293 the owner, so here the driver is fined two hundred (K.)

[2] Men or animals (Medh.)

[3] *Avicāritaḥ* (K.); *asandigdhaḥ* (Nand.); either *avicāritaḥ*, there is no application of fine (Medh., N.); or *vicāritaḥ*, a fine was set of old; there is a fine (G., Rāgh.)

[4] That is, his fine would be that of a thief, which is 1000 (*paṇas*), (K., Rāgh., Nand. or), as the thief is punished by *vadha*, death, so here; and the "half" means cutting off the hand, feet, etc. (Medh.)

[5] So K. Or "injury;" but the context requires here "death."

[6] Crow, parrot, etc. (Medh.); cat, etc. (Nand.)

[7] Different sorts of antelopes and deer, flamingos and parrots, etc. (Medh., K.) "Propitious" animals are those that bring good luck; "the jackal, crow, owl (etc.), are unpropitious animals" (Medh.)

[8] That is, one's younger brother, for he is as a son (Medh.)

[9] Cf. iv. 164.

[10] Lit. more elevated, *i.e.* the head, etc. (K.)

301. Thus has the decision concerning corporal injuries been completely established. Now I will proclaim the rule for determining the punishment of a thief.

302. In restraining thieves the king should exert the greatest possible effort, for the fame and realm of the king are increased by restraining thieves.

303. For that king who bestows security is ever to be honoured,[1] for this is (as it were) a sacrifice that ever increases unto him, whereat the sacrificial gift is the security (which he bestows).[2]

304. In consequence of the protection afforded by him, the king has a sixth share of the virtue (which comes) from all (the good deeds of his people), while in consequence of failing to protect them he receives a sixth share of the wrong (done by them).[3]

305. In consequence of the protection[4] (afforded by him), the king properly becomes partaker of a sixth share in (all) that (merit which is gained by the) study, sacrifice, liberality, or worship (of his people).

306. If the king protect all creatures with justice, and

[1] Or is worthy of honour (from all the gods)—(Medh.)

[2] That is, when he gives his people security from thieves, it is as if he were performing a great *soma* celebration, and the gifts usually given on such an occasion are represented by the gift of security; as Medh. says, he receives the fruit of a sacrifice.

[3] This is that famous "sixth" of good or evil (*dharma*, *adharma*) which the king draws upon himself by protecting or by neglecting his people; he receives, it may be, a sixth of the produce as tax (vii. 130), and in return must give security to the realm, or he gets the same proportion of the fruits of their bad deeds; or (cf. vs. 308) he takes all the sin of the world. Yāj. says he takes one-sixth of the fruit of their good deeds, but one-half their sin in case he does not protect them (Yāj. i. 334-336). Similarly, in viii. 35, 39, is the share of treasure the king receives, and again in vs. 18 (of spiritual sin) he receives a fourth of the fruits of the sin caused by a wrong decision in court. It must have been then through a confusion between these last rules, or perhaps from different texts in earlier versions, that we find in a case dealing wholly with general protection a different statement assigned to Manu by the Mbhā. (xiii. 61, 34, 35), where we read, "The king obtains a fourth of all the sin done by his people if he does not protect them; now some say the whole sin comes upon the king (Manu, viii. 308?), or again a half (Yāj. i. 336?); this is their decision, but we think it is one quarter, because we have heard the law of Manu (*caturthaṁ matam asmākaṁ Manoḥ çrutvā'nuçāsanaṁ*)": viii. 308 is thus tacitly excluded.

[4] *Pālanāt* (Medh.); *rakṣaṇāt* (K.); the meaning the same.

inflict corporal punishment[1] on those deserving it, he would (thereby) virtually perform day by day sacrifices accompanied by hundreds of thousands of gifts.

307. If a king while giving no protection (yet) levies a tribute (for grain on husbandmen) or a tax (on real estate), and receives tolls (or taxes, from merchants), (daily) gifts (of flowers, vegetables, etc.), and (moneys paid for) fines, he goes at once to hell.[2]

308. They say that king who takes a sixth share as the tribute (due him), but gives no protection, takes upon himself all the wickedness of the whole world.[3]

309. One should know that that king is treading the downward path who considers not the law, who is an unbeliever,[4] who acquires wealth by unjust means, who gives no protection, and who is a devourer (of his people's wealth).[5]

310. By these three means, imprisonment, fetters, and corporal punishment of various sorts,[6] let (the king) earnestly restrain the doer[7] of evil.

311. For by restraining sinners and by kindly treatment[8] towards good men kings are ever purified, as the twice-born (are) by sacrifices.

312. Constantly must the ruler who would make him-

[1] Or perhaps better, "kills those deserving death (*vadhya*)."

[2] The different words for tax or tribute are explained by K., Rāgh., as translated in the parentheses; so too Medh., who says that they are all names for taxes (*kara*), the general term.

[3] That is, of all his people (Medh.); cf. note to 304. For *rājānam* Medh. reads *attāram*, devourer, as in v. 309.

[4] *Nāstika*: "one who says there is not" another world (K.) The converse, *āstika*, "one who says there is" (a believer), occurs only in later literature.

[5] Nand. reads *vipralopakaṁ* (for *vipralumpakam*), and defines as "one who deserts a Brahman," while Rāgh. translates "taking property, etc., even from a Brahman" (*vipra*, priest); but Medh. and K. hold this word to be merely from the verb and prepositions. Medh. notes a *var. lec.* in (*b*) which changes slightly the meaning of the whole sentence (*asatyaṁ ca nṛpaṁ tyajet*), *i.e.*, "one should desert a king who is," etc. This *var. lec.* is found in Nand. Medh.'s own text differs a trifle from K. in having *adhogataṁ* for *adhogatiṁ*, with no material change of meaning.

[6] *Vadha*, (or) "death by various means" (Medh.) K. understands mutilation. Nand. reads *daṇḍena* (for *bandhena*), by (punishment of) fines.

[7] Or doers (Nand.)

[8] Nand. reads, "by protecting the good" (*rakṣaṇena ca*).

self happy exercise patience toward men who revile (him) when they are engaged in affairs; and also toward the young, the old, and those who are ill.[1]

313. On this account is one magnified in heaven, if, when he is reviled by those in distress, he bears it with patience; and on this account he departs to hell, if because of his sovereign power he (will) not meekly endure (reviling).

314. A thief[2] must, with loosened hair and a firm bearing,[3] approach the king and proclaim his theft, (saying), "Thus have I done; punish me;"[4]

315. (While he) bears to (the king) upon his shoulder a club,[5] or a staff of acacia wood, a spear sharp at both ends, or an iron rod.[6]

316. By being punished or by being released the thief is freed from (the crime of) theft; but if the king does not punish him, he (himself) receives the crime of the thief.[7]

317. Upon the eater of his food the killer of an embryo causes his guilt to pass;[8] upon the husband, the wife who

[1] These, too, are by Medh. included in the idea "when engaged in affairs" (cases at law). *Kāryin* Medh. illustrates in a very general way, however, "as if, when one had been executed, the relatives should revile the king."

[2] A thief of gold is meant—one who has stolen the gold of a Brahman (Medh., K., and Nand.)

[3] *Dhāratā*, "running," or *dhīmatā* (=*dhairyaratā*, Medh.) "steadfast;" Medh. notes the reading *dhāratā* as a *var. lec.*, but prefers *dhīmatā*, which is also found in Nand.

[4] In xi. 101 ff. we have a similar account, and from this the commentators draw their conclusions in regard to the caste of the parties. No such distinction is made in the text, nor in the early form of the law, which is very primitive. Cf. Yāj. iii. 257; Āp. i. 9. 25. 4; Gaut. xii. 44.

[5] The acacia staff is given in ii. 45 as that appropriate to a Kṣatriya. The club called *musala* is very likely beset with iron, as in the Mbhā. it is used as a telum missile (*ayasmayam . . . musalam . . . cikṣepa, parigho 'pamam*, xi. 14, 29).

[6] It is evident that the earliest explanation of these verses did *not* exclude the Brahman. Medh. says, "They think the club and other instruments are to be used in the order of the [four] castes. This is wrong, for the use of the word *or* precludes this, as well as the fact that this atonement is not intended for the Brahman."

[7] The punishment here meant is death. Medh. notes that, if the king does not strike, he should change the punishment to a money fine.

[8] The slayer of an embryo is the slayer of a Brahman (all Comm.); he who eats his food receives his guilt. So the complacent husband, the negligent teacher and priest, the king

has gone astray; upon the Guru, a pupil and one for whom sacrifice is made; and upon the king, the thief.

318. Those men who have committed sins,[1] but on whom punishment has been inflicted by the king, go to heaven with all their sins removed, as (if they were) worthy men who had acted well.

319. He who takes from a spring either the rope or the bucket, and he who breaks open a water-tank,[2] should receive a fine of one *māṣa*,[3] and replace it in this (place).[4]

320. Death[5] (is the penalty) if one steals more than ten measures[6] of grain; where the amount is less he must pay (a fine) eleven times (the value of the grain), and (in either case) be made to return the property to that (owner).

321. In the same way death (should be inflicted) for (stealing) more than one hundred (*palas*)[7] of things measurable by weight,[8] gold or silver, and the like, or (for stealing) the finest garments.[9]

322. But cutting off the hand[10] is enjoined for (stealing) (less than one hundred but) more than fifty *palas*; where the amount is less, however, one should ordain a fine eleven times as great as the worth (of the things stolen).

who fails to punish when he ought, all obtain the guilt caused by their carelessness; nevertheless the sinners themselves are not absolved from guilt (K.)

[1] *Rājabhir dhṛtadaṇḍāḥ* (Medh., Rāgh.), °*kṛtadaṇḍāḥ* (Nand.), "those who have borne punishment (caused) by kings."

[2] Where water is kept to be given (to travellers) to drink (K.)

[3] A *māṣa* of gold is meant (K. and Rāgh.), as always when not specified (K.) The kind is not declared, whether copper or silver (Medh.) Nand. says nothing.

[4] So Medh.; in this spring (K.)

[5] *Vadha.*

[6] According to K. the measure (*kumbha*) = 20 *droṇa*, between three and four bushels. Cf. Colebrooke, Essays, i. 534 (K., however, makes the *droṇa* = 200 *palas*). Medh. puts it at 20 *prastha*, but says that this amount depends on the place. Nand. gives the definition *dhānya-bhājanaṁ kuśūlāt kinnā* (?) *nyūnam*, and says this punishment is for Kṣatriyas and lower castes stealing grain from a Brahman.

[7] One hundred *palas* (Medh., K.), or *karṣas*, according to some (Medh.); N. says *niṣkas.*

[8] The kind of *vadha* is determined by circumstances (Medh.); silver, gold, etc. (Medh., K.; cf. Viṣṇu, v. 13), or copper, etc. (Rāgh.)

[9] Silk turbans and the like (Medh.)

[10] This shows that the *vadha*, translated "death" in the preceding, is not mutilation. Cf. Viṣṇu, *loc. cit.*

323. A man deserves death for stealing men of (good) family,[1] and especially (for stealing) women (of good family); and also (for stealing) very valuable gems.

324. After considering the time and the purpose,[2] let the king ordain punishment for the theft of large cattle,[3] weapons, and medicine.[4]

325. (For stealing) cows belonging to Brahmans, for piercing (the nostrils) of an (unfruitful) cow (used for draught), and for stealing (small) cattle, (the thief) should immediately have half his foot cut off.[5]

326. (For stealing woollen) thread cotton, stuff to cause fermenting, cow-dung,[6] molasses, sour milk, milk, butter-milk, water, grass,

327. Baskets of bamboo-cane and rattan, (any kind of) salt, (utensils) made of clay, clay and ashes,

328. Fishes, birds, oil, ghee, flesh, honey, and whatever has its origin in cattle;[7]

329. Other things of like sort, intoxicating liquors, broth, all cooked foods—(for stealing any of these) a fine double the worth of the article (stolen) should be paid.

330. For stealing flowers, green grain, brush, vines, creepers, and other[8] (kinds of grain) not purified,[9] a fine of five *kṛṣṇala*[10] should be set.

331. (But) for (stealing) grain (that has) been purified, and for vegetables, roots, and fruits, a penalty of one hun-

[1] If they are not of good family (or good character) he should pay, as before, eleven times their value (Medh.)

[2] Or "the use intended" (*kāryam*). It makes a difference whether it is done by day or night, with ill-will or not, and what the object of their use may be (Medh.)

[3] Elephants, horses, etc. (Medh., K.)

[4] Medicinal plants.

[5] Small cattle intended for sacrifice are meant (K.) The doubtful word *sthūrikā* (*sic*) in Nand. receives a different definition from that (given above) of K. (*Sthūrikā nāma pārṣneç caturaṅgulād ūrdhvapradeçaḥ*). This latter is alluded to by Medh. as the opinion of some (*anye*); and he upholds the idea that it is the goading of the draught-cow.

[6] Nand. has *āyasasya*, "iron."

[7] As leather, horns (K., Rāgh.)

[8] Medh. and Nand. read (*alpeṣu* for *anyeṣu*), *i.e.*, "a small amount of grain, or—"

[9] Where the bad grain has not been sifted out (K.); cleared of dust (Nand.)

[10] Of gold or silver (K.)

dred (*paṇas*) (should be imposed, if the thief) is not a relative;[1] if he is a relative the fine should be half a hundred.

332.[2] Any act (of robbery) done by force, in the presence (of the owner), would be an act of violence; if it should be done in secret, it would be (simply) a theft;[3] and where one takes anything, and (the act) is denied, (that also is theft).

333. If a man steal (these) things when they are prepared (for use),[4] or abduct fire from a house,[5] the king should have him fined one hundred (*paṇas*).

334. With whatever limb a thief executes his purpose among men, even that (limb) shall the king take from him, (that it may be) for an example[6] (to others).

335. If the father, teacher, friend, mother, wife, son, or domestic priest fail to attend to their own duties,[7] they should not go unpunished by the king.

[1] Or "connected in any way;" so K. and Medh., though the latter, while giving this explanation, says it may mean whether there is a guard or not; if there is a guard (*sānvaye*), the guilt is divided, and the thief's fine is less; or, again, it may mean, says Medh., whether he has any reasonable excuse or not. In vs. 198 we have similar explanations of these words, and Nand., as there, differs here from Medh. and K. in glossing *niranvaya* by *niḥçeṣā-pahāra*, *i.e.*, when one steals all the grain the fine is one hundred. Medh. and K. agree that the grain here meant is from the open field, on account of vs. 320.

[2] Omitted by Nand., and follows 333 in Medh. with (*a*) and (*b*) inverted.

[3] Instead of resistance or non-resistance (B. R.), K. understands open (robbery) or secret (theft). Medh. gives the same explanation, and paraphrases "an open assault on guarded property" (is violence); the opposite is theft; in Medh. (*a*) *kṛtvā nā'pahnute ca yat*, "and it is also theft (alone) when one commits theft and does not deny it" (while if he denies it it is violence). I think the verse was probably added as a gloss to explain the preceding—"A fine of 100 in a *niranvaya* case (what is *niranvaya*?), simple theft is *niranvaya*," etc. The position in Medh. is evidently wrong, though the hemistichs themselves are better transposed.

[4] So Medh. and K. (*These* are the thread, etc., of vs. 326.)

[5] "Sacred fire is meant, not, as Govind. says, any ordinary fire, for the fine is too heavy for that" (K.); but G. probably read, as Medh. and Nand. do, *çataṁ* for K.'s *ādyam*, *i.e.*, put the fine at 100 instead of 250. Medh. says no special fire is meant.

[6] *I.e.*, by frightening them he prevents a repetition of the crime in the future (Medh., K.); "for example, if one should trust to his feet to escape, believing none able to catch him, he should lose his foot; or if he slily cuts a purse, his hand" (Medh.)

[7] *Dharma*.

336. In any case where a private individual would be fined one *kārṣāpaṇa* in that case the king ought to be fined one thousand: this is the law.[1]

337. The crime of the Çūdra in theft is eightfold (that of a still lower man); sixteenfold is that of the Vaiçya; thirty-two-fold that of the Kṣatriya.

338. Sixty-four-fold is that of the Brahman, or even a full hundred; or twice sixty-four, if, indeed, he knows the quality of the sin.[2]

339. To take the fruit and roots of large trees, firewood, or grass to feed cows with, Manu said, (is) no theft.

340. If a Brahman seek for property from the hand of one who has taken what has not been given, (even if the man owes it to him) because of a sacrifice (performed) or instruction given, (then) this (Brahman) is even as a thief.[3]

341. If a twice-born man,[4] being on a journey, finds his provisions are exhausted, and takes two sugar-canes or two roots from the field[5] of another man, he ought not to pay a fine.

342. If one should fasten (cattle) which are not tied up, or release those that are tied up, and if one should take (away) a slave, a horse, or a chariot,[6] he would incur the sin of a thief.[7]

343. The king who by this rule secures the suppression of thieves shall obtain glory in this world and the highest happiness after death.

344. The king who longs to reach the home of Indra,

[1] K. refers to ix. 245, with the explanation that the king's fine is given to Brahmans or cast into water.

[2] This last clause is to be joined with each (K.)

[3] He is as a thief, and ought to be so punished (K.) Vs. 339 is in palpable contradiction to vs. 331, and is scarcely made better by referring to the *sūtras*; for though Medh. and K. would restrict this theft to "unenclosed" property by Gaut. xii. 28, yet this is not in the text, and another *sūtra* (Āp. i. 28. 2 ff.), ascribes a like rule to Vārṣāyaṇi, who makes this special exception to the general rule against theft.

[4] This excludes the Çūdra (Medh.)

[5] Even if it is fenced in (Medh.)

[6] Though "some" translate "a chariot yoked with horses" (Medh.)

[7] He ought to be punished, according to the enormity of the crime, with death, mutilation, or fine (K.)

and (his) eternal, never-dying glory[1] should not for one moment neglect[2] a man who commits violence.[3]

345. The man who commits violence should be regarded as the worst of evil-doers, (worse) than one who injures with the voice, or than a thief, or than one who smites with a stick.

346. If a ruler exercises patience towards a man occupied in an act of violence, he goes quickly to destruction and becomes hated.[4]

347. Neither for the sake of friendship nor for the sake of vast increase in wealth should a king set free those who commit acts of violence, (since) they subject all creatures to fear.

348. Wherever right[5] is oppressed, there may the twice-born take arms; (also) where, brought on by some (unlucky) time, calamity has come upon the twice-born castes.[6]

349. And in self-defence, in a struggle for gifts,[7] and when peril threatens a woman or a Brahman, he who (thus) kills a man in a just cause[8] does no wrong.

350. Thus let him, without hesitating, kill any one attacking him with a weapon in his hand,[9] (even if it be) a Guru, a child, an old man, or a Brahman who is very learned.[10]

[1] Or "a position like Indra's, and never-dying glory" (Medh.)

[2] *I.e.*, hesitate to seize (Medh.)

[3] Such as incendiaries or robbers (K.); or other reckless ruffians (Medh.)

[4] By his people (Medh., K.)

[5] *Dharma*, practically "their religious rites."

[6] When the king is dead, to save their own wealth or property, or, as "some" say, even for the sake of another, or when the enemy have come upon the land (Medh., K.), or when there is a famine (Nand.)

[7] When one attempts to rob them of cows and other sacrificial gifts, and a struggle ensues in consequence (K.); or, according to "some," *in war*. Nand. knows only the construction "in defence of self, and of his gifts, and in war."

[8] Or "in a just manner." Medh., Nand., and Rāgh. invert the order, *ghnan dharmena*.

[9] Nand. says *ātatāyin* means a "breaker of the rule of right, such as an incendiary;" cf. the seven kinds in Viṣṇu v. 190–192. Medh. and G. connect with vs. 249 as "one who comes *with a weapon in his hand*." K. says, with Kātyayana, that, though with one of high caste no corporal punishment is inflicted, a penance should be made, and that a low man must even suffer death.

[10] *Bahuçruta* = Çrotriya, a learned Brahman.

351. No sin comes at any time upon the slayer for causing, whether openly or in secret, the death of one who attacks him with a weapon in his hand,[1] for thus anger meets anger.[2]

352. Men busied with defiling the wives of others[3] the ruler should banish (from the realm), after branding them by punishments which cause fear.[4]

353. For, arising from this (practice), the mixture of the (different) castes among men is produced; whereby a wrong[5] that deprives (the kingdom) of its root arises, fit to destroy all things.

354. A man who holds a conversation in secret with another man's wife, if he has been previously accused[6] of (such) sins, should receive the lowest fine.[7]

355. But if one not previously accused should for some (good) reason hold (such) a conversation,[8] he ought to have no fault attached to him, for in him it is not a transgression.

356.[9] He who addressed the wife of another[10] at a watering-place, in a forest or wood, or at the union of rivers,[11] would incur (the sin of) adultery.[12]

[1] See vs. 350, note.

[2] Quoted Āp. i. 29. 7; from a "Purāṇa;" cf. Mbhā. xii. 34, 19, and 56, 30. This saying is found in all the rules pertaining to Kṣatriya. The explanation of Nand., based on his interpretation of *ātatāyin*, is "openly, that is, in open fight with a weapon." "Secretly, that is, by poison, magic," etc.

[3] Nand. offers a *var. lec.*, *paradāropasevāyām ceṣṭamānān narān nṛpaḥ* in (*a*), and *paricihnya* in (*b*), whereby the sense is not affected.

[4] Such as mutilation of nose or lip (Medh., K.); or castration (N.); cf. ix. 248.

[5] Or "lack of rites" (Medh., *adharma*).

[6] *Ākṣarita*, probably accused of adultery, cf. vs. 275 (note); so Medh. and Nand.

[7] Some say even if he does it for some good reason (Medh.)

[8] K. regards this as an open public conversation.

[9] Nand. places this verse after 358.

[10] This does not forbid conversation with one's mother, sister, or Guru's wife (Medh.)

[11] These imply any lonely place; *tīrtha* means a place to draw water (Medh., K.)

[12] The idea is, "he has committed adultery already in his heart," and the whole sentiment of the two verses is that if a man is really pure in heart he is not to be punished for the sin of conversing with another's wife; just as in Mbh. ii. 5, 104, we have the same verb employed in a similar thought. "A noble man of pure heart should not be killed when (falsely) accused of theft" (*kṣāritaç caurakarmaṇi*) In Nand.'s version *gṛhe* stands for *vane*, which seems preferable.

357. Attendance upon her,[1] sporting with her, touching her ornaments or clothes, sitting upon a bed with her, all this is called adultery.

358. If any man touches a woman upon an improper part (of her body),[2] or being thus touched by her submits to it with patience, this is all called adultery, (if done) by mutual consent.

359. One who is not a Brahman[3] deserves capital punishment for committing adultery. The wives of all the four castes must always be most carefully guarded.[4]

360. Beggars,[5] those who sing the praises (of the king), those who have been consecrated,[6] and working people may, unless (they have been) refused (the right to do so),[7] hold conversation with women.[8]

361. A man who has been forbidden (to do so) should not start a conversation with the wives of others; but if, having been forbidden, he should (still) converse (with them), he ought to be fined a *suvarṇa*.[9]

362. This rule[10] is not for the wives of strolling players,[11] nor for those who support themselves,[12] for these men prostitute (their own) wives, and, keeping out of sight (themselves), let (their wives) go astray.[13]

363. But a man who starts a conversation in secret with these women; with servant girls who have one master; or

[1] At the toilet (N.); or "polite attentions" (Medh., K.)

[2] Literally, "on (a place) not the (right) place." In distinction from the hand, etc. (Medh.)

[3] Nand. reads *smṛtā* for *sadā*. Cf. ix. 6.

[4] Medh. and Nand. say "a Kṣatriya and the other (lower castes)," while K. says "from the nature of the punishment a Çūdra (is understood)." So Ragh. K. also adds the crime is committed with an unwilling Brahman woman; and Medh. modifies the definition of a non-Brahman in speaking of the death penalty, which is for the "Çūdra alone on having connection with women of the twice-born castes."

[5] Religious mendicants.

[6] For some sacrifice, etc. (K.)

[7] By the husband. Or it may mean "they ought not to be forbidden" (Medh.)

[8] Who belong in the house, and the conversation must be in regard to their business (K.)

[9] Of 16 *māṣa* (K.) Some hold that this includes the beggars of vs. 360, but they cannot pay a fine (Medh.)

[10] That is, the rule of a fine of one *suvarṇa* (Nand.)

[11] Or dancers.

[12] *I.e.*, by their wives (Medh., K., Nand.), for the wife is one's self.

[13] Or, "they make women prostitutes, and, remaining concealed, make the women entice (the men) astray."

with wandering women,[1] should be fined merely some (small) fine.

364.[2] He who deflowers an unwilling girl ought to receive corporal punishment[3] at once; but a man of equal (caste) who deflowers a girl with her consent should not receive[4] corporal punishment.

365. (The king) should not cause a girl who tries to seduce a man of high (caste) to pay any fine at all; but he ought to compel a girl to live confined at home[5] if she make love to a man of low caste.

366. If a man of low (caste) make love to a girl of the highest (caste),[6] he deserves corporal punishment.[7] One who makes love to a girl of equal (caste)[8] should give the marriage-money if her father desires (it).[9]

367. Now, if any man through insolence forcibly dishonour[10] a girl, he ought instantly to have two fingers cut off, and pay a fine of six hundred (*paṇas*).

368. If a man of equal (caste) dishonour[11] a girl with her consent, he ought not to have his fingers cut off, but to prevent (another such) occurrence, he should be made to pay a fine of two hundred (*paṇas*).

369. And if a girl injure thus (with the finger another)

[1] Possibly Buddhistic nuns are meant. The "servant girls" are prostitutes.

[2] Some MSS. of Medh. change the position of the verses following to vs. 391.

[3] *Vadha:* K. does not understand death here, but mutilation; and he adds that if he goes to her a second time when she is willing, he should not be thus punished. The nature of the punishment excludes the Brahman (K.)

[4] *Prāptum arhati* (Medh., Nand.)

[5] Until her love for him is past (K.) The fine is paid by parent or guardian (Medh.)

[6] Whether willing or not (K.)

[7] *Vadha.* In accordance with the caste (of the offender) the punishment is mutilation or death (K.)

[8] With her consent (K.)

[9] "Give the marriage-money" means marry her. The consent of the father is (not to the marriage, but) to the receiving payment (for his daughter)! (Nand.) All commentators agree in taking the word "highest" to mean "higher," thus spreading the law over the three upper castes. The word *sev*, which I have translated "make love," probably, though not necessarily, implies sexual intercourse.

[10] A girl of equal caste is meant, and dishonour does not mean to deflower, but to commit bodily indignities, and (thence) the fingers offending are cut off (K.) Medh. gives two other explanations, both implying deflowering.

[11] K. as in vs. 367, apparently to add a new meaning to the (same) verb in vs. 364. Medh. renders as in vs. 367.

girl, she should be made to pay two hundred (*paṇas*) and give double[1] the marriage-price (of the injured girl) and receive also ten (blows with) switches.

370. But if a (married) woman injure a girl, she should have her head shaved at once, (or) two fingers should be cut off, (or) (she should be made to) ride upon an ass.[2]

371. If a woman, made insolent by (the rank of) her family, or by (her own) parts,[3] should prove false to her husband, the king should have her devoured by dogs in some much-frequented place.[4]

372. He should cause the evil man to be burned on a glowing hot iron couch, and they shall place pieces of wood about it till the evil-doer is consumed.[5]

373. Twofold should be the fine of a criminal sentenced within a year,[6] and just as much if one cohabit with a Vrātya woman or a Cāṇḍāla woman.[7]

374. A Çūdra cohabiting with (a woman of) the twice-born castes, whether she be guarded or not guarded,[8] is (to be) deprived of his member[9] and of all his property if she be not guarded, and of everything[10] if she be guarded.

375. A Vaiçya should (pay as) fine all his property after imprisonment for a year;[11] a Kṣatriya should be fined

[1] Treble, according to Nand. (*triguṇam*).

[2] Upon the king's highway; cf. for a like penalty, Vas. xxi. 1.

[3] Literally quality of any kind, as beauty or wealth (Medh., K.)

[4] A public square is meant. We read in the Mbhā. of a city with nine such squares (xiv. 66, 10, *navasaṁsthāna*).

[5] Gautama, xxiii. 15, states that the man is also to be devoured (by dogs), or, by another reading, simply killed. The offence in Gautama is expressly stated to be that of a man of low caste with a woman of rank, which in Manu are conditions merely implied. Rāgh. says the punishment is public as a warning to others. In Nand. the verb is in the singular; the same commentator lays stress on the fact that the man is a Çūdra.

[6] That is, if there is not a year's time between the two offences with the same woman.

[7] Also within the year; cf. vs. 385. Moreover, these cases are only cited *exempli gratia*, and the rule holds as a universal law that a penalty is doubled if an offender is convicted of the same offence a second time within a year (K.) For Vrātya see x. 20 (note).

[8] By her husband or other (relative)—(Medh., K.)

[9] Literally limb, but the meaning is plain by Gaut. xii. 2.

[10] That is, property and even life (K.)

[11] If he has had criminal intercourse with a guarded woman of the Brahman caste (K.)

one thousand (*paṇas*, or) should have his head shaved with urine.[1]

376. But if a Vaiçya, or one of the ruling caste (Kṣatriya), approach a woman of the Brahman caste when she is not guarded, the king should make the Vaiçya (pay) five hundred (*paṇas*) and the Kṣatriya one thousand.

377. But both of them, on committing adultery with a woman of the Brahman caste who is guarded, should be punished like a Çūdra,[2] or be burned in a fire of dry grass and straw.[3]

378. A Brahman should be fined one thousand if he force a woman of the priestly caste who is guarded; and five hundred if he have had a connection with (such a woman) when she consented to it.

379. Shaving the head is ordained as (the equivalent of) capital punishment[4] in the case of a Brahman, but in the case of the other castes capital punishment may be (inflicted).

380. Certainly (the king) should not slay a Brahman even if he be occupied in crime of every sort; but he should put him out of the realm in possession of all his property, and uninjured (in body).

381. No greater wrong is found on earth[5] than killing a Brahman; therefore the king should not even mentally consider his death.

382. If a Vaiçya have intercourse with a woman of the Kṣatriya caste who is guarded, or a Kṣatriya with a woman of the Vaiçya caste (who is guarded), they both ought to pay the fine (which is imposed for a similar offence) toward a woman of the Brahman caste who is not guarded.[6]

[1] Of an ass (K.) Literally, "and." Cf. vs. 384.

[2] That is (as stated in vs. 374), with death (Medh., K.)

[3] K. distinguishes the kinds of grass as used for Vaiçya and Kṣatriya according to Vas. xxi. 1–3.

[4] Not *vadha* here, but literally "punishment that makes an end of life."

[5] Or "is anywhere found" (*kvacit*), (Nand.)

[6] Namely, five hundred for the Vaiçya and one thousand for the Kṣatriya; cf. vs. 376. K. remarks that in consequence of the lightness of the penalty imposed on the Vaiçya for violating the guarded Kṣatriya woman, it is evident that a woman of bad morals must be meant; while the Vaiçya is a very good man, otherwise there would be a lower fine for adultery with a guarded Kṣatriya woman than with a guarded Çūdra woman (cf. vs. 383).

383. A Brahman should be made to pay one thousand (*paṇas*) if he have intercourse (with either of) these two women when they are guarded; and a fine of one thousand should also be (imposed) on a Kṣatriya or a Vaiçya (when they have committed a similar offence) toward a woman of the Çūdra caste (who is guarded).[1]

384. A fine of five hundred (*paṇas* should be imposed upon) a Vaiçya (who has intercourse) with a woman of the Kṣatriya caste, if she be not guarded; but a Kṣatriya must choose either to have his head shaved with urine or (to pay) the fine (of five hundred).

385. If a Brahman have intercourse with a woman of either the Kṣatriya or Vaiçya castes when she is not guarded, or with a woman of the Çūdra caste (who is not guarded), he should be fined five hundred, but one thousand if she be a woman of the lowest class.[2]

386. That king (shall) share in the world of Çakra in whose realm there is no thief, nor adulterer, nor libeller, nor any one who commits acts of violence or smites with a staff.[3]

387. The suppression of these five in his own realm gives a king supreme power over those who are his equals in birth,[4] and gives him glory among men (in general).

388. If a man for whom a sacrifice is to be performed desert the sacrificial priest, or if the sacrificial priest desert the one for whom he should perform sacrifice, they should each be fined one hundred (provided the other party) was able to (carry out) the ceremony, and had committed no sin.[5]

389. Neither mother, father, wife, nor son should be forsaken; one who forsakes them, although they have not

[1] (Medh., K., supplied from the first part); N. says also if unguarded.

[2] Such as a Caṇḍāla woman (Medh., K.), even lower than the Çūdra caste. Nand. reads *vaiçyarājanye*.

[3] Literally so, as complement of the libeller, "one with an injurious voice." The real meaning is, in general, one who commits corporal injury. Çakra is Indra.

[4] K. interprets, "over the kings of the same race."

[5] Cf. vs. 206. The conditions absolving from the fine are sufficient to excuse the one who gives the sacrifice, but by the verse referred to the one who makes the sacrifice is not excused from the work (by proxy) if already begun. Medh. takes *aduṣṭa* (sinless) to mean "not maimed in body."

been degraded (from caste), should be fined six hundred (*paṇas*) by the king.

390. When twice-born men mutually disagree in regard to (points of) duty in the different (ascetic) orders,[1] a king who desires his own happiness should not explain the law[2] (to them).

391. After paying honour to them in accordance with their deserts, let the ruler, together with Brahmans, first pacify them with kindly words, and then establish their rule of conduct.[3]

392. If a Brahman, when giving an entertainment to twenty people, fail to entertain his next neighbour and the next but one,[4] (although) they are worthy (of an invitation), he deserves a fine of one *māṣaka*.[5]

393. If a learned (Brahman) fail to entertain (another) worthy and learned (Brahman) at the religious ceremonies (of ordinary life),[6] he should be made to pay double the (cost of) the food, and (be fined) a *māṣaka* of gold.

394. A man who is blind, foolish, lame, an old man of seventy, and one who is serviceable to learned (Brahmans) should not be compelled to pay a tax by any (king.)[7]

395. The king should always cause a learned (Brahman) to be honoured; also one who is ill, or in distress, a child, an old man, a man without means, a man of important family, and a noble man (Ārya).

396. A washerman should wash the clothes[8] gradually upon a smooth board (made of the wood) of the *çālmalī* tree, and he should not mix the clothes (of one person) with the

[1] The orders of hermits (Medh.), householders (G.), or all four (K.) *Kārya*, though the same term as that used to designate disputes at law, K. here explains as the *meaning* of the law-books.

[2] Or, "should not decide against the right" (N.)

[3] Medh. says the verb "honour" may be taken with "with Brahmans."

[4] Or, the one opposite and the one next back (Medh., Nand.)

[5] Of gold (Medh.); of silver (K.); from vs. 393 either may be understood.

[6] "Ceremonies tending to goodness;" such as those of birth, marriage, etc. A neighbour is here meant (K.)

[7] "Any (king); even if the king has lost all his money (and is in need of taxes)."—K.

[8] If he does, he ought to pay a fine (K.) Medh. (in some MSS.) and Nand. omit *çanaiḥ*, and repeat *vāsāṁsi* (*nijyād vāsāṁsi nejikaḥ*).

clothes (of another), nor let the clothes (of one person) be worn (by another).

397. That which consists of ten *palas* a weaver should give back increased by one *pala;*[1] if he act otherwise, he should be made to pay a fine of twelve (*paṇas*).[2]

398. The king should receive one-twentieth of the cost price (as tax on market goods), in accordance with the worth which experienced men in (various) places for taxation, being well acquainted with all goods bought and sold, shall set upon (the goods).

399. The king should take away all the property of a man who, through avarice, exports[3] goods of which the king has a monopoly,[4] or which are forbidden (to be sold).

400. A tradesman who slips by the place of taxation at some improper time,[5] or gives a false statement in regard to the amount (of his goods), should be fined the eightfold fine.[6]

401. After considering the place of importation and exportation,[7] the storage,[8] the gain, and the loss of all goods bought and sold, let (the king) establish (the price of) purchase and sale.[9]

402. Every five days, or at the expiration of every fortnight, the king should settle the price (of the goods) in the presence of these men.[10]

[1] The same ratio in Yāj. i. 129, whence it appears that this is not a royal tax. In Manu only coarse cotton or wool stuffs are meant; fine stuffs are increased three per cent.

[2] Or *palas* (Medh.) And give satisfaction to the owner (K.)

[3] Literally, "goods proclaimed (to be) the king's."

[4] Or "sells" (Medh.) From Yāj. ii. 261 it appears that "all the property" is all that sold against the law.

[5] At night, for instance (Medh., K.)

[6] The fine (literally, transgression), is represented by the value of the tax laid and lied about. Medh. says, "As much as he denies, so much eightfold is the fine;" K. "the tax (denied to the king) made eightfold is the fine." Another interpretation suggested by Medh. as that of "some" is that the word *akāle* (at improper time) is to be connected with the word *krayavikrayī* (he who trades), *i.e.*, he who trades (referring to payment of taxes) at an improper time or in secret, as distinct from him who slips by the custom-house. Cf. Viṣṇu iii. 31.

[7] The distance traversed (Medh., K.)

[8] The length of time they are stored (K.)

[9] In such a way as not to oppress the parties trading (K.)

[10] Traders or experts. Vss. 402–406 fail in Medh.

403. Each balance and measure[1] should be carefully tested (by the king), and he should have them re-examined every six months.

404. One *paṇa* should be paid at a ferry for a waggon, half a *paṇa* for a load that a man can carry,[2] a quarter for a cow or a woman, and half a quarter for a man without luggage.

405. Waggons full of wares should be charged toll in proportion to their value, but (empty) waggons and men without escort[3] should be charged but a trifle.

406. The toll should be in proportion to the place and time[4] when the course is a long one; one should know that this (law) is for passage across a river, (while) at sea there is no particular rule.

407. A woman more than two months advanced in pregnancy, a (religious) wanderer, a sage (ascetic), Brahmans who bear the signs (of their religious order),[5] should not be made to pay toll at a ferry.

408. If anything be destroyed on a boat[6] through the fault of the sailors, it must be paid for by the sailors collectively, each (paying) a small part.

409. Thus is declared the decision in regard to (any) legal dispute among those who go in boats, (where an accident occurs) on the water in consequence of the fault of the watermen. (When accidents occur) by the act of the gods[7] there is no fine.

[1] K. gives as illustration *prastha-droṇādi*, a measure of quantity in distinction from the measure by balance. Ragh. divides into balance, measure, weight, and documents signed by himself (a doubtful *var. lec.*)

[2] In Nand. *bharaḥ* for *tare* at the end of (*a*) may have crept in from the commentary, as it expresses more clearly than the usual text the idea of the load. The waggon is an empty one (K.)

[3] K. Ragh. understand beggars poor people, and K. says "chests, etc.," for waggons.

[4] Whether the water is rough or not, whether it is in summer (the dry season) or the rainy season, etc. (K.)

[5] According to Medh. and K., the religious students; according to Nand., pilgrims to the *tirtha*. The word Brahman includes the "wanderer" (*pravrajita*) (Medh. and Nand.), for a Kṣatriya might also be one who has given up all and taken up this life (Nand.); and this rule does not apply to those who bear the signs of an excluded (or forbidden) life of wandering (*vāhyapravrajyā*)—(Medh.)

[6] Lost overboard in the water (Medh., K., Nand.)

[7] *Daivike*, divine act, *i.e.*, fate; shipwreck, etc., is meant (K.)

410. The king should make the Vaiçya practise trade, gold-loaning, agriculture, and cattle-tending; and make the Çūdra (act) as the slave of those who are twice-born.[1]

411. A Brahman should support both a Kṣatriya and Vaiçya whose means of livelihood have been diminished, making them attend each to his respective duties,[2] (but) without causing them any cruelty.

412. But if a Brahman through avarice, and because he possesses the power, compel twice-born men who have received the initiation (into the caste order) to do the work of a slave[3] when they do not wish it, he shall be fined six hundred (*paṇas*) by the king.

413. But a Çūdra, whether bought or not bought,[4] (the Brahman) may compel to practise servitude; for that (Çūdra) was created by the Self-existent merely for the service of the Brahman.

414. Even if freed by his master, the Çūdra is not released from servitude; for this (servitude) is innate in him: who then can take it from him?

415. A (man made) captive in war,[5] a (slave) who serves for food, one born in the house, one bought, one given, one (formerly) belonging to (the owner's) father, and one serving out a fine:[6] these are the seven kinds of slaves.

416. Wife, son, and slave, these three are said to be

[1] The twice-born means all the three upper castes (Nand.) Some interpret this to mean that the king shall exercise force to compel them; . . . but if it is a matter of necessity for them to do other work, to force them to do their own would be to contradict other statutes (Medh.)

[2] If the Brahman is wealthy and does not do this, he is to be fined (K.)

[3] Such as washing his feet (Medh., K.)

[4] Supported or not (K.)

[5] Literally, one seized beneath a war-standard.

[6] Cf. vss. 49, 177, and ix. 229. One unable to pay a fine to the king must work out the fine (Medh.) There is no reason for not supposing other castes than the Çūdra meant in the "one taken captive in war" and the one "serving out a fine," though Medh. objects to this. The "fine" is either punishment set by the king (as Nand. says his punishment is his slavery) or more probably one serving out a debt to another when he has no money; so K., and Nand. alludes to this as the opinion of some (*kecid*). Vs. 414 contradicts the spirit of vs. 415. According to the Mbhā., a captive in war should be released at the end of a year.

without property:[1] whatever property they acquire is his to whom they (belong).

417. A Brahman may take possession of the goods of a Çūdra with perfect peace of mind,[2] for, since nothing at all belongs to this (Çūdra) as his own, he is one whose property may be taken away by his master.

418. (The king) should with great care oblige the Vaiçya and the Çūdra to perform each his own occupation, for by departing from their own occupations these two would cause the universe to shake.

419. Every day (the king) should inspect the management of (different) affairs,[3] the (condition of his) steeds, (his) regular income and expenditure, (the receipts from) the mines, and the (state of his) treasury.

420. If the king thus completes all these matters of legal difference, he casts from himself every sin and attains the supreme course (of bliss).[4]

END OF THE EIGHTH LECTURE.

[1] The epic is fond of emphasising this rule; it occurs three or four times in the Mbhā. In brevity it resembles vii. 96. Medh. and K. say that this verse is intended to imply the absolute dependence of the woman and the others in spending money, since the son and slave are in this respect like the wife. Later writers explain the "property" as that earned by mechanical arts, in order to do away with the contradiction between this rule and that of ix. 194. Cf. Jolly, Recht. Stellung der Frauen, § 11.

[2] Instead of *viçrabdham*, the adverb, Nand. reads the adjective agreeing with *brāhmanaḥ*, and explains as "not afraid of taking from the Çūdra," while Medh. also understands it (the adverb) as not afraid that it is a wrong thing to take gifts from a Çūdra, remarking that this is not opposed to the rule of right. Nand. understands that "any one of the three castes" is meant by the word *brāhmaṇa!* K. says if in time of need, even force may be used.

[3] *I.e.*, by his overseers (Medh.)

[4] A *var. lec.* in the MS. of Nand. reads, "He is exalted in the world of Brahm" (*brahmaloke mahīyate*).

LECTURE IX.

CIVIL AND CRIMINAL LAW (CONTINUED).

1. I WILL declare the eternal duties of man and wife (when) abiding by duty's[1] path, (both) in union and in disunion.[2]

2. Day and night should women be kept by the male members of the family[3] in a state of dependence. In pursuits to which they are too devoted they should be restrained under the husband's power.[4]

3. The father guards them in childhood, the husband guards them in youth, in old age the sons guard them. A woman ought not to be in a state of independence.

4. The father who does not give (his daughter in marriage) at the (right) time is blamable.[5] Blamable too is the husband if he does not have intercourse with her (at the right period). The son who does not protect his mother when her husband is dead is also blamable.[6]

5. Women should be especially preserved from even the little (vicious)[7] inclinations, for if not preserved (from them) they would bring sorrow upon two families.[8]

6. Since they see this is the chief duty of all the castes,[9] husbands, even (if they are) weak, strive to keep guard over the wife.

[1] Duty's path is a course of life free from mutual infidelity (K., Nand.)

[2] The husband being dead or on a journey (Rāgh.)

[3] By their husbands, etc. (Medh., K.) Cf. v. 147; Vas. v. 2; Baudh. ii. 3, 45; Viṣṇu xxv. 13.

[4] So Medh. K. explains as "they should be confined by their own wishes," *i.e.*, allowed freedom in (small and sinless) hobbies.

[5] Before menstruation, according to the commentators (Baudh. iv. 1, 13; Gaut. xviii. 21).

[6] The widow, therefore, does not die with the husband. In Medh., No. 1551, *yāpya* for *vācya;* also in Nand.

[7] K. and Rāgh.

[8] The Kashmir MS. adds here another verse to the effect that guarding a wife guards the progeny, and so one's self.

[9] Cf. viii. 359.

7. For he who guards his wife with diligence guards his posterity, his (ancestral) usages, his family,[1] himself, and his own duty.[2]

8. The husband, entering into the wife and becoming an embryo, is born again on earth; for this is the wifeship of the wife (*jāyā*), in that (the husband) is born (*jāya-te*) again in her.[3]

9. Since the woman brings forth a son of like sort with (the man) whose love she shares, therefore (the man) should guard the woman with care, that he may obtain purity of offspring.

10. No man can guard women by using force, but they may be guarded by employing these (following) means:

11. One should keep her (the wife) occupied in collecting and expending money, in keeping things clean,[4] in (attending to her) duty,[5] in cooking food, and in looking after the things about the house.[6]

12. Women (are) not guarded (by) being confined at home by men,[7] (however) cleverly (they) attempt it. Those women who guard themselves through themselves (are alone) well guarded.[8]

13. Drinking (liquor), connection with bad people, living apart from their husbands, wandering about, (untimely) sleeping, living in the house of another man,[9] (these) are six things that bring shame on women.

[1] Probably his race, as an adulteress dishonours it all (Medh.), or his progenitors, as they can be saved only by legal offspring (Medh., K.)

[2] The husband of an adulteress cannot keep the sacred fire (K.)

[3] Cf. Ait. Br. vii. 13, 6, and frequently in the epic. The pun was probably, like many verses of our text, proverbial.

[4] Applicable to things or to her person (Medh., K.)

[5] *I.e.*, obeying her husband, etc. (K., Rāgh.)

[6] Or "the marriage goods" (*pāriṇāya*). *Vide* B. R. *s. v.* = *āsanayānādikam* (Nand., who has *pāriṇāhya*), "the furniture." Medh. (1551) has *pariṇāhya*.

[7] Guards of the harem (Medh.)

[8] This is a parody of the philosophical maxim, "Know thyself through thyself." The guarding of themselves here enjoined on the women is simply occupying themselves at home, which will prevent their gadding about and disgracing themselves; and the antithesis is merely between a woman who finds and loves occupation at home, and one who is confined there by force. No higher meaning is meant by "guarding through themselves."

[9] Any other man than her husband.

14. These (women) regard not beauty, nor do they care for youth. Whether the man be beautiful or ugly, they cry "It is a man," and enjoy (him).[1]

15. By running after men, by their fickleness of mind, by their natural lack of firm affection, these women, although carefully guarded, prove false to their husbands.

16. The husband, then, knowing the natural disposition of these women, as it was originally formed by the creation of Prajāpati,[2] should take the greatest pains in guarding them.

17. The bed, the seat, adornment,[3] desire, wrath, deceitfulness,[4] proneness to injure and bad morals Manu[5] ordained for women.

18. No religious ceremony for women should be (accompanied) by *mantras*,[6]—with these words the rule of right is fixed; for women being weak creatures and having no (share in the) *mantras*, are falsehood itself.[7] So stands the law.

19. There are a number of revelations (*çrutayaḥ*) of this sort sung[8] even in the (Vedic) *nigamas* in order to exhibit the distinguishing traits (of women). Hear the (verse of) expiation for (the sin of) these women.

20. "Inasmuch as my mother has gone astray and has sinned, being false to her husband, (therefore) may my

[1] Nand. reads *rūpavantam arūpaṁ vā*, "endowed with beauty or without it." Cf. the same, Mbhā. xiii. 38, 17, *virūpaṁ rūpavantaṁ vā*.

[2] That is, Manu, the son of the self-existent (Nand.)

[3] These three imply love of sleep, laziness, vanity.

[4] Or perhaps better (with some MSS.), "lack of nobility," *anāryatām* (so Nand.)

[5] Not the lawgiver, but the original creator, represented in vs. 16 by Prajāpati. According to the Mbhā. Manu gave weak and foolish women to men when he himself was on the point of going to heaven (xiii. 46, 8).

[6] Except marriage. Cf. ii. 67; Yāj. i. 13.

[7] From other texts, and supported by general statements in the Nirukta, another reading is possible, according to which the meaning of the last part of this verse would be, "women have no manly strength, and have no share in an inheritance," *nirīndrīyā adāyādāḥ striyo nityam iti çrutiḥ* (or . . . *striyo' nṛtam iti sthitiḥ*, as in the common version). Cf. vs. 201, where *nirindriyāḥ* (masc.) are excluded from a share in the heritage. This meaning is supported by the Sūtras (cf. the text and quotations given by Mandlik, May., ii. 366–367), but is not the reading of Medh. or of K. Cf. Baudh. ii. 3, 46; with Bühler's note.

[8] "A *var. lec.* gives *nigadā*, kind of *mantra*" (Medh.)

father keep far from me this seed (of the adulterer)."[1] These are the words that illustrate (his expiation).

21. And if in her thoughts she meditate anything displeasing to him who has taken her hand in marriage, (this verse) is declared to be in due form an expiation for that (mental) sin.[2]

22. Whatever qualities the husband has to whom the wife is lawfully wedded, she becomes possessor of just such qualities, even as the (river) flowing to the deep (when united) with the sea.[3]

23. Thus the Akṣamālā, though born of the lowest caste, when united to Vasiṣṭha, and the (bird) Sārañgī (when united to) Mandapāla, became worthy of honour.[4]

24. These and other women who have been born on earth in a lowly station have each obtained a high station through the noble qualities of their husbands.

25. Thus is declared the constantly pure everyday rule of life for man and wife. Learn now the rules concerning offspring, (rules) of which the result is happiness both after death and in this world.

26. When women (are found) blest because of offspring, worthy of honour, (true) lamps in the house, then there is not the slightest distinction in the homes (of men) between (them) and Happiness.[5]

[1] According to K. and Nand., "may my father take" or "purify," etc. The formula is found elsewhere (Gṛhya Sūtra of Çāñkhāyana), and is otherwise applied.

[2] This verse is for the son to say, not the mother (K., Rāgh.)

[3] The etymological meaning of the word river (*nimnagā*, going to the deep), strengthens the comparison, which is commonly used in philosophy to indicate the perfect union of the individual with the All. Cf., *e.g.*, Muṇḍ. Up. 3. 2, 8. The same figure has been used to denote the union of desire on the part of the people and king, viii. 175. It applies here more particularly to the qualitative difference, as the fresh water becomes salt.

[4] Akṣamāla is probably an epithet (wearing an *akṣa* wreath) of (the vine) Arundhatī, who, though a Cāṇḍālī (Rāgh.), attained heaven by her obedience to her husband, the renowned sage Vasiṣṭha. The Sārañgī or Çārañgī is the female Sārañga, a kind of bird, according to K. a sparrow (*caṭakā*). Mandapāla was a seer who became a male bird of this sort and had intercourse with her (cf. Mbhā. i. 229, 5), obtaining four sons; thereby she had the honour of rescuing him from hell, as till then he was sonless, and had gone to hell through this deficiency in spite of his piety.

[5] The similarity of sound probably occasions this sentiment, which is often repeated in the epic

27. To bear children, to take care of them[1] when born, and to oversee personally the ordinary affairs of life,[2] (these acts) each for each[3] depend on the wife.

28. Offspring, the due performance of religious duty,[4] obedience,[5] and the most profound voluptuous[6] joy are dependent upon the wife; so also the (attainment of) heaven for the (husband's) ancestors and for himself.[7]

29. She who, restrained in mind, speech, and body, is not unfaithful to her husband, attains the abode of (her) husband,[8] and is called virtuous by the good.

30. Now a woman from unfaithfulness to her husband gets blame in the world, is born of a jackal[9] (on being born again), and is tormented by evil diseases.

31. Learn now this holy utterance, applicable to all mankind, declared concerning a son by the good and by the great seers born of old.

32. They are well aware that a (legitimate) son belongs to the husband,[10] but in regard to the actual father (of an illegitimate son) there is a twofold explanation[11] (given)

and in other smṛtis (cf. Dakṣa's iv. *Çrīr eva strī*); since the woman (*strī*) gives happiness, she is said to be identical with Happiness (*çrī*), either as abstract condition or personification. The lofty sentiment is however restricted by the clause "because of offspring," which is the sole reason from the standpoint of the law-book why women deserve honour. The same expression in vs. 96 illustrates this. Cf. iii. 57, 61.

[1] *Paripālanam* (or *parirakṣaṇam*, Nand.)

[2] Such as providing for the entertainment of guests and friends (K.)

[3] *Pratyartham* (Medh.), or "oversee day by day" (*pratyaham*), (K.)

[4] The care of the sacred fire, etc. (K.)

[5] Attendance (K.)

[6] *Rati*, so Rāgh., "pleasure by union with woman."

[7] By bearing a legitimate son, who, as the law says, saves his progenitors from hell.

[8] Two MSS. Medh. have *lokam* (the world), the order in this and subsequent verses being in No. 935 much altered. So in the Mbhā.: The daughter of the king of Videha sang a song, "Never a ceremony at the sacrifice, no feast for the manes, and no fasting bring heaven to woman; but obedience to law and to husband, thereby may women conquer heaven." (Ref. Viṣṇ. xxv. 15, note). Cf. v. 155, and the same epithet *sādhvī* of the wife in the following. The verse is repeated by K. in v. 166; cf. note.

[9] The jackal was very low in the system of transmigration, but not the lowest; the dog, for instance, was more unworthy. This verse is found at v. 164; cf. note.

[10] Literally, "supporter;" here equal to owner (Nand.), *i.e.*, husband.

[11] Literally, "a doubleness of *çruti*." Cf. Vas. xvii. 6 ff.

by revelation (*çruti*); some say the progenitor (owns him), others think the owner of the land.[1]

33. The woman is said to have the nature of land; the man is said to have the nature of seed; the origin of all corporate creatures (is caused) by the union of land and seed.[2]

34. In some places the seed is the chief (factor);[3] in other cases the womb of the woman; when both are equal, the offspring is considered best.

35. (In a general comparison) between seed and womb the seed is called weightier, for the offspring of every created being is characterised by the characteristic of the seed.

36. Whatever qualities the seed that is sown in land which has been prepared[4] at the (proper) time possesses, the same sort of seed grows up in this (land), endowed with qualities of its own (parent seed).

37. For (though) this earth is declared to be the eternal womb of created beings, (yet) the seed exhibits in the things produced from it not a single one of the qualities of this womb.[5]

38. In the earth, even in one and the same (kind of) land, the seeds which spring up after being sown by husbandmen at the (proper) time are of various appearances, each according to its own natural qualities.

39. Rice, *çāli*,[6] *mudga*, sesame, beans, and barley sprout

[1] Even if he, the owner of the land (*i.e.*, the woman's husband), is not the progenitor (K.) Medh. (Nos. 935 and 1551) has *kartari* (maker, progenitor, "actual father") for *bhartari*.

[2] "The twofold explanation" is given in 32, to which 33 is added to explain the terms used: "he now (in 34) gives an opinion of his own" (Nand.) "All corporate creatures" mean the four classes born of egg, moisture, sweat, or seed (Medh.), *i.e.*, not animate alone.

[3] The chief factor in determining the qualities of the offspring. Cf. x. 72. The first is illustrated by the case of Vyāsa, the second by that of Dhṛtarāṣṭra (Medh.)

[4] By ploughing, etc. (K.)

[5] In the stems and bushes no dust, earth, etc. (Medh., K.) More probably to be taken literally, ignoring the effect of different earths on the products. Whether the earth is dry, wet, etc., the seed produces its like all the same.

[6] According to Nand., "rice or (other) grains, sesame, etc.," omitting *mudga*; by some *çāli* is taken as also a kind of rice.

forth according to their seed, and so do leeks and sugar-canes.

40. "One thing sown, another produced"—these words do not express what properly occurs; for whatever be the seed sown, exactly that (kind) alone sprouts forth.

41. Thence[1] a well-instructed man, aware (of this law) and understanding wisdom and science,[2] should never, if he desires long life, sow (seed) in the wife of another man.

42. Those who know the things of the past relate songs sung by the winds,[3] to the effect that[4] seed should not be sown by a man in the wife[5] of another.

43. Just as a dart is wasted if shot into a hole where (the hunter merely) wounds (an animal) which has been already wounded (by another hunter), so indeed is seed wasted at once when (sown) in the wife of another.[6]

44. Those who know the things of the past know that the earth (*pṛthivī*) is the wife of Pṛthu;[7] they say, too, that land belongs to him who clears off the timber, and a forest animal to him who owns the arrow (that first hit it).

45. It is said that the man is as much as his wife himself and his offspring;[8] so the priests declare this saying: What the husband is, that the woman is said to be.

[1] *Tad iti tasmād arthe* (Rāgh.)

[2] Wisdom (*jñāna*) is the treatises of the Vedāṅga (or Vedāṅga and (law) treatises); science (*vijñāna*) is logic (*tarka*), etc. (Medh.) Wisdom is the Veda, science its subsidiary branches (K.) *Çruti* and *smṛti*, according to Rāgh., represent these two, while Nand. defines wisdom as "worldly knowledge," and science as the "branches" (of law, etc., in general).

[3] Either as material or immaterial, *i.e.*, the god Vāyu.

[4] *Yathā* means "for which reason" (*yena hetunā*), and he then gives the song (= 43) (Nand.); so Medh.

[5] Enclosure, field, wife.

[6] According to another reading, "at once" (*kṣipram*) should be in parenthesis, and "sown" (*kṣiptam*) in the text. Medh. (No. 1551) has (*nikṣiptam*), and in (*a*) *kṣiptaḥ* (so 935). He also explains "a dart which wounds an animal already wounded by another dart shot by the same hunter."

[7] Cf. vii. 42. Although the earth was ruled by several kings before him, Pṛthu first got control of her (as it were, married her). The point of the verse is that he who marries is the owner, so that offspring belongs not to the progenitor, but to the woman's husband. The kings subsequent to Pṛthu, according to Medh., have no legitimate claim of possession.

[8] A *var. lec.* in Nand. suggests that this was not always given as a quotation (*prajeha ca*).

46. Neither by sale[1] nor by abandonment is a wife released from her husband; so we recognise this as a law laid down of old by Prajāpati.

47. Once only a share[2] falls (to a person's lot); once only is a girl given in marriage; once only one says, "Let me give."[3] These three (things) are in each case[4] (done but) once.

48. Just as in the case of cows, mares, female camels, slave-girls, buffalo-cows, goats, and ewes it is not the progenitor that owns the offspring,[5] even thus also (stands the rule) in (the case of) other men's wives.

49. Those who, not owning the land but possessing the seed, sow it in the land of another man, never at any time receive the fruit from the crop thus produced.[6]

50. As, should a bull beget a hundred calves by cows belonging to another owner, the calves (would) belong to those alone who own the cows, and the bull's seed (would be) cast to no purpose;

51. So even thus those who, when they do not own the land, sow their seed in the land of another man, do good to those who own the land, and the possessor of the seed receives no fruit.[7]

52. If there has been no agreement between those that own the land and those that own the seed, the advantage gained belongs plainly to those who own the land; the womb is more important[8] than the seed.[9]

[1] Cf. xi. 62. Sale of girls and even married women is known (Yāj. iii. 242). Even if one pays a thousand *niṣka* for her, he does not become her husband (Medh.)

[2] The division of property of one's father, etc., is referred to, with no allusion to a possible redistribution. Medh. says the division must hold, but if one complains afterwards that the division is unfair, he gets the same as the others; or if one is afterwards proved to have received a share illegally, it is still valid.

[3] General gifts, or "I will give (the girl)."

[4] Or, (*var. lec.*), "These three among the good are for once." The verse illustrates the preceding (K.)

[5] The one who lends the male animal is not the one who owns the young of the females (K.)

[6] This is quoted by Vas. xvii. 8, with a contrary opinion (cf. Ap. ii. 13, 7) in 9.

[7] Figuratively applicable to the wife as the land.

[8] The reading *balīyasi* (more powerful) of the Beng. MS. is supported by (Nos. 935 and 1551) Medh., the MS. of Nand., and the gloss of K. (*balavat*).

[9] The superiority of the "seed" in vs. 31 is due to the results produced

53. But both the owner of the seed and the owner of the land are known in this world to be (equal) possessors of all that which is produced in consequence of a special agreement respecting the seed.[1]

54. If seed carried by a stream or by the wind grow up in the land (of another), this seed belongs to the owner of the land alone;[2] the one who sows does not (in this case) receive the fruit.

55. This is the law[3] which should be recognised in regard to the offspring of cows, mares, slave-girls, female camels, goats, sheep, fowls, and buffalo-cows.

56. The value and worthlessness of the seed and the womb have been declared unto you: now I will next proclaim the chief duties of women in time of need.[4]

57. The wife of the eldest brother in respect to a later-born brother (is said to be) the wife of the Guru, and the wife of the younger (brother) is said (to be) the daughter-in-law of the eldest (brother).[5]

58. If, when there is no need,[6] the eldest brother have sexual intercourse with the younger brother's wife, or the younger brother with the wife of the first-born (brother), they both become degraded, even (if they have been) commissioned (to act thus).

59. When there is a lack of offspring the progeny[7] wished for may be procured by the wife being regularly

on the offspring; here ownership is alone in question.

[1] A special agreement regarding the sowing of the seed.

[2] So Nand., *var. lec.*, *tad jñeyaṁ kṣetrikasyaiva.* Medh. has *na vījī* (possessor of the seed) for *na vaptā* (sower).

[3] That is, this law of agreement (Medh., K.)

[4] That is, when in need of children, when there is no offspring (Medh., K., Rāgh., and Nand.)

[5] The daughter-in-law in one case implies as correlative mother-in-law, as Jones translates, but the text says only "wife of the Guru," towards whom the strictest propriety is required, and to corrupt whom is one of the cardinal sins. Rāgh. takes Guru to mean the father instead of the father-in-law.

[6] As in vs. 56. These verses, 52–58, are inserted in Burnell's copy of Medh. after vs. 58 of the eighth Lecture.

[7] *I.e.*, sons, who have the right of being heirs; in case other children are born the commission is, therefore, repeated (Medh.) The same commentator allows a *putrikā* (*vide* vs. 127) to take the son's place.

commissioned (to bear children generated) by the brother-in-law or some blood-relation of the husband's family.[1]

60. The (man who is) commissioned, being anointed with ghee, and with voice restrained, shall beget at night one son by the widow,[2] but never a second (son).

61. Some who understand this matter[3] think a second procreation by (such) women is in accordance with the law of right, as they consider the purpose of the commission (still) incomplete (if there be only one son).[4]

62. But when the purpose of the commission in regard to the widow has been completed according to rule, the two should act toward each other as (if they were) Guru (father-in-law) and daughter-in-law.

63. If the two who have been commissioned dispense with the rule,[5] and act[6] according to the promptings of lust, they would both be degraded; having (in theory) violated, (the one) the daughter-in-law, (or the other) the wife of the Guru, (mother-in-law).

64. A widow woman[7] should not be commissioned by twice-born men (to have carnal intercourse) with any other man (than her husband), for those commissioning (her to

[1] *Sapiṇḍa*, so Medh. This formally introduces the levirate law, which is both recognised as right, and again (64–68) denied by the law-book. The wife is commissioned by the (husband or) Guru (K.), and the brother of the husband or some other Sapiṇḍa performs the duty of raising up a child for the (dead) husband. The Sapiṇḍa is generally any one of the blood relations within six degrees (cf. v. 60). The practice is forbidden by Āpast. ii. 27, 2-7, if the husband is alive, but with the widow is expressly enjoined by Gaut. xviii. 4, and xxviii. 21–22, and Vas. xvii. 56. Nārada gives in his later law-book an elaborate account of the formalities. Our text speaks of the widow only, though the commentators understand as included "a wife without children." Cf. Jolly, Recht. Stellung, § 18, where this passage is discussed.

[2] Or wife, according to the commentators, if the husband lives without children (K.) *Vide* last note.

[3] *I.e.*, the law in cases of need (Nand.), or the rule for raising up offspring (K.)

[4] Gaut. xviii. 8 permits this in laying down the rule "not more than two sons." An expression quoted by Medh. and K. occurs often proverbially in the epic, "He who has one son has no son."

[5] The rule (cf. vs. 60) of anointing, etc. (K., Nand.)

[6] MS. of Nand. gives "if they raise up children by lust."

[7] *Vidhavā nārī* like *mulier vidua*.

have carnal intercourse) with any other man would violate the eternal law of right.[1]

65. In the *mantras* on marriage[2] (such) a commission is never mentioned, and the second marriage of a widow is not spoken of in the rule of marriage.

66. For this is reprehended[3] by the twice-born who are wise, as a law (fit only) for cattle; (but) it was declared (to be the law) even for men when Veṇa ruled over his kingdom.[4]

67. This supreme[5] king-seer, enjoying the possession of the whole earth long ago, produced a mixture of the (different) castes, his mind being destroyed by lust.[6]

68. From that time on the good blame any one who in delusion commissions a woman to raise up offspring when her husband is dead.[7]

69. If the (intended) husband[8] of a maiden die after troth has been plighted,[9] her own brother[10]-in-law should marry her according to the (following) rule.

70. Approaching her according to rule, she being clothed

[1] Vss. 64–68 contradict 59–64, and are probably a later addition.

[2] Verses from the Vedas contained in the house-rules for recitation at a wedding.

[3] Or, "This law of cattle is reprehended by the wise."

[4] No other authority exists for this statement.

[5] Not supreme because of virtue (K.)

[6] He is known as an impious king, claiming sacrifice for himself instead of the gods. *Vide* vii. 41. Some MSS. have Vena.

[7] K. and Nand. say: This denial of the commission declared by himself (Manu) appertains only to the Kali age, as Bṛhaspati says: The commission is proclaimed by Manu (v. Jolly, *loc. cit.*, p. 97) and forbidden by him, so this practice cannot now be performed on account of the weakness of the age. To this and other verses quoted from Bṛhaspati, K. adds a disapproval of Govindarājā: "Now Gov. not understanding the state of things caused by the difference in the ages, declared that not to have the commission was at all times better than to commission the widow. I have no respect for this opinion, which is made up out of his own head and contradicts the sage's opinion." Nand. does not notice this. It is probable that the original rule was acted on too freely and produced a nominal reaction; the custom has continued, however, without restriction to modern times in spite of widow-burning, and at the time of Mandeslo was in general acceptance.

[8] *I.e.*, the bridegroom, future husband, like the *çulkada* of 97, q.v.

[9] That is, after she has been promised in marriage.

[10] *I.e.*, of the woman. The own brother of the husband (K.) Nand. defines this as *patidevaraḥ*.

in white, and true to observance of purity, let (the brother-in-law) have intercourse with her once regularly at the proper seasons, until a child is conceived.[1]

71. A wise man after giving a girl to one man should not give her again (to another); for by giving her (once) and offering her a second time he is guilty of an untruth respecting man.[2]

72. Even after marrying a girl according to rule (the husband) may abandon her (if he find her) blameworthy, sickly, very corrupt,[3] or married to him by fraud.[4]

73. If a man give a girl (in marriage) when she has defects without telling of them, (the husband) may make void this (gift) of that evil-minded man who gave him the girl.[5]

74. A man[6] who has business to attend to (away from home) should take his journey (only) after establishing some means of sustenance for his wife; for a woman, even if inclined to abide by the law, may become corrupt if she is harassed by lack of means of sustenance.

75. When (the husband) has gone off on a journey after establishing means of sustenance (for his wife), she should live with strict adherence to vows of chastity; but if he take a journey without establishing means of sustenance, she should live by (any) blameless acts.[7]

[1] These two verses are an attempt at restricting the former law (without denying it) to cases where marriage is as yet not consummated. The connection ceases after the ceremony, and the son belongs to the dead.

[2] That is, he commits a sin equal to stealing a man (Medh.) or killing 1000 relatives (K.) Cf. viii. 98. The allusion is probably to deceit after receiving marriage money; cf. 99. Yâj. i. 65 says the girl may be given to another suitor (after being promised), if he is better than the first. Medh. and K. understand a second betrothal when the first bridegroom is dead.

[3] Or, with Medh., K., and Nand., "if she has already lost her virginity;" but the translation required in xi. 177 is as above.

[4] This is not to recommend divorce, but to inculcate the necessity of the wife's being blameless (K.)

[5] Cf. viii. 205: "It is no fault if he has declared her blemishes;" and *ib.* 224 the fine is 96 *panas* if he does not declare them. Yāj. makes the fine much higher. In Nand. MS. *prayacchati* for *'papādayet*; *tasyāpi* for *tasya tad*, and *kanyādānam* for *'dātur*.

[6] According to the Nand. MS. a twice-born man (*dvijah*).

[7] By spinning and the like (Medh.) The Nand. MS. places K.'s 95, 96, between 74, 75.

76. A man should be waited for (by the wife) for eight years when he has journeyed off in order to attend to religious duties; six years if he has gone to gain wisdom or glory; but (only) three years (if he has journeyed) for love's sake.[1]

77. The husband should wait[2] one year for a wife who hates him; at the end of the year he should take away what (he) has given her, and not live with her (any more).[3]

78. If a woman transgress (in her duty toward a husband when he is) either neglectful[4] of her, or a drunkard, or troubled with disease, she should (nevertheless) be set aside for three months without (the use of her) ornaments and (feminine) paraphernalia.[5]

79. (But if she transgress) because she hates[6] (a husband when he is) crazy, degraded, castrated, impotent, or afflicted with an evil disease, (that husband) has no right to set her aside, or take away the gifts (he has given her).[7]

[1] "Religious duties," *i.e.*, in obedience to a command of the Guru, or a pilgrimage, etc.; "wisdom," *i.e.*, by study; "love," *i.e.*, when he has left his wife for another woman (Medh., K.) Medh. quotes the opinion of those who permit a woman in five cases to marry a second time, and refutes this explanation for this passage (*vide* vs. 46), as a second marriage appears to him inadmissible. K. quotes Vas. to the effect that the wife of a husband absent on a journey should wait eight years and then go and hunt him up. (The received text of Vas. xvii. 75, 76, gives only five years.) In Gaut. xviii. 15 the six years are mentioned, with the addition attributed by K. to Vas. Yāj. i. 84 directs that when the husband is away the wife shall give up play, adornment, visiting, etc. Nand. says she may marry another husband at the expiration of this time, and his explanation seems correct. K.'s idea that she is to follow him rests on a later view in regard to second marriages; cf. 175. The text makes no distinction of caste.

[2] The same verb as in vs. 76, as if by hating she had separated from him, and he "looked forward" to her return.

[3] "Not live with her," *i.e.*, not have sexual intercourse with her (Nand.); "what he has given her" is simply the jewellery, ornaments, etc., that he has given her. These are to be taken away (K., Rāgh.); but by ix. 202 he must keep her supplied with food and clothes (Medh., K., and Rāgh.)

[4] Neglectful on account of his love for gambling (K.), or greed (Rāgh.)

[5] In this case her jewellery, bed, etc., are taken from her (K.); according to Medh., even her servants.

[6] The MS. of Nand. supports the reading *dviṣāṇāyā* (so both Medh. MSS., No. 935 and 1551).

[7] In this case, however, she has a right to leave her husband according to the Sūtras (Vas., Baudh.), and according to Nar. xii. 97, ought to do so.

80. If a woman indulges in intoxicating liquors or does sinful things, or opposes (her husband), or is diseased, or plagues[1] (her husband), or is always wasting his money,[2] she may be over-married.[3]

81. A sterile (wife) may be over-married in the eighth year (after marriage); if her children have died (she may be over-married) in the tenth (year); if she bears (only) female (children), in the eleventh (year); but instantly, if she says disagreeable things.[4]

82. A wife, if she be of a lovable disposition and endowed with virtue, should, when diseased, be over-married (only) with her own permission; and at no time should she be despised.

83. But if a woman having been over-married leave (her husband's) house in wrath,[5] she should instantly be put in confinement, or be set aside in the presence of the family.[6]

84. If a woman, even when she has been forbidden, go to (drinking) intoxicating liquor, even[7] on festal occasions, or go to an exhibition, (or into) a crowd, she ought to be fined six *kṛṣṇala*.[8]

[1] *I.e.*, beats her husband (and other relatives), (K.)

[2] Or (under these circumstances) she may always be, etc.

[3] "Over-married," *i.e.*, superseded by another wife (K.), who takes her place; but this does not force her to leave the house.

[4] The latter case should be restricted to wives who have no male offspring, for if the wife has a son, the husband, in accordance with Āpastamba's prohibition, must not over-marry her (K.) Cf. Āp. ii. 11, 12.

[5] That is, if she grow angry and leave the house. The superseded wife does not necessarily leave the house.

[6] In the presence of the family, beginning with the father (K.) Rāgh. translates *kula* (family) as a collection of people, and directs that regard be paid (in selecting them) to place, time, and family. Medh. refers the family to the relations of her husband and those on her own side.

[7] The ordinary fault is not so great, but the (first) word *even* (although) shows a greater crime accompanies the fault when the woman is forbidden, and the (second) word *even* shows that the fault is less on festal occasions (Nand.) "A woman," *i.e.*, of Kṣatriya (lower) caste; "forbidden," *i.e.*, by her husband; "intoxicating liquor," *i.e.*, the liquor forbidden (perhaps by law, as the Kṣatriya could drink certain kinds).

[8] "Exhibition," *i.e.*, an open show, at a dancing place or other show (K., who takes the compound as "crowd at a show"); "festal occasions," a birthday party, marriage, etc. (Medh., K.)

85. If twice-born (men) marry women both of their own (caste) and of another (caste), the pre-eminence, honour, and apartments[1] of these (wives) should be in accordance with the order of (their respective) castes.

86. Among all (men) the (wife who is of one's) own (caste) should alone attend both to the bodily service of the husband and to those regular occupations (of a wife) enjoined by duty.[2] (A wife) not of his own caste (should) at no time (perform these acts).

87. The man, however, who foolishly allows this to be done by any other (wife) than the one of his own caste when the latter is at hand, has been of old[3] looked upon as (no whit better than) a Cāṇḍāla of a Brahman.[4]

88. One should give a girl in marriage according to rule to that suitor who is of high (family),[5] handsome, and of like (caste),[6] even though she has not reached (the age of puberty).[7]

[1] Possibly "in the house" (*veçmani*); so the Nand. MS. Cf. Rāgh. Instead of "apartment" we may translate *house*, as Medh. and K. understand. The "honour" is shown by gifts of clothes, ornaments, etc. Cf. Mbhā. xiii. 47, 31 (attributed to Manu): "If a Brahman has three wives (of different castes) and marries a Brahman woman, she becomes the chief (*jyeṣṭhā*), the honoured one (*pūjyā*), etc. There is one name for *dārā* (wives), but a great difference between them."

[2] Such as giving food to beggar guests, attending to her part of the sacrificial preparations, etc. (K.) The Mbhā. in the passage just quoted gives an interesting review of the duties of the chief wife. The Brahman wife bathes and adorns her husband; she cleans his teeth and anoints him; the sacrifices (*havya* and *kavya*) ordained in the house are to be performed by her alone; and since she is the most venerable, she must give her husband his food, drink, wreaths, clothes, and ornaments.

[3] Medh., or "by the old seers" (K.)

[4] That is, although a Brahman he is considered as low as a Cāṇḍāla, the son of a Çūdra and Brahman woman.

[5] Medh., or simply "excellent," "in family and habits," etc. (K.)

[6] (K.), or "like in caste and other respects" (Medh.)

[7] The age of the girl differed according to the family and caste custom; for some twelve, for some eight years are recommended; others say she should be given to her husband while she still runs around the house naked (Vas. xvii. 70; Gaut. xviii. 23; Baudh. iv. 1, 11–14). K. quotes Dakṣa (cf. vs. 94) as approving eight years. Twelve years seem to be the limit. If unmarried at that age, the girl is disgraced and her father has sinned. Medh. objects to marriage at eight years, as such are contracted for money. The age of puberty is reached by women in India at ten or twelve years. The explanation of Nand. is different, "not fitted, *i.e.*, even if not similar

89. Better that the girl, even if she has arrived at the age of puberty, should remain at home till her death than that one should ever give her to a suitor lacking in (good) qualities.[1]

90. A girl having reached the age of puberty should wait three years[2] (for a husband);[3] but at the end of that time she should (herself) choose a husband of like (caste).[4]

91. If she should herself take a husband when she has not been given (in marriage),[5] she is guilty of no crime, nor (is he guilty) whom she takes (as husband).

92. A girl choosing for herself should not take with her the ornaments (received) from her father, nor those (she has received) from her mother, nor those given by her brothers: if she took them she would be a thief.[6]

93. But a man who takes a girl that has (already) reached the age of puberty should not give marriage money to (her) father,[7] for by (thus) hindering the natural exercise of the female functions (the father) would lose (his) ownership.

(to the husband) in age, beauty, and other respects." "According to rule," means with the customary ceremonies.

[1] "Good qualities," such as wisdom, bravery, etc. (Medh., K.) According to some this is denied; it is better for the girl to be married to somebody, no matter whom. Modern instances will be found in the Appendix to Mandlik's edition of the May., ii. p. 427.

[2] Elsewhere monthly periods. Cf. Viṣṇu xxiv. 40, and Jolly's note.

[3] That is, wait for her parents to get her one. (Nand. reads *upāsita*; so Medh. MSS., Nos. 935 and 1551).

[4] (Medh. and K.) The period of waiting begins at twelve (Medh.)

[5] *I.e.*, by her relatives. Rāgh. says her self-choice of husband is legal only when there is no one to give her in marriage; she is then blameless even if she choose a husband who is not excellent.

[6] Or, "it would be theft" (Medh. as *v. l.* Nand.) This self-choosing of the bride (*svayamvara*) was the ancient custom, well known by the epic tale of Damayanti and other cases; it is conceded here out of respect for the old custom, but was not practised at this date; and the restrictions in regard to property show it was not really approved of except as a last resort. Yaj. i. 64 and Nar. xii. 22 permit the *svayamvara* when there are no relatives to give the girl in marriage (cf. Viṣṇu, xxiv. 40–41). Vas. xvii. 68, Gaut. xviii. 20, among earlier writers, permit this without distinction of caste; in the epic it is confined to royal maidens; among later commentators it is restricted to the lower castes. In the text the gifts were given as marriage presents before the *svayamvara* was decided on (Medh., K.)

[7] The law-book is contradictory on the subject of marriage-money

94. At thirty years of age a man may marry a beloved girl of twelve years, or, (if) he is thrice eight years, (he may marry a girl) of eight years; if his religious duties would (otherwise) be unfulfilled (he may marry) at once.[1]

95. Should the husband marry a wife given by the gods, and desire to practise what is pleasing to the gods, he should, though himself without love,[2] always support her (if she be) virtuous.[3]

96. Women are created in order to bear children, and men (are created) in order to beget posterity;[4] therefore common religious duties (for the man) with his wife are declared in revelation (*çruti*).

97. If the giver of the marriage-money should die after the marriage-money for the girl has been given, the girl should, if she be willing, be given over to her (expected) brother-in-law.[6]

98. Not even a Çūdra (when) giving his daughter (in

(for such is meant by *çulkam*). Cf. iii. 23, 24, 51, 52; viii. 366; ix. 46. 71, 97, 98; xi. 62, etc. So Nar. xii. 23; Viṣ. v. 43. Cf. Jolly, Recht. Stell., § 7. Medh. thinks the verse is not Manu's (*amānavo'yaṃ çlokaḥ*). The purchase of the bride is the more ancient form, which the later writers sought to eradicate.

[1] K. refers this to the duties of the householder, as the Brahman must marry on completing his studentship, which may perhaps be ended before he is twenty-four years old. The verse is a general injunction that the bride should be about a third as old as the bridegroom; the time given in the text being only used as an illustration (Medh., K.)

[2] *I.e.*, even if he hate her because she hates him (Rāgh.) he must support her, for she is given by Bhaga, Aryaman, Savitar, etc. (K.), by Soma, and Gandharvas (Nand.)

[3] Cf. vs. 29, where the epithet is quoted as the title of a good wife. If he did not support her, the mutually given honour to the gods would fail, and so this would displease them (Medh.) Another reading is, "he marries a wife given by the gods, not by desire of himself." Medh. prefers the one translated above (*vindetā'nicchayā*).

[4] Or, mortals were created, female for bearing, male for procreating; literally, for (self-)continuation. Cf. vs. 27.

[5] K. The rules for laying on the holy fire, etc., are common to husband and wife (K.) The moral is that even disliked wives should not be deserted (Medh.)

[6] In vs. 69 no agreement on the part of the girl is necessary. Nārada (xii. 30) says in a like case that when the marriage-money has been given, and a better (richer, etc.) suitor comes, she is to be given to him. The Mbhā. lays down the rule (xiii. 44, 52) that when the suitor dies the woman may be given to his brother, or remain at home and perform penance. Nand. says, "or given to another" (if she does not consent to the brother-in-law).

marriage) should take marriage-money; for (by) taking marriage-money one makes a secret sale of one's daughter.[1]

99. Truly neither good men of old, nor good men of later times, have ever performed this (sin) of promising (a girl) to one man, and giving her over again to another man.[2]

100. For, truly, we have never heard that even in former ages a secret sale of a daughter (was made) for a settled price, under the name of a marriage-offering (*çulka*).[3]

101. Let there be mutual fidelity ending in death (alone); this, in few words, should be recognised as the highest law of duty for man and wife.

102. And ever thus should the man and wife who have been united by the ceremony (of marriage, etc.) give constant heed lest they mutually commit transgression.[4]

103. Thus has been declared to you this rule of right in regard to man and wife, (a rule) founded on love; and the (means of) obtaining offspring (have been declared): learn now the law [5] of inheritance.

104. After both the father and the mother (are dead), the brothers, having come together, should divide the paternal [6] inheritance; for while the two (parents)

[1] In Nand. the arrangement is 98, 100, 99, 101.

[2] Cf. vs. 71.

[3] The contradiction in the teaching regarding the *çulka* (97, 98) results from the probably later prohibition being inserted without modifying the original text permitting the practice. The *çulka*, in plain words, was money or goods paid for a wife. Such is the definition in the Mitākṣarā, and such is apparent in the use of the law-books. It was undoubtedly a common occurrence, and this denial of the fact as a usage is contradicted by other portions of this same work. From early times to those of Mandeslo and till to-day, the girl was sold as openly as cattle or grain. The pretence that it was an honorary offering was probably mere pretence. In the Mbhā. (xiii. 45. 18 ff.), "he who sells his son or gives his daughter for a *çulka* goes to hell. The sale of a daughter, although practised by some people, is not the eternal rule of right" (in the song of Yama). *Vide* note to vs. 93.

[4] Both the Medh. MSS. (No. 935, and 1551) have *niyuktau*.

[5] Some MSS. have *dāyabhāga*, partition of heritage; the MSS. of Medh. have *dharma*, so Rāgh.; some MSS. of K. and Nand. have *bhāga*.

[6] The word "paternal" seems to include maternal property, though explicitly denied by the Dāy. Bhāg. iii. 2. K. refers to Yāj. ii. 114 to

are alive the (sons) have no power (over the property).[1]

105. Now the eldest[2] alone may take the paternal property without leaving anything, and the remaining (brothers) may live supported by him just as (if he were their) father.

106. By means of the eldest (son) as soon as he is born[3] a man becomes possessed of a son, and is thus cleared of his debts towards the manes;[4] therefore this (eldest son) deserves the whole (inheritance).

107. (That son) through whom the father pays his debt, through whom he gains eternity—this son alone is duty-born;[5] the other (sons) they recognise (only) as (sons) born of desire.

108. As[6] a father would protect his sons, (so) should the eldest (brother protect) the younger brothers, and they should act in accordance with their duty toward the eldest brother, even as sons.

109. The eldest causes the family to flourish, or, again, he causes its destruction;[7] the eldest is most honoured among men; by good men the eldest is not disparaged.

110. That eldest (brother) whose conduct is that befitting an eldest brother should be (honoured) like a mother, like a father; but he whose conduct is not that befitting

show that if he pleases the father divides before death. In *ib.* 117 Yāj. directs the debts as well as property to be divided. If the mother is past child-bearing, Bṛhaspati says (cf. Gaut. xxviii. 2) that the property may be divided while she is alive. The Dāy. Bhāg. (ii. 2) limits this to ancestral wealth, not paternal wealth. Cf. Gaut. xxviii.; Āp. ii. 14; Vas. xvii.

[1] "Power (over the property)" means they have no right to divide it.

[2] *I.e.*, best (in point of age). Sometimes the *jyeṣṭha* is a variable term, referring not to the eldest, but to the one regarded as best, *i.e.*, receiving the privileges of primogeniture, because excelling in caste, etc. Cf. below.

[3] That is, even before he has become initiated into the caste order (K.)

[4] The Hindu has three debts—toward the gods, manes, and men; the first is paid by sacrifice, the second by offerings, the third by charity. K. quotes the *çruti*, "No world (of heaven) exists for one not possessed of a son." (Ait. Br. vii. 3, 9.)

[5] Born for the sake of duty, to fulfil a religious duty, which is the reason why he was begotten (K., Rāgh., and Nand.)

[6] This verse follows 109 in the Nand. MS.

[7] According to the qualities he possesses (Medh.)

an eldest brother should be respected like an (ordinary) relative.[1]

111. They may live either in this way together, or (let them live) apart (if influenced) by desire for religious duty; religious duty [2] is extended (by living) apart, therefore separate ceremonies are in accordance with religious duty.

112. One-twentieth (is) the portion to be taken out for the eldest, and (also) whatever (is) most desirable out of the whole property; [3] a half of that would be (the share of the middlemost, and a fourth (the share) of the youngest (brother).[4]

113. Thus both the eldest and the youngest should take to themselves (their portions) as (just) explained; if there are other (brothers) beside the elder and younger, they should have the middlemost property.[5]

114. The one born first should take the best [6] of all the things possessing any real value,[7] and also whatever

[1] The text means that the eldest born, if endowed with good qualities, is honoured as a father; a lack of virtue is entailed upon his posterity, and so he is the ruin of the family (K.) Cf. Gaut. xxviii. 4. The ordinary relative is a maternal uncle or other such relative (Medh., K., and Rāgh.)

[2] "Duty" (*dharma*) means here religious duty and ceremonial duties. A free translation would be: or let them live apart if influenced by a desire to fulfil certain duties, for thus ceremonial duties are extended; and consequently living apart and having separate ceremonies (instead of one ceremony for the whole family) is lawful and proper. Religion is extended by multiplying rites and spreading the five great sacrifices over a larger area. K. quotes from Bṛhaspati the remark that the honour given to gods, manes, and Brahmans by those who live and cook together (*i.e.*, form one household) is isolated; but if the brothers live apart, each branch of the family would show the same honour. The priests, it may be observed, would be better served by the family dividing into different households.

[3] *Atha vā dravyeṣv aparaṁ varam*, as *var. lec.*

[4] Or half of that, *i.e.*, of the half, according to the text in May. The same authority says that the *uddhāravibhāga*, portion deducted for the eldest, is not permitted in this (*kali*) age, p. 35. A point expanded to the application of local laws by Medh., who quotes this law as falling under the same restriction as that of cow-killing, and *niyoga* (commission of widow), namely, being, according to some, antiquated.

[5] That is, each would receive one-fortieth (K.)

[6] Literally, "the top-born takes the tip-top."

[7] Or, "of all the kinds of property" (Medh., K.)

is most excellent;[1] and from ten (cattle) let him take the most desirable.[2]

115. If (the sons are all) perfect in their own occupations, there is among ten (cattle) no (one) portion taken out (for the eldest), but some trifle only should be given to the elder (brother) to indicate an increased respect (for him).[3]

116. In case the portion to be taken out (for the eldest)[4] has been thus taken out, let one arrange equal shares; in case the portion to be taken out is not taken out, let the following be the arrangement of the shares of these (brothers):

117. The eldest should take (a share) increased by one (share),[5] then the son next born[6] (a share) with a half (share) added, and the younger (brothers) one share each; with these words the right rule is established.

118. Moreover, out of their respective shares the brothers should individually bestow a fourth part, each from his own share, upon the girls;[7] if they should be unwilling to give (such a portion) they would be degraded.

[1] As one garment or ornament (Medh.) Repetition of verse 112 (Medh., K.)

[2] Cf. Gaut. xxviii. 12. "Out of ten cattle (*daçataḥ*) let the eldest take one" (*sic* K.; the text received gives quite another meaning; cf. Bühler's translation and note, whereby he would receive ten), *i.e.*, if he is virtuous (K.) Medh. gives the same interpretation.

[3] The Dāy. Bhāg. remarks that, as now-a-days (younger brothers) have not much respect (for the elder brothers), the custom of taking out a share (one-twentieth, etc., *vide* 112) for the elder brother has died out, and equal partition is the rule (iii. 26–27.)

[4] That is, the twentieth part; cf. vs. 112.

[5] That is, two shares, while the next takes a share and a half, and the other younger brothers one share apiece. K. makes the whole arrangement liable to change if the necessary wisdom and virtue fail in the chief shareholder.

[6] Or, "the following" (*apara*) in May. Medh. MSS. (both Nos. 935 and 1551) have *anujaḥ*.

[7] The Dāy. Bhāg. makes this apply only when the wealth is comparatively small; if large, only enough to defray wedding expenses is to be given, and only when the number of sisters is equal to that of the brothers. Medh. says the sister is not to have a fourth of the wealth if the brother's is very small. K. remarks that the amount of the sisters' shares depend on their mother's caste; they receive their shares when they have not been married (so Medh.), and should take them from brothers of the same mother (or caste, Medh.) Cf. 149 ff. Although, if such brothers fail, the others should give her the share for the sake of the initiation, as Yāj.

119. One should indeed make no division[1] of goats, sheep, and animals with uncloven hoofs[2] when they do not fit into an equal division, but the goats or sheep (thus remaining over and) not fitting into an equal division are appointed for the eldest alone.

120. If a younger (brother) were to beget a son by the wife of the eldest, the division between them[3] should be equal: with these words the right rule is established.

121. The subordinate does not, according to law, take the place of the principal[4] (in respect to his legal rights); the principal (becomes) a father by this procreating; one should therefore have this (son) share (with his uncle), in accordance with the law of right.[5]

122. (Suppose) the youngest son (is born) by the eldest (wife),[6] and the first-born (son is born) by the youngest (wife), how should the division be between them? If a doubt should arise expressed in these words,

123. (We answer it thus): The first-born[7] should receive

says (ii. 124). The Dāy. Bhāg. (iii. 37) makes here the fine distinction that the unmarried girls do not get this property by right of inheritance (as the Mitākṣ. claims), or it would not be given by the brother out of his inheritance; which is only playing with terms (to prove that money to defray the wedding expenses is meant and no more); for if the daughter has a legal claim on one-fourth the brother's inheritance, then that is her inheritance defined and limited by the brother's.

[1] Not only are the animals left over after an equal division not to be divided, but no money equivalent should be received for them (Medh., K.) The reading of the May. repeats *sai'kaçapham* in (*b*).

[2] Horses, mules, etc. (Medh.)

[3] The division is equal between the son thus born and his natural father (really his uncle); the portion which would have been taken out for the father, *i.e.*, the eldest brother, is in this case not bestowed. These two verses recognise the *niyoga*, condemned in vss. 64–68.

[4] The subordinate is the representative, the son; he does not receive the extra share of the principal, *i.e.*, the (deceased) husband of the commissioned wife.

[5] *I.e.*, since his legal father became his father only by commission, he does not become superior to the younger brothers (of that father), one of whom is really his father; and not being superior (as was his legal father), he forfeits the right of the extra portion due to that father.

[6] *I.e.*, the wife first married (Medh., K.)

[7] Medh. and K. define *pūrvaja* as "the son born of the first wife, even if he is the youngest," and render *svamātṛtaḥ* "in consequence of their mothers," as explaining "inferior;" but Gaut. xxviii. 14, shows that the eldest son is intended, even when born by other than the first wife. This verse gives the rule for the eldest son, irrespective of his

one bull as his portion, to be taken out (of the general inheritance); after this the other bulls, not the best,[1] (belong), according to their mothers, (to his brothers who are) inferior to him (in point of age).

124. But when the eldest (son) is born of the first (wife), he should take fifteen cows and a bull;[2] then the rest may divide according to their mothers:[3] with these words the rule is fixed.

125. If sons are born by mothers of equal (caste, and consequently) without any distinction (of caste), the seniority is not according to their mothers,[4] (but) the seniority is declared (to be) according to (the time of) birth.

126. It is said that the invocation (contained) in the Subrahmaṇyā[5] (verses) (is settled by) primogeniture; and the superiority of a pair of sons (engendered at the same time) in (different) wombs is according to birth.[6]

127. One who is without a son should, by the following rule, make his daughter provide him a son:[7] "The offspring which may be hers shall be for me the giver of offerings to the manes."[8]

128. For of old Dakṣa himself, the primeval parent, in order to increase his race, made his daughters provide sons in the following manner:

mother; the next allots him a better portion if his mother is the first (eldest) wife.

[1] Or the next best bulls (K.); best, *i.e.*, in quality only (Medh.)

[2] Medh., K. Cf. Gaut. xxviii. 15.

[3] According as the mother is older or younger, or as she is married earlier or later (Medh.)

[4] *I.e.*, the time of the mother's marriages; for, in general, the priority of the mother's marriage indicates that she belongs to a higher caste.

[5] Verses (*mantra*) addressed to Indra (Medh.)

[6] *Sañjñāsu* is the inferior reading given in the May. text; but (as K. here correctly observes) where two sons by two wives are engendered at the same time, the first seen is the heir. Another belief is noticed in the May., that the first born of *twins* is the last conceived, therefore the (right of) primogeniture is given the twin born last.

[7] This formula of the Putrikā is said at the time the daughter is married, and with the consent of her husband (K. *Vide* K. to 136).

[8] That is, shall offer oblation to my manes (myself and ancestors) when I am dead. Medh. quotes here the verses of Gaut. xxviii. 17 ff.), noting an informal, secret commission of this sort on the part of the father (*vide* below, note to vs. 136).

129. Ten he gave to Dharma, and thirteen [1] to Kaçyapa, and twenty-seven to King Soma, treating them kindly and pleased in heart.

130. Even as the (man's) self, so is the son; the daughter is equal to the son; [2] how can any one, other than the daughter abiding in himself, receive his property?

131. All the personal property [3] of the mother should become the share of the daughter; [4] and the son of the daughter alone should take the whole property of (his mother's father if he dies) without a son.

132. And, indeed, since [5] the son of the daughter takes the whole inheritance (of his mother's) father (who) died without a son, he alone should give two funeral cakes, (one) to his father, and (one) to his mother's father. [6]

133. There is, according to the rule of right, no difference among men between the son of a son and the son of a daughter, [7] for the mother and father of these two are both born together from the body of this (common parent).

134. If, now, a son should be born (to a man whose daughter) has previously been appointed to provide a son, the partition would in that case be even, [8] for a woman has no right of primogeniture.

135. Now, if the daughter appointed to provide a son should at any time die without (leaving) a son, the husband of this daughter (who has been) appointed to provide a son may take her property without hesitation. [9]

[1] From these thirteen given to Kaçyapa, the whole world, men, gods, and demi-gods, were produced.

[2] The Mav. does not (as do Medh. and K.) refer this to the daughter appointed to provide a son, and adds that if there are several they divide.

[3] The property given her by her father, etc., at marriage.

[4] K. quotes Gaut. xxviii. 24; the woman's property goes to the unmarried or poor daughters.

[5] Some erroneously regard this as a mere repetition, reading "if he takes" (Medh.) (Cf. vs. 136.)

[6] Cf. 136 and 140. (Nand. reads *tat piṇḍam*); he has to play the part of son to each.

[7] Cf. vs. 139.

[8] That is, the portion ordinarily taken out for the eldest son should not be given to the daughter appointed to provide a substitute for this son (K.)

[9] This son is not the Kānīna of vs. 172, although no restrictions of this or any other sort are implied in the text; the girl has been actually married, as *bhartar* shows.

136. When a daughter not being appointed, or even being appointed, receives a son by a (man) of like (caste), the father of the mother becomes through him the possessor of a son, (and this son) should give the funeral cake and take the property.[1]

137. Through a son one conquers worlds,[2] through a son's son one attains endlessness, and through the son's son of a son one attains the world of the sun.

138. Since from hell, called *put*, the son (*putra*) preserves (*trā-yate*) the father, therefore, *putra* was he called, even by the Self-existent himself.[3]

139. Properly there is no difference among men between the son of a son and the son of a daughter, for even the son of a daughter, like the son of a son, causes him to be saved hereafter.[4]

140. The son of a daughter appointed to provide a son should cast down a funeral cake in the first place to (his) mother, and (he should cast down) a second to her[5] father, and a third to her father's father.

141. Now, if a man has a son-given endowed with every good quality, this (son) alone should receive the inheritance of that (man), even (if he has been) adopted out of another family (*gotra*).[6]

[1] The difference between this and vs. 132 is the fact that it makes no difference whether the formality enjoined in vs. 127 is gone through with, or whether the father, without repeating the formula, merely intends that his daughter should be authorised to provide a substitute. This view is alluded to by Gaut. xxviii. 19, who says it is on that account that a man is advised to marry no girl without brothers (cf. Yāj. i. 5, 3). K. remarks that Govindarāja wrongly interprets this to mean that any daughter's son has an equal right of inheritance with the Pautrikeya. Cf. Vas. xv. 6. Medh. says decidedly that the verse refers to the Pautrikeya only.

[2] Heaven (*svarga*) and other places devoid of sorrow (Medh.) Cf. Vas. xvii. 5.

[3] This pun is often repeated in legal and epic literature.

[4] Cf. vs. 133; the daughter is the one appointed to provide a son (Medh., K.)

[5] Medh. records that some read *pitus tasya* ("his father"), but compares vs. 132.

[6] K. and Medh. with Govind. disagree in regard to the conditions under which the son-given (cf. vs. 159) may take the property, opening a discussion as to whether this means the good qualities of the son-given are to have more weight than the claims of a son of the body not so endowed, or the claims of a wife's son, as a question not touched upon by the text, and apparently unknown to Nand., who dismisses the verse with a simple "self-evident." (Both Medh. MSS., Nos. 935 and 1551, read *dātrimaḥ*).

142. A son-given should at no time take[1] the family and inheritance of his progenitor. The funeral cake, (which) follows the family and inheritance, and the offering to the manes, (which would have been offered) for the giver (of the son), die out.[2]

143. Both the son of a non-commissioned[3] wife, and (a son) obtained (by a wife) from a brother-in-law, when (this wife already) has a son, do not deserve a share (in the inheritance), (as they are respectively) produced by a seducer and born of lust.[4]

144. Even if the wife has been commissioned, the male child not born in accordance with the set rule[5] has no right to the patrimony, for he is begotten by one (who by violating this set rule has become) degraded.[6]

145. The son born of (a wife who is) commissioned may inherit just like a son of the body; moreover, that seed and the progeny rightly belong to the owner of the land.[7]

146. He who maintains both the estate and the wife of a dead brother[8] should, after raising up a child for this brother,[9] bestow upon this (child) alone the property of this (brother).

[1] Medh. says some interpret *haret* as *hārayet*, "one shall (not) let him take." One Medh. MS. has *svadhām*, "of him who gives (?) the *svadhā*." The funeral cake, *piṇḍa*, means the funeral ceremony (Medh., K.); or, according to some, it means the *sapiṇḍa* relationship, and *svadhā* is the *çrāddha* and other ceremonies.

[2] The general meaning is that all connection with the first family ceases. Nevertheless, according to Kāty. and the later usage, if there is a special agreement to that effect, the son may belong to both fathers (*dvyāmuṣyāyaṇa*). Cf. May. p. 43. Along with this is quoted in May., p. 44, and the Datt. Mīm., ii. 8. This verse from Bṛhan Manu, "The relationship of the *given* and other sons to the progenitor is to the fifth and seventh degree; so also their family, which is, too, that of their adopter."

[3] Cf. vs. 59. The second case may be one where the wife is duly commissioned, but ought not to be, as she has a son already (K.)

[4] The Nand. MS. omits two verses after 143 and two after 146; but in 142 the gloss says, "He now says by three *çlokas* that even certain Kṣetraja are unworthy of inheriting." Then follow vss. 146, 149.

[5] As given in vs. 70 (Medh.), or better according to vs. 60 (K.)

[6] For both are in that case degraded by vs. 63.

[7] *I.e.*, the husband.

[8] Cf. vs. 190, which is probably a later addition, as it is not found in Medh.

[9] By the law of commission (Medh.)

147. If she who is commissioned should procure a son from any other source, or even from her brother-in-law, they declare this (son), (if) born of lust,[1] (to be) without share in the inheritance, and begotten in vain.

148. This should be recognised as the rule of partition among (sons) of the same origin. Learn now (the partition) among (sons) begotten of one (man) by many wives of several (castes).[2]

149. If a Brahman has four wives according to the regular order of the castes, the rule in (regard to) the partition (of the property) among the sons born of these (wives) is declared to be the following:

150. The ploughman,[3] the bull for cows, the waggon, the ornaments, and the house should be given to constitute the portion to be taken out for the Brahman,[4] and also a special part in consequence of (his) superiority.

151. The Brahman should take three parts of the inheritance, the son of the Kṣatriya woman two parts, the one born of the Vaiçya woman only one part and a half, the son of the Çūdra woman should take one part.[5]

152. Or,[6] after arranging the whole inheritance in ten parts, one who knows the law should make a just partition according to the following rule:[7]

153. The Brahman should take four parts, the son of the Kṣatriya woman three parts, the son of the Vaiçya

[1] So K. That is, without observing the rules of chastity as laid down by Nārada (xii. 80–88). Or if she should procure a son, etc., when *not* commissioned, he *is* born of lust and without share (Rāgh.) Medh. says this verse is to prevent the right of inheritance declared above, and construes (*aniyuktā*) as Rāgh does.

[2] Medh. and K. "Several wives" means the same as "of different castes," a mere repetition. Some make a distinction between them (Medh.)

[3] *Kīnāça*, ploughman (K.); workman (Nand.)

[4] The other sons are given by name. The son of the wife of Brahman caste is called simply the priest or the Brahman.

[5] A slight *v. l.* occurs in Nand. without change of meaning.

[6] Without taking out the special share for the Brahman (K.) (Two Medh. MSS. have *sarvathā*).

[7] This division was followed out systematically by the later writers, so that if a Brahman had three sons from the three highest castes, the property is divided into nine parts, and the sons receive in order four, three, and two portions, etc. Cf. Jolly, Ueber die Systematik des Indischen Rechts (Separatabdruck), s. 4.

woman should take two parts, the son of the Çūdra woman should take one part.[1]

154. Although (deceased) had, or even if he had not a (twice-born) son,[2] one may not, according to the rule of right,[3] give more than one-tenth to the son of the Çūdra woman.

155. The son of a Brahman, Kṣatriya, or Vaiçya by a Çūdra woman has no share in the inheritance. That only which his father may have given to him should be his property.[4]

156. Or[5] all the sons of the twice-born born of (women of) the same caste should give to the elder brother the part to be taken out (of the whole inheritance), and then the others[6] should divide (the remainder) equally.

157. It is a fixed rule that the wife of a Çūdra must be just (a woman) of the same caste (as himself) and no other. (The sons) born of this wife would have equal shares (in the inheritance) if he had (even) a hundred sons.

158. Six of those twelve sons which Manu, son of the Self-existent, declared belong to men (are) members of the family and heirs; six are not heirs, but members of the family.[7]

159. A son of the body, a wife's son,[8] a son-given, a son-made, a son-in-secret, and a son-rejected are the six heirs and members of the family.

[1] Land alone cannot be taken by the Çūdra son (Medh.)

[2] This implies that the Kṣatriya and Vaiçya sons take all but one-tenth when no Brahman son exists (K.)

[3] In Nand. *dhīmate* (to a pious son of a Çūdra) is probably a clerical error.

[4] That is, he has no legal claim on anything; it is only a matter of informal giving. Medh. and K. admit a seeming contradiction between this verse and the foregoing, but say it depends on the virtue of the Çūdra woman's son whether he be entitled to a share, or the prohibition in this verse refers only to the son of an *unmarried* Çūdra woman, according to some.

[5] *Samavarṇāsu vā* (Medh.), "the 'or' denotes a second method of division" (Medh.); *ye* (K., Rāgh.)

[6] That is, all the brothers divide equally; those other than the eldest receive no special share.

[7] This means they become, as members of the *gotra*, capable of performing the different family ceremonies (K., Rāgh.) To show Medh. what really constitutes such a sharer in the *gotra* alone, K. quotes Baudh. ii. 2. 3. 32.

[8] Literally, the one born on the land, *i.e*, the one by the commission described in vs. 59 ff.

160. A son by a girl,[1] a son taken with the bride, a son bought, a son of a twice-married woman, a son self-given, and a son by a Çūdra (woman),[2] are the six who are not heirs, (but) members of the family.

161. The sort of reward one gets on crossing water by means of bad boats is the sort of reward one gets on crossing the darkness (of the next world) by means of bad sons.[3]

162. If the two sons who together inherit[4] the property are the son of the body and the wife's son, he to whom any paternal inheritance comes should take that (inheritance); (and) the other (shall) not (take it).[5]

163. The son of the body is the one and only lord of the paternal wealth; but to do the others no harm he should afford (them something) to support life.[6]

164. The son of the body, dividing the paternal inheritance, should give to the wife's son one-sixth part of the paternal property, or even one-fifth.[7]

165. The two sons sharing the inheritance of the father are the son of the body and the wife's son; but the ten others,[8] according to their rank, have a share in the family (*gotra*) and a part of the inheritance.[9]

[1] The son of an unmarried girl (*Kānina*).

[2] Sometimes called Niṣāda; Baudh. ii. 2. 3, 29; Manu x. 8. Baudh. apparently distinguishes this Niṣāda from the Pāraçava (M. ix. 178, cf. note) by the former being born legitimately, the latter born of lust. This list is given with changes in Mbhā. i. 120, 33. Vas. xvii. 15 gives the appointed daughter as the third "son;" Āp. does not recognise these twelve kinds.

[3] Good sons are necessary to save the father from hell by means of offerings to the manes.

[4] *Ekarikthinau aribhaktadhanau* (Nand.)

[5] Cf. vs. 191. "He" is the son of the body; the "other" is the wife's son, who is here the first-born (K.) The permission given by Yāj. ii. 127, that the wife's son may inherit the property both of his natural and assumed father, is only to be understood as applicable to cases where the assumed father has no son of the body. Medh. and Gov. mistake when they assume the verse to have been added in reference to the son of the body and the son of a wife not commissioned. The son of a wife not commissioned is not a wife's son (K.) According to Baudh. ii. 2. 3, 18, the wife's son inherits from both fathers.

[6] Food and clothes (K.)

[7] In accordance with his good qualities (K.)

[8] That is, the sons-given, etc.; cf. vs. 159.

[9] They have share in the family, and each in the order named in vs. 159 shares the property when the one next higher does not exist (K.) *I.e.*, the presence of one higher in rank annuls the claim of each lower.

166. One should recognise as the son of the body, and first in rank, that son whom the (father) himself begets on his own land, (that is,) by a (wife) who has performed the ceremony (of marriage).[1]

167. If (a son is) born in the marriage-couch of a man who has died, (or) is impotent, or ill, after the wife has been commissioned in the proper manner, this son is called the wife's son.[2]

168. If a mother or a father should give a son, (to any one who is) in need, by the (ceremony of) water, (and if the son is) of like sort (with the family adopting him), and is filled with affection[3] (for the family), this son should be known as the son-given.[4]

169. If a man makes a (boy) of like sort (with himself) his son, (and this boy can) distinguish good and evil,[5] (and is) endowed with the good qualities of a son, this (son) should be known as the son-made.

170. If (a boy) is born in a man's house, and it is not known to what (father) he belongs, (he would be a son) born in secret in the house, and he would belong to him to whom the (son) born in the marriage-couch belongs.[6]

[1] From Baudh. ii. 2. 3, 14, it is clear that the wife must also be of like caste (K.)

[2] "Son-by-land," *i.e.*, wife.

[3] Or, with the commentators, "with desire;" that is, he is not to be given by fear, force, deceit, or magic (K., Rāgh., Nand.)

[4] Vas. xv. 2 grants the father and mother the right to give, sell, or desert a son; Ap. ii. 13, 11, denies it; K. says that the father or mother give him by mutual consent when the one receiving the son is in need of a son. The word "like" (*sadrça*) may mean either of like family, caste, or qualities (cf. vs. 174 note); a boy of any other caste, ex. vs. 92; a Kṣatriya may, according to Medh., be a son given to a Brahman. K. and Nand. restrict to caste; in the May. the latter is preferred. The general sense is preferable for our text, as special restrictions in regard to the definition of "like" are later. Madana thus explains the word "or": "the father may give him if the mother is dead, the mother if the father is dead; if both are alive, both" (May., p. 39).

[5] K. refers this to virtue or sin produced by performing or by not performing the *çrāddha* and other spiritual ceremonies; like sort, *i.e.*, quality or caste (Medh. or K.)

[6] That is, to the husband, the master of the house. Cf. vs. 167. Neither Yāj., Baudh., Gaut., nor Vas. say who the mother is. Apparently it is the wife, as K. says, who adds, this son must be presumed to be of the same caste if his parentage cannot be discovered.

171. If one adopts a son deserted by both father and mother, or by either of the two,[1] this son is called the son-rejected.

172. If an (unmarried) girl should secretly bear a son in her father's house, one should designate him by the name son-by-a-girl, being born of a maiden (and belonging) to (the future) husband.[2]

173. If a pregnant woman is married by the (regular marriage) ceremony, whether she is known (to be pregnant) or is not known, the unborn child belongs to the husband, and is called (a son) taken with the bride.

174. If a man for the sake of having offspring buy (a son) openly from the mother and father, this son is a son-bought, whether he is like or unlike this (father by purchase).[3]

175. If a woman being deserted by her husband, or being separated from him by her own desire,[4] bears a son after she has married a second time, this (son) is called (a son) of a twice-married woman.

176. Now if she is (still) a virgin, or even if she has returned (to her husband) after going away (from him),[5] she ought to go through the (marriage) ceremony a second time with her husband, (who thus) receives a woman twice-married.

[1] A son deserted at the death of one of the two parents by the other (K.)

[2] They know he is the son of the husband, not the son of the girl's father (Nand.) According to Yāj. (ii. 129) he is called son-by-a-girl, (not in respect to her (future) husband, but) in respect to her father; cf. Vas. xvii. 22. K. seems to understand that he belongs to his natural father after he has married the mother; so Viṣṇu, xv. 12. From vss. 172 to 179 is wanting in both MSS. Medh. (Nos. 935, 1551).

[3] K. says that here, because of *asadrça*, the reference is to like or unlike moral qualities, for in all cases in Manu the sons are to be understood as of like caste, and this is emphatically stated by Yāj. ii. 133; but the emphasis in Yāj. (*proktaḥ . . . mayā vidhiḥ*) would seem to show it was original with that law-book and not to be assumed for Manu.

[4] The woman, according to Vas. (xvii. 19, 20), who deserts a worthless husband and marries another, or who goes back to her original husband after leaving him, is a twice-married woman. Baudh. (ii. 2. 3, 27) recognises only the one who deserts a worthless husband.

[5] That is, if she deserts the husband of her youth, lives with another, and comes back again to the first (K.)

177. If (a boy should be) deprived of mother and father (by death), or be deserted (by them) without cause, and should (then) attach himself to any man, this (boy) is called (in respect to this man) a (son)-self-given.

178. If a Brahman through lust beget a son by a Çūdra woman, this (son), being as a corpse in saving, is (therefore) called a corpse-for-saving (Pāraçava).[1]

179.[2] If a son is born to a Çūdra by a slave-woman (or *dāsī*), or by a slave's slave-woman (*dāsadāsī*),[3] he may, if permitted,[4] take one share: with these words the rule of right is established.

180. Wise men say these eleven sons, beginning with the wife's son, as mentioned (in verse 160), are (only) substitutes for a son, (substituted) in consequence of the failure of religious ceremonies (which failure would ensue if there were no son).[5]

181.[6] Those who, begotten by the seed of another man, are on some occasions designated as sons, belong to that man from whose seed they are born, and (they do) not (belong) to anybody else.[7]

[1] Cf. x. 8. The meaning is, that he is no better than a corpse in saving his father from hell. K., Rāgh., and Nand. understand "he is, though living, a corpse." This fanciful derivation cannot be supplied by a certain one, though the Pāraçava were probably so called either because this mixed class carry axes (*paraçu*) or are born by another woman (*pārasara*). By a quotation from Yāj., which is not found in our text, K. endeavours, against the text, to prove that the Çūdra woman is not a concubine, but a wife (cf. note to vs. 160).

[2] The description of the list given in vs. 160 is not complete. A modification is now stated in regard to the last named, when the parent is not a Brahman but a Çūdra.

[3] K. refers to viii. 415; any one of the there-mentioned seven kinds of slaves is meant. The word "slave" may itself mean Çūdra, and *dāsī* has various meanings; but here the verse means merely that the Çūdra's son, (by wife or) by slave, is entitled to one share.

[4] "Permitted" means permitted by the father (K., Nand.) This is emphatic; for if he were not especially permitted by the father, he would have no claim on the estate (Nand.)

[5] The religious ceremonies devolving on the son would become extinct (K.) Through failure of religious ceremonies (iii. 63) families become extinct. The substitutes are to be created only when there is fear of the failure of these ceremonies (Nand.)

[6] From verse 181 to 202 fails in all MSS. of Medh., but some of the verses, *e.g.*, 182, 192, are found in the Mitākṣarā.

[7] Apparently flat contradiction of

182. If among brothers born of one (father)[1] one should have a son, Manu said (that) all these (brothers would be) possessed of sons by means of that son (alone).[2]

183. If among all the wives of one (husband) one should have a son, Manu said (that) all these (wives would be) possessed of sons by means of that son (alone).[3]

184. In the absence of each higher (in rank) the (son next) lower should receive the inheritance; but if there are several of like (rank),[4] (they should) all have a share of the inheritance.[5]

185. Neither brothers nor parents, (but) sons take the inheritance of a father;[6] the father should take the inheritance of (a son who dies) without a son,[7] and also the brothers.[8]

186. To three (ancestors) the water (libation) must be made; for three (ancestors) the funeral cake is prepared; the fourth (descendant) is the giver (of the water and the funeral cake); the fifth has properly nothing to do (with either gift).[9]

187. The property (of one deceased) should belong to

the foregoing, but K. quotes Vṛddha Bṛhaspati to show that this means only that when the son of the body and daughter appointed to procure a son exist, these others should not be adopted. Rāgh. quotes Yāj. ii. 132 to show each of the sons inherits in order, and it is only in the absence of the secondary sons that the wife, etc., have a right to the property.

[1] Brothers with the same mother and father (K.)

[2] This one son inherits and gives the funeral cake for all, and if he exists, other substitutes for sons should not be made (K., Nand.) K. also refers to Yāj. ii. 135 to show that on failure of (sons), wife, daughter, parents, and brothers, the nephew is heir. Nand. observes that this one son must be a son of the body, and so in vs. 183.

[3] Therefore, when one wife has a son, another should not adopt one (K.)

[4] *E.g.*, several sons of twice-married women (Rāgh.)

[5] The order in rank follows the list in vs. 159, and the one who is heir should, by Viṣṇu xv. 30, support the others (K.) Cf. vss. 163–165.

[6] Cf. vs. 217 and Yāj. ii. 135.

[7] And without wife or daughter (K.); grandson or great-grandson (Nand.)

[8] The brothers take possession in the absence of (father or) mother (K.) The additions of K. are based on a later standpoint in regard to female inheritance. Nand. and Rāgh. read "*or* the (own) brothers alone." Rāgh. marks the reading "*atra ca*" as a *var. lec.*

[9] And sonship, or the right to inherit by direct descent, to the exclusion of brothers, etc., ceases at the fifth, *i.e.*, goes no farther than the great grandson.

that (man) who (is) next after the Sapiṇḍa; next to him, one of the same clan[1] should be (the heir); (next) the teacher, or even a pupil.[2]

188. But in the absence of all (heirs),[3] Brahmans versed in the three Vedas, pure and subdued, take the inheritance; by these means the law of right fails not.[4]

189. The property of Brahmans must never be seized by the king;[5] this is a fixed rule; but the king may take (the property) of the other castes when all (other heirs) fail.

190. (If the widow) of a man who has died childless procure a son from a man of the same family (*gotra*),[6] she shall make over to this (son) whatever (property) has grown out of the inheritance.[7]

[1] Or those (pl.) of the same family (*kula*), *i.e.*, distant relatives (*samānodakāḥ* (Nand.)

[2] K. takes the Sapiṇḍas as male or female; for an explanation of Sapiṇḍa see iii. 5 and v. 60. In the text the word is masculine. K. begins by taking it generally as masculine or feminine, then, after giving the law of inheritance for the sons, he begins by taking the wife as the first female inheritor, quotes seven verses of Bṛhaspati and Vṛddha Manu (called Bṛhan Manu in Rāgh.) to prove the statement (also Yāj. ii. 135–136), and ends by giving a list of female Sapiṇḍas, after denouncing Medh. as "not fond of the opinion of the good," because he denies the wife the right of sharing the inheritance. He then gives wife, daughter not ordained, father, mother, own brother, his son, and (by vs. 217) the mother of the father—after these any male Sapiṇḍas. Cf. Āp. ii. 14, 2; Gaut. xxviii. 21; Vas. xvii. 81 ff.; Baudh. i. 11, 11; Viṣṇu xvii. In Append. iii. to his translation of the May. Mandlik has discussed the subject at large. In respect to the sons who inherit in order, K. says: by 163 the son of the body inherits; he should give one-fifth or one-sixth to the wife's son and son-given, but need only support the son-made and others (vss. 163, 164). If there is no son of the body, the next heir is the ordained daughter or her son, for by the son of vs. 131 is meant the son of the body (then *dauhitra* = *pautrika*); if these do not exist, the wife's son and other ten in order; the son by the Çūdra woman (if she is married) should, by vs. 154, take but a tenth, consequently the next heir takes all but this. In the absence of the sons, the wife inherits, etc. Nand. seems to know nothing of K.'s explanation and his attempts to construe Sapiṇḍa as inclusive of females, as he himself understands only the masculine, which he employs in his gloss several times, not suggesting the possibility of its embracing females, though in vs. 188 he makes "all" embrace "men and women."

[3] All these (just mentioned)—(K.)

[4] For they, like other heirs, give the funeral cake, etc. (K.)

[5] It must, in default of heirs, be given to other Brahmans only, while the king may take the property of a Kṣatriya, etc., when all heirs mentioned fail (K.)

[6] *I.e.*, bears a son through commission by the brother-in-law or others (Nand.)

[7] Cf. vs. 146. The wife must be commissioned; one of the same family is allowed by vs. 59 (K.)

191. But if two (sons) born of one woman by two (husbands) have a strife regarding the property, each of these should take what (comes) to him from his father, (and) the other (shall) not (take it).[1]

192. Now when the woman who bare them is dead, all the brothers of one mother should divide equally the maternal inheritance, together with the sisters-german.[2]

193. If these sisters have daughters,[3] something in accordance with their dignity should kindly be given even to them out of the property of their maternal grandmother.

194. That which is given over the (marriage)-fire,[4] that which is given in the bridal procession, that (which is given) for an act of love, and that (which is) received from brother, mother, and father, (all this) is called the sixfold property of woman.[5]

195. That which is received as a gift (by a married

[1] K. understands the own son by the first husband, and second son of the twice-married woman by a second husband, and compares the similar expression in vs. 162 referring to sons of body and wife. So Nand., "if a woman marry again having a son, and with property, and bears another son by the second husband, each son gets the property left by his own father." Rāgh. says, "or it may apply to the woman's property."

[2] That is, if these sisters are unmarried. If they are married, Bṛhaspati says a small present only is to be given them as a token of respect. A fourth part of the brother's share of the mother's property should be given the sister who is married, just as in vs. 118 the unmarried sister receives one-fourth of the brother's share in the father's estate (K.) But if there is no unmarried daughter, the married daughters share equally with the brothers (Kāt. in May., where the quotation from Bṛhaspati (though farther on attributed to him), is here said to be Manu's). Nand. knows no such distinction.

[3] Unmarried (K.)

[4] Or *prītitaḥ striyai* (in Dāy. Bhāg., iv. 4) "given out of love to the wife."

[5] Cf. Jolly, Stellung, p. 22, and note to iii. 52. This simple text in regard to women's property covers what in later writers is expressed with much greater fulness. According to viii. 416, the wife has no property at all, but this is explained by later writers as referring to wealth got by mechanical arts. The earlier writers allow her ornaments (Baudh.) and presents (Āpas., Vas.), while Viṣṇu adds *adhivedanikam*, given when the husband marries another wife, etc. For limits to this right of possession, cf. vs. 199 note. Nand. glosses this verse with (the quotation from Kāt. found in K., and) the remark, "woman's property other than this is the property of the husband gained by the wife, but not the property of the women." The commentators say that the "sixfold" is the lowest limit in kind, but she may have more.

woman) after her marriage, from the family of her husband or of her connections,[1] and that which has been given her by her beloved husband, shall become the property of (her) children, should she die while her husband is alive.

196. Whatever valuables (she receives) at the (marriages called) Brāhma, Daiva, Arṣa, Gāndharva, Prājāpatya, are declared to belong to her husband alone, if she die without children.

197. But if property be given her at the Āsura and other marriages,[2] it is declared to belong to her father and mother if she die without children.

198. Now if at any time property is given to a woman by her father, the girl of the Brahman caste would inherit it, or it would become (the property) of this (girl's) children.[3]

199. Women should not make expenditure[4] out of the family (property) belonging to several, or even out of her own wealth, without the consent of her husband.

200. The heirs should not divide among themselves such ornaments as are worn by the women while the husband is alive.[5] If they divide (them) they are degraded.

[1] *Anvādheyam*, a pledge to hand over. The translation is according to the definition of other law-writers.

[2] The Rākṣasa and Paiçāca marriages (K.)

[3] K. explains that the husband is supposed to be a Brahman and have several wives, and then the property, left by the Kṣatriya wife or those of lower caste when they die, becomes that of the daughter of the wife of the Brahman caste or of her children, and this case supposes the wife deceased to have left no children. The May. in annotating this verse says: "The word *or* means *and*, *i.e.*, the property is divided; there is a varied opinion as to whether the Brahman daughter who thus inherits may not refer to any one of higher or of equal caste" (p. 62).

[4] K. "Wives and other women should not make a hoard from the property of her kindred which is common to her and many (brothers, etc.), and not even from her husband's property without his consent, for this is not women's property." "Hoard" is, however, not the real meaning of *nirhāra* (cf. May., p. 60, *nirhāro vyayaḥ*, West and Bühler, ii. 73). This verse must be understood to limit the reach of vs. 194 in putting limitation of use even on *strīdhana*. Nand. supports the rendering "expenditure" as in May., "they should not make *expenditure* of the husband's goods even *for the sake* of the family, nor of their own goods," etc. The property called *saudāyaka* (than which has been given her by kindred out of affection) was regarded as her own to do with as she pleased.

[5] The text is ambiguous. Either "worn while the husband is alive,"

201. An impotent man and one degraded are without share (in an inheritance); so also those born blind or deaf, those (who are) crazy, idiotic, or dumb, and all who are without manly strength.[1]

202. But the rule is for a sensible man to give to each one of these, according to (his) ability, both food and clothes without end;[2] for should he not give (these) he would be degraded.

203. But if at any time desire for a wife seize hold of the impotent man and the others, and they should thus become parents, their offspring has a right to the inheritance.[3]

204. If the eldest (brother) acquire any property whatever[4] after the father has passed away, a share in that case (belongs) to the younger (brothers), if they have preserved their (sacred) learning.[5]

205. But if all the brothers, being unlearned, should acquire wealth from (their united) exertion,[6] in that case the division (of the property) should be equal, being independent of the paternal (wealth):[7] in these words the rule is expressed.

206. If any one possesses property (gained) by his learning,[8] this property should be his alone; so too (pro-

or "the heirs should not divide while," etc. Bühler upholds the latter, and has Nand. as authority (to Viṣṇ. and M.) Jolly (Viṣṇu, xvii. 22 note) supports K. and others in the former rendering. The women are of course the various wives.

[1] Cf. vs. 18; *nirindriya* may mean simply devoid of organs. So K. explains as "those lame in arm or foot," etc., and Rāgh. as "lacking a hand," etc., and Nand. "as lacking an organ" (*karmendriya*).

[2] As long as he lives (Medh., K.)

[3] A portion as great as the daughter's (Medh.) By commission the impotent man may become a father; cf. vs. 79. Such marriages appear to have been common. K. remarks that "at any time" is added because these people ought not to marry as a regular thing.

[4] By his own individual ability (K.)

[5] K. understands a partition made after the brothers have lived together, and restricts the extra share to those who keep up the study of sacred learning. The reading *vidyānupālinām*, noted as a *var. lec.* by Rāgh., is found in Nand. and implied by K. It may mean "pursuing any outside branch of study," as Medh. takes it. The eldest must put in his gains with the inheritance, and divide with the younger brothers.

[6] If they unitedly gain wealth by agriculture or trade (K.)

[7] No special portion is to be taken out (for the eldest)—(K.)

[8] Under the circumstances in vs. 204. There is one exception; if a brother recovers ancestral land by his own exertions, it is to be regarded as

perty received) through friendship, (that) gained at a marriage,[1] and (that received when one as a guest is honoured) by the honey-mixture.

207. But if any one of the brothers, being able (to support himself) by his own occupation, does not desire (his share of the) property, he may be excluded from his share after giving him something (in the way) of support.[2]

208. If one acquires anything by his industry without detriment to the paternal estate, that,[3] being gained by his own efforts,[4] he need not, unless he chooses, give up (to the other brothers).

209. Now, if a father acquires any wealth of which, (although) belonging to the paternal estate, one had not (before) got possession, he need not divide this with the sons unless he chooses, (as it was) acquired by himself (alone).[5]

patrimony, and is partible. The one who recovers it has a fourth, and it is then shared with the others in a common division (Çaṅkha in May., p. 47). Cf. vs. 209. The property gained by learning is defined by Kāty. as the proceeds of learning gained from another, or gained by disputation after betting on the result, or by being a priest, or as teacher (from a pupil), etc. K. says Medh. and Gov. are wrong in rendering *mādhuparkikam* (by the honey-mixture) as that gained by being priest, since this is included by the verse of Kāty. under property gained by learning. The simple explanation of Nand., that property gained by learning is "got by arts," etc., seems older and better than K.'s and Rāgh.'s elaborate explanation (from Kāty.), based on a technical term, probably unknown at the time of the text, and it is supported by Medh., who renders it "by teaching, or by skill in the arts."

[1] This means women's property (Nand.); it is more probably what a man receives when a guest at some one's else wedding (so Medh.)

[2] Some nominal portion of no great value is meant, as K. says, in order to prevent his sons making a fuss about losing the inheritance. Such a case could easily occur if one of the brothers were always away from home as a soldier.

[3] Cf. Yāj. ii. 118. A *var. lec.*, supported by the Mitākṣarā and by the May. (p. 47), for (*b*), reads "he need not give that to the heirs, nor that gained by learning." Such gain as that by agriculture, etc. (Medh., K.) The reading of (*b*) in Mbhā. xiii. 105 agrees with Medh. and K., though the labour is in (*a*) stated to be that gained by travelling (as merchant). Rāgh. defines *anupaghnan* as "not supporting himself by the paternal estate."

[4] (Medh., K. or) "and that given him by his own desire" (Nand. to Viṣṇu xviii. 42).

[5] Or perhaps better "provided it were" (as Nand. to Viṣṇu xviii. 43). Cf. Viṣṇu xvii. 1, "a father may dispose of self-acquired property as he sees fit." Yāj. ii. 119 says if one recovers, etc., he need not give it to the co-heirs;" from this K. and Rāgh. take the "son" as the subject of the first verb, and interpret

210. If, on living together after being separated,[1] they divide (the inheritance) a second time, in that case the division should be equal, (as) in that case no right of primogeniture occurs.

211. If the eldest or the youngest among several (brothers) be lacking[2] at the distribution of shares, or if either of the two die, his share is not lost.[3]

212. For the own brothers, and those who were reunited,[4] and the own sisters, should assemble together and divide this share equally.

213. If an eldest (brother),[5] through avarice, commit an injury[6] against (his) younger (brothers), he should be made a not-eldest and shareless, and be put under restraint by kings.[7]

214. None of the brothers who perform wrong acts[8] deserve (share in) the property; and the eldest shall not create a private property,[9] (by) not giving (their proper shares) to the younger.

"heirs" as the "sons" of the text (Rāgh.); even Nand. renders as above, which is the only meaning possible.

[1] Or *saṁsṛṣṭāḥ*, "reunited" (May., p. 56); *vibhaktāḥ* (our text), "having (separated the property and) divided." The May. (p. 56) says that this text expresses the custom, remarking that there is a saying to the effect that the law-book has its roots in custom.

[2] Be deprived of his share by being away, or being degraded (K., Nīl. in May.)

[3] This rule applies to brothers reunited or not reunited (Nand.)

[4] *I.e.*, those who have divided the property and afterwards come together again (Rāgh.); to be applied to the wife, father, paternal grandfather, etc. (beside the brothers) (May., p. 57). This rule applies when the deceased leaves no son, wife, daughter, etc. (K.) Nand. says in the absence of own brothers, the reunited; in their absence, the own sisters; making each exclude the following. Medh. makes the "reunited" apply to the brothers only (as K. says, "not all the own brothers"), paraphrasing "the reunited own brothers and own sisters," and adds that "and" includes sisters.

[5] That is, any one who takes the heritage (May., p. 49).

[6] Defraud him (K.)

[7] *I.e.*, be made an ordinary relative in the honour he receives (*bandhuvat pūjyaḥ*) (Medh.), or lose his right of primogeniture and be fined (K.) The Mayūkha quotes in this connection a verse from Manu, which says that after a division of property has been made, and some common property is discovered not known at the time of partition, a new partition must be made (p. 50), and another to the effect that a new division must be made if there is a doubt in regard to the partition (p. 51). Neither verse occurs in the text.

[8] Such as frequenting a gambling-house (K.); gaming and drinking (Rāgh.); acts accomplished by bad behaviour (*vivṛtti*)—(Medh., Nand.)

[9] *Yautakam*, usually the bridal gift of a woman; so taken here by

215. If there should be a common endeavour (to gain wealth)[1] on the part of brothers who (live together) without having divided (the property), the father should never make the share of (any one) son different (from those of the others).[2]

216. Moreover, a son born after partition[3] should receive only the paternal property; or if any (sons) should be reunited with this (father), he[4] should share it with them.

217. The mother should receive the heritage[5] of a childless son, and in case the mother also is dead, the father's mother should receive the property.[6]

218.[7] When everything, debts and possessions, have been divided according to rule, and anything[8] is afterwards

Nand., "he should not in this way make money for his daughter, but he should take his daughter's marriage portion out of his own share alone." With vss. 213–214 cf. Mbhā. xii. 105, 7–10.

[1] So Medh. and K., otherwise explained by Jimūta-vāhana (Dāy. Bhāg. ii. 86) as effort, *i.e.*, desire to have a division.

[2] At the time of division, *i.e.*, when they cease to live together (Rāgh.) The commentator to Mbhā. takes this to mean at the time of eating or division of food, *i.e.*, if they get their dinner by united toil, each shall have an equal share (xiii. 105, 12).

[3] The partition being made while the father is alive by the sons' desire, the son subsequently born after the father's death has a claim only on the property (subsequently held by the father)—(K.)

[4] *I.e.*, the son born after partition is made: if they reunite, he shares with them at the father's death (K.) By Yāj. ii. 122 and Viṣṇu xvii. 3, a son conceived before the partition, but born after it, has his share made up by contributions from the other brothers. The Medh. MSS. vary between *hared dhanam* and *dhanam haret* (latter in May., p. 37).

[5] *Dāyādam* (Medh.)

[6] Between this verse and vs. 185 (which is not in Medh.'s text) is a plain contradiction; the later law scheme arranged the succession as follows: son, grandson, great-grandson, wife, daughter, daughter's son, mother, father, brothers, brothers' sons, father's mother, etc. In vs. 185 we have the order father and brothers; to unite which with this and make both correspond to the later scheme has cost the commentators some labour. K. quotes Yāj. ii. 135, compares our text, ix. 185, and Viṣṇu xviii. 6 (Bṛhaspati, Vṛddha Manu, and Vṛddha Viṣṇu) (Rāgh.), to show that both parents are here intended. A discussion in May. (p. 53) settles against the Mitākṣarā that the mother's claim comes after the father's. If we take Nand.'s explanation of *apatya* as including son, grandson, and great-grandson, wife and daughter and her son, the last of which are of course not intended, we still have the father, brothers, and brother's son omitted between the mother and grandmother; and even if mother is, as K. says, an *ekaçeṣā*, *i.e.*, includes the (father) omitted, the brothers by vs. 185 should intervene.

[7] In the MS. of Nand. vs. 218 follows vs. 219.

[8] Whether property or debt (K.);

discovered, one should make an equal partition of all of it.[1]

219.[2] Clothes, vehicles,[3] ornaments, prepared food, water, women, religious wealth, and paths they declare[4] (are impartible.[5]

220. Thus has been declared to you the (rule of) partition and the rule of ceremony in respect to (all) the sons[6] in order, beginning with the wife's son. Learn (now) the rules of right respecting gambling.

221. Both gambling and prize-fighting the king should exclude from his kingdom. These two vices bring to an end the sway[7] of those who rule the land.

222. Gambling and prize-fighting are the same as open robbery; the king should always be active in his antagonism to these two (vices).

223. That (play) which is performed by means of things without life is called among men "gambling;" that which is performed by means of living creatures is to be known as "prize-fighting."[8]

probably here only property is meant, as in Yāj. ii. 126, though debts are included, *ib.* 117.

[1] That is, no special share should be given to the eldest (K.) The general rule is that debts descend to the heirs.

[2] From vs. 219 to vs. 228 fails in Medh. (MSS. No. 935, 1551) (*vide* note to vs. 228). A different version of this verse is attributed to Manu in the May. (p. 46), where also an ordeal (which is not found in Manu) is ordained in case one suspects that goods have been concealed.

[3] (Or) horses, etc. (Rāgh.) For *patram*, "vehicle" (or *vijñānam*, "document"), Nand. reads *pātram* (*udakapātram*), a receptacle for water.

[4] Women means slaves or mistresses. If of equal value, the garments and ornaments are not divisible; if some are more valuable than others, they must be divided (Bṛh. in K.) Water from tanks, etc., is to be used by all (Medh., K.) Religious wealth is defined variously as councillors, ascetics, or priests (Medh., K.), or wealth of sacrifices and good deeds (Laugākṣi in May., p. 48). *Pracāra* (*paths*) may be taken as pasture-ground (K.) In respect to the female slaves, it is said in May. that they are to be divided if of equal number, otherwise they must work by turns as they can (cf. K.), but the kept women of the father are not partible. Cf. Gaut. xxviii. 47.

[5] "And a book" is Viṣṇu's reading in the same verse (xviii. 44).

[6] Nand., *yogavidhiḥ sampādanavidhiḥ*.

[7] Or by *var. lec.* bring to those who rule the land the destruction of the king. (Nand. has *rājya°*.)

[8] "Gambling" with dice, etc.; "prize-fighting" (literally, challenging) fights (for bets) by cocks, rams, etc. (K.)

224. All such people as indulge in gambling and prize-fighting, or cause them to be carried on, the king should have corporally punished,[1] and (he should also corporally punish) Çūdras (who) bear the emblems of the twice-born.[2]

225. Gamblers, players,[3] cruel men,[4] men who abide in heresy, men who do wrong acts, and men who manufacture spirituous liquor (the king) should banish from the city[5] at once.

226. These robbers in disguise, living in a king's realm, constantly injure the worthy subjects by the performance of their misdeeds.

227. This gambling has been seen (to be) in a former age[6] a great maker of strife; therefore a wise man should not devote himself to gambling even for the sake of amusement.

228. If any man should devote himself to this (sport), either secretly or openly, he should receive an adjustment of punishment[7] such as is in accordance with the pleasure of the ruler.[8]

229. Now one whose caste is that of Kṣatriya, Vaiçya, or Çūdra, (when he is) unable to pay a fine, may absolve himself of debt by labour; a priest should pay little by little.[9]

[1] By cutting off a hand or foot (K.)

[2] The marks of caste, such as the sacred string, etc., etc. The addition to this verse given by May. (p. 95), "without the king's permission," rests on the fact alluded to in note on the next verse.

[3] Or "players and men of bad habits." K. defines the latter as dancers, singers, etc.

[4] For *krūrān* (cruel) Nand. reads *kailān* (!) from *keli*, and defines (*keliçilān*) "in the habit of sporting (with women);" cf. viii. 357, where *keli* is a proof of adultery. Another reading, *kerān*, is explained by Rāgh. as singers.

[5] That is, from the realm (K.) In later times the vice of gambling was turned to account, and royal gambling-houses were established, where play was legalised, and play without royal authority was fined. (Cf. Nārada xvi.)

[6] Not only now, but in ancient times (K.); in the case of Nala, Yudhiṣṭhira, and others (Nand.) It is very probable that these are the examples meant; at least, as Medh. omits most of this part on gambling, it must have been inserted long after the epic was completed.

[7] The punishment (*daṇḍa*) is not here, as in the following verse, a fine (cf. vs. 224).

[8] This verse is in the MSS. of Medh., and is referred by him to the sport mentioned in vs. 219, but the latter verse is not given in his text.

[9] Cf. viii. 49, 177, 415. K. says (cf. Yāj. ii. 43) in accordance with what he makes.

230. The king should ordain the correction of women, children, crazy people, old people, and (those who are) poor (or) ill (to be made) by a switch, (or) a split bamboo-cane, (or) a cord,[1] (or) by other (like means).

231. Now those who, on being commissioned (to look after[2] business) affairs, ruin the affairs of those engaged in (these) affairs, (because they are) cooked by the heat of money, the king should cause to be deprived of their property.

232. (The king) should slay those who make false proclamations,[3] those who seduce his ministers,[4] those who slay women, children, and Brahmans, and those who devote themselves to (his) enemies.

233. Whenever anything has been gone through with[5] and adjusted, let the (king) know that this has been done in accordance with the rule of right, (and) let him not have this (matter) reverted to any more.

234. If the ministers or a judge should perform any business in a wrong manner,[6] the king himself should attend to this (matter), and have these (officers) fined one thousand (*paṇas*).

235. A slayer of a Brahman, a drinker of intoxicating liquor, a thief, and one who defiles the couch of a Guru,[7] these men are all in turn to be regarded as the great criminals.[8]

[1] With the first two they are beaten, with the cord they are tied (K.) Medh. defines *vidala* as *vṛkṣa-tvac*.

[2] Commissioned, etc., means those appointed (*adhikṛtāḥ*) in the king's stead to examine suits at law, or more generally of any one appointed to oversee merely, and who thereby tries to injure his patron (Medh., K.) A *var. lec.*, endorsed by Medh. as such (*aniyuktāḥ*), would mean those who have no business with the affair or the uncommissioned assessors.

[3] This does not necessarily include the forging of documents, though naturally so understood by the commentators.

[4] K., "seduce," or "make dissensions among."

[5] (*E.g.*, a lawsuit.) *Tīritam* (Medh., K.), *tāritam* (Rāgh.), *nir-ṇītam* (Nand.) Nand. gives a technical definition from Kāty.

[6] Render an unjust decision in court, etc. (K.)

[7] Guru may mean father.

[8] Cf. xi. 55. Medh., K., Rāgh., and Nand. specify, without warrant from the text, that the thief (*taskara* in Medh., Nand., Rāgh.) is a stealer of gold from a Brahman; and K. says drinking intoxi-

236. And for these four (great criminals), if they have failed to perform expiation,[1] (the king) should ordain proper corporal punishment accompanied by (a fine of) money.

237. On the (defiler of the) couch of a Guru (the brand of) a cunnus should be made;[2] on a drinker of intoxicating liquor, (the brand of) a liquor (dealer's) sign; on a thief, (the brand of) a dog's foot; on the slayer of a Brahman (the brand of) a headless man.

238. (These), with whom indeed none may eat, with whom none may sacrifice,[3] with whom none may peruse (the sacred texts), with whom none may unite themselves by marriage, shall wander miserable about the earth, excluded from every law of right.[4]

239. And these (who) have the mark put upon them shall be abandoned by family and kindred, (finding) no pity and (receiving) no respect:[5] this is the ordinance of Manu.

240. Now, on completing the expiation as enjoined (for the offence), the (three) highest castes[6] should escape the

cating liquors is restricted to (any) twice-born man drinking arak, and a Brahman drinking either arak, mead, or rum (cf. xi. 95), whereas all kinds are forbidden here for all classes. The part from vs. 235 to vs. 256 occurs also inserted in the eighth lecture in Burnell's copy of Medh. (after viii. 46 and 198).

[1] Enjoined in xi. 72 ff. He says four, because he who associates with these and is the fifth (in the group of great criminals) does not deserve the same punishment (Nand.) The "fifth" is indicated by the word *api* (Medh.) Corporal punishment is here implied for all castes; Medh. says some make it apply to the branding, which is allowed even in the case of a Brahman.

[2] On the forehead, as is implied by vs. 240 (Medh., K.)

[3] *Asaṁyojyā* in Nos. 935, 1551, and Burnell's copy of Medh. (*saṁyojanaṁ . . . saṁyājanaṁ vā*).

[4] *Dharma* here means rites and rights. Excluded from all *dharma* is to be debarred from social privileges, excluded from sacred rites, denied legal rights, deprived of all the fruits of possible good works; in short, to be one for whom no statute of the law is valid save those that specially treat of him.

[5] No one shall pity them when ill, or rise up and salute them (Medh.)

[6] So Medh. (*pūrve*). K. has *sarve* (all castes); No. 935, Medh. *yathoditāḥ*. A *var. lec.* in Nand. gives *akurvāṇāḥ pūrve varṇā . . . aṅkyā rājñā lalāṭeṣu:* gloss, *pūrve* means the members of three castes; it is known by this saying, "A mark should be made on the forehead." Now when the great criminals have not performed expiation and are thus branded, (they should have) a distinction of punishment for a distinction of cause. He says this in (the next) two çlokas.

branding upon their foreheads by the king; but they should be fined the highest fine.

241. The medium fine should be imposed for crimes[1] by a Brahman alone; or he may be banished from the realm with his goods and chattels.[2]

242. But the others,[3] on committing these sins, deserve to have all their property seized (when they commit them unintentionally); but (if they commit them) intentionally, (they deserve) banishment.[4]

243. A good king should not receive the property of a great criminal; but if through avarice he receives it, he becomes smeared with that sin.[5]

244. Casting upon the water this (money paid as) fine, let him make it over to Varuṇa, or bestow it upon a Brahman (who is) endowed with learning and of good behaviour.

245. Varuṇa is lord of punishment,[6] for he holds punishment over kings. A Brahman who has gone through a Veda is the lord of all that moves.

246. Where a king avoids getting wealth from evildoers, there in (due) time[7] are born long-lived men;

247. And the (different) crops of the husbandmen are each raised as they were sown; the children do not die; and nothing distorted[8] is brought forth.

[1] Medh., K., and Nand. say for unintentional crimes the first arrangement, and for intentional ones the second. The highest fine must, however, be given to one without good qualities (Medh., K.)

[2] *I.e.*, he is not to be fined at all, but he is to be banished.

[3] *I.e.*, all except the Brahman, viz., Kṣatriya, Vaiçya, and Çūdra (Medh., K., Rāgh., Nand.) Medh. says some say even if they have performed penance.

[4] Banishment in this case the explainers read as meaning death (K.)! So some say, but this is not correct; because a twelve years' penance is enjoined even for one who is branded with punishment by the king, and this is not compatible with death (Rāgh.) Nand. does not notice any such meaning of *pravāsana*. Medh. confines this interpretation to the case of the Çūdra.

[5] With the sin the great criminal committed.

[6] Medh. and K. take *daṇḍa* here as fine, and paraphrase tamely enough, "Varuṇa is the owner of the money (paid as) fine by the great criminals."

[7] Nand. "among men" (*loke tu*).

[8] Medh. (MSS. Nos. 935, 1551) reads *vikṛtiḥ*, "distortion is not produced."

248. Now the king should punish,[1] by the various means of corporal punishment (which) cause terror, (any man) born of low caste (who) intentionally injures Brahmans.

249. A king becomes exposed to the same lack of spiritual merit[2] in releasing a man deserving corporal punishment as in punishing corporally one not deserving corporal punishment, whereas spiritual merit is seen (to exist in that king alone who) holds in check.[3]

250.[4] Thus has been declared at full length the determination of lawsuits under (any one of the) eighteen titles in the case of two persons mutually at strife.[5]

251. Thus the sovereign duly performing the duties which are enjoined by the rules of right,[6] should seek to get possession of districts not (yet) possessed, and exercise protection over (those already) in his possession.

252. Now with his land duly put in order, and his fortress made in accordance with the statute,[7] let (the king) constantly expend the greatest care in uprooting the thorns (from his kingdom).

253. By protecting those who follow the good customs

[1] Here and in the following verses we may translate either "slay" and "capital punishment" or "corporally punish" and "corporal punishment." The precise meaning is to be determined by the context. In this verse *hanyāt* would seem to mean "slay," and *vadhopāyaiḥ* "by means of death;" but the milder meaning is given in the similar verse, viii. 352, and so understood by the commentators (Medh., K., Rāgh.) In point of fact it makes little practical difference, as the following paraphrase from Medh. will show: "He should torment a Çūdra (so K., Nand.), who robs or frightens a Brahman, by impaling him, cutting his flesh, twisting his limbs, and mutilating him with knives, all which punishments shall cause terror (to others?) by the long torment they occasion." K. and Rāgh. suggest cutting off the hands, drinking hot oil, and so forth.

[2] *Dharma.*

[3] Holds (sinners) in check, or perhaps holds himself in check (as a middle voice). The commentators understand inflicting punishment in accordance with the statutes, or even by other means than those there laid down.

[4] This verse would be more in place after vs. 228, where the eighteen heads given in viii. 3 ff. are completed.

[5] Or "thus has been declared the decision in regard to two persons mutually quarrelling about one of the eighteen titles."

[6] *Dharmya.*

[7] *Çāstrataḥ*, as declared in Lecture vii. (Medh.) Cf. vii. 70 ff.

of noble men[1] (Ārya), and by clearing out thorns (from his kingdom), kings (who are thus)[2] wholly devoted to the protection of their people attain the threefold sky.

254. But if a king accepts tribute while he administers no punishment to robbers, his kingdom is shaken, and (he) is debarred from heaven.

255. For[3] if, relying on the strength of (his) arm, the realm of any king rests in security, it constantly increases unto him, even as a tree carefully tended.[4]

256. A king, whose eyes are his spies, ought to see[5] that robbers who steal others' goods (are) of two sorts, (the one) open, (the other) concealed.

257. Of these, those supporting themselves by the various (means of) trade are open cheats; while those people[6] who steal, and those who live in the woods, are hidden cheats.

258. Those who receive bribes, deceivers,[7] cheats,[8] and gamblers; those who make it their business to proclaim good luck; those who are fine (without and foul within),[9] together with fortune-tellers;[10]

259. And both elephant-breakers and physicians who act as they should not;[11] those engaged in the practice of manual skill;[12] and artful women (whose virtue) may be bought;

260. These and other similar undisguised thorns among

[1] Priests, or "those who have an honourable means of support" (Medh.); or simply the twice-born.

[2] Or "if they protect," as in vs. 254.

[3] *Hi* (Rāgh., Nand.)

[4] *Sevyamānaḥ* (Medh.); K. has "watered" (*sicyamānaḥ*).

[5] *I.e.*, he "ought to see" by employing his spies for eyes (K., Nand.) The Mbhā. says "cows see by smell, the Brahmans see by the Vedas, kings see by spies, other men by their two eyes" (v. 34, 34).

[6] Or "those who steal, live in the woods, and the like" (K.); Medh. has *janāḥ*, and is supported by Rāgh and Nand. Those who live in the woods are highwaymen. Rāgh. explains as *dasyu*.

[7] By false weights and measures (Nand.)

[8] Or magicians (Nand.)

[9] K.; so Nand., "those who wear fine clothes for the purpose of cheating others."

[10] By seeing the signs of a man's hand, etc. (K., Nand.)

[11] This clause goes with both substantives (K., Nand.)

[12] Such as painters, who get money for worthless work (K.)

men the king should learn to know, and (also all) others who act in secret, bearing the marks of noble men (Ārya), (while in reality they are) ignoble.

261. On discovering these by well-skilled secret (agents who are) engaged in the business of these (cheats), and by spies in several different forms,[1] let (the king) suppress them and get them into his power.

262. After he has, in accordance with the truth, exposed their sins in respect to each of their actions, let the king duly inflict chastisement[2] in proportion to the wealth (of the criminal) and (the enormity of) the crime.[3]

263. For without punishment the suppression of evil among evil-minded thieves, who roam in secret about the earth, cannot be effected.

264. Assemblies, reservoirs, cake-stalls, houses of prostitution, (places where) selling of liquor and food (takes place), places where four roads meet, trees belonging to temples, crowds and shows,

265. Old gardens, woods, houses of workmen, empty dwellings, woods, (artificial) groves—

266. Such sort of places let the king have inspected by stationary and movable guards, and even by spies, to the end that he may suppress the robbers.

267. The king should find them out, and suppress them by means of skilful (men), formerly robbers (themselves, who act as) companions of these (criminals) and associate with them,[4] knowing their various occupations.

268. By pretences of food and amusement, by (pretending) visits on Brahmans,[5] and by pretence of (seeing) deeds of valour,[6] (the spies) should make an assembly of these (cheats).[7]

[1] K. refers to vii. 154 for the fivefold sort (of spies).

[2] The chastisement is here a fine (K.), as is seen by the allusion to his wealth.

[3] From here to vs. 274 fails in Medh. (MSS., Nos. 935, 1551).

[4] (Or) "(who act as their) companions, (though really) obeying his own commands" (*svānugatair ātmavaçaiḥ*) (Nand.)

[5] Saying: This Brahman knows how to make our wished-for hopes succeed; let us visit him (K.)

[6] Saying: There is a certain man that is going to fight all alone with several; let us go and see (K.)

[7] In some place where they may be seized by the king's men (Nand.)

269. The king should secure and corporally punish[1] those who on this occasion do not come near (the designated place), and those who have been deterred by knowing (these tricks) of old,[2] together with their friends,[3] blood relations, and connections.

270. A just king should not cause a thief to be corporally punished without (the thief's possessing) the (goods he has) carried off; but he must corporally punish without hesitation (a thief taken) with (what he has carried off[4] and with his tools.

271. And (the king) should also have corporally punished all persons whatsoever who in the villages even bestow food on thieves, or who merely provide a place for their utensils.

272. If those (whom he has) appointed to protect his realm,[5] and the neighbours employed for the same purpose,[6] stand neutral during attacks by robbers when besought for help, (the king) should chastise them at once as (if they were) thieves.

273. If any man whatever lives by performing meritorious acts,[7] while he departs from (his own) bounden duty,[7] let the king consume him also by punishment (as) one (who has) departed from his duty.[8]

274. When a village is plundered, a dam[9] broken down, or a robbery is seen on the road, those (who do

[1] Literally, "smite." This expression here and in following, as in vs. 248 (v. note), may mean kill. The regular mode of punishment, as already described in the eighth lecture, was for the king to smite a thief with a club.

[2] So K., Rāgh.; and Nand. defines "those among whom the proofs are known" (*praṇihitamūlāḥ jñāta-kāraṇāḥ*).

[3] Or sons (Nand., Rāgh.)

[4] See the definition of this word in Mit. Y. ii. 5 as *loptra*, and cf. B. R. s. *hoḍha*. Cf. Vas. xix. 39.

[5] *Var. lec.* in Nand. MS., *rāṣṭre*[*vā*] *pure vā'dhikṛtān*, "appointed over realm or city."

[6] Rāgh. understands the neighbours who give a place for the thieves' utensils.

[7] *Dharma.*

[8] That is, if any man, even a Brahman, supports himself by performing sacrifice, etc., while he does not do the duties enjoined for his profession (K.) He is the same as a thief (Nand.)

[9] *Hitā* (K.), *baḍā* (Nand. = *setu*), and according to Medh. a "fence" (?), the breaking of which ruins the crops (K.)

not) hasten to (give what help) they can should be banished, (taking) with (them their) effects.

275. Those who steal the treasure of the king, and abide by (practices) repugnant (to his orders), he should have corporally punished[1] by various (means of) punishment; so, too, those who instigate (his) foes (to greater enmity).[2]

276. Now, if any robbers commit theft at night by cutting (a hole in) a wall, the king should cause both their hands to be cut (off), and have them fastened on a sharp stake.[3]

277. (The king) should cause the two fingers of a cut-purse to be cut (off) at the (time of his) first theft;[4] on his second (theft), a hand and a foot; on the third, he deserves capital punishment.[5]

278. The sovereign should slay as (he would) a thief,[6] (those who) give (them) fire, food, or places for (their) weapons, and those who aid in concealing the theft.

279. One should slay a man who destroys[7] a pool (by drowning him) in the water, or by simple death;[8] or (the

[1] By cutting off the hand, foot, tongue, etc. (K.); death may be meant.

[2] In Nand. *b.* 2 takes the place of *b.* 1 of K. with *vadhaiḥ* for *daṇḍaiḥ*. Nand. explains the expression *arīṇām upajāpakān* as above (like K.), "or it may mean those who instigate his allies (with whom he has a treaty of peace) to become his enemies." So Medh., "they make his allies foes."

[3] This punishment implies death, and appears to have been a general custom. In the Mbhā. we read of a seer caught along with some thieves; the king gave the order that they should be killed, and the seer was consequently "stuck upon a stake" (i. 117, 12). It was not confined to thieves, for in the same epic, on a special occasion, we are told that a king ordered that those who indulged in forbidden liquor should "mount the stake alive" (xvi. 1, 31). The text in the May. has *bhitvā* for *chitvā* (p. 89).

[4] Medh., K., and Rāgh.

[5] *Vadha;* the two fingers are said by K. and Rāgh. to be those indicated by Yāj. ii. 274, namely, the thumb and forefinger; so Nand.

[6] *Caurān* (Beng. MSS., Medh., Nos. 936, 1551, Nand. MS.), *i.e.*, as he would thieves.

[7] Literally, breaks, *i.e.*, destroys by breaking the dam (K.) Medh., K., *taḍāga*, but some MSS. (Nand., Rāgh.) have *taḍāka pond.*

[8] *Çuddha vadha, i.e.*, by the sword (Nand.) The word *vadha* here means "cutting off a limb" (Nand.), [or] his head, or other parts are cut off according to circumstances (Rāgh.) It probably means death without mutilation (cf. vs. 291, note). Medh. says that some regard the pool as a mere type for a graver offence; but this explanation is not

criminal) may (simply) put it to rights again; but he should (in that case) be fined the highest fine.

280. One should also slay without hesitation (those who) destroy a grainary,[1] an arsenal, or a temple of the divinities; and (those who) steal elephants, horses, (or) chariots.

281. Now he who steals water from a pool laid out long before, and also (he who) even diverts the course of the water,[3] should be fined the first fine.[4]

282. If any one, without pressing need,[5] emits impurities upon the king's highway, he should pay (a fine of) two *kārṣāpaṇa*,[6] and clear up the impurity at once.[7]

283. Now (if it is) an old man (who) finds it necessary, a pregnant woman, or a mere boy, they should receive a reproof;[8] and that (filth) should be cleaned up: so stands the rule.

284. A fine (is set) for all physicians treating (a case) incorrectly;[9] in (the case of creatures) not human[10] (this is) the first, but in (the case of) human beings the medium (fine).

285. One who destroys a stile,[11] a sign, a pole,[12] or the images (of divinities), should replace all that (he has injured), and pay (a fine) of five hundred (*paṇas*).[13]

necessary, as ruining a sacred pool is quite bad enough to warrant the punishment. From vs. 279 to vs. 282 fails in Medh. (Nos. 935, 1551).

[1] Belonging to the king (K.)

[2] The reason why death is ordained here and a fine in vs. 285 is that in the latter case the small earthen images of the divinities are meant, which are not so important as a temple (with the large idols in it (K., Rāgh.)

[3] If one takes or destroys the water of the whole pool, he suffers death, as said in vs. 279; in this case just (a little) water if taken from an old pool; diverting the water, *i.e.*, by a dam so as to hurt the pool (K.)

[4] The first fine is the lowest, *i.e.*, two hundred and fifty *paṇas* (Rāgh.)

[5] Through fear of a tiger, etc., or through illness (Rāgh.)

[6] Two copper *paṇas* (Rāgh.)

[7] Or pay a Caṇḍāla to do it (Medh.)

[8] *I.e.*, they should not be fined (Nand.); one should say, "Don't do it again" (Rāgh.)

[9] Not as enjoined in the treatises (Medh.)

[10] Animals, horses (Nand.), and cows, etc. (Medh., K., Rāgh.)

[11] Stile, or footbridge (Medh.); sign or ensign at the king's door (K., Rāgh.)

[12] Used like the sign for a symbol (Medh.); in a lotus-pond (K., Rāgh.)

[13] This is the "medium" fine; cf. note to vs. 280.

286. For injuring uninjured goods,[1] also for destroying[2] jewels, and for piercing (them) in the wrong place, the penalty is the first fine.

287. Now if any man acts unequally with (things) that are equal; or, again, (if he defrauds) by a difference in the price, he should receive the first, or even the medium fine.[3]

288. And (the king) should have all places for confining (criminals)[4] set by the king's highway; where evil-doers may be seen, miserable and maltreated.[5]

289. One who destroys the (city)[6] wall, one who fills up the moat, and one who breaks the gates, (the king) should at once banish.

290. A fine of two hundred (*paṇas*) should be imposed

[1] By putting worthless goods in with perfect articles (K.)

[2] According to the commentators (so B. R.), the meaning here is "for boring certain gems which ought not to be bored, and for boring other gems (pearls, etc), in the wrong place." This gives two meanings to *maṇi*, or a new word with a different and elaborate meaning must be supplied. *Bhedana*, like *bhedaka* in vss. 279, 280, may mean simply injure in general, or literally "for breaking or bad boring." Medh. defines *bhedana* here as *dridhā-karaṇam*. K. adds that in addition to the fine, satisfaction must be made to the owner, as is the case wherever another's property is destroyed. Medh. says some order in the fines is to be observed: for medium articles the medium, for the best the highest fine.

[3] K. says the weight of the fine depends on the deceiver's intention, and he and Rāgh. translate the first clause as meaning "one who employs different goods or different measures for those who give the same amount of money." Nand. explains "he who uses different weights and measures in (selling) the same goods, and does not demand the same price (for the same goods)." The translation above is based on the first explanation given by Medh., that is, that this represents a case where a limitation has been set by law on the rate of exchange between goods, and one tries to obtain, *e.g.*, for a little oil, which another needs, a larger supply of grain, etc., than is right; or again, if he sells goods at too high an advance on the price he paid, even if no limitation has been set by law.

[4] Medh. and K. take this to mean the houses of confinement where the prisoners are seen in fetters and bonds. Rāgh. explains as fetters, and Nand. (MS. has *bandhanāni ca kaṣṭāni*) explains by the same word. As it is doubtful if prisons were established at the time of the text, we may perhaps better understand stocks or something of the sort set up by the roadway, where, to be sure, the mutilated victims were better seen than in a "prison-house." Medh. suggests that torture-places may be anywhere "where(ever) the evil-doers may be seen; the author thus shows the variableness of the locality."

[5] By starvation, poison, etc. (Medh.)

[6] These are all the property of the king in the city (K.)

for all (cases of) bewitching;[1] and (the same) for a ceremony with roots, (performed) by those not attaining (their object);[2] and for the various (kinds of) magical rites.[3]

291. He who sells bad seed,[4] or improved (worthless) seed,[5] and also he who destroys a boundary,[6] should receive corporal[7] punishment accompanied by disfiguration.[8]

292. But the king should cause a worker in gold who acts in an unlawful manner—(he being) the most evil of all the thorns (infesting a kingdom)—to be chopped up into small pieces with sharp knives.

293. For abducting things (used) in ploughing, weapons,[9] or medicinal plants, let the king establish punishment after he has found out the time and purpose (of the act).[10]

294. The master[11] and his ministers, the (chief) city, the people,[12] the treasury and army,[13] likewise the ally[14]—

[1] By hymns (Medh.); oblations to ensure death (K.); such as the hawk-sacrifice (Rāgh.)

[2] The ceremony with roots is for the purpose of slaying an enemy, or getting property by certain roots having this power, such as those described in the Mbhā., which informs us that in the Ātharva (*sic*) it is ordained that plants which are prickly, and sting, and have red flowers, are to be used in bewitching one's enemies (xiii. 98, 20). The expression *anāptaiḥ* (construe with each clause) may mean bad people (K.), or unskilful people (Rāgh.), unless Nand.'s *var. lec.* (*anāpte*) be preferred, which gives practically the same sense as the last (*anāptaphale vaçīkaraṇe*) "unsuccessful ceremonies for gaining power over one."

[3] *Kṛtyā*, "any magic to remove enemies," etc. The fine is in all these cases for unsuccessful attempts to destroy life; successful attempts should meet with death, according to the commentators. Medh. distinguishes between designs on man or cattle, but either may be meant by the text.

[4] As good seed (Medh., K.)

[5] So K. Nand. paraphrases by *uptānāṁ bījānām uddhartā*, "one who pulls up seed sown." The *improving* of worthless grain is done, according to the commentators, by surreptitiously inserting good grain on the top of the bad, and declaring it is all good.

[6] Of village or town (K.); cf. Yāj. ii. 155. According to Medh., the boundary is a legal restriction, "he who breaks a law."

[7] *Vadha*; the commentators say the criminal is to have his nose cut off (Medh.), or hand, foot, etc. (K.)

[8] This *vadha* is opposed to that in vs. 279.

[9] Weapons of the king bring a greater, other weapons a lesser punishment (Medh.)

[10] That is, in such cases where a plough, yoke, etc., is stolen, there is no set punishment, but it depends on circumstances (Medh., K., Rāgh., Nand.) After this verse Nand. places K.'s vs. 312.

[11] The king.

[12] City is his capital, home of the king (Medh.); people (so Medh., literally, realm) means "country," according to K.

[13] *Daṇḍa*, better than the alternative meaning "system of punishment, courts," etc.

[14] Literally, friend.

these indeed are the seven elements (constituting what is) called a complete kingdom.[1]

295. Now (in case) a great calamity (is liable to occur) to these seven elements of the kingdom one after another, one should know (that it would prove to be) more severe (in the case of) the first (mentioned than in the case of the next), and so on (to the last).[2]

296. When in this world the kingdom of seven members stands firmly together like a threefold staff,[3] no one part then surpasses (another), through any superiority of the qualities of one over the other.

297. But this or that member is especially prominent (only) in the duties respectively pertaining to it; that member is in any given duty called the best by whom this duty is successfully performed.

298. By (means of) spies, by exercising his power, and also by carrying on (various) enterprises, let the king constantly learn his own strength and that of the enemy.[4]

299. Having (first) considered all the unfortunate accidents and injuries (liable to result from his plans),[5] and the relative importance (of these misfortunes), let one afterwards undertake what is to be done.[6]

[1] Medh., MS. No. 935, has *samastam;* No. 1551 has this altered in the margin to *saptāṅgam*, the reading in some K. MSS. Medh. paraphrases *kṣiptam*. Another *var. lec.* is *samagram* (so Rāgh. MS.) The reading *saptāṅgam* is prettier, "the seven elements" explaining the "seven-limbed kingdom," but Medh.'s reading is found in the Bengal and Bombay MSS. and in the Nandinī text. Cf. Viṣṇu, iii. 33.

[2] In other words, let the king first see to his own safety, then for that of his ministers, etc.

[3] Where each part mutually supports and is supported (K., Nand.) The relation is like that of earth, seed, and water, all necessary each to each for growth (Medh.)

[4] Medh. reads (for K.'s *mahīpatiḥ*) *parātmanaḥ*, and in this is followed by Nand. (who also has *kevalam* for *karmaṇām*, explaining exercising power as open, and *kriyā* as secret power, such as reflection). The sense remains the same, except in Nand., who renders *para* (enemy) as "any one else, a friend." Medh. says he must find out what power the other party has over himself and what he himself has over the other. He also renders *utsāhayoga* as "gifts," etc., *i.e.*, by the four means of subjugation enjoined for a king.

[5] This seems to be the meaning, and is so given by K.; so Medh., though he has another explanation.

[6] Nand. has an (unauthorised) *var. lec.*, without material change of meaning: (*mahīpatiḥ*) *gurulāghavato jñātvā tataḥ karma samacaret*. Medh. and K. regard *pīḍana* as of nature, *vyasana* as of man.

300. One should just keep on renewing his attempts again and again, however tired and weary (he may be); for fortune favours the man who keeps on renewing his attempts.[1]

301. The ages—Kṛta, Tretā, Dvāpara, and Kali—all (indicate) the actions of the king; for the king is called the age.[2]

302. Asleep he is Kali; awake, the Dvāpara age; (when) actively engaged in work, Tretā; but (when) advancing (against the enemy), the Kṛta age.[3]

303. The king should practise the glory and conduct of Indra (the storm-god), of Arka (the sun), of Vāyu (wind), of Yama (here god of the dead), of Varuṇa (here god of punishment), of Candra (the moon), of Agni (fire), and of Pṛthivī (earth).

304. As Indra rains down upon the people through the four rainy months, so should the king, practising Indra's rule, besprinkle his realm with favours.[4]

305. As the sun with its beams takes (to itself) the water during eight months, so let (the king) ever[5] take from his realm the revenue; for that is the sun's rule.

306. As the wind wanders about, proceeding among all created beings, so (the king) should proceed everywhere by means of his spies; for this is the wind's rule.

307. As Yama (the constrainer) constrains both friend and foe when their time has come, so the people[6]

[1] Cf. iv. 137. This verse is omitted by Medh. (Nos. 935, 1551).

[2] The four ages represent four periods of relative goodness and happiness. Kṛta is the perfect, Kali the worst and latest age. It is a point discussed in the Mbhā. (v. 132, 16) whether the king depends on the age in which he lives, or the age is dependent on the king for its character. The latter is considered the right doctrine; any king by good conduct can produce the age of bliss and perfection, or that of evil, etc.; the notion in vs. 302 is a variation of this.

[3] Literally "expanded;" *vikṛtas tu* is Medh.'s reading (Nos. 935, 1551).

[4] Cf. Mbhā. xiii. 102, 26 (the world), *yatra Çakro varṣati sarvakāmān.*

[5] Nand. MS. reads "take properly" (for *nityam* reads *samyag*).

[6] Nand. *sarve* (for *prajāḥ*), *i.e.*, *priyadveṣāḥ*.

should be constrained by the king; for this is Yama's rule.[1]

308. Just as one is seen (to be) bound fast by Varuṇa's cords,[2] so let (the king) seize hold of evil men; for this is Varuṇa's rule.

309. As human beings rejoice on beholding the full moon, so that king in whom the (ministers and other) elements (of the realm take delight) fulfils the rule of the moon.

310. Let (the king) be ever ardent and glorious in (consuming) evil-doers, and destructive to the enemies that surround him.[3] That is called the rule of fire.

311. As the supporting (earth) supports alike all creatures, so when (the king) supports all creatures (he follows) the rule of the earth.

312. Ever holding fast to these and other means (of procedure), let the king unweariedly seize hold of thieves in his own realm, and also (in that) of another.[4]

313.[5] Even if he has fallen into the greatest distress, let him never arouse the Brahmans to anger; for on being made angry they could destroy him with (all his) dependents, force, and equipment.

314. Who could escape destruction if he angered those

[1] Yama, the constrainer (by a false but old derivation), constrains men to die. The people are constrained to be punished or killed if sinful.

[2] Nand. has the whole verse slightly altered in my MS., *vāruṇena tu pāçaiçca baddhyate vāruṇair naraḥ.*

[3] *I.e.*, his inimicable ministers (Medh., K.), or his vassals.

[4] "The enemy," *eva vā* (Nand. MS.) Nand. places this verse more appropriately after vs. 293. "Other means," are those current in the world (Medh.), even if not specially declared by the law (K.)

[5] From vs. 313 through vs. 319 appears to be a late addition to the work, if we judge it by the language, and agrees closely with a portion of the epic that is also a late addition to that work. Cf. Mbhā. xiii. 152 adhy. (all the twenty-three verses); cf. also *ib.* ix. 36, 40; iii. 191, 21; and v. 40, 8, where it is said that "one angry Brahman destroys a realm." I have elsewhere pointed out this fact (Mutual Relations, p. 22 ff.), and the Nandinī shows a confusion in the verses (vss. 313, 314, being placed after vs. 319) indicative of perhaps local uncertainty. Nevertheless my former opinion must be modified to this extent, that these verses are by no means among those last added to the work, as Medh. has them all complete in proper order, and with few *var. lec.*

by whom the all-devouring[1] fire, the undrinkable sea, and the waning and waxing moon (were) made?[2]

315. Who could prosper if he injured those who could, when incensed, produce other worlds and (other) guardians of the world, and (other) gods and not-gods?

316. Who, if he had lust to live, would harm those, on whom[3] relying stand eternally the worlds and the gods, of whom also the wealth is *brahma* (the Veda)?

317. Wise or unwise, the Brahman is a great divinity;[4] just as fire is a great divinity, whether applied (to the sacrifice) or not applied.

318. Even in the places where corpses are burned the glowing purifier (fire) is not defiled, and when it has received the oblation in the sacrifice it is the more magnified.[5]

319. Thus, even if engaged in all (kinds of) occupations (which are looked upon) with disfavour, the Brahmans[6] should (none the less) be reverenced at all times, for that divinity is the highest one.[7]

320. Since the Kṣatriya caste arose from the Brahman, the Brahman caste alone should be the one to subdue[8] the Kṣatriya caste at all times, when it has grown overweening toward the Brahmans.

321. From water fire is produced;[9] from the Brahman

[1] The Bomb. MS., that of the Nandinī, and Medh. No. 935, has °*bhakṣo* for *bhakṣyo*. Nand. has also *asir* for *agnir*; the sword is synonymous, but this is probably a clerical error.

[2] *Kṣayīcavṛddhimāṁçce'nduḥ* (var. lec. No. 935, *yakṣi* (*sic*), and 1551) in Medh. gives same sense.

[3] Medh. (Nos. 935, 1551), Rāgh., and Nand. have *samāçritya* for K.'s *upa*° (in Medh's gloss); the worlds and gods rely on the Brahmans' offerings (Medh.); for *yeṣām* Medh. (No. 1551) has *teṣām*.

[4] Mbhā. iii. 200, 89, gives the same view.

[5] *Abhivardhate* (increases), K., No. 1551, Medh.; *abhivarttate*, No. 935, Medh.; *abhipūjyate*, Nand. (magnified in glory).

[6] The Brahman (Nand., singular throughout).

[7] That is the highest divinity, *i.e.* the Brahman is (Nand. has *saḥ*).

[8] Or "would be able" by means of incantations, etc. (Medh., K., Nand.)

[9] The water in plants and trees is meant, thence fire comes (Medh.). Nand. has the absurd explanation for *brahmataḥ* that it refers to Dakṣa, Marīci, and other creators.

caste, the Kṣatriya caste; from stone, iron. In their own birthplaces their all-pervading force is quenched.[1]

322. The Kṣatriya caste does not prosper without the Brahman caste; the Brahman caste does not flourish without the Kṣatriya caste; but when the Brahman and Kṣatriya castes are united they flourish both here and hereafter.

323. Now after giving to the priests the wealth that has been produced by all the fines,[2] and after committing the realm to (his) son,[3] let (the king) meet his death in battle.

324. The sovereign acting thus, ever[4] constant to the duties of a king, should also have all his dependents employed in (such) acts (as will be) beneficial to the world.

325. Thus has been declared the complete and eternal rule of action for a king; this (following) rule of action one should know is for a Vaiçya and Çūdra, one after the other.

326. Now a Vaiçya, after being initiated and having married a wife, should be always employed in gaining wealth[5] and in tending cattle.

327. For after Prajāpati had created cattle he gave them over to the Vaiçya, (while) he gave all the people to the Brahmans and to the king.

[1] Vs. 320 is found in Mbhā. xii. 78, 27, and vs. 321 is found *ib.* v. 15, 34, xii. 56, 24 (and in *ib.* 23 is ascribed to Manu, along with another verse not found in our text); also *ib.* 78, 22, and i. 137, 12 (*salilād utthito vahniḥ*), although in vs. 14 cases of "Brahmans born from Kṣatriyas" occur. Cf. Gaut. xi. 1; Çat. Br. iv. 1, 4, 4–6.

[2] All the fines except those paid by the great criminals (which must be given to Brahmans at once or thrown into the water). This verse refers to king ill or dying; and if to die fighting is impossible, he should burn, drown (Medh.), or starve himself (K.) Cf. Mbhā. vi. 17, 11, "It is *adharma* for a king to die of disease in a house."

[3] Nand. gives a slight change by reading (MS.) *sutam rājye samāveçya*, setting his son over the kingdom (cf. the reading of Medh., *samāsādya*, and the Bengal MS. *var. lec. samāsajya*); cf. iv. 257. Medh. says some interpret "fines" as including money got by taxes, etc., *i.e.*, his whole property.

[4] This is omitted in some MSS., and the word reads, "closely constant."

[5] *Vārtā* often includes cattle-tending; the term is general, and means all the work and activity by which the Vaiçya gained his living.

328. The Vaiçya should, moreover, never express any such desire as "I would not tend cattle;" and, when the Vaiçya is willing (to tend them), they should never be tended by another.

329. (The Vaiçya) should know the relative value[1] of gems, pearls, corals, ores, woven-stuffs, perfumes, and essences.

330. He should understand the sowing of seeds, know the defects and good qualities of land, and be well acquainted with the application of measures and of weights in all (their particulars);[2]

331. Also the comparative worth of goods, the good and bad qualities of (different) districts, the gain and lack of gain in different wares, and the propagation of cattle.[3]

332. He should know the support of his dependents,[4] the various languages of men, the means of preserving commodities, and also (all about) purchase and sale.[5]

333. He should expend the greatest effort in justly increasing his goods, and he should also take pains to bestow at least food[6] on all creatures.

334. Now the supreme duty of a Çūdra, and that which ensures his bliss, is merely obedience toward celebrated priests who understand the Veda and (live as) householders.

335. If he be pure, obedient to the higher (castes), mild in speech, without conceit, and always submissive to the Brahmans,[7] he attains[8] (in the next transmigration) a high birth.

[1] That is, in what districts they are valuable, etc. (Medh.)

[2] Such as how weights like the *droṇa*, *āṭhaka*, etc., are to be estimated, whether by hand, etc. (Medh.)

[3] *Ca vivardhanam* (Medh.)

[4] How much is necessary to support the cowkeepers (etc.) (Medh.)

[5] *Mālavaka - Magadha - Draviḍā - dideçabhāṣāḥ* (Medh.)

[6] Nand. says, "at least food even to Çūdras." "He must give much food" is what is meant by "take pains to bestow food," otherwise the king should be fined.

[7] "Finds refuge in Brahmans" is K.'s explanation. Medh. reads, both in No. 1551 and No. 935, *Brāhmaṇāpaçrayo*, explaining "*anyān apāçritasya, anyaçuçrūṣakasyc'ti.* Nand. reads *Brāhmaṇānām çreyaḥ (nityam)*, "everlasting bliss of Brahmans" he obtains.

[8] *Āpnuyāt* in Medh. No. 1551; *açnute* in No. 935.

336. Thus has been declared the pure rule of action for the castes (when) not in (time of) distress: learn (now) also in order the rule which they should follow in time of distress.

END OF THE NINTH LECTURE.

LECTURE X.

THE MIXED CASTES AND CLASSES: PROCEDURE IN TIME OF NEED.

1. THE (members of the) three twice-born castes, abiding by their respective occupations, should peruse (the holy texts); but among these a Brahman only, not (members of) the two other (castes), should expound (these texts): this is the decision.

2. The Brahman should understand the lawful means of livelihood of all (the castes); he should both expound (them) to the others and also be himself such (as the rule demands).

3. By reason of his excellence,[1] his pre-eminence of origin, his carrying the ordinances,[2] and because of the difference in his initiation, the Brahman is lord of the castes.

4. The Brahman, Kṣatriya, (and) Vaiçya (constitute) the three twice-born castes; but the fourth, the Çūdra, has only one birth.[3] There is no fifth (caste).

5. In all the castes those (sons), and those only, are to be recognised as born equal in caste[4] which are born in the caste order, of pure[5] wives, equal (in caste).

[1] Excellence in qualities, which then follow (Medh.); "Four causes" (Rāgh.); Pre-eminence in birth, *i.e.*, from the head of Brahmā (Medh., K.)

[2] So, or perhaps bearing vows of Snātaka (Medh.) Govindarāja explains as bearing vows of Snātaka, which is not correct, as that applies to the Kṣatriya as well (K.)

[3] He has no religious birth (Medh., K.)

[4] Or, family.

[5] Who are pure maids till married. Not uniting wife with *akṣatayoniṣu.* The ancients read *nārīṣu*, rejecting the word *patnī;* but "pure" merely means (except in the vernacular *rajakasya patnī*, where no real marriage occurs), an honourably wedded wife, married for the first time; not one gone and returned again (Medh.)

6. They call those sons (which are) born of the twice-born by women of the next (caste below) Similar,[1] being exposed to blame by the fault of the mother.

7. This is the eternal rule for those born of women of the next (caste below): one should know that this (following) is the lawful rule of right for those born of women (who have) one or two (castes) intervening.[2]

8. From a Brahman by a Vaiçya girl is born (a son) with the name Ambaṣṭha;[3] by a Çūdra girl (one named) Niṣāda, who is (also) called a Pāraçava.[4]

9. From a Kṣatriya by a Çūdra girl is born a creature called an Ugra (cruel), which has a nature partaking both of Kṣatriya and of Çūdra, and finds its pleasure in savage conduct.

10. (The sons) of a priest (Brahman) by (women of) the three (lower) castes, those of a king (Kṣatriya) by (women of) the two (lower) castes, and those of a Vaiçya by (women of) the one (lower) caste,[5] these six (kinds of sons) are called Rejected.

11. From a Kṣatriya by a girl of the priest(ly caste) is born a son (called) a Sūta; from a Vaiçya are born by women of the king(ly and) priest(ly caste) a Māgadha and Vaideha.

12. From a Çūdra are born by women of the Vaiçya, regal, or priestly castes, by[6] a mixture of castes, an Āyogava, a Kṣattar, and a Cāṇḍāla, (who is) the basest of men.

13. Just as the Ambaṣṭha and Ugra are said to be those

[1] K. gives the names and acts of these (from Yāj. and Uçanas; cf. Yāj. i. 91 ff., though the text does not specify them) as Mūrdhāvasikta (tending horse and chariots); Māhiṣya (dancing, etc.); Karaṇa (police).

[2] That is, two or three grades lower than the husband.

[3] Also called Bhṛjjakaṇṭha in another Smṛti (Gaut. iv. 20), (Medh.) (*vide* vs. 21 note).

[4] Cf. ix. 178. K. says, referring to the lost (?) verse of Yāj. (cf. ix. 178 note, and ix. 160), that the "girl" means one married. So Medh., "it means the wife (*strī*) of the Vaiçya," etc.

[5] Çūdra; in general of lower mothers.

[6] Medh. locative "in" (*Saṅkare*, in Nos. 989, 1551, and 935 (*palimpsest*).

(born) of women two castes below in the direct order (of the castes), so the Kṣattar and Vaidehaka are of the same sort in a birth which goes contrary (to caste order).

14. The sons of the twice-born which are born of women of the caste just (below) (as) declared, one after the other, they call Next, on account of the mother's defect.[1]

15. (A son called) Āvṛta by name is born from a Brahman by an Ugra girl; an Ābhīra (by name), by an Ambaṣṭha girl, and a Dhigvaṇa, by a female Āyogava.

16. The Āyogava, Kṣattar, and Cāṇḍāla, (who is) the basest of men, are born against the caste order from a Çūdra (as) the three rejected (of that caste).[2]

17. The Māgadha and Vaideha (produced) by a Vaiçya, and the Sūta alone from the Kṣatriya, these also are born against (the caste order) as three other Rejected.

18. (The son) begotten by a Niṣāda by a Çūdra woman is by birth a Pukkasa, and (the son) begotten by a Çūdra by a Niṣāda woman is called a Kukkuṭaka.

19. Moreover, (the son) of a Kṣattar by an Ugra woman is called a Çvapāka, while he begotten by a Vaidehaka by an Ambaṣṭha woman is called a Veṇa.

20. If the twice-born beget by (women of) the same caste sons (who do) not (undergo) the proper ceremonies[3] (*vrata*), one should designate these (sons) as Vrātya (inasmuch as they) are excluded from the *gāyatrī*.[4]

21. Now from a Vrātya priest is born (a son) whose soul is sinful (called) Bhṛjjakaṇṭaka, Āvantya, Vāṭadhāna, and Puṣpaçekhara.[5]

[1] Cf. vs. 6.

[2] Cf. vs. 10.

[3] The ceremonies prescribed at birth, etc.

[4] *Sāvitrī.* All the three MSS. of Medh. have *ity abhinirdiçet.*

[5] Medh. says the names are owing to difference of locality, but the ancients explained them as born from the preceding; thus the father of the Āvantya was the Bhṛjjakaṇṭa(ka), that of Vāṭadhāna was the Āvantya, that of Puṣpaçekhara the Āvantya. The different names of this one son depend on difference in locality (K.), *i.e.*, all these people are regarded as having their origin in some outcast priests. The wife is a Brahman woman (of the same caste, Medh., K.) Bhūrj° or Bhṛjjakaṇṭhaka (*sic*) (as in vs. 8); also Puṣpaçekhara (*sic.*) *eva ca* in the three Medh. MSS. (935, 989, 1551), which from his gloss, must be correct. The Vrātya is practically outcast, or outsider.

22. From a Vrātya member of the regal caste (is born) a Jhalla, Malla, Licchivi,[1] Naṭa,[2] Karaṇa, Khasa, and also Draviḍa.

23. Now from a Vrātya Vaiçya is born a Sudhanvan, likewise a Cārya, Kārusa,[3] Vijanman, Maitra, and Sātvata.[4]

24. The mixture of castes is [5] produced by adultery on the part of the (pure) castes, and by marrying those who ought not to be married, and by men deserting their respective occupations.

25. Now I will proclaim without omission those who are of mixed origin, born either in conformity with, or against the order of the castes, and those (whose birth is) mutually confused.

26. The Sūta, and Vaidehaka, and the Cāṇḍāla, basest of men; the Māgadha, and he (who is) by birth a Kṣattar; so also the Āyogava;

27. These six beget, by (women whose) origin is (the same as) theirs, castes (which are) similar; and they produce them by the mother's family, and by women of the higher (kinds of) origin.[7]

28. As a man's self is born of (women of) two of the three castes, and, when there is no (caste) intervening, (of women) of his own caste, so even thus is the order [8] among the outcasts.

[1] Licchivi (Medh., Nos. 935, 989, 1551), perhaps for Licchavi; K. has Nicchivi (?).

[2] The Naṭa as nom. *agentis* is a "play actor."

[3] (*Sic.* Medh.)

[4] All these in vss. 22, 23, are names of one person as before (K.)

[5] Medh. (*jāyate . . . saṅkaraḥ*, Nos. 935, 989, 1551).

[6] Cf. ix. 65.

[7] The similarity is in respect to the mother's, not to the father's family (K.). Medh. reads *jātyā*, (*jātau anye*). The last clause means they go against caste order (Medh.), as the mother's family of each is higher.

[8] *Ca . . . kramaḥ* is Medh.'s reading (Nos. 989, 935, 1551). K. (quotes incorrectly, and) refutes Medh.'s notion that this shows the twice-born-ship to inculcate initiation; for those born against the caste order have no right to this. The type at the beginning is the Brahman, the two out of three castes are Kṣatriya and Vaiçya (Medh., K.) But Medh. says twice-born-ship is produced thus against the order, and where that exists the initiation must be made (*sati dvijatve upanayanaṁ kartavyam*).

29. These two by each other's wives produce again many more debased and despised outcasts than themselves.

30. As a Çūdra begets outcast children by a Brahman woman, so an outcast produces (a son) more outcast (than himself) by (women of) the four castes.

31. Acting in a manner opposed to the caste order, the degraded outcasts beget again (those) degraded and still more outcast, (to the number of) fifteen.[1]

32. A Dasyu begets by an Āyogava woman a Sairandhra, who not being a slave, yet lives by slavery,[2] knowing how to adorn and to serve, and obtaining his livelihood by trapping.

33. A Vaideha begets a Maitreyaka,[3] whose voice is pleasant,[4] and who unweariedly extols men by striking a bell when morn arises.

34. A Niṣāda begets a Mārgava[5] (or) Daça, who lives by working in vessels, whom they that live in Aryavarta call Kaivarta (fisher).[6]

35. These three,[7] degraded in family, are severally born of Āyogava (women), who wear the clothes of the dead, are ignoble,[8] and eat forbidden food.

36. A leather-worker (called) Kārāvara is born of a Niṣāda, an Andhra, and a Meda, who live outside the village, (are born) of a Vaīdehika.[9]

37. From a Cāṇḍāla[10] (is born) a Pāṇḍusopāka, whose

[1] This refers only to cases against the caste order. Medh.'s (and Govind.'s) explanation including cases in caste order is wrong (K.); the fifteen are worked out by each. Medh. paraphrases *pratikūlaṁ vartamānāḥ* generally by *çāstraryatikrameṇa vartamānā mithunībhavanti*, "marry in opposition to the statutes."

[2] *Dāsyajīvana* (Medh., Nos. 989, 935, 1551).

[3] Or, Saireyaka (*v. l.*, Medh.)

[4] K. and Medh., also with a varied explanation.

[5] Like Mṛgayu, of hurtful occupation, because they who live in boats hunt fish (Rāgh.)

[6] As if a known but foreign district.

[7] One MS. (No. 989) Medh. has *ime trayaḥ*; the three are Sairandra, Maitreya, Mārgava (K.)

[8] *Anāryāsu* = *aspṛçyāsu*, "not to be touched" (Medh.)

[9] Same as Vaideha. The mother is a Vaideha, Kāravara, and Niṣāda woman in turn (Medh., K.)

[10] Perhaps by Vaideha woman

occupation is in reeds; an Āhiṇḍika is also born of a Niṣāda by a Vaideha woman.

38. From a Cāṇḍāla is produced by a Pukkasa woman an evil Sopāka, who gains a livelihood by the occupation of his progenitor,[1] and is always despised by the good.

39. A Niṣāda woman by a male Cāṇḍāla produces a son, Antyāvasāyin [2] (living among low people), occupied in places for burning the dead, and despised even by the outcasts.

40. These mixed classes (have been) explained according to their fathers and mothers; whether hidden or exposed to view they may be known by their respective occupations.

41. Six (sons) are said to have the twice-born's laws of duty,[3] (those) born in the same caste and those born of the next (caste),[4] but all those born of lower (father than mother) are said to have the same laws of duty as Çūdras.[5]

42. But [6] age by age they ascend by virtue of austerity and lofty seed to a high position here among men, or (descend by their opposites) to a low position, (all being) in accordance with their birth.

43. Gradually, through the loss of sacred ceremonies, and by not seeing Brahmans,[7] the following families of Kṣatriyas have reached the condition of Vṛṣalas among men:

44. Pauṇḍrakas, Oḍras, Dravidas, Kāmbojas, Yavanas

(Medh., K.), from *eva;* or with Medh. the Āhiṇḍika has just the same business to pursue.

[1] Like the Cāṇḍāla he kills criminals (Medh., K.; cf. vs. 56), or (Medh.) trades in wood he chops down (*vyasanam = vibhāgakaraṇam*).

[2] Proper name, or designates Cāṇḍāla, of which caste this is an epithet (Medh.)

[3] *Dharmin.*

[4] The natural explanation is: Brahmans', Kṣatriyas', Vaiçyas' sons by wives of their respective castes, or of the caste next below; but as this brings in the Parāçara, Medh. and K., violating the evident sequence, bring in the Brahman's son by a wife of any of the three upper castes (cf. vs. 14), and render *anantara* as *anuloma*.

[5] For Sutā (K.), *uktā* (No. 989, Medh.), corresponding to *smṛtā* in next verse.

[6] *Ca* (Medh., Nos. 935, 1551); *tu* (K.)

[7] Or by violating the rules ordained for the Brahmans (Medh.) Cf. Mbhā. xiv. 29, 15.

(Greeks), Çakaṣ (Indo-Scythians), Pāradas, Pahlavas (Persians), Cīnas (Chinese), Kirātas, Daradas, Khaças.[1]

45. Whatever classes (there are) among men outside of those born from the mouth, arm, thigh, and foot[2] (of Brahmā), all those (people) are called Dasyus, whether the language[3] they use be that of Mlecchas (barbarians)[4] or of Āryas.

46. (The sons) of the twice-born which are termed the Rejected and the Lowered[5] should occupy themselves only with such occupations as are blamed[6] of the twice-born.

47. Management of horses and driving waggons (is the occupation of Sūtas; the practice of medicine (that) of Ambaṣṭhas; attendance on women[7] (that) of Vaidehakas; the way[8] of the tradesman (that) of Māgadhas;

48. Killing fish (that) of Niṣādas; carpentry (that) of an Āyogava; killing forest animals (that) of Medas, Andhras, Cuñcus, and Madgus.[9]

49. Moreover, catching and killing animals that live in holes (is the occupation) of Kṣattars, Ugras, and Pukkasas; dealing[10] with skins (that) of Dhigvaṇas; making instrumental music (that) of Veṇas.

[1] Other than translated are probably Indian tribes; Kāmbojas, in the East; Yavanas, *probably* Greeks; possibly more generally applied to Alexandrians, etc. The last mentioned, Khaças, are not given in Medh., Nos. 935 like 989 and 1551 having *tathā*, but amended in the first to Khaṣāḥ (*sic.*) Pundraka, as in Bomb. MSS., in all three MSS. of Medh. Rāgh. follows K. in adding Khaṣāḥ.

[2] *I.e.*, the four regular castes.

[3] This means even those living in Āryavarta (cf. ii. 22), or who, like the Çabaras and Kirātas, are wild tribes and speak a barbarous language (the first = *āryavartanivāsinaḥ*), Medh. "Outside" means "degraded on account of lack of religious ceremonies" (K.); "by being of other caste than the four regular castes" (Medh.)

[4] Not the place but the language makes the Mleccha (Medh.)

[5] Cf. vss. 10 and 41.

[6] Disapproved for themselves.

[7] Guarding the harem (Medh., K.)

[8] Trading *on land* is specified by K. Medh. gives "the way" as on "land and water," etc.

[9] Cf. vs. 36. But the Cuñcu and Madgu are not otherwise mentioned; they are given (Baudh. in K.) as sons of Brahmans by a Vaidehaka woman and by the Bandistrī, who in turn is born of a Kṣatriya by a Çūdra woman = Ugra woman (cf. iii. 158). (Cuñcu, Bhūbhu, Medh., 989, 935, Vūca or Vūva (B°. ?))

[10] That is, the sale of leather to distinguish him from the Kārāvara in vs. 36 (K.), though not necessarily from the text (*carmakāra* and *carmakārya*).

50. These should live, being recognised,[1] occupied in their own several works, in places for burning the dead, around trees of temples, in the mountains, and in the woods.[2]

51. The dwelling of Cāṇḍālas and Çvapacas (should be) outside the village; they should be deprived of dishes[3] (*apapātra*); their property (consists of) dogs and asses;

52. Their clothes (should be) the garments of the dead, and their food (should be) in broken dishes;[4] their ornaments (should be) of iron; and they must constantly wander about.

53. A man who practises the rule of right should not desire intercourse[5] with these (people); their business transactions must be among each other; their marriages (should be only) with their equals;

54. Their food, (for which they are) dependent on others, should be given in a broken dish; they should not wander by night about the villages and towns;

55. They should go about by day to attend to their work, made known by the (signs of) punishments (inflicted) by the king;[6] and they should carry out the corpse of one (who dies) without relatives: so stands the rule.

56. They shall always slay those who are to be slain in accordance with the king's orders, and as the statute (has arranged); the clothes of those to be slain they may take, and (their) couches and ornaments.

[1] By carrying a mark of their order (Medh.)

[2] In artificial groves, according to the usual definition of *upavana*.

[3] Broken dishes or mean dishes must be supplied, or the dish is to be set down, not handed to them (Medh.). *Apapātra* in the Sūtras is synonymous with low caste, etc.

[4] K. Or, *bhinnabhāṇḍe ca* (Medh.), "given them in a broken dish."

[5] He must not stand, or sit, or sport in the same place as they do (Medh.)

[6] That is, they bear about banners and other tokens of their profession, or mount axes, etc., on their shoulders to proclaim that a criminal is to be killed (Medh.) Rāgh. thinks it means "branded on the forehead;" and K. does not understand the "work" to be that of vs. 56, but "business." In this sense we should have to translate *rājaçāsanaiḥ*, "by order of the king." This alternative meaning is also in Medh.

57. One should make known by (his) deeds (a man who), being shut out from his caste[1] and unknown, (and being) of impure origin and ignoble, has, as it were, a noble (*ārya*) appearance.[2]

58. Ignobility, coarseness,[3] savageness, laziness,[4] reveal here among men a man of impure origin.

59. Whether he assume the father's or the mother's character, or that of both, the base-born man never disguises his true nature.

60. Even if born in a high family, the man whose birth is due to a mixture of caste acquires, in small or great degree, a character (suitable to) this (impure birth).

61. That realm where these caste-debasing mixtures are produced goes right quickly to destruction, together with the inhabitants of the realm.

62. Desertion of life for the sake of a Brahman or for the sake of a cow, (if the act be) done without secondary motives,[5] or, again, losing life in coming to the rescue[6] of a woman or of a child, (are acts which) cause the ultimate bliss of outcasts.

63. Not to commit corporal injury, (to speak) the truth, not to steal,[7] to be pure, to restrain the senses, this condensed rule of duty Manu declared for the four castes.[8]

64. If (the caste) produced from a Brahman by a Çūdra

[1] By neglect of initiation (Rāgh.)

[2] Or "ignoble," (but), as it were, of noble nature (*āryabhūtam iva*, Medh.); or *ārya* is, perhaps, merely twice-born.

[3] Selfishness (Medh.)

[4] So B. R. Medh. and K., "neglect of prescribed ceremonies."

[5] So K. More specifically Medh. says, "without having received money."

[6] *Abhyava°*, Nos. 989, 935; *adhyava°*, No. 155 (Medh.); *abhyupa°* (K., Rāgh.)

[7] Or "not to be angry," *akrodhaḥ* for *asteyam* (Nos. 989, 935, 1551, Medh.)

[8] This rule, however, holds for all classes, the mixed as well as the pure (K.) Medh. notes that the first rule, not to do harm or not to kill (as *ahiṁsā* may mean) is in seeming contradiction to those statutes which enjoin fish-killing, killing animals in holes (vss. 48, 49), which is explained by some as having reference to gaining a livelihood only, while this includes also other cases. Others say not to kill animals is recommended as a negative means of obtaining bliss, but is not absolutely forbidden.

woman keeps reproducing itself by nobler (marriage), this ignoble attains a noble family at the seventh union.[1]

65. The Çūdra attains Brahmanship and the Brahman attains Çūdraship. This also one should know (to be the case with) the offspring of a Kṣatriya, and likewise of a Vaiçya.[2]

66. If there is (a son) born anyhow[3] of a Brahman by an ignoble (*anārya*) woman, and again one born of an ignoble man by a Brahman woman, and (the question) arises, "Where is the superiority?"[4]

67. (We answer): He (who is) born of a noble man by an ignoble woman might, by means of his good qualities, become noble, while he (who is) born of an ignoble man by a noble woman (remains) ignoble. Such is (our) decision.

68. But both of them are incapable of being initiated; with these words is the rule of right established, the former on account of his birth being devoid of good traits, the latter because (his birth is) against the caste order.

69. As good seed alone (when) sown in good land is successfully raised, so (the son) alone (who is) born of a noble man by a noble woman deserves complete initiation.

70. Some wise men extol the seed, others the land; others only seed and land combined; but on this point the fixed rule[5] is this:

[1] *Yuga* (here birth, generation; *yugaçabdo janmavacanaḥ*, Medh.), *i.e.*, if the woman of this class (called Pāraçava, by union of a Brahman and a Çūdra woman) marries a Brahman, and her daughter does the same, and so on to the seventh generation, this last generation acquires Brahmanship (Medh., K.)

[2] And in the fifth generation (of the caste produced from a Brahman) by a Vaiçya woman; in the third by a Kṣatriya woman; while the caste from a Vaiçya by a Çūdra woman attains in the third generation to Vaiçyaship, and from a Kṣatriya in the fifth, and from a Kṣatriya by a Vaiçya woman in the third (Medh., K.) Last word is *tu*, not *ca*, in Medh. (Nos. 989, 935, 1551).

[3] *Yadṛechayā = yathā katham*, *i.e.*, by an unmarried woman (Medh.)

[4] Or (Medh.) What, would superiority ever exist? *çreyas tu kiṁ, kvacid bhaved* (*kiṁçabdaḥ kṣepe*). Here and below "noble" is *ārya*.

[5] Cf. ix. 34. This was of equal wife with husband; the present discussion is whether the father exceeds the wife enough to make the son lose the bad influence induced by the evil land (field, womb), or *vice versâ*.

71. Seed sown in poor land is within that very (land) destroyed; land which has not even received seed (is) nothing but bare ground.[1]

72. Since (creatures) born of animals have become seers through the excellence of the seed, and (have been) both honoured and praised, therefore the seed is extolled.[2]

73. The creator on considering an ignoble man whose actions are noble, and a noble man who acts ignobly, said "The two are neither equal nor unequal."[3]

74. Those Brahmans who, abiding in Brahma as their source,[4] (are) established in their own occupations, should live by six occupations (one after the other) in order:

75. Giving instruction in, and perusing (the holy texts); giving sacrifice themselves, and also offering sacrifice (for others); giving and receiving (presents) also: (these are) the six occupations of (him whose) birth is highest.

76. Of his six occupations three occupations afford him a livelihood—offering sacrifice (for others), giving instruction (in the holy texts), and the reception (of presents) from a pure man.[5]

77. Three of the Brahman's duties[6] cease with the Kṣatriya—offering sacrifice (for others), giving instruction (in the holy texts), and third, the reception (of presents).

78. These (acts)[7] in the same manner should also cease with the Vaiçya. So stands the rule, for Manu Prajāpati said these duties (were) not (intended) for these two (castes).

[1] Whence no fruit is obtained (Medh.)

[2] Or, "is superior" (Medh.) Cf. ix. 35.

[3] Cf. iv. 224, 225.

[4] Brahmans who live in Brahm as their source. According to Medh. and K., those devoted to means of attaining (source) Brahma (viz., pious meditation).

[5] From one of the twice-born (K.)

[6] That is, in the outspoken words of Medh., the three which are employed by the Brahman for a livelihood are not permitted to the next caste, while the three that bring him no gain (*adṛṣṭārthāni*), sacrifice, study, generosity, are also for the Kṣatriya. "Giving instruction" means in the sacred texts, Veda, etc., but does not include the Dhanurveda (science of arms, implied vs. 79) and worldly sciences generally (Medh.)

[7] *Tathai'tāni* (Medh.)

79. In order to support life (it is the part) of a Kṣatriya to bear the sword and spear,[1] and of a Vaiçya (to) trade, (tend) cattle, and (practise) agriculture; but (their) religious duty is to give (presents), peruse (the holy texts), and (to give) sacrifice.

80. Among their respective occupations the most excellent (are) studying the Veda (in the case) of a Brahman, affording protection (in the case) of a Kṣatriya, and earning a living by industry (in the case) of a Vaiçya.

81. But a Brahman when not able to support life by his own proper occupation, as (it has been) declared, should live by the rules of duty (enjoined) for the Kṣatriya, since he (stands) next to him (in the caste order).

82. But if he (be) not able to support life by either[2] (course of life), and (if the question) should arise "What is he to do?" (then) let him live by the means of life (enjoined) for a Vaiçya, following agriculture and cattle-tending.[3]

83. But a Brahman, or even a Kṣatriya, when living by the means of life (enjoined) for a Vaiçya, should carefully avoid agriculture, (as it) causes great pain (and) is dependent on other (creatures).[4]

84. They[5] think agriculture is an excellent thing, (but) by the good this occupation is blamed, for the iron-faced block of wood smites the earth and also the (animals) dwelling in the earth.

85. But when one is forced to omit the fulfilment of these religious duties because his occupation is not sufficient to support life, he may multiply his wealth by selling

[1] This includes all knowledge of the Dhanurveda (Medh.)

[2] Literally, "both."

[3] This manner of supporting life, which includes selling and buying, is in case of need, and may be employed by the Brahman himself; when there is no need (distress) he is not to employ it (K.) There seems to have been an uncertainty if these occupations of the Vaiçya were really meant to be done personally, and include usury and trade in things not forbidden. Medh. says some quote the verses found in iv. 5, 6, against it. Cf. Gaut. x.

[4] As steers, etc. (K.)

[5] Some (K.); people generally (Medh.)

the things a Vaiçya is permitted to sell, with the exception of (what in his case also is usually) excepted.

86. One should avoid (to sell) all essences and made food, together with sesame, (precious) stones,[1] salt,[2] cattle,[3] and human creatures.

87. And all woven stuff dyed;[4] hemp, flax and woollen goods, even if not dyed; fruits and roots and (medicinal) plants;

88. Water, a weapon, poison, meat, soma, and perfumes under all circumstances; milk, honey, sour milk, ghee, sesame oil, sweets,[5] sugar, *kuça*-grass;

89. And all forest cattle, creatures that rend with the teeth,[6] (large) birds; intoxicating liquor, indigo, lac; also all creatures with whole hoofs.[7]

90. But if by farming a farmer has himself raised sesame for pleasure, he may sell that which is pure and has not been long kept in order to (fulfil) his religious duties.[8]

91. If he does anything else with sesame than to eat (it), anoint (with it), or make a present (of it), he with his ancestors sinks in the form of a worm into the excrements of a dog.[9]

92. A Brahman falls at once through (selling) meat, lac, and salt; in (the course of) three days he becomes a Çūdra through selling milk.

[1] According to Medh., stones of all sorts.

[2] The special mention of salt shows the special heinousness of the crime in selling it (K.); no special salt is mentioned, but Medh. says it is sea-salt.

[3] Belonging to town or wood (Medh.); such as cows and horses (Rāgh.); *mānuṣāḥ* (= *manuṣyāḥ*, Medh.) Cf. with this Yāj. iii. 39; Āp. i. 7. 20, 12 ff. Gaut. viii. 8 ff.; Vas. ii. 24 ff.

[4] Saffron (K.); red mantles, etc., according to Medh., who adds that *rakta* (dyed) generally is applied to red (*lohite varṇe raktaçabdaḥ prasiddhataraḥ*), but may mean any colour not white.

[5] Cf. Yāj. iii. 37 (K.); or *madhu* may be = *mādhvīka* (Medh., with other explanations, who also says *guḍa* (sugar) is mentioned as belonging to *rasa*, or, according to some, to permit candy.)

[6] As dogs and wild boars (Medh.)

[7] That is, many of them (*bahūn iti tathā-çabdasthāne paṭhanti*), it is no fault to see one only (Medh.)

[8] To aid religious rites, etc. Medh. observes that this, together with the words "pure" and "not long kept," mark the distinction between vs. 90 and vs. 86. (In Medh., Nos. 935, 989, *hastam* for *kāmam*).

[9] This refers to (*tila*) sesame in its natural state (Medh.). Cf. Vas. ii. 30.

93. But through the wilful sale of other commodities[1] a Brahman in (the course of) seven nights acquires here on earth the nature of a Vaiçya.

94. Essences[2] may be exchanged for essences, but not thus salt for essences;[3] and made food (may be exchanged) for unmade food, and sesame for grain, when equal to it (in value).

95. A man of the regal caste (Kṣatriya) may live by all these (means) when he has come to need, but he should at no time meditate (living by) a higher[4] occupation.

96. If any man low in birth should, through greed, live by the occupations of the exalted, the king should banish him at once, after depriving him of his property.

97. Better one's own duties incomplete than[5] those of another well performed, for he who lives by the duties of another falls from caste at once.

98. A Vaiçya,[6] if not able to live by his own duties, should support himself even by the occupation of a Çūdra, engaging in nothing that ought not to be done; and he should stop (as soon as he is) able.

99. Now when a Çūdra cannot slave for the twice-born, and has reached (the point where) his son and wife are dying, he may live by the work of a manual labourer;

100. (That is), that work of a manual labourer and those various arts by performing which the twice-born are served.

101. A Brahman not taking up with the occupation of a Vaiçya, (but) abiding by his own path, being in distress

[1] Other than those allowed. Medh. says "without necessity" must be added.

[2] Or, fluids.

[3] Or, "for sesame oil" (*tilaiḥ*, *var. lec.*, Medh.); "by this reading the exchange of salt with *tila* alone is forbidden, not with other essences."

[4] The priestly.

[5] *Paradharmāt svanuṣṭhitāt* (Medh. in Nos. 935, 989). This is a common proverb, occurring repeatedly in the epic. K.'s reading is, "his own . . . is a better (thing), not anothers . . . ." In Medh., No. 1551, the oldest of the three MSS., the following change of order occurs: 96, 105–115. 97–105, 115, etc., as the rest. This may indicate an old uncertainty in respect to the verses; from their character they may easily be believed to be late.

[6] But not the Brahman or Kṣatriya, which some say this includes (Medh.)

(because) harassed by lack of subsistence, may act in accordance with this (following) rule of duty:

102. A Brahman (who) has come to need may take (gifts) from everybody, for it cannot justly[1] be said that the pure becomes defiled.

103. Neither by giving instruction (in holy texts), nor by sacrificing (for others), nor by a receipt (of presents), (which is generally) censured, does any fault arise (on the part) of the Brahmans, for they are like fire (and) water.

104. If one eats food (procured) from any source whatever when he has reached (the point where) life (is) passing away, as the air (is not soiled) by dirt, so he is not besmeared by (this) sin.

105. Ajīgarta,[2] when desiring to eat, undertook to kill his son, and was not (on that account) besmeared with sin, (because) practising (this as) an antidote to hunger.

106. Nor was Vāmadeva besmeared (with sin) when he, well knowing right and wrong, wanted to eat dog's flesh in order to preserve animation, (because) oppressed with hunger.

107. Moreover, Bharadvāja, whose devotion was great, being oppressed by hunger in a lonely wood with his son, received many cows from Vṛdhu the carpenter.

108. Moreover, Viçvāmitra, well knowing right and wrong, being oppressed by hunger, proceeded to eat the rump of a dog, having received it from the hand of a Cāṇḍāla.

109. Of (all these three)—the receipt (of presents), offering sacrifice (for others), and, too, even giving instruction (in holy texts)—the receipt (of presents) on the part of a Brahman is lowest, and after death (is) censured.

110. Offering sacrifice (for others) and giving instruction are always done for (those who) have had their souls pre-

[1] *Pavitram*, "the Ganges is not defiled by filth, so the Brāhmaṇa (Medh.)." Medh. takes *dharmataḥ* as "in accordance with the law," referring to "the stream is purified by its motion" (v. 108) as an explanation of this.

[2] Ajīgarta, he who has nothing to eat, and his son Çunaḥçepha are well known from the tale in the Ait. Br. (vii. 15 ff.) The other sages are familiar in early and later epic. Vss. 105 to 115 are perhaps later than the rest; *vide* note to vs. 97.

pared (for it), but one receives (presents) even from[1] a low-born Çūdra.

111. Through prayer and sacrifice the guilt incurred by (improperly) offering sacrifice and giving instruction departs, but that which has its cause in the (improper) receipt (of presents departs) only by giving up (the gift) and by penance.

112. A Brahman may accept (the right to) glean ears and pick up kernels from any one whatever, when he cannot (otherwise) support life. To glean ears (is) better than to receive (presents), and to pick up kernels is even better than that.

113. The sovereign ought to be besought by Brahmans who have completed their studies, when they are in distress and want the (baser) metals or property; if he does not choose to give he ought to be deserted.[2]

114. (Amid) a (field) uncultivated, a cultivated field, cows, goats, sheep, gold, grain, and food, each preceding object is void of fault.[3]

115. The just modes of acquiring wealth are seven: inheritance, receiving,[4] purchase, conquering, earning by lending money or by labour, and also receiving (presents) from the good.

116. Science,[5] art, working for hire, (servile) attendance, cattle-tending, trade, agriculture, determination,[6]

[1] Medh. has the genitive case.

[2] The priest should leave his country (Medh., Govind.), or the king, if not inclined to give, should not be asked (K.). Cf. viii. 389. The first is noted in K., but Medh. really has another explanation, according to which *tyāga* = *hāni*, *i.e.*, *dharmahānim prāpnoti*, "he receives loss of virtue," a forced explanation. When it is said that a priest should not take presents from a king (iv. 84 ff.), the remark applies only to a bad king (Medh.)

[3] The earlier mentioned in order is less sinful than the following throughout the list; can be received with less sin.

[4] Receiving is to take a gift from a friend or depositor. The first three are for all the castes, the fourth for the Ksatriya, the two next for the Vaiçya, the last for the Brahman (Medh., K.); but Medh. quotes "some" who give a broader sense to the passage, *e.g.*, that conquering applies to all, and may include gaming, etc. Cf. Gaut. x. 39–42.

[5] *Vidyā*, Vedic knowledge (?); the commentators say all but this.

[6] Determination or firmness. K. says "contentment, for where this exists life is supported by even a little."

begging, and usury, (are) ten means of supporting life.[1]

117. A Brahman or even a Kṣatriya should not lend money at interest, but may indeed give at pleasure for duty's sake a little (interest) to the sinner (who demands it).[2]

118. A Kṣatriya (king) who takes even a fourth part (as revenue), in (time of) distress, is released from all sin (in so doing) if he protects the people with all his might.[3]

119. In his case victory is his special duty; he ought not to turn his face away in battle. When he has defended the people with his sword he may take to himself a rightful tax.[4]

120. (He may take) from the people[5] a tax of one-eighth on grain, (and a tax) of one-twentieth (on sums of money), down to one *kārṣāpaṇa* as the lowest (sum).[6] Çūdras, handworkers, and artisans render (him) assistance by (corporal) labour (only).

121. Now a Çūdra desiring some means of subsistence may serve a Kṣatriya,[7] so (is the rule); or the Çūdra, (if) anxious to support life, (may do so by) serving a wealthy Vaiçya.[8]

[1] In time of need all these acts may be performed by all men (Medh.)

[2] *Dharmārtham*; either when the object for which the money is borrowed appertains to religious duty, or when he thereby satisfies the lawful claims of the usurer (Medh.)

[3] Cf. vii. 130.

[4] The people are literally the Vaiçyas, from whom the tax is drawn. The word "victory" means the fruit of victory (is his right) (Medh.)

[5] *Viçaḥ*, here meaning people in general (Medh.) The tax of one-twelfth in Lecture vii. is not in case of distress, as this of one-eighth is (K.)

[6] On money (invested) the tax is one-twentieth. Cf. Vas. xix. 37, who quotes the restriction as that of Manu; cf. also vii. 127 ff.; Gaut. x. 27.

[7] Not for duty's sake, but to gain property (for support); whereas in serving the Brahmans both are united (Medh.) This is only when he cannot serve the Brahman (K.)

[8] Medh.'s reading, *ākāṅkṣan*, . . . *ārādhayed iti* . . . *jijīviṣuḥ*, does away with the awkwardness of K.'s reading, and presents a new thought. When seeking occupation, let him serve a Kṣatriya; reduced to seeking bare means of life, a Vaiçya. This is the reading of MSS. No. 1551 and No. 989; so too of No. 935 before (as is frequently the case in this copy) it was touched up by a later hand. Rāgh. has *ākāṅkṣan*, but with K. *jijīviṣet*, according to my MS.

122. But he should serve the Brahmans for the sake of heaven, or for the sake of both (heaven and livelihood); for by him (by whom) the word Brahman (is always) uttered [1] is thus (attained) the state of completing all he ought to do.

123. Merely to serve the Brahmans is declared (to be) the most excellent occupation of a Çūdra; for if he does anything other than this it profits him nothing.[2]

124. His means of life should be arranged by these (Brahmans) out of their own household (goods) in accordance with what is fitting, after examining his ability, cleverness, and (the amount) the dependents embrace.[3]

125. The leavings of food should be given (him) [4] and the old clothes; so too the blighted part of the grain; so too the old furniture.

126. There is not any commission of sin in a Çūdra, and he ought not to receive the initiation; he has no authority in respect to a rule of right, and no restraint in consequence of a rule of right.[5]

127. But (those Çūdras who are) desirous of (performing) meritorious acts,[6] (and) know the rules of right [6] (and)

[1] Literally, "who has produced;" but K. (from Çākapārthiva) explains "of whom it is said he is devoted from birth to the Brahman;" Medh., "(to repeat) the word 'he is a Brahman' is his best occupation," or as K.

[2] This does not exclude him from *pākayajña*, however (Medh.)

[3] "The number of dependents," ultimately the Brahman's; the proportion allotted to each slave being limited by the number of sons, etc.; said of the Çūdra slave, "dependents" must mean his family, and his portion is adjusted to its size (Medh., K., Rāgh.)

[4] Contradicted in iv. 80, which K. says refers to any Çūdra not de-dependent on him, (while this refers to the Brahman's own servant). Medh. defines *pulāka* as "bad grain" (*asāradhanyāni*); "furniture," couches, seats, etc. (Medh.)

[5] That the Çūdra does not sin means not in respect to the sins of vs. 63, but in respect to the rules laid down for those who have received the initiation regarding the eating of certain vegetables and such rules (K.) The last seems to repeat this thought; he has nothing to say in regard to the rules given the twice-born, and they do not apply to him in their prohibitions. K. says he should not be hindered from his own duty. Cf. ii. 16, paraphrased as "*na ca dharmam açnute na cā 'sya dharmapratiṣedhanaṁ smṛtam*" (Medh. to vs. 127); but the Comm. explain as "no prohibition from the *pākayajña* and other *dharma* of a Çūdra." Cf. Yāj. iii. 262; Mbhā. xiii. 165, 10.

[6] *Dharma*. Cf. Gaut. x. 50 (Bühler's note).

follow the custom of the good, except[1] (as regards) the *mantra*, do not do wrong but obtain praise.

128. Just in proportion as one pursues without complaining the mode of life (practised by) the good, so, free from blame, he gains both this and the other world.

129. Indeed, an accumulation of wealth should not be made by a Çūdra even (if he is) able (to do so), for a Çūdra getting possession of wealth merely injures[2] the Brahmans.

130. The rules of right for the four castes in times of distress have thus[3] been proclaimed, (by) pursuing which (rules) properly they attain the supreme path (of bliss).

131. This lawful (and) complete rule in respect to the four castes has been declared; now then I will next expound the pure rule for expiations.

END OF THE TENTH LECTURE.

[1] These Çūdras are forbidden to use the holy texts except the text for showing reverence, according to Yāj. i. 121 (K.) The texts for reverence alone are allowed them, not for laying on of the fire, etc.; it does not mean that the ceremonies prescribed for the twice-born are allowed the Çūdra provided he omits the texts (Medh.)

[2] "How can they injure the Brahmans by having a great deal of wealth? by making them receive too many presents; for receiving presents from a Çūdra is forbidden the Brahmans" (Medh.) K. has a more rational explanation, "they would cease to serve the Brahmans, and so distress them."

[3] Medh., Nos. 935, 989, 1551, *var. lec.*, *evam* for *ete*, and vs. 131, *varṇye prakīrtitaḥ*.

LECTURE XI.

PENANCE, EXPIATION, ETC.

1. (He who) desires offspring, (or) wishes to sacrifice, (or) goes on a journey, (or) gives away all (his) wealth,[1] (or) seeks wealth for the Guru, (or) seeks wealth for father (and) mother, (or) seeks wealth [2] for his own study, (or) is ill;

2. These nine Brahmans having returned home from their studies, one should know (are thus) beggars for virtuous reasons,[3] and gifts are to be given them in accordance with their learning (when they are) without possessions of their own.

3. To these foremost indeed of the twice-born food should be given with gifts (at a sacrifice); to others (it) is said (that) prepared food should be given outside the place of sacrifice.[4]

4. Now upon Brahmans acquainted with the Veda the king should bestow, as may be fitting,[5] all sorts of gems and (sacrificial) gifts also, for the sake of sacrifice.

5. A man married, who, after begging,[6] approaches

[1] As a sacrificial present (K.) at a *viçvajit* (all-conquering) sacrifice (Medh., K.), but not if it was for an expiation (Medh.)

[2] *I.e.*, seeks food, etc., as a student, or seeks instruction from one who has mastered a Veda (Medh.)

[3] All nine being learned (Snātaka is properly one who has bathed at completion of studentship), and being twice-born Brahmans, may lawfully beg food, etc., for the reasons given in vs. 1. Cf. iv. 251, and Āp. ii. 10, 1–3.

[4] That is, anywhere except in the place of sacrifice, reserved as the place of giving for the nine mentioned above; gifts of food to guests, etc. (Medh.)

[5] In accordance with the learning of the recipient (Medh.)

[6] To enable him to marry; a man may beg to defray marriage expenses (when desiring offspring, cf. vs. 1), and a Brahman has a right to a second wife, but no right to beg for money for this marriage as if it came under the first proviso. "After begging" means after getting money to defray the marriage expenses, cost of the wife.

(carnally) another wife, has sensual love alone as his reward, and the offspring (is his who) gives the wealth.

6. Now one should bestow upon the Brahmans wealth according to his ability, upon (those who are) learned in the Veda and freed (from earthly ties); after death (the giver) reaches heaven.[1]

7. He who has food enough to support his dependents for three years or more has a right to drink *soma*.

8. The twice-born man who drinks *soma* when his wealth is much less than this (amount) does not get the reward (that belongs) to it, even (if) he has drunk *soma* before.[2]

9. A man of means[3] giving gifts to strangers while his own family lives in wretchedness tastes poison (while) seeking honey;[4] he makes a counterfeit of right.

10. If any one[5] perform funeral rites by (means which entail) distress on his dependents, this (act) results in his woe, living and dead.[6]

11. If, where the king is a just man, a sacrifice should be interrupted through (incompleteness in) one article,[7] when (any one), especially a Brahman, is offering sacrifice,

12. One should take that article, to ensure the success of the sacrifice, from the household (possessions) of any Vaiçya who, (although) rich in cattle, does not perform sacrificial rites and does not drink *soma*.[8]

[1] Omitted by Medh. (Nos. 935, 989, 1551), and Bomb. MS., and Rāgh.; no doubt late.

[2] The *soma* is drunk at the first sacrifice; even after this he must not repeat it (Medh.)

[3] With the meaning "means" as ability or wealth.

[4] Somewhat similar in form is the remark made by the seers to the king in the Mbhā. (xiii. 93, 34), "Receiving presents from kings is tasting honey like to poison" (*madhvāsvādo viṣopamaḥ*).

[5] *Yaḥ* (Medh.), *yat* (K.)

[6] (*Karoti*)*aurddhvadehikam* is frequently used of making gifts at a funeral (cf. Mbhā. xii. 42, 7; xiii. 125, 73, etc.) This is a sumptuary law like the Roman, only restricted to where the expense injures the family. Literally, "if he does (an act) connected with one dead." Medh. and K. regard it as simply giving gifts to secure future happiness.

[7] Literally, "one limb" (of the whole).

[8] Cf. Gaut. xviii. 24 ff.

13. One may take, as he wishes, three or two (articles) from a Çūdra's house; for when sacrifices (are performed) a Çūdra has no (right of) possession.[1]

14. Without hesitation one may take (articles) from the household goods of these two, viz., (one) who, (although) possessing one hundred cows, does not build a (sacrificial) fire, and (one) who, (although) possessing one thousand cows, does not offer sacrifice.[2]

15. One may seize (property) from (one who) is always receiving but is not a giver, (if the latter) does not offer (it);[3] thus his fame becomes extended and his spiritual good increased.

16. So, too, at the seventh meal, (food) may be taken from a man who neglects ceremonies, by (a Brahman) who has taken on himself the rule of having no store for the morrow,[4] (after he has passed) six meal-(times) without eating.[5]

17. Whether (food) be taken from threshing-floor, from field, from (store)-house, or from any other place, if (the owner)[6] questions (the one who takes it), the thing should be explained to him questioning.

18. The property of a Brahman should at no time be taken by a Kṣatriya; but, having no means of life of his own, he has a right to take the property of a Dasyu or of one who does not perform ceremonies.[7]

[1] Or, "a Çūdra has no connection with sacrifices," the meaning given by the commentators; quite literally the words mean "has no hold upon," which may be taken absolutely. K. says this means that the Çūdra is to be forced to give up his property, as vs. 24 forbids the Brahman to *ask* for it. Medh. says "some declare that the property ceases to belong to the Çūdra if the Brahman appropriates it," so that it is thus pure for sacrificial use. Recourse to the Çūdra is to be had only when there is no Vaiçya (to get the articles from)—(Medh., K.)

[2] This applies to a Kṣatriya or a Brahman (Medh., K.); the one who takes the Brahman's goods must, however, be a Brahman.

[3] On being asked to do so (K.); this refers to all castes (Medh.) (Medh., Nos. 935, 989, have *yathā* for *tathā*.)

[4] Cf. iv. 17.

[5] (There are two meals a day), thus the seventh meal is the morning meal after a three days' fast (Medh., K.)

[6] Medh., K., Rāgh.; or (Medh.) "if the king questions . . . the thing must be explained to the inquiring owner."

[7] Similarly, that of a Kṣatriya cannot be taken by a Vaiçya or a Çūdra (K.)

19. He who takes goods from the unworthy and presents them to the worthy makes a boat of himself, and transports both.[1]

20. If those who are accustomed to perform sacrifice possess any property, the wise regard it as the possession of the gods; but if those who do not offer sacrifice possess any wealth, it is said to be the possession of demons.[2]

21. A sovereign who does what is just should not have punishment inflicted upon this man;[3] for (it is) through the foolishness of the Kṣatriya[4] (that) the Brahman is afflicted with hunger.

22. Out of his own household goods should the lord of earth (the king) arrange (for him) a righteous support, after learning (how large) a family has to be supported (by him),[5] and understanding his wisdom and character.

23. And, after arranging his support, (the king) should guard him on all sides; since it is by virtue of protecting him that the king receives a sixth part of his spiritual merit.[6]

24. At no time[7] should a Brahman beg property from a Çūdra for the sake of sacrifice, for on offering sacrifice after begging (from a Çūdra) he is born after death as a Cāṇḍāla.

25. The Brahman who, after begging goods for the sake of sacrifice, fails to offer the whole (in sacrifice), enters for one hundred years into the condition of a bird of prey or of a crow.

[1] The one who is unworthy (because not giving) is transported, rescued, from the sin of not giving, and the other from the woes entailed by lack of means (K.); perhaps better "transports (both) to heaven," as ix. 139 (*amutra*).

[2] *Deva* and *asura* are here opposed as god and devil; originally *asura* was any spirit, good as well as bad.

[3] The Brahman just described, who takes food to support life (Medh., K.)

[4] The king.

[5] The people dependent on him, his *familia*.

[6] Cf. viii. 307.

[7] Or, "a Brahman who knows the right" (*dharmavit*, in Medh., Nos. 935, 989, 1551). This is simply to forbid his begging; it is no sin to take the Çūdra's property without asking (Medh.); he supports this by quoting a proverb that "unasked-for goods make the best presents," which was evidently *not* intended to convey the meaning given by the commentator, but simply to recommend that one should not ask for goods at all; "such reception of presents one should know is virtually no reception."

26. The evil-minded man who, through greed, injures the possessions of the gods[1] or the possessions of Brahmans, lives in the next world on what a vulture leaves (in eating).

27. At the end of the year one should regularly offer the Vaiçvānarī sacrifice to ensure expiation, when the ordained rites with cattle and *soma* have not been performed.[2]

28. If a twice-born man, in (a time when there is) no distress, performs the (offices of) duty by the ordinance (appointed) for (times of) distress, he receives no benefit therefrom in the other (world): with these words is the rule settled.

29. The substitute for the (regular) rule was invented by the All-gods,[3] Sādyas, and great Brahmanic seers (when they were) in distress and fearful of death.

30. No benefit in the next world accrues to that evil-minded man who, when able (to act) according to the primary ordinance, acts in accordance with a secondary ordinance.[4]

31. A Brahman acquainted with the rule of right should not let anything be made known before the king;[5] by his own power alone he should punish those men (who) do (him) injury.

32. (In a comparison) between his own power and the power of the king, his own power is the stronger; therefore, by his own power alone should a twice-born man (Brahman) punish enemies.

[1] Cf. iii. 115. "Possessions of the gods" may be taken as belonging to the temples, etc., as K. says; or, according to the first explanation of Medh., they are here distinct from the Brahman's property (cf. vs. 20), and include that of all the three upper castes given to sacrifice; whereas the Brahman's goods must not be injured, even if he is not given to sacrifice.

[2] This sacrifice (*iṣṭi*) purifies from all sin; cf. Baudh. i. 1, 2, 17.

[3] Literally, "by all the gods," which means probably the *viçve devāḥ;* "the gods called *viçvadeva*" (K.)

[4] The secondary ordinance is one prescribed to take the place of the primary when the latter is impossible, and it is a sin to make a regular practice of what is ordained only for emergencies.

[5] *Rājani.*—"*Coram rege suo . . . tacentes plus poscente ferent,*" though with a different application.

33. He should employ without hesitation the verses of Atharvan and Aṅgiras. The Brahman's weapon is speech;[1] with this let the twice-born man slay his enemies.

34. The Kṣatriya may divert distress from himself by means of the power of his arm; the Vaiçya and Çūdra, moreover, by means of wealth; (but) the highest of the twice-born by muttered prayers and oblations.

35. The Brahman is called perfecter, teacher, speaker, well-wisher; one should not say to him what is inauspicious, nor excite an empty talk (with him).[2]

36. Neither a maid, nor a young woman, nor a man of small knowledge, nor a fool should be the officiating priest (*hotar*) at a fire-oblation, nor a sick man, nor one not initiated.[3]

37. For into hell they fall (by officiating in the) sacrificing, and (into hell falls) he whose (sacrifice) it (was);[4] therefore the officiating priest should be (a man) skilled in arranging the fire,[5] one who has reached the end of a Veda.

38. A Brahman who, when he has the means, does not give a horse dedicated to Prajāpati as a sacrificial present at the arranging of the fire, becomes (like) one that has no (sacred) fire arranged.

39. A man of faith and subdued senses may do other holy (acts), but here on earth let him at no time sacrifice with sacrifices that afford small sacrificial presents.[6]

[1] Cf. vs. 86. The Atharva-veda, as such, is not recognised in our text. Incantations, as a means of defence against enemies, are not forbidden (Medh.)

[2] *Vidhātar* (perfector, K., of acts appointed) may mean governor, or even creator (Rāgh.); disposer is perhaps as near as we can get to the idea "the disposer" of ceremonies of men, and of the world (Medh., creator). *Çuṣkāṁ giram irayet* (empty talk) may mean voice hoarse with passion (vox torrida); "one must not insult or get angry with him" (Medh., Rāgh. Cf. ii. 87, ii. 150 (*kartar = vidhātar?*); *çāsitar* also may mean punisher (Medh.), as the connection warrants.

[3] Some think the wife can, if she pleases, sacrifice morn and eve in the house-fire (Medh.)

[4] He for whom they performed the sacrifice.

[5] *Vitāno vihāraḥ, sa ca çrauteṣv agniṣu saṁbhavati* (Medh.)

[6] He may, for instance, go on a pilgrimage to ensure his after-bliss. This costs nothing, but he should not attempt to offer sacrifice unless he can afford to give the priest a handsome fee.

40. A sacrifice accompanied by small presents destroys (the giver's) organs of sense, reputation, heaven, long life, fame, children, cattle; therefore a man of small property should not offer sacrifice.

41. A Brahman fire-priest (who) neglects the fire on purpose should perform the moon-course (vow) for a month,[1] for that (sin) is equal to killing a man.[2]

42. If any (Brahmans), on receiving goods from a Çūdra,[3] assist at a fire-oblation, (they are) blamed among those who proclaim the Veda, as they (thus become) the priests of Çūdras.

43. The giver (alone) would escape miseries, treading with his foot upon the head of these ever[4]-ignorant worshippers of a Vṛṣala's fire.[5]

44. On failing to perform an act enjoined, and on practising (an act) prohibited, and on indulging in sensual pleasures, a man must perform a penance.[6]

45. The wise regard a penance (as intended) for a sin committed unintentionally; some, by (referring to) the ordinances of revelation (Çruti), declare (it is) even for (a sin) committed intentionally.[7]

46. A sin committed unintentionally is expiated by perusing the Veda, but when foolishly done on purpose (it is expiated) by penances of different sorts for different cases.[8]

47. The twice-born man who by fate,[9] or by an (act) formerly committed, has reached a condition where penance

[1] Some interpret "if he neglects the fire for a month." "Man" here means "son" (K.)

[2] Cf. Tait. Saṁh. i. 5. 2, 1 (K.)

[3] That is, on receiving them when given as a kindness by the Çūdra. It is no sin if he seize the Çūdra's goods without asking (Medh.)

[4] *Satatam*, according to K., means "in the next world" (he escapes).

[5] The Çūdra (Vṛṣala) who gives attains heaven, but the worshipper does not. The "Vṛṣala's fire" is one he has provided.

[6] Cf. Āp. ii. 12, 22; Mbhā. xii. 34, 2.

[7] As in the tale of Indra, Ait. Br. vii. 28 (Medh., K.) Cf. Vas. xx. 1-2.

[8] Medh. notices the other doctrine that there is no use in penance, "for the deed does not die." Cf. Vas. xxii. 2.

[9] "Fate." Medh. says done by "self-incurred carelessness," but notes that some read *mohād* instead of *daivād*, adding, "But a wrong act is done only through *moha* (delusion), for what sane person would violate the statute?" The opposition is evidently between acts done here and in a former existence, though *daiva* (divine, fate) is often a mere synonym of the former-birth cause still acting—as *daivamānuṣe* in vii. 205.

must be performed, ought not to come in contact with good men so long as the penance is unperformed.

48. Men of evil manners[1] receive an alteration of form, some through the evil (deeds) committed (by them) in this life, some also through (acts) formerly committed.

49. A thief of gold (receives) the disease of bad nails; a drinker of intoxicating liquor, (the disease of) black teeth; a slayer of a Brahman, consumption; he who violates the couch of the Guru, a skin disease;[2]

50. A slanderer, a foul-smelling nose;[3] a false informer, a foul-smelling mouth; a stealer of grain, the loss of a limb; and one who mixes (grains), a superfluity (of limbs);

51. One who takes food, dyspepsia; a thief of the voice, dumbness; a thief of clothes, leprosy; a horse-thief, lameness;

52. A stealer of a lamp would (in the next birth) become blind; an extinguisher (of a lamp), one-eyed; by (committing) injury (one would get) a condition of disease; by not (committing) injury, the condition of not being diseased.[4]

53. Thus, according to the difference in their acts, (men who are) blamed by the good are born dull, dumb, blind, and deformed in appearance.

54. Regularly, then, penance should be practised for purification, since those whose sins have not (thus) been done away with are (re)-born with (these) disgraceful marks attached.

55. Slaying a Brahman, drinking intoxicating liquor, theft, committing adultery with the wife of a Guru, (are), they say, the great crimes;[5] and association[6]

[1] *Durācārā* (Medh., Nos. 1551, 989, 935), or "evil-minded" (K.)

[2] Or, loss of fore-skin (K.)

[3] *Pūtināsatvam* (Medh., Nos. 1551, 989, 935).

[4] This verse was rejected by Loiseleur Deslongchamps. It has other readings, but that of the text is given in Nos. 1551, 989, 935, by Medh. (so the Bengal MS.), while, according to K., the last part reads "an adulterer (becomes) puffed out (in body)." Rāgh. says it is found in some texts (*kvacit*).

[5] Cf. ix. 235. K. repeats the restriction there noted; Medh. also specifies "the gold of a Brahman" as that stolen, "in accordance with another Smṛti."

[6] *Saṁsarga* (K.), or *saṁyoga* (Medh., Nos. 989, 1551).

with those (who commit these crimes is) also (a great crime).

56. Untruth in (respect to one's) superiority, slander brought before the king, and false accusation of a Guru (are) equivalent to slaying a Brahman.

57. Forgetting the Veda (*brahma*), abuse of the Veda, false testimony, slaying a friend,[1] eating (food that) has been forbidden and (things) which ought not to be eaten,[2] (are) six (crimes) equivalent to drinking intoxicating liquor.

58. Theft of a deposit, and of a man,[3] horse, silver, land, diamond, or gem, is said to be equivalent to stealing gold.

59. Carnal connection with (women who are) born of one's own mother, with maidens,[4] and with low-(born) women,[5] and with the wives of one's friend or son, they consider equivalent to (violating) the Guru's couch.[7]

60. Killing a cow, sacrificing for those for whom sacrifice ought not to be made, adultery with another man's wife, selling one's self,[6] deserting (one's) Guru, mother, father, study, fire, or son;

61. Being anticipated in marriage by a younger brother, and marrying before the elder, the gift of a daughter to either (thus married), and also performing sacrifice for either;

62. Also injuring[9] a girl, taking usurious interest,

[1] Or, corporally injuring (*vadha*); K. adds "if not a Brahman."

[2] *Parisāder adanam* (K.) Medh. is not quoted correctly by K.: (*anādyaṁ*) *manastuṣṭikaraṁ na bhojyam iti saṅkalpya yad bhujyate.*

[3] Of him who gives a daughter to one man, and then, though there is no fault in the one, gives her to another, it is said, "he receives the sin of a lie in respect to man" [*puruṣa*)—(Medh.)

[4] With sisters (*svayonyāsu*) and unmarried (Medh.) girls (too young to marry). Cf. vs. 171.

[5] Barbara or Caṇḍāla woman (Medh.)

[6] The expiation is not necessarily as severe in all cases because of the "equivalent" (Medh., K.); so Medh. in vs. 61.

[7] Into slavery. The *var. lec.* in the MSS. in respect to the first hemistich is specially noted by Medh. No essential change in the meaning results.

[8] Defaming or defiling (Medh.)

failure to perform a vow;[1] selling a pool, pleasure-garden, wife, or child;

63. Being a Vrātya, deserting one's kindred; also giving instruction by a hired (teacher) and receiving instruction from a hired teacher;[2] the sale of things which ought not to be sold;

64. Superintendence over all (sorts of) mines, undertaking great public works,[3] injuring (medicinal) plants, living by (prostituting one's) wife,[4] bewitching, and performing ceremonies with roots;[5]

65. Felling live trees to get firewood, undertaking ceremonies[6] for one's own sake, and eating forbidden food;

66. Living without having arranged the (sacred) fire, theft, non-payment of debts;[7] having recourse to the treatises of wicked (persons),[8] and doing (what) belongs (to the occupation of a) dancer and singer;[9]

67. Stealing grain, (base) metals, or animals; devotion to a woman who drinks intoxicating liquors; slaying a woman, a Çūdra, a Vaiçya, or a Kṣatriya, non-belief[10]—(are all) secondary crimes.

68. Doing harm to a Brahman,[11] smelling of (what) ought not to be smelt and of intoxicating liquors, deceit,[12] and carnal intercourse with a man, are said to cause loss of caste.[13]

69. Killing an ass, horse, forest animal, elephant, goat, or sheep should be known to cause (the same results as) mixing (castes); so too (killing) a fish, snake, or buffalo.

70. Receiving property from forbidden (persons), trad-

[1] Of chastity (K.) Medh. and K. read *vārdhuṣyaṁ vratalopanam*; Rāgh. notes this as *var. lec.*, but reads *vārdhuṣitraṁ vratācyutiḥ*.

[2] *Bhṛtakasya sato adhyāpakatvāt, yaçca bhṛtakād adhīte* (Medh.) See B. R. s. *bhṛti* and *adhyāpana*.

[3] So Medh. and K., of dykes, etc.

[4] Or simply by her wealth (Medh.)

[5] Bewitching, *i.e.*, killing an enemy with *mantra* or hawk-sacrifice (Medh.) Cf. ix. 290

[6] Sacrifices with the *pāka* (Medh., K.)

[7] The three debts (to god, manes, and men) with which man is born.

[8] *Asaçchāstra.*

[9] Medh., K., two MSS., Nos. 1551, 935, give *kauçilavyasanakriyāḥ*.

[10] In a next world (Medh., Rāgh.)

[11] With hand or staff (Medh., K.)

[12] When one thing is done, another said or thought in the heart (Medh.)

[13] *Jāti*, family or caste.

ing, serving a Çūdra, should be known to make (the receiver, etc.), a person unfit to receive presents;[1] also telling an untruth.

71. Killing worms, winged insects, birds; eating (what) accompanies[2] intoxicating liquor; stealing fruit, firewood, and flowers; and want of (mental)[3] firmness produce defilement.

72. Understand duly the various observances by which all these sins, as they have been declared one after the other, are removed.

73. The slayer of a Brahman should make a hut and live twelve years in a forest, eating food (which has been) given as alms, to purify himself, and making the corpse's head his sign.[4]

74. Or, by his own desire, let him be a mark for those that bear arms (and) know;[5] or cast himself three times headlong into a burning fire;[6]

75. Or let him offer sacrifice with the horse-sacrifice, or with (various sacrifices called) the heaven-subduer, the cow-celebration, the victorious, the all-victorious, or with the threefold (laud) or with the fire-laud;[7]

76. Or, muttering any one of the Vedas, let him go a

[1] *Apātrīkaraṇa*, "making unworthy," is the general meaning.

[2] Vegetables, etc., brought along in the same basket; not, as Medh. says, anything that has been in contact with it, for the penance is too heavy (K.) Medh. adds what K. does not note, "or accompanied by its smell." Cf. Viṣṇu, xli. 3 with Jolly's note.

[3] Medh.

[4] Cf. Āp. i. 25, 11; Vas. xx. 25; Gaut. xxii. This is only for a Brahman who unintentionally slays another Brahman; for according to the Bhaviṣya Purāṇa, the length of time is doubled for a Kṣatriya, trebled for a Vaiçya, and quadrupled for a Çūdra (K.); so Medh. K. also enjoins other restrictions from the same work, and from Yama and Angiras, in regard to the condition of the offender and his intent, none of which are even touched upon in the text. It may be the real head of the man slain or of some one else, or an effigy of it made of wood, as some say (Medh.) This skull is to be carried about on his stick like a banner (Rāgh.)

[5] That is, those who know his wish to be slain (Medh., K.), or know the science of the *Dhanurveda* (*i.e.*, know how to shoot) (Medh.)

[6] Till he die, says Āpast. (K.; but cf. Āp. i. 24). This and the first in vs. 75 is the threefold expiation for a Kṣatriya; also seen from Bhav. Purāṇa. These distinctions are due to the wish to make the sentiments of one authority agree with and amplify another often in fact contradictory.

[7] These are for three castes unintentionally slaying a Brahman, according to Bhav. Pur. (K., Medh.)

hundred yokings[1] to cast from him the slaying of the Brahman, eating moderately, with the organs of sense controlled;

77. Let him present his all to a Brahman (who) knows the Veda or property enough for life, or a house with its furniture;[2]

78. Or, eating sacrificial grains, let him follow up the Sarasvatī, (going) against the stream; or let him with restricted nourishment mutter over a collection of a Veda three times.[3]

79. After his head has been shorn, let him dwell on the border of the town, or in a place of cows, or in a hermitage at the foot of a tree, finding his pleasure in the happiness of cows and Brahmans.[4]

80. For the sake of a cow or for the sake of a Brahman[5] let him give up life at once;[6] the preserver of a cow (or) Brahman is released from the slaying of a Brahman;

81. Or he is released by making resistance (for their sakes) three times at least, or even[7] by recovering possession of all the property of a Brahman, or by loss of life from this cause.[8]

82. Thus always constant to his vow,[9] chaste (in body), and intent (in mind), at the completion of the twelfth year he dissipates the (sin of) slaying a Brahman;

83. Or he is released (from sin) after giving information in regard to his sin at a horse-sacrifice, in an assembly of

[1] The yoking, *yojana* (etymologically *jugerum*, but used as a measure of length), is a distance of about 2½ miles. The whole pilgrimage would be about 250 miles, or, according to another reckoning of this unit, 200 miles. K. says this again is for three castes who slay unintentionally a man who is a Brahman only by birth (Bhav. Pur.); so Medh.

[2] As in vs. 76, with difference in worth of the killer (Bhav. Pur., K.)

[3] Changes to murder of the first degree (Bhav. Pur.) with restrictions (K.) Medh. here notes that the "twelve years" no longer are applicable, and also enumerates the different cases to which each penance applies.

[4] This is distinct from the twelve years' penance and follows it (Medh., K.)

[5] Cf. v. 95. In Medh. *gavārthe* comes first.

[6] *Samyak* (Medh.); *sadyah* (K.) Cf. x. 65.

[7] *Apijitya* (Medh., Nos. 1551, 935, 989).

[8] Viz., dying to defend a Brahman or his property when attacked by robbers (Medh., K.) Cf. Gaut. xxii. 8.

[9] *Vrata*, vow or observance.

earth-gods, (brought together by) men-gods, and after taking the bath of purification.[1]

84. The root of (the system of) right[2] (is said to be) the Brahman; the top is said to be the Kṣatriya; therefore he is rendered pure by proclaiming his sin in an assembly of these men.

85. The Brahman by his origin alone is a thing divine even to the gods; so also (he is) the authority of (men in this) world, for in him (is found) the original source, (which is) the Veda alone.[3]

86. Of these (Brahmans), even three who know the Veda may declare the atonement for sins; and it shall be to them for a purification, since the speech of the wise (is) a purification.

87. Now a Brahman by pursuing either of the rules (for purification, and by being) intent (in mind), removes, through gaining the mastery over himself,[5] the sin caused by slaying a Brahman.

88. One should also practise these observances on having slain an embryo not distinctly known,[6] a Kṣatriya or Vaiçya (who are) offering sacrifice,[7] or a woman while in her courses.[8]

[1] The assembly made by the gods of men (the Kṣatriyas) consists also of the gods of earth (the Brahmans), who are assembled at the horse-sacrifice—the one to provide gifts the others to receive them. This is an independent penance taking the place of that for twelve years mentioned above (Medh., K.), and may be performed whether the other has been begun or not (Medh.) The Bhav. Purāṇa says a bath with sacrifice is for a worthy Brahman killing a worthless one without design, an explanation contradicted by Govind., who says this is the end of the penance completed without the sacrifice, and is to be performed after undertaking the twelve years' penance (K.) Medh. also notes other explanations, as that some say it is left optional like that in vs. 80, after the twelve years are entered on. Cf. Āp. i. 24, 22.

[2] *Dharma.* Kṣatriya, literally "regal."

[3] *Brahma* (Veda) is the source of knowledge. Since the Brahman explains the meaning of the Veda he is the authority, whose word no one doubts (Medh.)

[4] This excludes all secret penance (Medh., K.) Medh. discusses an apparent contradiction in xii. 111–113, where ten or one alone may declare the law as an assembly, but the "one" is not prohibited by *api*, which is not *avara* (at least). If three may, says K., how much more may a greater number? referring doubtless to the same verse.

[5] By knowledge of self (*ātman*) through the *çāstra* (Medh.)

[6] Not known in sex (Medh.)

[7] Medh. limits to those partaking of the great sacrifices, etc.

[8] Cf. Vas. xx. 35; Viṣṇu, l. 7, 9. Medh. says: *Ātreyīm striyam Atrigo-*

89. And even so on having uttered an untruth while giving testimony as a witness, and on having opposed one's Guru, stolen a deposit, or caused the death of a woman or of a friend.[1]

90. Thus is the purification declared (for those who) have slain a twice-born man unintentionally: for killing a Brahman intentionally there is no expiation appointed.[2]

91. A twice-born man having foolishly drunk spirituous liquor,[3] should drink (the same sort of) spirituous liquor (heated) red-hot; after his body has been burned out by it, he is released from that sin.

92. Or he may drink till he die red-hot cow's urine, water alone (thus heated), milk, ghee, or, again, the juice of cow-dung (thus heated).

93. Or he may eat once a night for a year kernels of grain or oil (cakes) to remove (the sin) of drinking spirituous liquor, having a hair-garment, with his locks braided, and bearing a sign.[4]

94. Spirituous liquor (is) indeed (said to be) the defilement of food, and defilement is said (to be) sin;[5] therefore the Brahman, the Kṣatriya, and the Vaiçya should not drink spirituous liquor.

trajātāṁ jāter aviçeṣāt strīpuṁsayor — adding that thence the killing of other women is a secondary crime (cf. vs. 67); but he says that other (commentators) take *ātreyī* as translated in the text (cf. Āp. i. 24, 9; Viṣṇu xxxvi. 1). To prove the *ātreyī* is here a Brahman woman in her courses, K. and Rāgh. quote Yama and Vasiṣṭha (xx. 36), while Aṅgiras gives K. ground for asserting that in vs. 89 is meant the "blameless wife of a Brahman who has the sacred fire." *Ātreyī* means, therefore, as above, a woman (bathing after) having menstrual discharge, or a woman of the race of Atri.

[1] Cf. vs. 57. Medh. and K. say the false testimony is in respect to gold or land, and the deposit, K. says, is one of a Brahman's goods except gold or land, or of gold belonging to those of other castes.

[2] Cf. Gaut. xxi. 7; Āp. i. 24, 25.

[3] "Spirituous liquor," *surā*. K. limits the general *surā* to *paiṣṭī* (vs. 95), after the Bhaviṣya Purāṇa, and often Bṛhaspati restricts the sin to intentional misdemeanour on account of the severity of the punishment (equivalent to death, cf. Āp. i. 25, 3); so too Medh., quoting xi. 147. In the latter point K. is undoubtedly correct.

[4] The sign is, according to K., the sign of a liquor dealer; something of the sort may be intended, but the text is general. K. also says an unintentional sin is here meant. Rāgh. makes it unintentional if the liquor is *paiṣṭī*, and intentional if *gauḍī* or *mādhvī*.

[5] The *mala* (defilement) means either *surā* in respect to food, or sin in general. Kṣatriya (as in vss. 84, 88, 128, etc.) is literally "one of regal (caste)."

95. Spirituous liquor should be known to be of three sorts: that made of sugar (molasses), of ground (rice), and of the (flowers of the) honey-tree;[1] just as each alone, so (are) all, (in that) they must not be drunk by the highest of the twice-born.[2]

96. Intoxicating drinks, meat, (and) *surāsava*[3] (form) the food of Yakṣas, Rakṣas, and Piçācas; this (food) must not be tasted by a Brahman who eats (what is) offered (in sacrifice) to the gods.

97. A Brahman might either fall on (something) impure (when) drunk, or even quote a (passage) belonging to a Veda, or do something else which ought not to be done when confused with drunkenness.

98. If the *brahma* that has entered any man's body is once overflooded with intoxicating drink, the Brahmanhood of that man disappears, and he descends to Çūdrahood.[4]

99. Thus the varied expiation for drinking spirituous liquor is laid down; now, then, I shall furthermore proclaim the expiation for stealing gold.

100. A Brahman (priest) who has committed a theft of gold should say, after approaching the king and declaring his act, "Sir, punish me."[5]

101. The king, seizing a club, should then in person

[1] Some sweet (*madhu*) drink from the flowers of a certain tree; the first two (*gauḍī*, *paiṣṭī*) are rum and arak.

[2] As the worst of these, that made of rice, is forbidden to all castes, so all of them are forbidden to the Brahman (K.); so Medh., who illustrates by an illustration from the Mbhā., where two (Kṣatriya) heroes are *madhvāsarakṣinau dṛṣṭau*.

[3] *Surāsava* is a kind of brandy. According to Pulastya (in K.) there are, beside the drinks of vs. 95, nine other intoxicating liquors; the *surāsava* not being included in the general *madya* (intoxicating drink) on account of its peculiar perniciousness. Medh.'s remarks at verse 92 support K., who here says it is an error of some to suppose that the law means men only as delinquents in drinking offences; the contrary is proved by Yāj. iii. 256 (K.) and Vasiṣṭha xxi. 11 (Medh.)

[4] *Āplāvyate*, over-flooded or drenched with (B. R.); *Brahma* is Veda, from vs. 97 (cf. vs. 122), or perhaps spiritual power.

[5] K. notes that this is gold stolen from a Brahman (so Medh.), as is stated by Çātātapa. Another version was given in viii. 314–316. The text makes the thief a Brahman, but not the injured person. Medh. says "priest" means all castes; K. says it is a type only, meaning any man;—that is to say, the priest is not intended! Cf. Gaut. xii. 43; Baudh. ii. 1, 16–17.

smite him once; the thief is rendered pure by the blow, or a Brahman by ascetic austerity alone.[1]

102. Now a twice-born man desirous of removing by ascetic austerity the defilement produced by stealing gold should, (being) clothed in rags,[2] practise in a forest the observances of one who has slain a Brahman.

103. By these observances a twice-born man should remove the sin caused by theft; but the (sin) caused by having (carnal) intercourse with the wife of the Guru, one should cast (from himself) by the following observances.[3]

104. One who violates the couch of (his) Guru[4] should, after declaring the sin, sleep upon a heated iron (bed), or embrace a red-hot (metal) cylinder;[5] by death he is purified;

105. Or, after himself amputating the penis and scrotum and carrying them in his bent hand, let him advance south-west,[6] going straight on till he falls (in death);

106. Or, carrying a club shaped like a bedpost (as a weapon),[7] clothed in rags,[8] with beard unshorn, in a deserted wood, let him, intent in mind, perform for one year the (*kṛcchra*) penance of Prajāpati;

107. Or, to remove (the sin of violating his) Guru's

[1] K. (Bengal MS.) has *vā*, "or," while other MSS. contain *tu*, so the Calcutta edition, and Medh. (Nos. 1551, 935). K.'s gloss shows *vā* to be his reading. If these two verses have any connection, the *brāhmaṇaḥ* of vs. 101 ought to represent the *vipraḥ* of vs. 100, in which case there is no opposition, but apposition in *steno brāhmaṇaḥ*, and the true meaning would be "the thief, (viz.) the Brahman, is purified by the blow, or even by austerity alone." This is, however, repugnant to the explanation of K., who has to reconcile this with viii. 380, which were not possible with the *vadha* (blow, resulting perhaps in death) impending over a Brahman. The Bhaviṣya Purāṇa aids him in his exposition. The *legal* punishment is put in here apparently by recollections of the law in viii. The *penance* is alone wanted, like that of the other great crimes, and the king's entrance is here really out of place, this representing a side with which the present portion of the work has nothing to do. Cf. Viṣṇu lii. 1-3.

[2] Or, "in bark."

[3] Cf. vs. 170, where this is repeated.

[4] K., "father." The Guru *may* always be the father, but not necessarily. Cf. Āp. i. 25, 1 ff., and i. 28, 15-16; Gaut. xxiii. 10; Vas. xx. 13; Baudh. ii. 1, 13 ff.

[5] Medh. and K. understand a metal image of a woman.

[6] Literally, "to the district of Nirṛti," genius of destruction; also, south-west.

[7] The weapon of Çiva.

[8] Or, "in bark." The penalty shows an unintentional sin is meant (Medh., K.)

couch, let him, with organs of sense restrained, practise for three months the moon-course (vow), by (eating such) grains (as are used) for sacrifice or weak barley-broth.

108. By these observances the great criminals may remove (their) guilt; and those likewise who commit the secondary crimes [1] (may expiate their sin) by the following observances of various kinds.

109. One who has contracted (the guilt of) a secondary crime (by) killing a cow should drink barley-(broth) [2] a month; having been shorn, let him dwell in the place of cows [3] enwrapped in that (cow's) hide.

110. Or [4] he should eat, at the fourth (meal)-time (only, food) without salt (and) moderate (in quantity), (and also) practise bathing [5] with cow's urine for two months, with the organs of sense restrained.

111. And by day let him follow after these cows; standing, let him drink the dust (they make) as it rises; showing them obedience and reverence by night, let him abide by the posture called manly.[6]

112. Let him stand behind them as they stand, and advance behind them as they advance, reclining,[7] too, when they recline; being restrained, and having selfish thoughts dispersed.

113. By all possible means [8] let him release (a cow that is) unwell, or threatened [9] by fear of robbers, tigers, etc., or one that is fallen or stuck in the mud;

114. In heat, rain, or cold, or when the wind blows strongly,[10] let him not make a shelter for himself before making (one) as best he can for the cow.

[1] Cf. vs. 67 and preceding.

[2] Or pounded grains, according to some, but grains without water one cannot drink (Medh.)

[3] The place of cows is where they pasture.

[4] Medh. Vss. 110–112 include one penance for the two months (Medh.)

[5] Bathing refers to the feet only (Medh.)

[6] An ascetic posture, literally "sitting;" the locative in Medh.

[7] Or, "let him recline," according to another reading (Medh., Nos. 935, 989, and Rāgh.)

[8] Or, "by (giving up his) life," according to Medh. and Rāgh. (*prāṇaiḥ* for *upāyaiḥ*).

[9] B.R. So Medh. (*gṛhītā*), "seized with fear caused by robbers," etc., though reading *abhiṣaktām*.

[10] Medh. connects with all; in fiercely (burning) heat, etc. Cf. iv. 122.

115. Let him not tell of (a cow) that eats or a calf that drinks in house, field, or threshing-floor, either of himself or of others.

116. Now if any man after killing a cow follows after the cows[1] in accordance with this rule, he removes in three months the sin caused by slaughtering the cow;

117. And, having strictly performed these observances,[2] he should give ten cows and a bull to those wise in the Veda; in case he has (them) not in his possession, he should bestow all he has.[3]

118. The twice-born who have (committed) secondary crimes, excepting him who breaks a vow of chastity, should perform this observance only in order to purify (themselves); or (they may) even (practise) the moon-course penance.[4]

119. But one who breaks a vow of chastity should make a sacrifice to Nirṛti by night, according to the rule for the house-sacrifice,[5] with a one-eyed[6] ass at a place where four roads meet;

120. Offering upon the fire the oblations according to rule, and at the end (of the ceremony), with the text beginning "Along with," let him offer oblations with melted butter to the wind, to Indra, to the Guru (Bṛhaspati), and to the Bearer (of sacrifice, viz., Fire).[7]

121. Those who know the rules of right, those who declare the Veda, call an effusion of seed on purpose by one twice-born and under the vow (of chastity) a violation of (that) vow.

122. The Brahmanic[8] glory of one who thus breaks a

[1] Medh., *gā anu*, etc.

[2] *Vrata*, or "having well performed his vow."

[3] Commutation to a money-fine is allowed by Rāgh.

[4] The verse is metrically defective, but none of the *var. lec.* found in the MSS. give a good reading.

[5] With the *pākayajña* rites; cf. ii. 86. Tait. Ār. ii. 18; I. S. x. 102; cf. Gaut. xxiii. 17; Vas. xxiii. 1–2; Āp. i. 26, 8 (Bühler's note).

[6] Or "black," according to a few MSS.

[7] *Kṛtvā* (Medh.), *hutvā* (K., Rāgh.) K. gives the first two words *samāsiñcantu māruta iti*; cf. Boht. Melanges Asiat. (R. V. vi. 49, 5), and one like K.'s in Yāj. iii. 282. Medh. and K. define the Guru as Bṛhaspati.

[8] Glory gained by restraint and reading the Veda (*brahma*); hence Brahmanic or Vedic glory (K.) Cf. Gaut. xxv. 2.

vow of chastity departs to the four (who) observe vows, viz., the Wind, the Much-called One (Indra), the Guru (Bṛhaspati), and the Purifier (Fire).

123. If this sin occurs, let (the sinner) clothe himself in the hide of an ass and go a-begging at seven houses, making known his act.

124. By eating the (food) received by begging from these (seven houses) once a day (only), and rinsing his mouth morning, noon, and night, he is made pure in the course of a year.[1]

125. On having voluntarily performed any act which causes loss of caste,[2] one should practise the (so-called) heating[3] penance, (or, if he has done it) involuntarily, (the penance) of Prajāpati.

126. In (the case of) acts which produce mixture (of castes), or make one unfit to receive presents, (one should practise) for a month the purification (regulated by) the moon;[4] in (the case of) acts productive of defilement, one should be burned three days (by drinking hot) barley (and water).[5]

127. In the murder of a Kṣatriya, one-fourth (part) of (the penance for) slaying a Brahman is declared (to be the proper penance); an eighth part (in the case of) a Vaiçya; and in (the case of) a Çūdra (who) lives virtuously, one-sixteenth part must be admitted (as the proper penance).[6]

128. But if one of the highest of the twice-born (a Brahman) slay a Kṣatriya involuntarily, he may, in order to cleanse himself,[7] give a thousand cows and a bull.[8]

129. Or let him for three years, (with senses) subdued

[1] Cf. vi. 24 (Dr. Burnell's translation) and vs. 217; literally, "three times," *i.e.*, morn, noon, and eve. Cf. Āp. i. 28, 19 (another crime).

[2] Such as in vs. 68 (K.)

[3] *Sāntapana kṛcchra.*

[4] Called generally the moon-course penance.

[5] K. refers in explanation of these respective acts to vss. 67, 70, 71.

[6] Cf. Gaut. xxii. 14; Vas. xx. 31 ff.

[7] K. Or (*var. lec.*), "having well performed his vow," as in vs. 117. Medh. gives the reading adopted by Lois. Desl., *çuddhyartham ātmanaḥ.*

[8] Give to the Brahmans (K.) Cf. Āp. i. 24, 1 ff.

and locks braided, follow the observance of one who has slain a Brahman,[1] living in (a place) rather far from the town, his dwelling-place the foot of a tree.

130. The highest of the twice-born (the Brahman) should practise just this expiation for a year on having slain a Vaiçya who lives virtuously, and[2] give one hundred and one (heads) of cattle.

131. The slayer of a Çūdra should practise exactly all this observance for six months; or he may give to a priest ten white cows and a bull.

132. On killing a cat, an ichneumon, a daw, or a frog, a dog, a lizard, an owl, or a crow, he should practise the observance (ordained for) killing a Çūdra;[3]

133. Or let him drink milk for three nights, or go a journey of a yoking,[4] or sprinkle himself in a stream, or mutter the text addressed to the divinity of the water.[5]

134. The highest of the twice-born (the Brahman), on slaying a snake, should give an iron-(pointed) staff;[6] in (case he kills) a eunuch,[7] a load of straw and a *māṣaka* of lead.

135. In (case he kills) a boar, a pot of ghee; in (case he kills) a partridge, a measure of sesame; in (case he kills) a parrot, a two-year calf; on killing a plover, a three-year (calf).

136. He must give a cow to a Brahman on killing a flamingo, crane (*balāka*), heron, peacock, ape, eagle,[8] or kite.

137. He must give clothes on killing a horse; five black bulls (on killing) an elephant; a steer (on kill-

[1] Cf. vs. 73.

[2] = "Or" (K.); Medh. has "but" (*tu*). Probably "or" is the meaning of *and* here; and the one hundred and one cattle are probably, as in the other cases, all cows, but one bull.

[3] If killed purposely (K.) Cf. Vas. xxi. 24 ff., and Viṣṇu l. 30 ff.; Yāj. iii. 270 ff.

[4] Cf. vs. 76.

[5] Cf. viii. 106 (R. V. x. 9, 1-13). This is for an unintentional act; if he cannot perform the former, he should do each succeeding penance in order (K.)

[6] Medh. and K.; or, perhaps, a hoe or pickaxe. Cf. Viṣṇu, l. 31.

[7] "Emasculated cattle," according to the interpretation of the commentator to Viṣṇu l. 35, but not thus Medh. or K.

[8] Or hawk (*çyena*).

ing) a goat (or) sheep; a one-year (calf) (on killing) an ass.[1]

138. On killing (forest) animals that eat raw flesh, he should give a milch-cow; (on killing animals) that do not eat raw flesh, a weaned calf; on killing a camel, a *kṛṣṇala*.[2]

139. On killing a woman of any of the four castes untrue (to her husband), he must give for purification a leather sack,[3] a bow, a he-goat, and a sheep, according to the caste.

140. A twice-born man, being unable to expiate the death of a snake and the other (creatures) by a gift, may perform in each case a penance[4] in order to remove the evil.

141. One should practise the observance (ordained) for killing a Çūdra on slaying a thousand animals which have bones, or on (slaying) a waggon-full of boneless (animals).[5]

142. But on killing animals with bones he should give some trifle[6] to a Brahman; while for slaying boneless (animals),[7] he is purified by suppressing the breath.[8]

143. And a hundred (repetitions of a) Vedic text must be muttered on cutting[9] trees which bear fruit, and (for cutting) bushes, vines, creepers, and plants which have blossoms.

144. And under all circumstances (on causing the death) of creatures born in rice-food, and of (those) born in liquids,[10] and of those of which the origin is from a fruit or flower, the purification (is) tasting ghee.

[1] K.

[2] Medh. and K. say this is a *rattikā* of gold; cf. viii. 134.

[3] Nos. 1551, 989, MS. Medh. have *jāla*, corrected (in Nos. 935 and margin No. 989) *jīrṇa*, defined as in K.; also sing. *narīm . . . anavasthitām*. Medh. gives a note on *hatvā* (killing), saying, "some here read *gatvā*," *i.e.*, "on committing adultery with a woman," etc. He observes, however, that this reading is not countenanced by the connection.

[4] Medh. and K. explain *kṛcchra* here as the "penance of Prajāpati."

[5] As *matkuṇa*, "bugs" (K.) Cf. Viṣṇu l. 46 ff.; Gaut. xxii. 20.

[6] K. (from a text of Sumantu) says one *paṇa*.

[7] Mosquitoes, etc. (Medh.)

[8] The suppression of breath defined by Vasiṣṭha (xxv. 13) is to repeat thrice with the Çiras (verses) the *gāyatrī* with *vyāhṛtis* and Om, the breath being held back (K.; so Rāgh.)

[9] So as to destroy them. Some say this is even for cutting wood as firewood (Medh.), but Medh. and K. dissent. According to Medh., the creepers are themselves branches of trees (*latā vṛkṣaçākhā*).

[10] Molasses, etc. (Medh., K.)

145. On pulling up for no purpose cultivated (medicinal) plants, and those that grow of themselves in a wood, one should follow after a cow for one day, performing the observance (of living on) milk (only).[1]

146. All the sin, whether caused wittingly or unwittingly, produced by destroying (animals or plants) may be removed by these observances: hear (the expiation) for eating things one should not eat.

147. On drinking brandy unwittingly one is purified by initiation[2] alone; (if one drinks) intentionally, the death penalty is not to be set:[3] so stands the rule.

148. On drinking water standing in a vessel (used) for spirituous liquors (*surā*), and (water which) has been put into a jar (used) for any intoxicating drink (*madya*),[4] one should for five nights drink milk cooked with the shell-plant.

149. On touching and on bestowing intoxicating stuff, on receiving it with the ordinary formula,[5] and on drinking water left by a Çūdra, one should drink *kuça*-water for three days.

150. Now a *soma*-drinking Brahman, on sniffing the odour of a spirit-drinking (man), is purified (by) drinking ghee (while) thrice suppressing his breath in water.[6]

151. The three twice-born castes should receive initiation a second time on unwittingly eating of fæces or urine, or (anything which has been) merely touched by spirituous liquor.

[1] Literally, having the milk-observance (or vow); Yāj. iii. 276, *kṣīrāçin*, for the same offence supplies the meaning. The offence is cutting down (analogous with Yāj.) or pulling up. Medh. reads *vṛthārambhe*, *i.e.*, "cutting without intending it for a cow," etc.

[2] K. quotes from Gautama (xxiii. 2) and the Bhaviṣya Purāṇa to show that before initiation there is a penance. Special kinds of the drink (*vāruṇī*, brandy) are intended in (*a*), viz., the first and third in vs. 95. The lighter penance in vs. 93 is enjoined, not that preceding (where the offence is for drinking *surā*, including the three of vs. 95).

[3] In regard to this, see vs. 91 and note.

[4] The *surā* in (*a*) K. limits to spirits of rice, and the *madya* is any other spirit. No difference is implied between that drunk wittingly or unwittingly. Cf. Viṣṇu li. 23.

[5] *Vidhivat*, according to rule, means taking it after saying, "It is well" (K.)

[6] Cf. Gaut. xxiii. 6.

152. But when this ceremony of initiation (is thus performed) for the second time, the shaving (of the head), the sacred cord, the staff, the begging for food (as performed by a religious mendicant), and the (various) religious vows do not take place.[1]

153. On devouring the food of those whose food one ought not to eat, and (food) left by a woman or a Çūdra, and (such) flesh (as) ought not to be eaten, one should drink (water and) barley for seven nights.

154. On drinking sour (juices of fruit) and distilled liquids (causing puckering), even if (regarded as) pure, a twice-born man remains unfit (for his duties)[2] so long as that (which he has drunk) does not pass down.[3]

155. A twice-born man should practise the moon-course (penance) on tasting of the urine or fæces of a pig belonging to the house,[4] of an ass, or of a camel, of a jackal, of an ape, and of a crow.

156. On eating dry flesh, mushrooms that grow on the ground,[5] and (anything) belonging to a slaughter-house, even if (the source was) unknown, one should practise the same observance.

157. On eating (the meat) of animals that eat raw flesh, (on eating the meat) of boars, camels, and hens, also of men, crows, and asses, the hot penance[6] is the purification.

158. The twice-born man who, before completing the time of study,[7] eats the food (given) in the monthly (sacrifice, *i.e.*, *çrāddha*), should fast three days, or[8] stay one day in water.

[1] The various observances which, like the acts mentioned, are performed at the first initiation (Medh.) This is quoted as Manu's rule by Vas. xx. 18; cf. Viṣṇu li. 5.

[2] Or, simply impure (Medh., K.)

[3] That is, as long as it remains in him.

[4] Cf. v. 19, from which this case, implying an unintentional act, differs.

[5] This rule, therefore, does not forbid one eating mushrooms that grow in the hollow of a tree (Medh.) Yama forbids both the earth-born and the tree-born (K.)

[6] *Taptakṛcchra*, explained in vs. 215.

[7] *Asamāvṛttika* (Medh.)

[8] *Vā* (Medh.), *ca* (K.), "at the end of his fast." Whether the partaking of the funeral feast is done by request or no is not touched upon by the text, but, according to Medh., is a question disputed by "some." Cf. Viṣṇu li. 43 ff.

159. That student who at any time eats honey (or) meat should complete the rest of his sacred observances (only) after performing the common penance.[1]

160. On devouring what has been left by a cat, a crow, a mouse, a dog, an ichneumon, or anything on which a hair-louse has fallen, one should drink (the plant) holy rue[2] (in water).

161. By one who seeks purity of soul that which ought not to be eaten should not be eaten, but (that which, being impure, has) been eaten unwittingly should be cast up, or, (if this is impossible), purification should be made at once by some expiatory means.[3]

162. Thus is declared the manifold rule of observances in respect of eating what ought not to be eaten. Let the rule of observances which take away crimes of theft be (now) heard.

163. One of the highest of the twice-born having purposely made thefts of grain, food, or property from a house of his own caste, is purified by a year's penance.[4]

164. And[5] for a theft of men, of women, of land, of a house, or of the waters of a (sacred) pool or pond, the moon-course (penance) is said to be the purification.

165. On making a theft from another's house of articles whose worth is small, one should, to purify himself, perform the burning penance,[6] after returning that (which he has stolen).[7]

166. For a theft of (sweet) eatables and (milk) food,[8] of a waggon, a couch, a seat, and of flowers, roots, and fruits,

[1] Viz., that of Prajāpati (Medh., K.) Cf. Āp. i. 4, 5–6; Vas. xxiii. 11–13.

[2] *Brahma suvarcatā.* The penance is for one day (Medh.)

[3] Some say that *çodhanāni* here means laxatives which he is to take (instead of vomiting)—(Medh.) Cf. Gaut. xxiii. 26.

[4] *Kṛcchra, i.e.,* the penance of Prajāpati (K.)

[5] *Ca* (Medh.) "Men and women" means slaves (Medh.)

[6] *Sāntapana* (*kṛcchra*).

[7] If he cannot return it the penance must be doubled (Medh.) The things meant are wooden pots, etc., as distinguished from iron.

[8] Medh. and K. divide: *bhakṣya*, are things pleasant to eat (as *çaṣkuli*) and *bhojya* as milk food (K.)

the purification (consists of) the five things belonging to a cow.[1]

167. (For a theft) of grass, wood, trees, dry food,[2] molasses, clothes, armour,[3] or flesh, there should be a fast for three nights.

168. Eating dry kernels of grain for twelve days (is the purification enjoined for stealing) gems, pearls, coral, copper, silver, iron, brass, or stone.

169. (Drinking) milk (only) for three days (is the purification enjoined for stealing) cotton, silk, wool, (animals) with cloven or single hoofs, birds, perfumes, (medicinal) plants, or a rope.[4]

170. A twice-born man should by these observances remove the sin caused by theft; but the (sin) caused by having (carnal) intercourse with those with whom one ought not to have intercourse he should cast from him by the following observances:

171. On having carnal intercourse with women who have the same mother (as oneself), one should perform the observance (enjoined) for (violation of) the couch of a Guru; also (on committing the same offence) with the wives of one's friend or of one's son, and with maids (or) low-born (women).[5]

172. On having (carnal) intercourse with her (who is equal to) a sister, (being) a (daughter) of one's father's sister, or a daughter of the sister of the mother, or a daughter of one's mother's brother, one should practise the moon-course penance.[6]

173. A wise man should not take (any one of) these

[1] Drinking-milk, sour-milk, butter, urine, and fæces. This is to last for one day (Medh.) Cf. Viṣṇu l. 23.

[2] Rice-corn, etc. (K.), or food without oleaginous matter (*anupalepanam*)—(Medh.)

[3] *Varma; kavacam* (Medh.) Leather, *carma* (K.)

[4] A well-rope is meant (Medh.) Cf. Viṣṇu lii. 11–13.

[5] Cf. vs. 104 ff. and cf. vs. 59. K.'s quotation from Yama enjoins death even in the case of wives of general *sapiṇḍa.* Cf. Gaut. xxiii. 12. By women who have the same mother, sisters are meant.

[6] The lightness of the penalty shows that the offence has been committed but once, and that unintentionally (K.) Medh. reads *āptasya* (= °*sodaryasya*) for *tanayām*, which he supplies.

three women to wife; they should not be (carnally) approached because of the kinship (with them), for he who has (carnal) intercourse (with them) falls down (to hell).[1]

174. If a man has expended his seed on females not belonging to the human (species), on a woman in her courses, elsewhere than in the female part, or (cohabited with a woman) in water, he should perform the burning penance.[2]

175. Now if a twice-born man practise carnal intercourse with a man or with a woman in a waggon (drawn) by cows, in water, and also (if he do it) by day, he should perform (the penance of) bathing with his clothes on.[3]

176. On having (carnal) intercourse with Cāṇḍala women or low-(born) women, on eating (their food) or receiving (presents from them), a Brahman, (if he has done so) unwittingly, falls; but (if he has done so) wittingly, he comes to an equality (with them).[4]

177. A wife who is very corrupt the husband should confine to a single house, and make her perform the same penance as (is enjoined) for a man (who has carnal intercourse) with another's wife.[5]

178. But[6] if she sins a second time, being seduced by a man of like (family), the simple penance (*kṛcchra*) and (in addition) the moon-course (penance) also is said to be that which gives her purification.[7]

[1] Medh.

[2] *Santāpana* (*kṛcchra*); the animals are a mare, etc.; for a like sin with the (sacred) cow Çankha and others ordain a heavier penance (K.)

[3] K. modifies the text only by making the rule apply to any circumstances in the case of a man, and limiting the case of a woman to the following expression, "in a waggon." Cf. Yāj. iii. 288–291.

[4] In the first case he should perform the penance of one degraded, but from the severity of the penance the receiving of presents and eating apply to cases done repeatedly (K.) Cf. with the above Viṣṇu liii.

[5] This is where the offence is done purposely, while Vasiṣṭha's rule (*strīṇām arddhaṁ pradātavyam*) is where the crime has been committed without intention (K.) In ix. 71 the man may desert the girl whom he has taken and finds "very corrupt," but this may be before marriage. The question of what this penance is must be answered according to the offender's caste; this is explained at length by Medh., while K. says simply "of one's own caste." The text itself ignores caste and differences of penance in consequence. Cf. Vas. xxi. 6–15, and xxviii. 2–3, also Viṣṇu liv. 33.

[6] Medh. reads *praduṣyeta* and *anumantritā* (*prārthitā*).

[7] *Kṛcchra*, *i.e.* of Prajāpati (K.)

179. That (sin) which a twice-born man commits by having carnal intercourse with a Vṛṣala woman for one night, he removes in the course of three years by eating constantly what is given in alms and muttering (holy texts).[1]

180. This is the expiation declared for the four (kinds of) evil-doers;[2] hear the following expiations for such as have connection with those who are fallen.

181. In the course of a year a man falls on associating with a fallen man; not by performing sacrifices[3] (for him), by giving (him) instruction, (or) by forming a marriage connection (with him), but by riding, sitting, (or) eating (with him).

182. If any man have intercourse with any one of those who have fallen (into sin), he should perform the penance of this same man to expiate (the sin of) intercourse with him.[4]

183. A water (libation) must be made for a fallen man

In explaining the "like family," which includes different penances for different degrees of relationship, Medh. quotes and explains the following verses without saying whence the list comes (similar to ii. 131): *Mātā mātṛṣvasā çvaçrur mātulānī pitṛṣvasā / pitṛvyasakhiçiṣyastrī bhaginī tatsakhīsnuṣā // duhitā cāryabhāryā ca sagotrā çaraṇāgatā / rājñī pravrajitā sādhvī dhātrī varṇottamā ca yā //.* All these degrees have to be arranged for according to the later scheme; in the time of the text the general rule probably sufficed.

[1] Cf. iii. 19, where "there is no expiation" enjoined for a similar act. K. quotes Āp. (i. 27, 11), where the words may mean "serving the black race." Cf. Baudh. ii. 2, 11; Vas. i. 22; Viṣṇu liii. 9, and xxxv. 3–5. Govind. limits it to unmarried Çūdra women (K.).

[2] Viz., those who kill, eat forbidden food, steal, and have carnal intercourse (K.)

[3] Or, "falls by performing sacrifice, etc., but not by riding, etc." K. notices two interpretations of the negative, one his own, supported by quotations from Devala, Viṣṇu (*loc. cit.*) and Baudhāyana, to the effect that the group "performing sacrifice," etc., causes degradation, *not* in a year, but at once, while degradation in a year's time is caused by "riding," etc.; the other opinion, that of Govindarāja, which K. scornfully discards, is that degradation in a year is caused by the first group, the second group, being lighter crimes, does not cause degradation till a longer period has elapsed. From the position of the words, the latter seems the sense, but Medh. and K. both support the former, and this has been followed in the translation, which, preserving the order of the original, would be: "In a year falls one associating with a fallen man through sacrifice, etc., not, however, through riding, etc." Cf. the references above and Baudh. ii. 2, 35. The "fallen one" is comprehensively used to embrace the four criminals of vs. 180 (Medh.)

[4] *Saṁsargasya çuddhaye* (Medh.)

by (his) *sapiṇḍas* (and distant) connections, outside (the town), on an unlucky day, in the evening, in the presence of a relative, a sacrificial priest (*ṛtvig*) and Guru.[1]

184. A female slave should, as if for the dead, overthrow with her foot a full waterpot; they, the *sapiṇḍas*, together with the (distant) connections, must remain impure a day and a night.

185. Now, too, must cease with this man conversation and sitting together, delivery of inherited property and the like, and indeed, also, (all) social intercourse.[2]

186. And (his right of) primogeniture must cease, together with the property[3] which falls to the eldest; and (his) younger (brother who) surpasses him in (good) qualities shall take this man's share-of-the-eldest.

187. But when the penance has been performed, they[4] should overthrow a new jar full of water, after bathing along with this same man in a pure pool.[5]

188. Then, after he has flung that jar into the water and returned to his own abode, he may perform, as before, all (the acts which) one related by blood has to perform.[6]

189. One should follow just the same rule also in (the case of) women fallen (from caste); but clothes, food, and drink should be given them, and they may live in the vicinity of the house.[7]

[1] K. says this relates to a great criminal, for whom, although living, the water-oblation of the dead is offered; for *sapiṇḍas* and connections (K., *samānodaka;* Medh., *sagotra*) see v. 60.

[2] Such as inquiring in regard to his health when meeting him (Medh.), or sending him an invitation at New Year's (K.)

[3] Medh. reads *vasu* for *dhanam*. Medh. alludes to a dispute as to whether the property be that of an undivided family, and what the real meaning of the property of the eldest may be. From the ordinary use in the text the *dhana* or *vasu* would be the inherited property, and the "share" is that added portion (lying outside the property divided among brothers) kept exclusively for the eldest.

[4] This is done by the man himself, not by the slave (as in vs. 184) (Medh.)

[5] Or, holy, sacred stream (Medh.); literally, a "place for water."

[6] All the obligations incumbent on a relative.

[7] The last clause indicates, perhaps, a milder punishment for women; it is not that they *must*, but they *may* live near their former home. This is for women even before performing penance; some say it is only women who have performed penance that receive these gifts; that is wrong (Medh.)

190. One should not have anything to do with sinners (who) have not washed away (their guilt); one should also at no time seek to avoid those who have performed the ablution (of their guilt).

191. One should not live with (such as) slay children and destroy (kindnesses) done to them,[1] nor with (such as) kill those who have sought their protection, nor with (such as) slay women, even if (these sinners) have been properly purified.

192. One should cause those twice-born men to whom the *gāyatrī* has not, according to rule, been repeated to perform three (common) penances,[2] and then have them placed under (a teacher) according to rule.[3]

193. And for those twice-born men who have committed a wrong and desire an expiatory penance, and for those who have given up the Veda,[4] one should ordain the same penance.

194. If Brahmans obtain any property by (means of) a forbidden act, they are purified by giving up this property), by muttering (holy texts), and by austerity also.

195. (By) muttering with minds intent three thousand (repetitions) of the *gāyatrī*,[5] (and by) drinking milk within the place of cows for a month, one is freed from (the sin of) receiving (presents) from a bad man.

196. Now this man, (after he has) returned from the place of cows, thin with fasting and bowed (before them),[6] they should address with the question, "Worthy man, desirest thou equality (with us)?"

[1] That is, those who, by forgetting (kindnesses) done to them, prove themselves thankless. Cf. Viṣṇu liv. 31 ff. This sin of forgetting favours is in the Mbhā. (xii. 172, 25) declared to be one for which no expiation is permitted.

[2] *Kṛcchra*.

[3] Yāj. (i. 37-38) provides a "Vrātya-sacrifice" as preventive of falling from the *sāvitrī* (rights of caste) for those who are not properly initiated at the right time. The *kṛcchra* is the penance of Prajāpati (K.) *After the penances have been performed* they are to be initiated (Medh.)

[4] (*Brahma*), *i.e.*, those who have not perused or have allowed themselves to forget the Veda (Medh., K.)

[5] Some say three thousand repetitions a day, some say a month, *i.e.*, one hundred a day (Medh.) For these secret penances cf. Gaut. xxiv.; Vas. xxv.; Yāj. iii. 300 ff.; Viṣṇu lv., etc.

[6] Resting on his knees (Medh.)

197. After he has said to the Brahmans "(Such is) the truth," he should scatter grass for the cows, and in the holy place[1] made by the cows they should consummate his readmission (among them).

198. By three simple penances[2] (*kṛcchra*) one removes (the sins caused by) performing either a sacrifice for Vrātyas, the last offices for strangers, magic rites, or the (sacrifice) of several days.[3]

199. A twice-born man (by) eating barley-grains for a year dissipates that sin (which is caused by) deserting a man who has sought refuge (with him) or (caused by) spreading abroad the Veda.

200. On being bitten by a dog, jackal, or ass, by village animals that eat raw flesh,[4] or by men, horses, camels, and boars, one is purified by suppressing the breath.

201. The regular purification of (such as are) not fit to enter the society of respectable people[5] is to eat for a month at the sixth meal-time only,[6] and[7] to repeat a collection of the Veda, and to make the oblation of the Çākalas.[8]

202. Now a Brahman, on having voluntarily mounted upon a waggon (drawn by) a camel, or a waggon (drawn

[1] *Tīrtha;* the idea is that the place is made holy by the cows eating the grass there given them (K.) *Tīrtha* is generally the sacred pool where cows and pilgrims drink; so Medh.: "At the crossing-place of the *tīrtha*, by the path where the cows go to drink the water of the river." Assuming this sense, the passage would be, "At the *tīrtha* used by the cows" (*viprebhyaḥ* in Medh.)

[2] The verb in some MSS. is "one is purified;" so Medh. (Nos. 935, 989).

[3] One should not officiate at the burning of the corpses of strangers, should not practise the incantations (of the Atharva, etc.), and should not perform the Ahīna (sacrifice of several days, "of two nights and more"—Medh.), which, according to the Çruti, causes impurity (K.) Cf. I. S. x. 355. In ix. 290 the legal penalty for bewitching is given (cf. xi. 64). All kinds of injury are hereby forbidden, either by bewitching enemies to death or by destroying fruits, etc., and the verse applies to the officiating priest (Medh.) The ceremony mentioned by the commentators is the famous "hawk-sacrifice."

[4] Such as cats, etc. (Medh.) Cf. Gaut. xxiii. 7; Vas. xxiii. 31.

[5] Apāṅktya.

[6] Once in three days.

[7] Medh., *ca* (so Rāgh.)

[8] Eight texts beginning with the one, "Thou art the expiatory sacrifice" (K.); so Medh. and Gov., but others give four; cf. Gaut. xxv. 10. (*Devakṛtasya'ty* (V. S. viii. 13) *ādibhir mantrair hūyate, sa çākalahomaḥ* (Medh.): *aṣṭau kāṣṭhaçakalahomāḥ*, Gov. Cf. vs. 257.

by) an ass, or on having bathed clothed by the air alone,[1] is purified by a suppression of the breath.

203. One who in distress emits[2] fæces without water (near), or in water, is purified (by) immersing himself with (his) clothes on outside (the village, and by) touching a cow.

204. Fasting is the expiatory penance on neglecting the regular ceremonies declared in the Veda, and on failing[3] in the observances of a student returned home.[4]

205. On saying "Hum!"[5] to a Brahman, and on (saying) "Thou" to one more venerable (than himself), one should appease (the one insulted by) saluting (him), after bathing and fasting the rest of the day.

206. On striking (him) even with grass, or on tying (him) by the neck with a cloth, or on overcoming (him) in a discussion, one should appease (the injured Brahman by) falling down before (him).[6]

207. Now on threatening (to strike), and on (really) striking with the desire of killing a Brahman, one goes to hell for a hundred years and for a thousand (years respectively).

208. As many (as are) the (grains of) dust (which) the blood of the twice-born man gathers up, so many thousand years shall its shedder remain in hell.[7]

209. On threatening (to strike a Brahman) one should perform the simple penance, and the extra-penance on knocking (him) down. One should perform (both simple) penance and extra-penance on drawing (a Brahman's) blood.[8]

[1] Stark naked.

[2] *Sannişevya tu* (for *sanniveçya ca*), Medh. (Nos. 1551, 989, 935).

[3] For one day (Medh., K.)

[4] A Brahman who has just completed his studentship or is a householder.

[5] *I.e.*, be quiet, stand still! (K.); *hūm* (*sic*) expresses anger or disdain (Medh.)

[6] Cf. iv. 165–169. Cf. Viṣṇu liv. 30.

[7] With 206–208 cf. iv. 165–169. Medh. has for *mahītale* (°*lāt*) with the Beng. MS. *drijanmanaḥ*, or *var. lec.*, "the blood collects on the ground;" or, like iv. 168, "from the ground." I suppose K.'s *bhūmau* is, like Medh.'s, an addition to the text, and he reads *dvijanmanaḥ*, paraphrasing in Medh.'s words *brāhmaṇasya rudhiram*.

[8] (Simple) penance, *kṛcchra*; extra-penance, *ati-kṛcchra*.

210. Now to remove sins for which no expiation has been declared,[1] one should ordain an expiatory penance, after considering both the ability (of the sinner) and the sin (he committed).[2]

211. I will explain to you those means practised by gods, seers, and manes through which a man[3] casts off crimes.

212. A twice-born man practising the penance of Prajāpati must eat for three days in the morning (only), for three days in the evening (only), for three days (what has been given him as alms) unasked, and for another three days he must not eat (at all).[4]

213. The burning penance[5] is said (to consist of) cow-urine, cow-dung, milk, sour milk, melted butter, *kuça*-water, and a one night's fast.

214. A twice-born man practising the extra-penance[7] should eat one mouthful every day (for) three (times) three days as before,[8] and the last three days he should fast.

215. A Brahman practising the hot penance[9] should drink for three days each hot water, milk, ghee, and air;[10] bathing once with (mind) intent.

216. A twelve days' fast by a man self-restrained and

[1] That is simply, "if the law has not provided an expiation," not "if the law admits none," as in vs. 90.

[2] The kind of sin and circumstances under which it was done (K.)

[3] Of any caste (Medh.)

[4] This Prajāpati or simple twelve-day penance is usually designated as "the penance" (*kṛcchra*) in the text. Cf. Āp. i. 27, 7; Viṣṇu xlvi. 10 ff.

[5] (*Kṛcchraṁ*) *sāntapanam.*

[6] These things are mixed together and eaten during one day without other food being eaten; then follows a fast of one day and night. If the fast continues seven days it is called by Yāj. the great burning penance (iii. 316)—(K.) Others say they are eaten separately (Medh.)

[7] *Ati-kṛcchra.* Cf. Vas. xxiv. 1 ff.

[8] "As before," *i.e.*, as directed in vs. 212; the added severity is in eating but a mouthful a day.

[9] *Taptakṛcchra.*

[10] But see B. R. Parāçara says the quantity of milk to be drunk is three times that of ghee, and the quantity of water twice that of milk (K.; *i.e.*, six *pala* of water, three of milk, and one of ghee). K. makes the penance one of twelve days, three days each devoted to hot water, milk, ghee, air. Yāj. iii. 318 gives one day each of water, ghee, milk, and a day's fast (like vs. 213). Medh. gives a verse which coincides with the fourfold division: *apāṁ pibet tu tripalam, palam ekaṁ tu sarpiṣaḥ, payaḥ pibet tu dvipalaṁ, tripalam, vo'ṣṇamārutān.* Cf. Viṣṇu, xxiii. 2.

not inattentive (constitutes) the penance (called) Parāka[1] by name, (which) removes all sin.[2]

217. When one diminishes (his food by) one mouthful (a day) in the dark (half of the month), and increases (it) in the bright (half in the same way), bathing three times a day,[3] this is called a moon-course (penance).[4]

218. (Or) one practising the moon-course penance may observe all these regulations in the barley-(shaped) middle (penance), beginning with the bright half of the month (to be) restrained (in his senses).[5]

219. One practising the moon-course (penance) of an ascetic should, self-restrained, swallow, when midday has arrived, eight mouthfuls of sacrificial grain (every day for a month).[6]

220. When a Brahman, intent (in mind), eats (for one month) four mouthfuls in the morning (and) four when the sun goes home, (the penance) is called the child's moon-course (penance).[7]

221. On eating for a month, whatever manner one adopts,[8] three (times) eighty mouthfuls of sacrificial grain with (mind) intent, one succeeds (after death) in sharing the world of the moon.

222. This observance the Rudras, the Ādityas, and the Vasus have followed for release from all inauspicious

[1] "Distant;" cf. Viṣṇu xlvi. 18.

[2] Cf. vs. 259.

[3] K. perhaps both this and rinsing the mouth. Cf. K. to vs. 224; cf. vi. 24, xi. 124 (translated rinsing the mouth by Dr. B.)

[4] *Cāndrāyaṇa.* Cf. Viṣṇu xlvii.; Vas. xxiii. 45.

[5] Each of these is termed moon-course (penance), as it continues the course of the moon. The one described in vs. 217 has an "ant-shaped" middle, because in performing it at the middle of the penance one eats least. This is, on the contrary, called the moon-course with barley-shaped middle, because, beginning the fast with the bright half, one gradually increases till the fifteenth day (the "middle") and then diminishes, so that the food is least at the extremities, greatest at the middle (K.)

[6] *Haviṣyasya* (Medh., Rāgh., and Beng. MS.) The words "for a month" are implied in the name of the penance (Medh., K.) Medh. and K. add that it here makes no difference whether one begins with the bright or dark half.

[7] Cf. Vas. xxiii. 43.

[8] (*Yathā kathaṁcid.*) In any order he pleases, only consuming two hundred and forty mouthfuls (balls) in a month (Medh.)

(things); so too the Maruts and the great seers (have followed it).[1]

223. An oblation must be made daily and personally, (accompanied) by the great Vyāhṛtis;[2] and one should practise not harming (any creatures), truth, freedom from anger, uprightness.[3]

224. Thrice by day and thrice by night should one enter the water with clothes on,[4] and also one should not at any time address women,[5] Çūdras, or fallen persons.

225. One should occupy (oneself) by (alternately) standing (and) sitting, or, being unable (to do this), one should lie down;[6] one should be chaste[7] and observant of his vows,[8] giving glory to the Guru, to the gods, and to the twice-born.

226. And one should regularly repeat the *gāyatrī* and (other)[9] purifying (verses) according to ability; strictly considering[10] in the same way the object of the expiatory penance in every one of these observances.

227. By these observances the twice-born (who) have revealed their crimes are to be purified; but those (who) have not revealed (their) sins one[11] should make pure by (means of) *mantras* and oblations.

228. A sinner is freed from sin by proclaiming (it), by repenting, by austerity, by perusing (the Veda), and also, in time of need, by gifts.

229. Just in proportion as he himself confesses[12] the

[1] All divine beings among the lesser divinities. Cf Viṣṇu xlvii. 10.

[2] Vyāhṛtis, the three words *bhūḥ*, *bhuvaḥ*, *svar*; cf. ii. 78.

[3] *I.e.*, in performing penances one must also observe the ordinary rules of piety.

[4] This Medh. and K. say is the explanation of the "both three times a day;" cf. vs. 217.

[5] Even Brahman women; but the wife, mother, and elder sister are excepted when it is a matter of necessity to speak to them (Medh.)

[6] Cf. vi. 22.

[7] *Brahmacārin.*

[8] K. explains by a verse from Yama to the effect that he must carry his staff, sacred cord, etc.

[9] "Other," *i.e.*, *aghamarṣaṇa*, *puruṣasūkta*, etc. (Medh.)

[10] Or, *with great care . . . for the sake* of expiation (*ādṛto*, *yatnavān*, Medh.)

[11] The assembly (K.) Purification for secret sin is by instructing pupils at the time for explaining the *çāstra* (Medh.)

[12] *I.e.*, of his own accord. This

wrong (deed) he has done is a man released from that wrong (deed), as a snake from its skin.

230. Just in proportion as his mind despises[1] the ill-done deeds is his body[2] released from that wrong (deed).

231. For (by) repenting (after) committing a sin one is released from that sin; and he[3] is purified by desisting (from the sin) with the words, "I will not act thus again."

232. Thus pondering in mind the result after death of acts (done in life), one should with mind, voice, and body[4] ever perform good acts.

233. When one has committed, either unwittingly or wittingly, a forbidden act, and desires release from it, let him not perform a second (like it).[5]

234. In whatever act done by him (he feels) no lightness of heart, let him practise (ascetic) austerity in (respect to) that (act) until it gives satisfaction.[6]

235. The whole happiness of gods and men has been declared by the wise expounders of the Veda to have its root in austerity, its middle in austerity, its end in austerity.

236. Knowledge is the austerity of a Brahman; protection (that) of a Kṣatriya; practice of business,[7] more-

implies self-infliction of penance, but the proportion rests on the self-confession.

[1] *Garhati* or *nindati* (Medh., No. 989).

[2] *Çarīram* (body) is the inner self (*antarātman*), not the corporal self (*bhūtātman*) (Medh.) K. says it is the soul (*jīvātman*).

[3] *Tu saḥ* (K.); *narah* (Medh., Rāgh.)

[4] Or, "deed" (*karma*); Medh. has *karmabhiḥ* in No. 1551 (the other MSS. altered); cf. vs. 242.

[5] The penance for the second offence should be doubled (K. from Devala. Rāgh. appears to have read *viçuddhim*.

[6] Another meaning is given by K. and Rāgh., viz., "in whatever *expiatory* act he fails to receive satisfaction, he should keep on performing penance," etc. But Medh. paraphrases the text thus: *duṣkṛte karmaṇi asya kāyikā vicikitsā yadi bhavati tataḥ kṛte 'pi prāyaçcitte*, etc., *i.e.*, if he has done wrong and feels no relief after performing the usual penance. One idea must be supplied whether we take *karma* as (evil) act, or act (of penance). Medh. slyly adds that the word austerity may include giving presents (to the Brahmans); cf. vs. 228.

[7] "Practice of business" or gain (*vārttā*) is a comprehensive expression including all the legal means by which a member of the third caste gains his livelihood (*vṛtti*); it might be paraphrased loosely by farming and trading, though "occupation" and "business" come nearer to the original idea in the word.

over, (make) the austerity of a Vaiçya; the austerity of a Çūdra (is) servile attendance.

237. The self-controlled seers, eating fruits, roots, (and) air, beheld, by (means of this) austerity alone, the three worlds, with (all therein) that moves (or is) immovable.

238. (Medicinal) plants, health, divine[1] wisdom, position[2] of various kinds, are perfected by (means of) austerity alone; for austerity is the requisite for success in these (things).

239. If there be aught hard to overcome,[3] hard to acquire, hard to reach, or hard to perform, these[4] things are all successfully completed by means of austerity; for austerity is hard to overpower.[5]

240. And even the great criminals, and others who do what ought not to be done, are released from these sins merely by austerity well performed.

241. Insects, snakes, winged insects, cattle, (large) birds, and existing (things that are) stationary,[6] attain heaven by the power of austerity.

242. Whatsoever sin (men) commit by the acts[7] of the mind, the voice, (or) the body, all this (they who are) rich in austerity quickly consume by (means of) austerity alone.

243. Those whose home is heaven receive the sacrificial gifts of a Brahman (who has been) made pure by austerity alone, and they cause (his) desires to be fulfilled.[8]

244. By (means of) austerity alone the Lord Prajāpati emitted this treatise;[9] even thus by (means of) austerity have the seers acquired the Vedas.

[1] B. R.

[2] Position in life, rank, or, with the commentators (connecting *daivī* with *sthitiḥ*), position of the deities in heaven.

[3] As sickness, etc. (Medh.)

[4] *Sarvam tat* (Medh., Rāgh., and perhaps K.)

[5] Cf. Mbhā. xiv. 51, 17, and elsewhere.

[6] *I.e.*, the vegetable world.

[7] Medh. has *mano-vāk-kāya-karmabhiḥ*; K., °*mūrtibhir janāḥ*; cf. vs. 232.

[8] Medh. adds another verse beginning, "The gods do not receive the offering of a man who has not practised austerity," to show the negative side of this teaching; austerity is, according to the same commentator, *yoga*.

[9] *Çāstram*.

245. The gods, since they see (that) the sacred birth[1] of this All (comes) from austerity, acknowledge this great importance of austerity.

246. Daily perusal of Veda according to ability, ceremonies with great sacrifices, and patience quickly cause sins to be destroyed, even if (these sins have) produced the great crimes.

247. As fire by its heat burns up in a moment the wood it has laid hold of, so a Veda-wise man by the fire of knowledge consumes all sin.[2]

248. Even thus is the expiatory penance declared according to rule for (open) crimes; now further learn the expiatory penance for secret (crimes).[3]

249. Sixteen suppressions of breath along with the Vyāhṛtis and Om, if performed every day, purify in a month even the slayer of an embryo (or Brahman).[4]

250. Even a drinker of spirituous liquor[5] is purified (by) muttering that (hymn) of Kutsa (beginning) with the words "Away," and the verse of Vasiṣṭha (beginning) with the word "Toward," the Māhitra, and the (texts) containing the word "Purified."[6]

251. Moreover, even on stealing gold, one is made spotless in a moment (by) muttering once (the

[1] *Udbharam* (Medh., with Beng. MS.); *sambharam* (Rāgh.)

[2] *Kṛtsnaṁ pāpam* (Medh., Rāgh.)

[3] "This verse is not in the text of Govind. but is in that of Medh." (K.) In the MSS. Medh. it follows verse 249, Medh. remarking, "Some read the following verse (248) before (249)," *i.e.*, K.'s order and that of Rāgh.

[4] K. reads (as these are the four great criminals) slayer of a Brahman (*brahmaghnan*), or means it shall apply only when the embryo is of Brahmanic origin. Cf. Vas. xx. 23. Medh. notes a difference of opinion in regard to the manner and times of restraining the breath and repeating *Om*. Some restrain the breath, say *Om*, and repeat the repression of breath, etc. The duration of the suppression is as long as there is no excessive trouble in holding the breath. Medh. mentions the three kinds given in K., "not like a mere *çvāsanirodha*." Çūdras and women are not allowed to perform this penance, as they cannot repeat the sacred texts (K.) Cf. Vas. xxvi. 4 ff.

[5] *Surā*.

[6] The text of the Māhitra is found Ṛg-V. x. 185; the texts containing the word "purified" (*çuddha*) are Ṛg-V. viii. 84, 7–9. The hymn seen and declared by Kutsa begins *apa naḥ çoçucad agham* (Medh., K.), Ṛg-V. i. 97, 1; the "Vasiṣṭha verse" means three (Medh.) verses of Ṛg-V. vii. 80.

hymn) beginning "Of him you,"[1] and also the Çiva-saṅkalpa.[2]

252. He who violates the Guru's couch is released (from the sin) (by) going over (the hymn) beginning "Drink the oblation,"[3] and that beginning with the words "Not him,"[4] (and by) muttering the Puruṣa hymn.[5]

253. On seeking something to remove crimes, (both) great (and) small, one should mutter for a year the texts (beginning) with the words "Off,"[6] or (the one beginning) with the words "Whatever," thus.[7]

254. On receiving (presents) which should not be received, and on eating forbidden food, a man is purified in three days (by) muttering (the hymn) beginning "Swiftly this pleasure-giver."[8]

255. Now one who has (committed) many crimes is purified (by) going over the (hymn) to Soma and Rudra[9] for a month, (while) practising bathing in a stream, and (by repeating) the three verses with the words "Of Aryamans."[10]

256. A criminal should for half a year mutter that collection of seven (verses beginning) with the word "Indra,"[11] and on putting (any) forbidden (substance) into water, he should sit for a month eating (food obtained) by begging.

257. A twice-born man (by) making for a year an oblation of ghee (accompanied) by the *mantras* which belong to the oblations offered according to the manner of the

[1] Ṛg-V. i. 164; "once" means once daily for a month (Medh., K.)

[2] V. S. 34, 1. In 250–251 occurs a *var. lec.* *vā* (or) for *ca* (and), *i.e.*, either, not both, being sufficient to ensure purity.

[3] Ṛg-V. x. 88. Every day for a month all sixteen verses (Medh., K.)

[4] Ṛg-V. x. 126.

[5] Ṛg-V. x. 90; daily for a year (K.)

[6] Ṛg-V. i. 24, 14.

[7] K. seems to imply Ṛg-V. x. 119, 1, in the *iti* ("whatever," thus), beside the other texts; Böhtlingk in Mel. Asiat. compares Ṛg-V. vii. 89, 5, and this is given by Rāgh. (and K.), and Medh. *yat kiṁc 'edam ititica.* (So Rāgh. and Medh., No. 989.) The texts are to be repeated daily for a year (K., Rāgh.)

[8] The *Tarat sa mandī*, Ṛg-V. ix. 58, four verses (K., Rāgh.) Cf. Gaut. xxiv. 1; Baudh. ii. 5, 8.

[9] Ṛg-V. vi. 74.

[10] Three verses beginning to Aryaman, (Varuṇa and) Mitra, (K., Rāgh.), Ṛg-V. iv. 2, 4 (?).

[11] *Indramitraṁ varuṇam agniṁ traya iti* (K.)

Çākalas,[1] or (by) muttering the text (beginning) with the words "Not of me,"[2] removes even a very heavy crime.

258. One who has committed a great crime should, intent in mind, follow after cows; by going over the *pāvamāni* (texts)[3] for a year and living on (food obtained) by begging he is made pure;

259. Or[4] by thrice going over a Veda collection in the woods, (with passions) controlled, and purified by three Parāka (penances),[4] one is released from all sins.

260. Again, one should fast three days properly, going down into the water three times a day, (and) thrice muttering the (hymn called) "Forgiver of impurity,"[5] one is released from all sins.

261. As the horse-sacrifice, king of ceremonies, is a dissipater of all sins, so the hymn (called) "Forgiver of impurity" is a dissipater of all sins.

262. A Brahman even (by) slaying these three worlds, even (by) eating (food) taken from anybody, receives no sin at all if he holds the Ṛg-(Veda) in memory.[6]

263. One is released from all sins (by) thrice going over with mind intent the collection of the Ṛg-(Veda), or (that of) the Yajur- or Sāma-(Vedas) with their mysteries.[7]

264. As an earth-clod falling into a great lake is quickly lost, so all evil acts sink (out of sight) in the threefold Veda.[8]

265. The texts (Ṛg-Veda), and the other[9] sacrificial

[1] Cf. vs. 201. Eight *mantras* beginning "Thou art the expiatory sacrifice" (Medh.)

[2] *Na ma Indraçca iti* (K.)

[3] Texts, chiefly from the ninth book of Ṛg-V., on the purification of *soma* when pressed.

[4] *Parāka.* Cf. vs. 216; *ca* or *vā.*

[5] *Aghamarṣaṇa*, Ṛg-V. x. 190. Cf. Baudh. iv. 2, 15; Gaut. xxiv. 10.

[6] Remembering the Ṛg-Veda prevents this sin from taking effect. Cf. ii. 118 with this and the following verse.

[7] The philosophical and other portions that, in addition to the hymns, go to constitute a Veda collection.

[8] *Kṣipraṁ loṣṭo* (sic) *vinaçyati* (No. 989), and *kṣiptaṁ loṣṭam* (No. 935); the like divergence in the Bomb. and Beng. MSS.

[9] The "other" are "different from the others" (*Sāma* and *Ṛg*) according to K.; but Medh. has *ādyāni* (*mukhyāni, brāhmaṇa madhye yāni paṭhitāni*) or "different" *sāmans* according to a division for village and jungle (*grāmāraṇyavibhāgena*).

formulas (Yajur-Veda), and the songs of various sorts (Sāma-Veda)—this must be known as the threefold Veda: who knows this Veda, he is Veda-wise.

266. That primordial *brahma*, consisting of three sounds,[1] in which the triple (Veda is) contained, (is) another threefold Veda (which is) to be kept secret: who knows it, he is Veda-wise.[2]

END OF THE ELEVENTH LECTURE.

[1] Essence of Veda, *a*, *u*, *m* = *Om* (*aum*)—(K.); cf. xii. 117.

[2] Some MSS. (Rāgh., Beng.) add another verse to this (cf. Lois.) not found in the best MSS. With *trayī* (*vidyā*) cf. iv. 125; cf. also xii. 117.

LECTURE XII.

EXPOSITION OF PHILOSOPHICAL PRINCIPLES AND THE ACQUISITION OF FINAL HAPPINESS.

1. THIS complete rule of right (action)[1] for the four castes has been declared by thee, Sinless (One)! Proclaim to us in verity the future accomplishment of the fruit of actions.

2. He, Manu's son,[2] Bhṛgu, whose self is virtuous,[3] said to the great seers: Listen to the judgment regarding the course of actions of this All.

3. An act, (whether its) origin (be) in the mind, the voice, or the body, has (its) fruit, pure or impure; the courses of men, (whether) high, low, (or) medium, (are) born of (their) acts.

4. Let one know the mind (to be) the instigator of this incorporate here (in the worlds), (which is), indeed, exactly threefold, resting on three (things), and joined to ten signs.[4]

5. Invidiously regarding the property of others, thinking with the mind[5] of forbidden things, and wrong inclination,[6] (constitute) the threefold (evil) act of the mind.[7]

[1] *Dharma-çabdaçcakartavyatā-vacanaḥ* (Medh.)

[2] *Mānavaḥ = manoḥ çiṣyaḥ*, "a disciple of Manu" (Rāgh.)

[3] *Dharmātmā* (cf. v. 3, *a*).

[4] *Dehin* = (act) of the body (K.) The act is threefold (*trividha*), for it results in (transmigrations), high, low, or medium; it rests on three things, viz., mind, voice, and body; the ten signs are given in the next verses (K.) But *dehin* generally means "soul," as distinct from *deha*, "body," and we may translate "know thinking (minds) to be the instigator to action of this incorporate person."

[5] This is the threefold impure act causing impure fruit (cf. vs. 3); so in the following verses. K. illustrates the first as pondering how to get unjustly another's goods; the word itself, *abhidhyāna*, has the same significance of preposition as our word (invidia) "envy."

[6] Thinking with the mind of forbidden things is defined by K. as desiring to kill a Brahman, etc.

[7] Wrong inclination is an inclination to scepticism. Had *manasā* more than its usual redundant

6. Abuse and untruth, as also malice, under any circumstances, and talking about what does not concern one,[1] would be the fourfold (evil act) done by the voice.

7. Taking (things which) have not been given, as also injury not (done) in accordance with (legal) injunction,[2] and adultery with another's wife, are called the threefold (evil) act of the body.

8. This (man) receives his reward in the mind alone[3] for a pure (or) impure (act) of the mind; in the voice for what is done by the voice, and so too in the body alone for (an act) of the body.

9. A man reaches the condition of stationary existence[4] through faulty acts done by the body; the condition of winged creatures or (wild) animals through (those) done by the voice;[5] the condition of low birth (among men) through (those) done by the mind.

10. Now (there is) a rod for the voice, a rod for the mind, and likewise a rod for the body; he in whose consciousness these (three rods) are treasured up is called the (man) of three rods.[6]

sense we would be inclined to take (2) as unconscious mental action, and (3) as volition. Medh. mentions that some supply *parasya* with the second clause, "Thinking of what is unfavourable *to another*." The third is a repetition of the foregoing idea, according to him, but others say it is *nitya nirāmiṣadveṣa*.

[1] Medh. has *anibaddha* for *asambaddha* (Nos. 1551, 935, 989). "Abuse" is illustrated by Rāgh. as saying "You're the son of a Mleccha (barbarian)."

[2] Injury to animals, except at authorised sacrifices, injuries to men, when not inflicted as legal penalties, etc.

[3] Medh. reads *upayuṅkte* for *upabhuṅkte* according to some MSS., and remarks a modification of the whole passage, saying, "Some declare that one does not receive mental grief through an act by which mental distress is caused to another person, but I say mental grief is got by all the so-called threefold (act) of the mind; (cf. vs. 5), and so with the two following (verses) also."

[4] Is reborn as part of the vegetable world.

[5] Birds or beasts. The grossest sins result in one becoming a vegetable, the next in becoming an animal (*tiryakjāti mātra pradarçanārthām*, Medh.), the least in becoming a low man.

[6] *Tridaṇḍin*, he of the triple rod (or staff); this is a play on words, for the rod is a symbol of subjugation, while "he of the triple rod" (staff) alludes to the Brahman who wore a staff of three pieces (cf. ix. 296) when he became an ascetic. The man is here called *tridaṇḍin* not so much on account of his triple "staff" [as on account of his *command* over thought, word, and act. (The MSS. of Medh. have *yasyaite niyatā daṇḍāḥ so tridaṇḍī va-*

11. A man (by) exercising this threefold rod in (respect to) all creatures, and [1] (by) suppressing desire and hate, obtains thereby a firm hold on happiness.

12. That which causes this self [2] to act they declare (to be) the conscious-(soul) ("thing-knower"),[3] but that which does the acts is called by the wise the elemental self.[4]

13. (There is) another, the inner self, (that) has the name (of) vital-(spirit), born at the same time with every incorporate (creature); through which is experienced all that is pleasant or unpleasant in (the various) births.[5]

14. Both those two, the Great one [6] and likewise the Conscious (soul), united with the existent (elements), abide, penetrating That one [7] (who) abides in (all) existent (things) high and low.

15. Innumerable forms [8] descend from the body of

vasthitah, but commentary *nihitā;* he explains in brief that the *tridaṇḍin* is he *yo na skhalati*, not he *yo gurukāṣṭadaṇḍam dhārayati*. Rāgh. notes the *var. lec.* as occurring somewhere.) The whole passage (cf. v. 165, ix. 29) has a Buddhistic appearance.

[1] *Ca*, Medh.

[2] *Ātman*, (self), here "body" (Medh., K.); the man's self *in toto* is meant.

[3] *Kṣetrajña*, "knowing the thing" or place, *i.e.*, what is done, or "conscious of the body."

[4] *Bhūtātman*.

[5] The vital (spirit), *jīva*, is other than the body: thus it is said, "There are two selves, the inner self and the self of the body;" the inner self is this called vital (*jīva*) spirit. The *jīva* is the vital soul as distinguished from the conscious one, and both from the body; both souls are really one, the individual.

[6] Mahān (masc.), "the Great one," for *mahat*, "the intellect." (K.)

[7] That one (masc.) is, according to the forced and false explanation of Medh. and K., the highest self, supreme soul, *paramātman*. The existent (*bhūta*) sometimes means "the elements," as apparently in the first part of the verse (so the comm.); sometimes "existent (things)," as at the end. I translate "the existent," and add what seems in each case to be the underlying meaning. In translating "That one," "Great one," etc., I mean to express that the pronoun or adjective is masculine. In the following "That one" is also applied to the individual (vital soul) after death. According to K.'s Vedantic note on this Saṅkhyan passage, the meaning of the verse is that intellect and the conscious soul (*mahat* and *kṣetrajña*), joined to the elements, exist, dependent on the supreme soul (*paramātman*) who (which) exists in all beings. (All the three MSS. of Medh. have *tau* for *tam;* Rāgh. has (*sthitam*) *deham vyāpya*, as another explanation instead of *paramātmānam*).

[8] Or, manifestations (*mūrtayaḥ*). According to K. this means that individual vital spirits descend from the Supreme (Paramātma) like sparks from fire (*vedāntoktaprakārena*) and animate soulless matter. After K.'s vs. 14 there is in Medh.

That one, which are for ever setting in motion (all) existent (things), high and low.

16. From just[1] the (same) five elements there is produced after death for men (who) have done evil another body, durable, intended for torture.

17. After passing through with that body here those torments (inflicted) by Yama, (they) are absorbed among just those (same) existent elements,[2] piece by piece.

18. That one,[3] after passing through sins ending in unhappiness (and) produced by contact with sensual (pleasure), goes, having had its stains removed, even unto both those two greatly powerful ones.[4]

19. Those two,[5] unwearied, look together upon the good

(all the MSS.) merely a quotation from Bhag. 15, 16 (*dvau puruṣau . . . kṣaraçcāraçca*, etc.), and the text continues with K.'s vss. 20–26, while vss. 15–19 appear after our vs. 26. *Niḥ-patanti* ("descend") means *prādur bhavanti* ("become visible") according to Medh. It is interesting to note that the (Vedantic) Medh. compares "like waves from the sea."

[1] *Eva*, *i.e.*, the body formed to endure torture after death is made of just (the same) elements as in life. The word "element," usually *bhūta*, is here *mātra*; in vs. 17, *bhūtamātrā* ("elementary substances"). Medh. says expressly that the body of this resurrection to torture is to be "no other body than (one made of) the five elements, but, on the contrary, one having blood," etc. (cf. vs. 21, note); when released entirely, his frame is such as is described in ii. 82 (Medh.) The "fine elements" as distinct from these are not known to the work.

[2] K. says among fine and coarse portions; he imagines the subject to be *jīvāḥ*, fine individual vital spirits suffering the torture of hell after the grosser body of this life is gone. Medh. says, "absorbed among the 'fine' elements" (*sūkṣmāsu*), and makes the subject of "absorbed those bodies."

[3] *Sa*; that individual (*jīva*) is meant, inhabiting on earth a single body.

[4] K. interprets the two as "intellect" and the "supreme soul" (*paramātma*); Medh. says "some" interpret so, but he prefers to regard the second of the two as the conscious soul (*kṣetrajña*), which seems more in accordance with vs. 14 (so Rāgh.) *Tāv eva' bhau* should be rendered "(to) those same two," *i.e.*, as in vs. 14, the *mahān* and *kṣetrajña*. The text gives no explanation of itself and is very uncertain.

[5] K. interprets as in vs. 18; he renders "that one" the "vital spirit," that is, the individual. Rāgh. says *jīva* or *sthūladeha*, and keeps *mahān* and *kṣetrajña* as the "two." Medh. gives the subject quite a discussion, which embraces "those two" and "that one," so that even in his time there seems to have been dispute as to the *kṣetrajña* gazing in this manner at the *jīva*, some identifying the two, and some not. (*Tasye' 'ti kaḥ saṁbodhyate? jīva iti kecid* (as K.) *uktaṁ ca sa eva kṣetrajña sa eva jīva iti*, etc.)

and evil of that one, united to which[1] two, (either good or evil, that one) receives, after death and here, happiness (or) unhappiness.

20. If[2] that one practises in the main (what is) right, in small degree (what is) not right, (that one) receives happiness in heaven, being encompassed by those existent (elements) only.[3]

21. But if that one cultivates in the main (what is) not right, in small degree (what is) right, (that one) receives the tortures (inflicted) by Yama, being deserted by those existent (elements).[4]

22. After receiving those tortures (inflicted) by Yama, that vital (spirit), having had its stains removed, goes again unto the same five existent (elements) piece by piece.

23. Beholding thus in his very own thought these courses of this vital spirit (resulting) from (practising) right and not-right, let one ever give[5] his mind to (what is) right.

24. Essentiality, passion, and darkness one should know (to be) the three threads of self,[6] by (means of) which

[1] Rāgh. alone makes this refer to *mahat-kṣetrajñau*, the others to "good and evil."

[2] *Yathā* ("when"), Medh., or *yadi* ("if")—K.

[3] Fine elements alone compose his frame; he cannot suffer as one can whose form is made of grosser elements. Here and below "right" and "not-right" are translations of *dharma* and *adharma*.

[4] He has a corporal frame and feels the torture; Medh. reads *ca* for K.'s *tu*; the *var. lec. saṁparityakto* is found only in No. 989; in the next, *abhyati* is also Medh.'s reading.

[5] *Dadyāt* (MSS. Medh. and Beng. MS.)

[6] *Sattva, rajas,* and *tamas* are the three *guṇa*. This verse goes to the bottom of the Sāṅkhya philosophy. These three *guṇa* are the substrata of all that exist; their equipoise is *urstoff*. It is difficult to find any words to convey at once the original and philosophical idea in *sattva* or in *guṇa*. "Essentiality" is the literal sense of *sattva*, that which preponderating makes goodness (as *sat* is "good"), hence sometimes translated "absolute goodness." *Guṇa* is literally "thread," but also employed, as in Ben Jonson, "(a man) of a most elegant *thread*," to denote "quality," "characteristic." It is generally translated "quality," but in the developed system *guṇa* was not quality but underlying substance; the union of the three *guṇa* produces the *urstoff*. In the text I have preferred to keep the original sense, as it corresponds sufficiently well to the original, and is certainly less misleading than "quality."

(three) the Great one,[1] penetrating without exception all these conditions,[2] abides.[3]

25. Whenever among these (threads) any one thread is completely predominant in (any) body, it makes that incorporate (individual) wholly its own.[4]

26. Essentiality is called knowledge; darkness, ignorance; passion, love and hate. This is their form, penetrating all and underlying all existent (things).

27. Whenever one observes in the self anything united with joy, perfectly clear (effulgence), at peace as it were one should regard that as essentiality.[5]

28. But whatever (is) united with grief and causes the self no joy, one should know (to be) irresistible passion, (which) for ever holds incorporate (beings).

29. And whatever (is) united with confusion,[6] undiscrete, the essence of which is the sensuous, undiscoverable, unknowable,[7] one should regard as darkness.

30. I will now declare without omission what is the final result of these three threads, (whether it be), the first,[8] middlemost, or last (result).

31. The sign of the thread belonging to essentiality (comprises) perusal of the Veda, (ascetic) austerity, knowledge, purity,[9] restraint of the senses, performance of the (rules of) right,[10] and meditation upon the self.

[1] The intellect.

[2] *Bhāva*, or "all existent things," as perhaps in vi. 80. The word may mean thing or condition. K. and Rāgh. take it as "thing," Medh. as (*vikāra*) "condition."

[3] In the epic *dharma* is described in the same way as *iha cā'mutra ca sthitaḥ sarvagaḥ sarvam vyāpya cārācaram* (Mbhā. xv. 28, 19, 20).

[4] Literally, "That (thread) makes it wholly that thread's."

[5] Medh. begins again with K.'s vs. 19 last preceding (*vide* vs. 15 n.)

[6] In respect to good and bad (K., Rāgh.)

[7] The last two epithets (literally, 'not to be imagined,' 'unrecognisable') have been employed (i. 5) to characterise the primeval darkness. According to another reading (perhaps K.'s, and found in all three MSS. Medh. and in Rāgh.), we should translate "undiscrete" as epithet of (*viṣaya*) sensuous, "the essence of which is the undiscrete sensuous." In translating *avyakta* by "undiscrete" I have preserved Dr. B.'s translation in i. 6, 7, etc.

[8] Best, middlemost, and worst (Rāgh.)

[9] Purity of body by bathing, etc. (K., Ragh.)

[10] *Dharma.*

32. The sign of the thread belonging to passion (comprises) desire for undertaking,[1] instability,[2] undertaking things not right to be done,[3] indulgence in sensuous (pleasures) again and again.[4]

33. The sign of the thread belonging to darkness (comprises) greed, sleep, lack of firmness (of will),[5] cruelty, unbelief, attention to many things,[6] fondness for begging, and carelessness.

34. The thread-sign of these same three threads, which abide in three (things),[7] should be known (to be comprised by) the short and orderly summary which follows:

35. Whatever act one feels ashamed of having done, of doing, or[8] of being about to do—every such act should be known by a wise man (to be) the sign of the thread belonging to darkness.

36. If by any act in this world one seeks extended fame, although not made unhappy by not succeeding, that act should be known (to be one) belonging to passion.

37. If one desires (that) any (act) be known[9] by everybody, if (there is) any (act) he is not ashamed (of) performing, and if by any (act) his self is pleased—(every) such (act is) the sign of the thread of essentiality.

38. The sign of darkness is called desire; (the sign) of passion, gain; the sign of essentiality, right; among these each follows in order according as it is better (than the preceding).[10]

[1] Undertaking things for a selfish purpose (K.) Medh. reads *ārambharatitā*, explaining as undertaking things selfishly and vainly (*vṛthārambha*).

[2] Discomfiture of mind at a little matter, according to Medh. and K.

[3] *Asatkārya*, not essential, not right, "practising forbidden acts" (Medh., K.)

[4] In the text there is a redundant syllable, avoided by omitting *ca* (Lois.); so originally in No. 989 Medh. Sensuous pleasures, *i.e.*, of sense, more specifically sensuality.

[5] Medh., K.,

[6] Neglect of good customs (K.)

[7] What things? K. and Rāgh. say in the three ages past, future, and present; Medh. says in the three worlds and in the three results, high, middle, or low (*phalodayeṣu*); the last agrees best with the threefold division in vs. 40.

[8] Literally, "and."

[9] Or, "desires with all his heart to know" (K.); *sarvene'cchati jñātum*, is as K. takes it, literally active. (Medh. has *yaḥ* for *yat*).

[10] There are two readings: *yathākramam* ("in order") or *yatho'ttaram* ("their superiority is as each is

39. I will tell briefly the transmigrations in due order of this All,[1] which one receives through (possessing) any one of these threads.

40. Always (those creatures) possessed by essentiality attain divinity; those possessed by passion, man's estate; those possessed by darkness, the estate of animals: the threefold course[2] (is explained) in these words.

41. But this[3] threefold course caused by the threads must be known (to be again) threefold—lowest, middlemost, and highest—according to the difference (both) in the act (and) knowledge (of the actor).[4]

42. (Things) stationary,[5] worms, insects, fishes, serpents, tortoises, cattle, and jackals[6] (are) the lowest course resulting from darkness.

43. Elephants, chargers, Çūdras, the abhorred barbarians,[7] lions, tigers, and boars, (are) the middlemost course resulting from darkness.

44. Vagrants,[8] birds, hypocritical men, Rakṣas, and Piçācas,[9] (are) the highest course among those resulting from darkness.

45. Pugilists, wrestlers,[10] play-actors, men who live by

subsequent"). K. probably read the latter; Medh. has the former. The meaning is that gain is better than desire, right (*dharma*) is better than gain (K.)

[1] Transmigrations throughout all the universe. The word *saṁsāra* (transmigration) means the same as course (*gati*)—(Medh.)

[2] Transmigration of three kinds. These individuals are not, however, supposed to be exclusively but predominantly possessed by the different threads; an individual may contain essentiality and passion; the preponderance of the latter places him in man's estate; of the former, in divinity, etc.

[3] Or, "of these" (*eṣām*).—Bomb. and Beng. MSS.

[4] As whether the act is good or bad, done wittingly or unwittingly (Medh.) Each of these three divisions is thus subdivided, so that we have in all a ninefold division.

[5] Masculine in the original; the vegetable world is meant.

[6] Or, "wild forest animals;" *çṛgālāçca* is the reading of Medh. and Beng. MSS., instead of *mṛgāç caiva* (so the MS. Rāgh.)

[7] *Mlecchāçca garhitāḥ*, "the despised Mlecchas or barbarian inhabitants." K. says the epithet repeats the Mlecchas' character, while Medh. says it limits *Çūdrāḥ* (!).

[8] Vagrants are strolling players; the regular actors are found in vs. 45; Medh.'s definition of the vagrants (*cāraṇāḥ*) is interesting: *Kathakagāyanakastrisaṁyojanakādayaḥ*.

[9] Rakṣas and Piçācas are evil spirits (the good are found in vs. 47). Cf. the translation in i. 43.

[10] *Jhallas* (K., "fencers,") and *mallas* (cf. x. 22, note); so Medh.; but

(making) swords, and those addicted to gaming and to drinking, (are) the lowest course resulting from passion.

46. Kings and Kṣatriyas, the domestic priests[1] of the king, (and men who) have pre-eminence in word-battles, (are) the middlemost course resulting from passion.

47. Gandharvas, Guhyakas, Yakṣas, and (all those) who (are) attendants of deities, as also all the Apsaras, (are) the highest course among (those) resulting from passion.[2]

48. Those who practise (ascetic) austerity, those who have renounced the world,[3] Brahmans,[4] the troops connected with the palatial chariot of the gods,[5] the stars, and Daityas,[6] (are) the first course resulting from essentiality.

49. Sacrificers, seers, gods, the Vedas, the constellations, the years, and also the manes and Sādhya s, (are) the second course resulting from essentiality.

50. Brahmā, the all-creators,[8] Dharma, the Great one, and also the Undiscrete (one)[9]—this the wise call the highest course resulting from essentiality.

to the former he adds *parihāsajīvino vā* ("or professional jesters"). Two variations occur in all MSS. Medh.: *prayuktāçca* for *prasaktāçca*, and *puruṣāçca kavṛttayaḥ* for *puruṣāḥ çastravṛttayaḥ*.

[1] *Purohita.*

[2] These are the good spirits: the Gandharvas are Indra's heavenly singers; Guhyakas, those who guard the treasures of Kubera, god of wealth; Yakṣas, servants of Kubera; Apsaras, the wives of the Gandharvas (cf. i. 37). Instead of *vibudha* all the MSS. Medh. have *vividhā*, "various". (No. 989 altered).

[3] *Yatayaḥ* ("religious mendicants," K.) Some say (and compare Ait. Br. vii. 28) that certain tribes on Mount Meru are called *yatayaḥ*, but really *parivrāja-kādayaḥ* ("wandering priests," etc.), are meant (Medh.)

[4] *Viprāḥ* ("priests in the last stadium of life")—(K.)

[5] The "palatial chariot" (*vimāna*) is the vehicle of the deities; these are the *accompanying* hosts (K.), or the gods of the ether, who ride therein (Medh.)

[6] The Daityas appear to be sun-divinities, possibly connected with the twelve zodiacal stations. It is uncertain whether *nakṣatrāṇi* (stars) mean the small stars or the twenty-eight moon-stations.

[7] The Sādhyas' "subtile host" are spoken of in i. 22 and elsewhere; they are divine beings of lower grade. "*Vedās tadabhi māninaḥ*" (K., Rāgh. is not authorised by the text.)

[8] These are the Marīci, etc., according to Medh. and K.

[9] Haughton's remark that the Undiscrete (Dr. B.'s translation for *avyakta*) is here better masculine than neuter (the MSS. vary between *avyakta eva ca* (so all MSS. Medh.) and *avyaktam eva ca*) seems well made, for these are all personifications, not *mahat* (intellect), and *avyaktam* (that Undiscrete, first principle), but *mahān*, the Great one, and so *avyakta*, the Undiscrete one; in the same way *dharma* seems

51. (Thus has been) explained all[1] this complete transmigration (resulting) from acts of three kinds, (transmigration which is) threefold (and again) threefold, (and) extends through all existent things.[2]

52. By indulgence of the organs of sense and by not practising right,[3] ignorant and low men enter upon base transmigrations.

53. Learn now in full by what different acts here this vital (spirit) enters into different births[4] one after the other[5] in this world.

54. After receiving (as punishment) horrible hells during many series of years, the great criminals at the end[6] of this (time) enter upon the following transmigrations.

55. The slayer of a Brahman enters the womb of dogs, boars, asses, camels, cows, goats, sheep, (forest) animals, birds, Cāṇḍālas and Pukkaças.[7]

56. A Brahman (who) drinks spirituous liquor[8] would pass (into the womb) of worms, insects, winged insects, winged (creatures) that eat manure, and beings delighting in destruction.[9]

57. A Brahman (who is) a thief (would pass) thousands of times (into the womb) of spiders, snakes, chameleons,

here (not = *vedārtha*, as Medh. suggests) to be personified as the deity. But I see no reason for insisting on absolute philosophical accuracy in the text; much more in harmony with the general tone of the philosophical portion would be just this absurd personification of the neuter *avyaktam*, as a *quasi*-deity alongside Brahmā, presupposing, of course, that at the time of the text the neuter was recognised as meaning this principle (the passage i. 6 has a doubtful text). The Great one, as in vs. 14 above, is *not* intellect, but apparently its personification. Johaentgen's doubtful suggestion (to supply *ātmā*) seems unnecessary and liable to mislead.

[1] Medh. has *dharmaḥ* for *sarvaḥ*, like the Beng. MS., at vs. 82.

[2] This tripled threefold transmigration is divided in short thus: Every act brings the actor into one of three states (essentiality, passion, darkness), each of which has three grades (lowest, middlemost, highest), the act itself being of three kinds in that it may be of the mind, speech, or body.

[3] *Dharma.*

[4] Literally, "womb."

[5] K. writes "learn . . . one after the other." Cf. with the following Viṣṇu xliv.; Yāj. iii. 207 ff.

[6] *Tatkṣaṇāt;* in Medh. (same idea).

[7] Which of these he enters depends on the circumstances under which the crime is committed (K.)

[8] *Surā.*

[9] Such as tigers, etc. (Medh., K.)

animals living in the water,[1] and Piçācas (who) delight in destruction.

58. (He who) violates the Guru's couch (would pass) hundreds of times (into the womb) of grasses, bushes, vines, (animals) that eat raw flesh,[2] ravenous (animals),[3] and (animals that) have done cruel acts.[4]

59. Those delighting in destruction become (animals) that eat raw flesh; those eating what ought not to be eaten (become) worms; thieves (become creatures) that devour each other; (those who) have had carnal intercourse with low women (become) ghosts.[5]

60. (By) forming a connection with fallen men, or (carnally) with another man's wife, or (by) stealing the property of a Brahman,[6] (one) becomes a Brahma-injuring (demon).[7]

61. (By) stealing through greed gems, pearls, coral, and the various (kinds of) jewels, a man is born (again) among the (birds called) gold-workers.[8]

62. (By) stealing grain, copper, water, honey, milk, essences, or ghee, (one) becomes (respectively) a mouse, a flamingo,[9] a water-bird, a gadfly, a crow, a dog, or an ichneumon.

63. (By stealing) meat, omentum, sesame, salt, or sour milk (one becomes respectively) a vulture, a *madgu*,[10] an oil-drinking (bird),[11] a cricket, or the bird (called) *balākā*.

[1] All the MSS. Medh. have *vāri°* for *c'āmbu* (like *vāricara*).

[2] Such as vultures, etc. (K.)

[3] Lions, etc. (K.)

[4] Whose nature it is to do cruel acts (Medh., K.)

[5] Ghosts (*pretāḥ*), a class of spirits, literally, "the advanced, the departed;" some of them are described farther on (cf. vs. 71 ff.). They are to be distinguished from the manes (the "fathers"), the progenitors of each individual. The *pretāḥ* appear to be originally the dead in general; to these no respect such as is paid to one's own dead ancestors is due. *Pretānte'ti sandhir ārṣaḥ* (Rāgh.)

[6] *Viprasvam*, "priest (Brahman's) property;" the MSS. Medh. have *brahmasvam*, which means the same thing, and explains *brahmarākṣasa*.

[7] *Brahmarākṣasa.*

[8] Or, he is born as a goldsmith, but some say this word (gold-worker) is the name of a bird (K.); this latter is Medh.'s explanation (*pakṣiṇaḥ*).

[9] *Haṁsa.*

[10] A species of water-bird.

[11] The MSS. Medh. have *tailaṁ vai tailapāyikaḥ* (cf. the feminine in B. R. and L.'s note on (Bomb. ed.) Mbhā. xiii. 104, 114: "*Gṛheṣu* . . . (parrots, etc.) *na pāpāya, tathā vai tailapāyikāḥ*," followed by other birds (not insects).

64. (By) stealing silk goods, linen goods, woven cotton goods, a cow, or molasses, (one becomes respectively) a partridge, a frog, a curlew, an iguana, or (the bird called) *vāgguda*.[1]

65. (By stealing) fine perfumes, vegetables with leaves prepared food of various kinds, or unprepared food, (one becomes respectively) a musk-rat, a peacock, a (boar called) *çvāvidh*, or a porcupine.

66. (One) becomes indeed a (kind of) heron[2] (by) stealing fire; a house-wasp (by stealing) a (house) utensil; (by) stealing dyed cloths (one) is born (again as) a (fowl called) *jīvijīvaka*.

67. (By stealing) a (forest) animal (or) elephant (one is born again as) a wolf; (by stealing) a horse (one is born) a tiger; (by stealing) fruits or roots[3] (one is born) an ape; (by stealing) a woman (one is born) a bear; (by stealing) water (one is born a bird called) *stokaka*;[4] (by stealing) waggons (one is born) a camel; (by stealing) cattle (one is born) a goat.

68. (By) taking forcibly any goods whatever (belonging) to another, a man reaches necessarily the estate of animals, and also (by) eating an oblation not offered (to a divinity).[5]

69. Women also in the same way would (by) stealing incur sin: these (women) pass into the condition of being wives to these same creatures.

70. Now indeed the castes, (by) deserting without neces-

[1] The reason for each change is not apparent, though some are easily seen to be from a similarity of attributes; others, again, appear meaningless, as these last (cow-thief becoming an *iguana*, molasses-thief, a *vāgguda*), till we see the original text, where it is apparent that the fate of these sinners is the result of a pun (*godhā gāṁ, vāggudo guḍam*). This "bird" (K.) is perhaps a bat, as it is probably identical with *vālguda* (Viṣṇu xliv. 30, where Nand. so renders the word *vālguda*; Gaut. xvii. 34, *vāgvada*, commentator's rendering of *māndhāla*). Dr. Bühler has suggested that the word is the same as Gūjarat *vāgul* or *vāgud*, "large bat." Medh., in MS. No. 1551, has this form with *l*, but here and in No. 935 *valguti* (*sic*).

[2] *Baka*.

[3] Or, flowers (Medh.)

[4] "That begs for a drop of water."

[5] "Offered," *i.e.*, on fire; sacrificial cakes, etc., are meant (K.)

sity their own proper occupations,[1] after migrating through evil transmigrations, enter a condition of servitude among enemies.[2]

71. A Brahman (who) has deserted his own proper (rules of) right[3] (becomes) the ghost (called) Ulkāmukha,[4] an eater of vomit; a Kṣatriya, the ghost (called) Kaṭapūtana,[5] an eater of impurity and corpses.

72. A Vaiçya (who) has deserted his own proper (rule of) right becomes the ghost (called) Maitrākṣajyotika, (that) eats what smells foul;[6] and a Çūdra becomes a ghost (called) Cailāçaka.

73. Just in proportion as those whose whole self is (devoted) to (pleasures of) sense[7] indulge themselves in (pleasures of) sense, is their proficiency in (these pleasures of sense) reproduced.

74. By repeating those sinful acts these (men) of little intelligence collect unto themselves woes among those different wombs here (on earth):[8]

75. Wanderings through horrible hells, that of darkness[9] and the rest, forest (hills) where the trees have swords for

[1] That is, their caste occupations (Medh.), or their proper religious ceremonies (K.)

[2] All the MSS. Medh. have a *var. lec.* *saṁvṛtya* and *bhṛtyatām . . . dasyuṣu* ("servitude amid Dasyus"), explained by Medh. as "amid thieves, ruffians," etc.

[3] *Dharma.*

[4] That is, "with a face like a firebrand." Cf. iii. 109.

[5] The meaning is not clear. *Kaṭa* is a mat, bier, corpse; *pūtanā*, the name of a female demon, perhaps "corpse-demon." Medh. says *kutsitagandhā nāsikā'sya bhavati*, "his nose has a disagreeable smell." He gives a *var. lec.* (*putana iti vā pāṭhaḥ*), explaining "invisible demons inhabiting cemeteries." The first explanation seems to imply *kūṭa*, to which the root *pūy*, "smell foul," is added. The MS. No. 989 has *kūṭa* in each case, partly erased and changed to *kaṭa*, and *kūṭa* is also found in No. 1551. In (*a*) *vipro bhavati vicyutaḥ* (Medh.)

[6] Medh. says on Maitrākṣajyotika that it is as before the name of a demon, or (as K.) "creatures of excrements," while others explain otherwise. K. explains the Çūdra's ghost (Cailāçaka) as one devouring lice or moths in clothes. Medh. here reads *Tailāçakas tu*, according to all three MSS., *i.e.*, "eating sesame oil."

[7] The three MSS. Medh. have, however, *viṣayaiṣinaḥ*.

[8] That is, (in these successive transmigrations and births in different) wombs, which, as K. says, become more and more despicable (till the sin ceases).

[9] Cf. iv. 88–90, *tāmisra*. Cf. Yāj. iii. 206.

leaves,[1] and the rest (consisting of) captivities and mutilations;

76. And tortures also of many sorts, being eaten by crows and owls; (hells) hard to withstand,[2] (of) hot sand (to be eaten) as grits, and (burnings like) the cooking of a pot;[3]

77. And forever births in base[4] wombs wholly of woe, beatings by cold and by heat, and terrors of many sorts;

78. Often an abode in the abodes of the embryo, and birth severe, and miserable captivities and also servitude under others;

79. And separations from relatives and dear (ones), and cohabitation with wicked men; the gaining of things and the losing (of them again), and the gaining of an enemy (thought) a friend;

80. And also an incurable[5] old age, and torturing by illnesses, and many distresses of various sorts, and likewise death, hard to conquer.

81. Now with whatever sort of disposition one cultivates any one act, with just that sort of body he reaps in each case its fruit.[6]

82. The origin and the result of acts has thus been explained:[7] learn the following rule of action[8] for a Brahman, (a rule) which brings deliverance.

83. Perusal of the Veda, (ascetic) austerity, knowledge,[9]

[1] *Asipatravana*. A *var. lec.* in Medh. (all MSS.) for *vivartana* (wanderings) is *pravartana* (progression).

[2] *Duḥsahān* (Medh.) or *dāruṇān*, "fearful;" and °*kās taptāḥ*, "heated."

[3] Cooked like food in a pot (Medh.), or burned as the clay is when made into a pot.

[4] Base, *i.e.*, born as animals, ghosts, or demons (Medh.)

[5] So B. R., literally, "without defence." "Revenge of kings" (*rājñāṁ caiva pratīkāram*), is the remarkable *var. lec.* in the three MSS. Medh.

[6] The future body is affected by the same thread as that under the influence of which an act has been committed (Medh., K.) Medh. has *sa tat tat phalam açnute* (same sense). Cf. i. 28, and cf. Mbhā. xv. 34, 18.

[7] Beng. MS. *var. lec. dharmaḥ*; K. *sarvaḥ . . . vaḥ* (cf. vs. 51); Medh. *sargaḥ . . . ca*.

[8] Or "learn this act (that) causes." The MSS. Medh. agree with Bomb. MS. (*karmavidhim*). Cf. i. 106. Dr. B.'s translation, *deliverance*. Cf. in general Mbhā. xiii. 112, 1 ff.

[9] Of Veda or self. Cf. vs. 31.

and controlling the organs of sense, doing no injury, and serving the Guru, (is) the highest source of deliverance.[1]

84. Is there then amid all these holy acts here (on earth) any one act declared (to be) yet more productive of deliverance for man (than the rest)?[2]

85. Amid all these holy acts, the knowledge of self is said (to be) the highest; this indeed is the foremost of all sciences, since from it immortality is obtained.[3]

86. Now amid all these six acts, that one more productive of deliverance (than the rest), both after death and here, should be known (to be) always the ceremony (taught) in the Veda:[4]

87. And in practising the ceremony (taught) in the Veda, all these without exception are comprised, one after the other, in this very rule of ceremony.[5]

88. The ceremony (taught) in the Veda is of two sorts, either selfish or disinterested, and, (according as it is of the former or the latter sort), it produces (worldly) happiness (only) or causes (final) deliverance.

89. A selfish ceremony[6] is explained (as) one connected with some desire (of benefit) here or hereafter; a disinterested (ceremony) is designated (as) one devoid of desire and (performed) after knowledge (has been acquired).

[1] Cf. vs. 104.

[2] This verse appears to be one of the awkward knots by which the whole work is tied together; it is supposed to be a question asked by the listening seers. No. 989 Medh. MS. has it inserted in the margin, but Nos. 1551 and 935 omit it altogether.

[3] The commentators of course take "self" in a Vedantic sense; this cannot be if we insist on the whole text representing Sāṅkhya ideas, but rather one's own self as a microcosm in contrast to the outside world. The commentators may, however, be right, if, as I suspect, vss. 84, 85, are Vedantic insertions into the original text. Medh. has *arcyam* (honoured) for *agryam* (foremost).

[4] This seems to be the meaning of *karma vaidikam* (literally, "the act of the Veda"), which the commentators explain as sacrifices, etc., as taught in the Veda. "Amid all" is "amid the former" according to some MSS. (*pūrveṣām*, Bomb. MS. and Medh. MSS.)

[5] Referring to the ceremony just mentioned (Medh.)

[6] *Karma*, as before, "ceremony," or perhaps "act" in general. A religious act is meritorious any way, whether done from interested motives or not; doubly so, however, when done without such motive by one "who has attained knowledge."

90. (By) practising a selfish ceremony one reaches equality[1] with the gods; but (by) practising a disinterested (ceremony) one overcomes in truth the five existent (elements).[2]

91. One who sees alike self in all-existent (things) and all-existent (things) in self, (as) a sacrificer of self attains absolute sway.[3]

92. The highest of the twice-born (the Brahman) having neglected the ceremonies as they have been declared, should be diligently occupied with knowledge of self, peace, and perusal of the Veda;[4]

93. For herein, especially to a Brahman, consists the whole end and aim of existence; since the twice-born man becomes perfect[5] (only by) attaining this,[6] (and) in no other way.

94. The Veda (is) the eternal eye of manes, gods, and men; (something) impossible[7] and immeasurable (is) the Veda treatise;[8] so stands the case.

95. Whatever traditions (Smṛtis) lie outside the Veda,[9] and whatever (works) are ill-revealed (heterodox), are all without fruit after death, since they are said to rest in darkness.[10]

1 K., *Sāmyatām;* Medh., *sātmyatām;* Rāgh. reads *sārṣṭitām* ("equality of power"), noting the other as a *var. lec.*

2 There appears beside *atyeti* to have been another reading, *abhyeti*, "enters into," by which not riddance of the elements, but absorption into them would be taught.

3 *Svārājyam;* cf. vi. 75. Johaentgen translates, "Zu dem im eigensten Glanze strahlenden Wesen," *i.e.*, Brahma, as in vs. 125. "Sacrificer of self" means that he identifies himself with all the divinities; so his sacrifice is to self (Medh.)

4 The neglect of ceremonies for one who desires perfection is laid down as a rule (*karmaṇāṁ parihānir vidhīyate*) according to Medh., though the participle might grammatically be construed as a concessive clause. The (rather strange) antithesis between *yatnavān* and *çama* is removed by Medh.'s text: *Ātmajñānaṁ samāveçya*, "laying aside ceremonies and entering completely into the knowledge of self, one should be diligently occupied with the perusal of the Veda" Rāgh. notes the *var. lec.*

5 *Kṛtakṛtyaḥ;* literally, "one who has done (everything) to be done."

6 Knowledge of self.

7 Impossible to be made by man alone (K.)

8 *Vedaçāstram.*

9 *I.e.*, are opposed to the teachings of the Veda.

10 Their fruit is hell (K.); their root is confusion (Medh.) The MSS. Medh. have *çrutayaḥ* for *smṛtayaḥ;* "ill-revealed" systems of philosophy are meant (*asattarkadarçana*), Medh. Cf. on this verse particularly Johaentgen, p. 79, note.

96. And all (systems) other than that, which are brought forth and disappear,[1] (are), on account of (their) being (composed) in time near (to us, proved to be) without fruit and without truth.

97. One by one the four castes, the three worlds, the four orders of life, the past, the present, and the future[2]—(in short) everything depends on the Veda for success.[3]

98. Sound, touch, form, taste, and fifth, smell, depend, according to (their) origin, mood, and action, upon the Veda alone.[4]

99. The eternal Veda-treatise supports all existent (things); therefore this I think the highest which ensures success to this creature (man).

100. One who understands the Veda-treatise deserves rule over armies, kingly power, the right to adjudge punishment, and the governorship of all the world.[5]

101. As fire (when its) strength is brought forth consumes even wet trees, so the Veda-knower consumes the act-born sin of self.

102. He who abiding in any order whatever knows the true inner meaning of the Veda-treatise, even while existing here in this world is fitted for *brahma*-existence.[6]

103. Those who have (perused many) literary compositions (are) superior to those who are ignorant; those who remember (what they learn are) better than those who have (perused many) literary compositions; those who understand (what they learn are) superior to those who remember (it); those who practise (what they learn are better) than those who understand (it).

[1] *Cyavante;* Medh. has *vyathante* (*vinaçyanti*); "other than that (Veda)," (Medh.)

[2] Literally, "(what) was, is, will be;" (*bharad*, var. lec. *bhavyam*).

[3] That is, their authority is found in Veda (K.)

[4] *Prasidhyanti* (*sic.*, Medh.; cf. Beng. MS.) There are two readings: *prasūtiguṇakarmataḥ* (according to the origin, nature, and use of sound, etc.), or *prasūter guṇadharmataḥ* (according to the goodness of the nature of their origin, *i.e.*, whether they result from the *guṇa* of darkness, passion, etc.—(Medh.)

[5] Vss. 100-105 follow vss. 106-108 in Medh.; his order being from here to end: 99, 106-108, 100-105, 109-122, 126; vss. 100-105 being perhaps interpolated.

[6] *Brahmabhūya*, existence in Brahmā, or existence as *brahma*, *i.e.*, as ethereal substance. Cf. vii. 23.

104. The best source of deliverance for a Brahman is (ascetic) austerity and (Vedic) wisdom; through (ascetic) austerity one slays sin,[1] through (Vedic) wisdom one gets immortality.

105. Immediate (visual) perception, inference,[2] the treatises (of law)[3] according to the various traditions, (this) triad must be well understood by one desiring clearness[4] in regard to (rules of) right.

106. He and no other knows the law who, by means of a philosophical system, not opposed to the Veda-treatise, intelligently follows (the works) of the seers and the regulations of the law.[5]

107. This, as has been declared without omission, (is) the act that causes deliverance; (thereby) the secret mystery of this Mānava-treatise[6] is explained.

108. If (a question) should arise (couched thus): "How (is one to act) in (case) no (rules of) right (are) handed down?" (The answer is), let that which well-instructed[7] Brahmans may declare be (regarded as) an undoubted (rule) of right.

109. And they (are) to be known as well-instructed Brahmans by whom the Veda, with (its) additions,[8] has been gone over according to law, (and who) possess proofs perceptible by the senses from revelation.[9]

110. That rule (of right) one shall not allow to be dis-

[1] Cf. vs. 183; *kilbiṣam* or *kalmaṣam* (cf. Mbhā. xiii. 69, 19: *Kalmaṣaṁ guruçuçrūṣā hanti*); this is the reading in all three MSS. Medh.

[2] Perception by the senses, inference, and the law, are the three means of knowledge; it is in the second that the affinity with the Sāṅkhya system is seen best.

[3] Law-treatise, apparently, as shown by *dharma*, "rule of right," following. "Traditions," *āgama*, are the different works *tradita ab antiquis*, constituting together the body of the law (*çāstram*, "treatise"). Cf. viii. 44. Possibly Veda is meant, as below (in 109) *çruti* takes the place of *çāstra*.

[4] Or, *var. lec.* "perfection in." According to Medh. (all three MSS.) we have *karmabuddhim abhīpsatām*, "for those desiring knowledge of an act."

[5] Medh. has *ārṣadharmo'padeçena*, which would give a very different force to the last half. "Law" (*dharma*) supplements the seers' work (Veda); philosophical system (*tarka*) is, according to Medh., *anumāna*, inference.

[6] *Mānavaṁ-çāstram*, or "treatise (of law) by Manu," as the commentators, of course, say. Cf. vs. 117.

[7] "Well-instructed," *i.e.*, Çiṣṭas; cf. Baudh. i. 1, 5, and Āp. i. 20, 6.

[8] Itihāsas, Purāṇas, even Smṛtis (Medh.)

[9] *Hetu = anumāna* (Medh.); revelation, *i.e.*, *çruti*, Veda.

puted, which an assembly shall establish, consisting of at least ten or of at least three men of good conduct.

111. One (learned) in (each of) the three Vedas, one who understands proofs,[1] a philosopher,[2] an etymologist, one who recites the (rules of) right, and three members of the first[3] orders, would constitute an assembly consisting of at least ten.

112. One wise in the Ṛg-Veda, and one wise in the Yajur-Veda, and one also learned in the Sāma-Veda, should be known (to constitute) an assembly consisting of at least three, in deciding a doubt in regard to a (rule of) right.

113. That rule of right which even one (of) the highest of the twice-born wise in the Veda shall propound must be known as the supreme rule of right, not (that) declared by myriads of ignorant (persons).

114. A genuine assembly is not found among men assembled (even) by thousands, (if they) have not (performed) the (proper) observances, have not (perused) the *mantras*, (and if they) live by virtue of their caste alone.

115. If fools, whose nature is darkness, declare any rule of right (when) they know nothing about it, the sin resulting therefrom, becoming an hundredfold (greater), enters into them who declared it.

116. All this,[4] the best cause of deliverance, has now been set before you; the Brahman who swerves not from this obtains the highest course.

117. This Lord, the divine one,[5] through a desire for the good of the worlds, has thus declared unto me all this (that follows, as) the highest mystery[6] of the law.

[1] One skilled in *anumāna* (Medh.), *hetuka* (or *haituka*); cf. *haituka* in iv. 30 (rationalist), and note on ii. 11.

[2] *Tarkin* (cf. Joh., p. 79, note), "one skilled in testing and reviewing a thing;" possibly "a logician," if the science was one then recognised, which seems improbable.

[3] "The three first" are the student, householder, and hermit. According to K., some MSS. have *sarve*, "all." Cf. Gaut. xxviii. 48; Vas. iii. 20; Baudh. i. 1, 7–16; Yāj. i. 9.

[4] All this teaching of the law is meant; *vihitam* in Medh., "explained."

[5] *I.e.*, Manu declared it to me, Bhṛgu (Medh., K.)

[6] "Mystery" is literally "(that which is) to be concealed" (*guhyam*);

118. In self should one behold the All, being and not-being,[1] with mind intent; for beholding in self the All one does not turn his mind to wrong.[2]

119. Self alone (are) all divinities;[3] the All is founded in self, for self begets the chain of action[4] in (all) these incorporate (creatures).

120. One should cause the ether to enter[5] in the hollows (of the body), the wind in movement and touch, supreme heat and effulgence in digestion and sight,[6] water in the fatty parts, and earth in the solid particles (of the body);

121. (Also) the moon in the mind, the quarters of the heavens in hearing, Viṣṇu in walking, Indra[7] in strength, Fire in voice, Mitra in excretion, and Prajāpati in procreation.[8]

122. Controller of all (things), (a being made) of particles finer than fine even, gold-glancing, comprehensible (only) by an intelligence asleep[9]—him one should know (to be) the supreme man (Puruṣa).

cf. vs. 107 and xi. 266. "Law" (*dharma*) here includes the whole treatise; above, in vss. 113, 115, *dharma* is a special "rule" (of right).

[1] Or, "with mind intent on being and not-being" (Johaent.), though the apposition above seems preferable.

[2] *Adharma* (so Medh.)

[3] "Self is indeed all divinities" (Johaent., who says, "Dem Gesetzbuche liegt nichts ferner als der Gedanke, die Götter seien reiner Geist," and finds the explanation to be that "self has a share in all the gods" (s. 57), as explained below. It is doubtful whether we should seek the "thought of the law-book" proper in this closing stanzas of the late and last book. *Ātmai'va* is not *ātmā hi*, and the words of the text, whether they agree with the tone of the work or not, mean that all the divinities are just "self," and nothing else.

[4] Literally, "causes the production of pursuance of acts of these incorporate."

[5] *I.e.*, "one should recognise the connection between the ether (*kha*) and the hollows (*kha*), between wind and movement," etc.

[6] *Tejas* implies heat and light both.

[7] Hari; in Rāgh.'s time the two *var. lec.* Hara (Çiva) or Hari (Indra) stood side by side. The three MSS. of Medh. have Hari (in No. 989 this was afterwards erased and changed into Hara).

[8] The exercise of the faculties are intended where the organs themselves are given; the connection between the two last divinities and the function is that of presiding geniuses. Viṣṇu is not strictly "god of walking," but his three great steps are referred to; the connection between speaking and fire is that the latter "calls" the gods to sacrifice. Cf. with this passage the parallel in Tattva Samāsa given by Johaent. (s. 58).

[9] Sunk into sleeplike meditation; this Puruṣa, "the highest, first principle," is spoken of in i. 11; in the

123. This one some declare (to be) Fire; others, Manu Prajāpati; some, Indra; others, breath; others again, the eternal *brahma*.[1]

124. This one, penetrating all-created (things) by (means of) the five elements,[2] for ever by (means of) birth, growth, and death, keeps up like a wheel (the course of) transmigrations.

125. Thus he who by (means of) self sees self in all created (things), after attaining equality with the All, enters into *brahma*, the highest place.[3]

126. The twice-born man who recites this Mānava treatise as it has thus been expounded by Bhṛgu, always becomes attached to (good) custom, and[4] shall obtain a course[5] (just such) as (shall be) desired (by him).

END OF THE TWELFTH LECTURE.

rest of the law-book it is ignored, and belongs consequently to the late philosophical portions.

[1] This verse with the two following Medh. omits; they are, therefore, probably the latest verses of the latest portion of our work.

[2] *Mūrti*, "elementary particles."

[3] Cf. Āp. ii. 21, 13 ff.

[4] Some MSS. have "eternal" (*sanātanam*) for "highest (best) place." "*Brahma*" is here neuter, and probably means the "world-substance," not "world-spirit."

[5] In the next life his existence shall be as he wishes it (K.)

THE END.

INDEX OF SUBJECTS.